THE ROUTLEDGE HISTORY HANDBOOK OF CENTRAL AND EASTERN EUROPE IN THE TWENTIETH CENTURY

Intellectual Horizons offers a pioneering, transnational and comparative treatment of key thematic areas in the intellectual and cultural history of Central and Eastern Europe in the twentieth century.

For most of the twentieth century, Central and Eastern European ideas and cultures constituted an integral part of wider European trends. However, the intellectual and cultural history of this diverse region has rarely been incorporated sufficiently into nominally comprehensive histories of Europe. This volume redresses this underrepresentation and provides a more balanced perspective on the recent past of the continent through original, critical overviews of themes ranging from the social and conceptual history of intellectuals and histories of political thought and historiography, to literary, visual and religious cultures, to perceptions and representations of the region in the twentieth century. While structured thematically, individual contributions are organized chronologically. They emphasize, where relevant, generational experiences, agendas and accomplishments, while taking into account the sharp ruptures that characterize the period.

The third in a four-volume set on Central and Eastern Europe in the twentieth century, it is the go-to resource for understanding the intellectual and cultural history of this dynamic region.

Włodzimierz Borodziej is Professor of History at Warsaw University, Poland.

Ferenc Laczó is Assistant Professor of History at Maastricht University, the Netherlands.

Joachim von Puttkamer is Professor of Eastern European History at Jena University, Germany and Co-Director of the Imre Kertész Kolleg, Germany.

The Imre Kertész Kolleg at the Friedrich Schiller University in Jena is an institute for the advanced study of the history of Eastern Europe in the twentieth century.

The Kolleg was founded in October 2010 as the ninth Käte Hamburger Kolleg of the German Federal Ministry for Education and Research (BMBF). The directors of the Kolleg are Professor Joachim von Puttkamer and Dr Michal Kopeček. Professor Włodzimierz Borodziej was the Kolleg's co-director from 2010 to 2016 and is now chairman of its advisory board.

SPONSORED BY THE

THE ROUTLEDGE TWENTIETH CENTURY HISTORY HANDBOOKS

The Routledge History Handbook of Central and Eastern Europe in the Twentieth Century
Volume 1: Challenges of Modernity
Edited by Włodzimierz Borodziej, Stanislav Holubec and Joachim von Puttkamer

The Routledge History Handbook of Central and Eastern Europe in the Twentieth Century
Volume 2: Statehood
Edited by Włodzimierz Borodziej, Sabina Ferhadbegović and Joachim von Puttkamer

The Routledge History Handbook of Central and Eastern Europe in the Twentieth Century
Volume 3: Intellectual Horizons
Edited by Włodzimierz Borodziej, Ferenc Laczó and Joachim von Puttkamer

For more information about this series, please visit: www.routledge.com/The-Routledge-Twentieth-Century-History-Handbooks/book-series/RHHC20.

THE ROUTLEDGE HISTORY HANDBOOK OF CENTRAL AND EASTERN EUROPE IN THE TWENTIETH CENTURY

Volume 3: Intellectual Horizons

Edited by
Włodzimierz Borodziej, Ferenc Laczó
and Joachim von Puttkamer

LONDON AND NEW YORK

First published 2021
by Routledge
2 Park Square, Milton Park, Abingdon, Oxon OX14 4RN

and by Routledge
52 Vanderbilt Avenue, New York, NY 10017

Routledge is an imprint of the Taylor & Francis Group, an informa business

© 2021 selection and editorial matter, Włodzimierz Borodziej, Ferenc Laczó
and Joachim von Puttkamer; individual chapters, the contributors

The right of Włodzimierz Borodziej, Ferenc Laczó and Joachim von
Puttkamer to be identified as the authors of the editorial material, and of the
authors for their individual chapters, has been asserted in accordance with
sections 77 and 78 of the Copyright, Designs and Patents Act 1988.

All rights reserved. No part of this book may be reprinted or reproduced or
utilised in any form or by any electronic, mechanical, or other means, now
known or hereafter invented, including photocopying and recording, or in
any information storage or retrieval system, without permission in writing
from the publishers.

Trademark notice: Product or corporate names may be trademarks or
registered trademarks, and are used only for identification and explanation
without intent to infringe.

British Library Cataloguing-in-Publication Data
A catalogue record for this book is available from the British Library

Library of Congress Cataloging-in-Publication Data
Names: Borodziej, Włodzimierz, editor. | Ferhadbegović, Sabina,
editor. | Puttkamer, Joachim von, editor.
Title: The Routledge history handbook of Central and Eastern Europe
in the twentieth century / edited by Włodzimierz Borodziej,
Sabina Ferhadbegović and Joachim von Puttkamer.
Other titles: Central and Eastern Europe in the twentieth century
Description: New York : Routledge, 2019- | Series: Routledge twentieth
century history handbooks | Volume 1 title information from publisher's
website. | Includes bibliographical references and index. | Contents:
[Volume 1. The Challenges of Modernity]—Volume 2. Statehood—
Identifiers: LCCN 2019049033 (print) | LCCN 2019049034 (ebook) |
ISBN 9781138301665 (hardback) | ISBN 9780367822118 (ebook)
Subjects: LCSH: Europe, Central—Politics and government—1989- |
Europe, Eastern—Politics and government—1989- | Post-communism—
Europe, Central—History—20th century. | Post-communism—
Europe, Eastern—History—20th century.
Classification: LCC DAW1051 .R68 2019 (print) | LCC DAW1051
(ebook) | DDC 943.009/04—dc23
LC record available at https://lccn.loc.gov/2019049033
LC ebook record available at https://lccn.loc.gov/2019049034

ISBN: 978-1-138-30165-8 (hbk)
ISBN: 978-1-003-05549-5 (ebk)
ISBN: 978-0-367-51865-3 (set)

Typeset in Bembo
by Swales & Willis, Exeter, Devon, UK

CONTENTS

Series introduction   vii
    Włodzimierz Borodziej and Joachim von Puttkamer
Acknowledgements   ix
List of tables   x
List of abbreviations   xi
List of contributors   xiii
Volume introduction: intellectual horizons   xvi
    Włodzimierz Borodziej, Ferenc Laczó and Joachim von Puttkamer

1   Spatial configurations: regional intellectual imageries in
    twentieth-century Central and Eastern Europe   1
    Diana Mishkova

2   Thinking dangerously: political thought in twentieth-century
    East Central Europe   69
    Balázs Trencsényi

3   A history of fiction in twentieth-century Central and Eastern Europe   132
    John Neubauer, with Endre Bojtár and Guido Snel

4   Writing history in twentieth-century Eastern Europe   194
    Maciej Górny

5   Nationalization vs. secularization: the Christian churches in East
    Central Europe   256
    John Connelly

Contents

6 Visual cultures: tele-visions   311
   Anikó Imre

Index   367

SERIES INTRODUCTION

Włodzimierz Borodziej and Joachim von Puttkamer

What were the central twentieth-century experiences for Eastern European societies? Depending on whom you ask and depending on which country their thoughts intuitively drift towards, the answer is likely to be quite different. The answer could refer to significant dates, such as the 1939 Molotov–Ribbentrop Pact, the 1956 Hungarian uprising, the Prague Spring of 1968 or the year of Solidarity in 1980–1981. It could also revolve around the experiences in various countries – the Stalinist deportations left deep scars in the Baltic states, as did the wars of the 1990s in former Yugoslavia. The thoughts of a Western European are likely to jump to 1989 and the collapse of communist rule – perhaps also to the disappointed (or at least unlikely) prospects of a unified Europe. Hopefully, he or she might learn something from this volume.

As that Western European will discover, there were particular as well as shared experiences. The volumes presented here focus on both, grouped around what the editors regard as central, overarching themes. To emphasize the experience of *Violence* (vol. 4) is just as obvious as prioritizing the manifold *Challenges of Modernity* (vol. 1) of a region that has often been described – and perceived by its own inhabitants – as the periphery of Europe. The need to address the transformation of *Statehood* (vol. 2) over the course of the century may initially seem less apparent, but it allows for an elucidation of profound changes and phenomena that are otherwise obscured in a discussion of the emergence and emancipation of modern nation states. *Intellectual Horizons* (vol. 3) reflects the wealth of self-descriptions and self-localizations in and about the region.

What do these volumes offer the reader? Not an encyclopaedia of Central, Eastern and Southeastern Europe in the long twentieth century, but a series of essays written from different perspectives and life experiences. The authors live in Bulgaria, Germany, Canada, Austria, Poland, Romania, Serbia, Czechia, Hungary and the United States. They belong to different generations and milieus and often have vastly different conceptions of historiography and the writing of history. Therein lies – according to the editors – the appeal of these volumes.

The shared goal of these contributions is to tell the story of *the suburbs of Europe* in the twentieth century; to tell how the story unfolded, how it was perceived within this region and how it can be interpreted today.

Series introduction

The authors were not given any methodological parameters to follow. Some contributions may seem conservative or even old-fashioned; others argue in the spirit of what, in many universities today, is considered mainstream. None of the authors, however, crosses the boundary beyond which they see traditional sources as nothing more than merely conceptual obstacles. If the present volumes provide a new impetus for a collective reflection on Eastern Europe, both in teaching and in research, then much will have been gained.

ACKNOWLEDGEMENTS

As part of the series 'Central and Eastern Europe in the Twentieth Century', this volume has been with us for several years, longer than we expected. We would like to thank all our contributors for their dedicated engagement and flawless cooperation throughout the years. The late John Neubauer made every effort to improve our joint project and, though gravely ill by the time, he even attended our last joint workshop in the summer of 2015. We are also deeply indebted to Guido Snel and to the late Endre Bojtár for completing the manuscript of John's chapter. Béla Abrányi Szabó translated Endre Bojtár's additions from the Hungarian. Daniela Gruber has supported us in completing and straightening out many bibliographic references. We would particularly like to thank Jaime Hyatt for her thorough language editing. Her patience with authors and editors is simply admirable.

The editors.

TABLES

5.1 Percentage of people who declare themselves Atheist or Agnostic   300

ABBREVIATIONS

AIESEE – The International Association of Southeast European Studies
ARD – Arbeitsgemeinschaft der öffentlich-rechtlichen Rundfunkanstalten der Bundesrepublik Deutschland/Consortium of public broadcasters in the Federal Republic of Germany
BBC – The British Broadcasting Corporation
CBC – Canadian Broadcasting Corporation
CISH/ICHS – Comité International des Sciences Historiques/The Committee of Historical Sciences
CNSAS – Consiliul Naţional pentru Studierea Arhivelor Securităţii/National Council for the Study of the Archives of Securitate
COMECON – The Council for Mutual Economic Assistance
Comintern – Communist International
DEFA – Deutsche Film-Aktiengesellschaft/German Film Studios Inc.
DFF – Deutscher Fernsehfunk/German Television Broadcasting
EBU – European Broadcasting Union
EGTA – European Group of Television Advertising
FRG – Federal Republic of Germany
HDZ – Hrvatska Demokratska Zajednica/Croatian Democratic Union
IBU – International Broadcasting Union
KOR – Komitet Obrony Robotników/Workers' Defence Committee
KP – Keresztényszocialista Párt/Christian Socialist Party of Hungary
MTV – Magyar Televízió/Hungarian Television
NDR – Norddeutscher Rundfunk/Northern German Broadcasting
NKVD – Narodnyy Komissariat Vnutrennikh Del/People's Commissariat for Internal Affairs, Interior Ministry of the Soviet Union
NSDAP – Nationalsozialistische Deutsche Arbeiterpartei/National Socialist German Workers' Party
OIRT – Organisation Internationale de Radiodiffusion et de Télévision/International Radio and Television Organisation
OZON – Obóz Zjednoczenia Narodowego/Camp of National Unity
PSB – Public Service Broadcasting
RAI – Radiotelevisione Italiana

List of abbreviations

ROC – Biserica Ortodoxă Română/Romanian Orthodox Church
RTF – Radiodiffusion-Télévision Française/French Radio and Television Broadcasting
SED – Sozialistische Einheitspartei Deutschlands/Socialist Unity Party of Germany
TVP – Telewizja Polska/Polish Public Broadcasting Corporation
UNESCO – The United Nations Educational, Scientific and Cultural Organization
USSR – Union of Soviet Socialist Republics
YLE – Yleisradio Oy/Finnish Broadcasting Company
ZDF – Zweites Deutsches Fernsehen/Second German Television

CONTRIBUTORS

Endre Bojtár was a literary historian, a translator and was one of the founders of the Central European University, Budapest. A member of the Institute of Literary Studies of the Hungarian Academy of Sciences from 1963 until his retirement in 2010, Bojtár published numerous books and articles. His publications include: *Foreword to the Past: A Cultural History of the Baltic People* (CEU 2000), *East European Avant-Garde Literature* (Akadémiai Kiadó 1993) and *Slavic Structuralism* (John Benjamins 1985). From 1991 to 1994, he was Director of the Comparative Literature programme at CEU, and throughout his career he held various international fellowships. Sadly, Endre Bojtár passed away in February 2018.

Włodzimierz Borodziej is Professor of Modern History at Warsaw University. He was Co-Director of the Imre Kertész Kolleg in Jena (2010–2016) and is currently the chairman of the Kolleg's academic advisory board. His books include *The Warsaw Uprising of 1944* (English translation, Univ. of Wisconsin 2006), a seminal twentieth-century history of Poland (*Geschichte Polens im 20. Jahrhundert*, C.H. Beck 2010) and many key studies of Polish and Polish–German history. The two-volume monograph, which he co-authored with Maciej Górny, *Nasza Wojna: Imperia 1912–1916* (WAB 2014) and *Nasza Wojna: Narody 1917–1923* (WAB 2018) has been published in German as *Der Vergessene Weltkrieg: Europas Osten 1912–1923* (wbg Theiss 2018) and offers the most comprehensive account of the First World War in Central and Eastern Europe. An English translation is forthcoming.

John Connelly is Professor of History at the University of California, Berkeley, and is the author of *From Peoples into Nations: A History of Eastern Europe* (Princeton 2020), *From Enemy to Brother: The Revolution in Catholic Teaching on the Jews* (Harvard 2012) and *Captive University: The Sovietisation of East German, Czech, and Polish Higher Education, 1945–1956* (Univ. of North Carolina 2000). He has published widely on Central and Eastern European political and social history, the history of nationalism and racism, and the history of Catholicism.

Maciej Górny is extraordinary Professor at the Historical Institute of the Polish Academy of Sciences. His recent publications include: *Science Embattled: Eastern European Intellectuals and the Great War* (Ferdinand Schöningh 2019), *The Nation Should Come First: Marxism and Historiography in East Central Europe* (Peter Lang 2013), and with Włodziemierz Borodziej he is

xiii

the co-author of *Der Vergessene Weltkrieg: Europas Osten 1912–1923* (wbg Theiss 2018, English translation forthcoming). Górny is also co-editor of the series *Discourses of Collective Identity in Central and Southeast Europe (1770–1945)* (CEU 2006–2014). He has published many other monographs, co-edited volumes, and articles on intellectual history, German–Polish relations, minority politics and Marxist historiography in Eastern Europe and the Balkans.

Anikó Imre is the author of *TV Socialism* (Duke 2016), *Identity Games: Globalization and the Transformation of Media Cultures in the New Europe* (MIT 2009) and editor of *A Companion to East European Cinemas* (Wiley-Blackwell 2012) and *East European Cinemas* (Routledge 2005). She is co-editor of Palgrave's Global Cinemas book series and is on the editorial boards of *Television and New Media*, *Studies in East European Cinema* and *NECSUS European Journal of Media Studies*. She is Professor of Cinematic Arts and Director of Undergraduate Studies in the Division of Cinema and Media Studies at the University of Southern California.

Ferenc Laczó has published widely on twentieth-century Hungarian Jewish culture, the Holocaust, memory studies, and Central and East European intellectual history. He is co-editor of the volume *Catastrophe and Utopia: Jewish Intellectuals in Central and Eastern Europe in the 1930s and 1940s* (De Gruyter 2017) and the author of *Hungarian Jews in the Age of Genocide: An Intellectual History, 1929–1948* (Brill 2016) and two Hungarian-language books: *Német múltfeldolgozás. Beszélgetések történészekkel a huszadik század kulcskérdéseiről* ('The German process of dealing with the past: conversations with historians on key questions of the twentieth century', Kijárat 2016) and *Felvilágosult vallás és modern katasztrófa közt. Magyar zsidó gondolkodás a Horthy-korban* ('Between enlightened religion and modern catastrophe: Hungarian Jewish thought in the Horthy Era', Osiris 2014). He is Assistant Professor of History at Maastricht University.

Diana Mishkova is Professor of Modern History and Director of the Centre for Advanced Study in Sofia, Bulgaria. Her latest books include: *Beyond Balkanism: The Scholarly Politics of Region Making* (Routledge 2018), *European Regions and Boundaries: A Conceptual History* (co-edited with Balázs Trencsényi, Berghahn 2017) and *Entangled Histories of the Balkans, Vol. II: Transfers of Political Ideologies and Institutions* (co-edited with Roumen Daskalov, Brill 2014). She has published widely on the history of Southeastern Europe and intellectual history and has taught at universities in the United States, Switzerland, Greece, Sweden and Hungary.

John Neubauer was the author of a wide range of publications on Central and Eastern European literature, German and European Romanticism, music and literature, cultural history and comparative literature, including the landmark four-volume *History of the Literary Cultures of East-Central Europe* (co-edited with Marcel Cornis-Pope, John Benjamins 2004–2010). Other works include *The Exile and Return of Writers from East-Central Europe: A Compendium* (De Gruyter 2009) and *The Fin-de-Siècle Culture of Adolescence* (Yale 1992). A leading figure in rethinking literary history from a global and transnational perspective, he was Professor of Literary Studies at the University of Amsterdam. Sadly, John passed away in October 2015.

Joachim von Puttkamer is Co-Director of the Imre Kertész Kolleg and Chair of Eastern European History at the Friedrich Schiller University of Jena. He has published widely on the histories of nationalism, state-building and statehood, education and security apparatuses, as well as on cultures of memory and political thought in the region. He is the author of the survey history *Ostmitteleuropa im 19. und 20. Jahrhundert* ('East Central Europe in the 19th and

List of contributors

20th centuries', Oldenbourg 2010), *1956- (nieco) inne spojrzenie* ('1956: A Somewhat Different Perspective', co-edited with Jerzy Kochanowski, Neriton 2016) and is co-editor of numerous publications including *From Revolution to Uncertainty: The Year 1990 in Central and Eastern Europe* (Routledge 2019) and *Catastrophe and Utopia: Jewish Intellectuals in Central and Eastern Europe in the 1930s and 1940s* (De Gruyter 2017).

Guido Snel is a writer, translator and a senior lecturer teaching in the department of European Studies, University of Amsterdam. He specializes in contemporary European literatures, with a specific focus on Central and Eastern Europe and the Balkans. He has recently contributed to *Claiming the Dispossession: The Politics of Hi/storytelling in Post-Imperial Europe* (Brill 2017) and *The Novel and Europe: Imagining the Continent in Post-1945 Fiction* (Palgrave Macmillan 2016).

Balázs Trencsényi is the author of *The Politics of 'National Character': A Study in Interwar East European Thought* (Routledge 2012), co-author of *A History of Modern Political Thought in East Central Europe: Negotiating Modernity: History of Modern Political Thought in East-Central Europe*, vols. I–II (Oxford 2016–2018) and co-editor of the series *Discourses of Collective Identity in Central and Southeast Europe, 1775–1945* (CEU 2006–2014) as well as *European Regions and Boundaries: A Conceptual History* (co-edited with Diana Mishkova, Berghahn 2017). Professor of History at Central European University, he has held fellowships at the Wissenschaftskolleg zu Berlin, the Institute for Human Sciences in Vienna and the Centre for Advanced Study in Sofia.

VOLUME INTRODUCTION: INTELLECTUAL HORIZONS

Włodzimierz Borodziej, Ferenc Laczó and Joachim von Puttkamer

When historians conceptualize horizons, they tend to draw on Reinhart Koselleck's famed distinction between 'space of experience' and 'horizon of expectations'. In Koselleck's spatial metaphor, as history remained essentially static prior to modernity, the 'horizon of expectations' used to be limited by the known past. It was only when this horizon expanded towards the hitherto unknown and became increasingly detached from the 'space of experience' that progress became conceivable at all. As a result, our sense of historical time fundamentally changed.[1]

For the purposes of the present volume, the editors and authors have conceptualized the notion of horizons in somewhat different ways. The volume rather addresses the range of interpretations by which Central and Eastern Europeans tried to assign meaning to their specific experiences within modernity, from which they in turn derived notions of historical trajectories – usually from a specific national or regional past to a similarly distinct national or regional future. More concretely, *Intellectual Horizons* presents interpretative overviews of six key areas in the intellectual and cultural history of Central and Eastern Europe in the twentieth century. The thematic fields – in strict alphabetical order – of history writing, literary cultures, political thought, religion, spatial conceptualizations and television are explored by reputed scholars from Central and Eastern Europe and countries farther west. The six main contributors, John Connelly, Maciej Górny, Anikó Imre, Diana Mishkova, Balázs Trencsényi and the late John Neubauer not only draw on the most recent scholarship in their respective areas to fulfil expectations raised by the handbook format, but repeatedly combine such coverage with original explorations into representative samples of primary documents. What they thereby accomplish are effective synopses that offer numerous original insights into the often-underestimated diversity of Central and Eastern European intellectual and cultural life in the twentieth century. It is hoped that the present volume as a whole may thus help attenuate the continued underrepresentation of local intellectual and cultural traditions in a pan-European context.

These six contributions to intellectual and cultural history pursue neither the type of regional approach that would depict Central and Eastern European countries as sharing essential similarities, nor a methodologically nationalistic one in which the particularisms of the individual countries would predetermine their interpretative agenda and the basic structuring of the material. While individual authors may follow one slightly more than the other, the overall approach of the volume is comparative and transnational in practically equal measure. While certainly not

---

1 Reinhart Koselleck, '"Space of Experience" and "Horizon of Expectation": Two Historical Categories', in idem, *Futures Past: On the Semantics of Historical Time* (New York: Columbia University Press, 2004), 255–76 (first printed in 1985).

xvi

Volume introduction: intellectual horizons

without valuable precedents in previous epochs, such a comparative and transnational history of Central and Eastern Europe in the twentieth century can currently be pursued under the significantly more conducive circumstances of European integration. This is not to deny that researchers who are committed to such a project continue to face daunting challenges – not least of all linguistic ones – in a widely heterogeneous area which lacks substantial mechanisms of regional scholarly integration.

The book begins with an overview of the twentieth-century intellectual history of a highly debated question: Diana Mishkova covers the attempts made within a host of Central and Eastern European countries to develop spatial concepts, describe the key characteristics of regional units (historical or otherwise) and delimit their boundaries. Mishkova's contribution draws on several major methodological currents in intellectual history while placing a clear emphasis on conceptual analysis. She not only explores a wide variety of spatial and, more concretely, regional conceptualizations, several of which continue to pose as alternatives in the early twenty-first century, but also reveals the repeated transformation of the primary contexts, basic ambitions and intellectual-political stakes of such discussions. Through drawing such a detailed and nuanced panorama, Mishkova makes an important contribution to the self-reflection and self-historicization of historians that is of special relevance for the entire series of handbooks on twentieth-century Central and Eastern Europe.

Balázs Trencsényi draws on a similarly impressive variety of intriguing and previously underexplored sources to offer a synopsis of Central and Eastern European political thought. While focusing on key topics in political ideological discourses of the twentieth century in a broad regional and comparative framework, Trencsényi also proves highly sensitive to the critical role of intellectual transfers as well as the recurrent discrepancies between their contents and local – political and social – realities. Beyond the plethora of specific insights his contribution offers, the author also shows the ways in which scholarship on Central and Eastern Europe may help us rethink the European tradition of political thought; his chapter, similar to Mishkova's preceding one, amounts to a major step in the direction of de-provincializing Western Europe.

After the loss of faith in the grand narratives of literary history, John Neubauer's study in the literary cultures of Central and Eastern Europe, which is delightfully humorous at times, evokes the exceptional creativity and key dilemmas of a fine selection of literary authors in an age largely defined by the brutal intrusion of history and politics. Tragically, John Neubauer's erudite contribution to this volume will serve as the ultimate statement of a great literary scholar; beyond all expectations, Neubauer made heroic efforts into the very last days of his life to improve his chapter manuscript and had very nearly managed to complete it by the time of his departure in the autumn of 2015. Based on agreements made prior to the author's untimely departure, the manuscript was subsequently further enriched through contributions by the late Endre Bojtár and was eventually completed with essential help from Guido Snel.

In the subsequent, fourth chapter on history writing, Maciej Górny chiefly pursues a transnational approach to explore the transfer to and adaptations of crucial historiographical innovations in Central and Eastern Europe. His marked interest in major waves of transfer, however, does not lead the author to a facile emphasis on the 'Europeanness' of these historiographic traditions. Górny is too sensitive to asynchronies for that and keenly aware how historians in Central and Eastern Europe often tried to make a virtue out of their theoretical and methodological eclecticism. Ultimately, the author rather conceptualizes Central and Eastern European historiography as a semi-peripheral area in relatively close contact with major continental centres of scholarship but which fall short of being an equal partner to them: openness, exposure and indebtedness are key ideas organizing his rich narrative of history writing.

If Górny had a somewhat stronger emphasis on the transnational dimensions of a key facet of intellectual activities in twentieth-century Central and Eastern Europe, John Connelly's chapter on religion proves more interested in comparing and contrasting the countries under scrutiny. In our post-secular moment when controversies about religions appear to have returned to the very heart of cultural and political argument, Connelly untangles the complex relation between religious institutions, local states, national identities and levels of modernization across the many ruptures of the twentieth century. With its focus on the dominant Christian Churches, Connelly's chapter finds original ways to place the remarkably diverse countries of Central and Eastern Europe on the global map and is thereby able to contribute novel arguments to the secularization debate.

Last but certainly not least, Anikó Imre adds a thorough coverage of television history, which clearly belongs among the most exciting new subjects in cultural history. Imre provides a multidimensional and in many ways original analysis, in turn tackling the foundational ideas and agendas, the institutional contexts, and the gradual evolution of television programming. By highlighting notable similarities and interconnections across the Iron Curtain in the post-war moment of stability, Imre's chapter counters a number of false conceptions, of anti-communist inspiration or otherwise, to arrive at a well-rounded and balanced assessment of Central and Eastern European television history during the rise of consumerism but before its thorough post-communist commercialization.

The preference given to these six major topical areas over others was very much the result of conscious choices. In accordance with the main ambition of the volume, i.e. to explore intellectual horizons, the primary focus is on key topics in intellectual history. At the same time, select themes in cultural history, such as religion or visual cultures, have been included as well. However, the final selection of subjects was also partly due to perceived balances of the volume and other similarly pragmatic considerations. In recent years, research efforts into Central and Eastern European history writing, literary cultures, political thought, religion, spatial conceptualizations and television have all reached impressive new heights. While our knowledge of all six themes has greatly increased as a result, and the study of these themes has also greatly diversified in the process, the tendency has been to publish on these topics in rather large formats, in volumes of many hundreds or even thousands of pages. Our guiding idea, therefore, was to invite leading scholars in their respective fields who have typically been involved in such larger and empirically more detailed projects and ask them to compose rather brief and accessible interpretative overviews. The themes explored in the individual chapters are to be understood as exemplary case studies – a volume of this scope could not hope to additionally cover such vast fields as the visual arts, the history of music, science and philosophy, or the formation and role of the intellectual classes and 'expert knowledge', all of which would be similarly deserving of comparable overviews. The hope is that the more accessible format of the chapters in this volume will prove useful to fellow professional historians and advanced students of Central and Eastern Europe and, more broadly, to all humanities scholars interested in modern and contemporary Europe.

1

SPATIAL CONFIGURATIONS

Regional intellectual imageries in twentieth-century Central and Eastern Europe

Diana Mishkova

This chapter explores supranational geographies, against the backdrop of dramatic developments in twentieth-century European history, produced by several generations of intellectuals in Central and Eastern Europe through consideration of the meaning they assigned to these regional concepts and the cultural-historical ('civilizational') self-identification and self-positioning associated with them. Underlying this is an understanding of space and borders as related to the premises of their social production, the ideological underpinnings behind such production and the various forms of interpretation and representation that they embody. Admittedly, such an approach underscores the intimate relation between space on the one hand and the formation of identities and identity politics on the other. Regionalizations in this sense can be described as the lexicalized expression of processes of self-reflection and self-description condensed into spatial terminology, and regions as broad spatial metaphors, semantic markers and ideologemes.

There have been various modes of spatialization: territorial but also cultural-linguistic (such as 'Slavic Europe'), federalist or pan-ideological (e.g. 'socialist world'), conceptualizations of liminal spaces (as captured by concepts or metaphors such as the bridge, in-betweenness or cultural synthesis) or central spaces (such as the myths of the middle or centre), as well as discourses of othering through spatialization (orientalism, occidentalism or Balkanism). This chapter takes into account all these forms of spatialization, however, it focuses on the meta-regions of 'Europe', the 'East' and the 'West' as well as the 'historical regions' of Eastern Europe: (East) Central Europe, the Balkans/Southeastern Europe and Slavic Europe. Its structure reflects the major turning points in the history of the region, which also signalled major shifts in terms of cultural and geopolitical orientation: the turns of the nineteenth and twentieth centuries, the interwar years, the post-First World War period and the post-1989 era.

The chronological span this chapter covers is broad enough to warrant a rigorous yet (hopefully) representative selection of authors whose work conveys some sense of the various forms of regionalization and the arguments that have supported them. It does not attempt to create a more or less comprehensive tableau of often highly individualized spatial representations and types of self-identification. For similar reasons, together with inevitable linguistic limitations, we have restricted our coverage of 'East Central Europe' mainly to Bulgaria, Czechoslovakia,

Hungary, Poland, Romania and Yugoslavia. Obviously, such constriction does not do justice to different nations that have traditionally been considered part of the region, such as Albania, Greece and the Baltic countries, while others, such as the German, Ottoman and Russian Empires, are only given consideration to the extent that they proved instrumental in generating (typically rival) spatial visions of their European successor states. The chosen sample of spatial conceptualizations of nations is nevertheless deemed illustrative enough to allow reflection on the way the region itself had previously been conceived and thus helps us to historicize and reflect more on our own usage of spatial terminology.

Turn-of-the-century spatial imageries

Fin de siècle visions of Europe and the East–West divide

Even if the East–West divide originated in Western Europe at the time of the Enlightenment, 'Eastern Europe' partook heavily in its semantic conceptualization, with the result that Eastern concepts about the West often preceded Western ones. Problems stemming from asymmetrical power relations were not the only reason for this. On the one hand, Europe and the West operated, especially before the First World War, as 'unmarked concepts', the contents of which were usually taken for granted and rarely specifically thematized. At the same time, however, the meaning of 'Europe' and its later hypostasis 'the West', supported and indeed came to constitute an integral component of debates on fundamental issues, such as modernization, (economic, political or social) reform, and above all, national identity. Definitions of Europe functioned primarily as a symbolic means or instrument for (re)defining and (re)constructing the nation, as a yardstick for national self-evaluation and a symbolic counterpoint to identity in which orientalism and occidentalism interacted dialectically. In this sense 'Europe', the 'East' and the 'West', operate as spatial categories of a formative symbolic order and at higher levels of abstraction when compared with categories such as (East) Central Europe, Southeastern Europe or the Slavic world, which were themselves defined with regard to these 'higher' concepts.

The nineteenth-century Eastern European conceptualizations of Europe and the West, which transcended or connected national and subnational readings, have had a controversial legacy. Part of this legacy created an image of Europe (and an attendant 'Occident') as a normative horizon and a metageographical notion: a metonymy of modernity and civilization or a set of values whose rejection could take place in the geographical West at the same time that 'the true West could be found wherever [these values] were seriously advocated and defended'.[1] Acts of regionalization in this context involved a complex, symbolic, geographical negotiation with the West and the 'further East'. Essentially this was a process of self-inclusion: Europe was considered to be 'our home', or was even created by 'us', and the various Eastern European nations performed important European missions (typically *antemurale Christianitatis*, or 'bulwark of Christianity', vis-à-vis 'Oriental' Russia and the Turks and/or creating a 'bridge' between the East and the West).

In parallel to this, the nineteenth century bequeathed a set of meanings that implied self-exclusion of Eastern Europe. 'Europe' often came to be viewed as the cultural 'other' and a quasi-colonial threat to Eastern European nations either in the form of destroying national

---

1 Zoran Milutinović, *Getting over Europe: The Construction of Europe in Serbian Culture* (Amsterdam: Rodopi, 2011), 71. Luisa Passerini speaks in this sense of 'Europe as an Elsewhere', in *Europe in Love, Love in Europe: Imagination and Politics in Britain between the Wars* (London: I.B. Tauris, 1999), 11.

Spatial configurations

'organicity' or the Great Powers obstructing national independence (or both simultaneously). Occasionally such notions of (Western) Europe also involved self-peripheralization, an 'exteriority complex'[2] and victimhood, in which 'we' represented the oriental, incomplete or non-European peoples, defenceless prey for the more powerful. In this configuration, the 'Slavic world' – yet another inheritance from the nineteenth century – functioned as a cultural and geopolitical alternative for pursuing a particular liminal 'space' that was both included in and maintained a certain distance from Europe.

In many ways, Jovan Skerlić's work, perhaps the most influential Serbian intellectual and literary scholar at the turn of the twentieth century, epitomizes this nineteenth-century tradition of conceptualizing Europe and the West, while it also anticipates some expressions of anti-Westernism that will surface in a considerably more radicalized form in the decades after the First World War.[3] For Skerlić, Europe – a term he used more frequently than any other Serbian author – was synonymous with modernity, and westernization was the only road to survival for the Serbs. Europe's intrinsic attributes – energy, initiative, work, democracy, socialism, optimism, rationalism, secularism, education and progress – were value-laden and absolute in the sense that everything he perceived as subverting these values (such as the 'Byzantine spirit and Russian theology', and also European Romanticism) was characterized as 'non-Western' and of the Orient, degenerative and doomed to death. For Skerlić, the East or the Orient, located in Asia and Russia (save for the Russian socialists), was an illness and an evil that should be fought against. Skerlić's East, in the words of the Serbian philosopher Vladimir Vujić, was 'lazy, fatalistic, dirty, indolent, regressive', a part of the world plagued by 'darkness, ignorance, slavery, sluggishness and filth'.[4] 'That gummed-up, sleepy, disgusting East is still in and around us', Skerlić wrote at the beginning of the new century, maintaining:

> We are suffocating in this passive, stale, Oriental spirit, and there is only one cure for us: to open wide the door to the West and its ideas, to the West which thinks, which acts, which creates, which lives a full and intensive life, the only life that deserves to be called human.[5]

Consequently, the war the Balkan countries waged against the Ottoman Empire in 1912 was described as the 'last act of a magnificent historical drama: the struggle between Europe and Asia, civilization and barbarity'.[6] By fully assimilating the West's basic values, Serbia would *become* the West; staying with the 'disgusting East' would spell not only its stagnation but its death.

On the other hand, the equation of a notion of Europe with a definite set of values conducive to modernity – that had a modern *mentalité* – made it possible for Skerlić to question the 'Europeanness' of Europe and expose her dark side whenever she acted against her own ideals, specifically a Europe of arrogant power, egoism and mercantilism. Recapitulating its policies towards the Balkans in the nineteenth century, he concluded the following:

---

2 Wendy Bracewell, 'The Limits of Europe in East European Travel Writing', in *Under Eastern Eyes: A Comparative Introduction to East European Travel Writing on Europe*, eds Wendy Bracewell and Alex Drace-Francis (Budapest: CEU Press, 2008), 112.

3 The following paragraphs draw largely on Milutinović, *Getting over Europe*, 59–80.

4 Vladimir Vujić, *Sputana i oslobodjena misao* [Hampered and liberated thought] (Belgrade: Algoritam, 2006 [1931]), 195.

5 Quoted in Milutinović, *Getting over Europe*, 73.

6 Ibid., 60.

> What is called Europe is actually a cluster of mutually envious, predatory and soulless bullies, who have not been able to agree upon how to share their booty, and who have their own interests in artificially keeping alive this living corpse called Turkey, which is a disgrace and permanent threat to civilization. ... Had it depended on the humanity of a Christian and civilized Europe, which masked its selfishness and greed with false claims in the interest of peace, the Balkans would today be one huge graveyard.[7]

The trope of Europe as the cultural self and the political other that is characteristic of Skerlić's work, as well as in contemporary Bulgarian debates, did not disappear completely after the First World War but was to a great extent marginalized by alternative and far more radically articulated critical visions of Europe.

The late nineteenth- and early twentieth-century Polish discourse on Europe and the West built upon a similarly controversial tradition. In the nineteenth century, one could identify two types of meaning in the Polish discourse on Europe. One identified Europe with the West and implied that Poland had a special role within it as a shield against 'Asian barbarism' and a transmitter to the Eastern Slavs of the West's values and ideals – a vision captured by the recurrent trope of *antemurale Christianitatis* (and related tropes like 'the knight of Europe' or 'the Christ of Europe'). A different cultural geography, rooted in Romantic ethnocentrism and Slavophilism, presented an image of a Europe as divided into the (Latin) West and (Slavic) East, in which Poland, as the purest incarnation of Slavic principles, functioned as the natural leader of all Eastern European nations, including the benighted empire to the east.[8] For many of those who went into exile after the 1830 and 1863 uprisings, the West became synonymous with egoism, cold rationalism, pursuit of economic gain, materialism and superficiality. In contrast, Slavic Europe stood for spiritual and moral integrity, a love of freedom, equality and social solidarity that had its roots in 'ancient Slavic communalism'.[9]

Polish positivism resolved this perceived dichotomy. The late nineteenth-century Cracow School of History promoted a vision of Europe that was allied to Western Christianity and Latin civilization. The founder of the school, Walerian Kalinka, wrote in 1879 that 'Just as Latin divides Europe from Asia and where knowledge of Latin ends, there was the border of real Europe, thus the difference in alphabets has pushed the nations which adopted them in different directions as to history and civilization'.[10] Notwithstanding some dissident voices such as Józef Szujski's that pointed to a rift between Polish and Western historical developments since the fifteenth century, the Cracow school instilled in the Poles the idea of the fundamentally Western and Latin character of Polish culture and Poland's state of belonging to Western European civilization, a thesis that endured unquestioned until the Second World War. In 1915 the renowned historian Oswald Balzer compellingly argued that Poland's history can only be properly understood as constituting not an unusual path of development but a variant of the Western pattern.[11]

---

7 Ibid., 60.

8 Jerzy Jedlicki, *A Suburb of Europe: Nineteenth-Century Polish Approaches to Western Civilization* (Budapest: CEU Press, 1999); and Barbara Törnquist-Plewa, 'The Complex of an Unwanted Child: The Meaning of Europe in Polish Discourse', in *The Meaning of Europe: Variety and Contention Within and Among Nations*, eds Mikael af Malmborg and Bo Stråth (Oxford: Berg, 2002), 217–22.

9 Andrzej Walicki, *Poland between East and West: The Controversies over Self-Definition and Modernization in Partitioned Poland* (Cambridge, MA: Harvard University Press, 1994), 20–3.

10 Quoted in Törnquist-Plewa, 'The Complex of an Unwanted Child', 227.

11 M.B. Biskupski, 'Marceli Handelsman (1882–1945)', in *Nation and History: Polish Historians from the Enlightenment to the Second World War*, eds Peter Brock, et al. (Toronto: University of Toronto Press, 2006), 352–85, here 358–60.

Spatial configurations

The salience of discourse on the East–West divide in Poland, with a certain degree of similarity to that in Romania, was inextricably bound up with the perceived necessity to differentiate the country from its immediate neighbours to the east and the west: Russia and Germany. The Polish discussions were characterized by the omnipresence of Russia as a point of reference for Poland's identity. Andrzej Walicki argues that, in the Polish context, the concept of Latin civilization itself marks the civilizational separation between Poles and Russians.[12] Mieczysław B. Biskupski speaks of two Polish 'Easts'. First, there is a large, amorphous East, posited rather than analyzed, which includes Islamic civilization, the Tatars and the Ottoman Empire. Second, there is another quasi- or 'attributed' East, which includes Russian civilization and to a considerable degree also the Orthodox world in general and, at times, the notion of a Slavic civilization, suggesting a prominent role for Russia.[13] More than a few nineteenth-century Polish historians took part in developing a cluster of spatial, temporal and civilizational Polish markers of identification, which drew upon binaries that essentialized the differences between Poles and Russians and in which the East–West dualism was often racially delineated. Consequently, Bronisław Trentkowski posited these differences within a larger 'struggle of Europeanism and Asianism', Franciszek Duchiński and Wincenty Lutosławski talked of a 'broader civilizational struggle' based on racial conflict between Aryan Poles and Turanian, and so non-Slav, Russians and Józef Szujski saw the cultural clash between East and West as 'one of the fundamental certainties of history'.[14] Civilizational antagonism between Poles and Russians continued to underwrite visions of West and East at the turn of the century and beyond the First World War in the works of historians such as Władysław Smoleński, Jan Kucharzewski, Wacław Sobieski and Bogumił Jasinowski.[15] These visions fit comfortably with the one espoused by Poland's leading political groups, both on the right and left, at the turn of the century. The ideological fathers of Polish ethnonationalism – Roman Dmowski, Jan Ludwik Popławski and Zygmunt Balicki – saw Europe as divided into eastern and western parts. East for them meant Russia, which belonged to Europe geographically but not culturally; it epitomized economic backwardness, poverty, disorder, alcoholism, sloth and debased manners. The West stood for technological progress, prosperity, order, a strong work ethic, respect for law – in a word, civilization. Ethnonationalists, conservatives and socialists were united in insisting that Poland's place was in Europe, and so the West.[16] By emphasizing its Western elements, however, Poland risked falling into a Central Europe dominated and shaped by Germany. The question of whether the greatest danger to Poland came from the east

---

12 Andrzej Walicki, *Rosija, katocicyzm, i sprawa polske* [Russia, Catholicism, and the Polish question] (Warsaw: Prószyński i S-ka, 2002), 366–7.

13 M.B. Biskupski, 'Polish Conceptions of Unity and Division in Europe: Speculation and Policy', in *Domains and Divisions of European History*, eds Johann Arnason and Natalie Doyle (Liverpool: Liverpool University Press, 2010), 95–6.

14 On the negative image of Russia in Polish thought, see Michal Bohun, 'Oblicza obsesji – negatywny obraz Rosji w myśli polskiej' [Faces of obsessions – the negative image of Russia in Polish thought], in *Katalog wzajemnych uprzedzen Polakow i Rosjan*, ed. Andrzeja de Lazari (Warsaw: PISM, 2006), 203–302 (also accessible at www.pism.pl/files/?id_plik=3374).

15 See Mirosław Filipowicz, *Wobec Rosji. Studia z dziejów historiografii polskiej od końca XIX wieku po II wojnę światową* [Against Russia. Studies in the history of Polish historiography from the late nineteenth century to the Second World War] (Lublin: Instytut Europy Środkowo-Wschodniej, 2000); and Rafal Sobiecki, 'Rosja i Rosjanie w polskiej myœli historycznej XIX i XX wieku' [Russia and Russians in Polish historical thought of the nineteenth and twentieth centuries], in de Lazari, *Katalog wzajemnych uprzedzen Polakow i Rosjan*, 159–201 (also accessible at www.pism.pl/files/?id_plik=3373).

16 On the Occidentalism of the socialist literary and social critic Stanisław Brzozowski, see Törnquist-Plewa, 'The Complex of an Unwanted Child', 229.

or from the west, and respectively whether Poland should pursue an active Eastern- or Western-oriented policy, was a major divisive issue among the politicians of the Second Polish Republic. Several generations of Polish intellectuals, therefore, felt an overwhelming compulsion to balance between the competing needs of drawing a stark contrast with the East on the one hand, and asserting Poland's non-German Westernness on the other.[17]

Romania's position between Russia and the Dual Monarchy spurred civilizational maps similar to the Polish map. The deeply entrenched idea that Romania is intimately connected to the West, especially to France – what Sorin Antohi has called 'geocultural bovarism' – was derived from several controversial sources.[18] One was the notion, compellingly cultivated since the eighteenth century, of the Roman origin of the Romanians. Another was the perceived threat to Romania as a Latin island surrounded by a Slavic sea, which was occasionally sublimated in a peculiar *mission civilisatrice* for the Romanians in the Slavic East. Yet another was the long-standing historical and cultural links with the 'Balkan Orient', including their Orthodox Christianity, which buttressed successive cycles of collective self-Balkanization, de-Balkanization and re-Balkanization. In both Romania and Bulgaria before the First World War, the East–West and European–Slavic points of reference in the mainstream cultural debate did not function out of the pros and cons of imitating the West per se, but around its mechanistic and superficial character, which was held respon-sible for the inorganic development of these societies. Significantly, this critical view unfolded against the backdrop of a general faith in evolutionary improvement and in the benefits – indeed inescapability – of overall Europeanization, provided that the 'rules of history' were observed, meaning the gradual synchronization of the nation's temporality with that of Europe.

Divergences in interpretations of the East and the West notwithstanding, the majority of intellectuals in East Central Europe – from Serbia and Bulgaria to Poland and 'Latin' Romania – referred to Europe as a natural, normative horizon for their nations, while taking for granted Europe's existence as a specific political, geographic, economic and cultural sphere. As has already been noted, before the First World War, Europe did not, as a rule, function as a *marked* concept – a label that allowed focused reflection on its nature or identity.[19] Discussing the Czech case, Miroslav Hroch has argued:

> The word 'Europe' was very frequently used as *terminus technicus* of geography or even politics, without being conceptualized as a classificatory scheme. Reflections on Europe as a quality, as a dimension of national identity were rather rare in Czech dis-course, compared for instance to similar reflections on the relationship with Germans, or on the Slavic identity. ... The concept of Europe never played a dominating, decisive role in Czech national discourse and not even in Czech political vocabulary. It never became a mobilizing slogan of politics, despite the fact that from the end of the nineteenth century the mostly spontaneously accepted European horizon strongly influenced the concept of Czech culture.[20]

---

17 Biskupski, 'Polish Conceptions of Unity and Division', 96.

18 On the notion of 'cultural bovarism', see Sorin Antohi, 'Romania and the Balkans: From Geocultural Bovarism to Ethnic Ontology', *Tr@nsit online*, no. 21 (2002), www.iwm.at/transit-online/romania-and-the-balkans/(accessed 29 January 2020).

19 Peter Bugge, 'Longing or Belonging? Czech Perceptions of Europe in the Interwar Years and Today', *Yearbook of European Studies* 11 (1999): 111–29, here 113.

20 Miroslav Hroch, 'The Czech Discourse on Europe, 1848–1948', in Malmborg and Stråth, *The Meaning of Europe*, 247, 259. 'This under-representation', Hroch adds, 'did not chance until the 1990s when, on the contrary, the concept of Europe became a very fashionable component of cultural and political rhetoric' (247).

Spatial configurations

The reasoning laid out by František Palacký and adopted by Tomáš G. Masaryk was simple: national aspirations are an expression of the development of European civilization towards a pluralistic civil society. Accepting European values, therefore, obliged the Czechs to carry on and strengthen their national movement.[21] This vision continued to inform the Czech national movement at the beginning of the twentieth century. It took the Europeanism of the Czechs for granted and asserted the historical agency of the Czech world, placing its struggle for national and civic freedom at the very vanguard of European events.

Yet the Czech mindset vis-à-vis Europe, similar to that of the Serbs, had another side that ultimately created a contentious, dualistic vision. This other side to the national mindset defined Europe as a different world to that of the Czechs – a foreign, hostile, even inhuman one with which a battle must be waged for the Czechs' independence. 'Both the acceptance of Europe as an appropriate context for Czech matters as well as the perception of Europe as a foreign and hostile world', the semiotician Vladimír Macura observes, 'served a single goal: to demonstrate the special and important values of the Czech question'.[22] His conclusion can be extended to the other national cases we have referred to here: 'The Czech world is simply obsessed with the desire to be seen and appreciated by Europe', yet 'On the other hand, when the "Czech world" declares itself to be "European", it does not try to hide its desire for dissimilarity and otherness.'[23] The distinctiveness in question, in all Slavic national contexts apart from the Polish one, drew on an imaginary space that was an 'improvement' to the European one: the 'world of the Slavs'. Macura rightly suggests that there is an interface with, rather than antagonistic relation to, the notion of Europe here in that the Slavic world was seen to possess a different value system, yet it was imbued with traditional European values: 'In fact, it personifies Europe in a more authentic and pure form, whereas modern Europe has abandoned these values.'[24] The idea of a new Slavic civilization was invoked as a return to original values, nature and fundamental human relationships; it symbolized the effort to replace the prestigious values attributed to Europe (technology, wealth, high culture and cognition) with 'another value, immeasurable and absolute'.[25]

It is easy to discern the influence of Russian Slavophilism in this 'patheticization of Slavism'. But there were important Czech specificities to it. Czech Slavism can only be understood against the backdrop of German cultural domination, in which the Slavic element entailed radical separation from the Germans, the creation of a different past and a different future. In indirect polemical relation to Leopold von Ranke's metaphor about Europe being the child of a 'Germanic–Romance marriage', the Czechs promoted the idea of a marriage between Europe and the Slavs.[26]

Neo-Slavism

The turn-of-the-century idea of a Slavic world was a geocultural image rooted in the pan-ideology of neo-Slavism, a term that was intended to distinguish it from the older pan-Slavism, which cut across 'territorial' regions. This notion capitalized on a scholarly discourse with a

---

21 Hroch, 'Czech Discourse on Europe', 249–51.
22 Vladimír Macura, *The Mystification of a Nation: 'The Potato Bug' and Other Essays on Czech Culture* (Madison, WI: University of Wisconsin Press, 2010), 15.
23 Ibid., 16.
24 Ibid., 17.
25 Ibid., 18.
26 Ibid.

long tradition in comparative ethnography and linguistics, which Ernest Renan once described as 'comparative philology transported into the political field'.[27] Its ideological underpinnings and dialectical relation to pan-Germanism, however, endowed it with meanings and aspirations that were only remotely connected with the agenda and actual findings of comparative Slavistics. Apocalyptic Romantic visions kept feeding into messianic images, such as the one that gave shape to the popular Czech poet Svatopluk Cecil's poem 'Slavie' (1884), which voiced the fervent belief that only a united Slavic world under Russia's leadership would be able to save Europe from impending catastrophe. But although the *fin de siècle* variant of pan-Slavism took on board many of the themes of its national-romantic pedigree, it was palpably more pragmatic. According to Stefan Bobchev, the most active Bulgarian proponent of the movement, although it was basically a 'development of the theories of the great Slavophil [sic] leaders', it also differed substantially in that

> the abstract and mystical doctrine of the old Slavophiles was replaced by a healthier and more practical outlook, and the earlier belief was relinquished, that the Slavs had a special mission to fulfil and possessed a peculiar type of character and civilization which set them apart from the Latin West and the Teutons. The new movement laid stress on the kinship of the Slavonic nations and the need for a cultural, economic and political commonwealth.[28]

The driving force and mastermind behind this new 'Slavic idea' was Karel Kramář, the leader of the national-liberal Young Czech Party that represented burgeoning Czech industrial interests in the Austrian Reichsrat. As conceived by Kramář and the Young Czechs, neo-Slavism was at once a strategy of creating a counterweight to the Germans in the Dual Monarchy and the wider region through a 'Slav policy' ('We Slavs must imitate [the Germans]', Kramář wrote[29]) and a quasi-colonial project of opening up Balkan and Russian markets to Czech banks and industry. The neo-Slav programme was formulated at the Petersburg Conference (1907) and the pan-Slav congresses in Prague (1908) and Sofia (1910), which came to the conclusion that the Slavs 'must regard themselves as equal members of the great Slavonic family', that each Slav nation must be 'enabled to develop its individuality freely, independently and in its own way', and that cultural and particularly economic cooperation between Slavic nations should be enhanced.[30] In his opening address to the Prague congress, Kramář formulated the stakes of Slav cooperation in the following terms:

> We bring to the world peace and love; we don't wish to overthrow any throne or to destroy any empire or state. We wish only to feel ourselves one great whole held together by common cultural interests, lest we fall, in disunity and discord, one after the other, under the pressure of an overly-powerful organized and planned cultural and economic expansion. This consciousness that it is to the advantage of all of us to join together for cultural and economic work, brought us here, and the iron necessity

---

27 Quoted in Paul Edward Corcoran, 'The Political Thought of Ernest Renan' (PhD diss., Duke University 1970), 234.

28 Stephen Bobčev, 'The Slavs after the War', *Slavonic Review* 6 (1927): 291.

29 Paul Vyšný, *Neo-Slavism and the Czechs, 1898–1914* (Cambridge: Cambridge University Press, 1977), 30.

30 Ibid., 291.

of the common danger will oblige us, not to separate ourselves but to work with all our force for the strengthening of the fraternity and solidarity of the Slav peoples, free and equal among themselves.[31]

Neo-Slavism was later criticized for its lack of a political programme and for overvaluing the benefits of stronger cultural and economic ties between the Slavic nations as a precondition for these nations' stronger civilizational representation in the European cultural and political arena. Its priorities and the rhetoric of mutual support, fraternity and unity were at times framed in racial and biological terms. However, accompanied by gestures of political loyalty, neo-Slavists proved ineffective in mitigating the contradictions and conflicts that weakened neo-Slav unity. The efforts to placate Russia led to the estrangement of the Ukrainians and the Poles; those who attempted to mollify Hungary estranged the Slovaks, while the idea of a rapprochement between Russia and Austria–Hungary as a precondition for the realization of the neo-Slav programme was deeply distasteful to the Balkan nations. An observation from Ukraine's leading historian at the time, Mykhailo Hrushevsky, illustrates the irreconcilable understandings of and approaches to the politics of Slav unity. He wrote:

> The basis of Neo-Slavism is a policy directed against the German people. This people has done no harm to the Ukrainians. Why should they who are oppressed by Russians and Poles act against the Germans? The anti-German Neo-Slavism is directed against Western civilization, which the Ukrainians will never abandon. Neo-Slavism is an instrument of reaction and we were and we always are on the side of progress.[32]

Russian reactions, on the other hand, were only weakly sympathetic, as only a few liberals supported the idea, whereas the majority of more conservative public opinion remained attached to the pan-Slavic ideas that focused on Orthodox Slavs. The ascendancy of the neo-Slav idea was, therefore, a brief one, extending from 1907 to 1910. In the post-war era, neo-Slavism's heritage would be exclusively claimed by the Czechs, while the South (Balkan) Slavs, especially the Serbs, would draw inspiration not from ideas about a 'cultural, economic and political commonwealth' but from the messianic philosophy of Russian Slavophilism.

Southeastern Europe as a cultural-historical space

By the end of the nineteenth century the Balkans had already emerged as a part of the political imagination within the Western mind. The military struggles for national unification, which culminated in the Balkan Wars (1912–13), stabilized the image of the Balkans as a violence-ridden region beset by ethnic conflict that posed a threat to European peace (an image that re-emerged during the wars of Yugoslav succession of the 1990s, reflecting back on a terminological distinction between the 'Balkan' wars and 'Southeastern European' peace). At the turn of the century, this negative representation was disseminated in numerous studies on Macedonia and 'the Macedonian Question', which presented the country as 'the Balkans in miniature'.[33]

---

31 Quoted in Hans Kohn, *Pan-Slavism: Its History and Ideology* (Notre Dame, IN: Vintage Books, 1960), 245–6.

32 Quoted in Kohn, *Pan-Slavism*, 244–5.

33 The book titles themselves were often evocative enough, e.g. Victor Bérard's *La Turquie et l'hellénisme contemporain. La Macédoine: Hellènes, Bulgares, Valaques, Albanais, Autrichiens, Serbes; la lutte des races* (Paris: F. Alcan, 1893).

The disintegration of the Ottoman Empire, the faltering modernization of small, weak, economically backward and dependent successor nation states, and the accompanying excesses of nationalism 'created a situation in which the Balkans began to serve as a symbol for the aggressive, intolerant, barbarian, semi-developed, semi-civilized, semi-oriental'.[34] Balkanism as a political (and popular) Western European discourse drew on this quasi-Orientalist metaphorical function of the term 'Balkan' and a great many local conceptualizations of the region took shape that were either in negotiation with or contested the term.

Remarkably, this largely external political deployment of the image of the Balkans at the turn of the century ran in parallel to the emergence of a local, cultural-historical conception of the region. It was spurred on by the rise of comparativist methodologies in a number of old and new disciplines (linguistics, philology, ethnography and folklore, ethnopsychology and sociology) and by political connections: the ultimate dismantling of 'Turkey-in-Europe', which ushered in the annexation of Bosnia-Herzegovina (in 1908) and the two Balkan Wars. It was also driven by a search for a larger, integrative cultural or civilizational space. Next to the creation of a state, the national culture had to be connected to its sister cultures in Europe and redraw, in the words of Mircea Eliade, 'the spiritual geographies of the world'.[35] For most of the nineteenth century the space in question was the Western world; from around the beginning of the twentieth century, alternative spaces, whether defined by genealogical affinity (e.g. the Slavic world) or with which the nation happened to have a direct and permanent interrelationship, began to be promoted in a more systematic way as possible mediators towards broader integration.

Promoting awareness of and research into Balkan linguistic communities and folklore/ethnography were the first areas where the concept of a Balkan historical common identity was deliberated. The 'Balkan linguistic area' or 'linguistic league' (*Sprachbund*) proved to be 'the first area of contact-induced language change to be identified as such' and *the* model prototype for language contact, interaction and convergence.[36] Indeed, it was linguists who first introduced the term 'Balkanism' to denote the opposite of fragmentation. In their use of the term, they referred to a lexical and, more indicatively, grammatical feature that was shared among the unrelated or only distantly related languages of the Balkans: the Balkan Slavic, Balkan Romance, Albanian, Greek and Balkan Turkish dialects. Although the notion (and the theory) of the linguistic union was only devised by Nikolai Trubetzkoy in 1920 – particularly in order to explain the internal coherence and external boundaries of 'Eurasia' – it drew from a long-standing linguistic tradition of viewing the Balkans as an area of confluence between disparate ethnicities and their tongues.

Generally speaking, ideas of migration, exchange and contact became fundamental for a number of academic fields around the turn of the twentieth century from linguistics and ethnology to literary studies and geography. Regional ethnographers and literary historians such

---

34 Maria Todorova, 'Balkanism and Postcolonialism or On the Beauty of the Airplane View', in *In Marx's Shadow: Knowledge, Power, and Intellectuals in Eastern Europe and Russia*, eds Costica Bradatan and Serguei Alex Oushakine (Lanham, MD: Lexington Books, 2010), 176; see also idem, *Imagining the Balkans* (Oxford: Oxford University Press, 1997).

35 Alexandru Zub, 'En quête d'une synthèse: l'historiographie roumaine au xixe siècle', *Nouvelle études d'histoires* 9 (1995): 99.

36 For Balkan linguistic unity, see Victor Friedman, 'Balkans as a Linguistic Area', in *Encyclopedia of Language & Linguistics*, ed. Keith Brown, 2nd edition, vol. 1 (Oxford: Elsevier, 2006), 657–72; and Jouko Lindstedt, 'Linguistic Balkanization: Contact-Induced Change by Mutual Reinforcement', in *Languages in Contact*, eds D. G. Gilbers, J. Nerbonne and J. Shaeken (Atlanta, GA: Rodopi, 2000), 231–46.

Spatial configurations

as the Bulgarian Ivan Shishmanov and the Romanian Ioan Bogdan contributed to this trend by undercutting a romantic belief in national uniqueness and substantiating the notion that the Balkans is an area of long-standing cultural interaction and exchange. Even so, their reflections on the points of transfer and the resultant similarities within this historical area did not produce a picture of a unified cultural space. Their implicit understanding of the region considered it to be a space in a state of flux where cultural osmosis took place based on long-standing processes of coexistence and interpenetration, the driving forces of which were national cultures.[37]

The Balkan scholar who has contributed the most to the cultural-historical definition of the region as early as the period before the First World War was Nicolae Iorga, the founder of the Institute of South-East European Studies (established in 1914). Iorga's 'Southeastern Europe' (as opposed to 'the Balkans' or the 'Balkan Peninsula' – geographical terms he deemed both inaccurate and unjustified for their lack of a unifying quality) included the area from the Carpathians to the Aegean and was thus coextensive with the 'Carpatho-Balkan' or 'Carpatho-Danubian' realm, incorporating the Romanians with the once Romanized inhabitants (the Vlachs) to the south of the Danube, that is, in the Balkans proper. In anthropogeographical terms, the region of Southeastern Europe was said to be the opposite of Eastern Europe, which Iorga considered to be identical with the 'Eurasian world'. Not only territorially but also semantically, Iorga's Southeastern Europe differed from the Ottoman and post-Ottoman Balkans; beneath its internal diversity and ethnic fragmentation there lurked a 'fundamental unity resting on archaic traditions', a historical, ethnographic and civilizational 'synthesis of a completely particular character common to the whole South-East of Europe'. This specificity, drawing upon the great Thraco-Illyrian-Roman tradition and epitomized by Byzantium, was taken over by the Ottoman Empire and constituted the heritage that all the Southeastern European peoples – Greeks, Bulgarians, Serbs, Romanians, Albanians and Turks – shared. At the same time, Iorga sought to dispel the idea of a Slavic world as a rival symbolic frame for the Balkan Slavs.[38]

The combination of national and regional registers and agendas was characteristic of these cultural-historical conceptualizations. While Iorga's *historical* notion of Southeastern Europe endorsed the unity of the Romanians from Transylvania in the north to Macedonia and Greece in the south, his *cultural* notion of Southeastern Europe emphasized the position of Romanians as the real transmitters of the Byzantine tradition after Byzantium had ceased to exist politically. His book *Byzance après Byzance* ('Byzantium after Byzantium') brilliantly exemplifies this synthesis of universal and national history through the mediation of regional history.[39]

Combining geomorphological, geophysical, geopolitical and ethno-psychological analyses, Jovan Cvijić, famous for being the founder of Balkan geology, geography and anthropogeography, outlined a scholarly interpretation of the inherent diversity of the Balkan Peninsula. What had typically been seen as an 'ethnographic museum', Cvijić reformulated into a much more complex

---

37 Ivan Shishmanov, *Izbrani suchinenia* [Selected works], vols 1–2 (Sofia: Izdatelstvo na BAN, 1965, 1966); and Ioan Bogdan, *Istoriografijia romană și problemele ei actuale* [Romanian historiography and its current problems] (Bucharest, 1905). See Diana Mishkova, 'Politics of Regionalist Science: Southeastern Europe as a Supranational Space in Late Nineteenth to Mid-Twentieth Century Academic Projects', *East Central Europe* 39 (2012): 1–38.

38 The above-quoted material features in a number of places throughout Iorga's work. See: Nicolae Iorga, 'Elements de communaute entre les peuples du Sud-Est Europeen', *Revue Historique du Sud-est européen* 12, nos. 4–6 (1935); idem, *Ce este Sud-Estul european* [What is the European Southeast] (Bucharest: Datina Romanească, 1940); and idem, *Generalități cu privire la studiile istorice* [Generalizations about historical studies], 4th edition (Iași: Polirom, 1999), 122–5, 135–7.

39 Nicolae Iorga, *Byzance après Byzance* (Bucharest: Institut d'études byzantines, 1935).

structure of geographic, historical, cultural, social and economic intraregional variations whose combination, somewhat paradoxically, turned into 'unifying structural characteristics' of the region. While such ontological fragmentation sealed the impossibility of Balkan cultural convergence and the existence of a unitary space, mobility or migrations (what Cvijić called 'metanastasic movements') acted as a powerful vehicle for intraregional 'penetration and connection'. Metanastasic movements, and the areas they came to shape, were what ultimately defined the prevailing civilizational and ethno-demographic profile of the region. Hardly surprisingly, the Serbs stood out as the largest and most dynamic force behind these movements; they were *the* vibrant Balkan metanastasic population par excellence and the natural unifiers of the greater part of the Balkan Peninsula.[40] The leading Bulgarian geographer at that time, and a disciple of Friedrich Ratzel, Anastas Ishirkov, used similar arguments to support the Bulgarian character of Macedonia while substantiating 'scientifically' the notion of the Balkan Peninsula as a distinct geographical area.

On the whole, the supranational regional *Denkfiguren* ('figures of thought') that we encounter at the turn of the twentieth century emerged as identity projects and distinct fields of study in a period of intensive nationalization that was coupled with the emergence of new universalist visions and comparativist methodologies. These spatial self-representations evolved in concentric national–regional–universal (or global) circles against the backdrop of 'civilizational' binaries of West and East, Europe and Asia, and were sometimes rooted in pan-ideologies, such as (neo-)Slavism. The modes in which the cultural-historical unity of these regions was conceptualized was strongly influenced by the pre-eminence of linguistic, folkloristic and ethno-psychological comparativism, especially in Slavic studies.

Interwar spatial configurations

The post-war identity crisis and the 'decline' of Europe

The First World War shattered faith in Europe as the centre of humanistic values and progress. In Central and Eastern Europe, where geopolitical dislocation was the most radical, the end of the war ushered in an era characterized by disorientation, faithlessness and identity crisis among both the winners and losers. 'Today', the Serbian writer Vladimir Velmar-Janković expressed in 1926, 'there is nothing to stir up great historical illusions that lead people through history … Today we live without idealism, without great ideas, without ideals.'[41] The 'catastrophic consequences' of the political events, bewailed the Bulgarian literary critic Boyan Penev, 'deeply affect our outlook, our notions of historical life and historical development'. He goes on:

> The war killed the faith of many, not only among the vanquished but among the vanquishers too – it killed faith in human virtue, in *human progress*. … Many of the old ideals have collapsed, while new ones have not emerged in their place. Many of the old deities were cynically rejected without being replaced by others. … Instead

---

40 The results of Cvijić's wide-ranging work on the human geography of the Balkans and his ideas in this domain were summarized in his famed *La peninsule balkanique: géographie humaine*, first published in French in 1918. Its impact on the interwar generation of French geographers can hardly be overestimated.

41 Vladimir Velmar-Janković, 'O ovom našem vremenu' [About our time], *Misao* 11, nos. 1–2 (May 1926): 2. Quoted in Branka Prpa-Jovanović, 'Između Istoka i Zapada Kulturni identitet i kulturno civilizacijska uporišta' [Between the East and the West. Cultural identity and cultural and civilizational orientations], *Tokovi istorije* 3–4 (1997), 10.

Spatial configurations

of the unshakeable inner strength, instead of the spirit of affirmation [and] creativity, today the spirit of negation, scepticism and disbelief dominates. There is no value that has not been dispelled.[42]

The overwhelming feeling of both a crisis and a turning point translated into a sense of urgency and the fervent search for new integrative ideologies, cultural orientations and collective identifications, which the Serbian writer and critic Rastko Petrović articulated in the following way:

Having entered into a close relationship with the modern world we, as a young and new race, cannot remain conservative in our national life and ... will be forced to gradually express the unity and the identity of our racial spirit through different, deeply peculiar gestures, which will be more suited to the modern life of the people.[43]

These 'deeply peculiar gestures' reorganized completely the erstwhile symbolic spatial order and demoted Europe and the West as *the* civilizational standard and normative horizon in favour of an indigenous (national) culture or a newly valued East. They created a number of Eastern or autochthonic alternatives to the West or alternative (Balkan, Eastern or Slavic) Europes, which were variously defined as 'young', 'new', or 'real'. Western critics took part in this process by deploying visions of the fall of the West in the same vein as Oswald Spengler's – a favoured point of reference for East Central European intellectuals across the board – and the rise of the Balkan (or Slav) East of the kind envisioned by José Ortega y Gasset when he argued that 'In the young and new Balkan countries modern thought and new ideas are understood with the greatest accuracy. The future of Europe is in these fresh and undeveloped countries.'[44]

Vladimir Vujić, a philosopher, literary critic and member of the Serbian expressionist group, vividly describes some of these radical shifts. The Serbs, he said, were not Europeans, since the feeling for life 'which [they] have developed is far removed from the one that has developed in Europe and has brought it to nothingness'. For him, Europe is the incarnation of brutal rational violence in contrast to Serbian culture, which represents 'spiritual love, humanity, and justice'.[45] Choosing between the West and the East, he wrote, was not about choosing between progress and modernity on the one hand and regression and traditionalism on the other. From this perspective, the scientific and technical advancement of the West was universally welcomed but its culture was not, as the West is spiritually and culturally bankrupt. A conspicuous aspect of this decline is Eurocentrism – the arrogance of imagining that Europe is a divinely appointed part of the world and the only one where progress occurs – which serves to legitimize imperialism: 'Europe shows the mark of its spiritual decline precisely in the imperialistic force with which it strives to seize the whole world.'[46] Why would a new culture such as that of the Yugoslavs need this element, Vujić asked. 'No, we are not Europe', he wrote, continuing that '[t]his can in no

---

42 Boyan Penev, *Literatura i inteligetsiya* [Literature and intelligentsia] (Sofia: Zahariy Stoyanov, 2003 [1925]), 48–9.

43 Quoted in Prpa-Jovanović, *Između Istoka i Zapada*, 11.

44 Bogdan Radica, *Agonija Evrope: razgovori i susreti* [The agony of Europe: talks and encounters] (Belgrade: Geca Kon, 1940), 221.

45 Quoted in Prpa-Jovanović, *Između Istoka i Zapada*, 16. See Vladimir Vujić, 'Vidovdanska razmišljanja o kulturi. Naša tragičnost' [St Vitus Day reflections on our culture: our tragedy], *Narodna odbrana* 24 (July 1929): 452; idem, 'Slovenski život. Odgovor "Obzoru"' [Slav life: answer to 'Review'], *Narodna odbrana* 14 (April 1929): 233.

46 Vujić, *Sputana i oslobodjena misao*, 194.

way be qualified as "backwardness" or "primitiveness" – it is the fresh and staunch feeling of our spirit'.[47] But nor could the notion of the East, Vujić argued, offer a direction for the masses of rural and religious Slavs. The metaphor of a Slavic bridge or East–West synthesis was also false: every point on the globe is somehow between the East and the West, while culture is not an aggregate of isolated features that can be combined at will, but rather an organic creation.[48]

Vujić thus refused to submit to both the binary logic of the East–West frame of reference and the possibility of their voluntaristic combination, a view that was also forcefully advocated by the Polish historiosopher Feliks Koneczny, which I will discuss later. Instead of offering a choice between geographical abstractions, the East–West debate in Vujić's reading was about the authenticity of Yugoslav culture and the future direction it would take. As a consistent autochthonist, he believed that the Serbs should concentrate on producing a new and vital culture of their own. What the Slavs (and the Yugoslavs in particular) had to do was disengage from the futile debate over whether they belonged to the East, to the West or somewhere in between, and rather become aware of, and develop, their own authentic culture by studying their past and specific worldview, their place in the world and ideas of life.[49]

The East and the West are equally alien to the Bulgarians, as the Bulgarian philosopher Yanko Yanev maintained. In a line of argumentation very similar to Vujić's, Yanev insisted that the Bulgarians were bound to follow their own path of self-reliance, which had nothing to do with either the mysticism of Slavdom or the intellectual mechanisms of the West. Slavdom was an abstraction and Russia was being industrialized and Americanized, to the extent that little remained of the mystery and profundity of its soul. Salvation was even less expected from the 'tired' West and decadent (and degenerating) European civilization than it was from the 'tractorized' East. For, as he put it, 'the West today has no foundation, no dogma, no religion. What can we expect from a world that is passing away?'[50]

Other Bulgarian intellectuals, however, perceived themselves as the vanguard in a different crusade: the reconciliation between East and West, understood as an organic synthesis between the native and the foreign, which must be accomplished 'intrinsically, between innermost principles, as a mystic marriage between two heterogeneous souls'. Konstantin Gălăbov was a leading figure in the influential Bulgarian literary circle Strelets ('Sagittarius'), which called for 'the elevation of the national to the level of the European but on an organic native basis', for the attainment of a unique 'synthesis between the native and the Western', 'the national and the supranational' (*plemennoto i nadplemennoto*). 'We want to be writers of the modern times – Bulgarian but at the same time European', Gălăbov wrote. What distinguishes the European is 'the organic link of the supranational and the national'. 'Our destiny is to be Europeanized', Gălăbov affirms. 'There are inevitabilities in life to which we must resign ourselves, and one of them is that we shall be Europeanized'. This 'intentional Europeanization' does not lead to depersonalization or estrangement from the native element. On the contrary, it seeks to 'activate the national principle', enabling it 'to reveal itself in higher forms' and generate 'a genuine cultural upsurge on a national basis'.[51] Europeanization in this conception becomes

---

47 Prpa-Jovanović, *Između Istoka i Zapada*, 16.

48 Milutinović, *Getting over Europe*, 109; See Vladimir Vujić, 'Vidovdanska razmišljanja o kulturi. Naša tragičnost' [Vidovdan reflections on culture: our tragedy], *Narodna odbrana* 24 (July 1929): 452.

49 Milutinović, *Getting over Europe*, 108–10.

50 Yanko Yanev, 'Iztok ili Zapad' [East or West], *Zlatorog* 14, no. 4 (1933): 174–80.

51 Quotes above found in Konstantin Gălăbov, 'Inteligentsiya i evropeizirane' [Intelligentsia and Europeanization] in idem, *Ornamenti. Filosofski i literaturni eseta* (Sofia: Hebros, 1934), 200–9.

Spatial configurations

the instrument through which the Bulgarian autochthonous culture, which itself contains the seeds of the universal, can fulfil its regenerative mission vis-à-vis Europe. 'The clever method', another Sagittarian explained, 'is to arm ourselves with their [the Europeans'] weapons in order to safeguard ourselves from oblivion and enable the manifestation of our personality'.[52] Raising national, cultural manifestations to the level of the European is the only way for Bulgarian culture to acquire 'international importance' – 'Then foreigners will stop treating us like a colony and will be appreciative of us'.[53]

The colonialist face of Europe was captured by the influential Croatian philosopher Vladimir Dvorniković's image of a 'civilized Viking' ('the greedy Viking soul, armed with civilization and culture'[54]). Dvorniković argued,

> Europeans want to bring a bit of culture, some happiness and freedom to the poor little peoples. And then cannons start to roll. And then comes mobilization, occupation and protectorate, or whatever they choose to call it. But if you peer behind these noble words proclaimed from high podiums, you'll see oil, rich mines, strategic points, and quite coincidentally all of it happens to be in the lands of these small peoples singled out to receive happiness and civilization.[55]

A new conception of the East as a means for cultural criticism began to support an unusually wide spectrum of cultural orientations and interpretations, including avant-gardist movements. For the modernists and avant-gardists of the 1920s, such as the literary circle Zenit in Yugoslavia or the Strelets circle in Bulgaria, anti-hegemonic critique of Europe was only a steppingstone on the way towards the assertion of a new type of man, a new notion of universal culture and a new place for the small nations and peripheral cultures in this new universe. The Serbian avant-gardists' radical rupture with the normative past was coupled with a similar rupture from the normative West through a new universal culture that drew upon an 'aestheticized dynamism on a racial basis, something which is distinctively ours: Balkanic', as literary critic Boško Tokin put it.[56] Imperialism, Catholicism and materialism had killed the European man, so the mission of Zenitism and the Zenitists, according to Ljubomir Mičić, editor of the Yugoslav avant-garde literary journal *Zenit*, was the creation of a New Man. The anthropological archetype that was able to accomplish this regenerative mission was first found on the Balkans and then expanded to include the whole of Eastern Europe, extending to the Urals and the Caucasus.

> The beginning of the great [twentieth] century is marked by the fiercest combat between the East and the West: A DUEL OF CULTURES. The Zenitists' position is one against Western civilization. The idea of the East is broad. It has the largest and widest part of the sky. Under this *Eastern* sky we, unfortunately, feel proud that in our yellow fields alien *Western* culture, of which we are faithful and blind guardians, is germinating. ... Are we to be merely guards defending the West? Are we still to remain

---

52 Asen Zlatarov, 'Kulturnostta v sluzhba na rodinata' [Culturedness in the service of the Motherland], in *Literaturen krăg 'Strelets'*, ed. Sava Vasilev (Veliko Tarnovo: Slovo, 2000), 90.

53 Konstantin Gălăbov, 'Nashite kulturni zadachi' [Our cultural tasks], in idem, *Ornamenti. Filosofski i literaturni eseta*, 22.

54 Vladimir Dvorniković, 'The Cultural Isolation of Slavs', in *Borba ideja*, idem (Belgrade: Službeni list SRJ, 1995), 111–12, quoted in Milutinović, *Getting over Europe*, 103.

55 Ibid.

56 Quoted in Prpa-Jovanović, *Između Istoka i Zapada*, 22–3.

servants for a long time, defending Lloyd George, Briand, Focha or D'Annunzio? *No! Latins out!* It is time for heroism! Therefore: *we can only be pioneers and participants in the creation of a universal culture which the eastern Man of the Urals, the Caucasus and the Balkans brings with him …*[57]

Mičić went further in this direction with his defiant image of the 'Barbarogenius' that initially encompassed all Slavs and later included only the Serbs. Overturning the original image, the 'barbarians' appeared here as positive actors, free of the burdens of civilization and full of vitality, strength and self-confidence, who would rejuvenate an exhausted Europe and save it from itself by 'Balkanizing' it. While this resignification of the barbarians was a broader European, avant-garde phenomenon, Mičić actually drew inspiration from an indigenous Balkan source: the 'primitive' Dinaric type described by the previously mentioned Serbian anthropogeographer Jovan Cvijić and praised by the German folk psychologist Gerhard Gesemann.

This 'modernist' conceptualization of the ontological antagonism between East and West exhibited fundamental similarities to the thinking of political orthodoxists, such as the theologist and professor at the Faculty of Orthodox Theology at Belgrade University, Justin Popović, who took an anti-European stance essentially of religious hostility towards Western humanism and rationalism. For Popović, humanistic and rationalistic civilization, with its anthropocentric view of life, its science and technology – in the name of progress – is responsible for the biggest regression in human history: bloody war and the barbarian transmutation of the human being. Between this European culture and what Popović called 'the culture of *svetosavskij Bogočovek*', there can be no reconciliation. The former proclaims that man – European man in particular – is the standard measure for all things. His Eurocentric culture is materialistic, his ethics fetishistic; by killing God he was left without a soul. In opposition to this culture of the West stood *Bogočovečanska* culture, which

> transforms humans from the inside, flowing from the inside to the outside, from the soul to the body; it regenerates the soul, and through the soul the body. … The purpose of Orthodox culture is not only to transform man and mankind but through them [to transform] the whole of nature.[58]

For Popović there was no dilemma when deciding in which direction one should go: moving towards the position of European man turns one into a 'fleeting moth', while moving towards the *svetosavskij Bogočovek* turns one into 'an immortal creator, a creator of the Orthodox culture'.[59]

In a certain sense, post-war Poland and Czechoslovakia offer a contrasting case in that their faith in Western civilization continued to hold sway, and the solutions applied to the 'crisis of European culture' did not dismantle the normative European space. Through the work of certain intellectual groups, however, the West's intrinsic values underwent a considerable change. In Poland, faith in Europe went hand in hand with denying the right to European citizenship

---

57 Ljubomir Mičić,'Delo zenitizma' [The work of Zenitism], *Zenit* 8 (October 1921): 2, quoted in Prpa-Jovanović, *Između Istoka i Zapada*, 22 (italics and emphasis in original text).

58 Jeromonah Justin, 'Između dvaju kultura: evropske-čovečanske i svetosavske Bogočovečanske' [Between two cultures: the European-Human and the Saint-Sava Godman], *Narodna odbrana* 45 (November 1928): 723, 747–8, quoted in Prpa-Jovanović, *Između Istoka i Zapada*, 12–13.

59 Ibid.

Spatial configurations

not only to Bolshevik Russians ('this locust of the East' and 'dustbin of the world') but also to Germans ('the Prussian brigands', as historian Jan Karol Kochanowski described them).[60] Poland's repelling of the Red Army in 1920 revived both the idea that the country was a 'bulwark' and the idea of Polish messianism of the Romantic period; and many Polish intellectuals considered their country to be the only rightful member, as well as protector, of Western European civilization east of the Rhine. The result was that, as writer Jerzy Stempowski put it in 1929, 'In Poland the Great War did not raise those questions and moral conflicts which at that time sowed apprehension and confusion in the minds of old Europe.'[61]

On this common ground, however, opinions that had prevailed since the late 1920s began to lean increasingly toward anti-liberal readings of European culture and its system of values. In 1929 Władysław Leopold Jaworski, professor of law and one of Poland's leading conservatives, wrote the following:

> We think the crisis of European culture consists in the hegemony of rationalism. In the political field, it has brought the system which under the name of democracy means the atomization of society on the one hand and its mechanization on the other.[62]

For the intellectuals espousing such views, especially among the young generation of nationalists in the 'national–democratic camp', authentic Western European culture was one of Christian values associated with the Roman Catholic Church. In these circles, the emergence of Italian fascism augured the end of the crisis of Latin, or West European, culture. Identified with rationalism, liberalism, communism, freemasonry and the Jewish people, this crisis was caused by Western Europe's departure from its original medieval values and had been exacerbated since the Age of Enlightenment. The founder and chief ideologue of National Democracy in particular, Roman Dmowski, viewed fascism and National Socialism as responses to the dangers threatening Western European civilization. Right-wing nationalist and ecclesiastical diagnoses of the nature of the civilizational crisis (attributing it to a departure not from a liberal system of values of the nineteenth century but from primeval Christian values) were practically identical.

One of the most elaborated visions of Europe in interwar Poland – and one that transcended the West–East binary – was advanced by Feliks Koneczny, a conservative historian and philosopher of history known for his pluralistic theory of civilizations. In his main work, *On the Plurality of Civilizations*, Koneczny distinguished between civilizations according to their attitudes to law and ethics, from which differences in values and institutional structures derive.[63] In view of this criterion, Europe in his time was a battlefield between four types of civilization: Latin; Byzantine (exemplified by the bureaucratic civilization of Germany under Bismarck – hence, Koneczny talked, following Edgar Quinet, of 'German Byzantinism' – but also by post-revolutionary France and Protestantism); Turanian (represented by the militaristic civilization of Russia and the Ottoman Empire); and Jewish (epitomized by the communist states).

---

60 Kochanowski quoted in Roman Wapiński, 'The Question of Civilizational Options in Polish Political Thought', *Polish Western Affairs* 33, no. 2 (1992): 221.

61 Quoted in Wapiński, 'The Question of Civilizational Options', 222–3.

62 Ibid., 225.

63 Feliks Koneczny, *O wielości cywilizacyj* (Cracow: Gebethner & Wolf, 1935). The book was translated into English in 1962, with an acclaimed preface by Arnold Toynbee, as *On the Plurality of Civilizations* (London: Polonica Publications, 1962) (also accessible at www.scribd.com/doc/4464979/ON-THE-PLURALITY-OF-CIVILIZATIONS-Feliks-Koneczny-Entire-Book). Outside of Poland, however, his work remains largely unknown.

Koneczny did not link his types of civilization to any particular race or nation, but since his theory was also a normative project, the civilizations could not be considered equal in the ethical sense. In his book, he argues that Latin civilization holds the highest value and is the best for the fulfilment of man's freedom and 'unalienable dignity'. Its survival depends on its purity which is under threat; for there is no single European or Western civilization but that, under the surface of culture and public life, the four civilizations compete for our souls. Just as Vujić had done, Koneczny claims that elements of a particular civilization cannot mix with those of another, arguing that 'between civilizations a synthesis is not possible ... there are only poisonous mixtures', therefore, 'it is not possible to be civilized in two different ways.'[64] Each civilization is a separate, closed whole. Syntheses between two or more civilizations lead to a state of 'un-civilization' – lower moral standards and ultimate failure. Russia exemplified the fruitless, indeed impossible, attempts to merge various cultural influences into a coherent organic whole, which led instead to social chaos and regression. Only civilizational purity can ensure vitality, harmony and the stability of society. Therefore, the contemporary crisis is not, as Spengler claimed, characterized by the decline of the West, but is rather a symptom of the coexistence of four civilizations. For Koneczny, this was the real source of Europe's crisis and ethical and political chaos.

The possibility that Poland and Central Europe could bring about a synthesis between East and West was thus forestalled. This 'literary cliché', Koneczny claimed, would only result in a 'civilizational caricature':

> Geographically we cannot stop being between East and West, but in terms of civiliza-
> tion it is not at all possible to be between East and West. ... For Poland, hidden in the
> desire for an East–West civilizational synthesis is cultural and political nothingness.[65]

A 'Polish' geopolitical agenda loomed large behind all of this. Koneczny described Latin Poland as positioned between 'Byzantine German' and 'Turanian' civilizations rather than post-Byzantine Russia, in each of which 'the moral element is subordinated to material strength'.[66] He thus completely overturned the idea that religion is a major civilizational marker and Byzantinism is intrinsically linked to Greek Orthodoxy. Needless to say, this move made it possible to count Ukraine and Belarus among the cultures of the same 'Latin' civilization, and to present Turanian Russian civilization, in both its Tsarist and Bolshevik incarnations, as the exact opposite of the Latin Western one.[67]

In Czechoslovakia, the philosopher and president Tomáš G. Masaryk's image of Europe – which was intended as much to boost his domestic position as to impress Western governments[68] – was founded on the premise that the Czechs were unequivocally tied to the West, both

---

64 Koneczny, *On the Plurality of Civilizations*, 25–6.

65 Feliks Koneczny, *Polska między Wschodem a Zachodem* [Poland between East and West] (Lublin: Onion, 1996 [1st ed. 1928]), 1–2, 51.

66 Quoted in Andrew Kier Wise, 'Russia as Poland's Civilizational "Other"', in *The East-West Discourse: Symbolic Geography and its Sources*, ed. Alexander Maxwell (Oxford: Peter Lang, 2011), 86.

67 Present-day conservative adherents to Koneczny's legacy like to stress his role as a precursor to Samuel Huntington and to describe the European Union as a Byzantine, bureaucratic project, alien to Latin values and institutions.

68 On the importance attributed to foreign and domestic propaganda in Masaryk's political thought and action, and in founding the myth of a historically democratic Czech nation, see Andrea Orzoff, *Battle for the Castle: The Myth of Czechoslovakia in Europe, 1914–1948* (New York: Oxford University Press, 2009).

Spatial configurations

culturally and politically. In his understanding, the West, comprising France, Britain and the United States, the Netherlands, Belgium and the other Romance peoples, constituted 'one cultural whole'. By contrast, he argued, Czech contact with the Byzantine and Russian East had always been unsubstantial. In terms of Germany, it was omitted from this model, as, according to Masaryk, it had increasingly isolated itself from the (Western) European cultural community since the Middle Ages.[69]

In 1918, during a time of war, Masaryk formulated his concept of the post-war European order in his pamphlet 'New Europe'. Central to this idea was democracy: Europeanization meant democratization. Masaryk went to great lengths to prove that, like its Western patrons, Czechoslovakia was staunchly democratic and committed to the protection of its minorities. Under the circumstances, such a normative definition was instrumental: if Europe was defined by the plurality of fully fledged democratic nations, then the (envisaged) construction of Czechoslovakia would help to protect 'European principles' of democracy against anti-democratic (and hence anti-European) Pan-Germanism. The basic and inevitable condition for this democratization was the moral re-education of nations in the principles of rationality, tolerance, humanity and Christian spirituality – virtues said to be represented by the West.[70] Thus, the narrative of Czechoslovakia as an outpost of liberalism and democracy and an island of stability, prosperity and tolerance amidst the chaos and backwardness of the rest of East Central Europe was connected to the Czechs' unequivocal filiation with the West in terms of culture and values. The principles of rationality and spirituality were crucial and being European meant sharing this common culture. Such definitions implicitly subverted the idea of regional, East Central European unity.

Masaryk also ventured into the cultural regionalization of Europe, but his propositions in this respect were contradictory. In 1922, he claimed that 'quite evidently Europe politically and to a large extent even culturally falls into three zones': Western (in this case including Germany); Eastern (Russia); and Central European, 'that special zone of small states and nations between the West and the East' stretching from Scandinavia to the Balkans.[71] Three years later, Central Europe had disappeared as a cultural entity:

> If the concept of Central Europe is defined not only geographically, but also culturally, then Western Germany with Switzerland and Italy belong to Western Europe. But even Bohemia and Austria belong culturally to the West. Culturally, the West and the East are divided so that the former Russia, Galicia and Hungary, Rumania and the Balkans belong to the East.[72]

For Masaryk, then, the West was not synonymous with Europe: America was part of it, while the eastern parts of Europe were not. At the same time, the tension between already *being* European and *becoming* European – as in most other East Central European cases – was intrinsic to the Czech debate.

The Czech foreign minister and political economist Edvard Beneš held a somewhat different view on this issue. At the beginning of the 1920s he interpreted differences between East and

---

69 Tomáš G. Masaryk, *Světová revoluce – za války a ve válce 1914–1918* (Prague: Orbis, 1925) [English edition, *The Making of a State: Memories and Observations (1914–1918)* (London: Allen & Unwin, 1927)], 512–16.

70 Miroslav Hroch, 'Czech Discourse on Europe', 251, 254.

71 Bugge, 'Longing or Belonging?', 119.

72 Masaryk quoted in Bugge, 'Longing or Belonging', 119.

West in Europe from a temporal perspective, identifying what he saw as the 'substantial lagging behind' of Eastern Europe and the Slavs. He analyzed various historical indicators of this lag and described how it had asserted itself in the mentality and philosophy of the Slavs as an inability to organize their political and economic life in a practical way. But the Czechs did not suffer from such deficiencies, as they had an advantage among the Slavs, which was that 'their geographical position brought them into immediate contact with the Germans and with Western Europe, and this influence soon manifested itself in their more rapid cultural, economic and social development.'[73] A few years later, Beneš no longer considered the Czechs to be *closest* to the West, for as 'the only ones among the nations of Central Europe', they were a *part* of it: 'Both before the war and during the war, our nation in the Czech lands stood in the camp of Western Europe with its historical development, its whole psychology, its philosophical concepts, and its spiritual and social structure.'[74]

The conceptual other to this notion of Europe was above all Soviet Russia, either due to its refusal to participate in European culture (František Václav Krejčí) or as the 'Asian threat' it posed if it chose to remain 'Eurasian' (Ferdinand Peroutka). The Catholic writer and editor Josef Dostál, on the other hand, perceived a double threat to Europe in the form of a 'yellow invasion from the East' and 'the extortion of the American moneybags'. In stark contrast to Masaryk's admiration for America, he maintained:

> We are against spiritless internationalism, at whose cradle stood liberalism with capitalism and socialism. The Czech nation, if it remains its own ... will not shrink from working for a just Europe, free intellectually and economically. The barbarians from the East and from the New World are a grave danger.[75]

Dostál predicted that 'the charity of American civilization will little by little turn European man too into an automaton, the mechanical product of a technical era.'[76] Karel Čapek, a liberal intellectual appreciative of the benefits of modern civilization, was similarly horrified by the thought of an American civilizing onslaught on 'old Europe', arguing that 'The Creator of Europe made her small and even split her up into little parts, so that our hearts could find joy not in size but in plurality. America corrupts us with its preference for size.'[77] Here the aestheticization of 'Czech smallness' supported the very identity of Europe as a primeval site of cultural variety.

The literary critic František Václav Krejčí's book, *Czechhood and Europeanness* (1931), is a unique attempt to analyze systematically the relationship between Czech and European identities. Krejčí's Europe is not a geographical concept, but a 'qualitative concept of culture'. The first criterion of Europeanness, for him, was a given community's (or nation's) level of participation in the consumption of European culture.[78] The second criterion was an active contribution to the improvement of European culture. Thus defined, cultural Europe was

---

73 Beneš quoted in Bugge, 'Longing or Belonging', 121.
74 Ibid. The discourse that Czechoslovakia is part of the West, combined with the myth of Czechoslovakia during the First Republic, was also propagated by the 'Castle circle' ('Hrad' in Czech), an informal political organization set up by Masaryk and Beneš, which included many intellectuals who were engaged in depicting Czechoslovakia as a model, Western-style democracy and were involved in struggles over the meaning of Czech history within the lineage of the best European traditions.
75 Dostál quoted in Bugge, 'Longing or Belonging?', 125.
76 Ibid.
77 Čapek quoted in Bugge, 'Longing or Belonging?', 125–6.
78 Hroch, 'Czech Discourse on Europe', 252.

Spatial configurations

significantly smaller than geographical Europe: it stretched along the historical Athens–Rome–Paris–London axis with the Western parts of Central Europe (Bohemia included) lagging not far behind, whereas to the east, this 'most European Europe' gradually gave way to Eurasia.[79]

By incorporating the dichotomy of (deep and spiritual) 'culture' and (superficial and mechanical) 'civilization' in his analysis of Europe, Krejčí contended that only in Western and Central Europe, and neither in mechanized America nor communist Russia, had culture and civilization become one, and it was only there that Europe had become a 'lived experience'.[80] Regarding the difference between Western and Central Europe, Krejčí argued that while the French believed that they *were* Europe, for the Germans and the other Central Europeans, Europe was an idea, a programme, rather than a reality – a distinction that will be taken up again in the 1980s by Central European dissidents.

Generally speaking, the interwar Czechoslovak outlook, which also arose from Czech conceptualizations of Slavdom and Central Europe, was a mixture of pragmatic parochialism and universalism, points on which Masaryk and Beneš insisted. In light of this, the birth of Czechoslovakia appears to be a product of an evolutionary European process in the direction of democracy and national emancipation. Czech history was inseparable from European history, most notably in its spiritual dimension; to Masaryk, the Enlightenment in Germany, France and England was only a continuation of 'the main ideas of the Czech reformation'.[81] Not without parallels elsewhere in East Central Europe, discussions about Europe were usually directly linked to the Czech national question coined by Masaryk as part of a national-pedagogic debate about the country's future and state of belonging, which thus usually took the form of debates about Czech 'Europeanness' (*evropanství*).

The Slavic world

The indiscrete charms of Slavdom: Balkan visions

As a criticism of Europe, the Slavic idea was a genuine nineteenth-century phenomenon, in which the European and the Slavic functioned as antithetical or alternative concepts. In interwar East Central Europe, the idea of Slavdom, a *sui generis* geocultural category, as an alternative to Europe, or an integrative space that fused the West and the East together, thrived. Hopes of a bright Slavic future that were prophesied by some conservative Western thinkers (Oswald Spengler, Hermann Keyserling and Arthur Möller van den Bruck) appeared to be fulfilled after the First World War by the independence or joint foundation of states carried out by many Slav peoples (Poles, Czechs and Slovaks, Croats and Slovenes). This utopian 'Easternism' had various sources: Russian messianism, Eurasianism, but also the cultural critique of European modernism in the first decades of the twentieth century, Spengler's philosophy of culture, Henri Bergson's critique of scientific rationalism and 'intellectualism', and to some degree the influence of the Indian 'spiritualist' critique of modernity.

In the Slavic countries of East Central Europe, discussions on the relationship between Slavdom and the West had a long history and were constitutive of these countries' cultural

---

79 Bugge, 'Longing or Belonging?', 126–7.
80 Ibid.
81 Piotr S. Wandycz, 'East European History and Its Meaning: The Halecki-Bidlo-Handelsman Debate', in *Király Béla emlékkönyv: Háború és társadalom: War and Society: Guerre et société: Krieg und Gesellschaft*, eds Jonás Pál et al. (Budapest: Századvég Kiadó, 1992), 318–19.

self-definition. They expressed a variety of combinations and modalities, ranging from a complete schism and irreconcilability between the two cultural archetypes to their amalgamation or overlapping. In post-war East Central Europe, the portrayal of the East as the cultural antithesis of Europe and the idea of Slavic messianism were closely linked with Spengler's prophecy of the civilizational collapse of Europe and the 'dawn' of the East and the Slavic culture. In the Balkans, this resonated with autochthonist anti-Western trends that were connected to resistance to imitation and the fear of identity loss, resentment of Western superiority in the technological, economic, military and scientific spheres, critiques of Western imperialism, and hostility towards Eurocentrism, all of which led to a new wave of messianic Slavic self-projections. As Miloš Milošević described it,

> Slavic psychology and Slavic thought are deeply penetrated by messianism, by the mystic belief that the Slavs are the 'newly chosen people of God' who have a special mission to fulfil in the life of humankind. They are a 'God-bearing' people [*bogonosac*] carrying in their pure womb the new testament of the Spirit to be yielded when the time comes. At the boundary of East and West, the Slavic world had been splashed by waves from all sides, which deposited in it both sand and pearls. The Slavs adopted and preserved deep in themselves all that was precious. And they hope that one day, enriched by all this, they will step onto the stage of world history.[82]

The interwar projections of the Slavic world, therefore, had much more in common with the 'abstract and mystical doctrine of the [nineteenth-century] Slavophiles' than with the 'healthier and more practical outlook' of turn-of-the-century neo-Slavdom.[83]

In Yugoslavia, the construction of Slavdom as the cultural opposite of (Germanic and Romanic) Europe, in combination with Slavic messianism, was directly linked with the question of the national (self-)identification of the new Yugoslav state, which brought together Slavic cultures and nations whose cohesion was anything but clear. In an important sense, the Slavic idea in the Yugoslav context was not only a response to the 'crisis' of Europe and the West, but it was seen as a powerful resource capable of transcending and overturning the cultural-historical divergences (or rather cultural *tabula rasa*) between Serbs, Croats and Slovenes — an integrative formula that fused Slavophilism and pan-Slavism with a Yugoslav vision of integration.[84] Thus the notion of the civilizational collapse of post-war Europe and the idea that Slavdom could provide both the solution to this crisis and an alternative to Western civilization converged within the Yugoslav nation-building project, which explains the spectacular flourishing of various forms of Slavic messianism in the tripartite kingdom, especially among the Serbs, during the interwar period. While it involved Russia, this Slavic idea, on the

---

82 Miloš M. Milošević, 'Pad Zapada i sveslovenski mesijanizam — Prilog problemu naše kulturne orijentacije', [The fall of the West and Slavic Messianism — a contribution to the problem of our cultural orientation], *Raskrsnica*, 3 June 1923, 30, quoted in Prpa-Jovanović, *Izmedu Istoka i Zapada*, 18.

83 See Bobčev, 'The Slavs after the War', 291.

84 It is important to point out that when Serbian intellectuals spoke about 'our culture' or 'our nation' it was generally unclear whether they meant the Serbian or Yugoslav culture/nation. The overall ambivalence must have had a clear function — the dominant Slavic narrative was intended to subvert the strong religious divisions within the new composite kingdom, while at the same time smuggling in particular Serbian conceptions and definitions of Slavic identity.

Spatial configurations

other hand, barely made reference to the Czechs, Slovaks or Poles, which once again highlights its Slavophile genealogy.

The Slav–West dichotomy was particularly fashionable among the young intellectual group of Serbian Expressionists (and philosophical Bergsonians). Some of them, like the modernist and avant-gardist from the right, Svetislav Stefanović, conceived of the Slavs and the West as radical opposites:

> Slavs are against the West. Deep in his soul, in the fundament of his being, a Slav is, as an individual as well as a member of his race, an antagonist of the West, which he finds lacking in soul, and whose technique threatens his soul. And since the West is Christianity, Christ's cult and his church, but not his faith and love, being against the West a Slav is also against Christianity.[85]

Besides ensuring the triumph of a 'higher, more humane religion' over Roman Catholicism, the Slavs' next task is

> to destroy the second, heavy and cursed inheritance of Rome, which is imperialism, a 'system of robbery and enslavement of smaller and weaker peoples', whose latest horrible deed is the current bloody World War. Slavs have a deeply engrained racial yearning for freedom, independence and equality. While struggling for their freedom, they struggle for ... the freedom and equality of all peoples.[86]

Serbian Expressionists, in the words of Zoran Milutinović,

> conceived the triumph of Slavdom to be the triumph of universalism, and its ascendancy a new civilizing mission which would uproot injustice and suffering by bringing equality, justice and liberty for all. ... [Their intention was] the creation of a cultural universalism which would not be simply Eurocentric or West-centred, but would encompass non-European traditions as well.[87]

The Serbian Expressionists and Bergsonians combined the Slavic idea, which had roots in Russia and its Orthodox thinkers (Dostoyevsky, Solovyov and Tolstoy), with an infatuation for India – portrayed as spiritual, intuitive and religious – and posited both as an antidote to the rational, soulless and atheist West. For the (expressionist) philosopher and classicist Miloš Đurić, East was essentially synonymous with Russia and India. It stood for 'ethics' and the 'soul', for integral thought and a meaningful life; it valued renunciation, gentleness and quietness, and leaned on irrationalism, intuitivism and spiritualism. The West, on the other hand, stood for 'technics' and 'reason', logical speculations and abstractions; it epitomized rationalism, positivism and materialism, and valued courage, strength and heroism. Đurić did not seek to substitute Slavic spirituality for European culture but aspired to combine the two worlds, West and East, Europe and Asia, 'in an organic way'. These two worlds looked to each other, but they could not meet. In order to come together, they needed a middleman; the Slavs, who were neither

---

85 Svetislav Stefanović, *Pogledi i pokušaji* [Views and attempts] (Belgrade: Geca Kon, 1919), quoted in Milutinović, *Getting Over Europe*, 90.
86 Ibid., 90–1.
87 Ibid., 91–2.

East nor West, neither Asia nor Europe, even if they had certain elements of both, were the perfect intermediary. Their culture was a 'child of the father West, representing the male principle, energy and technology, and the mother East, which represents the female principle, harmony and ethics'.[88] The Slavs' mission was thus to produce a higher cultural synthesis, harmonizing the two contrasting cultures, which Đurić called 'panhumanism'.

> We, the Slavs, who are neither East nor West but live between the East and the West, have the mission to merge, in a high cultural synthesis, these two kinds of life: the life of the East in space and the life of the West in time; to knit together the Western practice and rumbling with the Eastern splendid listening and peace. To yield a vivid culture, a rich syntagma, in which, in an organic way, are joined the eternal contents of Eastern and Western cultures. To raise alongside the Tree of Knowledge the Tree of Life.[89]

Similarly, according to the foremost Bulgarian Slavicist and public intellectual Boris Yotsov, the 'Slavic–European dualism' and the longing for an 'organic synthesis' between the Slavic and the European underpinned Bulgarian culture in the twentieth century. Turning to Slavdom – 'not as a political, cultural and literary, but as an ethical and mystic idea' – is tantamount to turning to the Bulgarian inner self and 'national consciousness, which is only a moment in the all-Slavic [consciousness], a moment in that universal cosmic current that portends the solution of world problems.'[90] In the same vein, the Bulgarian essayist Georgy Tomalevski wrote that 'the pregnant womb of Slavdom will give birth to the new Jesus, who destroys and rebuilds, for no element is closer to Jesus the destructor, the revolutionary in the human spirit than the Slavic [element]'.[91] The philosopher Nayden Sheytanov also linked the fortunes of Bulgarian culture to the expected upsurge of Slavdom, which was seen as uniting 'the old magic South and East' and the new world of Europe.[92]

While adopting Spengler's conclusion about the 'fading Western world', the previously mentioned Bulgarian philosopher Yanko Yanev rejected the prophecies of the Spenglerians for the future of the Slavic world. To him, Slavophilism was an entirely obsolete category of historiosophic thinking. In his eyes, the Slavic soul had completely changed, having lost its metaphysical power, the power of religious depth, national romanticism and the living, God-bearing word.[93] Elsewhere, however, Yanev praised Slavdom for its alleged 'closeness to life', 'sense for the mystic and the sacred' and its 'child-like innocent principle, life-giving force, primordiality and inspiration', in contrast to the rationality, formalism, technicism and bureaucratism of Europe.[94] He saw potential for the Slavs' world-historical role as it was unaffected by the 'herd period', one characterized by petty-mindedness and European uniformity, as the last period of Western culture. Slavdom shunned the bourgeois European mentality. Inasmuch

---

88 Ibid., 87–90.

89 Miloš Đurić, *Pred slovenskim vidicima. Prilog filosofiji slovenske culture* [Toward Slavic perspectives: contribution to the philosophy of Slavic culture] (Beograd: Knjižara M.J. Stefanovića, 1928), 64–5. Quoted in Prpa-Jovanović, *Između Istoka i Zapada*, 14–15.

90 Boris Yotsov, *Slavyanstvoto i Evropa* [Slavdom and Europe] (Sofia: Universitetsko izdatelstvo 'Sv. Kliment Ohridski', 1992), 44.

91 Georgy Tomalevski, *Chovek, priroda i Bog. Eseta* [Man, nature and God: essays] (Sofia, 1934), 84–5.

92 Nayden Sheytanov, 'Sădbata na slavyanstvoto' [The fate of Slavdom], *Zlatorog* 11, no. 2 (1930): 95–107.

93 Yanko Yanev, 'Iztok ili Zapad?' [East or West?], *Zlatorog* 14, no. 4 (1933): 174–80.

94 Yanko Yanev, 'Probuzhdane' [Awakening], *Zlatorog* 11, nos. 5–6 (1930): 273–83.

Spatial configurations

as the Slavic world could be thought of as a separate historical category, Yanev stated, it had always sought ways to implement the great ideas of Western culture.[95]

On the other hand, the above-mentioned influential Croatian philosopher and proponent of an integrated Yugoslavia, Vladimir Dvorniković, believed neither in Slav civilization nor in its regenerative cultural mission:

> Slavdom never existed as a historical, cultural, national or moral entity. History deeply refutes so-called 'Slav solidarity' and a common 'Slav consciousness'. ... hence every idea of a 'Slav mission' in the future is but a chimera, a Fata Morgana.[96]

That 'which gives Slavdom its immediate content', Dvorniković maintained, is 'a subjective-psychological basis, a feeling of family relationship and similarity'.[97] This 'non-existent reality' was of Europe's making: Western Europe isolated and excluded the Slavs, so their only choice was to react through stronger and more visible solidarity and cultural integration. This reaction, he argued, should not be the result of sentimentality or romanticism, but be borne out of the understanding that it is an imperative. Dvorniković's *ressentiment* sprang from 'the cultural isolation of the Slavs in Europe', meaning their being pushed into 'the vestibule, on the threshold or on the border of Europe', 'reek[ing] of Asia, of the Orient, and that means – cultural inferiority.' He added that 'Only Germano-Romanic Europe is [said to be] the real Europe'.[98] In fact, Dvorniković needed the idea of Slavdom in order to mount a counter attack on the West:

> The Slav spirit never completely sunk into the European one, and it fortunately does not recognize as its own all that which in reality is specifically European: for example, the bloodthirsty and sadistic Inquisition, which is unknown even in the deepest Orient; or, closer to our time, that disgusting imperialist greed and brutal technical materialism concealed under the shiny surface of civilization. We Slavs can easily live without the pride of belonging to such a family.[99]

Serbia's foremost geographer Jovan Cvijić added an anthropological dimension to this discussion. He subsumed the Balkan Slavs' 'original way of self-expression in the organization of the state, in the mode and direction of their social and economic work, and especially in science and art' under the concept of 'Slavic civilization', which he saw as 'a new type' of civilization drawing on 'the kinship of deepest psychic specificities'. As he put it, it 'will not be a copy of any of the existing types of European culture but will grow organically from the [Slavic] peoples' spirit and will be based on its most original and most fertile properties.' Cvijić envisaged this 'Slavic civilization' as being 'closer to truth, to pious life and to God than the present European civilization.'[100]

---

95 Yanko Yanev, Geroichniyat chovek [The heroic man] (Sofia: T.F. Chipev, 1934), 32–3.

96 Vladimir Dvorniković, *Naša kulturna orijentacija u današnjoj Evropi* [Our cultural orientation in today's Europe] (Zagreb: GSSZZ, 1930), 81, quoted in Milutinović, *Getting Over Europe*, 98.

97 Ibid., 99.

98 Ibid.

99 Ibid, 100.

100 Jovan Cvijić, 'Osnovi jugoslovenske civilizacije' [The bases of Yugoslav civilization], *Nova Evropa* 6, no. 7 (November 1922): 212–13, quoted in Prpa-Jovanović, *Između Istoka i Zapada*, 20.

Central European 'Slavic' visions

Although inspired by Russian Slavophilism, Central European Slavism had its specific background in being largely a reaction against the Germanic and Roman Europe of German nationalist propaganda. After 1918 the legacy of both Romantic Slavism and neo-Slavism had an enduring focus on Russia, and there was not a continued need to assert the Czechs' Slavic identity and the Slavs' domination in Eastern Europe to counter German claims. Jaroslav Bidlo's 1927 magisterial history of the Slavs was part of this climate.[101] The periodical *Slovanský Přehled* ('Slavic review'), founded in 1898 and re-established in 1924, promoted a kind of 'republican' Slavism. The presence of a sizeable number of Belarusian and Ukrainian emigrants (with their universities in exile in Prague), plus a plethora of Slavophile publications, the agrarian party's creation of the Union of Slav Agrarians, and the traditional use of Slav slogans by the nationalist *Sokol* movement all combined to present Czechoslovakia as the leading exponent of Slavdom.[102] The founding father of pre-war neo-Slavism, Karel Kramář, the leader of the National Democratic Party, continued to propagate openly his sympathy and admiration for Russia. However, the notion of a 'Slavic community' that was so crucial in the pre-war decade – 'our ultimate refuge', as Kramář put it – did not translate into a real programme of action, either foreign or domestic, and the term itself started to wane. As some Czech historians argue, 'in the conditions of independent statehood the Slav idea (*Slovanská mišlenka*) lost its former central place in the system of political thought of the Czech and Slovak nation.'[103]

As in Poland, both the place and 'belonging' of Russia played a central role in the discussions not only about the 'Slav idea' but about the Czechs' proper European identity. In his enormous monograph published on the eve of the war, *Russia and Europe* (1913), Tomáš G. Masaryk did not exclude Russia from Europe but regarded it as a specific part of it: 'Europe is not essentially foreign to Russia, but Russia still did not master it totally.'[104] Russia represented 'the childhood of Europe'; Russia is what Europe was, both decadent and theocratic, but with the potential to become, should it cure its sickness, the most powerful state in Europe.[105] The creation of Czechoslovakia, however, led to a strong sense of 'Czech' political and cultural identification with Western Europe, heralded by Masaryk's early post-war writings in which he outlines the search for Western patronage for the envisaged Czecho-Slovak state, emphatically dissociating Czech history from 'the Byzantine and Russian East'.[106]

The long Western European tradition of not considering the Slavs to be fully European, however, was a painful problem for the Czechs, and this disrespect and disinterest contributed to the difficulty of achieving unequivocal identification with the West.[107] Masaryk and Edvard Beneš often talked about 'Slav politics'. Beneš accepted as an 'existing fact' the 'feeling of kinship between Slav nations' and the 'similarity of at least some part of their national cultures'; in

---

101 Jaroslav Bidlo, *Dějiny Slovanstva* [History of the Slavs] (Prague: Vesmír, 1927). Even before the war, Bidlo advocated the idea of a distinct history of the 'Slav World as a whole'. See his article 'O historii slovanstva jako celku' [History of Slavdom as a whole], *Český časopis historický* 17 (1911): 143–51.

102 Several important institutions were founded in the 1920s – the Slavic Institute, the Slavic Library, the journals *Slavia* and *Byzantinoslavica*, to name a few – with the support of the state and with significant help from Russian, Belarusian and Ukrainian political emigration.

103 Wandycz, 'East European History', 318.

104 Hroch, 'Czech Discourse on Europe', 258.

105 Ibid.

106 Masaryk, *Světová revoluce*, 512.

107 Bugge, 'Longing or Belonging?', 124.

Spatial configurations

spite of all the diverging interests, there existed among the Slavs 'certain economic and cultural interests in common'. His stance, however, was fundamentally pragmatic and realist. The commonality of interests, he said, is a question of foreign policy, where no emotionalism is permitted; 'an independent state cannot allow itself to be romantic or sentimental' but is governed by its international interests and obligations. The knell had sounded for Slavophilism, he opined; for him, there was now no room for neo-Slavism, and the idea of Slavdom must be looked at in the same way as any other idea, from the angle of democracy and humanity.[108] The spheres where Beneš envisaged a 'broad Slav cooperation' were the 'literary, scientific and artistic fields and generally culture, as well as in the domain of technical and economic organizations'. The 'chief object of a practical Slav policy', in his opinion, was to acquire such a place among the European nations that 'nobody should look down on Slavonic peoples as less worthy'.[109] Beneš, however, was no believer in the idea of 'Slavonic agrarianism', namely cooperation between all Slav agrarian parties as promoted by the Slovak Dr Milan Hodža. This idea required an intrusion of politics and party interest into economic relations. The economic basis of such a cooperation would be questionable as the agrarian interests of different Slav states, all of which were agrarian, are a source of conflict rather than cooperation.[110]

The political aspects of Beneš' idea of a Slavic union did not go much further than this. In principle, he agreed that there were no 'serious obstacles' to a union between Yugoslavia, Poland and Czechoslovakia, which Bulgaria and Russia could join one day, pending the settlement of discord with both Yugoslavia and Poland. This union, however, had nothing to do with 'the old idea of a Slav federation or Slav Empire', that is with a political formation based on state law. He rather envisaged it as a sort of 'little League of Nations', reproducing its main features.[111] But even this he considered premature as it was likely to 'create misunderstandings and thus endanger the consolidation of Europe'; an incorporation of Russia into a Slavic union, in particular, could even 'bring about a catastrophe' if such a union were understood by the European states as a renewal of pan-Slavist imperialism.[112]

For the Slavs to be strong, Karel Kramář countered, they had to lean on Russia. Kramář did not believe in the viability of Bolshevism and thought that soon Russia would return to what it had been before the war, only that then the chief role would be played by the emigrants who had come to know the other Slavs and become more realistic and practical. Russia, Kramář maintained, would return to her Slav policy, but not only for sentimental reasons. She should be 'compensated' for her self-sacrifice and for providing protection: the Slav nations should accept her primacy over them and should enter into a union with her based on her leadership in questions of foreign policy and military defence. It is only in this way that the small Slav nations can get 'beyond the narrow limits of the possibilities which are now open to them' and 'become influential members of the great whole' and thus 'take part in the general life of the World'.[113]

The above-mentioned Bulgarian legal scholar and neo-Slavist Stefan Bobchev described the controversial debate between Beneš and Kramář in the following terms. The former exemplified a realist type of thinking in politics and diplomacy that prevailed after the war, which was

---

108 Beneš quoted in Paul Milyukov, 'A New Slavonic Policy', *The Slavonic and East European Review* 6, no. 18 (1928): 486. See also, Bobčev, 'The Slavs after the War', 293.

109 Milyukov, 'New Slavonic Policy', 487, 489.

110 Ibid., 487.

111 Ibid., 488.

112 Ibid., 488, 493.

113 Ibid., 489–90.

'entirely devoid of any appreciation of the racial kinship of the Slavs and run counter both to the best teaching of the earlier Slavophils and to the continuation of their work at the Prague and Sofia Congresses.' The latter stood for 'the great scheme for Slavonic reciprocity' – a legacy of Slavophile teaching and neo-Slavism, which were driven by the conviction 'that no Slav nation can hope to prosper if it ploughs the furrow of culture, economics and policy, alone and sundered from its fellows.'[114] The virtue of Slav solidarity or reciprocity, according to Bobchev, sprang from the Slavs' 'profound consciousness that they are members of one and the same great family or community.'[115] Like Kramář, Bobchev assigned Russia the place of 'first among equals'[116] by virtue of its size and population as well as its contribution to the Slavs' advancement, aggrandizement and liberation.[117] Russia and its Communist International organization (Comintern), however, made collaboration with her on behalf of the neo-Slav aspirations impossible; the only hope resided with 'the national and democratic Russia of the future'.[118] In the opinion of Bobchev:

> The efforts to secure the union of the Slavs must be, above all, of a cultural, economic, social and political nature. Full account must be taken of local, national characteristics, and these must receive their due recognition as part of the great Slav civilization, for even small nations of Slav descent can add something peculiarly their own to the rich treasure-house of European civilization. Those Slav nations and governments, whether great or small, which stand aloof from, and look askance at, the cause of Slav solidarity, cannot be strong enough to play the part in the civilization of the world to which their mere size entitles them. In order that their intellectual cooperation in the work of the Slavs and the world may be of real value, it must merge with the great stream and flow along the one channel of Slavdom.[119]

In interwar Poland, the Slavic idea, in both its 'realist' and neo-Slavist versions, was censured even by Roman Dmowski's nationalist camp, which focused instead on the contest with Germany and reconciliation with Russia. The praise of Western European civilization in political rhetoric, in schools and the media, and the promotion of Poland as belonging to the West – a view authorized by the historians of the Warsaw School – undeniably had an anti-Soviet and anti-Russian component. As has already been noted, the position of (Turanian) Russia as Poland's civilizational 'Other' and of Poland as an integral part of the cultural sphere of 'Latin (i.e. Catholic) civilization had been firmly established by the outbreak of World War I.'[120]

In a critique of Jaroslav Bidlo's major work on the history of the Slavs, one of the most distinguished historians of the Second Polish Republic, Marceli Handelsman, expressed serious doubts about whether the Slavs could be singled out as a valid object for universal treatment. Despite a certain 'common, primitive, ethnographic patrimony' and a consciousness of affinity and kinship, Handelsman argued, they do not share a single language, have no geographic or ethnic unity and no joint political past or culture. Methodologically, a comparative history of all Slavs, and thus a syncretic history of the Slav world, is impossible, and Bidlo's work is proof of

---

114 Bobčev, 'The Slavs after the War', 293, 297.
115 Ibid., 294.
116 Ibid., 299.
117 Ibid., 294.
118 Ibid., 295.
119 Ibid., 298.
120 Andrew Kier Wise, 'Russia as Poland's Civilizational "Other"', 73–92.

Spatial configurations

this;[121] one must part ways with the notions of origins, race and a unique civilization and replace or at least supplement them with the 'incontestable one of geography':

> The western Slavs of Latin civilization [and] the southern Slavs of pure Byzantine civilization, geographically linked with the Romanians and the Hungarians on the one side and the Italians and Germans on the other, are closer in history and civilization to their neighbours of different race than to their so-called brothers in race, whose fatherland is situated in Eastern Europe.[122]

Therefore, what was needed, Handelsman concluded, was a comparative history of Eastern Europe, where the Slavs would occupy a place of honour but not of isolation. Handelsman thus put geographical proximity at the centre of his conceptualization of both comparative history and historical regions. His younger colleague, Oskar Halecki, was no less averse to referring to anything that smacked of a Slavic unit. He took it upon himself to explain 'why central-eastern Europe, with its predominantly Slavonic population and so many centres of Slavonic political life, could never find any real unity based on the Slavonic element.'[123] On a more general level, he rejected the use of racial or ethnic criteria in defining a cultural-historical space.

The Polish Slavist and linguist Jan Niecisław Ignacy Baudouin de Courtenay held the same view: 'There is no special Slav civilization common to all Slavs at present and probably never has been and never will be', he wrote. There was Slav unity as far as language was concerned, but there was no Slav 'race', no community or even kinship forming a Slavonic 'soul', no common history, no common literature and no possibility of Slav solidarity from a simple emotional point of view. The dream of Slav unity was only dreamt of by intellectuals.[124] For his part, literary scholar Wenceslas (Wacław) Lednicki, another Polish Slavist, refuted the idea that there was a 'common [cultural] patrimony' among the Slav nations. According to him, the diversity of the main paths of history, the epochs of common feuds and struggles, the dissimilarity of their poetical and literary creations and artistic production, and their differing moral and religious ideologies make any general synthesis of Slav culture 'a purely philosophical speculation'.[125]

Generally speaking, the concept of Slav solidarity remained underdeveloped in interwar Poland. Polish intellectuals' and especially historians' critique of the Slav world construct was essentially aimed at delegitimizing an interpretative frame, which would have posited 'Slavdom' as a meaningful organizing unit in European history and privileged Russia and Prague (often seen as 'pan-Slavic' and 'Russophile') within such a construct. In the case of Handelsman and Halecki, who aspired to reinstate the regional role of pre-partition Poland after 1918, any Slavic organizing principle to conceptualize the East, as M. Biskupski aptly described it, would contradict the very element in the Polish experience that was central to their most cherished suppositions, namely 'that Poland was an idea, a multi-sourced collectivity, and not an ethnic

---

121 The periodization of Slav history as proposed by Bidlo, Handelsman pointed out, is valid for the western and the southern but not for the eastern Slavs.

122 Marceli Handelsman, 'Monde slave ou l'Europe Orientale?', *Bulletin d'information des sciences historiques en Europe Orientale* 3 (1930): 124–31, here 130.

123 Oskar Halecki, 'The Historical Role of Central-Eastern Europe', *Annals of the American Academy of Political and Social Science* 232, no. 1 (1944): 10–11.

124 Milyukov, 'A New Slavonic Policy', 482–3. The author comments on an article by Baudouin de Courtenay published in *Le Monde Slav* in July 1925.

125 Milyukov, 'A New Slavonic Policy', 484–5. Before the Second World War, Lednicki taught in Poland and Brussels; in 1940 he emigrated to the United States.

(or religious) community.' Thus, the liberal Handelsman and the conservative Roman Catholic Halecki joined hands in defending a vision of Poland that would transcend ethnic and religious definitions and, in the words of Handelsman, would infer 'the connection and influence of Polish life on the development of its neighbouring peoples of central, eastern, and southeastern Europe.'[126]

To better understand interwar Slavism (and its various autochthonist or regionalist ramifications) one needs to incorporate its contemporary conceptual counterpart: Eurasianism. The Eurasian movement (launched in the early 1920s) drew on a 'morphological conception' of the development of cultures similar to Spengler's and signified, in the words of one of its proponents, 'a fierce vindication of the rights of the non-European civilizations against the presumption of Europe in identifying herself with Mankind, and regarding her civilization as the highest and only human civilization in general.'[127] The main premises of the Eurasian doctrine, which in different ways influenced the symbolic reformulations of space in interwar East Central Europe, were that Russia is not part of Europe, European civilization is alien to Russia, Russia has a civilization of her own and that the Russian Revolution of 1917 'was in its subconscious essence the revolt of the Russian masses against the domination of an Europeanized and renegade upper class.'[128] In their identification of Russian civilization with the true Christianity of the Orthodox Church and opposition to juridical and rationalistic Western Christianity (or Romanism), the Eurasians were successors in faith to the Slavophiles. Unlike them, however, they saw little in common between the Russian people and the western Slavs – above all the Czechs and the Poles, whom they regarded as no better than second-rate Europeans.[129] Ironically, in the Eurasianist conception the Slavic element in the Russian make-up itself became subordinated to the Turanian one, and Slavophile ideas about Slavic unification were completely abandoned. The Eurasianists and the East Central European critics of post-war Europe from Slavic or autochthonist positions shared a large pool of common references and concepts. (Turanism in Hungary and Hunnism in Bulgaria were other geocultural projections that resonated with Eurasianism.) Even the 'turn to the homeland' and what some contemporaries called the new 'intellectual national romanticism' that pervaded interwar national debates about regional and European identity were often seen as the 'products of the influence of Eurasianism'.[130]

The 'new' Eastern and (East) Central Europe of the interwar period

The space that will be discussed in this section has been labelled differently in the scholarly literature – as Central, East Central and Eastern Europe – and each of these concepts evokes specific connotations, inside and outside the respective designated area. As long as the area thus

---

126 Biskupski, 'Marceli Handelsman', 368, 372.

127 D.S. Mirsky, 'The Eurasian Movement', *Slavonic Review* 6 (1927): 312. An original 'manifesto' of sorts for the movement was outlined in Nikolay Trubetskoy's pamphlet *Europe and Mankind* (1920), where he launched a severe critique of what he called 'Romano-Germano centrism' (in *The Legacy of Genghis Khan and Other Essays on Russia's Identity*, ed. A. Liberman (Ann Arbor: Michigan Slavic Publications, 1991), 1–64.)

128 Mirsky, 'Eurasian movement', 312.

129 *Ishod k Vostoku. Predchuvstviya i sversheniya. Utverzhdenie evraziytsev – Stat'i St. P.Savitskogo, P.Suvchinskogo, N.S. Trubetskogo i Geogriya Florovskogo* [Exodus to the East: premonitions and accomplishments; Position of the Eurasians – articles by S.P.Savitski, P.Suvchinski, N.S.Trubetskoy and Georgiy Florovski] (Sofia: Balkan, 1921), 103.

130 Georgi Konstantinov, 'Retsenziya za K. Gălăbov. "Zovăt na rodinata"' [Review of K. Gălăbov's 'The Call of the Homeland'], *Filosofski pregled*, no. 2 (1931): 213–14.

Spatial configurations

named was divided between four empires – Habsburg, German, Russian and Ottoman – there was little need for a collective meso-regional label or even to imagine these diverse lands as one region.[131] In both academic and political discourses, especially in Germany and France, Eastern Europe was identified with the Russian Empire (and only occasionally the Slavs generally) and was thus the subject of Slavic studies. After the war, the Roman Instituto per l'Europa Orientale (and its journal *l'Europa Orientale*) and the German publication *Osteuropa: Zeitschrift für die Gesamtfragen des europäischen Ostens* concerned themselves with the entire Russian, Polish, Baltic, Danubian and Balkan region.[132]

Within the region, terms like Central, Eastern, Central-Eastern Europe and the European East were gaining wider currency, while demonstrating at the same time the lack of stability in regional terminology. Journals like *L'Europe Centrale* (founded in 1926) and the *Central European Observer* (1923–48) were published in Prague; *L'Est Européen* appeared in Warsaw, in whose pages its contributors often used the phrase 'Central and Eastern Europe'. Terminological inconsistency reflected both different national-political agendas (or geopolitical imageries) and different cross-national disciplinary cultures. Simultaneously, among historians from the region the interwar years featured a lively discussion on the extension of Eastern Europe, the historical relationship between East and West and the scope of 'Eastern European history'. Many of these discussions, both academic and public, evolved in dialogue that engaged with the German notion of *Mitteleuropa*, as it had originally been envisioned by Friedrich Naumann in 1915 and the interwar school of *Ostforschung*.

The Halecki–Handelsman–Bidlo debate

The above-mentioned Polish historian Oskar Halecki was the first to raise these issues at the fifth International Congress of Historical Sciences held in Brussels in 1923.[133] In his talk, 'The History of Eastern Europe: Its Division in Epochs, Its Geographical Milieu and Its Fundamental Problems',[134] Halecki refuted the simple bifurcation of Europe into East and West. In his opinion, the territory beyond Germany's eastern border may be called Eastern Europe only in a geographical sense (*sens purement géographique*). In terms of cultural belonging, 'a great part of what is commonly called Eastern Europe has always indisputably belonged to the realm of Western civilization'.[135]

---

131 Peter Bugge, "'Shatter Zones": The Creation and Re-creation of Europe's East', in *Ideas of Europe since 1914: The Legacy of the First World War*, eds Menno Spiering and Michael Wintle (Houndmills, Basingstoke and New York: Palgrave Macmillan, 2002), 52–3; Hans Lemberg, 'Zur Entstehung des Osteuropabegriffs im 19. Jahrhundert: Vom "Norden" zum "Osten" Europas', *Jahrbücher für Geschichte Osteuropas* 33, no. 1 (1985): 48–91.

132 Wandycz, 'East European History', 309.

133 Jerzy Kłoczowski, 'Oskar Halecki (1891–1973)', in Brock et al., *Nation and History*, 429–42; Hans-Jürgen Bömelburg, 'Zwischen imperialer Geschichte und Ostmitteleuropa als Geschichtsregion: Oskar Halecki und die polnische "jagiellonische Idee"', in *Vergangene Größe und Ohnmacht in Ostmitteleuropa: Repräsentationen imperialer Erfahrung in der Historiographie seit 1918*, eds Frank Hadler and Mathias Mesenhöller (Leipzig: AVA, 2007), 99–133; and Biskupski, 'Polish Conceptions of Unity and Division', 93–111.

134 Oskar Halecki, 'L'histoire de l'Europe Orientale: Sa division en époques, son milieu géographique et ses problèmes fondamentaux', in *La Pologne au Ve Congrès international des sciences historiques de Bruxelles 1923*, ed. Aleksander Birkenmajer (Warsaw: Comité national polonais du Ve Congres d'histoire, 1924), 73–94.

135 Halecki, 'L'histoire de l'Europe Orientale', 76–7.

Halecki rebutted both the identification of Eastern Europe with Russia, which pervaded Western historiography, and the existence of a common Slav history or heritage. Instead, he sought to demonstrate the heterogeneous character and historic lack of unity of Eastern Europe. His aim, thereby, was to disentangle the histories of the Polish–Lithuanian Commonwealth and Tsarist Russia on the maps of Western political thought and historiography, and to assert the unique status and contribution of Central Europe, particularly Poland, to Europe. Since the thirteenth century, when Russian territory was conquered by the Tatars, Eastern Europe, Halecki argued, was divided into two parts 'clearly distinct and usually opposed to each other'. The emerging state of Moscow became 'definitely a different world' in comparison to the realm from which it originated and to the rest of European civilization. The western hemisphere of the geographical area Eastern Europe – made up, according to Halecki, of Poland, Ukraine and Belarus (thus excluding the Czechs, Slovaks, Hungarians and the population of the Balkans from his concept of Eastern Europe) – constituted an organic part of European history and, therefore, Western civilization. The eastern (Russian) zone, which was more primitive, evolved more slowly and consolidated later, exhibited the characteristics of Eurasia. Halecki strongly insisted on the need for the historical understanding of 'the profound divergence between these two parts' in order to explain the contrast in his own day between the Union of the Soviet Socialist Republics and the 'several independent states with a parliamentary regime'.[136]

Before the Second World War, Halecki assigned no name to the non-Russian part of Eastern Europe. He only adopted the concept of Eastern-Central Europe during the Second World War and applied it to a considerably expanded space, which included Bohemia, Hungary and Southeastern Europe.[137] Halecki kept on writing and publishing on this topic in the 1930s and – after his emigration to the United States in 1940 – during the 1950s.[138] Whereas in the early 1920s he argued that Eastern Europe consisted of two hemispheres, 'Occidental' and 'Oriental', in his later writings he altogether excluded Russia after the thirteenth century from European history. Following the rule of the Tatars and Russian autocracy, the Bolshevik Regime finally alienated this part of the world from Western civilization and its 'eastern borderlands', that is, East Central Europe.[139]

At the seventh International Congress of Historical Sciences held in Warsaw in 1933, the Czech Slavist and Byzantinist Jaroslav Bidlo proposed a model for Eastern Europe that differed dramatically from Halecki's.[140] He called Halecki's conceptualization 'geographical and ideological' and his own theory 'cultural and political, or political-cultural'. By the 1930s, Bidlo had abandoned the Slavic paradigm in favour of another one, which effectively identified Eastern Europe with the Orthodox domain. Following the tradition of Ernst Troeltsch's

---

136 Ibid., 81, 83, 91–2.

137 Halecki, 'The Historical Role of Central-Eastern Europe', 9–18.

138 Oskar Halecki, 'Der Begriff der osteuropäischen Geschichte', *Zeitschrift für osteuropäische Geschichte* 5 (1935), 1–21; idem, *The Limits and Divisions of European History* (London: Sheed & Ward, 1950); idem, *Borderlands of Western Civilization: A History of East Central Europe* (New York: Ronald Press, 1952).

139 Halecki, 'Begriff der osteuropäischen Geschichte', 18; idem, *Borderlands of Western Civilization*, 3. See also Robin Okey, 'Central Europe/Eastern Europe: Behind the Definitions', *Past & Present* 137/1 (1992): 107.

140 Jaroslav Bidlo, 'Ce qu'est l'histoire de l'Orient Européen?', *Bulletin d'information des sciences historiques en Europe Orientale* 6 (1934): 11–73; Jaroslav Bidlo, 'L'Europe orientale et le domaine de son histoire', *Le Monde Slave* 12 (1935): 204–33. See also Otto Hoetzsch, 'Begriffsbestimmung und Periodisierung der osteuropäischen Geschichte', *Zeitschrift für Osteuropäische Geschichte* 8 (1934), 92–100; and Wandycz, 'East European History', 308–21.

Kulturkreistheorie, Bidlo's Eastern Europe, or the 'European East' as he preferred to label it, was a space that epitomized a distinct culture: a Greco-Slavic Orthodox Europe with roots in the Byzantine world. Western and Eastern Europe, in Bidlo's view, had embarked on different paths of historical development as early as the year 330, when Constantinople was founded and Western and Eastern Christianity started to drift apart. Eastern Europe, comprising all the peoples of Orthodox faith, differed drastically from the West in that it had experienced no scholastic philosophy or heresies, no Reformation nor counter-Reformation. Bidlo summoned the anti-Western opinions of the Russian Slavophiles in defence of his thesis, while point-ing to their close connections and solidarity with non-Slavic peoples such as the Romanians, Georgians and Armenians. The traits he ascribed to this Slavo-Byzantine Eastern Europe were overwhelmingly regressive and stood in stark contrast to the rationalism, dynamism and lib-eralism of the West. These were: delayed cultural development; limited urbanization (hence weak crafts and industries); a certain spiritual apathy; and finally, an absence of innovative spirit, which resulted in social conservatism, the tyranny of the clerical element, political submission to the despotism of the state and an absence of civic virtues. Political events were of secondary importance in this interpretation, while culture and religion were the determining factors in historical evolution: 'the history of Eastern Europe, or better still the European East, is the his-tory of the Greco-Slav cultural world'.[141] Even though Orthodox culture had historically been on the retreat, as the state-driven modernization that began at the end of the eighteenth century brought these societies closer to the West, important differences nonetheless remained.[142]

In Bidlo's model, even though it was influenced, as previously mentioned, by Russian Slavophilism and the writings of the German religious philosopher Ernst Troeltsch, the west-ern Slavs (Poles and Czechs) and some groups of South Slavs (Croats and Slovenes) could be considered part of the Western world due to their affiliation with the Catholic and Protestant Churches. The Hungarian historian Imre Lukinich, who in 1935 began publishing *Archivum Europae Centro-Orientalis* ('The archive of European Central Asia'), the periodical of the Institute of East European History at the University of Budapest, relied on the same regionalizing crite-ria; for him, the territories that fell into Western Christianity's (Catholicism and Protestantism) area of influence form a region with a common civilization, whereas the states whose model in terms of political ideology and religion was the Byzantine Orthodoxy of the Middle Ages form another one.[143] Obviously, the idea of Eastern Europe as a space that encompasses both Western and Eastern Slavs – a concept that had also been promoted by Bidlo in the 1920s – was increasingly losing support among historians from East Central Europe in the 1930s.[144]

In his polemical piece with Bidlo, Halecki's colleague Marceli Handelsman, who had pre-viously criticized Bidlo's major work on the Slavs, expressed delight that the Slavic scheme, especially the treatment of the Slavs as a separate race and unified culture, had been abandoned. What really matters in the process of defining a historical region, he maintained, is not civiliza-tion (religion) but showing how geography and proximity result in various ties. Handelsman stressed the relativity of any historical-geographical notion, which he saw as being contingent

---

141 Bidlo, 'Ce qu'est l'histoire de l'Orient Européen?', 21.

142 Wandycz, 'East European History', 311–12; and Jerzy Kłoczowski, *East Central Europe in the Historiog-raphy of the Countries of the Region* (Lublin: Institute of East Central Europe, 1995), 11–12.

143 Imre Lukinich, 'Inaugural Address of the Bulletin Commission, Riga, 21 July 1928', *Bulletin d'information des sciences historiques en Europe Orientale* 1–2 (1928): 260.

144 Cf. Handelsman, 'Monde slave ou Europe orientale?', 124–31; Josef Pfitzner, 'Die Geschichte Osteur-opas und die Geschichte des Slawentums als Forschungsprobleme', *Historische Zeitschrift* 150 (1934): 21–85.

upon geographical location, point of view (*centre d'appreciation*) and a 'socio-psychological' element. In the light of this, the ideas of Western Europe and Eastern Europe, historically speaking, continuously changed meaning and territorial scope. This did not prevent him from arguing that, since the Polish–Lithuanian Commonwealth had constituted the centre of Eastern Europe for nearly a thousand years, it was 'in the history of Poland that one must look for the integrating element [the *principe organisateur*] of the history of Eastern Europe as a whole'.[145] At the end of the day, Handelsman's notion of East Central Europe was at once a counterproposal to the concept of the Slavic world and a reification of an ideal: the resurrection of a multi-ethnic and multi-confessional Poland as the regional *principe organisateur* capable of bringing about a solution to the fragmentation and vulnerability of the European East.[146]

Handelsman was also instrumental in asserting Poland's dominant position during the institutionalization of comparative regional studies. In 1927 he helped to found an international Federation of the Historical Societies of Eastern Europe, and an institute for East European research followed in 1930. The Federation's organ, *Bulletin d'information des sciences historiques en Europe Orientale* ('Eastern European historical sciences newsletter'), became an influential forum for scholarly exchange and theoretical debates on transnational methodologies. The study area of Eastern Europe charted by the institution was much more inclusive than Halecki's idea of Eastern Europe at that time, as it encompassed the entire small-state area from the eastern borders of Germany and Italy to the European boundaries of Russia and from Finland in the north to Greece in the south.[147]

Halecki's response to Bidlo concurred with but also extended Handelsman's argument. He conceded the merits of a broader concept of Eastern Europe that included the Southeastern part, but also stressed the existence of major differences between this area and the north. He took this as evidence that, as Handelsman had also argued, Eastern Europe could accommodate very different definitions and as such was a relative concept that could be approached from diverse viewpoints. Halecki took issue with Bidlo's concept of Eastern Europe on three points. First, he rejected the usage of geopolitical criteria for defining a cultural community. There was no immutable line that divided the European continent into West and East. Instead Halecki endorsed the notion of a 'geographic milieu' of Eastern European history, viewing it as a framework of interaction for unfolding historical processes. Second, while Bidlo had rightly abandoned Slavic history as a valid frame of reference, he had now gone to the other extreme, excluding some Slavs (such as the Poles) from Eastern Europe. This, in Halecki's opinion, smacked too much of a revived Slavophilism, even if it was devoid of a political bias. Finally, and most importantly, Halecki rejected a dualism in European history based on a dichotomy between Byzantium and Rome. In reality, the picture, he argued, was far more complex and involved: (i) transitional or mixed regions where Eastern and Western influences had intermingled for centuries; (ii) considerable differences within both the Orthodox and the Catholic/Protestant worlds, in which neither was immune to influences that stemmed from the

---

145 Marceli Handelsman, 'Quelques remarques sur la définition de l'histoire de l'Europe Orientale', *Bulletin d'information des sciences historiques en Europe Orientale* 6, nos. 1–2 (1934): 74–81. Handelsman had by then developed his views on this issue. See Handelsman, 'Monde slave ou Europe orientale?', 124–31. See also Wandycz, 'East European History', 313–14; and Kłoczowski, *East Central Europe*, 13.

146 Biskupski, 'Polish Conceptions of Unity and Division', 101–2.

147 *Bulletin d'information des sciences historiques en Europe orientale* 1, nos. 1–2 (1928): 5–8. The editorial committee of the federation's organ comprised Poles, Czechs, Hungarians, Romanians, Balts, Yugoslavs, Bulgarians and Greeks. For more on the activities of the federation, see Kłoczowski, *East Central Europe*, 6–10.

Spatial configurations

other; and (iii) Asiatic influences on Russia and Byzantium. What mattered for Halecki were not the divisions between Christians but the gap between the civilizations of Europe and Asia that had been visible since antiquity. He took on board the Turanian arguments of the Russian Eurasianists and relegated Russia to a part of Eurasia:

> More than the schism [between Orthodoxy and Catholicism], these Asiatic influences detached Byzantium from Rome, ultimately separating the two with an impassable barrier: the conquering of the Eastern Empire by the Turks. More than the Orthodoxy, the equally long Tartar domination dug a chasm between Muscovy and the rest of Europe, thus preparing the future Russian empire to become Eurasia.[148]

Elsewhere he states: 'The European part of the Soviet Union constitutes, together with its Asiatic part, a Eurasian world power with its own culture, dominated by the Russian element, and its own way of life, the Soviet system.'[149] The chronological and geographical divisions of European history, Halecki concluded, should take physical conditions and ethnic divisions into account (without becoming identified with them) and be justified by the existence of defining issues that determined the historical evolution of a given region.[150]

The Halecki–Handelsman–Bidlo exchange triggered a good deal of discussion not only on the pages of the *Bulletin d'information* but also in the *Zeitschrift für Osteuropäische Geschichte* ('Journal of Eastern European history') and the *Historische Zeitschrift* ('Historical magazine').[151] Within Czechoslovakia scholarly opinions were divided; some, like František (Frank) Wollman, a leading scholar in comparative literary Slavic studies, questioned the dualist view of European history, while others, like the historian Milada Paulová, sided with Bidlo's division of European historical evolution into Roman–Germanic and Greek–Slavic currents. Bidlo himself, in defence of his thesis, insisted that a historical conception of territory was 'but a necessary metaphor designed to describe not the territory itself, but the human society which lived there'.[152] Poland in this sense, although part of the geographic region of Eastern Europe, was not part of Eastern civilization. He emphatically denied that the latter concept signified a repudiation of his former synthesis of the Slav history. One could present a different synthesis, he maintained, and in his work on the Slavs he took into account their positions as close neighbours with similar living conditions and so on, rather than their common origin. Although preoccupied with finding out what the Slavs had in common, Bidlo adamantly challenged the concept of political unity based on Slavdom as being both impossible and detrimental to the individual Slav nations.[153]

The political implications and the academic 'afterlife' of the debate were significant. Halecki's regional conception of Eastern Europe had a very strong impact on subsequent historical

---

148 Oskar Halecki, 'Qu'est-ce que l'Europe orientale', *Bulletin d'information des sciences historiques en Europe Orientale* 6 (1934): 92.

149 Halecki, 'The Historical Role of Central-Eastern Europe', 18.

150 Halecki, 'Qu'est-ce que l'Europe orientale', 81–93. See Wandycz, 'East European History', 314–15; and Kłoczowski, *East Central Europe*, 13–14.

151 Wandycz, 'East European History', 315.

152 Jaroslav Bidlo, 'Remarques à la défense de ma conception de l'histoire de l'Orient européen et de l'histoire des peuples Slaves', *Bulletin d'information des sciences historiques en Europe Orientale* 6 (1934): 95–119.

153 Ibid.

scholarship both in Germany and the West.[154] From a Polish point of view, his and Handelsman's historical geography had a special significance. It avowed not only Poland's essential Westernness but its distinctive role in the Western tradition due to the country's borderland position. At the same time, it upheld what the Russian historian Ivan Aksakov dubbed 'the Eastern mission of the old Commonwealth', where Poland, in the words of M. Biskupski, 'was not just a country but a civilization'; while being Western, this civilization had produced a unique, local, multi-variant society (the Jagiellonian model), which had been able to influence a very considerable geographical space that was coextensive with the pre-partition boundaries, if not greater in scope. According to Biskupski, 'This process of diffusion created an essentially Polish portion of Europe, which is the key to Poland's historic role in Europe.'[155] In such a context, Poland was predestined to become an area of coalescence for much of the European East, which also included Ukraine, Lithuania and Belorussia; however, it did not act as a dominating but rather as an organizing power, in contrast to intolerant Russia. The belief in Polish leadership inspired by the Jagiellonian model – in other words, the Polish semantics of East Central Europe – forestalled both the ideas of Slav unity and broader regional cooperation.[156]

Bidlo's notion of Eastern Europe, on the other hand, despite criticism from his student Josef Macura in the 1940s, underwent a revival in the 1980s during the heyday of Central European dissident discourse. Not only Milan Kundera, whose opinion that Russia is ontologically different from Europe is well known, but also Václav Havel, who took issue with Kundera on other points, agreed that the Byzantine tradition of purportedly conflating church and state and spiritual and secular authorities is alien to European traditions, and is a major contributing factor in the distortions of the post-war experience.[157]

The 'virtue of the middle'

In Czechoslovakia, outside the small circle of historians that were involved in the Halecki–Handelsman–Bidlo debate, regional discourses employed different terminology and conveyed different meanings. They developed around the notion of the 'centre', whose genealogy dated back to the nineteenth century. Remarkably, German and Czech scholarship identified the 'virtue of the middle' or the 'golden mean' at the same time (in the mid-nineteenth century) – a simultaneous discovery that was made without apparent connection but with a similar purpose: to counter the threat of exclusion from European civilization, which at that point had a well-established location in France and Britain. A major part of the concept's attraction was in the

---

154 Werner Conze, *Ostmitteleuropa: Von der Spätantike bis zum 18. Jh*, ed. Klaus Zernack (München: C.H. Beck, 1993); and Klaus Zernack, *Osteuropa: Eine Einführung in seine Geschichte* (München: C.H. Beck, 1977).

155 Biskupski, 'Polish Conceptions of Unity and Division', 96–7, 102. As early as 1935, Halecki wrote that the nation and the state 'are looking for a new guiding idea and intuitively turn toward the old but always fresh Jagiellonian idea' (Wandycz, 'East European History', 317).

156 Wandycz, 'East European History', 317–18. Tellingly, when Józef Beck, the Polish foreign minister from 1935 to 1939, came up with the concept of a 'Third Europe' – a bloc composed of Poland, Hungary, Romania, Yugoslavia and Italy for the sake of opposing both German and Russian expansion – he postulated, as a prerequisite for its formation, the establishment of a common Polish–Hungarian frontier through Hungarian annexation of the territory it had lost to Czechoslovakia (Slovakia and Subcarpathian Ruthenia).

157 Kundera interview in *Cross Currents* (1982): 16; Tony Judt, 'The Dilemmas of Dissidence: The Politics of Opposition in East-Central Europe', *East European Politics and Societies* 2, no. 2 (1988): 223.

Spatial configurations

semantic ambiguity of the 'middle', which could signify both an affinity with and an alternative to the West, while serving as a mediator and organizer of European connections.[158]

According to Vladimír Macura, the Czech conception of Central Europe was heavily indebted to two previous stratagems with roots in the Czech and Slovak national revival culture and rhetoric: one was related to Slavdom and the other concerned the special significance attributed to the notion of the 'centre'. In a geographical sense, the Slavs lived between the Greeks and the Germans, thus blending the best qualities of classical antiquity and contemporary modernity, aesthetics and logic. Connected to the application of the concept of the centre in its geographical sense was the role of cultural mediation or brokerage of the unification of various cultural influences. This idea of the centre as a supreme value can be traced to František Palacký, the founder of modern Czech historiography, and his monumental book, *The History of the Czech Nation in Bohemia and Moravia* (1836–67), where he defines Bohemia as 'the centre and heart of Europe' and the Czech nation as

> the centre, in which the various elements and principles of modern European national, state and church life have met and fused, though not without strife. Here it is explicit and clear to see both the long conflict between and mutual penetration of Roman, German and Slav elements in Europe.[159]

This central position endowed the Czech nation with the historical role 'to serve as a bridge between the Germans and the Slavs, between the East and the West in Europe in general'.[160] Significantly, the Czechs' appropriation of the centre was contemporaneous with the emergence of *Mitteleuropa* in the German political, if not yet scholarly (e.g. geographical), discourse in the late 1840s.[161] This once again highlights what Vladimír Macura calls the 'translatorial' construction of Czech spatial imagery in relation to German processes, at a time when the two nations had been competing, both conceptually and physically, over the right to claim Central Europe.[162]

We should also bear in mind that such spatial projections often targeted a foreign audience and pursued geopolitical agendas and, as such, were adopted as means of cultural diplomacy and foreign propaganda. The writings that appeared during and shortly after the war of the founding fathers of Czechoslovakia – the philosopher president Masaryk and his lieutenant

---

158 Peter Bugge, 'The Use of the Middle: Mitteleuropa vs. Střední Evropa', *European Review of History* 6, no. 1 (1999): 18–19.

159 František Palacký, *Dějiny národu českého v Čechách a v Moravě, dle původních pramenů* [The history of the Czech nation in Bohemia and Moravia, according to original sources], vol.1 (Prague: J.G. Kalve, 1848), 9.

160 Ibid., 13. See Vladimír Macura, *Znamení zrodu: české národní obrození jako kulturní typ* [Sign of birth: Czech national revival as a cultural type] (Prague: Československý spisovatel, 1983), 198–207. Palacký, however, did not connect his thoughts on the centre with any concept of Central Europe – neither did he deny a natural German hegemony in Central Europe – and located the nations needing Austrian protection from the Russian Empire 'in the Southeast of Europe'. Jan Křen, *Konfliktní společenství: Češi a Němci 1780–1918* [Conflicting communities: Czechs and Germans 1780–1918] (Toronto: 68-Publishers, 1989), 127–37; Bugge, 'The Use of the Middle', 20.

161 Bugge, 'The Use of the Middle', 20–1. The term, in its expansionist reading, only became popular among geographers during the First World War.

162 In his study on 'The Use of the Middle', Bugge pays attention to the numerous 'constituent elements' that the interwar Czech notion of Central Europe adopted from the older German discourse of *Mitteleuropa*.

Beneš, a political economist – and those produced by the informal political-intellectual circle around them present perhaps the most conspicuous case. The concept of Central Europe, which they promoted, was predominantly political and economic and had few residual cultural characteristics.[163]

During the First World War, when he addressed Anglo-American experts and an intellectual audience, Masaryk had already come up with the idea of a 'New Europe' that encompassed the 'small nations' between Germany and Russia, while excluding both. In his 1918 book, *The New Europe*, Masaryk applied a straightforward East–West division to Europe, defining the Czechs as the westernmost non-German nation in the East. After the war, he introduced the concept of *Střední Evropa* ('Central Europe'), designating 'that special zone of small states and nations between the West and the East'.[164] Masaryk's Central Europe was thus a political and not a cultural entity, whereas his visions of the cultural divisions of Europe, as previously noted, were contradictory. The notion of Slavic Europe, which was popular among Czech and South Slavic scholars, overlapped to some extent with *Mittel* or *Zwischeneuropa*, but was geopolitically opposed to them, excluding the Germans altogether.

Indeed, Masaryk's notion of a 'small-nation Central Europe' was a direct reaction to and rebuttal of Friedrich Naumann's vision of a post-war *Mitteleuropa* that united Germany, the Austro-Hungarian Monarchy and the nations 'that belong neither to the Anglo-French western alliance nor to the Russian Empire'.[165] The rationale for this definition of *Mitteleuropa* was socio-economic and political: for the liberal nationalist Naumann, bigger was better, more efficient and more viable, and the very opposite of the principle of self-determination, since small nations were badly equipped to exercise political sovereignty and economic rationality.[166]

In an article surveying the first ten years of the existence of what he called the 'new Central Europe', which implicitly refuted Naumann's scepticism, Edvard Beneš described the region as 'a political expression of the national idea' but also as one characterized by an 'extreme intermixture of races and languages', which had made the complete implementation of the right to self-determination unfeasible. The countries that formed this new Central Europe were Czechoslovakia, Poland, Romania and Yugoslavia, states that were at once 'national', that is 'brought into existence by the will and efforts of nations once oppressed by Austria–Hungary', and 'mixed', containing 'fragments of other nations which were incorporated in them either on geographical or economic grounds.'[167] Hungary and Austria's 'admission' into this Central Europe was made contingent on their acceptance of post-war borders and abandonment of revanchist 'empty dreams' – a condition underscoring an unequivocally functionalist definition of the region. States of this kind, Beneš claimed, may be complicated from an internal perspective, but their international role is significant:

---

163 According to Bugge ('The Use of the Middle', 22), three factors catalysed the emergence of the Czech idea of Central Europe after 1918: a weakened German hegemony in the region and over the period; the correspondingly weakened attractiveness of pan-Slavic solidarity; and the need for a new designation for the former Habsburg community of nations and for some form of political and economic cooperation between them.

164 Masaryk, *Světová revoluce*, 563.

165 Friedrich Naumann, *Central Europe*, trans. Christabel M. Meredith (New York: Knopf, 1917) (original publication: Friedrich Naumann, *Mitteleuropa* [Berlin: Reimer, 1915]), 9.

166 Naumann, *Central Europe*, 33, passim.

167 Edvard Beneš, 'Central Europe after Ten Years', *Slavonic and East European Review* 7, no. 20 (1929): 245–60, here 250.

Spatial configurations

These States may serve as bridges between the east and the west, between the north and the south of Europe; they must incorporate the new ideas and methods of international co-operation. This is their special Central European function, on the comprehension of which obviously depends the whole stability of their international position.[168]

In addition to reifying national and democratic principles on the basis of the preservation of the post-war status quo, the notions of cultural 'intermixture' and 'bridging' are reinstated here as characteristic of Central Europe, notions that hark back to the Czech national Revivalist visions of the centre. At the same time, neither Beneš nor Masaryk favoured Central European (Danubian) federalization or any form of regional integration that could affect the political or economic sovereignty of Czechoslovakia.

The sole influential visionary of a Central European economic union, comprising the small states between Germany and Russia, was the Slovak politician and political theorist Milan Hodža. Hodža saw a common denominator and a unifying factor in the agrarian character of the region, which also implied a common mission:

Central Europe is the continuation of Western European civilization. What Central Europe once was for the West, i.e. a consumer of ideas and goods, the Orient will to a large extent become for our new Central Europe. Against American and Western European over-capitalistic mechanization Central Europe will defend itself – and perhaps also Europe's civilization – with the cooperative democracy of its small-scale farmers.[169]

The political ideal underpinning Hodža's regionalist project was peasant (agrarian) democracy; its economic justification was the need to overcome economic nationalism, which prevented the development of a mutually beneficial division of labour, and to stimulate agricultural productivity and exports. Consequently, Hodža called for a Central European Union – a multinational powerhouse in the heart of Europe – extending from the Baltic to the Aegean (and thus corresponding to Halecki's East Central Europe). Besides its economic and political justification, a federated Central Europe, in Hodža's plan, was intended as an independent geopolitical player between Germany and Russia. 'The East begins where Russia begins', he wrote, continuing that 'The old pan-Slavist conception, which counts above all on a great and powerful Russia ... could no longer be a basis for either culturally or politically positive work'. In his eyes, a Danubian federation – and a strong Central Europe – would become a pivotal element in a new balance of power and security in post-war Europe. Viewed from a long-term perspective, an integrated Central Europe was to be a steppingstone towards a united Europe.[170]

Other Czech intellectuals were busy upgrading the normative position of the middle, which was said to be essentially Czech, and qualifying the Czechs' affinity with the West. Ferdinand Peroutka stated that 'The West is attractive, but in a way also too hectic and wild for the little Czechs.'[171] In his article from 1935, 'Czechness and Europe', František Xaver Šalda, the

---

168 Beneš, 'Central Europe after Ten Years', 251.

169 Milan Hodža, *Články, reči, štúdie. Zväzok IV: Cesty sredo-evropskej agrárnej demokracie 1921–1931* [Articles, speeches, studies. Volume IV: the paths of European agrarian democracy 1921–1931] (Praha: Novina, 1931), 383, quoted in Bugge, 'The Use of the Middle', 22.

170 Milan Hodža, *Federation in Central Europe: Reflections and Reminiscences* (London: Jarrolds Publishers, 1942).

171 Quoted in Bugge, 'Longing or Belonging?', 123.

premier Czech literary critic of the time, wrote 'It may happen someday that we may strike the European balance. ... I believe in the mission of the centre in Europe.' Šalda prognosticated a future merger of Russian collectivism and Western individualism into a form of 'synthetic thinking', and asked rhetorically if this might not be a type of 'Central European thinking, and especially our thinking?'[172] In his previously quoted book, *Czechhood and Europeanness* (1931), František V. Krejčí arranged European cultures on a scale, at one end of which were

> the countries open to the Atlantic Ocean and the North Sea, [and] not far below them is the civilizational and cultural level of the more western parts of Central Europe (where also Bohemia belongs), but from there on eastwards the level visibly declines ...[173]

He then proceeded to define the main tasks of the Czechs, namely mediation between East and West and catching up with the most progressive Western nations. In Czech terminology, therefore, the concept of Central Europe remained firmly anchored to the normative connotations of the middle, although as a political programme the idea of Central European unity was supported by a few figures.

In interwar Hungary, the Central European lexicon was less prominent. In political parlance, it faced competition with other, partially overlapping spatial conceptualizations, such as the 'Carpathian Basin' of the integral nationalist political mainstream or the 'Eastern European peasant nation' of the populists. The linguist and writer Dezső Szabó was a representative of the latter group. While advocating an organicist ethno-cultural version of Hungarian nationalism, Szabó suggested that the new-fangled 'homogenous peasant nation states of Eastern Europe and the Balkans' were the models to follow. He also envisioned a federation based on the principles of 'new democracy' and 'new nationalism', two creative forces supposedly able to unify these peoples in regional cooperation against external imperialist pressures, especially those from Germany.[174]

As a scholarly notion, Central Europe appeared in the short-lived periodical *Apollo*, which, by stimulating regional cultural dialogue, aspired to become the platform for 'Central European humanism'.[175] In the latter half of the 1930s, *Archivum Europae Centro-Orientalis*, the periodical of the Institute of East European History at the University of Budapest, became a focal point for the young historians who focused on the history of the neighbouring peoples. István Hajnal, a member of this circle and the leading Hungarian social historian of the period, launched a project that pursued a transregional comparative history of the European 'small nations' in Central Europe, the Balkans and Scandinavia. Hajnal did not develop a regional narrative and instead contrasted the 'big' European nations, with their established territorial and social frames, to the 'small nations', which were characterized by late nation formation and the persistence of archaic social structures.[176] Many of the scholars in this area would go on to contribute to the creation

---

172 Ibid., 124.

173 František V. Krejčí, *Češství a evropanství: Úvahy o naší kulturní orientaci* [Czechhood and Europeanism: reflections on our cultural orientation] (Prague: Orbic, 1931), 28, quoted in Bugge, 'The Use of the Middle', 23.

174 Dezső Szabó, 'Tomorrow's Nationalism', in *Discourses of Collective Identity in Central and Southeast Europe (1770–1945)*, vol. 4, *Anti-Modernism: Radical Revisions of Collective Identity*, eds Diana Mishkova, Marius Turda and Balázs Trencsényi (Budapest: CEU Press, 2014), 110–14.

175 Balázs Trencsényi, 'Central Europe', in *European Regions and Boundaries: A Conceptual History*, eds Diana Mishkova and Balázs Trencsényi (Oxford: Berghahn Books, 2017), 171.

176 István Hajnal, 'A kis nemzetek történetírásának munkaközösségéről' [About the commonality of history of small nations], *Századok* 1–2 (1942): 1–42, 133–65. See Trencsényi, 'Central Europe'.

Spatial configurations

of a strong tradition of transnational historical research in Hungary during the short democratic interlude after the Second World War.

The Balkan utopia

In politics as well as academia, both inside and outside of the region, the period between the two world wars witnessed the peak of supranational scheming around the Balkans and Southeastern Europe. The terminological bifurcation is interesting here. On the one hand, references to Southeastern Europe (and Southeastern European studies) grew not only among the German practitioners of *Südostforschungen* but also in the official French and British nomenclature. Meanwhile, the Balkans and popular discourse on Balkanism, which was charged with fully negative connotations, continued to inform the Western understanding of the region and was dominant in journalistic, travel and political literature.

Against this backdrop, it is all the more striking to witness the systematic efforts within the region to rehabilitate, indeed the pursuit of a veritable renaissance for, the Balkans as a receptacle for positively charged cultural-historical and political imagery during the interwar years. Such revaluation was central to several parallel international and supranational undertakings: the communist project of Balkan federation, the liberal one for a Balkan union and the new 'science of Balkanology'. It was animated by various artistic and intellectual trends, notably the avant-gardist movements of the 1920s (e.g. the Zenit literary circle in Yugoslavia) and the various autochthonist, anti-liberal visions of the 1930s.

A series of academic institutions and publications emerged in the 1930s that framed their remit in explicitly regional terms. The 'new science of Balkanology' aimed to orient national academic research 'towards the study of a Balkan organism that had constituted one whole since the most distanced times'[177] and at creating a regional 'synthesis drawing on the elements of Balkan interdependence and unity'.[178] For medievalist Victor Papacostea, founder of the Bucharest-based Institute for Balkan Studies and Research in 1938, the adoption of the very idea of the nation state (one that was 'created in the West and for the West') had catastrophic consequences for the Balkans – a region that, unlike Western Europe, was marked by a unity of economic geography and by 'the same community of culture and civilization born by long coexistence'.[179] Papacostea talked instead of 'Balkan nationality' and 'Balkan society', as well as a '*homo balcanicus*',[180] and of the status of nationality as precarious and uncertain, 'in reality a notion, not ethnic, but mostly political and cultural'.[181] Against the tendency to frame the Balkans in terms of nationalist strife, Papacostea underscored the challenges nationalism faced in the region.

Balkanology contains an interesting blend of concepts and views. On a certain level, its 'immanently comparative', and cross-disciplinary methodology was remarkably enlightened. Informing this transnational agenda, on the other hand, was a metahistorical Balkanistic discourse

---

177 The subject and methodology of this new discipline were outlined for the first time by the two editors of the Belgrade-based *Revue internationale des études balkaniques* – the Croat Petar Skok and the Serb Milan Budimir. See M. Budimir and P. Skok. See in particular idem, 'But et signification des études balkaniques', *Revue internationale des études balkaniques* 1 (1934): 1–28 (here 2–3).

178 Victor Papacostea, 'Avant-Propos', *Balcania* 1 (1938): vi.

179 Ibid., iii–vii.

180 Victor Papacostea, 'La Péninsule Balkanique et le problème des études comparées', *Balcania* 6 (1943): iii–xxi.

181 Victor Papacostea, 'Balcanologia', *Sud-Estul și Contextul European* 6 (1996): 69–78.

that borrowed heavily from the discourse of (national) autochthonism. The Balkanologists discussed the profound cultural differences between the countries in the region and the Occident, the region's self-reliance and self-sufficiency; they began to vindicate 'strong and irreducible Balkan individuality', which they saw as a testament to the region's 'historic function' of safeguarding humanism, heroism and 'unity in variations'.[182] Balkanistic literature, especially that which was intended for domestic consumption, was explicit in its anti-Western and anti-capitalist leanings. Not only the rivalries and bloody wars between the Balkan peoples, but also the political, economic, social and cultural backwardness of the Balkan nations were said to be the product of the selfishness and greed of the Great Powers, and interferences in the region. Where the discourse on Balkanism contrasted the 'primitive' Balkans with a 'civilized' Europe, Balkanologists saw the primitivism of the Balkans as a consequence of European domination.

Here was a genuine orientalist critique *avant la lettre*. But where did it lead? More radically than Iorga, interwar Balkanologists redeemed the region by projecting the imagery of the nation onto it:

> The Balkans is more than the European Southeast. It is a world clasp. This clasp has a greater responsibility and heavier duty than Europe. ... Thus, the Balkans is something authentic within the old continents: neither Europe nor Asia ... neither European East nor Asian West, but a unique area with specific characteristics and specific assignment. This position of the Balkans also defines the fate of the Balkan peoples. They thus become intermediaries and warriors, defenders of the West against the East, protectors of the North against the South, keepers of the Balkan threshold in front of the Western people and main intermediaries between the fresh and coarse North and the warm, early blooming and faded South.[183]

Balkanology was but one attempt to devise a missionary discourse centred on the humanistic rejuvenation of the West. Ideals related to 'the Balkanization of Europe' were encapsulated in various vitalist imageries of the Balkans, such as Vladimir Dvorniković's 'epic man' or the 'Balkan Barbarogenius', a mythic hero within the most influential Yugoslav avant-garde movement called *Zenit*, which resurrected a Balkan ethos and authentic existence capable of generating a new European culture to combat Western degeneration.[184] Extra-regional, particularly

---

182 Budimir and Skok, 'But et signification des études balkaniques', vi.

183 *Balkan i Balkanci* [The Balkans and the Balkaners] (Belgrade: Izdanje Balkanskog instituta, 1937), 26.

184 Dvorniković's 'epic man' (*epski čovek*) of the Balkans represented the last refuge of old European values – traditional, elevated and heroic (Vladimir Dvorniković, *Karakterologija Yugolovena* [Characterology of the Yugoslavs], [Belgrade: Kosmos, 1939]). From his perspective, the Bulgarian philosopher Yanko Yanev praised the Balkan man as the 'eternal warrior, the most valiant man that history has ever known' (Yanko Yanev, *Der Mythos auf dem Balkan* [Berlin: Kulturpolitik, 1936]). The Zenit avant-garde movement attempted to universalize the local, which was 'Balkan' or 'Southeastern'; it conceptualized the Balkans as the epicentre of global creative energy, and the Balkan man as the embodiment of the authentic and all-embracing human spirit: the ultimate 'Barbarogenius'. See Vidosava Golubović and Irina Subotić, *Zenit 1921–1926* (Belgrade: Narodna biblioteka Srbije i Institut za književnost i umetnost; and Zagreb: Srpsko kulturno društvo 'Prosvjeta', 2008); and Darko Šimčić, 'From Zenit to Mental Space: Avant-Garde, Neo-Avant-Garde, and Post-Avant-Garde Magazines and Books in Yugoslavia, 1921–1987', in *Impossible Histories: Historical Avant-Gardes, Neo-Avant-Gardes, and Post-Avant-Gardes in Yugoslavia, 1918–1991*, eds Dubravka Djurić and Miško Šuvaković (Cambridge, MA: MIT Press, 2003), 294–330.

Spatial configurations

German, scholarship participated in this construction of a unique Balkan world and a Balkan man endowed with 'heroic life forms' and a proper cultural consciousness as a means 'to retrieve the Balkans for Europe'.[185] In clear defiance of the popular reading of Balkanization, this notion of Balkanness endeavoured to indigenize and devour the historical teleology and cultural authority of Europeanness.

A striking feature of all this was the complete volte-face that the power of the signifier 'the Balkans' – and of being Balkan – underwent within a large sphere of converging scholarly and political discourses in the 1930s. The movement towards the Balkan Conference and Balkan Pact, and the founding of Balkan institutes to conduct Balkan research came together around the slogan 'the Balkans for the Balkan peoples', which, as a contemporary observer noted, 'aimed to create a new political concept of the Balkans by the Balkan countries themselves' and 'an autonomous organization of a part of Southeastern Europe'.[186] From the perspective of Balkan scholars and intellectuals, their conception of what was Balkan in the 1930s had an emancipatory emphasis. On the one hand, it was a response to an awareness of frail state sovereignty and small-state status in the geopolitical environment of the 1930s. On the other, its manifest objective was to turn the orientalist semantics of the Balkans on its head – hence the insistence on the loaded term 'the Balkans' at the expense of the neutral but also faceless 'Southeastern Europe'.

Considering the prevalence of autarchic, nationalist projects at the time, the proliferation and variety of supranational spaces in the interwar period is indeed striking. The complexion of these projects that aimed to create such spaces differed considerably: from (sometimes radical) cultural-morphological redefinitions of Europe, the East–West relationship and the Slavic world to geopolitical or economic federalist schemes for Central European and Balkan unions with explicit anti-hegemonic implications; from (often contentious) mappings of historical regions derived from shared legacies and experiences, which also created new intraregional divides, to *sui generis* regionalist autochthonisms. Notwithstanding this variety, what united these supranational projects was that not only were they all connected to, and dependent upon, political contingencies, but they were deeply politicized and often subordinated to national geopolitical agendas.

Post-Second World War

The immediate post-Second World War period brought about a momentous reconfiguration in the discourse on symbolic geography, both political and scholarly, across the continent and within the region. It was signalled by the temporary disappearance of Europe from regional imagery, the decline of Central and Southeastern Europe/the Balkans, and the rise of Eastern Europe and the West as hegemonic frameworks. If there was any continuity, it was in that the formation of the Soviet bloc on the larger part of the region stabilized the Western interwar definition of Eastern Europe on the post-war mental map, as portended in Konrad Adenauer's

---

185 See, in particular, Franz Thierfelder, *Schicksalsstunden des Balkan* (Wien: Wiener Verlagsgesellschaft, 1941) and Gerhard Gesemann, *Heroische Lebensform: Zur Literatur und Wesenskunde der balkanischen Patriarchalität* (Berlin: Wiking-Verlag 1943). Gesemann eulogized Balkan patriarchal life and spoke of Balkan *humanitas heroica*. He also came up with an anti-Orientalist programme couched in the then fashionable völkisch paradigm.

186 Franz Ronneberger, 'Der politische Südosteuropabegriff', *Reich Volksordnung Lebensraum* 6 (1943): 75–6.

words that 'Asia stands on the Elbe'.[187] Later generations of regional intellectuals will see in this the destruction of the 'originality of this particular, stormy, tragic and vital subcontinent', so that, as Czech historian Jan Křen maintained: 'the concept still remains in meteorology, otherwise Central Europe is only a point of contact between the two social systems, their frontiers.'[188]

The brief ascent of the Slavic East: Czech cultural re-spatializations

A striking phenomenon of the Stalinist period in the history of the eastern part of the continent was the almost complete disappearance of the concept of Europe from intellectual and political discourses. As in the wake of the First World War, Europe after 1945 was largely divested of positive connotations: Nazism, fascism and war, colonialism and the Holocaust combined to strip Europe of the modicum of allure it had continued to preserve between the wars. The war and its aftermath led to a deep crisis in the European consciousness with regard to the Czechs and the Poles. Interwar ideas about their place and role in Europe were declared to be a tragic illusion; the Western European Allies had left them and other Eastern European countries to their fate. Once again, the opinion prevailed that Europe had betrayed the ideals and values it had defended, specifically freedom and democracy. It was not only Europe's foreign and defence policies that were called into question, but its moral and political authority also collapsed, and this had a particularly strong effect on intellectuals, many of whom lent their support to the communist system.[189]

The public debate in Czechoslovakia on the nation's cultural orientation in the immediate post-war period, explicitly framed in terms of East or West, bears witness to the magnitude of the discursive shift in the definitions of Europe, the East, the West and the Slavic world. The communist intellectuals' position in the debate was encapsulated in the article 'East and West' (1945) by the Marxist literary scholar Ladislav Štoll. Štoll's conceptualization rested on two main arguments. Firstly, he formulated the thesis that authentic European values had moved from the West to the East and Russia:

> It was the Russians who became not only the true inheritors of the great cultural traditions of the West, but who also took the initiative and ran ahead of the West ... They became the defenders of European culture and civilization because their culture was stronger, more vigorous and more powerful.[190]

Another communist writer, Lumír Čivraný, put this even more emphatically: 'The East, led by the Soviet Union, is the inheritor of [the progressive culture of the West] and the realizer of the world's best spiritual values.'[191] In 1950, the then Minister of Culture and Education, powerful manager of post-war Czech culture, historian and music critic Zdeněk Nejedlý, wrote that 'The true Europe, the Europe of the best and highest traditions, exists today in the Soviet Union, which took as its foundations the greatest and historically most significant achievement

---

187 Iver Neumann, *Uses of the Other: 'The East' in European Identity Formation* (Minneapolis, MN: University of Minnesota Press, 1999), 102.

188 Křen, *Konfliktní společenství. Češi a Němci*, 7.

189 Törnquist-Plewa, 'The Complex of an Unwanted Child', 233–5.

190 Bradley F. Abrams, *The Struggle for the Soul of the Nation: Czech Culture and the Rise of Communism* (Lanham, MD: Rowman & Littlefield, 2004), 159–61.

191 Quoted in Abrams, *The Struggle for the Soul*, 161.

Spatial configurations

of nineteenth-century European culture – the teachings of Marx and Engels.'[192] Related to this claim was another one, namely that while the past belonged to the West, the future belonged to the East. The bearer of that radiant future of the East was 'the great Slavic world', which was finally going to hold 'a respected place in European civilization, where the culture of the Slavic nations had often been looked down upon'.[193]

Significantly, these arguments had a strong resonance among non-communist intellectuals of various politico-ideological hues, from President Beneš, who proclaimed the main goal of a 'new Slavic politics' to be 'the gaining of a new place for all Slavic nations and cultures in Europe and in the world', to the intellectual and spiritual leadership of the Czechoslovak Church with their calls for a process of '[unifying] the Slavs and placing them on the foundation of pure Christianity', marked by 'a synthesis between religion and scientific endeavours'.[194] In their efforts to compensate for the nation's smallness and to counter potential peripherality, intellectuals often came up with distinct messianic and implicitly racist ideas that were highly reminiscent of those voiced by their Balkan peers between the wars.

The most coherent alternative position was formulated by the leading literary critic of that time, Václav Černý, on behalf of the democratic non-communist opposition. While he readily admitted that in the modern era the Czechs had drawn cultural inspiration from Russia and Slavdom, Černý believed that Czech culture was essentially Western. The Czechs' universalist mission – pointing to a *sui generis* 'Czech socialist humanism' – was to synthesize East and West not by a 'temporary compromise', but on the basis of their critical reception and by uniting them 'in a new, internally consistent higher organism'. Since post-war Czechoslovakia, he argued, is 'the only nation expressly "Western" in culture entering into a sphere decidedly under the politico-cultural influence of Russia', it has been privileged to perform this 'task of great honour' and serve as a 'supranational example [which has] supranational validity.'[195] The rhetoric here is no longer concerned with a 'bridge', but rather with a synthesis between the two cultures, and as such it won the wide support of democratic ('national') socialist intellectuals. At the end of the day, however, it was the communists' more coherent and emotive concoction of Marxism and nationalist Slavism, clad in the normative veneer of a rejuvenated Europe, which won the day.

For some time after the war scholarly literature outside Eastern Europe kept the interest in Slavdom alive. The work of the émigré Czech Slavist František (Francis) Dvorník – who, in a similar vein to Bidlo a few decades earlier, focused on Slavic early medieval history, Christianization and state formation – is characteristic of this climate.[196] But although Dvorník attributed a number of commonalities to the Slavs – from language and mentality to civilization and political history – his Slavic world was not confined to ethno-cultural boundaries, but placed within the broader regional context of Eastern Europe.

---

192 Macura, *The Mystification of a Nation*, 19–20.

193 Abrams, *The Struggle for the Soul*, 161.

194 Ibid., 165–6. For more on the Soviet discourse of Slavic unity in the 1940s, see Sergey Radchenko, 'Joseph Stalin', in *Mental Maps in the Cold War Era, 1945–68*, eds Steven Casey and Jonathan Wright (New York: Palgrave, 2011), 9–31.

195 Abrams, *The Struggle for the Soul*, 167–70. See also Carlos Reijnen, 'For a True Europe and a New Patriotism: Europe and the West from a Czech Stalinist Perspective', in *Europa im Ostblock. Vorstellungen und Diskurse (1945–1991)*, eds Christian Domnitz, José M. Faraldo and Paulina Gulińska-Jurgiel (Köln, Weimar and Wien: Böhlau, 2008), 113–14.

196 Francis Dvorník, *The Slavs in European History and Civilization* (New Brunswick, NJ: Rutgers University Press, 1962).

Other émigré Slavists, however, dismissed any notion of Slavic commonality and envisaged Eastern Europe itself as a battlefield between the irreconcilable East and the West. In his book, *Russia, Poland and the West* (1954), the previously mentioned Wacław Lednicki argued:

> The Russian-Polish conflict is a focus in which is concentrated the essence of Eastern and Western historical trends. Around this conflict are crystallized the chief Eastern and Western principles and conceptions of individual and collective life. … Geographically and historically, during the thousand years of her existence, Poland has been an outpost of the West, to which she was allied by her own free will as well as by circumstances. Her geographical situation, her political development and activities, her cultural traditions made of her a missionary of the West; she was preserving and spreading the ideas of Western civilization. For these reasons, after centuries of fighting for this civilization, although having been so often betrayed by Europe, Poland's ties with the West resulted in a particularly deep and indestructible attachment to Europe, to her ideals, concepts and beliefs. In a sense, therefore, Poland has always been more Western in her feelings than the most thoroughly Western nations. This tense Europeanism is generally characteristic for every Polish intellectual. Joseph Conrad is an excellent example of the phenomenon: he is much more devoted to the West than any purely English writer could be. … Eastern Europe became a battlefield on which two different, opposed, and even conflicting civilizations met.[197]

The dialectics between a prima facie alliance of Poland to the West and the act of distancing the nation from the Slavic world is clearly evident here, as is the intimate relationship between political views and scholarly conceptions.

From the 1960s to the 1980s, comparative Slavic linguistics and literature were almost the only domains in which the concept of a Slavic world still survived as a meaningful category; in all other areas, it was its *history* as a political movement or intellectual tradition rather than its function as a relevant contemporary category of analysis that prevailed. This was the case to the extent that in 1983 the leading British historian of Eastern Europe, Hugh Seton-Watson, could write the following: 'Today … the category Slav has lost virtually all meaning. There are Slav languages, there is Slav philology, and that is it … Slav solidarity is a lifeless corpse, and Slav culture never had any existence at all.'[198]

Eastern Europe

The concept of Eastern Europe, on the other hand, received an unprecedented boost after the war, most conspicuously in Western discourses. The bipolar East–West logic of the Cold War equated to some degree the Soviet sphere of interest (variously labelled as the 'Soviet/ Communist bloc', the 'countries of the Warsaw Pact' or the 'Eastern Bloc') and Eastern Europe, the latter of which was seen now as not only a common but also to a large extent homogeneous space, overwriting the previous Central, Southeastern and Slavic spaces. In Western

---

197 Wacław Lednicki, *Russia, Poland and the West: Essays in Literary and Cultural* History (London: Hutchinson, 1954), 13–14. During the Second World War, Lednicki emigrated to the United States, where he taught Slavic literatures at Harvard and Berkeley.
198 Hugh Seton-Watson, 'On Trying to be a Historian of Eastern Europe', in *Historians as Nation-Builders*, eds Dennis Deletant and Harry Hanak (London: Macmillan, 1988), 5–6.

Spatial configurations

public discourse, the term 'Eastern Europe' was assigned a predominantly political meaning, while discrete scholarly disciplines endowed it with structural-historical characteristics. This reconfiguration was accompanied by a veritable boom in academic institution-building and multidisciplinary 'area studies', focusing on Eastern Europe in many Western countries, especially the United States.

For scholars in the region, the relocation of its larger part into Eastern Europe was a political act with far-reaching military and economic consequences, which totally restructured the terms of geopolitical affiliation. However, in terms of the actual spatial categories with which they engaged, its impact was far less straightforward. At no point did the concept of Eastern Europe become a focus for self-identification or a powerful frame of reference (with the exception of economic history). Any sense of 'East Europeanness' that its inhabitants might have had, the Slovak political scientist Miroslav Kusý wrote, 'is tantamount to the feelings shared by an eagle and a lion living alongside each other in a zoo'.[199] (Nor were Eastern Europe or the East used as conceptions of collective identity by official Soviet and national propaganda.[200]) Europe, if not at all times the West, was soon restored to its position as a measuring rod, whether used to assert one's identity, to engage in differentiation or to contrast the levels of historical modernization and the civilizational profile of these societies. In the socialist states, this was mediated by ideologically recalibrated concepts of 'progress', 'historical laws' and 'progressive social forces' within a correspondingly readjusted teleological frame. But the core of the social-scientific vocabulary related to 'feudalism', 'capitalism', 'nationalism', 'social classes' and 'stages of economic development' remained palpably Euro- or Western-centric.

On the whole, after 1945, there were two trends that elaborated non-nationalist and regionally anchored, specifically East European, historical visions: one stressed common or comparable historical experiences of nation formation and the other was based on common or comparable patterns of socio-economic development. Hungarian academics, most of whom had gravitated before the war to the aforementioned Institute of East European History in Budapest, were at the forefront of comparative regional research in both these areas as early as the 1940s and 1950s. In his essay on 'The Misery of the Eastern European Small States' (1946), the political theorist István Bibó strove to historically reconstruct 'failed' nation-state formation in the region, which he saw as one of its defining and wide-reaching characteristics.[201] In the subsequent Marxist generation, the historian Emil Niederhauser was a prominent figure, whose work focused on the comparative history of national awakenings and who also framed his object of analysis in terms of a broadly conceived Eastern Europe from the Baltic to the Aegean.[202] One may add here the comparative study of Eastern European historiography written in the early post-war period (1946) by the Czech historian Josef Macůrek, who rejected the dualist vision and cultural determinism of his teacher, Jaroslav Bidlo, opposing the Latin–German and Greek–Slavic

---

199 Miroslav Kusý, 'We, Central-European East Europeans', in *In Search of Central Europe*, eds George Schöpflin and Nancy Wood (Cambridge: Polity Press, 1989), 93.

200 György Péteri, 'Introduction: The Oblique Coordinate Systems of Modern Identity', in *Imagining the West in Eastern Europe and the Soviet Union*, ed. György Péteri (Pittsburgh, PA: University of Pittsburgh Press, 2010), 5–6; Frithjof Benjamin Schenk, 'Eastern Europe', in Mishkova and Trencsényi, *European Regions and Boundaries*, 193, 200.

201 István Bibó, *A kelet-európai kisállamok nyomorúsága* [The misery of Eastern European small states] (Budapest: Új Magyarország, 1946).

202 Emil Niederhauser, 'Zur Frage der osteuropäischen Entwicklung', *Studia Slavica* 4 (1958): 359–71; idem, *A nemzeti megújulási mozgalmak Kelet-Európában* (Budapest: Akadémiai Kiadó, 1977; abridged English edition, *The Rise of nationality in Eastern Europe* [Budapest: Corvina Kiadó, 1981]).

spheres. Eastern Europe, Macůrek argued, was a product of multiple factors related to geography, culture, politics and economics, among other areas. However, with echoes of Halecki, he added that 'undoubtedly, the political features played a much bigger role in the European East and in the history of Eastern Europe than other forces and circumstances'.[203]

Eastern Europe was the preferred paradigm for economic historians. There is good reason to argue that Marxist scholarship should be credited with having supplied the political East–West divide of Europe with a socio-economic 'base'. The Eastern European paradigm, which was dominant during the Stalinist and immediate post-Stalinist periods, emphasized the 'pre-socialist' economic and political backwardness of the region in comparison to Western capitalist development. Focusing mainly on the study of agrarian history, these analysts identified a number of common features in the 'deviant' socio-economic – and by extension political – development of the countries located to the 'east of the Elbe', which thus created a common historical space that included, remarkably enough, not only Russia but also Prussia. The Hungarian historian Zsigmond Pál Pach was the first to develop such a historical model that employed Engels's concept of 'second serfdom' as the original point of divergence between East and West.[204] The early modern historian József Perényi also considered the socio-economic, rather than the 'cultural' or 'civilizational' development to be the critical factor in substantiating any 'historical region'. In arguing for long-standing dissimilarities between East and West, he sought to prove that the development of Eastern Europe was not simply a belated repetition or imitation of the 'Western model' but the manifestation of a 'substantive, qualitative difference'.[205] From the 1960s to the 1970s some of these authors were linked to contemporary, Western, neo-Marxist theories of underdevelopment, centre–periphery and the world economy. In Hungary, Iván Berend and György Ránki's *Economic Development in East-Central Europe in the 19th and 20th Centuries* (1974) surveyed the peculiarities in the genesis and development of capitalism across the region that stretched between Russia and Germany, while their *The European Periphery and Industrialization 1780–1914* (1982) sought to establish a typology of the Industrial Revolution in three nineteenth-century 'peripheral' zones: Eastern Europe, the Mediterranean countries and Scandinavia.

A series of studies stemming from Polish historiography from the 1960s onwards also placed Poland in an Eastern European regional framework, while linking the country to core–periphery and world-system spatial perspectives. Work conducted in this conceptual frame by economic historians such as Witold Kula and Marian Małowist, with its focus on the socio-economic history of the early modern period, was introduced into global academic debates by Fernand Braudel and Immanuel Wallerstein. Kula developed elaborate comparisons between Eastern Europe and the Americas in the colonial period (comparing slavery in colonial America to servitude in Europe), and between Eastern Europe and Latin America in the period of 'unsuccessful industrialization' in the nineteenth and twentieth centuries. The basic socio-economic

---

203 Josef Macůrek, *Dějepisectví evropského východu* [Historiography of Eastern Europe] (Praha: Nákl. Historického klubu, 1946), 126. Macůrek wrote on nearly all Eastern European nations.

204 Zsigmond Pál Pach, 'The Role of East-Central Europe in International Trade', in *Hungary and the European Economy in Early Modern Times*, ed. Zsigmond Pál Pach (Aldershot: Variorum, 1994 [1st ed. 1970]), 217–64.

205 József Perényi, 'L'Est Européen dans une synthèse d'histoire universelle', in *Nouvelles études historiques publiées à l'occasion du XIIe Congrès International des Sciences Historiques par la Commission Nationale des Historiens Hongrois*, eds D. Csatári, L. Katus, and Á Rozsnyói, vol. 2 (Budapest: Akadémiai Kiadó, 1965), 379–405.

Spatial configurations

features of pre-socialist Eastern Europe were thus serfdom, which lasted until the nineteenth century, and failed attempts at industrialization – a definition that made Russia part of Eastern Europe, although Kula did not specifically define the geographical scope of the region he was talking about and largely extrapolated from the Polish experience.[206] Małowist held a different view on this issue as he did not count serfdom among the essential features of Eastern Europe. For him, reliance on the export of raw materials since the late medieval period, and hence involvement in the unfavourable division of labour and dependence on foreign markets, constituted the defining feature of the region which, for that reason, extended from the Baltic to the Aegean, thus including the Ottoman Balkans where serfdom had not existed.[207]

One might argue that the picture of Eastern Europe drawn by Marxist economic historians, alongside and in tune with Berend and Ránki's work, has continued its dominance within global economic history. Within this picture, Eastern Europe appears, from the sixteenth century to the end of the Second World War, as one of the earliest peripheral regions in the world capitalist economy with its centre in north-western Europe. Its defining characteristics, according to domestic Marxist and foreign neo-Marxist authors, were the protracted presence of particularly oppressive feudal institutions, socio-economic modernization 'from above', delayed industrialization and attendant social tensions in preparing the ground for socialist transformation. Following this description, before the advent of socialism the region, economically weak and politically oppressive, never succeeded in pulling out of its backwardness. The reasons for this failure, which many such explanations treated as deeply interrelated, were both local in the form of domestic socio-economic structures and external in the shape of unequal terms for international trade and colonial exploitation.

(East) Central Europe

As much as Eastern Europe was popular among post-Second World War economists (and unpopular among nearly everybody else within the region), so Central Europe had been, since the 1960s, the favoured paradigm for humanities scholars and intellectuals and historians of culture. According to the literary historian Endre Bojtár, the reason for this is the peculiar hybrid that Central and Eastern Europe represents in that

> the region's culture, especially its 'elite' culture, is mostly 'Western', while its political-economic structure and general life is Eastern. This explains why economic historians who privilege the 'base' include the largest part of the region in Eastern Europe, while humanists count it, with equal justification, as part of the West.[208]

However, certain national nuances should be kept in mind. In an article from 1988, Tony Judt paid attention to the difference between the Hungarian and the Czech approaches to Central

---

206 Witold Kula, 'Some Observations on the Industrial Revolution in Eastern European Countries', *Kwartalnik Historii Kultury Materialnej* 1–2 (1958): 239–48.

207 See, in particular, his *Wschod a Zachod Evropy w XIII-XVI wieku: Konfrontacija struktur spoleczno-gospodarczych* [East and West of Europe in the XIII-XVI centuries: confrontation of socio-economic structures] (Warsaw: PWN, 1973). See also Anna Sosnowska, *Zrozumieć zacofanie. Spory historyków o Europę Wschodnią (1947–1994)* [Understanding backwardness. Disputes of historians about Eastern Europe (1947–1994)] (Warsaw: Wydawnictwo Trio, 2004); idem, 'Why is Eastern Europe Backward?', *Aspen Review* 4 (2013): 78–80.

208 Endre Bojtár, 'On the Comparative Study of the Region's Literatures', *Neohelicon* 29, no. 1 (2002): 28.

Europe. The Hungarian approach, he wrote, is dominated by historical sociology and is prone to set Central Europe in a concrete historical context as a term that describes the peculiar experience of a certain part of the continent that is different from the West and the East. (Judt saw the work of Mihály Vajda, which treated the historical location of fascism in Central Europe as crucial to its specificity, as exemplary in this sense.) For post-war Hungarian scholars, 'Central Europe is thus not a project ... so much as a critical tool of enquiry.'[209] (Indeed, one might add here the historical-sociological work of Jenő Szűcs or Ferenc Fehér that delves into deep-seated, historically anchored regional characteristics.) Among the Czechs, by contrast, a cultural approach to the historical specificity of Central Europe prevailed, and the Hungarian debate was barely mentioned. In the Czech case, 'Europe is a cultural, not a sociological category'; 'like Kundera's Europe, it is an ontological creation' undergirded with considerable enthusiasm for the Dual Monarchy.[210]

National divergences concerning the space of Central Europe were also considerable. On the whole, the Poles tended to identify (East) Central Europe with the Polish–Lithuanian Commonwealth and thematically orient it towards discussions on the place of Russia and Ukraine. The Czechs' concept rarely went beyond the former Habsburg realm and was marked by a certain fixation with Germany, while Hungarian authors frequently extended (East) Central Europe in a southeastern direction towards the Balkans.

The re-emergence of Central Europe as a paradigm after the war is linked to two important publications by Oskar Halecki, at that time an émigré historian in the United States, who reverted to his interwar ideas but modified them according to the Cold War context. In his *The Limits and Divisions of European History* (1950), Halecki openly confronted the widespread practice of speaking about a Western civilization in a way that excluded the eastern part of the continent. He reformulated and rescaled his interwar, two-fold division of Europe into a four-fold one, delineating between the following: Western (or Romance–Germanic) Europe; West Central Europe comprising the German lands (without Austria); East Central Europe made up of the 12 independent smaller states of the interwar period, with the addition of Austria, situated between Scandinavia, Germany and Italy to the west and the Soviet Union (without the three Baltic countries) to the east. The fourth part, Eastern Europe, included Russia, Ukraine and Byelorussia: the latter two from the fall of the Polish state to the Russian Revolution of 1917 and the former one from Peter the Great to the Revolution (before and after these dates the Eastern Slavic lands did not belong to Europe). For most of her history, therefore, Russia proper was not Eastern Europe but some kind of 'quasi-Europe' – a 'Eurasian empire under Russian control'.[211]

Halecki's East Central Europe, in turn, comprised three subregions: post-Byzantine Southeastern Europe (which, during the period of Ottoman domination, was only temporarily 'excluded' from Europe),[212] Danubian Europe (Hungary and the Habsburg lands) and Northeastern Europe (which originally consisted of Poland and Kievan Rus, and later the Polish–Lithuanian Commonwealth).[213] In this model, the distinction between Eastern and

---

209 Judt, 'The Dilemmas of Dissidence', 223.
210 Ibid., 223–4.
211 Halecki, *The Limits and Divisions*, 98–9.
212 According to Halecki, the medieval Balkan Orthodox kingdoms had already achieved cultural consolidation prior to their subjection to the Turks. Hence, in contrast to Russia, as a result of the Mongol caesura, Balkan Christians retained European identity, as they represented the part of Eastern Europe that emerged from the Byzantine Empire.
213 Halecki, *The Limits and Divisions*, 118 passim.

Spatial configurations

East Central Europe was the most problematic. In his later book, *The Borderlands of Western Civilization: A History of East Central Europe* (1952), Halecki posited that there were 'no permanent boundaries' between the two nor dramatic territorial fluctuations over time, yet insisted that the differentiation between these two regions was 'a prerequisite for a correct understanding of European history'.[214] What held these different parts together – and what explained the exclusion of (Soviet) Russia – was a conception of European culture that sought to strike a balance between freedom and authority as opposed to anarchy and nihilism. In contemporary terms, this meant respecting democratic independent units, which, nevertheless, join together into federations with efficient executive rule.[215] At the same time, Halecki made it clear that his East Central Europe was, firstly, decidedly Western in cultural and historical orientation; secondly, due to its exposure to German and Russian encroachments, it was *the* key to European stability, and the means to achieve such stability was the creation of a powerful Poland, which as 'the largest of the whole group, occupies a key position'.[216] Halecki thus bestowed on Poland a new mission – a secular and geopolitical version of its historic role in saving Europe.

The next generation of Polish regional historians, like the medievalists Jerzy Kłoczowski and Aleksander Gieysztor, followed in the footsteps of Halecki while reconceptualizing somewhat the regional divisions in his work. In his research Kłoczowski utilized the concepts of Slavic Europe and Eastern Europe, subdividing them into East Central Europe, Southeastern Europe and Kievan Rus. This division derived from his analysis of the processes of Occidentalization and Byzantinization, which he sees as two parallel processes through which European culture was diffused. The stress which he and Gieysztor place on the common spiritual roots and institutional traditions of East Central Europe was subversively intended to highlight the 'unnatural division' of Europe into politically defined blocs. At the same time, Kłoczowski stressed the 'enormous significance' of the Polish–Lithuanian Commonwealth as the major meeting ground of 'the Latin and the Byzantine civilizations which together constitute the great cultural tradition of Europe'.[217]

Józef Chlebowczyk, a Polish historian who analyzed the Central European experience through the lens of the processes of nation formation, was one among the very few Polish scholars whose definition of East Central Europe encompassed the whole area between Russia and Germany, bordering the Baltic, Adriatic, Aegean and Black Seas, and who considered the territories of the Habsburg Monarchy to be the core of the region. What for Chlebowczyk justified this demarcation of the region as a coherent analytical unit was the category of borderland, denoting 'areas where different linguistic-ethnic groups, nationalities and ethnic communities come into contact and coexist' and, as such, 'develop in a specific way'.[218] Overall, however, Polish scholars who employed the term East Central Europe rarely had Hungary, Czechoslovakia and Slovakia, not to mention the Balkan countries, in mind. As was the case in the 1930s, the region that really concerned them, and to whose transnational legacy they turned time and time again, was that of the Polish state.

---

214 Halecki, *Borderlands of Western Civilization*, 3; Biskupski, 'Polish Conceptions of Unity and Division', 99.
215 Halecki, *The Limits and Divisions*, 185 passim; Kłoczowski, *East Central Europe*, 18.
216 Biskupski, 'Polish Conceptions of Unity and Division', 99.
217 Kłoczowski, *East Central Europe*, 28, 32. Aleksander Gieysztor produced few monographs but many articles that situated Polish medieval history in a regional context, as well as on women and Jews in Central Europe and the use of the comparative method.
218 Józef Chlebowczyk, *On Small and Young Nations in Europe: Nation-Forming Processes in Ethnic Borderlands in East-Central Europe* (Wrocław: Zakład Narodowy im. Ossolińskich, 1980), esp. 9–40.

In Hungary, the Central European framework, which declined after the war, only resurfaced in the 1970s in tandem with a new round of intellectual discussions about the country's place in Europe. The recuperation of a common Austro-Hungarian heritage, similar in some ways to that of Byzantium in Southeastern Europe at around the same time, was one of the remarkable outcomes of this search for symbolic, geographical self-positioning. The work of cultural historian Péter Hanák played an important role in this sense in that it pursued a genuinely transnational reconstruction of the Dual Monarchy's cultural, political and economic setting, thus challenging deep-rooted nationalist assumptions and stressing the role of the German and Jewish bourgeoisie in the modernization of the Empire.[219] In some ways this work was related to the rise of historical interest in post-Habsburg cultural and intellectual heritage during the 1960s, as exemplified in the groundbreaking study by the Trieste-based literary scholar Claudio Magris on the 'Habsburg myth'.[220] Such transnational tendencies and the 'cultural turn' in Habsburg studies during the 1970s and 1980s, which harked back to the post-First World War retrospective utopias of Joseph Roth or Stefan Zweig, provide the scholarly context for the 1980s debate on Central Europe and the nostalgic Habsburg flair that infused it. It made possible the formulation of questions such as the one the Romanian émigré playwright Eugène Ionesco devised in 1985: 'The Austro-Hungarian Empire: Forerunner of a Central European Confederation?' It was used as a banner for his advocacy for the creation of a 'confederation of a new *Mitteleuropa* ... [made up of] Austria, Hungary and Romania, but also Croatia and Czechoslovakia.'[221]

Among the work of other comparativist literary scholars, Endre Bojtár's synthesis of the rise of Enlightenment and Romanticism mapped out a much more extensive East Central European space.[222] He even included Russian developments in his analysis, but he considered the Russian context to be rather different to those in East Central Europe, mainly on account of Russia's imperial state structure, which had made the Russian nation-building project incomparable to those of the vulnerable 'small cultures'. For Bojtár, the common traits that characterized East Central European cultures were the impeded national and economic development, the hypertrophied role of the intellectual as a national prophet and a heightened sensitivity to absurdity.

The convergence of the discourse of backwardness and Habsburg cultural studies is noticeable in the work of Jenő Szűcs, whose 'Sketch on the Three Regions of Europe' has been widely, although retrospectively, acknowledged as having foregrounded a new Central European discourse.[223] Making reference to historical structures of longue durée from the Middle Ages to modernity, Szűcs developed a system of five European regions: Scandinavian Northern Europe, Mediterranean Southern Europe, Western Europe, East Central Europe and Eastern Europe.

---

219 Péter Hanák, *A Kert és a Műhely* [The garden and the workshop] (Budapest: Gondolat Könyvkiadó, 1988); idem, *Jászi Oszkár dunai patriotizmusa* [The Danube patriotism of Oszkár Jászi] (Budapest: Magvető, 1985).

220 Claudio Magris, *Il mito asburgico nella letteratura austriaca moderna* (Turin: Einaudi, 1963).

221 Eugène Ionesco, 'The Austro-Hungarian Empire: Forerunner of a Central European Confederation?' *Cross Currents* 4 (1985): 4,7.

222 Endre Bojtár, *'Az ember feljő...': A felvilágosodás és a romantika a közép- és kelet-európai irodalmakban* ['Man shall come up ... ': Enlightenment and Romanticism in Central and Eastern European literatures] (Budapest: Magvető, 1986); idem, *Kelet-Európa vagy Közép-Európa?* [Eastern Europe or Central Europe?] (Budapest: Századvég, 1993). The second volume contains his essays from the 1980s.

223 Jenő Szűcs, 'The Three Historical Regions in Europe', in *Civil Society and the State: New European Perspectives*, ed. John Keane (London and New York: Verso, 1988 [originally published in Hungarian in 1983]), 291–332.

Having gone to some length in order to describe the 'aberrational' development of Eastern Europe vis-à-vis Western Europe, Szűcs elaborated on the need to acknowledge the existence of a region in-between 'the Western and the Eastern model' – a transitional zone, which combined both Western and Eastern structures and developments,[224] but which was nevertheless clearly distinct from the Eastern pattern. In the subsequent debate, Péter Hanák, arguing from the perspective of cultural history, proposed a triangular model in which Central Europe, including Austria and Switzerland, would be equidistant from East and West. Szűcs, on the other hand, insisted that East Central Europe, that is historical Bohemia, Hungary and the Polish–Lithuanian Commonwealth, were peripheral to the West.[225] Szűcs's essay had an enormous influence in Hungary, well beyond historical circles, and launched a public debate on the place of Hungary in relation to the Soviet-dominated Eastern camp that endured until the early 1990s.

'Becoming European by being Central European': the 1980s debate on Central Europe

Significantly enough, these discussions in Hungary and beyond proceeded at the same time as West Germany turned towards *Mitteleuropa* from the late 1970s. This turn was spearheaded by the historian Karl Schlögel, who was among the first to revive the idea of a cultural *Mitteleuropa* that included Germany and Austria. Schlögel talked of pre-Second World War *Mitteleuropa* in terms of a web of human contact and interaction that stood for a 'homogeneity of the cultural space which, however, has always been endangered by various nationalities.'[226] His book about the Germans and their *verlorener Osten* ('lost East') is a nostalgic look at the vanished 'chequerboard and interlaced territory of Central and Eastern Europe', which closely resonates with Hanák's vision from the other side of the geopolitical border. In this 'torn apart fabric that a whole continent had woven for centuries', the Germans' integrative role had only one parallel: the Jews of Central and Eastern Europe. Schlögel continues: 'In the destruction of the Central European Jews, who with the Germans served as the integrative strength of this region, the old *Mitteleuropa* perished.'[227] Yet, like Szűcs, Schlögel believed that this common heritage offered an alternative to the East–West dichotomy that dominated the continent.[228]

Stressing the 'apolitical' cultural aspects of *Mitteleuropa* was characteristic of Austrian approaches as well. For Erhard Busek, who later became chairman of the Institute for the Danube Region and Central Europe and then an Austrian vice chancellor, the area's 'constantly moving borders' resulted from the fact that *Mitteleuropa* was 'not an instrument of power politics, but rather more of an intellectual-cultural principle. It will not and should not have to do with state borders, because it should indeed be about border crossing'.[229]

---

224 Diana Mishkova, Bo Stråth and Balazs Trencsényi, 'Regional History as a "Challenge" to the National Frameworks of Historiography: The Case of Central, Southeastern, and Northern Europe', in *World, Global and European Histories as Challenges to National Representations of the Past*, eds Matthias Middell and Lluis Roura y Aulinas (London: Palgrave Macmillan, 2013), 292–3.

225 Ibid.

226 Karl Schlögel, *Die Mitte liegt ostwärts: Die Deutschen, der verlorene Osten und Mitteleuropa* (Berlin: Siedler, 1986), 17.

227 Schlögel, *Die Mitte liegt ostwärts*, 79, 81.

228 Joshua Hagen, 'Redrawing the Imagined Map of Europe: The Rise and Fall of the "Center"', *Political Geography* 22, no. 5 (2003): 489–517, here 498.

229 Quoted in Hagen, 'Redrawing the Imagined Map', 499.

Participants in the debate on Central Europe that emerged in the 1980s on the other side of the Wall were mainly Hungarians, Czechs and Poles, and occasionally some Romanians, Slovenes, Croats and Lithuanians. Most of them were writers, 'critical intellectuals' looking for ways to disassociate mentally the countries of what Kundera famously called the 'kidnapped Occident' from the Soviet Union and a politically defined Eastern Europe. On this common ground, their views differed on a range of basic issues concerning the space of Central Europe, the definition of its essential elements, its historical embeddedness and strategies for the future. Polish intellectuals were the least ready to rally under the banner of Central Europe; they seemed to display 'scant inclination toward any notion of a Central European cultural identity grander than that of the Polish nation'.[230] A notable exception was the writer Czesław Miłosz, who was born in Lithuania, was a long-term resident in the West and whose vision of a Central European literary tradition, like that of the Hungarian literary scholar Csaba Kiss, was highly inclusive, embracing the Balkan literatures as well. Beyond internal differences, in the following discussion an attempt will be made to identify recurrent themes within this work and analyze some salient characteristics of the 1980s notion of Central Europe.

At the core of this notion, as P. Bugge has pointed out, was the distinction made between an authentic Central European *culture* and an alien, implanted *politics*.[231] What the Hungarian novelist György Konrád called 'anti-politics' should not be taken literally, though. Metapolitics, as Melvin Croan has suggested, is perhaps more applicable to what is at stake. The invocation of anti-politics is meant to convey a total rejection of what Konrád called the 'Jacobin–Leninist tradition', which contradicts all Central European cultural aspirations. Propagating anti-politics is thus itself a political tactic.[232] Kundera formulated some of the implications of this metapolitical character of Central European discourse when he stated that

> Central Europe is not a state: it is a culture and a fate. … Central Europe therefore cannot be defined and determined by political frontiers (which are inauthentic, always imposed by invasions, conquests, and occupations), but by the great common situations that reassemble peoples … along the imaginary and ever-changing boundaries that mark a realm inhabited by the same memories, the same problems and conflicts, the same common tradition.[233]

'Central Europe', Miłosz wrote,

> is hardly a geographical notion. It is not easy to trace its boundaries on the map … The ways of feeling and thinking of its inhabitants must thus suffice for drawing mental lines which seem to be more durable than the borders of the states.[234]

---

230 Melvin Croan, 'Lands In-between: The Politics of Cultural Identity in Contemporary Eastern Europe', *East European Politics and Societies* 3, no. 2 (1989): 188.

231 Bugge, 'The Use of the Middle', 27.

232 Croan, 'Lands In-between', 189–90.

233 Milan Kundera, 'The Tragedy of Central Europe', *New York Review of Books*, 26 April 1984, 35. Indirectly, Kundera gives an indication of whom he considers to be 'Central European' by making reference to the Hungarians, Czechs, Slovaks, Poles, Croats, Slovenes, Romanians, Jews and Austrians.

234 Czesław Miłosz, 'Central European Attitudes', in Schöpflin and Wood, *In Search of Central Europe*, 116–17.

Spatial configurations

György Konrád called Central Europe 'a cultural counter-hypothesis',[235] by which he meant a cultural or moral realm beyond state involvement and geopolitical consideration (hence its vaguely defined territorial basis). Its political objective – emancipation from the Soviet realm – derived from its basic cultural and moral assertions. Central Europe was a means of 'returning to Europe', not a goal in its own right. It was primarily a geopolitical tool intended to challenge Soviet hegemony, critique the West's apathy towards the 'other Europe', and subvert the division of the continent.[236] As Kundera, echoing Bidlo's bipartite division of half a century earlier, put it:

> 'Geographic Europe' (extending from the Atlantic to the Ural Mountains) was always divided into two halves which evolved separately: one tied to ancient Rome and the Catholic Church, the other anchored in Byzantium and the Orthodox Church. After 1945, the border between the two Europes shifted several hundred kilometres to the west, and several nations that had always considered themselves to be Western woke up to discover that they were now in the East.[237]

In this sense, one should not overemphasize the region-building or identity-building aspects of the idea. Central Europe was never intended to be about the construction of a separate space but to facilitate movement from one geopolitical region to another by challenging the established regional geography of Cold War Europe. As Hagen points out, 'Rather than a step toward the destruction of the East–West division of Europe, perhaps it is more useful to view the revival of a new European centre as a transitional stage in defining a new East–West divide …'[238]

The determining role of culture led to a tendency to locate Central Europe in the past and to include strong mythopoetic elements in these historical references. The term itself, in Konrád's words, conveys 'the allure of nostalgia and utopia'.[239] Such a use of the past and the counter-positioning of politics and culture points to the romantic roots of Central European ideology. Its retrospective focus was not the independent states of the interwar years, but the polyglot urban culture of the pre-1914 Habsburg Monarchy: small nationhood, understood as an awareness of the precariousness of the nation's existence, and diversity overlaid by a common culture and a common fate were the main characteristics of this Central European world. Jews rather than healthy peasants were its social glue ('integrating element' and 'intellectual cement', in Kundera's words) and scepticism, irony and absurdity its unifying cultural traits. European values were generally said to be better preserved by the marginalized Central Europeans than in the complacent, consumerist West.[240]

According to Vladimír Macura, 'After August 1968, the Revivalist mythologization of the "centre" became a natural breeding ground for Czech rhetoric pertaining to "Central

---

235 György Konrád, 'Is the Dream of Central Europe Still Alive?' *Cross Currents* 5 (1986): 115.

236 Hagen, 'Redrawing the Imagined Map', 500.

237 Kundera, 'The Tragedy of Central Europe', 33.

238 Hagen, 'Redrawing the Imagined Map', 507; See also Bugge, 'The Use of the Middle', 27. Miroslav Hroch, on the other hand, has argued that 'almost all this discussion proceeded outside of the Czech territory and never became a part of the *internal* Czech national discourse: it was and continued to be an international discourse among cosmopolitan intellectuals, such as Kundera, Konrád, Miłosz and Havel. As a consequence, the concept of Central Europe in the Czech discourse of Europe played a less relevant role than was the case in Western Europe' ('The Czech Discourse on Europe', 256).

239 Konrád, 'Is the Dream of Central Europe Still Alive', 118.

240 Okey, 'Central Europe/Eastern Europe', 127; and Ivo Banac, 'Milan Kundera i povratak Srednje Evrope' [Milan Kundera and the return of Central Europe], *Gordogan* 9, nos. 23–4 (1987): 40.

Europe".[241] The beginning of the debate was initiated that same year by Kundera when he wrote that, by seeking to fuse socialism and civic freedoms, the Czechs had placed themselves 'in the centre of world history', thus fulfilling 'the Czech fate', which history had ascribed to them as a 'small nation in the middle of Europe'.[242] During the course of the critical debate that followed, in which several Czech intellectuals took part (including Havel, who accused Kundera of 'ridiculous provincial messianism'), Kundera emphatically reiterated what he saw as the irretrievable fact that 'Man is mortal, and Bohemia is in Central Europe. The Czech nation has always been a crossroads of European traditions, so that to de-Europeanize it ... means to unhinge it from its own history.'[243] The normative interpretation of the nation's geographical centrality thus morphed into a metahistorical argument about the singular cultural qualities and cultural role of Central Europe.

The vitality of Central Europe drew, in Kundera's view, from its 'passion for variety', which he considered to be quintessentially European:

> Central Europe longed to be a condensed version of Europe itself in all its cultural variety, a small arch-European Europe, a reduced model of Europe made up of nations conceived according to one rule: the greatest variety within the smallest space.[244]

The Czech philosopher Milan Šimečka also perceived the uniqueness of Central Europe in its composite nature, where nations lived in an amalgam of 'influences, languages, and traditions', which 'created the values of Europe's previous greatness'.[245] For György Konrád, 'The Central European idea entails the flourishing variety of the parts, the self-consciousness of diversity'. To be Central European entails having an 'aesthetic sensibility ... for the *Mehrsprachigkeit* of views'.[246] The polymorphism of Central Europe, perceived almost as a hereditary property, was invoked in opposition to both the cultural unification of Western Europe and monolithic, muzzled Russia.[247] By turning its back on Central Europe, thus irretrievably losing its centre, Europe itself seemed to be losing its meaning:

> The post-war annexation of Central Europe (or at least its major part) by Russian civilization caused Western culture to lose its vital centre of gravity. It is the most significant event in the history of our century, and we cannot dismiss the possibility that the end of Central Europe marked the beginning of the end for Europe as a whole.[248]

The real 'tragedy' of Central Europe in Kundera's mind was the 'barbarization' of the West, mainly due to American political and cultural domination, which put Europe on the road to

---

241 Macura, *The Mystification of a Nation*, 22. Martin Schulze Wessel also sees in Czech discussions of Central Europe 'the continuation of the ideology of the middle'. See: 'Die Mitte liegt westwärts: Mitteleuropa in tschechischer Diskussion', *Bohemia* 29 (1988): 327.

242 Milan Kundera, 'Český úděl' [The Czech deal], *Listy* 7–8 (December 1968).

243 The entire debate can be accessed at https://is.muni.cz/el/1423/jaro2011/SOC403/um/Cesky_udel.pdf.

244 Kundera, 'The Tragedy of Central Europe', 33.

245 Quoted in Macura, *The Mystification of a Nation*, 21.

246 György Konrád, 'Mein Traum von Europa', *Kursbuch* 81 (1985): 186, 189.

247 Macura, *The Mystification of a Nation*, 21.

248 Milan Kundera, 'Afterword: A Talk with the Author', in *The Book of Laughter and Forgetting* (New York: Penguin, 1981), 230.

Spatial configurations

'losing its own cultural identity'. Central Europe from this perspective was hemmed in on two sides by the 'big, oppressive neighbour' to the East and modernity – 'the subtle, relentless pressure of time, which is leaving the era of culture in its wake' – to the West. Hence the intellectual's 'task is to find the sources of value and inspiration from within their own threatened cultures.'[249] Kundera made no secret of the counter modern – 'conservative, nearly anachronistic' – but also messianic pathos of his *cri d'appel* in that it was 'desperately trying to restore the past, the past of culture, the past of the modern era',[250] namely, a truly conservative utopia of a new Central Europe. As Croan puts forth:

> Soviet Russian political hegemony is one thing … But much deeper and more complex wellsprings are tapped with respect to aspirations to recreate anew a distinctive, real or imagined, indigenous cultural milieu of ostensibly surpassing moral excellence. In some instances, this … gloss on the Central Europe construct tends to go hand in hand with a neo-romantic reaction against the Enlightenment and a concomitant renunciation of the 'rationalist illusion'.[251]

At times, this view took on a dystopian aspect in relation to Europe, as it did when Václav Havel wrote that East Central Europe contained 'deeply instructive information about the West's *own* crisis' that pointed to the 'moral future' of the West. In Havel's eyes, it was Europe – democratic Western Europe in particular – that bore the responsibility for modern science, rationalism, scientism, the Industrial Revolution and the idea of revolution itself as an abstract form of fanaticism. And now this Europe, for Havel, must face the consequences of its 'ambiguous exports'.[252]

The spatial 'others' of this idea of Central Europe were rather obvious. The conspicuous absence of Germany from this list deserves attention. Generally speaking, the Central Europe of the 1980s appeared in two versions: with and without Germany. The former was more popular among writers and literary scholars with a predilection for the cultural legacy of the Habsburg Empire. Before 1989, Konrád (like Schlögel) used Central Europe and *Mitteleuropa* interchangeably. The Czech art historian Josef Kroutvor defined Central Europe not by countries, since that would smack of nationalism, but by its main cities, and his list featured Munich, Dresden, Vienna, Budapest, Cracow and Lviv, and in the middle 'lies Bratislava, Brno and finally Prague as the ideal centre of the Central European space'.[253] The more restrictive version of Central Europe was used more frequently among historians and was also employed as a framework for discussing and reinterpreting Czech–German relations (see, for example, the work of Jan Křen).

On the self-professed 'anti-political' level, the exclusion of Germany from Central Europe made possible the exclusion of Nazism (and other hegemonic ideologies), as well as the entire recent past of 'ethnic homogenization', from the historical 'traditions' of the region. Kundera could then proceed with the self-gratifying observation that 'the people of Central Europe are not conquerors', and even ironic 'demystifiers' like Kroutvor could picture a Biedermeier Central Europe where 'everything is flat, neatly levelled, subordinated to the general mean.

---

249 Kundera, 'The Tragedy of Central Europe', 36–8. See also Judt, 'The Dilemmas of Dissidence', 225.
250 Kundera, 'The Tragedy of Central Europe', 38.
251 Croan, 'Lands In-between', 183.
252 Václav Havel, 'Politika a svědomi' [Politics and conscience], *Svědectví* 18, no. 72 (1984): 627, quoted in Judt, 'The Dilemmas of Dissidence', 233–4. According to Judt, Havel 'is certainly more consistently rigorous in his attack on the Enlightenment tradition in European thought than any other [East Central European] writer' (Ibid., 237).
253 Quoted in Bugge, 'The Use of the Middle', 32.

People avoid extremes and display no interest in them. ... The golden middle route is the route of Central Europe.'[254]

Russia, Eastern Europe or the East formed one counter-conceptual cluster. For Kundera, Russia was 'an *other* civilization'; the 'totalitarian Russian civilization ... anchored in the Byzantine world' was 'the radical negation of the modern West' and of 'the Central European passion for variety'.[255] Unlike Konrád, who spoke of the need for freedom and reforms in the whole of Eastern Europe, Russia included,[256] Kundera strongly warned against any association of the term 'central' with ideas of a bridge between Russia and the West since, as Martin Schulze Wessel remarks, one cannot build bridges between a civilization and its absolute negation.[257] Kundera also defied what he called 'the ideology of the Slavic world' as 'a piece of political mystification invented in the nineteenth century', which constituted a major 'error' in Central Europe.[258] The absurdity in Central European history, Kroutvor seconded, resided in its being caught between the historicity of the West and the ahistoricity of the East, that is Russia: 'From West to East history seems to wane, passing into the immobile Asiatic eternity.'[259] 'The freedom inborn in us [the Central Europeans]', Ionesco added, 'was wholly contrary to and in conflict with the spirit of servitude characteristic of every Russian, because every Russian is born more or less a slave, both socially and spiritually.'[260] Mihály Vajda, a philosopher and significant representative of the Hungarian New Left at the time, went just about as far when stating that 'There are crucial differences of human behaviour between Central Eastern Europe and Eastern Europe proper. ... Central Eastern Europeans are fundamentally Europeans ...'[261] There were some critics of this vision, though. The above-mentioned Czech philosopher Milan Šimečka cited the role of Nazism in 'the beginning of the end of the Central European tradition', the Czechs' own responsibility for their 'fate', the doctrine of communism as cultivated in the West and pleaded not to exclude Russia from Europe and European civilization.[262]

Although they identified Central Europe with it, the dissident intellectuals' attitude to the West was not unequivocal. The Czechs were particularly critical of the Western cults of consumption, materialism, self-centredness and growing 'post-cultural' mediocrity, so much so that Šimečka warned of letting this distaste for material goods and the benefits of modernity get out of hand.[263] But the ambiguity had a function, since against this backdrop Central Europe could 'stand in as a metaphor for this other Europe' that intellectuals sought to create. As such it had considerable success among the French intelligentsia.[264]

---

254 Quoted in Macura, *The Mystification of a Nation*, 21.
255 Kundera, 'The Tragedy of Central Europe', 34 passim.
256 György Konrád, *Antipolitics: An Essay* (San Diego: Harcourt, Brace, Jovanovich, 1984), 130.
257 Schulze Wessel, 'Die Mitte liegt westwärts', 339.
258 Kundera, 'The Tragedy of Central Europe', 34. The Russian poet Iosif Brodski retaliated by calling Central Europe 'Western Asia'.
259 Quoted in Bugge, 'The Use of the Middle', 29.
260 Eugène Ionesco, 'The Austro-Hungarian Empire: Forerunner of a Central European Federation', *Cross Currents* 4 (1985): 6
261 Mihály Vajda, 'Central Eastern European Perspectives', *East European Reporter* 1, no. 1 (1985): 6, quoted in Hagen, 'Redrawing the Imagined Map', 507.
262 Milan Šimečka, 'Another Civilization? An Other Civilization?', in Schöpflin and Wood, *In Search of Central Europe*, 157–62.
263 Milan Šimečka, 'A World with Utopias or Without Them?' *Cross Currents* 3 (1984): 26.
264 Tony Judt, 'The Dilemmas of Dissidence', 225, 234. Judt also points to the similarity of this discussion to the communist language of the late 1940s, in both Eastern and Western Europe, on the consumption-based 'Americanization' of Europe.

Spatial configurations

There was still a third 'other' to this Central Europe, which had originally been less apparent but became conspicuous after 1989: the Balkans. Indeed, much of Central Europe's self-promotion to membership in European civilization (and later the European Union) was executed by means of symbolic dissociation – backed by cultural, political and religious arguments – from the 'dark' Balkans.[265] The phenomenon was aptly captured by the Hungarian sociologist Ferenc Miszlivetz, who, in 1991, wrote the following:

> To be a Central European means to be neither an East European, nor a citizen of a Balkan state. It means to be better than the Russians, the Bulgarians, the Montenegrins. Central Europe became a programme which allowed one to distinguish oneself from the 'barbarians'.[266]

As has been noted by Peter Bugge, Central Europe was not about deconstructing Eastern Europe, but was rather about escaping it by pushing it further to the East.[267]

Between particularism and cohesion: the Balkans and Southeastern Europe

In contrast to the interwar decades, the late 1940s and the 1950s produced little enthusiasm for the Balkans. The spatial classifications after the Second World War along the East–West axis did away with the Balkans/Southeastern Europe as a separate (geo)political or economic area. In terms of geopolitical affiliation, we can roughly distinguish between three categories of states: NATO members Greece and Turkey; communist Romania and Bulgaria; and non-committed Yugoslavia and maverick Albania. In terms of symbolic-cultural imageries and spatial self-identifications, however, discrete national viewpoints tended to override such groupings.

It is therefore significant that despite their different, at times contradictory, objectives all these countries were involved in the Southeastern European academic movement. Research on Southeastern Europe resumed in the 1960s in an atmosphere of decolonization and political détente between the two blocs, when the Balkans was advertised as a zone of 'peaceful co-existence between the two world systems' (which did not mean, in Marxist–Leninist vocabulary, an ideological respite but 'a peculiar form of class struggle').[268] What distinguished this period was the strong drive towards state-sponsored academic institutionalization of the field across the region on both sides of the Iron Curtain. The International Association of Southeast-European Studies (AIESEE) was founded in Bucharest in 1963 under the auspices of UNESCO, which was briefly followed by the (re-)establishment of national institutions for Southeastern European/Balkan Studies in Romania (1963), Bulgaria (1964), Yugoslavia (1967) and Greece (opened as early as 1953), and of specialized chairs at the major universities.[269]

---

265 Maria Todorova, 'Hierarchies of Eastern Europe: East Central Europe versus the Balkans', *Southeast European Monitor* 5 (1955): 5–45.

266 Ferenc Miszlivetz, 'Mitteleuropa – Der Weg nach Europa', *Neue Gesellschaft/Frankfurter Hefte* 38/11 (1991), 975.

267 Bugge, 'The Use of the Middle', 34.

268 Voin Božinov, 'Peaceful Co-existence in the Balkans and the Policy of the People's Republic of Bulgaria', in *Actes du Premier Congrès International des Etudes Balkaniques et Sud-Est Européennes*, vol. 5 (Sofia: AIESEE, 1970), 535–6.

269 The terminological mélange in naming these institutional venues is clear: the association and the institute in Bucharest were concerned with 'Southeast-European Studies'; the institutes in Sofia, Belgrade and Thessaloniki dealt with 'Balkan Studies'; while the congresses engaged with 'Balkan and Southeast-European Studies'.

Beginning in 1966, the International Congresses of Balkan and South-East European Studies were convened every four years. This proliferation of regionalist organizations involved distinct political and cultural-diplomatic agendas. To the extent that one can speak of a common ideology, the aspiration was to highlight the universal contribution of the individual Balkan nations through the mediation of Southeastern European cultural-historical heritage – an ambition already stirred by the 1930s generation of Balkanologists, whose legacy was not only fully rehabilitated, but served to chart a respectable lineage for the newly institutionalized 'discipline' of Balkan/Southeastern European Studies.

The conceptualization of the Balkans that crystallized through this institutional web and scholarly exchange revolved around the meta-ontological binaries of diversity and unity, individuality and synthesis. Diversity and individuality were said to revoke 'homogeneity' and were epitomized by the Balkan nations, each one of which, out of the common font, 'selects, interprets and creates new meanings in accordance with its own particular conditions and with a view to its own genius.' Balkan unity and civilizational synthesis were European in their cultural morphology but were neither Western nor Eastern, being instead endowed with 'the special vocation of facilitating the mutual understanding between the East and the West'.[270] The emancipatory potential of such a notion unfolded on two levels: it displayed the originality of regional national cultures, and it upturned the established image of the Balkans as alien to Europe. A cluster of additional antinomies came to underscore the unique relationship between particularism and integration: 'oscillating movements from synthesis to differentiation', 'affinity vs. homogeneity', 'permanent interdependence of national history and regional history', 'interlocking local, regional and global circles', and so on.[271] This was a convenient formula in several ways: it provided a venue for the heightened international visibility of the national while eschewing parochialism; it sought to assert a modicum of autonomy in a hegemonic world and a distinctive Balkan Europeanness; it granted access to cultural universalism and to a specific modern mission that transcended the Iron Curtain; and it also operated across different registers depending on circumstances and audiences.

The actual research behind this self-asserting, regionalist ideology was even more equivocal. In some disciplinary fields, such as history, the analytical horizon was only nominally Southeastern European and was, in reality, ethnocentric. Cross-national relations and exchanges were usually dealt with on a bilateral basis, with the individual national historiographies tending to stress particular aspects of 'common Balkanness/Southeastern Europeanness' where they could claim a special contribution from the respective nation: 'Byzantine synthesis' and Greek influence in the Ottoman Empire in the Greek case; the Daco-Roman substratum and the post-Byzantine heritage in the Romanian case; and the 'Byzantino-Slavic' tradition, South-Slav solidarity and national liberation movements in the Bulgarian and Yugoslav cases. The comparative regional approach, to the extent that it was employed, did not affect the writing of national history, which remained a self-contained, didactic and parochial field.

Advances in social and economic history in the rest of Europe and the imposition of Marxist methodology in large parts of the region failed to yield a socio-economic 'synthesis' of the area –

---

270 Tudor Vianu, 'Les régions culturelles dans l'histoire des civilisations et le colloque de civilisations balkaniques', *Actes du Colloque International de Civilisations Balkaniques (Sinaia, 8–14 juillet 1962)* (Bucharest: Commission Nationale Roumaine pour l'UNESCO, n.d.), 11–14.

271 Denis Zakythinos, 'Etat actuel des études du Sud-Est européen (objets, méthodes, sources, instruments de travail, place dans les sciences humaines)', *Actes du IIe Congrès international des études du Sud-Est européen* 1 (Athens: AIESEE, 1972): 5–22; and Mihai Berza, 'Les études du Sud-Est européen, leur rôle et leur place dans l'ensemble des sciences humaines', *Revue d'Etudes Sud-Est Européennes* 13 (1975): 1, 5–14.

Spatial configurations

a strange failure considering both the burgeoning neo-Marxist comparativist approaches of the 1960s and 1970s, and the strong preoccupation with the economic unity of the region before the war. As had previously been the case, 'softer' disciplinary fields and subfields, such as linguistics, ethnography, cultural and literary history, classical archaeology and the history of ideas, fared better in terms of integrative perspectives and regionalist research, and the communication in these areas with fruitful developments outside of the region (e.g. history of mentalities, anthropology and Byzantine studies) was more productive in creating some elements of a Balkan cultural-historical ontology. Yet here one too often encounters the phenomenon of doublespeak: celebrating national exceptionalism for domestic consumption and endorsing solidarities in international meetings. Since the mid-1970s, furthermore, nationalist discourses in all of these states were becoming increasingly radicalized, self-centred and xenophobic. The mythopoetic vision of the Balkans was declining at precisely the time when that of Central Europe was on the rise.

Émigré scholars, especially in the US, continued to deploy the Balkans and, more rarely, Southeastern Europe as a cultural-historical or civilizational space (in the Annales School sense), which usually included Greece and the Ottoman Empire, but rarely Turkey. In the 1970s and 1980s it was underpinned by discussions of longue durée, socio-economic trends and predicaments of modernization in light of the neo-Marxist centre–periphery and world-economy paradigms, and family patterns and political trajectories typically associated with the 'peculiarities' of nation-building.[272] A critical strain in the 'history of ideas', on the other hand, chose to place the regional variants of nationalism, authoritarianism, fascism and communism in an Eastern European, rather than a Balkan or Central European, frame.[273]

The post-1989 reshuffling of space

The fall of the Berlin Wall, the disintegration of the USSR and the wars of Yugoslav succession were indications of dramatic shifts in the symbolic configuration of space in and outside the broader East Central European region. Eastern Europe and Slavdom all but disappeared from both political and scholarly discourses, and the rationale of some academic disciplines associated with their study was put into question. Some academics, especially in Poland, dramatized the departure from previous canonical works. Thus, the literary scholars Joanna Rapacka and Maria Bobrownicka took on the project of deconstructing the 'narcotizing myth' of a 'Slavic culture' as an ideological construct of nineteenth-century pan-Slavists grounded in (mostly invented) folklore.[274]

---

272 Daniel Chirot, *Social Change in a Peripheral Society: The Creation of a Balkan Colony* (New York: Academic Press, 1976); Ivan Berend and György Ránki, *The European Periphery and Industrialization 1780–1914* (Cambridge: Cambridge University Press, 1982); Huri Islamoglu-Inan, ed., *The Ottoman Empire and the World Economy* (Cambridge: Cambridge University Press, 1987); Robert F. Byrnes, ed., *Communal Families in the Balkans: The Zadruga* (South Bend, IN: Notre Dame Press, 1976); Charles Jelavich and Barbara Jelavich, *The Establishment of the Balkan National States, 1804–1920* (Seattle, WA: University of Washington Press, 1977).

273 Peter Sugar and Ivo Lederer, eds, *Nationalism in Eastern Europe* (Seattle, WA: University of Washington Press, 1969); Peter Sugar, *East European Nationalism, Politics and Religion* (Collected Studies) (Aldershot: Ashgate Variorum, 1999); Robin Okey, *Eastern Europe 1740–1980: Feudalism to Communism* (London: Hutchinson University Library, 1982).

274 Joanna Rapackka, *Śródziemnomorze, Europa Środkowa, Bałkany. Studia z literatur południowosłowiańskich* [The Mediterranean, Central Europe, and the Balkans: studies on South Slavic literatures] (Cracow: Universitas, 2002); Maria Bobrownicka, *Narkotyk mitu. Szkice o świadomości narodowej i kulturowej Słowian Zachodnich i Południowych* [The drug of myth: sketches of the national and cultural awareness of the western and southern Slavs] (Cracow: Universitas, 1995).

The 'fate' of Central Europe was a more chequered one. The hitherto ephemeral region-building potential of Central European discourses suddenly appeared close to fulfilment in the early 1990s with the creation of the Visegrád Group (Czechoslovakia, Poland and Hungary), which, in the words of Havel, took up the 'chance to transform Central Europe from a phenomenon that has so far been historical and spiritual into a political phenomenon'.[275] This period witnessed the emergence of perhaps the most ambitious historical synthesis of Central Europe, written by the Polish-American scholar Piotr S. Wandycz: *The Price of Freedom*.[276] Wandycz described Central Europe as a 'semi-periphery' and identified a number of common traits that characterized the development of Central European nations, especially Poland, Czechoslovakia and Hungary, which he considered to be Central European par excellence. These features included delayed state formation in the Middle Ages, a divergence between intellectual, institutional and socio-economic development between Central and Western Europe since the sixteenth century, a persistent gap between the elites and the masses, the presence of an ethnically diverse (predominantly German and Jewish) urban bourgeoisie and an ethnonationalist collective self-understanding. Yet the most important common trait of these nations, according to Wandycz, is their heroic struggle for freedom, especially in the period when they became subordinate parts of empires, a struggle Wandycz saw as decisive for the historical trajectory of the region.

By the latter half of the 1990s, however, the debate about Central Europe was toned down and the efforts of the Visegrád states to build separate structures for political and economic cooperation receded before the alternative project of 'returning to *Western* Europe'. Many intellectuals within the region, not to mention politicians, began to envision in Central Europe the spectre of provincialism and marginality and were eager to demonstrate instead their country's credentials as a historic and intellectual part of Western Europe. Once again, the idea of Central Europe proved more efficient in reconfiguring and ultimately buttressing, rather than subverting and relativizing, the dominant East–West framework. By 2000, Romanian historian Sorin Antohi observed that

> Central Europe appears to have lost its attraction, and to be relapsing willingly into posthistorical routine. ... The Kunderian mythology of the region survives in the latter's margins, enjoying a provincial afterlife. From Hungarian and Czech authors, the cultural motif of *Mitteleuropa*, especially its emancipatory potential, migrates to Romanian, Slovakian, and Western Ukrainian writers and audiences. Consequently, the centrality of Central Europe is gradually supplanted by its liminality, while its fashionable relics become the Banat, Bukowina, Galitia, or cities such as Temeswar, Czernowitz, and Lemberg (to use their nostalgic German names ...).[277]

In Hungary, the initial spurt in Central European discourse – especially in history and literary studies, a tide that was marked by a certain de-ideologization of regionalist terminology and the abandonment of the normative connotations of Central Europe – was swiftly followed by a

---

275 Václav Havel, 'President Václav Havel's Speech to the Polish sejm and senate, January 12, 1990', *East European Reporter* 4, no. 2 (1990): 56, quoted in Hagen, 'Redrawing the Imagined Map', 504.

276 Piotr S. Wandycz, *The Price of Freedom: A History of East Central Europe from the Middle Ages to the Present* (London: Routledge, 1993).

277 Sorin Antohi, 'Habits of the Mind: Europe's Post-1989 Symbolic Geographies', in *Between Past and Future: The Revolutions of 1989 and Their Aftermath*, eds Sorin Antohi and Vladimir Tismaneanu (Budapest: CEU Press, 2000), 65.

Spatial configurations

gradual dissolution of the concept and the emergence of allegedly less loaded or more encompassing spatio-terminological competitors like 'in-between Europe', the 'Danubian region' or East Central Europe.[278] As had been the case before, the Polish interest in (East) Central Europe remained marginal and was subordinated to preoccupations with Ukraine, Lithuania and Belorussia, while the mainstream was Western-oriented.

Ironically, as Antohi noted, 'Central Europe' owed its survival to intellectuals from the one-time peripheral provinces of the Habsburg Empire. In fact, the cultural programme of the Romanian *A Treia Europă* ('The third Europe') research group based in Timişoara (in Banat) tried not just to resurrect their region's Central European identity but to redefine Central Europe by repositioning the 'imperial margins' as its cultural centre, detached from the '*Mitteleuropean* dictate' of Vienna and Budapest, with the former Habsburg provinces of Bukovina (now part of Romania and Ukraine) and Banat now appearing as the quintessential Central European zones of interethnic, multilingual and cultural convergence.[279] On the whole, stemming from the historically composite character of modern Romania, Romanian debate since the 1990s has developed according to contestation between three spatial self-identifications: Central European (or post-Habsburg), Southeastern European (or post- Byzantine–Ottoman) and a syncretic one that defines Romania as the meeting point of the European and Byzantine spaces.

The wars of Yugoslav succession in the 1990s once again made the Balkans a powerful symbolic concept by rekindling, both outside and inside the region, Balkan imagery characteristic of pre-Second World War Western representations. This period witnessed a veritable boom in publications on the region, which searched for the roots of the Yugoslav wars and reanimated discussions of the Balkan *Sonderweg* and the region's otherness within the European project due to the purported endemic violence and incessant conflict it endured. Both popular media and academic sociopolitical analyses of the region revolved around the category of nationalism as 'the quintessential feature of an unchangeable Balkan condition' predicated upon its dissociation from sociopolitical developments in the rest of Europe.[280]

Resistance to this mode of representation, and concomitant attempts to 'normalize' the Balkans, became noticeable from the late 1990s and proceeded in different directions. The most impactful one in academia was the critical reformulation of the Balkans as a discursive concept inspired by Saidian Orientalism – not as a historical region, but as an imagined space and simplified representation in the Western mind, drawing on a hierarchical relationship between the West and the Balkans and performing crucial functions in discourses of collective identity. The Bulgarian–American historian Maria Todorova's *Imagining the Balkans* has been justly credited with compellingly embedding this Orientalist (or rather Balkanist) critique into the concept of the Balkans. Yet, her position is less unequivocal than often assumed in that she sees the Balkans as possessing not just 'imaginary' but also 'ontological' aspects, which she defines in terms of continuity and the perception of the Ottoman legacy.[281]

Constructivist conceptualizations of the Balkans were countered by 'structural' ones. The German historian Holm Sundhaussen saw the Balkans as an 'analytical category' defined by a

---

278 Maciej Janowski, Constantin Iordachi and Balazs Trencsenyi, 'Why Bother about Historical Regions? Debates over Central Europe in Hungary, Poland and Romania', *East Central Europe* 32, nos. 1–2 (2005): 16–22.

279 Adriana Babeţi and Cornel Ungureanu, eds, *Europa Centrală: Nevroze, dileme, utopii* [Central Europe: neuroses, dilemmas, utopias] (Iaşi: Polirom, 1997); Janowski et al., 'Historical Regions', 40–2.

280 Pavlos Hatzopoulos, *The Balkans Beyond Nationalism and Identity: International Relations and Ideology* (London & New York: I. B. Tauris, 2008), 41–66.

281 Todorova, *Imagining the Balkans*; idem, 'Balkanism and Postcolonialism', 177.

cluster of nine defining characteristics (*Merkmalcluster*), which, in their specific combination and high levels of correspondence over time and space, distinguished the region from the Byzantine era to the present day.[282] Two among these – the Byzantine–Orthodox and the Ottoman–Islamic heritage – he viewed as decisive for bringing about such political, economic and intellectual structures that had set the Balkans on a distinct path of development in comparison with other European regions. Only the countries that share this heritage, rather than the entirety of wider Southeastern Europe, constitute, according to this view, a 'historical region'.[283]

From a broader perspective, the conflict between constructivist and structural conceptualizations fed into the discussion on the definition of historical regions, which gathered momentum in the wake of the spatial and transnational turns in the human and social sciences that have occurred since the 1980s. Within this frame, the definition of Southeastern Europe – the prevailing regional term since the 1990s – becomes unstable, informed by neither objective criteria nor essentialist characteristics, but exposed to contestation, 'its boundaries seen as intellectual constructs, provisional, open to question and overlapping. This would have the advantage of interrogating definitions, traits and boundaries, rather than letting them pass unexamined.'[284] Meanwhile, however, the quest to locate the specificity and scope of the Balkans/Southeastern Europe *qua real* (as opposed to an 'invented') space has continued. A number of studies conducted since the 1990s have sought to rethink the unity of the region in terms of total history in a Braudelian vein (Traian Stoianovich),[285] or as a specific linguistic and ethno-cultural *mixtum compositum* (Victor Friedman, Raymond Detrez, or Klaus Roth),[286] a historical-anthropological zone (Karl Kaser) or according to common mental structures and normative categories of a 'Balkan model of the world' (Tat'jana Civ'jan).[287] All in all, despite certain important

---

282 These are: 1) the instability of population relations and ethnic mix in a very small space; 2) the reduced and late reception of the heritage of antiquity; 3) the Byzantine–Orthodox heritage; 4) a fundamental anti-Western disposition and cultural distancing from Central and Western Europe; 5) the Ottoman–Islamic heritage; 6) social and economic 'backwardness' in the modern period; 7) patterns of nation building; 8) mentalities and myths; 9) the Balkans as an object in the policies of the Great Powers. Holm Sundhaussen, 'Europa Balcanica: Der Balkan als historischer Raum Europas', *Geschichte und Gesellschaft* 25 (1999): 4, 626–53.

283 Holm Sundhaussen, 'Was ist Südosteuropa und warum beschäftigen wir und (nicht) damit?', *Südosteuropa Mitteilungen* 42, nos. 5–6 (2002): 93–105.

284 Wendy Bracewell and Alex Drace-Francis, 'South-Eastern Europe: Histories, Concepts, Boundaries', *Balkanologie* 3 (1999): 2, 61.

285 Traian Stoianovich, *Between East and West: The Balkan and Mediterranean Worlds*, 4 vols (New York: Aristide D. Caratzas, 1992–5); idem, *Balkan Worlds: The First and Last Europe* (London: Routledge, 1994).

286 Victor Friedman, 'The Place of Balkan Linguistics in Understanding Balkan History and Balkan Modernity', *Bulletin de l'Association des études du sud-est européen* 24–5 (1994–5): 87–94; idem, 'Balkans as a Linguistic Area', 657–72; Raymond Detrez, 'Pre-National Identities in the Balkans', in *Entangled Histories of the Balkans, Vol. 1: National Ideologies and Language Policies*, eds Roumen Daskalov and Tchavdar Marinov (Leiden: Brill, 2013), 13–66; and Klaus Roth, 'Ethnokulturelle Gemeinschaft der Balkanvölker: Konstrukt oder Realität?', in *Der Balkan: Friedenszone oder Pulverfaß?* eds Valeria Heuberger, Arnold Suppan and Elisabeth Vyslonzil (Frankfurt a.M.: Lang 1998), 63–78.

287 Tat'yana Tsiv'yan, *Lingvisticheskiye osnovy balkanskoy modeli mira* [Linguistic foundations of the Balkan model of the world] (Moscow: URSS, 1990), reprinted in a revised and enlarged version as *Model' mira i eë lingvisticheskiye osnovy* [Model of the world and its linguistic foundations] (Moscow: URSS, 2006); and idem, *Dvizheniye i put' v balkanskoy modeli mira* [Movement and road in the Balkan model of the world] (Moscow: Idrik, 1999).

post-structuralist advances that draw on the spatial turn, the debate between Southeastern Europeanists and (post-)structuralist theorists continues.[288]

With the 'securitarization' of the region and Romania and Bulgaria's accession to the EU (in 2007), both the political relevance of the concept and the scholarly interest in the Balkans/Southeastern Europe decreased dramatically. A number of spatial alternatives emerged based on new European fault lines or reassessments of historical interconnections. The German historian Stefan Troebst advocated a 'circum-Pontic' regional concept of the Balkans–Black Sea–Caucasus;[289] the Austrian anthropologist Karl Kaser devised the notion of 'Eurasia Minor', incorporating the historical space between the Danube and the Tigris Rivers;[290] while French geographers conceived of the concept of *Europe médiane*, which included Hungary and Romania but excluded 'Balkan Europe' (former Yugoslavia, Albania, Greece and Bulgaria).[291]

On the whole, the influence of the 'cultural turn', with its critical re-evaluation of grand theories, narratives of modernity and backwardness, and the breakthrough of alternative approaches to cultural history and historical anthropology, have been the most tangible since the 1990s. In addition to the ongoing interrogation of the theoretical and historical foundations of regions and regionality, the cross-cultural methods of historical anthropology have helped to formulate alternative spatial contexts for research, including the Black Sea area, the Mediterranean and the Near East.[292]

Conclusion

By now the inherent spatial and semantic instability of the regional imageries found in the work of East Central European intellectuals should have become obvious. The geographical coverage and definitions of East, West, Eastern Europe, Central Europe/*Mitteleuropa*, East Central Europe, Southeastern Europe, the Balkans, (Carpatho-) Danubian space and so on exhibit great volatility and are subject to contestation between parallel intellectual projects and change over time. The roots of this diversity can be found in the multiplicity of political agendas, academic and disciplinary subcultures, in geopolitical as well as generational shifts and divergent national traditions. Accordingly, the ideological implications (and underlying value systems) of spatial categories also differ greatly.

Most of the above-surveyed regional projections not only depend on political contingencies but are strongly politicized. Politicization could result from attempts to counteract geopolitical challenges (as was clearly the case in the interwar period, which witnessed a proliferation of 'regions' in the face of mounting 'extra-regional' hegemonic pressures). A more common source, though, was the fusion of regionalist and nationalist strategies. The drive for methodological rescaling beyond the national often originated from essentially nationalist agendas, and the outcome was profoundly ambivalent: regional imageries could at one time subvert and, at another, buttress national narratives, and they sometimes extrapolated nationalist and

---

288 Todorova, 'Balkanism and Postcolonialism'; and Vangelis Calotychos, *The Balkan Prospect: Identity, Culture, and Politics in Greece after 1989* (New York: Palgrave Macmillan, 2013) 26–33.

289 Stefan Troebst, 'Schwarzmeerwelt: Eine geschichtsregionale Konzeption', *Südosteuropa Mitteilungen* 46, nos. 5–6 (2006): 92–102.

290 Karl Kaser, *The Balkans and the Near East: Introduction to a Shared History* (Vienna: LIT Verlag, 2011).

291 Laurent Carroué and Valerè Oth, *L'Europe médiane* (Paris: Armand Colin, 1997).

292 This trend was evidenced in some of the panels at the CISH congress in Sydney (2005) that presented recent historiographical developments regarding the meso-regions of Europe (Central Europe, the Balkans, the Mediterranean and so on).

even autochthonist visions of society onto the wider region. Comparative methodologies could function both ways: playing down national differences or reinforcing the national framework.

The regional similes discussed here indicate that as powerful as the post-Enlightenment 'Western discourse' (or rather different national western discourses) of the European east and southeast had been, it was neither the sole, nor, at all times, the dominant 'agent' of regionalization. Local regional narratives conjured up their own mental maps, symbolic geographies and maps of civilization, and pursued their own political-ideological agendas. There were thus parallel, Western and local, external and internal processes of regionalization, which were not necessarily connected. Transfer of regional concepts and semantics, at that, was not a unidirectional, West to East traffic, but a two-way flow, overriding on occasion preoccupations with the margins' asymmetric conceptualization and enforcing alternative definitions and classifications.

Regionalist ideas did not exist merely to underpin political projects, though. While disclosing the politico-ideological implications of region-building, the historicization and contextualization of spatial imageries should not be seen as an attempt to rebut their cognitive potential. Many attempts at regionalization seek to create models of interpretation capable of making sense of the (often fierce) competition between neighbouring cultures with shared pasts and legacies. A wide range of academic disciplines have participated, with different degrees of force at different points in time, in producing regionalities. This, however, has never solved the question of the scholarly definition of regions, as different human and social sciences tend to provide different, often discordant, regional conceptualizations and disagree over what might lend coherence to the political, religious and linguistic diversity that characterizes these areas. This is conspicuously the case in historical studies, where one witnesses different history-embedded conceptualizations of a region, different 'stories' and ways of conceiving it as a 'unitary space'. Epistemological transformations and critical 'turns' are inherent to such plurality.

In the final analysis, the attraction of such regional projections seems to have resided in the symbolic resources that they provided for posing questions about modernity and negotiating the nation's relationship to the transnational cultural, social and economic processes. Basic notions of modernity are embedded in spatial categories, and spatial projections themselves are indicative of the coexistence and competition of different layers and visions of modernity. All this makes it spurious asking whether such spaces are 'real' or not. As Hans-Dietrich Schultz notes

> What is at stake here is rather whether they do what they are expected to do, and which chances, problems or even dangers are conveyed by certain conceptions of space, by those who proffer them, and by those to whom they address.[293]

Further reading

Abrams, Bradley F. *The Struggle for the Soul of the Nation: Czech Culture and the Rise of Communism* (Lanham, MD: Rowman & Littlefield, 2004).

Antohi, Sorin, and Vladimir Tismaneanu, eds. *Between Past and Future: The Revolutions of 1989 and Their Aftermath* (Budapest: CEU Press, 2000).

---

293 Hans-Dietrich Schultz, 'Halbinseln, Inseln und ein "Mittelmeer": Südeuropa und darüber hinaus in der klassischen deutschen Geographie', in *Metropolitanes & Mediterranes: Beiträge aus der Humangeographie*, ed. Hans-Dietrich Schultz (Berlin: Geographisches Institut, 2006), 147.

Spatial configurations

Arnason, Johann, and Natalie Doyle, eds. *Domains and Divisions of European History* (Liverpool: Liverpool University Press, 2010).

Berend, Ivan, and György Ránki. *The European Periphery and Industrialization 1780–1914* (Cambridge: Cambridge University Press, 1982).

Bracewell, Wendy, and Alex Drace-Francis, eds. *Under Eastern Eyes: A Comparative Introduction to East European Travel Writing on Europe* (Budapest: CEU Press, 2008).

Brock, Peter, et al., eds. *Nation and History: Polish Historians from the Enlightenment to the Second World War* (Toronto: University of Toronto Press, 2006).

Byrnes, Robert F., ed. *Communal Families in the Balkans: The Zadruga* (South Bend, IN: Notre Dame Press, 1976).

Calotychos, Vangelis. *The Balkan Prospect: Identity, Culture, and Politics in Greece after 1989* (New York: Palgrave Macmillan, 2013).

Casey, Steven, and Jonathan Wright, eds. *Mental Maps in the Cold War Era, 1945–68* (New York: Palgrave Macmillan, 2011).

Chirot, Daniel. *Social Change in a Peripheral Society: The Creation of a Balkan Colony* (New York: Academic Press, 1976).

Chlebowczyk, Józef. *On Small and Young Nations in Europe: Nation-Forming Processes in Ethnic Borderlands in East-Central Europe* (Wrocław: Zakład Narodowy im. Ossolińskich, 1980).

Daskalov, Roumen, and Tchavdar Marinov, eds. *Entangled Histories of the Balkans. Vol. 1: National Ideologies and Language Policies* (Leiden: Brill, 2013).

Dennis, Deletant, and Harry Hanak, eds. *Historians as Nation-Builders* (London: Macmillan, 1988).

Djurić, Dubravka, and Miško Šuvaković, eds. *Impossible Histories: Historical Avant-Gardes, Neo-Avant-Gardes, and Post-Avant-Gardes in Yugoslavia, 1918–1991* (Cambridge, MA: MIT Press, 2003).

Dvorník, Francis. *The Slavs in European History and Civilization* (New Brunswick, NJ: Rutgers University Press, 1962).

Gilbers, D. G., J. Nerbonne, and J. Shaeken, eds. *Languages in Contact* (Amsterdam: Rodopi, 2000).

Halecki, Oskar. *Borderlands of Western Civilization: A History of East Central Europe* (New York: Ronald Press, 1952).

Halecki, Oskar. *The Limits and Divisions of European History* (London: Sheed & Ward, 1950).

Hatzopoulos, Pavlos. *The Balkans beyond Nationalism and Identity: International Relations and Ideology* (London and New York: I. B. Tauris, 2008).

Hodža, Milan. *Federation in Central Europe. Reflections and Reminiscences* (London: Jarrolds Publishers, 1942).

Islamoglu-Inan, Huri, ed. *The Ottoman Empire and the World Economy* (Cambridge: Cambridge University Press, 1987).

Jedlicki, Jerzy. *A Suburb of Europe: Nineteenth-Century Polish Approaches to Western Civilization* (Budapest: CEU Press, 1999).

Jelavich, Charles, and Barbara Jelavich. *The Establishment of the Balkan National States, 1804–1920* (Seattle, WA: University of Washington Press, 1977).

Kaser, Karl. *The Balkans and the Near East: Introduction to a Shared History* (Vienna: LIT Verlag, 2011).

Keane, John, ed. *Civil Society and the State: New European Perspectives* (London and New York: Verso, 1988).

Kłoczowski, Jerzy. *East Central Europe in the Historiography of the Countries of the Region* (Lublin: Institute of East Central Europe, 1995).

Kohn, Hans. *Pan-Slavism: Its History and Ideology* (Notre Dame, IN: Vintage Books, 1960).

Koneczny, Feliks. *On the Plurality of Civilizations* (London: Polonica Publications, 1962) (also accessible at www.scribd.com/doc/4464979/ON-THE-PLURALITY-OF-CIVILIZATIONS-Feliks-Koneczny-Entire-Book).

Konrád, György. *Antipolitics: An Essay* (San Diego, CA: Harcourt Brace Jovanovich, 1984).

Kundera, Milan. *The Book of Laughter and Forgetting* (New York: Penguin, 1981).

Lednicki, Wacław. *Russia, Poland and the West: Essays in Literary and Cultural History* (London: Hutchinson, 1954).

Macura, Vladimír. *The Mystification of a Nation: 'The Potato Bug' and Other Essays on Czech Culture* (Madison, WI: University of Wisconsin Press, 2010).

Malmborg, Mikael, and Bo Stråth, eds. *The Meaning of Europe: Variety and Contention within and among Nations* (Oxford: Berg, 2002).

Masaryk, Tomáš G. *The Making of a State: Memories and Observations (1914–1918)* (London: Allen & Unwin, 1927).

Maxwell, Alexander, ed. *The East-West Discourse: Symbolic Geography and Its Sources* (Oxford: Peter Lang, 2010).

Middell, Matthias, and Lluis Roura y Aulinas, eds. *World, Global and European Histories as Challenges to National Representations of the Past* (London: Palgrave Macmillan, 2013).

Milutinović, Zoran. *Getting over Europe: The Construction of Europe in Serbian Culture* (Amsterdam: Rodopi, 2011).

Mishkova, Diana. *Beyond Balkanism: The Scholarly Politics of Region Making* (London and New York: Routledge, 2018).

Mishkova, Diana, and Balázs Trencsényi, eds. *European Regions and Boundaries: A Conceptual History* (Oxford: Berghahn Books, 2017).

Mishkova, Diana, Marius Turda, and Balázs Trencsényi, eds. *Discourses of Collective Identity in Central and Southeast Europe (1770–1945)*, vol. 4, *Anti-Modernism: Radical Revisions of Collective Identity* (Budapest: CEU Press, 2014).

Naumann, Friedrich. *Central Europe*, trans. Christabel M. Meredith (New York: Knopf, 1917).

Neumann, Iver. *Uses of the Other: 'The East' in European Identity Formation* (Minneapolis: University of Minnesota Press, 1999).

Niederhauser, Emil. *The Rise of Nationality in Eastern Europe* (Budapest: Corvina Kiadó, 1981).

Okey, Robin. *Eastern Europe 1740–1980: Feudalism to Communism* (London: Hutchinson University Library, 1982).

Orzoff, Andrea. *Battle for the Castle: The Myth of Czechoslovakia in Europe, 1914–1948* (New York: Oxford University Press, 2009).

Pach, Zsigmond Pál, ed. *Hungary and the European Economy in Early Modern Times* (Aldershot: Variorum, 1994).

Pál, Jonás, et al., eds. *Király Béla emlékkönyv: Háború és társadalom: War and Society: Guerre et société: Krieg und Gesellschaft* (Budapest: Századvég Kiadó, 1992).

Passerini, Luisa. *Europe in Love, Love in Europe: Imagination and Politics in Britain between the Wars* (London: I.B. Tauris, 1999).

Péteri, György, ed. *Imagining the West in Eastern Europe and the Soviet Union* (Pittsburgh: University of Pittsburgh Press, 2010).

Schöpflin, George, and Nancy Wood, eds. *In Search of Central Europe* (Cambridge: Polity Press, 1989).

Stoianovich, Traian. *Balkan Worlds: The First and Last Europe* (London: Routledge, 1994).

Stoianovich, Traian. *Between East and West: The Balkan and Mediterranean Worlds*, 4 vols (New York: Aristide D. Caratzas, 1992–5).

Sugar, Peter. *East European Nationalism, Politics and Religion* (Collected Studies) (Aldershot: Ashgate Variorum, 1999).

Sugar, Peter, and Ivo Lederer, eds. *Nationalism in Eastern Europe* (Seattle, WA: University of Washington Press, 1969).

Todorova, Maria. *Imagining the Balkans* (Oxford: Oxford University Press, 1997).

Walicki, Andrzej. *Poland between East and West: The Controversies over Self-Definition and Modernization in Partitioned Poland* (Cambridge, MA: Harvard University Press, 1994).

Wandycz, Piotr S. *The Price of Freedom: A History of East Central Europe from the Middle Ages to the Present* (London: Routledge, 1993).

2

THINKING DANGEROUSLY

Political thought in twentieth-century East Central Europe

Balázs Trencsényi

Introduction

The history of political thought in East Central Europe is among those subjects which have not been studied in a comparative regional framework even though there are many country-based case studies available as well as a certain amount of works focusing on transnational ideological transfers. The existing volumes usually subordinate political thought to a general narrative of political or socio-economic history,[1] or bring together nation-based case studies without creating a common narrative.[2] Simultaneously, the literature on the global history of political thought offers very limited insights on East Central European topics and thinkers.[3] It is only very recently that more focused works started to appear on the topic.[4]

Most of the works seeking to devise a broader interpretative framework for the history of modern political thought in the region opted for a model based on the binary opposition of

---

1 See, e.g. Piotr S. Wandycz, *The Price of Freedom: A History of East Central Europe from the Middle Ages to the Present*, 2nd ed. (London: Routledge, 2001); Andrew C. Janos, *East Central Europe in the Modern World: The Politics of the Borderlands from Pre- to Postcommunism* (Stanford: Stanford UP, 2000).

2 A case in point is Michel Maslowski and Chantal Delsol, eds, *Histoire des idées politiques de l'Europe centrale* (Paris: Presses universitaires de France, 1998).

3 In the volume edited by Terence Ball and Richard Bellamy, *The Cambridge History of Twentieth-Century Political Thought* (Cambridge: Cambridge University Press, 2003), the sections dealing with East Central Europe are predictably the one on anti-communist dissidents ('The literature of revolt against communism') and the one on Georg (György) Lukács.

4 A recent overview covering the period from the eighteenth to the twenty-first century is Ulf Brunnbauer and Paul Hanebrink, 'Political Ideologies and Political Movements', in *The Routledge History of East Central Europe since 1700*, eds Irina Livezeanu and Arpad von Klimo (London: Routledge, 2017), 323–64. The author of this chapter also co-authored *A History of Modern Political Thought in East Central Europe*, vol. 1, *Negotiating Modernity in the 'Long Nineteenth Century'* (Oxford: Oxford University Press, 2016), vol. II/1: *Negotiating Modernity in the 'Short Twentieth Century and Beyond'* (1918–1968) and vol. II/2: *Negotiating Modernity in the 'Short Twentieth Century and Beyond'* (1968–2018) with Maciej Janowski, Mónika Baár, Maria Falina, Luka Lisjak-Gabrijelčič and Michal Kopeček (Oxford: Oxford University Press, 2018).

pro-Western and autochthonist discourses. This obviously bears the stamp of the grand narrative of Russian intellectual history, going back to the classic studies of Alexandre Koyré[5] and Isaiah Berlin.[6] While the mutually exclusive nature of these two positions has also been questioned by these authors themselves, as well as by other scholars such as Andrzej Walicki, who looked at the interplay of these discourses of identity in the nineteenth-century Russian and Polish contexts, the opposition still remains an implicit – often even subconscious – organizing principle of presenting the political thought of the region. This is also evident from the attention accorded to two mirroring features of ideological production in the region: the manifestations of ethnonationalism, preparing the periodically recurrent waves of political violence, and the 'shortlist' of dissident thinkers in the 1970s–80s, who argued for the cultural and spiritual reintegration of their countries to a common European framework (from István Bibó and Jan Patočka to Václav Havel and Adam Michnik) and rejected both the local ethnonationalist traditions and the oppressive ideological framework of 'actually existing socialism'.

While not completely negating the relevance of the aforementioned interpretative framework, this chapter seeks to offer an alternative reading of the various local discussions as part of a multi-level dialogue on key issues of modern European political thought. Along these lines, the chapter seeks to offer a 'soft' regionalist narrative. While rejecting an essentialist definition of East Central Europe or the search for a set of 'original characteristics' of political thought in the region, it still hopes to identify certain 'local' factors, which in themselves might not be characteristic solely of this region, but their combination nevertheless lends a rather recognizable physiognomy to political discourses stemming from this part of the world.

One of the key features of political thought in the region is the constant overlap and frequent clash of different historical layers: a sort of asynchronic synchronicity of socio-cultural and ideological phenomena that is clearly rooted in the deeply differentiated social structure of these countries (e.g. the cleavage between urban and rural societies). The second key feature is the overlap of different transformations: the simultaneous breakthrough of modern social, cultural, economic and legal-institutional structures (a phenomenon that in the German context was described by David Blackbourn, Geoff Eley and Jürgen Kocka in their reconceptualizations of the *Sonderweg* debate).[7] The pressure created by this overlap challenged, in a particularly dramatic way, the established patterns of politics in East Central Europe as well. Finally, political thought in the region was characterized by a highly ambiguous relationship with the 'West': on the one hand, by constructing it as a homogeneous normative system of values and practices, on the other hand, by permanently grappling with the problem of the transferability and applicability of these patterns to the local context. Importantly, the 'external' and the 'local' reference points were equally dynamic: 'the West' could be the source of democratic and anti-democratic – as well as modernist and anti-modernist – ideas, and the domestic cultural and institutional traditions could be used to support highly divergent political projects, ranging from national liberalism and agrarian populism to various types of socialism and radical nationalism. Consequently, rather than searching for two mutually incompatible ideological positions (the

---

5 Alexandre Koyré, *La philosophie et le problème national en Russie au début du XIXe siècle* (Paris: Gallimard, 1976 [1929]).

6 Isaiah Berlin's key essays are collected in *Russian Thinkers* (London: Penguin, 1978).

7 David Blackbourn and Geoff Eley, *The Peculiarities of German History: Bourgeois Society and Politics in Nineteenth-Century Germany* (Oxford: Oxford University Press, 1984); Jürgen Kocka, 'Asymmetrical Historical Comparison: The Case of the German *Sonderweg*', *History and Theory* 38, no. 1 (February 1999): 40–50.

one arguing for the wholesale adaptation of these putative Western norms and another one categorically rejecting them), it is more productive to perceive this relationship in terms of a permanent reconfiguration of auto- and hetero-stereotypes and legitimizing constructions based on cultural transfer and the clash of competing visions of modernity.

Along these lines, this chapter revisits a set of thematic discussions that reflected the processes of socio-cultural and institutional transformation of this region throughout the twentieth century. The subchapters are organized on two axes: chronological and ideological, i.e. they present the evolution of the discussion on a given issue and the key ideological positions and discursive traditions. The main thematic hubs to be analyzed are as follows: the problem of overlapping nation-building projects, the role of the state, the social question, the relationship of politics and religion, the political thought *of* and *on* totalitarianism, and finally, the permanent crisis of identity characterizing the East Central European intellectuals, prompting them to search for various frameworks of identification that could weave the divergent threads of the past, present and future into a coherent narrative.

As for the temporal axis, the conventional narrative tends to follow the changes of the social-cultural-political context, proceeding from the pre-1914 belle époque, through the interwar period with its ambiguity of cultural boom and socio-political implosion, the period of communist domination starting immediately or almost immediately after the Second World War and, as a moderately optimistic coda, reaching the post-communist period after 1989 (or, in some cases, 1991). However, with regard to intellectual history, this periodization needs to be adopted with caution as many of the most interesting phenomena bridged these political-existential watersheds. Thus, the rise of integral nationalism and cultural anti-modernism that came to dominate the interwar period is rooted in the fin-de-siècle context, while many of the étatist homogenizing and modernizing policies implemented after 1945 by the communists had their intellectual roots in the expert communities of the right-wing authoritarian regimes in the late 1930s and early 1940s. Similarly, the dilemmas dividing these political cultures after 1989 cannot be understood unless their roots in the oppositional subcultures of the 1970s–80s are located.

To make all this more tangible – and because it is impossible to give a comprehensive account of all the national contexts in the region within one chapter, no matter how extensive – every subchapter presents a number of key individuals who shall exemplify the main trends and debates. Their work is briefly discussed in relation to their intellectual context, their socio-cultural background, personal itinerary, and involvement in intellectual and cultural transfers. Needless to say, the list is far from exhaustive and does not represent any imputed 'top list' of thinkers; it is rather meant as a 'group portrait' of men and women in 'dark times'. Rather than a definitive master narrative, what this chapter seeks to achieve is a mapping of intellectual traditions and key concepts, linking them to a kaleidoscopic image of formative experiences, transnational networks, personal and intellectual connections and affinities, and last but not least, a reflection on the often-tragic destinies of intellectuals during the highly eventful and equally traumatic twentieth century.

The 'national question', supra-nationalism and the perspectives of interethnic coexistence

This subchapter is concerned with the cluster of questions that has traditionally been the focus of research dealing with Central and Eastern Europe, namely the problem of the multi-ethnic composition of the region and the divergence of the state boundaries and ethnocultural communities. The first issue that deserves mention is the ambiguity of the drive of nationalization and national homogenization, which has been a permanent factor of political thought and practice throughout the twentieth century, and the concomitant reflection about the alternatives to nation statehood. An important point of departure here is the breakthrough of integral nationalism at the turn of the century. While the liberal nationalism of the nineteenth century was shaped by a vision of the ultimate harmony of different national projects (as is clear from the ideology of such 'nationalist internationals' as Giuseppe Mazzini's Young Europe, or *Giovine Europa*), the turn of the century brought a new type of national ideology that perceived the relationship of national projects to each other in terms of a 'zero sum game'. This is articulated in a paradigmatic way in the works of Roman Dmowski, whose *Thoughts of a Modern Pole* (first published in article form in 1902) can be considered one of the most original manifestos of integral nationalism in the region.[8] Drawing on a positivist episteme, Dmowski challenged the historicist liberal and radical democratic supra-ethnic concepts of the nation:

> The subject of this patriotism, or, to be precise, of this nationalism is not some set of liberties, referred to in the past as the homeland, but the nation itself, that is, a living social organism whose spiritual distinctiveness and culture are built on historical and racial grounds, and whose insistence on national language, culture, and tradition finds its source in the urge to be one and united as a nation.[9]

Importantly, this vision of national mobilization that was deeply rooted in Social Darwinism also entailed a certain emphasis on 'civil society', seen as detached from the 'alien' state structures and thus offering a socio-economic basis for the struggle for national survival. This ideological framework, focused as it was on the ethnonational community and proposing a homogeneous nation state as the only viable political entity, was to have a considerable influence all over the region and shaped various ideological projects, from the palingenetic nationalisms of the interwar period to some of the national communist experiments of the 1970s–80s and the post-1989 neo-conservative nationalist discourses.[10] Its focus on organic social activism can also be linked to the tradition of anti-politics that came to play a considerable role in the political cultures of the region. Integral nationalism thus provides an excellent illustration for the very ambiguity of the notion of civil society which has been somewhat one-sidedly hailed as the real core of a democratic political framework in the local dissident culture of the 1970s–80s as well as by the Western observers who were looking for an antidote to the routinization and formalism of democratic life in their own countries. Dmowski's National Democracy movement ('*Endecja*'), as well as the Central European *völkisch* subcultures at the beginning of the twentieth century, however, exemplify the potential 'dark side' of civic activism in the context of the ethnicization of the public sphere.

---

8 Roman Dmowski, *Myśli nowoczesnego Polaka* [Thoughts of a modern Pole] (Lviv: nakł. Towarzystwa Wydawniczego, 1904).

9 Roman Dmowski, 'Thoughts of a Modern Pole', trans. Zuzanna Ladyga, in *Discourses of Collective Identity in Central and Southeast Europe 1770–1945: Texts and Commentaries*, vol. 4, *Anti-Modernism – Radical Revisions of Collective Identity*, eds Diana Mishkova, Marius Turda and Balázs Trencsényi (Budapest: CEU Press, 2014), 61–9, here 65.

10 On the impact of integral nationalism in the region see Brian Porter, *When Nationalism Began to Hate: Imagining Modern Politics in Nineteenth-Century Poland* (Oxford: Oxford University Press, 2000); and Miklós Szabó, *Az újkonzervativizmus és a jobboldali radikalizmus története (1867–1918)* [The history of neo-conservatism and right-wing radicalism] (Budapest: Új Mandátum, 2003).

Thinking dangerously

It was not only the conservative right that became more nationalistic after 1900. The simultaneous engagement of the left with nationalism produced a number of alternative projects which sought to bring together social and national emancipation. One can even talk of an ideological tradition of 'national socialism' as it came to be called in the political system of the Czech lands at the turn of the century. (This should not in any way be confused with Nazism, even if it was not entirely accidental that the predecessor of the National Socialist German Workers' Party, NSDAP, emerged in the Bohemian German context.) Representatives of this stream sought to link a non-Marxist leftist agenda to an ethno-linguistically framed national programme.[11]

Before 1917, especially in the Western regions of the Russian Empire, the doctrine of self-determination had a distinctly leftist tinge and most of the important articulations of this idea came from socialist or *Narodnik* milieus. An early example is Iulian Bachynsky's *Ukraina Irredenta* from 1895, but in the same context one can place various Polish, Latvian, Estonian and Belarusian works written in connection with the 1905 Revolution. What was common in them is the strong emphasis on autonomy as a principal human aspiration, which could be interpreted in a collectivist way as well, extending the subject of self-determination from the individual to the national community. Importantly, however, the idea of national self-determination remained compatible with a federalist vision as most of these thinkers thought about some sort of democratic federation as a desirable state framework capable of replacing the autocratic tsarist empire.

A similar dynamic could also be observed in the South Slavic contexts, where the Yugoslavist discourse assumed the functions of a palingenetic national ideology. As the Dalmatian activist and writer Vladimir Čerina, one of the founders of the Croatian *Nacionalistička omladina* ('Nationalist youth') argued, the way to overcome the decadence of bourgeois life was to appropriate

> the notion of Nation not as a no-party but an all-party concept, not as being exclusive but unitary, not as being chauvinist but humane, not as being aristocratic and class-bound but democratic and racial; love for a fulfilling and comprehensive life, for a life free of all chains should be preached here more than anywhere else, where the intelligentsia is in the process of going totally bankrupt![12]

This type of discourse merged different components in an intricate manner, in many ways comparable to the Italian national radicalism that eventually gave birth to Benito Mussolini's fascism. While before 1914 it could be qualified as an unconventional leftist project, such biological nationalism opened the way for the subsequent extreme rightist turn in the interwar period.

Responding to the radicalization of nationalism, various thinkers tried to offer an alternative to the logic of nation statehood. One can identify two important trends that evolved simultaneously, but in certain contexts also intersected. One is a reformist conservative imperial supra-nationalism, most obviously present in the thought of the 'Belvedere Circle' around Franz Ferdinand in Vienna. The federalism cherished by the politicians gathering around the crown prince focused on strengthening the imperial centre but at the same time offered the

---

11 T. Mills Kelly, *Without Remorse: Czech National Socialism in Late Habsburg Austria* (New York: Columbia University Press, 2006).

12 Mishkova, Turda and Trencsényi, *Discourses of Collective Identity*, vol. 4, 91.

possibility of national development for the various national groups of the monarchy. The ideological backgrounds and agendas of the key thinkers were rather divergent (Aurel C. Popovici, a Banat Romanian, was a radical conservative who came under the influence of racialist ideas, while Milan Hodža, a Slovak, was an agrarian populist, much more democratically inclined and also influenced by Tomáš G. Masaryk's 'realism'), but their suggestions had a common ground, namely, the idea of establishing territorial units with relative national homogeneity and delimiting the federal and the local competences.[13]

An influential alternative trend was represented mainly by socialist and left-liberal political thinkers influenced by Austro-Marxism. They also sought to keep together the supra-national political entities but rejected the territorialization of nationalities and were more inclined to a conception of personal autonomy. However, in contrast to Otto Bauer, who was perhaps the most consequent theoretician separating nationality from the territorial principle, East Central European authors often mixed elements of personal and territorial conceptions of autonomy. A case in point is the federal project of Oszkár Jászi, who started from a position close to Austro-Marxism and originally considered that a consistent democratization could resolve most of the tensions that were articulated in national terms, but in 1918 moved towards federalism, arguing for the reorganization of the Habsburg Monarchy while still rejecting the territorial division of Hungary along ethnic lines.[14]

These theoretical discussions continued also in the interwar period, especially in the context of the problem of the status of non-titular nationalities in the successor states. The idea of personal autonomy had a considerable impact on the representatives of the minority groups that came to form an umbrella organization, the European Nationalities Congress, which sought to provide practical and theoretical assistance to the nationalities without directly challenging the post-First World War territorial arrangements.[15] A symbolic figure in this discussion was the liberal Baltic German journalist, Paul Schiemann, who was an ardent promoter of the model of personal-cultural self-government. Representing this position, he clashed with the radical pan-German and socially conservative factions of his own community, but also with the Estonian and Latvian nationalist political forces who considered the Germans to be their arch-enemy.[16]

An interesting parallel debate on the federalist paradigm occurred in the Balkans, ravaged by a series of bloody national conflicts (the 1876–78 anti-Ottoman movements and uprisings, the 1885–86 Bulgarian–Serbian War, the 1903 Ilinden Uprising, the two Balkan Wars and finally the First World War). At certain moments, this debate intersected with the developments in the post-Habsburg and post-Romanov imperial spaces. Balkan socialists were split between two positions: one arguing for the creation of small, nationally homogeneous states, which then would merge into some sort of new federation, while the other tried to transform the existing imperial frameworks into transnational federations. A key figure of the debate was the Bulgarian socialist theoretician, Krastyu (Christian) Rakovski, who argued against the nationalization of socialist movements and the subordination of the social question to the national agenda; however, he became increasingly aware of the importance of the national question in the region.

---

13 Aurel C. Popovici, *Naţionalism sau democraţie* [Nationalism or democracy] (Bucharest: Albatros, 1997).

14 Oszkár Jászi, *A Monarchia jövője – A dualizmus bukása és a Dunai Egyesült Államok* [The future of the monarchy: the fall of dualism and the Danubian United States] (Budapest: Új Magyarország Rt., 1918). On Jászi's thought see György Litván, *A Twentieth-century Prophet: Oscar Jászi, 1875–1957* (Budapest: CEU Press, 2006).

15 Sabine Bamberger-Stemmann, *Der Europäische Nationalitätenkongreß 1925 bis 1938. Nationale Minderheiten zwischen Lobbystentum und Großmachtinteressen* (Marburg: Verlag Herder Institut, 2000).

16 John Hiden, *Defender of Minorities: Paul Schiemann, 1876–1944* (London: Hurst & Company, 2004).

Thinking dangerously

His vision was in many ways comparable to the Austro-Marxist programme: he considered nationalism to be a means of dominance of the newly emerging national elites and argued instead for a more encompassing multi-ethnic socialist federal framework. In this respect, he hoped that the Young Turk revolution would enhance the possibility of overcoming national particularisms and federalizing the Balkans:

> In fact what has up till now prevented a Balkan alliance, or to call it by its correct name, a Balkan federation, is the struggle of the peoples of the East over their Turkish inheritance. The consolidation of Turkey would make this quarrel pointless. So the only serious and lasting guarantee of peace in Eastern Europe is on the one hand, internally, reform on the basis of equality between Christians and Turks and on the other, externally, a close alliance with the Balkan States.[17]

One of Rakovski's most spectacular gestures in this context was the organization of a parallel event during the 1910 Slavic Congress held in Sofia, where he sought to offer an alternative to the prevailing ideological mix of Slavic solidarity and ethnoculturally based nation statehood.

During the First World War, Rakovski pursued this programme further and became one of the most important protagonists of the (failed) anti-war mobilization in Southeastern Europe, to re-emerge as a member of the Bolshevik leadership in 1917–18. The period when he served as the head of government in Soviet Ukraine (between 1919 and 1923) coincided with the emergence of the indigenization ('*korenizatsiya*') programme, which he originally looked at with suspicion (as it was in many ways similar to the nation state-building agendas he struggled against at the turn of the century). However, his concern with the national issue made him open for dialogue with Ukrainian national communists. His fall from grace was not due to this, but rather his close connection to Leon Trotsky, whose clash with Joseph Stalin led to Rakovski's gradual marginalization, persecution and eventual murder in 1941.

As can be seen in the case of Rakovski, the interwar period brought a new factor into the dynamic relationship of the national ideology and socialism, namely the rise of the Soviet project. This raised a powerful challenge to socialists in East Central European countries who had to choose between their loyalty to the local state-building agenda and to the 'land of socialism'. At the same time, it also offered a model to deal with the national question in the form of the indigenization policies, creating national elites, institutions, symbols, cultural canons, and linking them to a certain territorial entity.

The stereotypical anti-communist narrative tends to emphasize the 'national insensitivity' of communists in the region, but one can find many interesting intersections which challenge this schematic judgment. A case in point is the dominance of the 'Popular Front' ideology, which was both encouraged by Moscow as a way out of the impasse caused by the takeover of Nazism in Germany and by the traumatic experience of the right-wing authoritarian turns all over East Central Europe (with the sole exception of Czechoslovakia). At this particular moment, the communists, who during the Stalinization of their parties in the early 1930s alienated many of their intellectual followers, embarked on mobilizing national references and thus expanded their ideological attractiveness and possible basis of cooperation with other 'anti-fascist' forces.

These efforts had very different outcomes depending on the local context. For instance, in the Yugoslav case, the complex entanglement of the Croatian, Slovenian, Serbian, etc.

---

17 Christian Rakovsky, 'The Eastern European Question and the Great Powers', *Revue de La Paix* (November 1908): 1–2, www.marxists.org/archive/rakovsky/1908/11/x01.htm (accessed 29 April 2019).

identities and the Yugoslav nation-building project catalyzed a number of new modalities, such as the return to a more emphatically Croatian radical leftist agenda, as in the writings of August Cesarec and Miroslav Krleža, but also a tentative Yugoslav communist patriotism. The latter was to have an impact on the emergence of the partisan ideology during the Second World War. Another interesting case is that of Hungary, where the catastrophic collapse of the 'kingdom of St. Stephen', coinciding with the revolutions in 1918–19, seems to have delegitimized the left, however, the Popular Front ideology offered a new possibility for cooperation between some of the young communist intellectuals and the left-wing agrarian populists. A document of this convergence is the manifesto of the March Front in 1938, demanding 'full self-determination' for the Danubian peoples as well as the establishment of a 'Danubian confederation' against the 'pan-Slavic and pan-German imperialist strivings'.[18] Needless to say, these demands were far from being uncontroversial: they challenged the territorial integrity of the neighbouring states even though they clearly rejected the mainstream revisionist agenda of the Horthy regime, which, at least on the propaganda level, aimed at the full restoration of 'historical Hungary'. All this may have had limited immediate relevance, but by providing a common ideological framework for young radical leftists such as Ferenc Donáth or Géza Losonczy, and agrarian populists such as Ferenc Erdei, Imre Kovács, Gyula Illyés and István Bibó, it had a long-term impact on the Hungarian 'national communist' subculture that came to play such an important role in the 1956 Revolution.

These examples also indicate the deep roots of national communism in the region, reaching back well before the end of the Second World War. After 1941, the trend also gained a new impetus from the Soviet leadership, both in terms of the Russian national turn of the war propaganda (which included a revival of Orthodox symbols), as well as the considerable pressure exerted by Stalin on the East Central European communists to fashion themselves as independent actors and appear sensitive to the 'national peculiarities' of their societies. All this figured into a discourse of 'national paths to socialism' which became extremely important for the political left after 1945 and provided a platform for dialogue with other 'progressive forces', but was also a useful tool to challenge the legitimacy of competitors from the Left and the Right for being 'non-national'.

A peculiar justification for this tentative nationalization came from the Hungarian-born Soviet economic theorist, Jenő (Eugen) Varga, who in 1945 argued for a relatively long trajectory towards socialism in Eastern Europe which would consider local socio-economic specificities.[19] A more typical strategy, however, was the instrumentalization of certain elements of the ethnonationalist tradition to legitimize the communists' patriotic self-positioning. This was the case with the strong support enacted on the part of Czech and Slovak communists for the expulsion of Germans and Hungarians, the Polish communists' self-legitimization as the main guarantors of the 're-integration of the Western territories', or the Hungarian communists' vocal support for the expulsion of the Danube Swabians ('*Donauschwaben*').

Another, arguably less common, but nonetheless theoretically important direction was the attempt to construct the post-war communist vision in terms of a framework capable of accommodating various national communities. Here the inspiration of the Soviet indigenization

---

18 The programme of the March Front is available at http://nol.hu/archivum/archiv-439083-247508 (accessed 18 April 2019).

19 Evgeniy Varga, *Izmeneniya v ekomomike kapitalizma v itoge vtoroy mirovoy voyni* [Change in the capitalist economy after the Second World War] (Moscow: Gosudarstvennoe izdatelstvo politicheskoy literaturi, 1946).

Thinking dangerously

project was evident, but there were important local intellectual sources as well. An exemplary case is that of the Slovenian Edvard Kardelj, who was to emerge as the leading Yugoslav Marxist theorist on the national question. As early as the 1930s, Kardelj sought to bring together the communist agenda with an emancipatory stance toward the non-Serbian national communities in Yugoslavia, thus going against the centralist stream in the Yugoslav communist party.[20] During the Second World War, he was also the chief engineer of the nationality policies of the partisan movement, rejecting the pre-war Yugoslav state as oppressive and projecting a socialist federation which would respect the national rights of all its components. After 1945 he was one of the key members of the party leadership, participating in the Sovietization of his country in 1944–5, but also in the process of de-Stalinization after Tito's break with Moscow in 1948. In the ideological framework that emerged in Yugoslavia, which was set on a special path toward socialism, Kardelj linked national autonomy with the principle of workers' self-management, thereby turning the idea of self-government into a central legitimating principle of the Yugoslav socialist project. It was into this exact context that another key figure of the Titoist leadership, Milovan Djilas, relaunched the idea of 'national communism' as radical reformism, aiming at the complete de-Stalinization of the party, as it were. While Djilas eventually became one of the most visible dissidents, Kardelj remained faithful to Tito and belonged to the reformist wing of the leadership. Kardelj played an important role in the liberalization of the 1960s, which also implied a de-centralization in national terms, i.e. leaving more competences with the republics, but his theoretical texts turned out to be increasingly abstract and more and more out of touch with the pressing social and political problems of the country.

Yugoslavia was far from being the only country where the stress on national peculiarities provided the ideological framework for de-Stalinization. We can find similar developments in Hungary and Poland after 1953, as well as in Czechoslovakia, especially in the mid-1960s. In these contexts, one can find many interferences between Marxist revisionism and the revival of national identity politics. Thus, in his writings from the late 1960s, the Czech philosopher, Karel Kosík, sought to devise a specific Czech progressive tradition to counter the re-imposition of Soviet hegemony, while the Belgrade-based members of the Yugoslav Praxis school after 1968 opted increasingly for a nationalist position against the Titoist 'consolidation', which from their perspective only meant the multiplication of the conservative bureaucratic apparatuses at the expense of the genuine structures of self-management.[21]

At the same time, an anti-reformist version of national communism emerged in countries that refused de-Stalinization after 1953 (such as Albania), or at a later point when some of the leaders turned to a national mobilization to supplant the increasing deficit of legitimacy of the communist regime (such as in Poland in the late 1960s, in Romania especially after the 1971 'July Theses', in Bulgaria from the mid-1970s onward, as well as in the Slovak half of Czechoslovakia after the Soviet intervention in 1968). While one can hardly discern a national communist 'grand theory', one may find a plethora of intellectuals who openly supported the new ideological course. Perhaps the most peculiar trend along these lines is Romanian 'protochronism', which sought to subvert the symbolic hierarchy subordinating Romanian culture both to the West and the Soviet Union by creating an alternative 'politics of time', stressing that Romanians were always ahead of other nations in producing cultural-political values

---

20 Edvard Kardelj, *Razvoj slovenskega narodnega vprašanja* [The development of the Slovenian national question] (Ljubljana: Naša Založba, 1939).

21 Karel Kosík, *The Crisis of Modernity: Essays and Observations from the 1968 Era*, ed. James H. Satterwhite (Lanham, MD: Rowman and Littlefield, 1995).

of universal significance (such as the principle of nation statehood, Renaissance humanism, Baroque and – by supposedly anticipating the French Revolution with the Transylvanian peasant uprising of Horea and Cloşca in 1784 – even the modern revolutionary spirit).[22] One might also argue that this modality was a radicalization of a trope already present in every nationalist project in the nineteenth century, for instance, in the claim of the existence of pre-modern democratic traditions (i.e. extolling the self-governing traditions of the gentry in the Polish-Lithuanian Commonwealth or Hungary) constructed as precursors of modern representative democracy and liberalism.

Last but not least, the region has been a testing ground not only for various nationalist conceptions, but also various models of interpreting nationalism. One might even argue that Nationalism Studies, as an academic field, has distinctive East Central European roots. It is possible to identify a cohort of historians and political theorists maturing in the interwar period who subsequently either became the founding fathers of Nationalism Studies in the Western hemisphere or contributed to the formation of local canons of comparative history. The emergence of these approaches can be linked to a series of constitutive experiences, most importantly, the disintegration of multinational empires, the coexistence and territorial overlap of competing nationalizing projects, the reconfiguration of Europe on the principle of national self-determination and the ensuing post-Second World War nationality conflicts.

Looking at the list of names participating in debates concerning these subjects, Prague stands out as a veritable laboratory of Nationalism Studies. Many of these discussions can be linked to the theoretical work of Tomáš G. Masaryk. At the turn of the century, Masaryk set out to rethink the 'meaning of Czech history' from a perspective highly critical of the liberal nationalists' increasing reliance on ethnocultural arguments (in an anti-German as well as anti-Jewish direction). At the same time, he himself in many ways perpetuated the ideological construction of romantic nationalism (e.g. relying on František Palacký's historical narrative concerning the universal significance of Hussitism). Masaryk's ideas had strong repercussions all over the region, starting with the cohort of young Slovak intellectuals grouped around the journal *Hlas* ('Voice') who looked for a way out of the debilitating conflict of traditionalist Slovak nationalism and the seemingly liberal, but in national terms highly intolerant, Hungarian nation-building project. Beyond the Czechoslovak context, the political ideas and image of Masaryk also had a powerful impact on the South Slav intellectual circles. His attempt to problematize the ethnoculturalist versions of nationalism from a universalist moral position, while reconfiguring rather than abandoning the national romantic framework, proved very attractive to some intellectual circles, especially in Croatia and Slovenia, who often became supporters of a democratic variant of Yugoslavism.

In the multi-ethnic milieu of interwar Prague, the study of nationalism became the main preoccupation for a group of scholars, including Eugen Lemberg, Eduard Winter, Hans Kohn and Karl Deutsch. These figures were all linked at some point to the German University and had divergent stances on national identity and politics – the first two belonging to the German minority, the latter two having Jewish roots. Further, they were subsequently destined for very divergent careers, although they all became famous theoreticians of nationalism as émigrés (Lemberg in West Germany, Winter in the GDR, Kohn and Deutsch in the USA). Almost

---

22 Katherine Verdery, *National Ideology under Socialism: Identity and Cultural Politics in Ceauşescu's Romania* (Berkeley, CA: University of California Press, 1991); Alexandra Tomiţă, *O istorie 'glorioasă' – Dosarul protocronismului românesc* [A 'glorious' history – the dossier of Romanian protochronism] (Bucharest: I.C.R., 2007).

Thinking dangerously

simultaneously, the Czech historian and agrarian activist, František Kutnar, who also specialized on the problem of nationalism, developed a complex theory of 'national awakening'. A perhaps less known but equally interesting figure in this context is the philosopher Emanuel Rádl. Linked to the Masarykian project, Rádl had some idiosyncratic features, such as his parallel adherence to social democracy and Protestantism, as well as his dual intellectual commitment to the science of biology and social philosophy. His most relevant work for our purposes here is his essay 'The War of Czechs and Germans', which analyzed the national policies of the Czechoslovak Republic from a highly critical perspective, arguing for a more consequent application of the principle of political nationhood to incorporate the non-Slavic (German and Hungarian) groups as well, and provide them with a symbolic as well as an institutional framework they could consider their own.[23]

Representing a parallel, and at points, an intersecting intellectual trend, the Polish historian, Marceli Handelsman, was at the forefront of the comparative social and intellectual history of Eastern Europe in the interwar period, in dialogue with the founders of the Annales School. Handelsman also studied the development of national movements. Identifying three phases of the emergence of modern nationalism, he expressed his hope that they would be followed by a fourth phase that would restore nationalism's original universalism.[24] Belonging to a subsequent generation maturing in the mid-1930s, Hungarian political thinker István Bibó also pointed to the tension between the democratic/universalist and the anti-democratic/particularist components of nationalism. According to Bibó, the process of creating a modern national community by extending the liberties of the privileged estates to the entire population unfolded without serious difficulties in the West, where nationalism and democracy thus remained closely linked. In Central and Eastern Europe, however, the multi-ethnic empires blurred the incipient national frameworks. Thus, the linguistic-cultural criteria became the central problem for national ideologies and the emerging 'nation states' opted for linguistic homogenization of their territories, which triggered permanent conflicts with other nation-builders. The ensuing feeling of existential threat led to the pathology of 'anti-democratic nationalism', which mobilized the masses against the democratic political agenda – in Bibó's interpretation, fascism constituted the most extreme version of anti-democratic nationalism.

In the South Slavic context there was also a theoretical interest in the morphology of nationalism, as witnessed by the work of the Slovenian social historian focusing on the history of national movements, Fran Zwitter, who was inspired by German *Volksgeschichte* in the 1930s but converted this methodology after 1945 into a historical legitimization of the territorial claims of Yugoslavia against Austria and Italy. Last but not least, coming from a different background, the Jewish Romanian-born British theoretician of agrarianism and international relations, David Mitrany, wrote a number of texts on the problem of nation state-building and minority questions in Southeastern Europe in the 1910s and 1920s, but eventually became world-famous as the author of the functionalist theory of international relations.[25]

The work of these authors was so multifarious that it is practically impossible to encapsulate their theoretical contribution in a couple of sentences. What seems to connect their efforts is

---

23 Emanuel Rádl, *Válka Čechů s Němci* [The war of Czechs and Germans] (Prague: Čin, 1928). See also his *O německé revoluci. K politické ideologii sudetských Němců* [On German revolution: the political ideology of Sudeten Germans] (Prague: Masarykův ústav AV ČR, 2003).

24 Marceli Handelsman, *Rozwój narodowości nowoczesnej* [The development of modern nationality] (Warsaw: Gebethner i Wolff, 1923).

25 David Mitrany, *The Effect of the War in Southeastern Europe* (New Haven, CT: Yale UP, 1936).

three basic observations and analytical strategies: the historicization of nationalism (that is, a rejection of the unproblematic vision of continuity and indicating various phases of the formation of both the nationalist doctrine and the social process of nation-formation); the analytical distinction (following the work of Meinecke and other German and French theorists) between political and ethnocultural types of nationalism; and, a tentative spatialization of these different national concepts – sometimes organizing them according to a binary opposition of Eastern and Western types, in other cases offering a more refined model. The fusion of the last two points, i.e. the construction of an Eastern ethnocultural and a Western civic-ideal type was to become central to Hans Kohn's theoretical contribution and strongly shaped the global discussion on nationalism after 1945.

While the Second World War and the ensuing communist takeovers amounted to a watershed and ended some of these discussions, there was a certain revival of them in the academic cultures and broader public spheres of these countries from the mid-1960s onwards. Although the genealogic threads were often rather complicated, it is evident that the interwar debates impacted the historiographical perspective of a new generation of historians influenced, in one way or another, by Marxism, such as Miroslav Hroch, Jenő Szűcs, Emil Niederhauser, Józef Chlebowczyk and Vlad Georgescu. While their intellectual and scholarly agendas were divergent, what was common in their work is that they all studied the emergence of modern nationalism in Central and Southeastern Europe from a comparative perspective. It is important to stress that in the context of a restricted public sphere of 'actually existing socialism', the audience, as well as the relevance of their analyses, went well beyond the academic community and thus can be linked to the sphere of political thought. Their comparative gaze had an obvious political message because it questioned the discursive autarchy of nationalist ideologies but also stressed the importance of the – often convoluted – processes of nation-formation in the history of the region. A case in point is the work of the Hungarian historian Jenő Szűcs whose essays on the problem of the continuity of pre-modern and modern forms of national identity challenged both the ethnonationalist ideology, prevailing in the interwar period and existing as an undercurrent also after 1945, and the 'vulgar Marxist' interpretation that completely subordinated the questions of identity to the evolution of the forces of production.[26]

The richness and complexity of these interpretative traditions makes the post-1989 East Central European reception of Western 'Nationalism Studies' all the more intriguing. The translations of Ernest Gellner (himself coming from Prague), Anthony D. Smith, Eric Hobsbawm and Benedict Anderson were often propagated as a completely new set of ideas as against the supposed *tabula rasa* of local intellectual traditions. However, one might surmise that the general enthusiasm and eager transfer of their ideas to this part of the world was due partly to the fact that the local historiographical debates were already preparing the ground for them, and that, as I argued above, at least some of these ideas were actually rooted in the East Central European cultural space and were thus much less unfamiliar than acknowledged at the time.

This situation achieves further irony in that the interpretative divergences in this corpus of texts came to be heavily politicized in the post-1989 setting. While the predominant employment of this branch of literature served to deconstruct the national communist ideological heritage, some neo-conservative subcultures in the region attempted to merge the local ethnonationalist ideological tradition with Smith's ethno-symbolism. However, these relatively complex intellectual endeavours became overshadowed by the rise of popular ethnonationalist para-histories all over the region, which profited both from the general relativization of

---

26 Jenő Szűcs, *Nemzet és történelem* [Nation and history] (Budapest: Gondolat, 1974).

Thinking dangerously

professional authority during and after the transition, as well as from the widespread craving for a stable point of orientation in a period of permanent change. Reverting to a unique national past, preferably a deeply archaic one, and proving the autochthonous presence and cultural superiority of the given nation over its neighbours became a surprisingly common compensatory mechanism, which in some cases (like in Hungary and Poland) shifted from being a marginal subculture to a booming intellectual counterculture, with increasing institutional support from the political elites as well.

Theories of the modern state: between impotence and omnipotence

In this subchapter I intend to analyze different conceptions related to the functions of the modern state and, in particular, those concerning the relationship of the state and the citizen. These issues were particularly pertinent in the case of new states, which had to define not only their territorial and governmental form, but also the underlying principles of the new state institutions. Significantly, as the discussions about statehood were always linked to questions of nationhood and social order, there was little space for abstract state theory comparable to the nineteenth-century German tradition of normative *Staatslehre* ('theory of state'). Instead, there was a vivid ideological contention about the geopolitical, socio-cultural and national factors of the state-building project.

A case in point is the Albanian debate on statehood in the 1910s and 1920s. Arguably, the Albanian case was rather extreme in the sense that here the pre-independence society had practically no experience of modern state infrastructure (particularly in the mountainous regions, where the population lived in secluded communities, interacting with the Ottoman bureaucracy only sparsely and following a customary law tradition). The two major Albanian political thinkers of the time, socialized in Western Europe and in the United States, Faik Konica and Fan Noli, both had a remarkable double-perspective, being familiar with their own society, but also with the institutions of Western modernity. As a result, they both engaged in theorizing on the tasks of the modern state in the context of general backwardness.

Konica's vision was comparable to the late nineteenth-century 'organic evolutionary' thinkers of the region, such as the Romanian *Junimists* or the Cracow Positivists, who envisioned a modern state structure as desirable but could only imagine its piecemeal development, simultaneously with the political education and mental transformation of the population. From this perspective, imitating Western institutional practices without a people who 'really understood' them might become counter-productive. In his political articles from 1923, Konica castigated the government of Ahmet Zogu:

> Who are the people who govern today's Albania? Just a group of thieves who have stolen, murdered, and spied for the enemies of Albania – and may even still be doing so today. Is it possible to open the doors of the Sing-Sing prison and give its prisoners the authority to govern America? No way! And yet this happened in Albania.[27]

However, after Zogu consolidated his power, Konica's position became more nuanced: on the one hand, he was painfully aware of the anti-democratic nature of the government, and on the

---

27 Faik Konica, 'The Political Crisis in Albania', in *Discourses of Collective Identity in Central and Southeast Europe 1770–1945: Texts and Commentaries*, vol. 3, *Modernism – The Creation of Nation-States*, eds Ahmet Ersoy, Maciej Górny and Vangelis Kechriotis (Budapest: CEU Press, 2010), 179.

other, he considered it some sort of modernizing authority which reinforced the state institutions and was practically unavoidable in the given geopolitical situation of being surrounded by expansive neighbours such as Italy and Yugoslavia.

A more radical position was represented by the Orthodox Bishop, Fan Noli, who emerged as the leader of the Republican movement that opposed Zogu and played a key role in the democratic coup of June 1924. Noli's discourse was based on the contrast between Western modernity, considered the only possible future for the country, and the parochialism of Albanian society, self-secluded in its ethnic and religious particularisms. Noli called for the dynamization of these identities in a modern democratic mass movement that would eventually realize the idea of the modern state. Noli's main models were the civic republicanism of the French Third Republic and the Greek republican movement led by Alexandros Papanastasiou (founder of the leftist intellectual group, the 'sociologists', and an ally of Eleftherios Venizelos in the 'National Schism'). The Albanian republican project was, however, short-lived as Zogu returned to power with Yugoslav military help and established an authoritarian regime which combined traditionalist and modernist elements of legitimization and governmental practice.

The Albanian story shows the entanglement of ideological and geopolitical visions. This was also the case in the Western borderlands of the Russian Empire, which experienced a deep crisis in 1905–6. The Russian Revolution of 1905 opened up the public sphere for articulating previously suppressed social and national demands, but the radicalization of social and political tensions threatened the complete collapse of the established order. In this context, most national movements in the region (those of Poles, Latvians, Lithuanians, Estonians, Belarusians, Ukrainians, as well as Jews and Bessarabians) faced new challenges and entered a new phase of activism. This was most visible in the case of the Baltic nations and the Belarusians, whose national activism in the nineteenth century had been comparably limited. Importantly, the social and national causes were closely connected, and it was the Marxist socialist and *Eser* ('socialist-revolutionary') subcultures that came up with a general political solution envisioning the democratic federalization of Russia. In contrast, local conservatives were usually much less daring in envisioning radical changes in the imperial framework, fearing the concomitant social disorder. Likewise, during the First World War, when the Russian Empire was already dwindling, it was usually from a centre-left position that the idea of statehood was launched. At the same time, complete independence remained difficult to imagine for a long time to come, and even in 1918 many Latvian and Estonian social democrats insisted on the conditional nature of state independence: it was to be sustained until a progressive democratic multinational federation was set up in the territories of the former tsarist empire.

Nevertheless, the Bolshevik Revolution changed the situation fundamentally, in the sense that it now became possible for the right to argue for independent statehood in the interest of fencing off the revolutionary wave. The most creative conservative theorist of statehood in this context was the Ukrainian Vyacheslav Lypynsky, who became a key ideologist and advisor of Hetman Pavlo Skoropadsky (the head of a short-lived conservative state-building project supported by the Germans which took power in April 1918 with a coup against the leftist-dominated Central Rada). The new regime tried to build on the support of the traditional social and economic elites and also on the wealthier peasants, as opposed to the poor peasants and the urban proletariat mobilized by the Bolsheviks and the Ukrainian Left.

While the Hetmanate collapsed by the end of the year as a result of the withdrawal of German troops, the ideological framework of the regime was revisited by Lypynsky in his Viennese emigration. Drawing the lessons of the collapse of Ukrainian independent statehood both in its leftist and conservative versions, Lypynsky developed an innovative theory of state-building. His main intellectual adversary was the post-Romantic Narodnik/populist vision of

Thinking dangerously

history; in contrast, Lypynsky insisted on the need for an elite that would serve as the spinal column of the state. What he suggested was a kind of *Ständestaat* ('corporatist state') where the most important productive social class was the peasantry, however, instead of the purported egalitarian/communitarian features of the rural world, he stressed the natural differentiation of the countryside and the social role of rich peasants as natural leaders of their local community. From this rural elite, he proposed the creation of a new type of nobility that would run the state not as an alien bureaucracy but as an organic leadership.[28]

In the context of more successful state-building projects after 1918, a multi-volume chronicle of the formation of Czechoslovakia, by the liberal Ferdinand Peroutka, is perhaps the most paradigmatic.[29] The young journalist Peroutka was part of the broader Masarykian political stream but at the same time he tried to devise his own agenda. In his work about state-building he commented on the efforts of creating a functional democratic system and gave a penetrating analysis of the contending political and social forces. Most importantly, he stressed that the complexity of the Czechoslovak undertaking was due to the interference of nation- and state-building tasks and the simultaneous presence of heightened social pressure, the latter a consequence of the post-war socio-economic crisis. Taking the side of Masaryk and the *Hrad* (i.e. the informal circle around the president), he criticized the radicalization of the former liberal nationalist ('Young Czech') circles as epitomized by the political thought of Karel Kramář. Instead, the liberalism he envisioned was rooted in the respect for human dignity which entailed not only the rejection of the fashionable collectivist ideologies of the time, such as fascism and communism, but also the unfettered rule of capitalism.

While the Czechoslovak political realities are usually described as atypically democratic when compared to other polities in interwar East Central Europe, it is instructive to bear in mind that this project also had a darker side. This is most obvious in the 1938 discussion on the 'Second Republic', taking place in the traumatic aftermath of the Munich decision where the British and the French, considered to be the chief protectors of the Czechoslovak state idea after 1918, consented to Hitler's demands on the country's territory. The projects of renewal, born as a reaction to the crisis, rejected the Masarykian–Benešian political model and turned its system of values upside down. Thus, in the manifesto entitled 'How to Build the Second Republic' that came out of the agrarian intellectual circle which centred around the journal *Brázda* ('Rut'), edited by the aforementioned František Kutnar among others, the envisioned state had primarily an ethno-protectionist function with the previous civic understanding of nationhood relegated to the background.[30] Furthermore, political competition was to be restricted and parliamentary democracy was to be replaced by a corporatist arrangement. Remarkably, in the discussion about the political system of the Second Republic, the agrarian right-wing – which prepared to take over the leadership – proposed an ingenious dual system in-between democracy and dictatorship. It would have consisted of a permanent governing party to be based on the conservatives and a permanent opposition to be recruited from the

---

28 Vyacheslav Lypynsky, *Lysty do brativ-khliborobiv pro ideyu ta orhanizaciyu ukrains'koho monarkhizmu* [Letters to fellow farmers concerning the idea and organization of Ukrainian monarchism] (1919–1926), ed. Yaroslav Pelensky (Kiev: Inst. skhidnoievropeiskykh doslidzhen Natsionalnoi akademii nauk Ukrainy, 1995).

29 Ferdinand Peroutka, *Budováni státu* [The building of the state] (Prague: Academia, 2003).

30 'Jak budovat druhou republiku' [How to build the Second Republic], *Brázda* 19, no. 44 (1938): 1–16. For the context see František Kutnar, *Generace Brázdy* [The generation of the journal, *Brázda*] (Prague: Historický klub, 1992). On the political culture of the 'Second Republic' see Jan Rataj, *O autoritativní národní stát* [On an authoritarian nation state] (Prague: Karolinum, 1997).

'nationally conscious' part of the former Left. All this was in manifest contradiction to the Masarykian state ideology although not completely unlike the informal practices of perpetuating the power of the Masarykian circle.[31]

In other cases, the issue of formal democracy was much less central, as the political elites had already decided against it before the final crisis of the interwar geopolitical order in 1938–9. The intellectual starting point of the Polish politician, Adam Skwarczyński, who emerged as the chief ideologist of the étatist turn of the political camp around Józef Piłsudski, is in many ways comparable with that of Peroutka. Thus, he had similar progressive modernist convictions and a more integrative stance in the national question than the ethnonationalist *Endecja* (the 'national democrats' led by Piłsudski's arch-rival, Roman Dmowski). However, as the parliamentary system became instrumental to the Right in the form of a coalition of the national democrats and the right-wing branch of the agrarians, there was a growing alienation of Piłsudski's camp from the institutions of representative democracy. All this was reinforced by the wartime experience of Piłsudski's legions, who considered themselves to be the avant-garde of the national cause abandoned by the undecided majority of the population (not to mention the *Endecja*, which had been pro-Russian and anti-German, thus assuming a diametrically opposed position). This revolutionary romanticism stressed personal heroism instead of the 'selfishness' of the masses and focused on the personality of the leader contrasted to the 'soulless' institutions well before the coup of May 1926.

In Skwarczyński's writings from the early 1920s one can follow the growing disappointment with parliamentary democracy and his craving for a charismatic leader who would be able to assume responsibility and implement the governmental measures efficiently. While in 1919–20 he described his position as part of the socialist tradition and stressed the interests of workers and peasants, he subsequently openly rejected the idea of class struggle and attacked the right with geopolitical and historical arguments.[32]

Yet another post-First World War 'new state', that of the Yugoslavs, produced equally interesting debates about statehood. Here, the central question was whether the state was to be a genuine federation, as pre-war Yugoslavists in the Habsburg Monarchy wished, or an 'enlarged' Serbian Kingdom, which made certain tactical compromises to accommodate a culturally and denominationally heterogeneous population while retaining its original national focus. The writings of the Serbian liberal nationalist, Slobodan Jovanović, who moved between Yugoslav and Serbian state-building agendas, exemplify the ambiguities of this state-building project. At the turn of the century, Jovanović was one of the main theorists of the state as a central agent of politics, arguing against the Radicals' anti-institutionalist vision of popular sovereignty. Such a focus on the strong state did not mean authoritarianism but squared well with the nineteenth-century liberal nationalist doctrine on the centrality of the rule of law to political modernity. After 1918, Jovanović welcomed the creation of the Kingdom of Serbs, Croats and Slovenes, but argued against a federal arrangement. He claimed that federal states always emerged as a result of the unification of several previously independent states, however, this was not the case here. Among the entities that formed the new state, only Serbia was a fully fledged modern state before 1918, while the others had no pre-existing state apparatus.[33]

---

31 Andrea Orzoff, *Battle for the Castle* (New York: Oxford University Press, 2009).
32 Adam Skwarczyński, *Od demokracji do autorytaryzmu* [From democracy to authoritarianism] (Warsaw: Wydawnictwo Sejmowe, 1998).
33 Slobodan Jovanović, *Sabrana dela* [Collected works], vols 1–12, eds Radovan Samardžić and Živorad Stojković (Belgrade: Srpska književna zadruga, 1990).

Thinking dangerously

In the late 1930s, after a decade of political violence and a regicide, followed by the increasingly authoritarian government under Milan Stojadinović – which to some extent co-opted the different national elites but failed to find common ground with the Croatians – Jovanović became a key voice in the discussion on the future of Serbia. As it became obvious that the survival of the common state depended on a thorough reorganization, which would satisfy at least part of the national aspirations of the non-Serbs, there was also a growing dissociation of the Serbian cause from the common state. This situation gave birth to such initiatives as the Serbian Cultural Club, founded in 1937. As a leading ideologist of the Club, Jovanović aimed at creating a political ideology involving a return to the nineteenth-century liberal nationalist tradition while focusing on the democratic nation state as the ideal political framework. The only problem was that in the context of the actual intermingling of populations and overlapping conceptions of national territory, the creation of such a homogeneous democratic nation state seemed to require radical – certainly anti-democratic and arguably even totalitarian – intervention.

The late 1930s indeed made the idea of the totalitarian state fashionable all over the region, as it seemed to offer a straightforward and easy solution to the chronic national and social incoherence of these polities. One should, however, not confuse the ideological references with fully fledged totalitarian regimes. As a matter of fact, even the ideological frameworks of the wartime regimes were rather haphazard and aimed to mix barely compatible elements: radical ethnonationalism with the idea of regional geopolitical integration under the aegis of the Nazi-dominated *Neues Europa*, legal formalism and the craving for anti-institutionalist charismatic rule, the idea of popular sovereignty and technocratic elitism as well as occasional support for 'national capitalism' combined with an anti-bourgeois rhetoric.

Consequently, there were relatively few comprehensive totalitarian state theories developed during the war in the region – partly because of the lack of time and partly due to the hybridity of regimes which were often struggling with an ideologically more 'coherent' and even more radical fascist internal opposition. Major exceptions are constituted by two thinkers who, during the Second World War, developed their interwar considerations further towards a comprehensive totalitarian theory of the state. In his theoretical writings from the early 1930s, the Romanian economic theorist, Mihail Manoilescu, distinguished 'pure corporatism' from party regimes using corporatist elements such as Italian fascism.[34] Originally, Manoilescu clearly opted for the first variant: he rejected the total concentration of power and favoured a complex web of competences and duties compartmentalized by almost autarchic corporations that were to be delegated all three traditional branches of power. In this framework, the state had a double function: it was considered a corporation in terms of its bureaucratic apparatus, but also a super-corporation mediating among the other corporations. From the mid-1930s, however, Manoilescu became a supporter of the extreme right, becoming an important proponent of the Iron Guard. Along these lines, his political journal *Lumea nouă* ('New world'), offered a mixture of corporatist and totalitarian political ideas. It is indicative that his book from 1937, *Le parti unique* ('The single party'), revised his original distinction between pure corporatism and fascism and put forward an 'evolutionist' model, considering the fascist system as a transitional phase toward 'pure corporatism'.[35] Eventually, in 1938, in the context of the introduction of the royal dictatorship of Carol II, he published the programme of turning Romania into a national-corporative state, which now implied a fusion of ethnonational exclusion and a corporatist-étatist transformation of the economy. Remaining close to the political leadership of

---

34 Mihail Manoilescu, *Le siècle du corporatisme* (Paris: Félix Alcan, 1934).
35 Mihail Manoilescu, *Le parti unique* (Paris: Les Oeuvres françaises, 1937).

the country, Manoilescu reached the peak of his political career as minister of foreign affairs in 1940. However, this turned out to be a rather ill-fated position because he had to negotiate and eventually accept the territorial losses of his country to Hungary and Bulgaria under the pressure of the two totalitarian powers Manoilescu cherished so much: Nazi Germany and fascist Italy.

Coming from a markedly different intellectual background, Štefan Polakovič, the Slovak Catholic ideologue, studied philosophy and theology in Rome and was influenced by Western philosophical trends, especially French personalism. During the independent Slovak state, he worked for the propaganda office and emerged as the key theorist of the authoritarian regime. Seeking to formulate an ideology of Slovak statehood, he tried to bring together the Christian heritage with some elements of German national socialist ideology, arguing that every nation had its own fitting ideological composition and thus it was not advisable to commit the whole-sale takeover of the other's national ideology. Along these lines, his ideal was a strong authoritarian regime rooted in Christianity, ethnonationalism and corporatism. After 1945, Polakovič went into exile, eventually settling in Argentina, while remaining committed to the ideals of the wartime state. He kept producing new theoretical works about Slovak nationhood and the theory of nationalism. Although he lived long enough to see the break-up of Czechoslovakia in 1993 and his ideas had a certain resonance among the Slovak nationalists of the time, his strong personal connection to the wartime regime made his figure a rather uncomfortable one even to those otherwise positively disposed towards his ideas.

Up until 1945, the debates on statehood were relatively straightforward. In the post-1945 period, it is much harder to isolate these discourses because state-building was inseparably linked to the socialist agenda of transformation. However, one can identify a number of phases characterized by different questions and conceptualizations. Thus, the immediate post-war debate on popular democracy questioned to what extent the new regime was different from 'bourgeois democracy'. Some key aspects of this differentiation were the nationalization of 'great capital', the extension of the sphere of state intervention in social affairs going way beyond the limits set by the 'bourgeois' doctrines, and the debate on the very nature of the post-war transition. Obviously, in this context the continuities or discontinuities with the wartime regimes deserve special attention, not only in terms of the persons involved but also in view of the étatist practices and obsessions with economic planning as well as the shared anti-individualist and anti-capitalist ideological references.

The second phase can be described as the climax of Stalinist state theory, marked by the disappearance of the hybrid 'popular democratic' stage from the model of transformation and its replacement with a voluntarist stance towards economic and social change. Stalinist political thought in Central and Eastern Europe linked the image of the 'new man' to that of the 'new state'. It also combined a future-oriented projection of a communist society resolving all the social contradictions with a vision of the ever-intensifying class struggle provoked by the seemingly defeated former ruling classes, the latter of whom had to be defeated again and again in order to create the conditions for the final harmony.

The phase of de-Stalinization after 1953 also contained strong projections of the future with regard to the socialist state but now the core was not so much the ideal socialist order but a welfare-centred ideology which explicitly aimed at 'catching up' and eventually overtaking the West both in technology and in living standards. The socialist state was supposed to disappear sometime in the future, but in the meantime, it was expected to catalyse the development that created the conditions for its eventual disappearance. A manifestation of this framework of ideas was the emerging socialist futurology, drawing on, but also criticizing, its Western counterpart. Similarly, theories of socialist legality and socialist patriotism were part of this new ideological framework.

Thinking dangerously

Standing alone in the region, the Yugoslav leadership already produced its own variant of de-Stalinization after the 1948 split with the Soviets. After a transitional period of reinforced political control and widespread repression – in many ways mirroring the Stalinist patterns while using them to politically combat Stalinism – it created an ideological framework which allowed for certain local specificities to be expressed. The most important development from the perspective of political thought was doubtlessly the doctrine of workers' self-government linked to Edvard Kardelj, already mentioned above. Although originally meant as a more practical solution to the very real problems of managing the Soviet-style planned economy, gradually it became a legitimizing ideology of the entire Yugoslav project and also an increasingly ritualized framework of actual and symbolic negotiations of power and resource allocation.

One alternative agenda of de-Stalinization, which eventually turned into a dissident position, emerged in Yugoslavia upon Milovan Djilas' break with the Titoist leadership in the early 1950s. Djilas' criticism focused on the embourgeoisement and bureaucratization of the socialist state and appealed to the idea of self-management, asserting that only a 'real' self-management could liberate the state from the grasp of these bureaucratic groups. However, it went beyond the variant promoted by Kardelj in the sense that it posited a necessary divergence of interests between the state bureaucracy and the self-governing workers. In a way, this perspective became a recurrent alternative modality of political representation in the form of workers' councils that surfaced in Hungary in 1956 and also in Poland, culminating during the times of the Solidarity ('Solidarność') movement.

Throughout Central and Eastern Europe in the 1970s and 1980s, the main modality of oppositional discourse dominating the scene – the focus on civil society – was similarly anti-statist but from a different perspective. Emerging in the post-1968 context when the original supporters of reforms were increasingly resigned to the irreformable nature of 'actually existing socialism', the discourse on civil society got entangled with two important political and ideological developments. One was the Helsinki process with its stress on human rights, while the other was the ongoing transformation of the world economy and the prevalent ideological mode of economic thinking in the 1970s, which undermined the étatist-welfare state-oriented consensus dominating Western Europe in the wake of the post-war boom. Furthermore, the discourse of civil society also resonated with pre-1945 local intellectual traditions and ideologies of 'anti-politics' and passive resistance, as well as the various doctrines of 'organic work' which also stressed the importance of small-scale communal action when the state was considered to be an 'alien' force.

The interplay of these ideological traditions led to a number of unintended and surprising consequences. First, one could observe a relatively swift transition on the part of thinkers trained in (revisionist) Marxism towards liberalism. The anthropological turn of Marxism focusing on praxis, the transformative power of human agency and the anticipation of the eventual death of the state made it possible to redirect the ideological vectors from a class-centred Marxist narrative to a framework seeking to emancipate society from the tutelage of the authoritarian state. Second, it resulted in the formation of competing modalities of reformism, which may have agreed on the need for liberalization but had very different underlying philosophical and political assumptions and, consequently, rather divergent visions of the future.

A particularly interesting group here is that of the technocrats, typically gathered around planning and research institutions. They closely followed the deepening economic crisis in the 1970s, aggravated by the reluctance of the political leaders to take radical decisions affecting the redistributive welfare policies, which functioned as the last remaining and arguably most powerful means of legitimization. Equally critical of the regime, the revisionist Marxist, and in some cases also Christian, personalist adherents of the human rights doctrine had a limited understanding of the economic sphere. This was due to the fact that their engagement with economic issues was often based on moral arguments, for instance castigating the nominally egalitarian 'workers' state' for introducing market mechanisms which generated social and economic differentiation. In contrast, the technocratic 'neo-liberals', who were fascinated with the neo-classical doctrine of the Chicago School, focused primarily on the self-regulating mechanisms of the market and appeared rather uninterested in social and political rights. It is characteristic that Augusto Pinochet's Chile was a model country in these circles, a regime which introduced deregulation while using the repressive mechanisms of the military dictatorship to prevent social unrest.

In multinational/federal states, the debate on statehood had another evident direction, namely the desirable transformation of the polity to accommodate the demands of the respective national communities. The turn of the 1970s saw the extension of the autonomy of the constitutive units both in Czechoslovakia and Yugoslavia, which was not unrelated to the social and political crisis of these regimes. In the former case, the extension of the national competences of the Slovak leadership turned out to be a way to guarantee the loyalty of Slovaks towards the post-1968 *normalizace* ('normalization') regime. In Yugoslavia, following the conflicts that culminated in the student unrest in 1968 and the clashes between the technocratic reform communists and the centralist bureaucratic and military elites that resulted in the dismissal of the reformists both in Serbia and Croatia, the new constitution of 1974 seemed to offer a wide-range of prerogatives to the republics. However, the extensive powers delegated to the level of the constituent republics went hand in hand with the efforts to suppress political dissent. The ensuing dynamic of debate came to shape the political framework of Yugoslavia in the final 15 years of its existence: while the push for democratization in Croatia and Slovenia was increasingly linked to the demand of national self-determination, Serbian dissidents, who originally cooperated with their Croatian, Bosnian and Slovenian peers on a common human rights agenda, came to link the defence of human rights with the assertion of the national rights of their 'endangered' ethnic Serb kinsfolk who were faced with the prospect of finding themselves in a minority status in the other, increasingly nationalized republics, especially Croatia, Bosnia and Herzegovina, and the autonomous province of Kosovo.

After 1989 the problem of statehood and citizenship became once again highly topical. Notably, the collapse of multinational federal states brought along the emergence of more than a dozen new (or 'new-old') independent states in East Central Europe. Consequently, one of the most important discussions related to statehood in the early 1990s focused on the reorganization of these multinational polities. The negotiation process about the future of Czechoslovakia, which eventually resulted in a peaceful separation and came to be dubbed a 'velvet divorce' focused mainly on constitutional issues.[36] In contrast, the much more violent disintegration of the Soviet Union and Yugoslavia triggered debates on the persistence of national hatred in the region as well as on the links and similarities between the (post-)communist and the nationalist mindset.

In the entire region, the post-1989 socio-economic and political-ideological transformation was closely linked to the task of state-building. Various models emerged to cope with the new and old challenges facing these societies. In this respect, a central issue was whether to define the subject of popular sovereignty in ethnocultural terms or to opt for a supra-ethnic or unspecified 'political nation'. This dilemma was particularly vital for the Baltic states where a

---

36 Eric Stein, *Czecho/Slovakia: Ethnic Conflict, Constitutional Fissure, Negotiated Breakup* (Ann Arbor, MI: University of Michigan Press, 1997).

Thinking dangerously

very substantial amount of their population in 1991 was actually settled after 1945 by the Soviet authorities – partly as a side-effect of the wide-ranging industrialization programmes, but also as the result of a conscious effort to cement the Soviet power in these 'unruly' republics. The ensuing policies and ideological frameworks were highly divergent: in Lithuania (with a significantly smaller Russian-speaking population) the citizenship policies were non-discriminatory, in Estonia and especially Latvia citizenship was conditioned primarily on the knowledge of the official language. This also implied highly divergent conceptions of the relation of state and nation, ranging from the vision of a mono-ethnic liberal democracy to various models of co-opting the 'non-indigenous' population, including a formally bi-national solution (with only limited appeal in practice).

The social question: overcoming backwardness

Exposed to the effects of global socio-economic crises and deflected modernization projects, the twentieth-century history of East Central Europe was shaped by various waves of social conflict and projects of social emancipation. The complexity of these issues generated a variegated literature on the 'social question', bringing together authors of different ideological persuasions, generations and levels of theoretical abstraction. As in the case of the debates on statehood, the social question also had national, cultural and economic implications, and these different aspects tended to be difficult to separate.

At the turn of the twentieth century, one paradigmatic debate where the social and cultural issues intersected concerned the role of the intelligentsia. Practically every national public pursued such a debate, at the core of which lay the ambiguity of modernization: while, on the one hand, the rise of a local intelligentsia indicated the capacity of the given nation to enter the cultural circulation of Europe, the emergence of a new cultural elite was also often held to be the cause of a 'fatal division' in society; one which eliminated the previous common referential system based on folk culture and thus supposedly undermined social solidarity. An additional aspect of the discussion concerned the competition between different foreign models. Some observers at the turn of the century were fascinated with the German model of combining a conservative political system with progressive social politics, while others preferred the French or British cultural and political influences. In certain parts and ideological subcultures of the region (for instance, the neo-Slavic movement but also among some of the agrarian populists), Russia could also be perceived as an important point of orientation, even though before 1917 its social and political structures were hardly ever extolled as an example to follow. The different models could have multiple political implications (e.g. the parallel existence of a reform conservative German model and a social democratic German model; or a republican French model and an integral nationalist French model) and offered different patterns of intellectual behaviour – for example, the more 'systemic' German expert/social reformer or the French *intellectuel* characterized by a strong critical voice. In view of this multiplicity of models it is not surprising that most attempts to define the role of the intelligentsia also had multiple political references. This is particularly evident in the work of 'civic radicals', such as the Polish thinker Stanisław Brzozowski, who started as a socialist and ended up as a Catholic modernist.[37] The polyphony of the ideological and political self-positioning of intellectuals in East Central Europe, together

---

37 Stanisław Brzozowski, 'Legenda Młodej Polski' [The legend of young Poland], in *Eseje i studia o literaturze*, vol. 2, ed. H. Markiewicz (Wrocław: Ossolineum, 1990); see also Andrzej Walicki, *Stanisław Brzozowski and the Polish Beginnings of 'Western Marxism'* (Oxford: Clarendon Press, 1989).

with their recurrent attempts to transcend the social divisions of their respective societies, had an impact on the most famous conceptualization of the social position and value orientation of intellectuals, namely that of 'free-floating', by the sociologist Karl Mannheim, a Hungarian-Jewish émigré to Germany and later England.[38]

The sharpest social issue of the first half of the twentieth century all over East Central Europe was, however, the agrarian question. This topic was approached from different ideological angles and had very different formulations. The main positions could be broadly defined as the socialist, conservative and agrarian populist ones, but there were also liberal (or liberal-conservative), and – in the interwar period – fascist discourses on 'solving' the question of the peasantry. Importantly, the position of certain intellectuals cut across these ideological dividing lines, such as the Romanian socialist theorist with Ukrainian-Jewish roots, Constantin Dobrogeanu-Gherea, who was active in the *Narodnik* movement before he escaped from the tsarist empire and eventually settled in Romania. At the turn of the century he was one of the most remarkable voices challenging the official line of the Second International on the agrarian question, a line which stressed the need for industrialization and had very limited space for incorporating specific peasant interests into its scheme of development.

Operating in an environment in which the industrial proletariat was minuscule compared to the masses of landless rural population, Gherea was eager to devise a Marxist framework which was capable of incorporating the peasants and could thus offer a point of orientation for Eastern European socialists, however, his position left open the question of peasant property. Although he was less adamant than the Bulgarian Marxist theorist Dimitar Blagoev and the socialist stream that surrounded him (commonly referred to as 'Narrows', who categorically rejected the cooperation between the socialists and the peasants), Gherea's anti-feudalism also did not imply much sympathy for protecting small-scale rural property.[39] Rejecting the *Narodnik* cult of the peasant community perceived as an alternative to modern patterns of social organization, Gherea's theoretical framework was built around the concept of 'neo-serfdom'. This implied that in peripheral countries like Romania one could not speak of the 'proper' development of capitalism because certain feudal structures were integrated into the capitalist system and created a hybrid configuration.[40] Importantly, Gherea's analysis could be taken in different directions. One possible reading was that socialists needed to fight for a more democratic and modern bourgeois society in some sort of cooperation with the democratic parts of the middle classes against the feudal-liberal 'oligarchy'. This was the main thread followed by the socialist theorists of the 1920s, such as Şerban Voinea, who tried to find a new identity for social democracy after the Bolshevik Revolution.[41] Another possible direction taken by, among others, Gherea's own son Alexandru, was to draw a Leninist conclusion and opt for a total negation of the post-feudal realities of Southeastern Europe. Following the Russian example, they put their faith into a revolutionary transformation which would sweep away the corrupted *ancien régime*. In the long run, this position incurred extremely high costs as the agents of world revolution became agents

---

38 Karl Mannheim, 'The Problem of the Intelligentsia: An Enquiry into its Past and Present Role', in *Essays on the Sociology of Culture*, ed. Bryan S. Turner (London: Routledge, 1992), 91–170.

39 On the debate of socialists and agrarian populists in Southeastern Europe, see Augusta Dimou, *Entangled Paths towards Modernity* (Budapest: CEU Press, 2009).

40 Constantin Dobrogeanu-Gherea, *Neoiobăgia: Studiu economic-sociologic al problemei noastre agrare* [Neo-serfdom: economic-sociological study of our agrarian problem] (Bucharest: Socec, 1910). On the broader context of the debate see Jochen Schmidt, *Populismus oder Marxismus: Zur Ideengeschichte der radikalen Intelligenz Rumäniens 1875–1915* (Tübingen: Verlag der Tübinger Gesellschaft, 1992).

41 Serban Voinea, *Marxism oligarhic* (Bucharest: I. Brănişteanu, 1926).

Thinking dangerously

of Soviet foreign policy and were eventually destroyed by the paranoid terror machinery of 'high Stalinism'.

The leading alternative to Gherea's socialist conception was formulated by the agrarian populists. Gherea's main partner in debate was Constantin Stere who was from a Bessarabian noble family and was another scion of the Russian *Narodnik* movement. In his key theoretical text, titled 'Social-democratism or Populism?', Stere also began by contrasting the Eastern and Western European patterns of development, stressing that the 'orthodox' Marxist position represented by Kautsky made no sense in Eastern Europe where the emergence of a modern capitalist economy was hindered exactly by the global distribution of labour, which relegated these countries to being agricultural *Hinterlands*.[42] Stere rejected the relevance of the Marxist doctrine regarding the 'big fish eating the small fish' in the agricultural sector, arguing that there was no reason to expect the concentration of the land in the hands of a few. He cited the example of Scandinavia with its labour-intensive farmer economy being more productive than the Eastern European countries with their huge latifundia. Stere's practical conclusion from this analysis was to opt for cooperation with the national liberals whose étatist economic policies could have been extended to a protectionist modernizing agenda involving the rural society, creating cooperatives and certain state-driven welfare provisions.

However, other agrarian theorists went well beyond this position and worked out the concept of a 'peasant state'. The Bulgarian Aleksandar Stamboliyski envisioned a political system serving the interests of the peasantry, protecting the landed property of the smallholders, while at the same time propagating peasant cooperativism.[43] Given the numerical preponderance of the peasantry in Southeastern Europe, Stamboliyski considered a regime which was seeking primarily to satisfy the social needs of the peasantry to be democratic by default. However, in practice – during the period of rule by the Bulgarian Agrarian National Union (1919–23) – enforcing the interests of the peasantry meant a clash both with the urban middle classes and the industrial proletariat. This contributed to the radicalization of the opposition and also the somewhat paradoxical neutrality of the Communist Party during the right-wing coup of Aleksandar Tsankov in 1923, which ended the agrarian regime and also led to the violent death of Stamboliyski.

The interwar period witnessed the continuation of these debates, with the concomitant rise of a new generation of agrarian theorists. The leading Romanian political economist and peasantist politician, Virgil Madgearu, developed a highly original position, seeking to answer the dilemma of how to bring together economic modernity with a predominantly rural society. His critique focused on the autarchism of the national liberals who used protectionist measures to create a national entrepreneurial elite. Madgearu pointed out that this was extremely unfavourable to the peasants who had to buy the industrial products necessary for their lives at higher prices than they were available on the international markets while the value of agricultural products was kept artificially low. From this analysis, Madgearu drew the conclusion that free trade was perfectly compatible with agrarianism.[44] He argued for the liberalization of the economy,

---

42 Constantin Stere, *Social-democratism sau poporanism?* [Social-democratism or populism?] (Galaţi: Porto-Franco, 1996).

43 Aleksandar Stamboliyski, *Politicheski partii ili saslovni organizatsii* [Political parties and corporatist organizations] (Sofia: Al. Stamboliyski, 1909).

44 Virgil Madgearu, *Agrarianism, Capitalism, Imperialism. Contribuţii la studiul evoluţiei sociale româneşti* [Agrarianism, capitalism, imperialism: contributions to the study of Romanian social evolution] (Cluj-Napoca: Dacia, 1999).

including the buying and selling of land within a regulative framework, thus encouraging a degree of social differentiation within the peasant class. However, the project floundered at the outbreak of the Great Crisis, which reinforced the protectionist tendencies all over Europe and hit the agrarian sector extremely hard, undermining the social and political legitimacy of the peasantist movement that had its social basis in the more well-to-do layer of the peasantry.

A typical genre of the 1920s–30s favoured by the agrarian populists was sociographic literature, which combined empirical-descriptive aspects with strong political engagement. A paradigmatic case is the work of Rudolf Bićanić on the 'passive regions' of Yugoslavia in the 1930s.[45] Depicting the everyday life and economic conditions of the peasants in these areas, he argued that not only was there no sign of economic and social modernization, but there was in fact a decline in living standards compared to the pre-1918 state of affairs, resulting in a desperate migration away from these areas. There was also a national implication to such an analysis because Bićanić described these regions as being inhabited mostly by Croats, whose economic marginalization was also due to the centralist policies of the Serbian bureaucratic elite who had no interest in the economic development of the non-Serbian parts of the country.

In the Romanian context the sociographic literature had strong institutional backing in the form of the 'monographic school' of Dimitrie Gusti. The well-established sociology professor could rely on state resources to engage a growing number of young social scientists on various projects mapping the social, economic and mental conditions of Romanian villages. In ideological and generational terms, a Romanian counterpart to Bićanić was Henri H. Stahl, who belonged to the left-leaning branch of the 'Gusti School'. In contrast to the 'metaphysical' nationalists talking about an 'atemporal' Romanian peasant culture, Stahl aimed at historicizing rural society and thus traced the long survival and eventual dissolution of collective forms of land-ownership in specific areas in the country which were comparable to the South Slavic *zadruga*. Rejecting the regressive utopia of the radical right, which aimed at the restoration of a lost 'golden age' of archaism, he posed the question of how it was possible to 'domesticate' economic and political modernity so that it capitalized on the peasants' specific skills and mentality and did not ruin village life.

A comparable rural sociographic school emerged in Hungary in the mid-1930s which was to a considerable extent directly inspired by Gusti's monographic method. One of its protagonists, the sociologist and writer Ferenc Erdei, was also searching for rural communities where the cooperative tradition could lift the peasants out of the general misery that characterized the countryside. He was eager to point out that these cooperatives also had a function of political education because their members had a democratic-patriotic oppositional stance towards the Horthy regime, a position he linked to the liberal democratic tradition of the 1848 revolution.

While rejecting the nationalism and 'neo-feudal' social ethos of the 'Christian-national' regime, Hungarian agrarian populists sought to position themselves as the spokesmen of the 'common people', claiming to represent a more authentic but also more democratic national tradition. A case in point is Erdei's book about a specifically Hungarian pattern of urbanization, which he contrasted to the Western model.[46] He argued that while Western urbanization was based on a strong legal and social dividing line between the city and the countryside, the Hungarian 'market town' emerged in the early modern period as a much more permeable structure, where the rural and urban mentalities amalgamated. Erdei identified a certain

---

45 Rudolf Bićanić, *Kako živi narod. Život u pasivnim krajevima* [How the people live: life in the passive regions], vol. I (Zagreb: Tipografija, 1936).
46 Ferenc Erdei, *A magyar város* [The Hungarian town] (Budapest: Athenaeum, 1938).

Thinking dangerously

'peasant-burgher' stratum in the society which emerged from this habitat and linked them to the progressive independentist (and predominantly Protestant) oppositional cultural-political tradition. The lesson he drew from this image was that in contrast to the state-induced cult of the apolitical and subservient peasant living an authentic folkloric existence, the classical 'peasant life form' was in a profound crisis and the only way out was through a modernization of the peasantry which would close the gap between the rural and urban lifestyles. This, however, did not only mean the urbanization of the peasantry, but also, along the populist programme, the revitalization of the middle class drawing on the rural resources. In Erdei's case the ethnicist overtones of this programme were not so poignant, however, in general the agrarian populist rhetoric in Hungary as well as in other East Central European countries frequently employed the image of the 'authentic peasant' versus the urban 'alien' (Jewish, German, etc.) and Erdei's own scheme was not completely free from loaded ethnic distinctions either.

Erdei's writings on 'market towns' notwithstanding, one problem with the agrarian political projects all over the region was that, due to their roots in a polemic with the socialist theorists whom they accused of being insensitive to the specific needs of the village, most agrarian leaders actually tended to be similarly insensitive to the plight of the urban proletariat. While some of the agrarian parties, such as the Romanian or the Czech, had strong links to the urban petty bourgeoisie, they described the industrial metropolis as an unnatural space, contrasting the more holistic agricultural work to the 'alienated' and mechanistic industrial production process. As a result, with the exception of some cases like Slovenia where some of the social democrats of the 1910s moved closer to the agrarian movement after 1918, there was surprisingly little intellectual interference between those who focused mainly on the peasantry and those who claimed to represent the workers.

In this context, socialists had to face a double marginalization by the Right, who rejected the idea of class struggle in favour of an integral nationalist vision of social harmony, and by the peasantists, who had a similar class-based agenda but considered the socialists' stress on the industrial workers completely misplaced. As a result, many socialist thinkers and movements continued the tradition of the late nineteenth-century social democrats who expected the 'proletarization' of the peasantry. Nevertheless, there were some authors who sought, particularly in the 1930s, for ways to integrate the peasantry into the socialist agenda. An exemplary case of this reorientation is provided by Illés Mónus, the most important theorist of the Hungarian social democrats in the 1930s, who after 1933 became impatient with the defensive position of his party that focused only on the everyday concerns of industrial workers and sought to reframe its social agenda in a more encompassing way. This naturally implied addressing the agrarian question. Mónus argued for a focus on the rural poor and demanded a land reform similar to the one envisioned by the agrarian populists. Furthermore, he had an intuition comparable to that of Antonio Gramsci about the importance of creating a dynamic socialist national culture that could break the hegemony of the Christian conservative/ethnonationalist regime. In accordance with these considerations, in the late 1930s he became a fervent supporter of collaboration with other anti-fascist forces, including both the liberals and the agrarian populists.[47]

The attitude of the communists was even more ambiguous due to the oscillation of Soviet policies. Because the Leninist revolutionary strategy was built on the distribution of the land, they were eager to propagate this idea in the early 1920s (also having learned from the failure of the Hungarian Soviet Republic which insisted on collectivization and thus alienated the

---

47 Illés Mónus, *Válogatott írásai* [Collected works], eds Ágnes Szabó and István Pintér (Budapest: Kossuth, 1988).

peasantry). The collectivization campaign of the late 1920s undermined this position, yet in the mid-1930s, in the context of the Popular Front ideology, certain authors again tried to reconsider the communist ideological position and create some sort of common platform with the agrarian populists.

The most inventive leftist conceptions of the agrarian problem were typically developed by intellectuals at the margins of their respective parties, such as the young Bulgarian sociologist Ivan Hadzhiyski.[48] Relying mainly on ethnographic material, he entered the debate on national psychology. His aim was not to give a normative image of the national self but to devise a history – framed in Marxist analytical categories – of Bulgarian society's engagement with economic and political modernity. Hadzhiyski argued that an indigenous proto-bourgeois social layer emerged in the mid-nineteenth century mainly from the artisanal class. As its thrust for economic emancipation coincided with the crisis of the Ottoman state, the struggle for social and national liberation went hand in hand for some time. This implied that instead of an individualistic striving for self-gratification this proto-bourgeois movement had a collectivistic ethos rooted in social and national solidarity. However, Hadzhiyski identified a growing rupture after 1878: the bourgeoisie now conquered the state and turned it into the instrument of its own class rule, suppressing further social mobility. This criticism was a fusion of the Marxist analysis of the dialectic of bourgeois revolutions and the populist tradition focusing on the state bureaucracy as an 'alien' social force blocking the social mobility of the peasantry. What Hadzhiyski added to these schemes, apart from his perceptive use of sources with which he anticipated modern historical anthropology, was a rather specific vision of the social revolution: it was not the various nationalist ideological subcultures but the communist party that was the authentic follower of the national tradition, i.e. the communist agenda of social emancipation was implying a return to the abandoned emancipatory collectivism of the national revival period.

While liberalism is often considered to have been completely out of the political game in the interwar years, in some countries one can find ingenious intellectual efforts to redefine it both in the context of the reconfiguration of the European state system during the early 1920s, and in the face of the totalitarian danger especially after 1933, and to rethink it from this perspective of the social role and history of the bourgeoisie. Romanian 'neo-liberalism' was an attempt to reconsider the liberal programme of the turn of the century in the post-First World War context. The key figure of this stream was Ştefan Zeletin, an unconventional thinker who relied on Werner Sombart's theory of the origins of capitalism to create a model of the rise of the Romanian bourgeoisie.[49] Importantly, Zeletin did not consider the specific étatist and nationalist features of Romanian national liberalism as a deviation but rather as the natural result of the peculiar social composition and political aims of the liberal movement. He argued that the protectionist measures implemented by Romanian liberal nationalists in the late nineteenth and early twentieth century were in line with the mercantilist logic characterizing the first phase of capital accumulation in every society. In a similar vein, while he explicitly rejected xenophobia, in the context of the newly created multi-ethnic Greater Romania, he supported the idea of national homogenization. His ambition was the creation of a strong, ethnic-Romanian middle class which would serve as the engine and become the main beneficiary of modernization.

---

48 Ivan Hadzhiyski, *Bit i dushevnost na nashiya narod* [The existence and spirituality of our nation] and *Optimistichna teoriya za nashiya narod* [The optimistic theory of our nation] (Sofia: LIK, 2002).

49 Ştefan Zeletin, *Burghezia română – Neoliberalismul* [Romanian bourgeoisie – neoliberalism] (Bucharest: Nemira, 1997).

Thinking dangerously

While state interventionism and a planned economy seemed to emerge as dominant ideas on the Left as well as the Right in the wake of the Great Depression, there were also dissenting voices. A case in point is the Polish-Jewish socio-economic theorist Ferdynand Zweig.[50] In the 1920s he had already published polemic articles on socialism, and in the 1930s, he entered the transnational debate on economic planning. Akin to Friedrich August von Hayek and Ludwig von Mises, he stressed the importance of the self-regulating mechanisms of the market and the economic inefficiency of planning and redistributive measures. At the same time, Zweig also emphasized the necessity of assuring a certain level of welfare for the whole population.

With the radicalization of politics in the context of the economic crisis there emerged yet another discursive modality, that of technocratism, which castigated the 'inherent' demagogy of politicians for preventing truly professional decision-making on social and economic questions. What these theorists offered instead was to move beyond ideological polarization. One of the most interesting examples is the oeuvre of Jan Antonín Baťa, brother to the founder of the Baťa Shoe Company, which was the pride of interwar Czechoslovak industry. Combining the Fordist methods of rationally organized production with impressive welfare provisions for its employees, the Baťa system seemed to offer a suitable model for the rational reorganization of the entire society.[51] Baťa's language merged pragmatism with a perfectionist moral philosophy, conceiving of politics as a *techne* that helps one to get closer to truth:

> The road to growth is a road to truth, to reality. Truth and reality are the only base for building a decent business. Nice sounding words are a good thing and may even be useful, as for example to politicians whose principal investment are electoral ballots. But beautiful words are not going to help you make money, because we are living in a world where nobody is willing to give something for nothing. In a world where each 'Income' column must have an 'Expenses' counter-item.[52]

Aiming to strike a common ground between capitalism and étatism, Baťa considered it the task of the state to create the general conditions (supporting education and research, building infrastructure, training an efficient bureaucracy) while the capitalist enterprises were to act as the principal actors of economic production.

Étatist social policies that came to dominate the region during the Second World War drew on these technocratic ideas but their ultimate aims were markedly different. While for Baťa the task of rationalization was to find a balance between economic freedom and social welfare measures which could trigger the growth of production, the aim of the technocrats preparing for, and managing the war economies, was to create a certain level of social peace which made it possible to concentrate the forces of the society on the war effort. What is more, the engagement of this technocratic elite with ethnonationalism meant that it became possible to imagine and implement a grand-scale redistribution of property from the excluded 'aliens' to the preferred 'native' lower classes and eventually also the biopolitical engineering of the society.

---

50 See Ferdynand Zweig's books: *Zmierzch czy odrodzenie liberalizmu* [Twilight or the revival of liberalism] (Lwów: Atlas, 1938), and *The Planning of Free Societies* (London: Secker & Warburg, 1942).

51 Jan Antonín Baťa, *Budujme stát pro 40 000 000 lidí* [Let us build a state for 40,000,000 people] (Zlín: Tisk, 1936).

52 Jan Antonín Baťa, 'Freedom of Trade: A speech in 1928', in *Reflections and Speeches*, trans. Otilia M. Kabesová, available at www.tomasbata.org/wp-content/uploads/download/reflections_and_speeches. pdf (accessed 29 April 2019).

This interplay of redistribution with ethnic homogenization was stimulated by the conception and practice of mass population exchange that had already become fashionable in the early 1920s – at the time of the triangular resettlement processes involving Turkey, Greece and Bulgaria. However, in the late 1930s, even the seeming mutuality of these measures was abandoned as certain minority groups came to be the target not only of ethnic violence but also state-designed policies of expropriation. An illustration of this propensity can be found in the writings of the Hungarian economic expert Mátyás Matolcsy, who started as a supporter of the agrarian populist movement, arguing for land reform in order to create a broader class of propertied peasants.[53] However, in the late 1930s, in the context of the boom of anti-Semitism, he changed the direction of his arguments and now envisioned grand-scale redistribution, social mobilization and the creation of a new middle class not on the basis of eliminating the latifundia but by nationalizing the property of the Hungarian Jews. The further destiny of a population who were to be cut off from any means of subsistence and thus made 'superfluous' was not specified by him, but the inherent logic of the argument pointed to the necessity of changing the demographic situation and assisted in opening the horizons of expectation for the deportation and eventually physical elimination of these 'undesirable' groups.

The intersection of programmes of social emancipation and biopolitics can also be observed in the various discourses focusing on 'the woman question'. Drawing on the late nineteenth-century positivist critical discourse which underlined the importance of education and social integration, activists aiming at the social and also political enfranchisement of women became increasingly active in the region from the turn of the century onward. Importantly, around 1900 the agenda concentrating on the right to education was already found to be too self-limiting and the issue of political participation came to the fore. Arguments for political participation were often framed in nationalist terms (such as in the case of Božena Viková-Kunětická, the first female elected member of the Bohemian Diet). A characteristic argument from this perspective concerned the specific local traditions empowering women (e.g. asserting that the local customary law traditions regulated inheritance more favourably than the Napoleonic Code). At the same time, the emerging socialist feminist discourse conceived of the oppression of women in social terms and was concerned with issues of labour conditions and public health. It raised the question whether the bourgeois feminists could legitimately represent their proletarian 'sisters'. As a result, the feminist 'grand debate' of the early twentieth century was about the primacy of layers of identification: should women of different social backgrounds and ideological persuasions strive to achieve emancipation together 'as women', or should they incorporate the specific aspects pertaining to the woman question into the agenda of their respective political-ideological camps.[54] While the debate remained undecided, it is important to note that before 1918 there was a relatively broad common ground where representatives from the different camps could meet and discuss. This common discursive and institutional space shrank considerably in the interwar period when every political movement from liberals to conservatives, or from communists to fascists, developed its own discourse about women and also tried to create its own specific women's organizations.

---

53 Mátyás Matolcsy, *Az új földreform munkaterve* [The plan of the new agrarian reform] (Budapest: Révai, 1934).

54 On the paradigmatic Bulgarian debate, see the anthology and introductory study by Krasimira Daskalova, ed., *Ot syankata na istoriyata. Zhenite v balgarskoto obshtestvo i kultura (1840–1940)* [Out of the shadows of history: women in Bulgarian society and culture (1840–1940)] (Sofia: LIK, 1998).

Thinking dangerously

The rise of a radical nationalist version of feminism is indicative of this ideological polarization. While eugenics was politically neutral or had a leftist tinge before 1918, in the interwar period the eugenic arguments were, first and foremost, chiefly used to support national self-reproduction. On the other end of the ideological spectrum the radical leftist branch of feminism linked the revolutionary rhetoric to the agenda of the social and political emancipation of women. However, the relationship of the radical left and the feminists was also not without its problems because the issue of women's emancipation was often overshadowed by the focus on class struggle and because the hierarchical nature of the communist movement implied a gender hierarchy with merely auxiliary functions being allotted to women. Although some of the female activists of the communist exile in the Soviet Union rose to leading positions during the Second World War, such as Wanda Wasilewska from Poland and Ana Pauker from Romania, their subsequent side-lining confirmed the persistent gender bias in the communist movement.

An interesting example of this ambiguous relationship is offered by the case of the Slovene Angela Vode who was part of the radical leftist cultural and political scene in the 1920s and 1930s. Vode wrote important leftist theoretical texts, including a study titled 'Women and Fascism' in 1935, but became alienated by the Stalinist radicalization of the communist party. Nevertheless, she joined the resistance during the Second World War where she clashed again with the communists who sought to suppress any difference of opinion. Arrested first by the Italian, and then by the German occupying authorities, she spent the last months of the war in a German concentration camp. Upon her return, Vode became a vocal critic of the totalitarian measures of the emerging communist regime, and as a result she was eventually sent to prison in 1947 after a show trial that targeted a group of prominent socialist and liberal intellectuals who had become increasingly critical of the system.

After 1945, the social question naturally remained central to the political discussion all over the region. There was a broad consensus on the need to nationalize 'big capital' and to implement agrarian reforms, giving land to the landless rural masses and providing the means for social mobility for the non-elite social layers. However, the blueprint and time-frame of the transformation was far from being consensual, as different forces alternatively defined the acceptable limits of private property, as well as the final aim of the transformation. Thus, for instance, agrarian parties generally held that small-scale landed property was not an instrument of exploitation. Furthermore, there was considerable disagreement within the communist parties themselves concerning the socio-economic order corresponding to the transitional phase of popular democracy, as well as the desirable length of this phase. However, with the consolidation of communist rule, which took place at different rhythms in the various countries between 1945 and 1948, it became practically impossible to point to any social conflict apart from the ones ideologically constructed by the regime (the fight against the 'former elites', kulaks, and in some cases also certain ethnic minorities designated *en masse* as reactionaries). Highlighting the continued existence of 'contradictions' would have been perceived as a challenge to the regime's legitimacy.

Social questions returned to the fore in the context of the debates on de-Stalinization when the situation of the peasantry, the workers and the intelligentsia (the three recognized 'social components' of socialist society) was increasingly debated everywhere, even if the terms and intensity of the debate varied country by country. While this veritable outbreak of discussions was silenced in more or less violent ways – in the case of Hungary and Poland it led to revolutionary events but in other cases remained constrained to certain intellectual forums, typically the writers' unions, as well as to internal party fora – the 1960s saw the rebirth of an analytical language on society triggered by the relaunching of sociology as an academic discipline. In most countries – with the exception of Poland, where sociology managed to preserve a certain modicum of autonomy in the 1950s – the Stalinist period meant a rupture in institutional terms. Nevertheless, the key figures relaunching the sociological paradigm could appeal to pre-existing 'progressive traditions', such as the Gusti School in Romania, the Brno School in Czechoslovakia, the heritage of civic radicalism and populist sociography in Hungary, or the historical ethno-psychology of Hadzhiyski in Bulgaria. In comparison to the interwar period, what represented a crucial shift was that the agrarian question was no longer the key preoccupation; while the agrarian population continued to be of considerable magnitude and there was a notable discussion on the possibilities of combining private and collective property in agriculture, the main debates increasingly concerned the situation of the working class and the intelligentsia.

A critical argument – which was extremely sensitive from the perspective of the regime – was that the workers' state was turning the actual workers into a low-paid and socially marginalized mass. The climax of this critique was at the turn of the 1970s, which was when the doctrines of the 'New Left' arrived in East Central Europe, including the most radical and at least verbally violent manifestations, such as Maoism. At the same time, a favoured discursive strategy of the local revisionist Marxists was to contrast the ideology of the socialist regime with its practice, pointing to the persistence of class exploitation and alienation within these societies.

A similar dynamic of contrasting the egalitarian ideology of the regime to the considerable extent of social differentiation characterizing the realities of 'actually existing socialism' can be found in the critical discourse on the intelligentsia as well. A paradigmatic case is the famous book by György Konrád and Iván Szelényi, *The Intelligentsia on the Road to Class Power*, which drew both on the theoretical sources of the new class theory from within the region, such as Milovan Djilas, and the current Western Marxist analyses. As the authors argued:

> Left-wing social theory must face up to the fact that socialist transformation – the nationalization of the means of production – has not brought about the results expected by nineteenth-century thinkers. Not only has it failed to abolish alienation and inequality, or to produce a more democratic system; it has in fact invented new methods of political oppression and economic exploitation.[55]

Along these lines, the book intended to prove that in contrast to the official propaganda, workers were far from constituting the ruling class, as the real power was increasingly in the hands of the intelligentsia (which in the authors' conception encompassed the technocratic managerial elites and the party apparatchiks as well).

The economic hardships in the 1970s and 1980s saw the growth of poverty and social differentiation and triggered a social crisis in most of these countries. It was in such a context that the Polish group KOR (Workers' Defense Committee), and the ensuing independent trade union and political movement Solidarity, sought to fuse the struggle for human and civil rights and the assertion of the economic interests of workers. In other countries too, there were dissident intellectual subcultures concerned with poverty and social marginalization, such as the Hungarian critical sociological school around István Kemény. On the whole, however, the mainstream of oppositional activism in the region did not target the social issues but focused more on civil rights and existential liberation from (post-)totalitarian indoctrination. As the

---

55 Iván Szelényi and György Konrád, *Az értelmiség útja az osztályhatalomhoz* (written in 1973/74), in English: *The Intellectuals on the Road to Class Power*, trans. Andrew Arato and Richard E. Allen (New York: Harcourt, 1979), xv.

Thinking dangerously

moment of the regime change drew nearer, the main questions to be debated came to be closely linked to the transformation of the constitutional order. There was also increasing support for economic liberalization, anticipated to be unpopular but seen as necessary in order to turn the economy and the society in a Western direction. One of the main reasons for the silence surrounding social issues in 1989 was that the intellectual groups at the forefront of the transition seem to have taken to heart the Arendtian lesson about the dangers of mixing the social issue with the constitutional revolution (without having necessarily read Hannah Arendt's book, *On Revolution*). Another reason was the lack of an adequate language because the discourse of civil society proved rather insensitive to socio-economic issues. Typically, it referred to a 'parallel polis', an alternative public sphere where questions of social hierarchies and economic policies were often relegated to the background.

As a result, after 1989 the most emphatic political discourse on the social question came from intellectual subcultures which considered the entire transition process illegitimate, e.g. either from post-Marxist circles, who kept to the language of class one way or another and interpreted 1989 as a cunning move of the elites to marginalize the working class, or from the emerging populist right, which contrasted the globalized 'winners' to the local 'losers'. Finally, at the turn of the millennium, another critical position emerged which positioned the social as a primary category: namely, the local subcultures of the worldwide anti-globalist movement that assimilated certain elements from the post-Marxist and national populist criticism of the transition, although they definitely rejected the ethnonationalist implications of the rightist position and also sought to reformulate the Marxist analytical categories to fit the new type of global economic interdependence.

The latest wave of the 'New Left' emerging after 1989 sought to extend the framework of inclusion not only to the groups that had been commonly identified as economically exploited and/or marginalized, but also to relations of gender. However, contrary to the expectations of the early 1990s that the democratization and Europeanization processes would give an impetus to the feminist movement in the region, these efforts proved to be of limited success. There are two major, though also only partial, exceptions to this rule. The first seems to be the former Yugoslavia, where the pre-1989 theoretical debates and women's activism, developing in a dialogue with Western feminism, were followed up by a strong anti-war activism in the early 1990s. The second is in Poland, where feminist discourse was well-integrated into the New Left ideological camp, had a certain intellectual prestige, and could thus be capitalized upon in the fervent debates with Catholic neo-conservative circles.[56]

Politics and religion: sacralized and desacralized power

The second half of the nineteenth century saw the gradual loss of the political importance of religion and the emergence of a public sphere that was increasingly independent of church structures. Significantly, many of the important East Central European clergymen of the time, such as the Metropolitan of Belgrade, Mihailo, were entering the political field as secular political actors. While the 'high church' in most cases was integrated into the mainstream liberal nationalist or conservative political establishment, it also had to face notable challenges from different ideological directions. There emerged, especially in the Catholic context, a new model of social and political engagement based on Leo XIII's *Rerum novarum* (or, *Rights and Duties of*

---

56 See Agnieszka Graff, *Rykoszetem. Rzecz o płci, seksualności i narodzie* [Ricochet: on gender, sexuality and nation] (Warsaw: WAB, 2008).

Capital and Labour). From the turn of the century, this model also had a considerable impact on other denominations, such as the Orthodox and the Lutherans. The spectacular political mobilization around the Mayor of Vienna, Karl Lueger, also provided inspiration for a new generation of East Central European Christian-socialist political actors. The influence of this doctrine was itself rather diffuse: while many of its followers developed a vocally anti-liberal and often anti-Semitic ethno-religious ideology, contrasting the uncorrupted countryside to the alienated urban elites (as opposed to Western Christian socialism, their interest in the industrial proletariat remained rather limited), there was also a more leftist variant which intersected with social democracy and/or with agrarian socialism.

For the former option one might cite the ideology of the Hungarian Catholic People's Party, emerging in the context of the *Kulturkampf* of the 1890s around civil marriage. They had limited political weight before 1918 in a political system marked by a restrictive electoral census, but their political rhetoric in many ways prepared the way for the interwar Christian conservative ideology. In its early phase, the People's Party went against the dominant assimilatory paradigm of Hungarian nationalism both in the sense of allowing political propaganda in the Slovak language, and in the sense of vocally rejecting the integration of the Jews – who were identified as the main culprits both of the process of secularization and the collapse of the old corporative socio-economic structures under the pressure of capitalism. For the second direction, a case in point is the Slovenian Janez E. Krek whose People's Party was extremely successful in combining the programme of social emancipation with Christian references. As a result, in the Slovenian context, the part of the leftist intelligentsia that were grouped around the Social Democratic Party remained in intellectual dialogue with Christian socialism also in the interwar years. Arguably, this was to have a long-term impact on the Slovenian ideological landscape, giving birth to a left-wing Catholic modality which had a special importance during the Second World War when some of these Catholic networks were to enter the anti-fascist resistance led by the communists.

These new forms of political mobilization and polarization intersected at the turn of the century with the transformation of theological discourse under the influence of modernist streams. The Hungarian Catholic Bishop of Székesfehérvár, Ottokár Prohászka started with a strong commitment to enter into dialogue with the modern world, accepting the importance of modern science in offering compelling explanations for various aspects of natural and human life. Reflecting on this new *Zeitgeist*, Prohászka sought to make the Catholic faith relevant also for an audience which had diverged from a more traditional lifestyle. However, during the First World War, with the ensuing democratic and communist revolutions, and the traumatic dissolution of 'historical Hungary', Prohászka became increasingly anti-intellectual and ethnonationalist, blaming mainly the Jewish middle class and the intelligentsia for the cataclysmic fate of the country. As a result, he emerged as one of the main ideologists of the new, official 'Christian course' in 1919, which combined neo-traditionalist social and cultural politics and ethnonationalism with an anti-Semitic edge.

The ideological trajectory of the Serbian Orthodox Bishop of Ohrid and Žiča, Nikolaj Velimirović was in many ways comparable, denominational and institutional differences notwithstanding. Educated in St. Petersburg and Switzerland, Velimirović was among the first Serbian clergymen whose theoretical horizons were similar to those of his Western counterparts. He was particularly influenced by the ideas of ecumenism that had a powerful upsurge at the turn of the century all around Europe. When the First World War broke out, he was sent to Britain and the US to represent the Serbian cause. In his wartime publications, he fused this ecumenical language (targeting mainly the Protestant audience, he repeatedly stressed the affinities of Orthodoxy and Protestantism) with an interpretation of Serbian history in a Messianic key, describing the nation as a martyr that in various historical moments sacrificed itself for universal liberty.[57]

After the First World War he was nominated the bishop of Ohrid in Macedonia, a recently acquired borderland in the crossfire of competing national projects. It is in this context that Velimirović assumed a radical nationalist position that was critical of a political establishment trying to elevate itself over the denominational and ethnic conflicts that were threatening the new Kingdom of Serbs, Croats and Slovenes with dissolution. Going against the politically more restrained church leadership, Velimirović was ready to cooperate with the charismatic-revivalist mass movement, the *bogomoljci*, and also got closer to the extreme right-wing ideologist, Dimitrije Ljotić. During the Second World War, he positioned himself between the collaborationist Nedić regime and the Chetniks. As a result, he was distrusted by the German occupiers who detained him in Dachau, albeit his living conditions were incomparably better than those of the common inmates of the camp. Tellingly, Velimirović wrote his most controversial text during his stay in Dachau, a pamphlet on the reasons for the tragic fate of the Serbs, blaming the Jews as principal culprits.

What connects the intellectual trajectories of these two charismatic clergymen, their denominational divergence notwithstanding, is that both started with a reformist agenda to turn towards a radical conservative and nationalist direction after the First World War. In intellectual terms this might be described as a *volte-face*, but there was also an underlying element of continuity: while both Prohászka and Velimirović abandoned the more liberal tenets of modernism, it was exactly their unconventional position when addressing some aspects of modernity that made their social-political involvement more straightforward and self-confident. In other words, it was partly their former modernist aspirations that enabled them to turn to modern strategies of political mobilization which their churches strongly opposed in the second half of the nineteenth century.

The interwar period saw the reinvigoration of religious aspects of politics all over the region, with the simultaneous emergence of a much more politically engaged clergy, as well as the proliferation of political discourses saturated by references to the sacred sphere. One can trace this in most national and denominational contexts. A paradigmatic case is the Romanian poet and journalist, Nichifor Crainic, who formulated a doctrine of 'political Orthodoxism' in the 1930s. Similar to Velimirović or Prohászka, his neo-traditionalism was the product of an encounter with modernist cultural trends, in his case with symbolism and Expressionism, as reflected by the journal *Gândirea* ('Thought'), which he co-edited from 1926 onwards. Crainic also had an interest in Russian religious philosophy and tried to transfer some of the key notions and ideological patterns from this literature (such as the idea of *sobornost*, or spiritual harmony). He linked all this to the crisis literature of the interwar period, arguing that Orthodoxy might offer a point of orientation for the world challenged by the heresy of materialism.[58] Crainic located this Orthodox doctrine not in the theological discussions but in the traditions of popular spirituality of the Romanian – and, more generally, the Balkan – peasantry. However, he considered the role of the neo-traditionalist intelligentsia to be crucial in articulating this doctrine and turning it into a proper ideological framework for the whole nation, whereby the religious and the national identification would merge into an unproblematic unity:

---

57 Nicholai Velimirović, *Serbia in Light and Darkness* (London: Longmans, 1916).
58 Nichifor Crainic, *Puncte cardinale in haos* [Cardinal points in the chaos] (Bucharest: Timpul, 1996).

Based on the same faith, on the same hope and the same love, the national community is found in a transfigured version in the community of the Church. Its local and temporal order is transposed in the eternal universal order. What deep insights does the cult of the ancestors gain through the cult of the saints, the cult of national solidarity through the cult of Christian love, faith in our vitality through faith in resurrection and in immortality, the sense of culture through the spiritualist sense of the cult![59]

From the mid-1930s onwards, this metaphysical neo-traditionalism had to face the challenge of the much more directly political Iron Guard, which also merged religious references with extreme nationalism. Crainic indeed moved closer to the Iron Guard, although he tried to retain his symbolic position of an autonomous thinker, as was reflected in his book on the 'ethnocratic state'.[60] This diffuse ideological position made it possible for him to be co-opted by the joint government of Ion Antonescu and the Iron Guard. After the break between the two forces and the destruction of the Iron Guard by Antonescu's military dictatorship, he continued to serve as an ideologist of the wartime regime, and for some time, also as a minister of propaganda.

Importantly, in different Orthodox cultures of the region the politicization of religion had a different dynamic: while in the case of Crainic or Ljotić political Orthodoxism merged with the extreme right, in the Bulgarian case the fusion was much less obvious. Neither the authoritarian regime of King Boris III, nor its extreme right-wing opposition appealed to Orthodox Christianity as the main constitutive factor of national identity. Likewise, the tentative merger of Orthodoxy and nationalism in the writings of Stefan Tsankov did not have explicitly totalitarian components. It is thus not by chance that some members of the high clergy, such as Metropolitan Cyril of Plovdiv, while assuming a nationalist ideological position, played an important role in preventing the deportation of the Bulgarian Jewish community.

In most countries where Catholicism was the dominant religion, the entanglement of nationalism and religion gave birth to various political movements of national conservative orientation in the interwar period.[61] There were, however, also intellectual projects of political Catholicism which were not easy to classify in terms of political camps. A case in point is the work of the Czech poet and essayist Jaroslav Durych.[62] Durych rejected the political and intellectual status quo of the Czechoslovak Republic. Representing a revolt against the self-complacent bourgeois order, in the early 1920s he even expressed his sympathy for the communists. In contrast, he idealized the medieval world supposedly permeated by heroism, spirituality and solidarity. While some of his peers from the radical Catholic subculture around the journal *Rozmach* translated this into a fascist political orientation at the turn of the 1930s, Durych retained his anti-institutional position and kept out of party politics. In other contexts, the Catholic/totalitarian fusion became a more attractive modality, as can be seen in the ideological references of Bolesław Piasecki's ONR-Falanga, the most radical branch of the Polish extreme right-wing nationalist organization of the 1930s. Piasecki fused the classical fascist ideological components, such as corporatism, anti-Semitism, the *Führerprinzip* and mass mobilization with

---

59 Crainic, *Puncte cardinale*, 126, English trans. in *Discourses of Collective Identity*, 4: 305.

60 Nichifor Crainic, *Ortodoxie și etnocrație* [Orthodoxy and ethnocracy] (Bucharest: Cugetarea, 1936).

61 See also John Connelly's contribution to this volume.

62 See Jaroslav Durych, *Naděje katolictví v zemich českých* [The hopes of Catholicism in the Czech Lands] (Prague: Ladislav Kuncíř, 1930).

Thinking dangerously

a religious symbolism and referential system, thereby arguing for the compatibility of fascism and Catholicism.[63]

The interwar politicization of religion was not only relevant in the context of Christian denominations but also to some extent in the Jewish identity debates, pitting various subgroups of Zionist, socialist and Orthodox streams against each other. In certain cases the spiritualist revival happened within the originally overwhelmingly secular Zionist framework, as it can be seen in the Czech case where the 1909/10 Prague lectures of Martin Buber had a catalyzing impact.[64] A similar intellectual negotiation can be seen in the case of some Hungarian Zionists, such as Béla Tábor, who tried to conceptualize the contents of the Jewish tradition in spiritual categories, and ended up reformulating Jewishness in terms of a simultaneous ethnocultural and religious-metaphysical engagement. This implied rejecting the secularizing and assimilatory construction of Jewish identity prevalent at the turn of the century, but it did not mean the return to traditional religiosity. In other cases, orthodox Judaism entered the political arena, such as in post-1918 Slovakia where the Agudat Yisrael party cooperated with the Czechoslovak agrarians and conservatives against the secular Zionists linked to the Czechoslovak left.

Likewise, one can speak of the rise of 'political Islam' in the interwar period, particularly in Bosnia. Within the larger Bosnian Muslim intellectual sphere, there were two distinct streams: reformists who claimed that Islam should enter into a dialogue with modernity, and traditionalists or revivalists who aimed at the revitalization of a 'more authentic' Islam. The reformists around Džemaludin Čaušević originally supported the Yugoslavist project. But, in the 1930s, when it became clear to them that Yugoslav nation-building implied Christian – an especially Orthodox – dominance, they increasingly distanced themselves from it. In contrast, the revivalists, led by Mehmed Handžić, an alumnus of the Al-Azhar University in Cairo and thus well connected to the global Islam revivalist movement, focused more on defining 'Bosnianness', merging ethnic and religious markers. He thus tried to link a historical narrative about the specificity of Bosnian Islam with a moral theology stressing the importance of intra-community solidarity, acts of charity and following the teachings of religion in everyday life.

After 1945, the direct political influence of the churches was curtailed all over the region, but this did not mean that political discourse as such was completely devoid of religious motives. As a matter of fact, both the directly oppositional subcultures and the tolerated alternative (but not directly oppositional) intellectual networks were often linked to religious traditions. One of the most interesting of such milieus was the post-war Polish Catholic modernist project led by such intellectuals as Jerzy Turowicz and Stanisław Stomma and grouped around the journals *Tygodnik Powszechny* ('Universal weekly') and *Znak* ('Sign'). They criticized the conservative attitude of the Church in post-war Poland, which, in their eyes, was reverting to the mere ritualization of religion. They proposed a moral and intellectual revival instead, which in the context of communist rule also implied a critical dialogue with the regime, assuming certain common values like solidarity and progress. The main aim of these intellectuals – who came to be labelled as 'neo-positivists' with reference to the organicist reformism of Polish Positivism after the failed January Uprising of 1863–4 – was to carve out a space for their own cultural and institutional existence, thus creating the framework for the parallel cultural, and eventually also

---

63 On the Polish debates concerning the relationship of nationalism, modernism and Catholicism, see Brian Porter-Szűcs, *Faith and Fatherland: Catholicism, Modernity, and Poland* (Oxford: Oxford University Press, 2011).

64 On the Bohemian context, see Kateřina Čapková, *Czechs, Germans, Jews: National Identity and the Jews of Bohemia* (Oxford: Berghahn, 2012).

political institutions, supported by the Church that came to define the Polish intellectual scene from the 1960s to the 1980s.

There were even more radical attempts to create a common ground between socialism and Christianity, as attested by the work of the Czech Protestant Josef L. Hromádka, a key figure of the international ecumenical movement. In his texts he pointed to the roots of progressive social thought in the Christian tradition. His acceptance of the official ideological framework was also evident in his move from the Lutheran Church to the Czech Brethren, a 'national' denomination promoted by the communist regime in line with its pro-Hussite and anti-German politics of history. The attempt to modernize the Church could have different practical consequences with regard to cooperating with the regime: Hromádka subordinated his ecumenism to the state interest, whereas Stomma and Turowicz may have opted for a depoliticized stance in the 1950s, but they gradually moved towards a more critical position, which culminated in their involvement in the council of cultural-political advisors around Cardinal József Glemp, who played a mediating role between the regime and the opposition during the 1980s.

An interesting, albeit highly idiosyncratic case is that of the Hungarian émigré Jesuit, Töhötöm Nagy. Nagy was involved in the Christian socialist movement in Hungary in the 1930s, and after 1945, sought to find common ground between the Catholic Church and socialism, allowing the Church to retain its liberty in exchange for its engagement in social reforms. In this process of negotiation, he clashed repeatedly with Cardinal József Mindszenty, who assumed an uncompromising stance towards the communists, but also towards the calls to modernize the Church. When his position became untenable in Hungary due to the escalating conflict between the church and the state, Nagy moved to Argentina, where he left the Jesuit order and became a freemason.[65] Nevertheless, he continued to agitate for a dialogue between the Church and socialism, and in the 1960s he published texts in Spanish which can be linked to the emerging doctrine of Liberation Theology. In 1968 he returned to Hungary, and once again became involved in the negotiations between the Vatican and the communist authorities aiming at the 'normalization' of their relationship. While he assisted the Hungarian government and secret services in their efforts to monitor the interaction of the clergy and the Vatican, he failed to create the envisioned ideological synthesis between communism and post-Second Vatican Council Catholicism, and he eventually became completely marginalized.

The national communist framework offered another possible track to negotiate with the communist regime for the representatives of religious ideological traditions. A case in point is Piasecki, who was co-opted by the post-war Polish authorities to lead the pro-regime Catholic PAX Association, which supported the regime throughout the 1950s in its conflict with Cardinal Stefan Wyszyński. It played a particularly infamous role in 1968 when it vocally endorsed the anti-Semitic purges. One can compare these developments to the ideological recycling of Romanian Orthodoxists. Although Crainic was imprisoned for his wartime political engagement, when he was released in 1962, he was immediately co-opted by the propaganda machine of the communist regime just as it took an increasingly nationalist orientation. Likewise, the political writer and theologian Dumitru Stăniloae, also belonging to the radical right intellectual milieu of the late 1930s, made a large contribution to the development of Romanian theological thought after 1945 and in some ways his work also entered into a dialogue with the national communist stream within the regime. Thus, in his writings he legitimized the Orthodox Church as the bastion of national continuity against the 'alien' (Habsburg,

---

65 Töhötöm Nagy, *Jezsuiták és szabadkőművesek* [Jesuits and freemasons] (Buenos Aires: Danubio S.C.A., 1965).

Thinking dangerously

Ottoman, Hungarian, etc.) state. Along these lines, he also supported the destruction of the Greek Catholic Church in 1948, labelling them a 'Western infiltration' into the spirituality of the nation.

The discussion on the role of religion in modernity was also pursued in the Muslim context after 1945. While the Young Muslims – who sought to combine Muslim spiritual revivalism with a conspiratorial oppositional organization in the immediate post-war period – were violently crushed by the Yugoslav communist authorities in 1949, these themes reappeared in the writings of one of their former members, Alija Izetbegović, who was to re-launch many of these debates from an oppositional position in the 1970s and was to emerge as the leader of the Bosnian Muslims during the 1990s. Izetbegović's *Islam between East and West* argued that in Europe there was a contradiction between materialism and religion, and Islam was the third option that could transcend this conflict.[66] In this sense, he considered Islam not so much a religion in the Western sense of the word, but a way of life. Whereas Christianity focused on individual spirituality, and materialism destroyed the human personality, Islam, which he described as rational and non-mystical, offered a way out of the cultural crisis of the world because it brought together communal existence and a respect for nature and spirituality.

In the 1980s most anti-communist oppositional subcultures included prominent intellectuals who sought to rethink the relationship between church, nation and modernity. The most intensive discussion took place in Poland due to the efforts of the 'neo-positivist' stream and the dialogue between the revisionist Marxists, such as Leszek Kołakowski, and Catholic intellectuals, such as the philosopher and priest Józef Tischner, who later became an important member of the Solidarity movement. Tischner drew on the personalist and existentialist philosophical traditions to offer a framework of dialogue which also held appeal for non-believers, while at the same time seeking to re-position religion from its pre-modern dominant status, conceiving of religiosity in terms of individual commitment and the result of self-reflection.[67] Above all, he sought to develop an ethical theory focused on human dignity, mediating between the two fundamental human tendencies: the craving for freedom and the thrust for rationalization. Human dignity, which was at the core of his 'ethics of solidarity', was rooted in the transcendent sphere, but Tischner conceived of this transcendence in a rather personal and non-institutional sense, assigning conscience a central role:

> Conscience is the knack of reading the road signs. Only conscience knows which road sign one should turn attention to, here and now ... a God who does not speak through the human conscience is not a true God but an idol.[68]

Comparable intellectual projects could be found in other countries too, such as in the writings of Tomáš Halík in Czechoslovakia.[69]

However, after 1989, instead of the intensification of dialogue promoted by these dissidents, the Church hierarchies were busy consolidating their social and economic power and marginalized the intellectual and clerical subcultures calling for modernization. Thus, rather than building on the syncretic traditions emerging out of the spirit of dialogue during the *aggiornamento*

---

66 Alija Izetbegović, *Islam between East and West* (Plainfield, IN: American Trust Publications, 1984).

67 Józef Tischner, *The Spirit of Solidarity* (New York: Harper & Row, 1984).

68 Ibid., 7.

69 Tomáš Halík, *Night of the Confessor: Christian Faith in an Age of Uncertainty* (New York: Doubleday/ Image, 2012).

of the 1960s, or on the theological links to dissident subcultures, the post-communist Church hierarchies were reverting to a softened version of the interwar conceptions of politicized religion with their anti-modernist moral theology and cultural visions, as well as a focus on collective rituals and symbolism at the expense of intellectual argument and individual conscience.

Political thought in the age of the extremes

The following subchapter deals with one of the most important intellectual discussions witnessed by this part of the world during the twentieth century, namely, that which concerns the nature of totalitarianism and the possibilities of resisting it. It introduces some of the most interesting and sophisticated intellectuals who, at some point, succumbed to the totalitarian temptation as well as those who developed critical interpretations and pleas for resistance. In fact, many of the most vocal and knowledgeable critics of totalitarianism were themselves tempted by its leftist or rightist forms at earlier stages of their lives. Furthermore, there are also intriguing examples of the opposite trajectory – critics of totalitarianism who eventually themselves became 'true believers'.

Such an act of conversion, symbolic for the entire twentieth century, is that of the Hungarian philosopher, György (Georg) Lukács. Coming from a Hungarian-Jewish elite social background, Lukács became part of the German intellectual scene of the 1910s, staying in Berlin and Heidelberg and frequenting the circles of Max Weber, Georg Simmel and Thomas Mann.[70] While his position before 1914 could be described as elitist aestheticism, during the war he participated in various cultural and political ventures of the Hungarian intellectual left and was increasingly radicalized. Lukács was originally in support of the democratic revolution of October 1918 while being critical of the Bolshevik political ideology and practice, drawing a strict theoretical line between ethical and political action. In his article 'Bolshevism as a Moral Problem', he contrasted democratic and Bolshevik commitments, arguing that the former implied the acceptance that the ideal order could not be imposed from above but required a long-term political education, while the latter implied committing acts of violence and thus compromising the noble cause of universal emancipation.[71] While at this point he still clearly leaned toward the former option, within a month he reversed his position and entered the Communist Party, becoming a prominent figure of the Hungarian Soviet Republic proclaimed in March 1919. His new political and philosophical stance was encapsulated in the volume *Tactics and Ethics*, published during the Soviet Republic.[72] Articulating a secularized Messianism as it were, Lukács depicted the socialist revolutions sweeping Eastern Europe as a new beginning, reconfiguring the entire past and future of humankind. In contrast to his pre-1919 texts, this perspective clearly legitimized the use of violence as a necessary evil, as his famous quote from Friedrich Hebbel's play, *Judith*, indicates: 'Even if God had placed sin between me and the deed enjoined upon me – who am I to be able to escape it?'

---

70 On the young Lukács, see Mary Gluck, *Georg Lukács and His Generation, 1900–1918* (Cambridge, MA: Harvard University Press, 1985).

71 György Lukács, 'A bolsevizmus mint erkölcsi probléma' [Bolshevism as a moral problem], *Szabadgondolat* (December 1918), available on the Marxists Internet Archive: www.marxists.org/magyar/archive/lukacs/bmep.htm (accessed 8 March 2019).

72 György Lukács, *Taktika és ethika* [Tactics and ethics] (Budapest: Közoktatásügyi Népbiztosság kiadása, 1919).

Thinking dangerously

After the collapse of the Hungarian Soviet Republic, Lukács was helped by his family to escape to Austria and then spent the 1920s mostly in Germany. In his philosophical works written in this period, he attempted to create a philosophy of history for the communist movement, trying to fuse Leninism with Hegelianism. He was also engaged in the internal opposition within the Hungarian communist exile, blaming the leader of the 1919 Soviet experiment, Béla Kun, for disregarding the local political and social conditions, such as the agrarian question. In the 1928 'Blum Theses' he put forward a number of recommendations for the Hungarian, and by implication the international communist movement, to consider 'national specificities', anticipating the Popular Front ideology of the mid-1930s. In 1930–31 he stayed for some time in Moscow, being employed by the Marx–Engels–Lenin Institute. He returned to Germany briefly in 1931, but after the collapse of the Weimar Republic, Lukács definitively settled in the Soviet Union, arriving there at the very moment of the radicalization of Stalinist terror. His main philosophical project at the time was offering a reinterpretation of Hegel to fit the ideological requirements of the regime. Importantly, his aesthetic penchant for classicism and his rejection of the avant-garde fit well with the socialist realist aesthetic canon imposed in the 1930s. Nevertheless, in the second half of the 1930s he was on the verge of being repressed, and so he destroyed most of his manuscripts in fear that they might serve as evidence against him.

In 1945, Lukács returned to Hungary as one of the chief ideologists of popular democracy. He clashed with the intellectual representatives of the populists and social democrats who argued for a more balanced distribution of power. This did not save him from criticism during the period of Stalinist hegemony after 1949, when his arguments in favour of popular democracy and a gradual transition to socialism were turned against him and he was accused of 'revisionism'. In 1956 he was co-opted into the revolutionary government of Imre Nagy for rather symbolic reasons, and after the repression of the revolution he came under attack for 'ideological deviation' once again. In the 1960s he was allowed to continue his work within the confines of the official cultural policy, occasionally demonstrating his loyalty to the Kádárist establishment. At the same time, his students emerged as a hub of criticism targeting the everyday realities of 'goulash communism', attacking what they saw as the 'unphilosophical' and petty bourgeois culture of the regime.

The dynamic of intellectual engagement and disengagement with communism of leading avant-garde figures in other East Central European cultures is comparable to that of Lukács, even though he was himself a fervent critic of avant-gardism. The young Czech visual artist, architect and theoretician Karel Teige enthusiastically identified himself with the distant but fascinating Soviet revolutionary experiment, perceived as a kind of avant-garde *Gesamtkunstwerk* that unleashed creative energies both in the political and the aesthetic spheres. Along these lines, many young Czech, Polish and South Slav artists and intellectuals projected their own anti-bourgeois existential revolt on the communist movement and became vocal supporters of the newly formed communist parties, which were desperately in need of cultural legitimacy and thus eagerly welcomed these intellectuals within their ranks.

What is more, these intellectuals often provided the most radical pressure group, a veritable Stalinist avant-garde, within these parties, clashing with the former social democrat activists who sought to keep to a more moderate political course. However, with the consolidation of the international communist movement under Moscow's tutelage, and the gradual marginalization of avant-garde artists in the Soviet Union towards the late 1920s, the situation was reversed. Now the party apparatchiks who emerged with the first wave of Stalinization, defeating the more moderate and locally embedded cadre, set out to purge the party of the 'unreliable' intellectuals. It was usually at this point around the early 1930s that these artists realized the mismatch between their aesthetic and political commitments, and gradually came to rethink their political position, asserting the importance of individual artistic liberty and intellectual autonomy.

The rise of Nazism and of the Popular Front ideology of the Communist International once again changed the situation because many of those who were castigated for 'formalism' and excluded from the party were reintegrated as leading representatives of the progressive intelligentsia with an essential role to play in the common struggle against fascism. The dilemma of such intellectuals was aggravated further by the fact that the peak of their enthusiasm about the Popular Front practically coincided with the climax of the Stalinist terror (1936–8), destroying most of the key figures of the party's former Leninist 'avant-garde'. As a result, many of them, such as Teige, who published the pamphlet *Surrealism against the Current* in which he bitterly criticized Stalinist cultural and judicial policies, broke with the party once again.[73] Those who lived until 1945 faced the painful dilemma of how to come to terms with communist dominance after the Soviet 'triumph over fascism'. Teige tried to assume a leftist but critical position, supporting progressive art and social politics but distancing himself from Stalinist dogmatism. It is not by chance that after 1948 he became a principal target of the anti-formalist campaign. He died soon afterwards of a heart attack.

There were other intellectual strategists on the cultural and political left who aimed to draw a thicker line between themselves and the communist ideological matrix. Karel Čapek, the popular left-liberal Czech writer and political journalist, whose position increasingly became identified with that of Masaryk, formulated perhaps the most cogent anti-totalitarian arguments in interwar Czechoslovakia. Čapek accepted the moral legitimacy of radical social criticism but considered the calls for violent resistance self-defeating since they undermined the mechanisms of social solidarity.[74] This position was also typical among the social democratic intellectuals in the region, however, the deterioration of the situation in the 1930s, with the rise of authoritarian regimes almost everywhere except for Czechoslovakia (at least until 1938), made this argument much less compelling. All the more so, as the alternative to violent class struggle was not a relatively benign liberal democratic state with fairly inclusive welfare provisions, but rather corporatist authoritarianism which offered certain measures of redistribution in exchange for complete political subservience. It is not by chance that the 1930s and early 1940s, and especially the outbreak of the war, saw the disintegration of the social democratic ideological framework in most of these countries, with some of the main ideologists (like the Bulgarian Sotir Janev or many of the Baltic leaders, such as the Latvian Miķelis Valters) eventually becoming co-opted by the national authoritarian regimes, while others like the Czech Zdeněk Fierlinger or the Hungarian Árpád Szakasits ending up as 'fellow travellers' of the communists during and after the Second World War.

Travelogues concerning the Soviet Union provided a crucial means to negotiate the merits and downsides of the communist ideology and reality. While there were a number of officially organized, mediatized and carefully controlled visits of 'progressive intellectuals' from East Central Europe, comparable to the more famous cases of Western 'fellow travellers', such as the French Radical Édouard Herriot, there was perhaps a higher rate of disenchantment due also to the relative socio-cultural proximity of some of these travellers to the rural world in the USSR.

---

73 Karel Teige, *Surrealismus proti proudu* [Surrealism against the current] (Prague: Surrealistická skupina, 1938).

74 Karel Čapek, 'Proč nejsem komunistou' [Why I am not a communist], *Přítomnost* 1, no. 47 (1924): 737–9.

Thinking dangerously

This made it harder for the Soviet authorities to make East Central Europeans completely disregard the disturbing signs of poverty and repression. The most famous case is doubtlessly that of the Paris-based Romanian writer, Panait Istrati, who originally travelled to the USSR intent on praising the Soviet achievements. Visiting the Russian and Ukrainian countryside as well as the Caucasus on two occasions, in 1927 and in 1928/9, and establishing close links with the anti-Stalinist opposition (people such as Christian Rakovski, Boris Souvarine and Victor Serge) his travelogue turned out to be highly polemic, attacking both the exploitative and the bureaucratized nature of the regime and anticipating the work of André Gide.[75]

Istrati's aesthetic and political interest in the peasantry, which he developed in his native Dobruja, made him receptive to the argument that the Soviet regime reproduced a strict, quasi-feudal relationship between the leading bureaucratic elite and the rural masses. When he expressed his increasing doubts, he was ostracized by his leftist French friends and former supporters, like Romain Rolland, and he became the target of a campaign of defamation. Eventually, he lost the support of the left-wing intellectual public completely. Returning to Romania, he tried his luck with a splinter party of the extreme right, that of Mihail Stelescu, whose ideology might be compared to the 'national Bolshevism' of the Strasser brothers in Germany. As a result, Istrati lost his credentials and died in desolation in 1935. A year later, the movement itself met its bitter end in a similar way to its German counterpart, its leader being murdered by a death squad of the Iron Guard.

Needless to say, the totalitarian temptation did not only overwhelm leftist intellectuals, but had an equally powerful grasp on the right. Actually, for many radical intellectuals of the 1920s it was, for a while, almost impossible to tell whether their sympathies lay on the left or the right because they were equally fascinated by the communist and fascist versions of ritualism and the submersion of the individual into the collective. It is not by chance that the members of the Romanian 'Young generation' ('*Tânăra generaţie*'), grouped around the Criterion association in Bucharest, dedicated a popular debate session in 1932–3 to Benito Mussolini and Vladimir Ilyich Lenin (as well as to less politically charged figures, such as Charlie Chaplin or Jiddu Krishnamurti). While this might be considered a jocular gesture, confirmed by the fact that some members of the group assumed a leftist position at one event and a rightist one at another, soon the polarization of political allegiances set in and most of the members had to decide where they stood.

One of the most brilliant members of the group, the young philosophy student from Southern Transylvania with an extensive but also very eclectic – though mostly German – cultural package, Emil Cioran, exemplified a new type of radical intellectual who would fall for a right-wing totalitarian position for philosophical reasons. Cioran spent some time in Berlin on a Humboldt fellowship (1933–5) and became overwhelmed by the pathos of 'national revolution' he claimed to have experienced. In the early 1930s, he published a series of idiosyncratic philosophical essays, which originally had limited political referentiality, although they also reflected his scorn for modern institutions and a search for authentic experiences to be found outside the confines of modern institutions. Influenced by Oswald Spengler and Ludwig Klages, Cioran was both abhorred and fascinated by what he saw as the age of decadence. He asserted that when living during such periods there was nothing one could do but to endure, with heroism, the fatal unfolding of a historical cycle.[76]

---

75 Panait Istrati, *Confession pour vaincus: Aprés seize mois dans l'URSS* (Paris: Rieder, 1929).

76 For the intellectual sources of Cioran's early works, see Marta Petreu, *An Infamous Past: E.M. Cioran and the Rise of Fascism in Romania* (Chicago, IL: Ivan R. Dee, 2005).

With the general political radicalization in the mid-1930s, Cioran became increasingly politicized, which means that he started to project a palingenetic solution as the escape from endemic decadence. His answer to the question preoccupying most members of the Romanian 'Young generation', namely how their own generational experience could be valorized as a catalyst of national regeneration, turned out to be a call for 'creative destruction'. Cioran considered the creative epochs of history to be linked to the cult of primitivism and the enthusiasm of youth deriving from their admiration for spontaneity and irrationality.[77] The new collective identity had to be formed through radical negation: great cultures emerged through radicalism, since only exclusivity and uniqueness could gain the status of universality.[78] The existential revolt in Cioran's vision thus turned into a plea for a new national beginning, a 'Romanian Adamism', which would unfold through the apocalyptic fight against the 'dictatorship of the rheumatic', and involved craving for a new St. Bartholomew's Night to eliminate the corrupted older generations.[79]

Cioran's most important and most idiosyncratic pro-totalitarian political-philosophical pamphlet is titled *Transfiguration of Romania* (1936). Its argument is anchored in a framework of cultural morphology and focuses on the 'small cultures' whose only historical chance to become valuable was defeating 'their own laws of existence'.[80] He looked for guidance mainly in the two cultures he identified as inherently eschatological, the German and the Russian. Importantly, this double referentiality indicates a divergence from the neo-traditionalist regressive utopias that were so common on the Romanian radical right, saturated by political Orthodoxism. Cioran talked about Byzantine 'spiritual damnation' and a self-deceiving traditionalism, which does not give meaning to the people. His vision of *totale Mobilmachung*, or 'total mobilization', fused left- and right-wing elements, thus the ethno-centric radicalism of the European radical right (going so far as to explicitly envision national purification through the 'removal' of Jews and Hungarians from the 'national body') and the voluntaristic industrial modernism of the Soviet project merged in his vision.

Due to its syncretism and anti-traditionalist radicalism this metaphysical version of totalitarianism did not perfectly overlap with the discourse of the Iron Guard. However, Cioran moved politically close to the movement especially after the murder of its leader, Corneliu Zelea Codreanu in 1938. In 1940, during the coalition government of Antonescu and Horia Sima, he accepted a position at the Romanian embassy in Paris. His Paris experiences, which remain mostly undocumented, and can be reconstructed largely from anecdotal evidence, seem to have been mixed: on the one hand, he was spending his time with German soldiers; on the other, he was genuinely traumatized by the deportation and death of his friend, the Jewish-Romanian writer Benjamin Fondane (Fundoianu). At the end of the war, he decided to remain in Paris, abandoning the Romanian and German linguistic and cultural milieus, and he started a new intellectual career in French. He kept a low profile even after 1949 when the publishing of his first French collection of essays brought him sudden literary fame, in an effort to repress the memory of his nefarious political engagement.

---

77 Emil M. Cioran, 'Sensul culturii contemporane' [The sense of contemporary culture] (1932), in *Revelațiile durerii*, eds Mariana Vartic and Aurel Sasu (Cluj-Napoca: Echinox, 1990), 64–5.

78 Cioran, 'Necesitatea radicalismului' [The necessity of radicalism] (1935), in *Revelațiile durerii*, 138–9.

79 Cioran, 'Crima bătrînilor' [The crime of the old] (1937), in *Revelațiile durerii*, 170.

80 Emil M. Cioran, *Schimbarea la față a României* [The transfiguration of Romania] (Bucharest: Vremea, 1941), 12.

Thinking dangerously

In the context of a leftist-dominated post-war French cultural scene, Cioran assumed an aristocratic stature, wittily criticizing European modernity and championing rather outmoded conservative references, such as Joseph de Maistre. Ironically, the 1960s counter-cultural wave discovered him as a critic of bourgeois civilization and like his peer from the 'Young generation', Mircea Eliade, he became a cultural icon of leftist anti-bourgeois thought. Through this process of re-positioning, he also changed his stance with regard to his former political engagement: while he never made it abundantly clear, for those who understood his allusions it became obvious that he distanced himself from the violently anti-Semitic and anti-Hungarian stance of the Iron Guard. This culminated in his ambiguous re-editing of the text of the 'Transfiguration' after the Romanian Revolution: he simply purged the ethnonationalist passages from it.

The demise of right-wing totalitarian ideology after 1945 was a common phenomenon in Eastern and Western Europe, but the trajectory of those who fought against it from a democratic position could be strikingly divergent. Namely, most East Central European anti-fascist thinkers and activists were forced to take a stance on the communist ideological framework that came to dominate the political culture of the region falling under Soviet geopolitical dependence. Beyond the power politics of having to choose between Hitler and Stalin, from the point of view of intellectual history the feeling of the collapse of the bourgeois world order and the craving for a radical transformation of these 'backward' societies seemed to be an equally powerful intrinsic reason for the acceptance of the communist arguments. This was true even in contexts which retained a modicum of political pluralism, such as Czechoslovakia between 1945 and 1948. This made the intellectual position of those thinkers who placed themselves on the progressive left of the political spectrum, but rejected the communist ideological tenets and practical methods, all the more complicated.

The Serbian agrarian democrat Dragoljub Jovanović, who turned from a left-wing critique of the interwar Yugoslav authoritarian regime into a defender of democracy in the face of the communist monopolization of power after 1945, had a particularly dramatic personal and intellectual path. In the 1930s he emerged as the most original ideologue of Serbian peasantism, anchoring the party firmly on the left of the political spectrum. Along these lines, he argued for a compromise with the Croatians and, during the Second World War, supported the partisans.[81] In 1944, Jovanović declared his support for the new communist-dominated government but sought to safeguard the separate existence of the Peasant Party to represent the rural masses. Later on, however, he became increasingly critical of the communists. Although he accepted the key aspects of their economic programme, he was to raise his voice against their monopolization of power in a number of memorable parliamentary speeches and articles. However, it soon became clear that the communists aimed at total political dominance and Jovanović became involved in the negotiations seeking to bring together the potentially oppositional forces in a common electoral bloc. In this Jovanović failed, however, which eventually led to his expulsion from parliament and long-term imprisonment.

In other contexts, there was somewhat more time and space in the aftermath of the Second World War for devising a democratic anti-totalitarian discourse. A good example is the Czech Catholic conservative-liberal journalist Pavel Tigrid, who between 1945 and 1947 acted as the key figure of a small but vocal subculture of Czech Catholic democrats. This group distanced themselves from the interwar and wartime corporatist-authoritarian propensities of the

---

81 For his journalism and political texts see Dragoljub Jovanović, *Sloboda od straha – izabrane političke rasprave* [Freedom from fear – selected political essays] (Belgrade: Filip Višnjić, Naučna knjiga 1991); idem, *Seljak – svoj čovek* [Peasant – his own man] (Belgrade: Institut za noviju istoriju Srbije, 1997).

conservative camp but also from the progressivist consensus that claimed to have aims similar to the communists (socialization of the means of production, pro-Soviet geopolitical engagement and a planned economy), even if remaining critical of the communists' 'impatience'.[82] Escaping to the West in 1948, Tigrid became an important figure of the Czechoslovak political emigration with his journal, *Svědectví* (Testimony), launched in 1956. The journal had an especially strong impact in the 1960s when it promoted a 'gradualist' stance towards the socialist regimes, i.e. creating a broad common platform of different exile forces while encouraging the more reformist policies and factions of the party.

The shift in Tigrid's opinions, who in 1946–7 attacked the leftist 'fellow travellers' but after 1956 was willing to extend the dialogue to the socialist internal critics of the regime, was to a large extent due to the rise of a new intellectual position, which in philosophical terms was often described as 'revisionist Marxism' (even though originally, this was more of an accusation then a self-assumed appellative). The most paradigmatic author in this vein was Leszek Kołakowski, who started his academic career during Stalinism as part of the official communist academic establishment, although his pre-1947 cultural experiences also lent him a certain level of familiarity with the classics of 'bourgeois philosophy', especially German idealism. He capitalized on the latter after 1953 when he gradually distanced himself from the official Marxist–Leninist doctrine and started to look for a more complex theoretical framework.

A key element in this search was the effort to historicize, i.e. to reinsert the Marxist philosophical system into its original nineteenth-century context. Kołakowski thus re-evaluated Marx's relationship to Hegel, making Marxism not so much the culmination but a variant of the Hegelian system, and also linked (especially the young) Marx and Engels to a broader Romantic-radical democratic ideological milieu with various intellectual and political aims but a rather common style of thinking. This historicization entailed the relativization of the Marxist doctrine, undermining its status as an atemporal and unchangeable doctrine. It also made it possible to argue for a need to involve other philosophical traditions in the study of problems which were not yet visible from the horizons of the mid-nineteenth century (such as philosophy of science in the 'atomic age').

At the same time, the 'revision' suggested by Kołakowski and his colleagues in Poland (Bronisław Baczko, Adam Schaff), Hungary (Ágnes Heller, György Márkus, Ferenc Fehér), Czechoslovakia (Karel Kosík) and Yugoslavia (the Praxis school: Predrag Vranicki, Gajo Petrović, Rudi Supek, Milan Kangrgra, Mihailo Marković, Ljubomir Tadić, Svetozar Stojanović) did not mean a rejection of Marxism as a key source of inspiration. On the contrary, the aforementioned thinkers asserted that Marxism was actually an open-ended system of thought, challenging rather than confirming the powers that be, and thus it was a grave error of the Stalinists to freeze it into a legitimizing doctrine. Kołakowski's intellectual development led him toward the idea that for any perspective on history to confer meaning on the seemingly unrelated and meaningless sequence of occurrences, one first needs to take a normative perspective and such a normative position can only be rooted in some sort of existential commitment, an act of faith, as it were.[83] This made it possible for him to bring the Marxist engagement onto the same epistemological level as the religious one. After the late 1960s this determined his general philosophical programme, leading him from Marxist revisionism towards a philosophically

---

82 Bradley F. Abrams, *The Struggle for the Soul of the Nation: Czech Culture and the Rise of Communism* (Lanham, MD: Rowman & Littlefield, 2004).

83 Leszek Kołakowski, 'Historical Understanding and the Intelligibility of History', in *A Leszek Kołakowski Reader*, ed. Charles Newman (Evanston, IL: Northwestern University, 1971), 103–17.

Thinking dangerously

rather eclectic and politically liberal position. This led to his polemic with the Western Marxist critics, eminently E. P. Thompson, who accused him of having betrayed critical Marxism. In his polemic with Thompson, Kołakowski pointed to the blindness of Western Marxists toward the actual experience of Eastern Europeans where Marxism was tried on 'actual people'. He also rejected the New Left emerging around 1968 for being dogmatic, asserting instead the importance of institutions of democracy and the protection of human rights as the only safeguards against the unfolding of Soviet or Nazi-type repressive dictatorships. His intellectual break with Marxism was made complete with his masterwork, *Main Currents of Marxism*, which he finished in his English emigration in 1978. In it he explicated the links between the Marxian philosophical foundations, the Leninist strategy and the Stalinist practice.[84]

In Poland, as well as in the other East Central European countries where revisionist Marxism was intellectually present, the 1960s witnessed yet another important development, namely the search for alternative left-wing intellectual references, rejecting not only Stalinism, but also the linear Marx–Lenin axis. This meant a search for 'indigenous' socialist thinkers with different intellectual preoccupations and emphases. An eminent example here is provided by Karel Kosík who looked at the nineteenth-century Czech radical democratic tradition for inspiration. However, 1968 meant a global turning point in the sense that the collapse of the belief in the reformability of the socialist system, caused by the occupation of Czechoslovakia, made this search for an alternative socialist tradition problematic and increasingly irrelevant. At the same time, the field was open for radically different philosophical references that had nothing to do with the Marxist framework. This is also detectable in Kosík's intellectual reorientation as he entered into a dialogue with the nineteenth-century liberal nationalism of František Palacký with the hindsight of knowing much more about the ambiguities of political modernity. Seeking to localize his intellectual project, Kosík turned to the concept of Central Europe, conceiving of it as a zone of civilizational in-betweenness, torn by the alternative of 'uniformity and "Gleichschaltung" on the one hand and variety and plurality on the other'.[85]

A paradigmatic work indicating this intellectual reorientation after 1968 was 'The Power of the Powerless', by Václav Havel.[86] Known as an author of absurd drama pieces, Havel emerged as a political figure in the stormy months of 1968 when he clashed with the reform communists, criticizing them for believing that their 'socialism with a human face' was a 'third way' between liberal democracy and bureaucratic socialism. He argued for the return to the liberal democratic tradition instead with its institutions, defence of rights and civic virtue. Influenced by the phenomenological works of Jan Patočka, Havel's famous essay written in autumn 1978 zoomed in on the figure of a greengrocer who placed the slogan 'Proletarians of the World, Unite!' above his fruits. Havel used this seemingly meaningless act of conformism to conceptualize a fundamental contrast between the inauthentic mode of existence in a system based on frightening and deceiving the population and the possibility of an authentic existence for those who dared to break with the collective lie. All this enabled Havel to create a common symbolic and ideological framework for very different groups detaching themselves from the official norms of the regime, from critical intellectuals to religious dissidents and members of artistic and musical countercultures.

Havel's vision had a strong impact on the Czech dissident movement in particular, but it was far from being a dominant, let alone exclusive, vision. The reform communist position

---

84 Leszek Kołakowski, *Main Currents of Marxism*, vols 1–3 (Oxford: Clarendon Press 1978).

85 Karel Kosík, 'What is Central Europe?' (1969), in Kosík, *The Crisis of Modernity*, 179.

86 Václav Havel, 'The Power of the Powerless' (1978), in *Open Letters: Selected Writings 1965–1990*, ed. and trans. Paul Wilson (New York: Alfred A. Knopf, 1991).

continued to co-exist with various alternative leftist (anarchist, Trotskyist, social democrat, ecological), liberal (and often liberal nationalist), and rightist (Christian conservative, nationalist) ideological versions. This was the case with all dissident movements. Arguably the more sizeable ones, like the Polish example, had more space for ideological differentiation, while the much more 'compressed' oppositional subcultures, like the Romanian and Bulgarian ones, displayed less variety. The latter were usually divided between the disaffected communist internal dissent and the anti-systemic, mostly conservative and nationalist circles. Importantly, the ideological debate between these camps, which became an important structuring element of the post-1989 political systems, already started before 1989, even though the opposition to the regime to a certain extent attenuated such differences.

On the surface, the largely unexpected implosion of the Soviet bloc in 1989 brought a total victory to the political vision of the dissidents, while in reality, they already had to face serious existential and political dilemmas at the onset of the post-communist transition. Most importantly, they were confronted by the choice between perpetuating the more inclusive and ideologically heterogeneous movement-type organizations based on a common ethical imperative rather than a common political agenda, or opting instead for political polarization along the lines of the party system preceding the Sovietization or new ideological patterns (following the Western taxonomies). This was one of the questions where the dissident leaders, such as Havel, who were committed to the anti-political tradition, clashed with the emerging new type of politicians (often coming from the technocratic 'grey zone' in-between the party state and the opposition), who urged the 'normalization' of the party system and often actively undermined the unity of the anti-communist opposition movements.

Torn by these ambiguities, the key intellectual figure of Solidarity, Adam Michnik, pondered the relationship between the ethical and the political:

> We know how fragile are the bases of democratic order in Poland, and we know that to denounce continuously the slippages in our democracy will make it even more fragile. We face, in these circumstances, a peculiar conflict of loyalties. What is more important, we ask ourselves, the fragile democratic order or the defenceless truth? None of us has a ready answer to the question of which of these two loyalties should prevail. We are doomed to inconsistency.[87]

Yet Michnik thought that there was a certain common normative framework:

> We are the children of our Judeo-Christian culture, and we know that this culture, which recommends loyalty toward the state, commands us to bend our knees only before God. We know, therefore, that we should put faithfulness to truth above participation in power. ... We reject the belief in political Utopia. We know that our future is an imperfect society, a society of ordinary people and ordinary conflicts – but precisely for this reason, a society that must not renounce its ethical norms in the name of political illusions.[88]

---

87 Adam Michnik, 'After the Revolution', *New Republic* (18 April 1993), reprinted in *Letters from Freedom*, ed. Irena Grudzińska Gross, trans. Jane Cave (Los Angeles, CA: University of California Press, 1998), 155.

88 Ibid.

Thinking dangerously

All this was further complicated by the question of the relationship to the former communist elites and common party members. Many leading dissidents opted for what was called in the Polish context the 'thick line', i.e. the regime change marked a caesura and they thereby considered the former communists to be legitimate members of the pluralist political framework, provided that they accepted this democratic framework themselves. This was also connected to the changing assessment of the main source of potential threat against the democratic order after 1990, especially in the context of the radical nationalist upsurge in Yugoslavia. As Michnik himself warned:

> Among the many traps lying in wait, nationalist conflict is especially dangerous. It is easy to see Yugoslavia, with its proliferating internal conflicts, as a post-totalitarian Central Europe in miniature. This European mosaic of nationalities could be swept by a conflagration of border conflicts. These are unhappy nations, nations that have lived for years in bondage and humiliation. Complexes and resentments can easily explode. Hatred breeds hatred, force breeds force. And that way lies the path of the Balkanization of our 'native Europe'.[89]

From this perspective, post-communist technocrats, interested as they were in the rule of law and the swift economic and institutional integration of their countries into the Western frameworks, seemed to pose less danger than some of the anti-communists whose main motivation behind the rejection of communist rule was their conviction that communists were 'alien' to the body of the nation.

These ambiguities also contributed to the politicization of the memory of the communist past: both its former opponents and supporters 'remembered' the workings of the system and their own role within it in a variety of ways. Former reform communists now had the choice between identifying themselves with the communist regime – for being at least partly emancipatory – and rejecting it completely. The second option implied refashioning themselves as clandestine revolutionaries who from the very beginning fought to undermine the regime 'from within' – a discursive strategy chosen for instance by some Baltic, Hungarian and Yugoslav former communist cadres. Simultaneously, the leading dissidents of the 1970s and 1980s, who were usually members of the intellectual elite before they came to clash with the regime, were often accused by the newly emerging radical anti-communists (many of whom were rather apolitical before 1989 or came from the 'second echelon' of the opposition movements of the late 1980s) of being the very products of the regime they repudiated, thus denying their moral legitimacy. All this was aggravated by the dual totalitarian heritage of most of these societies which made the categories of collaboration, freedom fight or liberation, extremely contested and often resulted in an unsavoury competition between competing victimologies.

Such conflicts were skilfully exploited by neo-conservative populists to create an alternative memory culture with an anti-elitist thrust. Focusing on the heroic anti-communist resistance of the 'people' in general, they relieved members of society from engaging in the more painstaking and self-reflective work of coming to terms with their often-ambiguous relationship with communist power (and often also the previous right-wing authoritarian regimes). Rather than pondering on complex processes of co-opting and the grey zones, which would have hardly fit the dichotomy between authentic and inauthentic existence, the real and virtual 'greengrocers'

---

89 Adam Michnik, 'Notes from the Revolution', *New York Times* (11 March 1990), reprinted in *Letters from Freedom*, 150.

Identity politics: between national essentialism and critical traditions

could now publicly consider themselves as victims of history while continuing to praise in private the 'good old times' when the state provided for 'everything'.

Identity politics: between national essentialism and critical traditions

Throughout the nineteenth and twentieth centuries, East Central Europe was a region of chronic political, social and territorial instability. It is therefore unsurprising that questions of collective identity have been at the very centre of political discussions. The key theme of these discussions concerned the spatial and temporal place of the given nation in a European or global framework of developmental hierarchies. Significantly, these debates were two-sided: one encounters both hypertrophic texts of identity built on essentialist theories of a national mission as well as deconstructions of these theories in the form of critical discourses of identity.

A central feature of these discourses of identity was the double-bind of *critique* and *crisis*. In Reinhart Koselleck's memorable interpretation – developed mainly on the example of the French Enlightenment and in many ways inspired by Carl Schmitt – the language of crisis was an instrument used by a new social group disentangled from the traditional estates society to assert its symbolic position and thus eventually to reconfigure power relations.[90] It would be reductionist to analyze the East Central European crisis discourses based solely on this model; nevertheless, there seems to be a powerful link between these two core concepts also in the case of political discourses stemming from this region.

East Central European crisis discourses may have become especially prevalent in the interwar years, but they clearly did not appear from nowhere: they in fact had strong links to the critical discourses of the nineteenth century. From the 1860s onwards, these discourses were usually linked to the positivist episteme, and they challenged national romanticism as a *cul-de-sac* of national cultural and political development. Critical voices, such as the *Junimists* or the Cracow Positivists, accused the romantic generation of having pursued superficial Westernization instead of organic progress. A key element here was the problematization of the 'primitive democracy' discourse of the romantic liberal nationalists which linked the pre-modern self-governing structures to modern liberal institutions and thus articulated an elliptic model that reached from archaism to modernity. In contrast, the linearist–organicist model of the positivist critics was based on consecutive legal and socio-economic stages, making it impossible to believe in a jump like the one advocated by the romantics.

There was another, potentially darker, side of this critical discourse which focused on the detrimental effects of importing ideas and institutions. From an organicist perspective, it was neither possible nor desirable to introduce the structures of modernity from above. This critical motif would at times be ethnicized: rejecting 'foreign' ideas and institutions could easily accommodate a polemic against those inorganic (alien or 'alienated') members of the society who mediated these values. The locus of the crisis discourse in this framework was the temporal gap between 'not any more' and 'not yet': the society lost its pre-modern bonds of solidarity (which were seen as rough and often downright oppressive but still creating a certain societal cohesion) without reaching the 'safe haven' of bourgeois modernity. This perception of an abyss, which could only be bridged by a radical change in elite thinking, became a recurrent trope of East Central European political and cultural thought throughout the twentieth century.

---

90 Reinhart Koselleck, *Critique and Crisis: Enlightenment and the Pathogenesis of Modern Society* (Cambridge, MA: MIT Press, 1988). The first German edition is from 1959.

Thinking dangerously

Moreover, at the turn of the century we see yet another clash, this time between the positivist episteme linked to the bourgeois lifestyle and a neo-Romantic stream, which was often championed by young intellectuals with a bourgeois background, turning against their 'fathers' word'. This conflict had many variants but what was common to them was the problematization of linear models of historical development and a new sensitivity toward the irrational and heroic, often encapsulated in discourses of crisis and decadence. However, in various cultures the logic and temporality of this clash was different. For instance, in Polish political culture it implied a revolt against the dominance of the positivist historical and aesthetic narratives; while in Hungary, the *fin-de-siècle* post-positivist generation revolted chiefly against the dominance of 'national classicism', combining a rationalist analytical language with a preference for modernist aesthetic streams, such as symbolism. It is also important to bear in mind that various ideological subcultures mixed these post-Romantic and post-positivist elements in different ways and there were also interesting common references – such as the discourse of decadence – shared by thinkers representing radically divergent political positions.

Hence, the crisis discourse emerging at the turn of the century had many faces and could be instrumentalized by the Right as well as the Left. The neo-conservative projects seeking to create an organic modernity were often genealogically linked to positivist critical discourses even though their aims were rather different. For instance, the Romanian social-political thinker Constantin Rădulescu-Motru and the Hungarian historian Gyula Szekfű both fused a *Völkerpsychologie*-inspired characterological discourse with a local version of the *Sonderweg* theory. The key elements of their discourse were the criticism of liberal voluntarism, the rise of an alienated political class which had lost touch with 'reality', the concomitant collapse of social coherence, and last but not least, the rise of an 'inorganic' bourgeoisie signalling dissolution in ethnic terms. These elements may not have been so different from key elements of the positivist critique, however, their temporal horizons varied. In contrast to the 'linearist' historical vision of the positivists, the early twentieth-century neo-conservatives suggested that the way to remedy the distorted national character was by turning back to a pre-existing configuration that had been marginalized by the self-deluding and self-destructive liberal mainstream.

Having studied in Leipzig, Rădulescu-Motru was influenced mainly by Wilhelm Wundt's vision of *Völkerpsychologie*. His breakthrough in political pamphleteering was his book, *Romanian Culture and Politicking*, published in 1904,[91] which was a sweeping criticism of the political infrastructure of his country in view of its distorted adaptation to Western moral and institutional patterns. In contrast to Western social cohesion, he asserted that in the East, the concepts and institutions of Western political reality (parliament, democracy, popular vote, etc.) were merely borrowed, and served to mask the existing attitudes of egotism and undermine any societal coherence. According to Rădulescu-Motru, Romanian society existed in a state of archaism up to the early nineteenth century, and the ancestral culture accomplished its final aim in 1859 with the emergence of a unified Romanian state. This framework, however, was being destroyed by *politicianism* (taken from the French term *politicisme*), the pointless fight of political factions, using the subterfuge of modern institutions but essentially following their barbarian and antisocial instincts of self-gratification. This criticism of the superficial and insufficient modes of Westernization, however, did not mean rejecting the very aim of adapting to Western culture. By analyzing the question of developing an authentic culture in terms of the Wundtian duality of institutions and ethnocultural predispositions, Rădulescu-Motru's normative model

---

91 Constantin Rădulescu-Motru, 'Cultura română şi politicianismul' [Romanian culture and politicking] (1904), in *Scrieri politice*, ed. Cristian Preda (Bucharest: Nemira, 1998), 65–183.

remained the Western nation-building process which he linked to the ideal of racial and socio-economic unity.

Gyula Szekfű began his career with a resounding attack on the romantic nationalist tradition (*Rákóczi in Exile*, 1913), but his main works written in the interwar period took a more forgiving stance towards 'political romanticism'. After 1918–19, Szekfű's context was dramatically transformed; he did not reflect on the relative failure of liberal modernization like Rădulescu-Motru, but instead on the catastrophic collapse of historical Hungary and the experience of the two revolutions. His key work from the period titled *Three Generations* (the first edition came out in 1920; the expanded edition, in 1934) sought to link the crisis discourse to a generational perspective and the rhetoric of national characterology. The book is an analysis of the supposed shift from the revivalist political programme of the 1830s–40s that was still rooted in 'authentic' national identity, to the 'self-indulgent' liberal discourse of the second half of the nineteenth century, which reached its final phase of dissolution in the early twentieth century.[92]

The First World War and the propaganda campaigns around it turned such national character discourses into major legitimizing tools all over the region. As such, they were in dialogue with and often directly integrated into the 'grand narratives' of war aims formulated outside of the region – German *Kultur*, the entente civilizational discourse and, finally, the Wilsonian vision of self-determination. References to a normative national character had strong resonance all around, but especially in those cases where the very existence of the nation state had been a central bone of contention. As a result, various approaches were devised: from scientific self-documentation in a descriptive mode (especially in anthropogeography, but also ethnography, sociology, etc.) to more essayistic works describing the 'national mentality' based on subjective observations (the latter was often done from the position of an 'educated' officer watching the peasant soldiers representing different regional types within the national community).

Defining the national body became a central issue for intellectuals linked to political elites, especially towards the end of the Great War and during the peace negotiations. In this context, the crisis of the war and the immediate post-war period was often conceived of as crucial for transformation, a 'now or never' moment through which the nation could achieve its regeneration – or be doomed. This became all the more imperative in the negotiation about the future borders of the emerging nation states as the growing disenchantment with inflated statistics exposed the need for seemingly more reliable cultural-anthropological arguments.[93]

One of the outcomes of this conjuncture was the boom of the curious genre of national metaphysics in East Central Europe and beyond. The intellectual ambition of nationalizing philosophy had nineteenth-century antecedents in the region, being present in the para-Hegelian speculations on the itinerary of the absolute spirit that eventually reached the Slavs and achieved new impetus in the first half of the twentieth century. In addition to the romantic inspiration, it also employed the positivist method of building 'national sciences' from folklore to anthropometrics. However, the shift in the late 1910s towards a more deductive, metaphysical modality was fostered by the growing disaffection with positivist inductive methods of describing the nation. The inductive approach proved increasingly counter-productive as the symbolic unity of the nation was threatened by observations which tended to prioritize local variations. As a

---

92 Gyula Szekfű, *Három nemzedék és ami utána következik* [Three generations and what followed] (Budapest: ÁKV-Maecenas, 1989), 295.
93 Glenda Sluga, *The Nation, Psychology, and International Politics, 1870–1919* (Basingstoke: Palgrave Macmillan, 2006).

Thinking dangerously

result, there emerged a demand for an 'ontological turn', which would be able to establish the underlying unity beyond the seeming multiplicity of forms.

A case in point is the Lithuanian philosopher Stasys Šalkauskis who developed an idiosyncratic discourse on national specificity which nonetheless came to inspire an entire cohort of young intellectuals in the interwar period. Influenced by French and Russian intellectual streams alike, Šalkauskis considered it the mission of his nation to create a synthesis between Western and Eastern spirituality. However, similar to the liberal constructions of national psychology at the turn of the century, for which the work of the Romanian Dumitru Drăghicescu might stand as an example, Šalkauskis also argued that the main character trait of his nation was its plasticity and ability to assimilate influences of different cultural provenance. One could say that, according to him, Lithuanians lacked a fixed character and they were thus especially prone to pursue such a new synthesis.

In the interwar period, as the above-mentioned book by Szekfű also indicates, the crisis discourse and the search for a new civilizational synthesis was closely intertwined with the debate on the conflict of generations. The generational issue already had an upsurge at the turn of the century in Western Europe too, as is attested by the famous 'Agathon report' from 1912, by Gabriel Tarde and Henri Massis, or in the ideology of the different German and Austrian *Jugendbewegungen* ('Youth movements'). This discourse had a particularly strong resonance in contexts where the modernist cultural movement overlapped with a palingenetic nationalist ideology, such as the case of the Czech *Omladina* ('Youth'), *Mlada Bosna* ('Young Bosnia'), *Mlada Hrvatska* ('Young Croatia'), or the Transylvanian Romanian 'tineri oțeliți' ('Steely youth'). By the early twenties, such generational mobilization had been reinforced by the common experience of the war, and consequently a huge variety of political projects framed themselves in categories of a generational ideology. There was a considerable discursive similarity between statements stemming from seemingly diametrically opposed ideological camps and often there was a conscious effort to go beyond previous divisions. One can identify roughly three waves – the early 1920s, the late 1920s to the early 1930s, and the late 1930s – marked by different experiences and ideological affinities. The first generational discourse usually had the war experience and the social radicalization after the war at its centre, the second was mainly concerned with the collapse of previous ideological alternatives and the search for a new matrix, while the last one was already reacting to the emergence of leftist and rightist totalitarian regimes.

A paradigmatic case for the merging of cultural, political and generational crisis discourses is the above-mentioned Romanian 'Young generation' or 'Generation of 1927', which brought together a plethora of highly original young intellectuals who later had a formative impact on their national culture and beyond.[94] The first articulation of their ideology is usually considered to be Mircea Eliade's *Spiritual Itinerary* from 1927.[95] Eliade defined the agenda of the new post-war generation as the search for spiritual experience, stressing the openness of his generation toward a new orientation. The crisis he detected at this point was existential rather

---

94 Matei Călinescu, 'The 1927 Generation in Romania: Friendships and Ideological Choices (Mihail Sebastian, Mircea Eliade, Nae Ionescu, Eugène Ionesco, E. M. Cioran)', *East European Politics and Societies* 15, no. 3 (2001): 649–77. On the politicization of the generational discourse see Leon Volovici, *Nationalist Ideology and Anti-Semitism: The Case of Romanian Intellectuals in the 1930s* (Oxford: Pergamon Press, 1991).

95 Mircea Eliade, *Itinerariu spiritual. Scrieri de tinerete* [Spiritual itinerary: youthful writings], ed. Mircea Handoca (Bucharest: Humanitas, 2003). On Eliade's intellectual career see Florin Țurcanu, *Mircea Eliade: Le prisonnier de l'histoire* (Paris: La Découverte, 2003).

119

than political. However, his texts from the early 1930s already framed the crisis related to the very nature of modern European culture – which, being based on historicism, had supposedly lost touch with its spiritual origins – in meta-political terms. Eliade took a Nietzschean stance: not only did the sense of historicity contain the seeds of its own negation but it was already a sign of the agony of culture. 'Whatever will happen after the cataclysm-to-come, the forms of European life and thought, created by the Renaissance and the industrial and social revolutions that followed it, will be definitely buried and surpassed.'[96] In the second half of the 1930s, he became increasingly convinced that the crisis of historicism meant a 'monumental chance' for peoples without a glorious history: 'symbols are present, beside other original phenomena, and are expressed, sometimes even more neatly and richly, in zones without history, but with lots of prehistory'.[97]

Eliade became ever more passionate about the theme of linking the ahistoricism of Romanian ethnicity to the vision of a supra-historical mission. In a paradigmatic article, titled 'Romania in Eternity', he stressed that only the presence of eternity can overcome corrupted politics.[98] Jumping beyond history required a frenetic belief and a total identification with the programme of national regeneration. Eventually, Eliade projected the spiritualist discourse, originally devised as a generational identity programme, onto the Iron Guard.[99] In this framework, the Legionaries became the principal catalysts of a spiritual revolution, while the Romanian mission in Europe was to manifest the primacy of the spiritual, to create the 'new man' uncontaminated by the corrupting influence of historical progress characterizing the West.

A comparable generational project with a diffuse political programme connecting aesthetic modernism and the search for individual self-assertion with national mobilization was *Neoshqiptarizëm* ('neo-Albanianism'). Its main ideologist, Branko Merxhani also started with the assertion of a crisis in Albanian society that rendered it unable to go beyond the feudal stage. Consequently, he called for releasing the creative energies of the society via a programme of radical modernization. His fascination with elites imposing a full-fledged modernization programme was tempered by his need to distance himself from totalitarian solutions, be it fascism or communism. The model he praised the most and found most suitable for Albania was Mustafa Kemal Atatürk's Turkey, a secular-modernist nation-building programme with some elements of democracy.[100]

The rise of national ontologies was linked to a shift in the image of history as the evolutionist vision gave way to a range of models stressing cyclicality, discontinuity and a return to earlier configurations. A key feature of this new regime of historicity emphasized the rupture of development and the arrival of a liminal period threatening the community with dissolution but also carrying the promise of renovation. The work of yet another member of the Romanian 'Young generation', Mircea Vulcănescu, may illustrate this. As Vulcănescu pointed out in 1937, reality was at a crossing point between metaphysics and history, and thus the task of the philosopher

---

96 Mircea Eliade, 'Protoistorie sau ev mediu' [Proto-history or middle ages], in *Fragmentarium* (Bucharest: Humanitas, 1994), 41.

97 Eliade, 'Protoistorie', 45–6.

98 Mircea Eliade, 'România în eternitate' [Romania in eternity] (1935), in *Textele 'legionare' şi despre 'românism'*, ed. Mircea Handoca (Cluj-Napoca: Dacia, 2001), 138–40.

99 Mircea Eliade, 'Ion Moţa şi Vasile Marin' [Ion Moţa and Vasile Marin] (1937), in *Textele 'legionare' şi despre 'românism'*, 36–8.

100 Branko Merxhani, *Formula të neo-shqiptarismës* [The formula of neo-Albanianism] (Tirana: Apollonia, 1996).

Thinking dangerously

was to create the image of the Romanians of all times.[101] From a phenomenological point of view the nation exists in a supra-historic sphere because the historicity of the national character is not evolutionary, but relates to cognition, or recognition – a kind of collective anamnesis that realizes the hidden potential of the nation in temporal self-projection. Hence, national regeneration is to be based on the return to these metaphysical roots of national existence. The specifically Romanian perspective of the world was rooted in the sentiment of universal connection of entities and the dynamic plurality of modes of existence – not an existential rupture between positive reality and unrealized potential but a coexistence of these modalities. For Vulcănescu all this indicated that the Romanians preserved the original, dynamic, meaning of existence, rooted in the notion of 'becoming' ('*devenirea*'), abandoned by the West.

Characterological and *Sonderweg* theories were also present on the left-wing of the political spectrum. For such authors, the normative framework was the Marxist vision of the development of capitalism, which they localized in the Western European trajectory. By comparison, they considered their own social conditions not only on a lower developmental stage, but also 'distorted'. A key issue here was the survival of feudalism, which under the seemingly bourgeois conditions of production continued to determine both the social and the economic relations of the country. Dobrogeanu-Gherea's above-mentioned concept of 'neo-serfdom' is a case in point: a specific socio-economical and mental configuration occurring in societies where the bourgeois transformation was incomplete and their integration into the world economy was based on extensive agriculture.

In the leftist debates of the first half of the twentieth century the question of the normative image of the community was less crucial, although national character as an explanatory model was also present in Marxist discussions of the time, for instance, in Otto Bauer's highly influential theoretical writings on nationalism. Nonetheless, it was usually considered socially constituted and thus not really a key factor in causal explanations. Such a discourse did not negate the linear developmental model but implied the hope of a more robust modernity that could reshape society, opening the doors to a socialist transformation.

In the relatively liberal atmosphere of Czechoslovakia, for instance, the fusion of generational ideology, crisis discourse and national characterology was inserted into a progressive matrix. In 1924, Ferdinand Peroutka published a paradigmatic essay titled 'What are we like?' with which he launched an intense debate.[102] In this essay, Peroutka criticized the 'official' culture of post-romantic nationalism. He pointed at the romantic implications of the Masarykian conception, describing some of the key tenets of Masaryk's vision as mere mythologemes. The core of Peroutka's argument was the claim that Czech national ideology was chronically lacking creative originality because it was based on hundreds of years of self-defence against foreign influence. He therefore considered the search for the constitutive elements of national character in history as being entirely mistaken, claiming instead that only the present could serve as a source of grasping the 'national essence'. Peroutka's text was thus highly ambiguous – on the one hand, he challenged the official narratives of 'Czechness', while on the other hand, he still devised some kind of a normative identity discourse. This can be considered a typical strategy of many critical intellectuals who sought to undermine the post-romantic tropes and the images of the nation derived from certain metaphysical or biological markers, but also believed in the

---

101 Mircea Vulcănescu, 'Omul românesc' [Romanian man] (1937), in *Către fiinţa spiritualităţii româneşti. Dimensiunea românească a existenţei*, vol. 3, ed. Marin Diaconu (Bucharest: Eminescu, 1996), 116–29.
102 Ferdinand Peroutka, *Jací jsme* [What are we like?] (Prague: Fr. Borový, 1924).

importance of creating a certain characterization of the nation as a regulative idea sustaining the liberal democratic institutional framework.

István Bibó's essays can also be read as an internal polemic with the essentialist streams of national characterology. As a young intellectual, who entered the public sphere in the mid-thirties as a supporter of the populist movement, he was strongly influenced by the post-war crisis discourses and turned to the characterological narrative. The most important motive that prepared the way for Bibó's break with the discourse of 'normative characterology' was his encounter with sociographical literature (especially the writings of his friend, Ferenc Erdei). Bibó described the tradition of 'populist sociography' as the Hungarian version of crisis literature – fusing literature, science and politics. From this perspective, the importance of Erdei's sociographic writings was that they dismissed 'the illusion of peasantry living in an idyllic natural setting, being healthy and a reservoir of forces for the society'.[103] This meant that the peasant culture, as it actually was, could not serve as the normative basis for the reconstruction of the community.

At the root of his redefinition of characterology was Bibó's peculiar conception of 'collective psyche' based on collective experience and not on any pre-existing biological propensity. From his perspective, 'political hysteria' is the avoidance of 'real' problems, offering a 'coherent explanation of the world', something like a *magic* interpretation of politics and therefore a manifestation of 'collective infantilism'. Drawing inspiration from the works of Bibó's teacher in Geneva, Guglielmo Ferrero, Italian anti-fascist historian, for the Hungarian thinker, the counter-concept to hysteria was 'balance' – the 'ordered emotional structure' of the individuals and the community. Its continuous existence 'creates a specific human type who dedicates himself to the preservation of the conventions and traditions of the whole order'.[104] In Bibó's interpretation, as Eastern Europe was lacking proper institutional frameworks, the people (*Volk*) and its specificity became a crucial point of reference in defining the political community below the state frameworks – the guardian of the 'real national essence' in contrast to a supra- or un-national elite. The subversive message of this interpretation was that the core of the ethnonationalist characterology, i.e. the fixation on the *Volk*, was an indicator of the 'distortion' of national development.

Ferrero's ideas also inspired his own nephew, the Croatian political thinker Bogdan Radica, whose work provides yet another example of the democratic use of the crisis discourse in the region.[105] Radica referred to the classical roots of European civilization, which he considered to be a synthesis of Athens, Rome and Christianity. He argued that the contemporary 'chaos of Western thought' was due to its departure from this tradition and he consequently talked about the death of 'old Europe'. At the same time, he vigorously criticized the totalitarian recipes for regeneration. In the spirit of Ferrero, Radica sought a principle of legitimacy that might consolidate the European political system, which he believed was entering a vicious cycle of revolutionary and counter-revolutionary violence. Therefore, Radica's political analysis was equally critical of the fascist and communist regimes and his efforts were directed to finding cultural and ideological resources that might enable the restoration of the liberal democratic political regimes on a 'higher' level.

---

103 István Bibó, 'Erdei Ferenc munkássága a magyar parasztság válságának irodalmában' [The oeuvre of Ferenc Erdei in the literature on the crisis of Hungarian peasantry], in *Válogatott tanulmányok*, vols 1–3, ed. Tibor Huszár (Budapest: Magvető, 1986), 1: 190.

104 István Bibó, 'Az európai egyensúlyról és békéről' [On European balance and peace], in *Válogatott tanulmányok*, 1: 320.

105 Bogdan Radica, *Agonija Europe: razgovori i susreti* [The agony of Europe: conversations and encounters] (Zagreb: Disput, 2006 [1940]).

Thinking dangerously

Although both Radica and Bibó were silenced after the communist takeover (the former emigrated while the latter withdrew from public life), their anti-totalitarian characterological constructions were transmitted to the generations of critical intelligentsia maturing in the 1960s. Bibó's work on the 'meaning of European social development', which he resumed after 1963 (when he was amnestied after six years of imprisonment for his participation in the 1956 revolutionary government), can be considered a bridge between the interwar debates and the critical discourses of the 'democratic opposition' of the 1970s. Likewise, Radica was an important member of the Croatian exile. His memoirs helped to recover the intellectual atmosphere of Croatian democratic cultural and political traditions that offered an alternative to both the communist and fascist narratives. Focusing on the Mediterranean aspects of Croatian culture, he also contributed to the rise of a symbolic geography that rejected Yugoslav communist federalism, but also sought to overwrite the anti-democratic and anti-modern orientation of the Ustasha exile.[106]

Another case of mediation was the oeuvre of Jan Patočka. Importantly, in the late 1930s and early 1940s, influenced by Husserl's interpretation of the philosophical crisis of Europe, Patočka engaged in a critical dialogue with the Masarykian tradition and linked the metaphysical crisis to the crisis of liberal democracy. The Czech émigré philosopher Erazim Kohák summarizes the position Patočka took in these early works: 'The problem is the ontological significance we have attributed to the constructs of our sciences, the solution is to be sought in a radical bracketing that gives us access to the apodictic certainty of primordial, pre-reflective experience.'[107] In 1968, after two decades of social marginalization spent with more technical and historical investigations, Patočka re-emerged as the main non-Marxist philosophical voice in Czechoslovakia. Through revisiting the reasons for the failures of the Czech political community in 1938, 1948 and 1968, he provided an intellectual basis for the criticism of the regime but also for collective self-criticism.[108]

Patočka devised a phenomenological analysis of the Czech political character, contrasting two models of nation-building in modern Czech history: the Jungmannian linguistic nationalism and Bernard Bolzano's political nationalism. A crucial element of his criticism of the post-romantic ethnocultural tradition was the rejection of the myth of continuity, a myth which he linked mainly to the work of Palacký. What he proposed instead was an alternative tradition based on the political understanding of the nation, going back to Bolzano and to be found also in Emanuel Rádl.[109] The conflict between the political vs. ethnocultural conceptions of the nation also had a link to the debates on the German question, which connected the post-war expulsion of the Germans to the collapse of democracy and pointed to the moral distortion of the community.

The essays of the Czech literary scholar Vladimír Macura, who was not part of the dissident milieu but rather belonged to the 'grey zone', represent an alternative take on the romantic heritage. His position was shaped by structuralism and especially semiotics (being a student of Yurii Lotman in Tartu) rather than phenomenology. As a result, he conceived of the cultural-linguistic understanding of the nation as being natural and not pathological. This, however,

---

106 Bogdan Radica, 'Sredozemni povratak' [Mediterranean return] (1971), *Živjeti nedoživjeti*, vols 1–2, (München: Knjižnica Hrvatske revije, 1982–84).

107 Jan Patočka, 'Edmund Husserl's Philosophy of the Crisis of Science and his Conception of a Phenomenology of the "Life-world"', trans. Erazim Kohák, *Husserl Studies* 2, no. 2 (1985): 129–55, here 132.

108 Miloš Havelka, *Dějiny a smysl. Obsahy, akcenty a posuny 'české otázky' 1895–1989* [History and meaning: contents, accents and shifts of the 'Czech Question', 1895–1989] (Prague: Lidové noviny, 2001).

109 Jan Patočka, *Náš národní program* [Our national program] (Prague: Evropský kulturní klub, 1990); idem, *Co jsou Češi?* [What are the Czechs?] (Prague: Panorama, 1992).

does not imply that he held an uncritical stance towards national romanticism. Macura's interpretation was two-fold: on the one hand, he registered the imitative nature of the national revivalist cultural production which sought to create functional equivalents for all genres of Western high culture, often yielding almost parodic results.[110] At the same time, he pointed at the self-critical voices within the very same cultural system who reflected on the artificiality of such cultural efforts. Macura argued that it was exactly this second-level critical position that constituted a fully fledged national culture: acts of self-critical reflection pointing to discontinuities can be retrospectively organized into a continuity of achieving self-consciousness and cultural maturity. In this vision, where self-critical reflection belongs to the core of national culture, one can easily recognize the author's idealized image of the 'critical intellectual'.

Yugoslav (Montenegrin-Hungarian-Jewish) writer and essayist Danilo Kiš articulated another critical take on the national canon during 'late socialism'. His passionate *Anatomical Lesson* (1978) was based on his own experience of 'exclusion', after his magical realist works on the dilemmas of identity under totalitarianism were met by an orchestrated campaign merging apologetic communist and nationalist perspectives. Nationalism for Kiš was the product of the loss of individual orientation, an ideology of banality purportedly conferring meaning on human actions but eventually trapping the individual at an impasse. Nationalist culture, even though it claims to be the result of a sacrificial self-abnegation of the artist, amounts to kitsch. Nationalism is the 'negative category of the soul' rooted in the negation of culture, thinking, and eventually the very presence of another nationality.[111] Detecting the merger of communist orthodoxy, social conservatism and ethnic nationalism, this passionate text pointed to the deep crisis of Yugoslav identity and to a certain extent anticipated the political and ideological implosion of the 1990s.

While the political context and intellectual roots of Bibó, Patočka, Macura and Kiš were markedly different, what is common in their perspective is their critical stance toward the instrumentalization of national romantic identity narratives and by implication the communist use of ethnocultural nationalism. What they proposed instead is a 'healthier' form of national consciousness based on critical self-reflection. At the same time, many intellectuals in the 'grey zone' opted for a more emphatically nationalist position, entering into a dialogue with the national communist ideology and often relaunching the Westernist-autochthonist debates of the interwar period.

A paradigmatic case of the ideological transfer between interwar national metaphysics and national communism is the philosophical oeuvre of the Romanian Constantin Noica, a close friend of Eliade, Cioran and Vulcănescu. Marginalized as a former extreme rightist after the Second World War and imprisoned in 1958 as a result of the campaign against the 'nationalist intelligentsia', Noica was released from prison in 1964 and was allowed back to the periphery of intellectual life by paying the price of ideological concessions to the regime. By the mid-1970s he was already at the centre of attention with his philosophical essays that returned to the themes of interwar 'national ontologies'. He fused his Heideggerian inspiration with references to the Romanian philosophical tradition, drawing especially on Vulcănescu's ideas, to focus on the metaphysical implications of language and devise a normative discourse on the universal cultural mission of the nation.[112]

---

110 Vladimír Macura, *Znamení zrodu: České obrození jako kulturní typ* [Birthmarks: the Czech revival as a cultural type] (Prague: Československý spisovatel, 1983).

111 Danilo Kiš, *Čas anatomije* [The anatomy lesson], (Belgrade: Nolit, 1978), 29–33.

112 Constantin Noica, *Sentimentul românesc al fiinţei* [The Romanian sense of existence] (Bucharest: Humanitas, 2000 [1978]).

Thinking dangerously

While in purely material terms Romanians might have been backward compared to the West, according to Noica, they had a considerable advantage on the ontological level, because their relationship to Being – which he illustrated with an analysis of the Romanian peasant idiom, the poetry of Mihai Eminescu and the unconventional visual language of the sculptor Constantin Brâncuşi – was much more complex and open-ended than the 'impoverished' occidental understanding. Noica thus projected the interwar contrast between an 'inauthentic' bourgeois West and Eastern European rural archaism onto the clash of the capitalist West and the autarchist Romanian national communist project, envisioning his native country as a potential catalyst of universal regeneration. Such a position could be read as a straightforward legitimization of the Ceauşescu regime just as it was becoming increasingly isolated from the world in its nationalist fervour. However, there is another possible reading of Noica's thought if one tones down the anti-Western implications. This was popularized mainly by the young intellectuals gathering around the philosopher in the 1970s–80s to study and discuss ancient Greek and classical German philosophy.[113] These intellectuals, who after 1989 came to play a major role in the reorganization of cultural life in Romania, asserted that Noica's project aimed at preserving those national and universal cultural values which were threatened by the dogmatic official ideology of Marxism–Leninism and, tactical compromises notwithstanding, it thus deserved to be qualified as 'resistance through culture'.

The central dilemma of identity politics, which occupied both the dissident subcultures and the more mainstream intellectual milieus in the 1980s, concerned the relation of the individual to the national community. The key Polish debate on patriotism went back to the quandaries of the dissidents in the 1970s on whether to instrumentalize or reject the Polish nationalist tradition. In a *longue durée* perspective it referred also to the clashes between the internationalist and national revolutionary wings in the Polish socialist movement at the turn of the century. In his famous essay, Jan Józef Lipski,[114] a literary scholar and former fighter of *Armia Krajowa* ('Home Army'), who was involved in the left wing of the dissident movement, differentiated between a self-centred and an open-minded patriotic attitude: 'Patriotism is not only awe and love for the tradition but rather a selection of elements of this tradition, an obligation of intellectual work in that area.'[115] From this perspective 'critical patriotism' required a willingness to enter into a dialogue with the ethnic and national 'others'. In the Polish case, for Lipski, the most important partners of this dialogue were the Jews and the Eastern neighbours, especially the Ukrainians and the Lithuanians. Similar to the circle around the Paris-based émigré review *Kultura*, edited by Jerzy Giedroyc and Juliusz Mieroszewski, Lipski also stressed that the only way to abolish Soviet domination was through the efforts of oppressed nations, including the Russians, to overcome their historical traumas and dissensions and develop new forms of solidarity.

After 1989 the quest for critical patriotism focused on the question of collective responsibility versus self-victimization, reaching its peak in the debates on the Warsaw Uprising (and its musealization) and the Polish involvement in the Holocaust, triggered especially by Jan Tomasz Gross' book on the Jedwabne mass murder. Similar debates about the pre-communist and communist past erupted in all countries of the region, which tended to be closely related to the

---

113 Gabriel Liiceanu, *The Păltiniş Diary: A Paideic Model in Humanistic Culture* (Budapest: Central European University Press, 2000). The original Romanian edition was published in 1983.

114 Jan Józef Lipski, 'Dwie ojczyzny – dwa patriotyzmy' [Two fatherlands – two patriotisms] (1981), available at http://otwarta.org/wp-content/uploads/2011/11/J-Lipski-Dwie-ojczyzny-dwa-patriotyzmy-lekkie3.pdf (accessed 9 May 2019).

115 Lipski, 'Dwie ojczyzny', 14–15.

legal instruments and institutional structures designated to establish historical justice and document the crimes committed by the communist regime. Contrary to expectations, however, the period after the regime changes did not witness the emergence of a new consensus about the past but rather led to the politicization of recent history and the fragmentation of 'collective memory'.

The transition also led to the reconfiguration of the symbolic geographical imaginary, as the bipolar imaginary of the Cold War, which had been taken for granted even by those who tried to escape its logic, was finally superseded by a more complex and dynamic framework with a plurality of geopolitical centres and (semi-)peripheries.[116] Hence, an important topic for debate concerned the exact relationship between sub-national, national, meso-regional and European identity layers. A central issue here was the uniqueness of the historical experiences and political culture of certain communities. Along these lines, the Romanian historian Lucian Boia's essays after 1989 sought to contextualize the apparent belatedness of his country's transformation in a regional comparison. Boia's work is highly significant because it once again fused the crisis discourse and a critical-deconstructive position with a characterological narrative.[117] Even though his writings on Romanian 'historical myths' have often been perceived as a local variant of the postmodern stream of demythologization, drawing on Eliade, Boia repeatedly stressed that myths formed part of the cognitive framework of the mind, which we cannot simply leave behind, and thus, their historicization could never lead to their destruction. That said, he debunked some of the most commonly shared historical narratives rooted in the national communist indoctrination, starting with the extravagant ethnogenetic theories and including such sensitive questions as the 'collaboration' with the Germans during the First World War, or the 'union of the Romanian provinces' in 1918.

The matrix of critique, crisis and characterology, which emerged at the beginning of the twentieth century, thus continues to impact the East Central European discourses of collective identity. Moreover, it still transcends the actual political and ideological divisions and it is also impossible to describe it in terms of a duality of pro-Western and anti-Western streams because Western references could appear in very different contexts (e.g. in certain moments a fascist position could also be framed as pro-Western). However, one can still identify competing discursive traditions. According to the (post-)romantic model of identity discourse, the crisis of orientation can be resolved by the demiurgic intellectual who extracts the hidden potentiality of the national character from the depth of the national soul (folklore, language, etc.) and contrasts it with the actual inauthenticity of the community's existence, thereby mobilizing the creative minority to a self-sacrificial act of collective regeneration. In contrast, the critical model is based on rejecting the myth of continuity and prefers to emphasize the ruptures of the national tradition. While representatives of the latter position were not immune to the dramatizing rhetoric of the *Sonderweg* (i.e. they often presented the path of their nation as highly specific), they tended to reject metaphysical schemes and identified mistaken collective choices as the root of the crisis. Consequently, instead of contrasting 'inauthentic actuality' with 'authentic potentiality' they usually called for a critical engagement with the historical path of their nation. Their diagnosis of a crisis of values and social functions thus implies a need to collectively assume responsibility for the past and the future.

---

116 See Diana Mishkova's contribution to this volume.
117 Lucian Boia, *History and Myth in Romanian Consciousness*, trans. James Christian Brown (Budapest: CEU Press, 2001). The original Romanian edition was published in 1997.

Thinking dangerously

Conclusion

By observing from a distance, one needs to compare the East Central European developments to those of Western Europe and the other European peripheries, such as Southern Europe and Scandinavia or even to non-European political cultures, in order to establish some recurrent themes and debates characteristic for this part of the world. This is not to deny that, one way or another, most of these issues are also present in other regional frameworks. While the focus on the peasantry in the twentieth century emerges as an important feature of East Central European political thought when contrasted with its Western European counterpart, the tropes of 'peasant nation' were equally present in Scandinavia and many political cultures outside Europe, from India to Mexico. Similarly, interwar crisis discourses and constructions of national metaphysics were far from specific to this region as one can find analogous texts from Spain to Japan. The nationalization of communism was another global phenomenon, eminently present in non-European regimes, most conspicuously those of North Korea and China, but also in countries without an 'actually existing socialist' regime, such as Greece or even Iceland.

What might perhaps still be considered a constitutive East Central European feature is the experience of consecutive rightist and leftist authoritarian regimes, which lasted more than 50, and in some cases even more than 70 years, thus leaving permanent marks on the political culture of these countries. At first glance, this experience is far from incomparable with the case of such non-European 'socialist' countries as North Korea, China, Cuba or Ethiopia. However, the dynamic of East Central Europe was markedly different because the local dictatorial regimes were born out of a specific entanglement with an overlap of the Italian/German and Soviet models and corresponding geopolitical zones of influence. Hence, political thinking in East Central Europe has been 'dangerous' in multiple senses: it often meant a desperate search for a way out of the omnipresent authoritarian realities and heritages, scanning and reformulating various local cultural-political traditions to support a project of emancipation. At the same time, one should not forget that as a reaction to the apparently backward social and cultural status of these countries and to the traumas caused by the encounter with the 'other' version of totalitarianism, many intellectuals in the region fell for various totalitarian recipes.

Consequently, it would be difficult to draw an unequivocal moral from the story told above: it is both a story of human resilience and fragility, of emancipation and exclusion; of generous conceptions of multi-ethnic coexistence and equally powerful visions of national homogenization; of ecstatic moments of freedom and deeply ingrained reflexes of collaboration; of carefully engineered agendas of reform and a capacity to adapt to wholly unexpected changes in geopolitical realities; of a sweeping politicization of everyday life and ingenious anti-political practices and doctrines. These are markers of a specific in-betweenness – repeatedly pointed out by various self-reflective political thinkers from Masaryk and Bibó to Kosík and Kiš – not so much in a geographic, but rather, in a moral and existential sense.

In the eyes of many enthusiastic commentators, the 'annus mirabilis' of 1989 was meant to close the geopolitical gap between East Central Europe and 'the West' and thereby offer a way out of these ambiguities. However, the developments following the regime changes, especially the implosion of Yugoslavia and the re-emergence of radical nationalism across the region, served as a premonition to those who hoped to 'erase the past' through a geopolitical re-alignment. Rather than declaratively rejecting or simply ignoring it, the only practicable way to come to terms with the past seems to be to critically engage with it. As this chapter hopefully demonstrates, East Central Europe can boast a powerful stream of such critical engagements. The imperative of contextualization, however, makes it impossible to emulate them uncriti-

127

cally. Nor is it possible to engage with them in the sense of Meinecke's *Gipfelwanderung*, i.e. in terms of an exclusive dialogue with a limited number of 'great minds'. What we may nonetheless learn from the authors discussed above and their works is how to scrutinize the different traditions and intellectual positions in a critical but empathic manner, in order not to take any of the purportedly predetermined past and present trajectories for granted, but to reflect instead on their contingencies, ambiguities and complementarities.

Further reading

Abrams, Bradley F. *The Struggle for the Soul of the Nation: Czech Culture and the Rise of Communism* (Lanham, MD: Rowman & Littlefield, 2004).

Apor, Balázs, Péter Apor, and Edward Arfon Rees, eds. *The Sovietization of Eastern Europe: New Perspectives on the Postwar Period* (Washington, DC: New Academia Publishing, 2008).

Bibó, István. *The Art of Peacemaking: Political Essays by István Bibó*, ed. Zoltán Iván Dénes (New Haven, CT: Yale University Press, 2015).

Biondich, Mark. *Stjepan Radić, the Croat Peasant Party, and the Politics of Mass Mobilization, 1904–1928* (Toronto: University of Toronto Press, 2000).

Boia, Lucian. *History and Myth in Romanian Consciousness*, trans. James Christian Brown (Budapest: CEU Press, 2001).

Bolton, Jonathan. *Worlds of Dissent: Charter 77, the Plastic People of the Universe, and Czech Culture under Communism* (Cambridge, MA: Harvard University Press, 2012).

Bucur, Maria. *Eugenics and Modernization in Interwar Romania* (Pittsburgh, PA: University of Pittsburgh Press, 2002).

Cabada, Ladislav. *Intellectuals and the Communist Idea: The Search for a New Way in Czech Lands from 1890 to 1938* (Lanham, MD: Lexington Books, 2010).

Călinescu, Matei. "The 1927 Generation in Romania: Friendships and Ideological Choices (Mihail Sebastian, Mircea Eliade, Nae Ionescu, Eugène Ionesco, E. M. Cioran)," *East European Politics and Societies* 3 (2001): 649–77.

Čapková, Kateřina. *Czechs, Germans, Jews? National Identity and the Jews of Bohemia* (New York: Berghahn Books, 2012).

Congdon, Lee. *Seeing Red: Hungarian Intellectuals in Exile & the Challenge of Communism* (Chicago, IL: Northern Illinois University Press, 2001).

Cornwall, Mark, and Robert John Weston Evans, eds. *Czechoslovakia in a Nationalist and Fascist Europe, 1918–1948* (Oxford: Oxford University Press, 2007).

Daskalov, Roumen, Tchavdar Marinov, Alexander Vezenkov, and Diana Mishkova. *Entangled Histories of the Balkans*, 4 vols (Leiden: Brill, 2013–17).

Deák, István. *Europe on Trial: The Story of Collaboration, Resistance, and Retribution during World War II* (Boulder, CO: Westview Press, 2015).

Dimou, Augusta. *Entangled Paths towards Modernity* (Budapest: CEU Press, 2009).

Djilas, Milovan. *The New Class: An Analysis of the Communist System* (London: Thames and Hudson, 1957).

Djokić, Dejan. *Elusive Compromise. A History of Interwar Yugoslavia* (London: Columbia University Press, 2007).

Dragović-Soso, Jasna. *Saviours of the Nation? Serbia's Intellectual Opposition and the Rise of Nationalism* (Montreal: McGill-Queen's University Press, 2002).

Ersoy, Ahmet, Maciej Górny, and Vangelis Kechriotis, eds. *Discourses of Collective Identity in Central and Southeast Europe 1770–1945: Texts and Commentaries, vol. 3, Modernism – The Creation of Nation-States* (Budapest: CEU Press, 2010).

Falk, Barbara. *The Dilemmas of Dissidence in East-Central Europe* (Budapest: CEU Press, 2003).

Fehér, Ferenc, Ágnes Heller, and György Márkus. *Dictatorship over Needs: An Analysis of Soviet Societies* (Oxford: Blackwell, 1983).

Feinberg, Melissa. *Elusive Equality: Gender, Citizenship, and the Limits of Democracy in Czechoslovakia, 1918–1950* (Pittsburgh, PA: University of Pittsburgh Press, 2006).

Gal, Susan, and Gail Kligman. *The Politics of Gender after Socialism: A Comparative-Historical Essay* (Princeton, NJ: Princeton University Press, 2000).

Thinking dangerously

Gluck, Mary. *Georg Lukács and His Generation, 1900–1918* (Cambridge, MA: Harvard University Press, 1985).

Górny, Maciej. *The Nation Should Come First. Marxism and Historiography in East Central Europe* (Frankfurt: Peter Lang, 2013).

Havel, Václav. *Open Letters: Selected Writings 1965–1990*, ed. and trans. Paul Wilson (New York: Alfred A. Knopf, 1991).

Havel, Václav. *Summer Meditations on Politics, Morality and Civility in a Time of Transition* (Boston, MA: Faber and Faber, 1992).

Havel, Václav, et al., *The Power of the Powerless: Citizens against the State in Central-Eastern Europe*, ed. John Keane (Armonk, NY: M. E. Sharpe, 1985).

Held, Joseph. *Populism in Eastern Europe: Racism, Nationalism and Society* (Boulder, CO: Columbia University Press, 1996).

Heller, Ágnes, and Ferenc Fehér. *The Postmodern Political Condition* (Cambridge: Polity Press in association with B. Blackwell, 1988).

Janos, Andrew C. *East Central Europe in the Modern World: The Politics of the Borderlands from Pre- to Postcommunism* (Stanford, CA: Stanford University Press, 2000).

Jedlicki, Jerzy. *A Suburb of Europe: Nineteenth-Century Polish Approaches to Western Civilization* (Budapest: CEU Press, 1999).

Jowitt, Kenneth, ed. *Social Change in Romania, 1860–1940: A Debate on Development in a European Nation* (Berkeley, CA: University of California Press, 1978).

Judt, Tony. *Postwar. A History of Europe since 1945* (New York: Penguin, 2005).

Kardelj, Edvard. *Democracy and Socialism* (London: The Summerfield Press, 1978).

Kołakowski, Leszek. *Main Currents of Marxism*, vols 1–3 (Oxford: Clarendon Press, 1978).

Kopeček, Michal, and Piotr Wciślík, eds. *Thinking through Transition: Liberal Democracy, Authoritarian Pasts, and Intellectual History in East Central Europe after 1989* (Budapest: CEU Press, 2015).

Kopecký, Petr, and Cas Mudde, eds. *Uncivil Society? Contentious Politics in Postcommunist Europe* (London: Routledge, 2003).

Kosík, Karel. *The Crisis of Modernity: Essays and Observations from the 1968 Era*, ed. James H. Satterwhite (Lanham, MD: Rowman & Littlefield, 1995).

Krastev, Ivan. *Democracy Disrupted. The Politics of Global Protest* (Philadelphia, PA: Penn Press, 2014).

Kubik, Jan. *The Power of Symbols against the Symbol of Power. The Rise of Solidarity and the Fall of State Socialism in Poland* (University Park, PA: Pennsylvania State University Press, 1994).

Lampe, John R., and Mark Mazower, eds. *Ideologies and National Identities: The Case of Twentieth-Century Southeastern Europe* (Budapest and New York: CEU Press, 2004).

Lilly, Carol S. *Power and Persuasion: Ideology and Rhetoric in Communist Yugoslavia 1944–1953* (Boulder, CO: Westview Press, 2001).

Lindheim, Ralph, and George S. N. Luckyj, eds. *Towards an Intellectual History of Ukraine: An Anthology of Ukrainian Thought from 1710 to 1945* (Toronto: University of Toronto Press, 1996).

Litván, György. *A Twentieth-century Prophet: Oscar Jászi, 1875–1957* (Budapest: CEU Press, 2006).

Livezeanu, Irina. *Cultural Politics in Greater Romania: Regionalism, Nation Building and Ethnic Struggle, 1918–1930* (Ithaca, NY: Cornell University Press, 1995).

Livezeanu, Irina, and Arpad von Klimo, eds. *The Routledge History of East Central Europe since 1700* (London: Routledge, 2017).

Mark, James. *The Unfinished Revolution: Making Sense of the Communist Past in Central-Eastern Europe* (New Haven, CT: Yale University Press, 2010).

Michnik, Adam. *Letters from Freedom*, ed. Irena Grudzinska Gross, trans. Jane Cave (Los Angeles, CA: University of California Press, 1998).

Michnik, Adam. *Letters from Prison and Other Essays*, trans. Maya Latynski (Berkeley, CA: University of California Press, 1985).

Michnik, Adam. *The Church and the Left* (Chicago, IL: University of Chicago Press, 1993).

Miller, Nick. *The Nonconformists: Culture, Politics, and Nationalism in a Serbian Intellectual Circle, 1944–1991* (Budapest and New York: CEU Press, 2007).

Miłosz, Czesław. *The Captive Mind* (London: Secker and Warburg Ltd, 1953).

Milutinović, Zoran. *Getting over Europe: The Construction of Europe in Serbian Culture* (Amsterdam: Rodopi, 2011).

Mishkova, Diana, ed. *We, the People. Politics of National Peculiarity in Southeastern Europe* (Budapest: CEU Press, 2008).

Mishkova, Diana, Marius Turda, and Balázs Trencsényi, eds. *Discourses of Collective Identity in Central and Southeast Europe 1770–1945: Texts and Commentaries, vol. 4, Anti-Modernism – Radical Revisions of Collective Identity* (Budapest: CEU Press, 2014).

Motyl, Alexander. *The Turn to the Right: The Ideological Origins and Development of Ukrainian Nationalism, 1919–1929* (New York: Columbia University Press, 1980).

Mudde, Cas, ed. *Racist Extremism in Central and Eastern Europe* (London: Routledge, 2005).

Narkiewicz, Olga A. *The Green Flag. Polish Populist Politics, 1867–1970* (London: Croom Helm, 1976).

Newman, Charles, ed. *A Leszek Kołakowski Reader* (Evanston, IL: Northwestern University, 1971).

Orzoff, Andrea. *Battle for the Castle* (New York: Oxford University Press, 2009).

Patočka, Jan. *Heretical Essays in the Philosophy of History*, trans. Erazim Kohák (Chicago and La Salle, IL: Open Court, 1996).

Perica, Vjekoslav, and Darko Gavrilović, eds. *Political Myths in the Former Yugoslavia and Successor States: A Shared Narrative* (Dordrecht: Republics of Letters, 2011).

Petreu, Marta. *An Infamous Past: E.M. Cioran and the Rise of Fascism in Romania* (Chicago, IL: Ivan R. Dee, 2005).

Plach, Eva. *The Clash of Moral Nations: Cultural Politics in Piłsudski's Poland, 1926–1935* (Athens, OH: Ohio University Press, 2006).

Plamínková, Františka. *The Political Rights of Women in the Czechoslovak Republic* (Prague: Gazette de Prague, 1920).

Pollack, Detlef, and Jan Wielgohs. *Dissent and Opposition in Communist Eastern Europe: Origins of Civil Society and Democratic Transition* (Farnham: Ashgate, 2004).

Popov, Nebojša, ed. *The Road to War in Serbia* (Budapest: CEU Press, 2000).

Porter, Brian. *When Nationalism Began to Hate: Imagining Modern Politics in Nineteenth-Century Poland* (Oxford: Oxford University Press, 2000).

Porter-Szűcs, Brian. *Faith and Fatherland: Catholicism, Modernity, and Poland* (Oxford: Oxford University Press, 2011).

Pynsent, Robert B. *Questions of Identity: Czech and Slovak Ideas of Nationality and Personality* (New York: CEU Press, 1994).

Ramet, Sabrina. *The Radical Right in Central and Eastern Europe since 1989* (University Park, PA: Pennsylvania State University Press, 1999).

Rév, István. *Retroactive Justice: Prehistory of Post-Communism* (Stanford, CA: Stanford University Press, 2005).

Satterwhite, James. *Varieties of Marxist Humanism: Philosophical Revision in Postwar Eastern Europe* (Pittsburgh, PA and London: University of Pittsburgh Press, 1992).

Sher, Gerson S. *Praxis: Marxist Criticism and Dissent in Socialist Yugoslavia* (Bloomington, IN: Indiana University Press, 1977).

Shkandrij, Myroslav. *Modernists, Marxists and the Nation: The Ukrainian Literary Discussion of the 1920s* (Edmonton: Canadian Institute of Ukrainian Studies Press, 1992).

Shore, Marci. *Caviar and Ashes: A Warsaw Generation's Life and Death in Marxism, 1918–1968* (New Haven, CT: Yale University Press, 2006).

Skilling, Gordon H. *Samizdat and an Independent Society in Central and Eastern Europe* (Columbus, OH: Ohio State University Press, 1989).

Staniszkis, Jadwiga. *Poland's Self-limiting Revolution* (Princeton, NJ: Princeton University Press, 1984).

Szacki, Jerzy. *Liberalism after Communism* (Budapest: CEU Press, 1995).

Tischner, Józef. *The Spirit of Solidarity* (New York: Harper & Row, 1984).

Tismăneanu, Vladimir. *Stalinism for All Seasons: A Political History of Romanian Communism* (Berkeley, CA: University of California Press, 2003).

Tismăneanu, Vladimir, and Bogdan Iacob, eds. *The End and the Beginning: The Revolutions of 1989 and the Resurgence of History* (Budapest: CEU Press, 2012).

Trencsényi, Balázs, Maciej Janowski, Mónika Baár, Maria Falina, Michal Kopeček, and Luka Lisjak-Gabirjelčič. *A History of Modern Political Thought in East Central Europe*, vols 1–2 (Oxford: Oxford University Press, 2016, 2018).

Turda, Marius, ed. *The History of East-Central European Eugenics, 1900–1945. Sources and Commentaries* (London: Bloomsbury, 2015).

Verdery, Katherine. *National Ideology under Socialism: Identity and Cultural Politics in Ceauşescu's Romania* (Berkeley, CA: University of California Press, 1991).

Thinking dangerously

Volovici, Leon. *Nationalist Ideology and Anti-Semitism: The Case of Romanian Intellectuals in the 1930s* (Oxford: Pergamon Press, 1991).

Wachtel, Andrew Baruch. *Making a Nation, Breaking a Nation: Literature and Cultural Politics in Yugoslavia* (Stanford, CA: Stanford University Press, 1998).

Walicki, Andrzej. *Stanisław Brzozowski and the Polish Beginnings of 'Western Marxism'* (Oxford: Clarendon Press, 1989).

Wandycz, Piotr S. *The Price of Freedom: A History of East Central Europe from the Middle Ages to the Present*, 2nd ed. (London: Routledge, 2001).

3

A HISTORY OF FICTION IN TWENTIETH-CENTURY CENTRAL AND EASTERN EUROPE

John Neubauer, with Endre Bojtár and Guido Snel[1]

Preliminary reflections

Traditional national histories have become outdated and the very concept of writing a continuous literary history is under fire. How is one to write, then, a literary history of a multilingual and multinational region? The following reflections outline ideas that have shaped this brief history.

For a long time, 'European literature' meant only English, French, Italian and Spanish literature. Central Europe's German literature was added at the end of the eighteenth century and Eastern Europe's Russian literature in the second half of the nineteenth. While the designations 'Scandinavian' and 'Balkan' reasonably cover two of the three remaining areas, the third one, labelled in this project as 'Central and Eastern Europe' remains problematic, for Central and Eastern Europe also covers, as noted, German and Russian literature respectively.

The present chapter covers the rich but geographically and linguistically vague literary region between Central Europe and Eastern Europe. It has profited from the four-volume *History of the Literary Cultures of East-Central Europe* edited by Marcel Cornis-Pope and John Neubauer,[2] but differs from it essentially. In search of cohesion and due to space limitations, we have excluded the Baltic and Balkan states, as well as virtually all poetry and drama. The spatial restriction brings the coverage closer to the former Austro-Hungarian Monarchy, but we retain

---

1 This chapter is chiefly the product of the late John Neubauer (1933–2015). John Neubauer very nearly managed to complete his manuscript prior to his departure and entrusted the remaining work to his colleague Guido Snel. Based on a previous agreement between John and Endre Bojtár, the latter has added three parts to the texts which deal with Jaroslav Hašek, Czesław Miłosz and Péter Nádas.

2 Marcel Cornis-Pope and John Neubauer, eds, *History of the Literary Cultures of East-Central Europe: Junctures and Disjunctures in the 19th and 20th Centuries*, 4 vols (Amsterdam: Benjamins, 2004–2010).

A history of fiction

the term 'East Central Europe' for our region in order to distinguish it from a Vienna-centred or German-speaking Central Europe.

East Central Europe's multilingual and multicultural richness is indicated by the fact that until 2019, 12 out of the 116 literary Nobel Prize winners were born here: Ivo Andrić, Elias Canetti, Günter Grass, Imre Kertész, Czesław Miłosz, Herta Müller, Władysław Stanisław Reymont, Jaroslav Seifert, Henryk Sienkiewicz, Isaac Bashevis Singer, Wisława Szymborska and Olga Tokarczuk; to these we ought to add the Nobel Peace Prize recipient Elie Wiesel. Canetti, Grass and Müller are now regarded as Central-European German writers. As we shall show in the penultimate section, some writers and intellectuals from the region in the 1980s wanted to call the region 'Central Europe', but this desire to move the region to the heart of Europe was resented by representative Russian and Balkan writers and scholars.

Instead of using canonized concepts like modernism and post-modernism, we use headings like 'The Monarchy disintegrates', 'The interwar decades' and 'The Holocaust', but we focus on fiction in each case. Each historical event generated sets of fiction, which we interconnect across languages and nations via narrative perspectives, metaphors and character portrayals. Literary fiction usually reacted later to the events than newspaper articles, diaries, witness accounts, poems and short stories. We shall indicate how fiction about the Wars or the Holocaust shifted as time went on, and how the distance between experience and writing lengthened.

We take a broad cultural and political approach, but repeatedly focus on select geographical sites, just as archaeologists choose a spot to dig down in search of past cultures. As in archaeology, we shall not limit the site to its present official national language but include all the literatures in all languages written there. Hence, we also include select German fiction that was written in the region. The result should be multilingual and transnational *lieux de mémoire*, not only within the region itself, but also based on works written in exile, in Paris, London, Buenos Aires, New York and Toronto.

Urbanization and ruralism 1900–1914

Westward Ho?

In 1889, the young Pole Stanisław Przybyszewski went to study in Berlin. There, he became inspired by Friedrich Nietzsche and a number of Scandinavian artists, and he gathered around him bohemians in the pub 'Zum schwarzen Ferkel'. Looking westwards for inspiration and actually heading for one of the great metropoles was quite typical. The Vienna of Hermann Bahr, Hugo von Hofmannsthal and Sigmund Freud between 1898 and 1909 became the home of Slovene writer Ivan Cankar, though he sarcastically rejected its social and political condition:

> A fat drunken Philistine lies in a naked shirt under the Kahlenberg; drops of sweat on the forehead, drops of sweat under the nose; occasionally, a heavy sigh frees itself from the burned lungs; the eyes are closed; only the right upper eyelid raised itself a bit, and the dull eye in sleep looks tired and imbecile … This is Vienna today.[3]

Next to Vienna, Paris held an attraction for writers and artists of the region which intensified with the rise of Symbolism, Secessionism, Decadence and Naturalism. The Romanian poet Ion

---

3 Ivan Cankar, 'Dunaj poleti' [Vienna in the Summer], *Zbrano delo*, vol. 9, ed. Anton Ocvirk (Ljubljana: Državna založba slovenije, 1970), 267–71, here 267.

Minulescu studied law at the University of Paris between 1900 and 1904, became intensely devoted to Symbolism, and when he returned to Bucharest, he became the colourful bohemian figure to whom the young poets were drawn. The Hungarian poet Endre Ady went to Paris in 1904 and returned there seven more times before 1911; his younger penniless compatriot Lajos Kassák took a vagabond voyage from Budapest to Paris in 1909. The artist Josef Čapek spent a year in Paris, and his brother Karel visited him there for a longer time. Modernism made a deep and lasting impression on both of them.

Such literary itinerants immersed themselves in the latest Western literary and artistic currents and tried to open a window westward upon their return home. Yet, their imported goods underwent profound transformations when confronting not just traditional realism but also powerful currents of nationalism and populism. Returning writers like Ady were deeply impressed by the French symbolists and modernists but their aestheticism and cosmopolitanism could not ignore native nationalist movements. Many of them became national modernists; modernist manifestos like Artur Grado Benko's *Mlada Hrvatska* or Artur Górski's *Młoda Polska* ('Young Croatia' and 'Young Poland' respectively; both published in 1898) spoke of a national type of youth.

Modernist journals

The first Western-inspired modernist journals of the region did promise, however, that only artistic quality would shape their publications. This was the orientation of Prague's *Moderní revue pro literaturu, umění a život* ('Modern review for literature, art and life', 1894–1925), of *Życie* ('Life', 1897–1900) in Cracow and later in Lwów, and of *Nyugat* ('West', 1908–41) of Budapest. The editors of the *Moderní revue*, Arnošt Procházka and Jiří Karásek, declared the journal to be open without bias:

> *Moderní revue* will neither be expressly Symbolist, nor expressly Naturalist, nor Neo-Romantic, nor any of the existing fine-sounding labels. Rather, it will be open to anything modern. *Moderní revue* will translate from foreign literatures artistically highly distinguished authors as yet unknown in our country. *Moderní revue* will treat the questions of modern life in a thoroughly theoretical and scientific way, readily allowing space for the expression of different opinions.[4]

The poet and artist Karel Hlaváček, a key figure in the early years of the journal's publication, openly rejected chauvinism in 1897:

> National chauvinism is quite obviously the work of *coolly calculating minds* and therefore the very assumption that it might have anything to do with the *psyche* does not hold up, even if we were to concede the existence of separate Czech, German or French psyches. But in fact such separate souls do not exist. There is but one soul, and that cannot be divided into pens like a flock of sheep.[5]

---

4 Jiří Karásek ze Lvovic, *Vzpomínky* [Memoirs], eds Gabriela Dupačová and Aleš Zach (Prague: Thyrsus, 1994), 69.

5 Karel Hlaváček, 'Nationalism a Internationalism' [Nationalism and internationalism], *Moderní revue pro literaturu, umění a život* 5 (1897): 110, italics appear in the Czech original.

A history of fiction

Indeed, Procházka and Karásek corresponded with many international artists, and they published works of Stanisław Przybyszewski, who still lived in Berlin and mainly wrote in German. When Przybyszewski was repatriated from Berlin to Cracow and became the editor of *Życie* in 1898, Hlaváček designed its cover,[6] and the two journals began exchanging texts regularly.

Under Przybyszewski's editorship, *Życie* attracted not only prominent Polish writers but also French, Czech and Scandinavian ones. Its artistic director, Stanisław Wyspiański, saw to it that it became richly illustrated with contemporary works. The 10 January 1899 issue published Przybyszewski's essay 'Confiteor', which restated in Polish his theory of the 'naked soul'.

Censorship confiscated several issues of *Życie*, which contributed to the journal's bankruptcy in 1900. The *Moderní revue* lived on until Procházka's death but became increasingly conservative and anti-Semitic both during and after the First World War, losing touch with the new developments.

Nyugat was launched later than *Moderní revue* and *Życie* but was closed down only when the rightist regime withdrew the publication permit after the death of its editor-in-chief Mihály Babits in 1941. The founders, Miksa Fenyő, Ignotus (Hugo Veigelsberg) and Ernő Osvát, gave this journal a Western orientation in response to nationalist trends that accentuated Hungary's Eastern origins. Ignotus's lead article in the first issue used István Széchenyi's book title *Kelet népe* ('People of the East', 1841) to argue 'that the nations of Eastern Europe should preserve their uniqueness while assimilating Western thought and achievement'.[7] The journal criticized the 'National Classicism' of the critics Pál Gyulai, Zsolt Beöthy and János Horváth.

Originally, *Nyugat*'s Western orientation placed regional connections on the backburner. However, the editors published Pável Konstantin's article on the evolution of Romania's language and literature, announcing in a footnote that they planned to print more articles in the future on the literature and culture of the other nationalities, stating 'we live under the same roof'.[8] Most lively was the contact with the Romanian Emil Isac from Cluj. Ignotus wrote a warm open letter to him about the new Hungarian literature,[9] while *Nyugat* printed Isac's plea for a friendly treatment of the Romanian Transylvanians.[10] The following year, the journal printed Isac's farewell to Romania's King Carol,[11] and his somewhat naïve article about peace between Romania and Hungary.[12]

Urban cultures

Literary cafés and cabarets appeared in the decades around 1900 at the centre and the periphery of cities. The cafés provided the literati not only with domestic and international newspapers, but often also with game-, card- and chess rooms. They hosted editorial gatherings and

---

6 Neil Stewart, 'The Cosmopolitanism of *Moderní Revue* (1894–1925)', in Cornis-Pope and Neubauer, *History of the Literary Cultures*, vol. 3, *The Making and Remaking of Literary Institutions*, 63–70, here 66.

7 Ignotus, 'Kelet Népe', *Nyugat* 1, no. 1 (1908): 1–3; József Szili, 'The Uncompromising Standards of *Nyugat* (1908–1941)', in Cornis-Pope and Neubauer, *History of the Literary Cultures*, vol. 3, 70–9, here 71.

8 Pável Konstantin, 'Hatások a román irodalom fejlődésében', *Nyugat* 6, no. 22 (1913): 723–4.

9 Ignotus, 'Az új magyar irodalom: Levél Isac Emilhez' [The new Hungarian literature: Letter to Emil Isac], *Nyugat* 6, no. 6 (1913): 496–8.

10 Emil Isac, 'Új románság' [New Romanianness], *Nyugat* 6, no. 12 (1913): 900–03.

11 Idem, 'Carol: A román király halála alkalmából' [Carol: on the occasion of the death of the Romanian king], *Nyugat* 7, no. 21 (1914): 448–9.

12 Idem, 'A román–magyar béke' [The Romanian-Hungarian peace], *Nyugat* 7, no. 24 (1914): 650–1.

John Neubauer et al.

discussions, while encouraging drinking and occasional debauchery. Ferenc Molnár held them responsible – tongue-in-cheek – for the decline of family life, and their homosociability did indeed lure husbands and fathers away while offering only limited hospitality to women. Only by 1930 did Budapest's Centrál kávéház become a gathering place of women writers as well.

Cafés

The availability of current information turned the literary cafés into modern agoras, where public opinion and judgment were generated and disseminated. Dezső Kosztolányi regarded Budapest as a 'coffee city' (*kávéváros*) where everything beyond 'this wretched life' emerged from the cafés.[13] In Arthur Koestler's eyes, however, the cafés were 'Budapest's literary ghettos'[14] – perhaps because they also hosted so many Jews.

The literary cafés occasioned innumerable anecdotes, melancholy recollections, and even obituaries about headwaiters. In a touching farewell, Ernő Szép remembered how often the headwaiter at the New York Kávéház paid for the coffee that destitute writers could not afford, while Emil Artur Longen recollected that the legendarily blunt headwaiter of Prague's Café Union always warned him when the police were looking for him.[15] František Langer lovingly recalled the small rooms, the special atmosphere and the odd artists and writers of this Café Union,[16] while Zdeněk Kratochvíl made fun of its odd owner.[17] After the war, the 'Narkav' (=*Národní kavárna*, or 'National café') became the gathering place of the leftist avant-garde group Devětsil.[18] Each literary café had its own physical complexion, its luxury or nonchalant disorder, its own clientele with a particular political orientation. The café Casa Capşa in Bucharest was originally associated with avant-garde poet and causeur Ion Minulescu. The Polish café Pod Pikadorem ('Under the sign of the Picador') opened in November 1918, when Poland regained its independence.

Cabarets

The cabarets emerged in Paris in the 1880s and in Berlin with the venue Überbrettl in 1901. The first Polish cabaret, the Zielony Balonik ('Green balloon'; 1905–12), was improvised entertainment by Cracow bohemians, among them the writers Tadeusz Żeleński-Boy and Adolf Nowaczyński, who gathered in the Jama Michalika, or Jan Michalik's den. In Warsaw, Arnold Szyfman founded the artistic and literary cabaret Momus (1908–12). The Czech cabaret turned from light entertainment to intellectual presentations after 1910, staging parodies of theatre classics, political and satirical songs and poetry recitation involving Jaroslav Hašek and Egon Erwin Kisch, as well as a number of actors, singers and designers.[19] The leading Prague cabarets were the Lucerna ('The lantern', 1910–23), the Montmartre (1911–22) and the Kabaret U kuřího oka ('Cabaret at the chicken's eye', 1913–15).

---

13 Dezső Kosztolányi, 'Budapest, a kávéváros' [Budapest, the coffee city], *A Hét* (15 March 1914).

14 Arthur Koestler, *The Invisible Writing* (London: Collins, 1954), 193.

15 Karl-Heinz Jähn, ed., *Das Prager Kaffeehaus: Literarische Tischgesellschaften* (Berlin: Volk und Welt, 1988), 54.

16 Jähn, *Das Prager Kaffeehaus*, 7–30.

17 Ibid., 170–5.

18 Veronika Ambros, 'Prague: Magnetic Fields or the Staging of the Avant-Garde', in Cornis-Pope and Neubauer, *History of the Literary Cultures*, vol. 2 (Amsterdam: Benjamins, 2006), 176–82, here 178–81.

19 Ambros, 'Prague: Magnetic Fields', 179.

A history of fiction

Budapest's first cabaret, the Fővárosi Cabaret Bonbonnière ('Capital Cabaret Bonbonnière') opened on 1 March 1907 with Endre Nagy, a genius of the new genre. The following year, he opened a cabaret under his own name. The key figure on his stage was the *konferanszié*, a master of ceremonies who commented with bitter but engaging irony on the events of the day and announced the next sentimental *kuplé* (an ironic-humorous ditty), or short dialogue. Nagy had studied and worked in Oradea, where he met his lifelong friend Ady, who later wrote poems for Nagy's cabaret, as did Babits, Kosztolányi, Molnár and others. Nagy himself wrote novels, novellas, plays and an autobiographical novel of the genre, *A kabaré*.

Urban spaces: Molnár's *The Paul Street Boys*

The rapid growth of Budapest was a painful process and became the subject of numerous literary works. Gyula Krúdy's short stories often melancholically portrayed Budapest's declining old neighbourhoods, as did Molnár's *The Paul Street Boys* ('*A Pál utcai fiúk*', 1907), a novel about two high school gangs fighting over an area called 'the *grund*', one of the last vacant lots in a lower-middle-class district. The *grund* is the territory of the Paul Street Boys, but their rivals, the Redshirts, want to claim it for themselves since they are not allowed to play ball on their own territory, an island in the botanical gardens. János Boka, the leader of the Paul Street Boys, has a strategy for defending the *grund*, yet when their defence is on the verge of collapse during the crucial battle, little Ernő Nemecsek, the smallest and weakest member, surprisingly captures the great leader of the Redshirts. It is a pyrrhic victory: Nemecsek dies of pneumonia in the days following the battle and the Paul Street Boys are told that a tenement house will be erected on the *grund*.

Both gangs model themselves on the Indian war heroes in Karl May's popular *Winnetou* novels and they also adhere to the nationalist slogans of the day. The Redshirts put their ears to the ground to listen for their enemy, they use wooden weapons for ceremonial purposes and follow the rules of wrestling.[20] Their leader refuses to 'take over the plot when nobody is there' for he wants to fight 'in a proper way'.[21] Their war declaration is coupled with an agreement about the weapons and the modes of fighting. After the battle, the Redshirts visit Nemecsek, who behaved so heroically when he was captured and forced to jump in the lake. Furthermore, the gang war also reveals disconcerting political attitudes. When a Redshirt declares that they want to own a football field, the narrator adds that

> their motives for war were exactly the same as those which make real soldiers fight. The Russians needed the sea space, so they waged war against the Japanese. The Redshirts needed a football pitch and having no other alternative, set out to acquire it by war.[22]

On the contrary, the cheer, 'Hurrah for the grund!' sounded like 'Long live our Fatherland!'[23]

Molnár hints at class differences by assigning the Paul Street Boys to a classical gymnasium and the Redshirts to a lower 'real-gymnasium',[24] and by reporting that a callous rich customer

---

20 Ferenc Molnár, *The Paul Street Boys*, trans. Louis Rittenberg (Budapest: Corvina, 2010), 139.
21 Ibid., 55.
22 Ibid., 57.
23 Ibid., 37.
24 Ibid., 126.

insisted that Nemecsek's father quickly deliver his suit though he was aware that the child was dying. It remains unclear whether Nemecsek is a loner because of his physical weakness, his lower social standing or his ethnic background.

Ruralism and populism

While the emerging urban literature of the region was largely cosmopolitan and Western, literature from and about the countryside was ethnically and nationally oriented. The spectrum of rural culture was broad. In music, for instance, the nineteenth-century nationalist current in reviving folk songs, folk music and folk culture took new directions in the early twentieth century when composers like Leoš Janáček, Béla Bartók and Zoltán Kodály rejected 'inauthentic' folk music and unearthed deeper layers. Bartók came to learn that folk music was transnational rather than national.

Fiction about the poor peasants and their culture flourished in the whole region in the pre-war years. Most famous at the time was Władysław Stanisław Reymont's four-volume *Chłopi* ('The peasants', 1904–9), which won the author the Nobel Prize in 1924. In *The History of Polish Literature*, Czesław Miłosz writes that the early years of the twentieth century were a time of the *chłopomania* ('peasant mania') with political undertones. The village signified the untapped resources of the nation. What the intelligentsia lacked, it recognized in the illiterates or half-literates that were unspoiled by cultural decadence.[25] Reymont idealized the elementary power of the peasants, including their ability to feast and drink, and he devoted long passages to nature and work in the fields.

Octavian Goga, an influential Romanian populist and anti-Semitic writer and politician, had studied in Hungary and spoke the language well. When he was jailed for two months in 1912 for nationalist agitation, Ady defended him in a newspaper article. They met the following year, and Ady introduced Goga to some of the contributors to *Nyugat*. When a Hungarian minister declared that the state would only tolerate Hungarian culture,[26] Goga responded ironically claiming that in Hungarian literature, the dying race of Hungarians had been replaced by Jews. Cabarets, and the 'jargon of the [Jewish] Dohány street obscenities' dominated the nights in contemporary Budapest. After Sándor Petőfi and János Arany, Goga contended, Hungarian national poetry yielded to the more popular Jewish literature of Budapest.[27] Ady replied that Goga spoke out of envy, for Hungary 'had lived its life always a bit with Europe', and Jewish-Hungarian literature was part of this.[28]

In 1914, Goga moved to Bucharest, agitated for Transylvania's transference to Romania and enlisted in the Romanian army. Since he was a citizen of the Monarchy, he was condemned to death for this in absentia. In his 1915 open letter to Goga in the journal *Világ* ('World'), Ady admitted that the Romanians faced a dilemma, but he disagreed with the response that Goga and the 'old romantics' gave. Goga did not respond, but his journal sent an open letter to *Világ*. After the war and Ady's death, Goga bought Ady's castle in Csucsa (Transylvania), translated some of Ady's poems into Romanian and embarked on a chauvinistic and anti-Semitic political

---

25 Czesław Miłosz, *The History of Polish Literature*, 2nd ed. (Berkeley, CA: University of California Press, 1983), 370.

26 Endre Ady, *Összes prózai művei* [Complete prose works], vol. 11 (Budapest: Akadémiai Könyvkiadó, 1982), 198.

27 Ibid., 205–7.

28 Ibid., 17–19.

A history of fiction

career. Jews were stripped of their Romanian citizenship during his two-months Romanian Prime-Ministership in 1937–8.

The Monarchy disintegrates

Writers and writing in wartime

Until recently, studies of the First World War in literature have covered only a single nation while transnational approaches tended to neglect Eastern Europe. New transnational approaches to the War have been explored in Margaret Higonnet's anthology of European women writers and Geert Buelens's anthology and study of European poetry.[29] Yet comprehensive studies of war fiction are still urgently needed: Ernst Jünger, Ernest Hemingway or Erich Maria Remarque's canonized Western novels do not thematize the disintegration of countries or the existential agony that soldiers experienced when forced to fight, often against their own people.

Slavic and Romanian writers automatically became suspects when the war broke out; many of them were arrested or drafted. Ivan Cankar was interned for two months in the Ljubljana Castle without concrete charges. Ivo Andrić was arrested in Belgrade, while his countryman Miloš Crnjanski served two years on the Galician front until he was hospitalized. Jaroslav Hašek, Janko Jesenký, and other Czech and Slovak writers deserted the Austro-Hungarian Monarchy's army and joined the Czecho-Slovak Legion (*Družina*) on the Russian side.

The Croatian Miroslav Krleža and the Romanian Liviu Rebreanu present more complex cases: both attended The Royal Hungarian Ludovica Defense Academy in Budapest. Krleža was enrolled in a preparatory military school in Pécs before he went to Ludovica. During the Balkan War of 1912, he volunteered for the Serbian army but was rejected as they suspected him of being a spy. He then served as a non-commissioned officer in the Royal Croatian Home Guard belonging to Croatia-Slavonia, then part of the Austro-Hungarian Monarchy. He developed tuberculosis in 1916, recovered, was sent to Galicia, fell ill again, and was finally allowed to get treatment in Budapest. Rebreanu, born in Transylvania, attended the Ludoviceum from 1903 to 1906 and then served as a lieutenant until 1908. He started his literary career writing in Hungarian but was soon falsely charged with embezzling military funds and publishing anti-Hungarian articles in Romanian. He resigned and illegally crossed the border to Romania. He volunteered for the Romanian army when the war broke out but was rejected for having been born in Transylvania. He was arrested as a Hungarian deserter in 1918 but managed to escape. The texts discussed in the following section reveal such divided loyalties and existential agonies, yet all fiction by such 'nationality' writers rejected the war, hoping that the Monarchy's disintegration would lead to the independence of their country.

As members of the Monarchy's junior partner, Hungarian writers had mixed feelings about supporting the Austrians, but they also remembered that the Russians had a decisive role in suppressing the Hungarian revolution in 1849. According to Ignotus, it was preferable to live in Austro-Hungary than in a decimated independent Hungary.[30] Accordingly, *Nyugat* first tried to balance pro- and anti-war publications, though by 'West' the editors meant France and England rather than Germany.[31] Béla Balázs and Ferenc Molnár wrote patriotic war diaries and

---

29 See Margaret R. Higgonet, ed., *Lines of Fire: Women Writers of World War I* (New York: Penguin Plume, 1999); Geert Buelens, *Europa Europa! Over de dichters van de Grote Oorlog* (Amsterdam: Ambo/Manteau, 2008).

30 Ignotus, 'Háború' [War], *Nyugat* 7, no. 15 (1914): 129–32.

31 Szili, 'The Uncompromising Standards of Nyugat', 73–5.

notebooks, but Ady painfully agonized at home about his inability to share the war enthusiasm: 'and yet, and yet, and yet … I am not allowed to join you, believers'.[32] The other great contributor to *Nyugat*, Mihály Babits, lost his teaching job when his lyrical 'I' ended a love poem with the words that he would prefer shedding 'gurgling blood' for the little finger of his beloved 'than for a hundred kings and banners'.[33] His poem 'Húsvét előtt' ('Before Easter') miraculously slipped through censorship, though it echoed Ady's repetition: 'enough, enough, enough: let there be peace!'[34] However, the March 1917 *Nyugat* issue was confiscated because of his poem 'Fortissimo' (which was reprinted in 1918 in issue 23). Babits's poems, as well as the following stories by Margit Kaffka and Zsigmond Móricz, oppose the war for social and personal reasons rather than political concerns.

Kaffka's 'Az első stációnál' ('At the first station', 1916) shows how the war sharpens class differences. Protagonists Feri and Jóska share in their war miseries until both are wounded while retreating. Jóska's minor wound kindles his hope of being sent home, for he comes from a rich family. Feri on the other hand, a poor schmuck, becomes severely ill, and Jóska no longer responds to him: injuries on the front serve to extinguish the camaraderie that once allowed them to temporarily bridge their class differences. Arguably, social injustice rather than the war itself is the primary subject here.

Móricz's 'Szegény emberek' ('Poor folk', 1916) shows how the war brutalizes the poor. When a soldier on furlough discovers that he is unable to feed his family and repay his wife's debts, he breaks into a wealthy person's house and kills a young girl and her babysitter. Within hours, he is arrested. The story is shocking not only because of the detached description of the brutal murder, but also because of the murderer's simple-minded, confused, yet logical reasoning. As he recalls his first war murder (that of a young girl) and his subsequent murders, it becomes evident that his training in the war had made killing appear like a natural thing to him. He used to look away when his mother or wife killed a chicken, but the war taught him many things he cannot easily forget once he returns home. Furthermore, his desperate financial situation opens yet another front at home between the rich and the poor: instead of it being the Russians on the opposite bank, it's the wealthy people who are over there. He claims that everyone on his side – the poor folk – has 'a stinking hovel' and that the sun only seems to shine on the other side, on the officers' mess hall.[35] The murderer is thus no nationalist.

Anti-war fiction

Liviu Rebreanu, *The Forest of the Hanged*

The Forest of the Hanged ('*Pădurea spânzuraţilor*', 1922) opens with the gruesome hanging of a Czech deserter from the Austro-Hungarian army.[36] The novel's Romanian artillery officer, Apostol Bologa, spontaneously voted for the death sentence, but he soon begins to agonize over his decision. His uncertainty and divided loyalty are shared by the other minority soldiers serving in his unit. Bologa remembers that his father tried to instil in him duty and pride for being a Romanian. Bologa refuses the idea of a nationalist 'holy war' as well as the naïve

---

32 Endre Ady, 'Mégsem, mégsem, mégsem' [And yet, and yet, and yet], *Nyugat* 7, no. 21 (1914): 405.

33 Mihály Babits, 'Játszottam a kezével' [I played with your hand], *Nyugat* 8, no. 16 (1915): 884–5.

34 Idem, 'Húsvét előtt' [Before Easter], *Nyugat* 9, no. 7 (1916): 391–4.

35 Zsigmond Móricz, 'Szegény emberek', *Nyugat* 9, no. 24 (1916): 850–73.

36 Liviu Rebreanu, *The Forest of the Hanged*, trans. A.V. Wise (London: G. Allen & Unwin, 1930).

'internationalism' of Lieutenant Varga, who calls on all nationalities to fight for the Empire. When Bologa's unit is called upon to fight the Romanian army, he asks for a transfer but is rejected. He falls in love with a Hungarian peasant girl, abandons his post and aimlessly starts to walk around in the no-man's land between enemy lines. He would like to stay in this suspension but is caught by a patrol and is hanged for desertion, just as Liviu Rebreanu's brother Emil was in 1917.

Joseph Roth, *Radetzky March*

Though written in German by a cosmopolitan writer who became associated with Austria, *Radetzky March* ('*Radetzkymarsch*'), first published in 1932, is about the grandfather, son and grandson of a Slovenian family, and the plot leads to the former multicultural Galicia, where Joseph Roth (in Brody), as well as Bruno Schulz (in Drohobycz) and other important writers were born and raised.

A few days into the war, Lieutenant Carl Joseph Trotta stumbles into a forest of hanged deserters at Galicia's easternmost border. Using his sword, he cuts the rope of three cadavers and buries them. Trotta's ancestors were simple peasants in the fictional Slovenian village Sipolje until his grandfather saved Emperor Francis Joseph's life in the battle of Solferino and was awarded the title of Baron. The novel follows the lives of the Baron's son, who is a civil servant in Moravia, and his grandson, the aforementioned Carl Joseph Trotta, who serves as a military officer, first in Bohemia and then in Galicia. The Baron's stiff and formal son is totally devoted to the Monarchy, but his grandson is unable to find his place in the disintegrating order. He is obsessed with premonitions of death and is killed in the war a few days after burying the cadavers.

The Monarchy's death is foreshadowed in an eerie sequence of scenes. Carl Joseph's Galician military unit holds a great military parade, to be followed by dancing and drinking. While a devastating storm gathers outside, unconfirmed news about the assassination of Archduke Franz Ferdinand rouses dormant conflicts among the nationalities. The Hungarian Baron Jenő Nagy, of Jewish descent, regards the Hungarians 'as one of the noblest races of the Monarchy', and skips a Hungarian *csárdás* (a dance) due to rumours that he regards as betrayal. The other Hungarians share his dislike of the Archduke who is said to favour the Slavs,[37] and they start to converse agitatedly amongst themselves in Hungarian. This outrages the Slovenian Captain Jelačich who loves the Monarchy and hates the Hungarians and the Serbs: slamming the table with his hand he demands that the Hungarians speak German.[38] Trouble arises when the Hungarian Benkyö responds in German that he and his fellow countrymen agree: 'we can be glad the bastard is gone'.[39] Trotta, who had always anticipated such a splintering of his fatherland, threatens, in vain, to shoot anybody who offends the Archduke. When the Archduke's murder is confirmed, Benkyö delightfully shouts that the bastard is now really gone, while the other drunken guests start a funeral march to Chopin's music. Trotta submits his resignation the following day, but the war breaks out and all the men are mobilized. Trotta's devoted servant hides in his neighbouring village as a deserter, but Trotta slips into his uniform again and soon dies. Roth's novel ends by depicting a Monarchy already shattering at the start of the war. The deaths of the Emperor and Carl Joseph's father follow in the epilogue.

---

37 Joseph Roth, *The Radetzky March*, trans. Joachim Neugroschel (New York: Overlook Press, 1995), 297.
38 Ibid., 299.
39 Ibid.

Miloš Crnjanski, *The Journal of Čarnojević*

While Rebreanu and Roth deal with issues of disintegration in a realistic and coherent style, Miloš Crnjanski narrates the catastrophe in *The Journal of Čarnojević* (*Dnevnik o Čarnojeviću*, 1921) through fractured characters and a disordered plot. In 1690, Archbishop Arsenije III Čarnojević led a large migration of Serbs to Hungary, but his relevance to the title of the novel is left vague. Some critics identify the narrator as a Čarnojević, while others stress that the nametag on the protagonist's hospital bed says Petar Raitch, so that Raitch must be the narrator.[40] Much of the novel is actually about an unnamed Dalmatian sailor, whose adventures blur into the life of Raitch's character. There is no firm plot and in a similar manner, the Raitch/Čarnojević character does not express any strong emotions either about himself or about others, even when he is in love. The war seems to have sapped all of his passion for life, so he simply drifts around. His hesitation and indecision are rendered in a broken narrative style; more than Carl Joseph Trotta, he is a broken person. What he loves in nature, the war has consistently turned into dead wood and mud.

Crnjanski went on to publish *Migrations* (*Seobe*) in 1929, a nationalistically tinted account of what happened to the Serbians that Archbishop Arsenije III Čarnojević led into exile. He himself stayed in London during and after the war but eventually returned to Yugoslavia in 1965.

Miroslav Krleža, *Croatian God Mars*

Miroslav Krleža began sketching the novellas in this volume when he was back in Zagreb and no longer in active service. The stories were published in 1917 but only appeared as the book *Croatian God Mars* (*Hrvatski bog Mars*) in 1922. They follow the life and death of 'domobrani', or, the home guard. In contrast to other ethnic soldiers of the Monarchy, the *domobrani* were under the command of Croatian officers, who were in turn under the command of their co-national Croatian officers. However, these officers were often loyal to the Hungarians and Austrians, and they had career goals in the war. Hence, Krleža's stories have two different orientations: they either ridicule the officers, their bureaucracy, their corruption, their addiction to exercise and their yearning for medals, or they show the suffering and miserable deaths of the common *domobrani*.

In the decades following the publication of *Croatian God Mars*, Krleža became the most distinguished Croatian novelist. In one of his main works, *Messrs. Glembay: A Drama in Three Acts from the Life of One Agremerian Patrician Family* (*Gospoda Glembajevi*, 1932), he presents a panoramic history of a family, whose decline is related to the First World War and the disintegration of the Monarchy.

Ivan Cankar, *Dream Visions*

In 1917, Ivan Cankar managed to publish his final collection of short stories, *Podobe iz sanj*, by deceptively calling it *Dream Visions*, as if the earlier-published sketches in it had nothing to do with reality. Actually, many of the short texts are passionately conveyed moral and religious allegories that show contempt for the war while they confirm a belief in human values. Occasionally, they even reveal openings to a better world. In 'Idiot Martin', the protagonist wanders around after having been dismissed from the army and tells how a weeping Christ

---

40 Miloš Crnjanski, *Dnevnik o Čarnojeviću* [The journal of Čarnojević] (Belgrade: Nolit, 1983 [1921]), 58; see Miro Mašek, *Nation und Narration im literarischen Werk Miloš Crnjanskis* (Frankfurt a.M.: Peter Lang, 2004), 97.

A history of fiction

accompanies him one night.[41] In 'The Solemn Mass', the Lord brightens the sombre service offered to the crippled and famished members of a parish church: 'He stretched forth His almighty hand and thrust all the doors and windows ajar. And into this darkness, into this gloom, the heavenly light poured its mighty rays in gigantic billows, full of song and gladness'.[42] If Martin's vision is a product of the idiot's imagination, the narrator sighs at the brightened mass, 'Oh my dreams, what do you behold!'[43]

There are no consoling images in 'Children and Old Folks'[44] and 'The Extinguished Lights'.[45] The former tells how the children's happy playing is interrupted by a message that remains unintelligible to them:

> Something strange and incomprehensible reached with its brutal hand from a strange foreign land, snatched that heavenly light from them, and blotted out their stories, holidays and fairyland. A letter came from the War Department announcing that their father had fallen on the Italian front.[46]

The latter story is about a famished lonely soldier amidst corpses. He finds 'crumbs of zwieback soaked in his blood and seasoned with that pungent smell. But I devoured that jumble to the last crumb.'[47] None of these sketches, however, explicitly addresses the political issue of whether Slovenia should join the state of united South Slavs – a matter that Cankar discussed in his wartime lectures.

Jaroslav Hašek, *The Good Soldier Švejk*

Jaroslav Hašek wrote only one novel, *The Good Soldier Švejk* (*Osudy dobrého vojáka Švejka za světové války*), which itself remained unfinished as he intended to write six parts, but only completed three before he died. Although his genius occasionally glimmers in his other works, none of them matches the brilliance of his novel. In 1911, he published his first five short stories as *The Good Soldier Švejk and Other Great Tales*. In 1917, he published the novella *The Good Soldier Švejk in Captivity* in Kiev as part of a legionnaire series. Both are rather didactic, and the latter is further tinted by a disturbing chauvinism that reflects Hašek's disposition at that time. The jump from these early works to the Švejk of the novel was the result of Hašek's life experiences, whereby we should not think of Hašek's incredible adventures (such as the time the Czechoslovak Legion condemned him to death for treason in Samara and he escaped to the Red Army by pretending he was congenitally imbecile); rather more important was that the earlier figure of Švejk was developed from the perspective of the war and of world history.

The theme of the 'little man in the turmoil of history' had a strong tradition in literary history, especially in the picaresque novels of the sixteenth and seventeenth century. Švejk's most direct ancestor is Simplicius, the hero of Hans Jakob Christoffel von Grimmelshausen's *Simplicius Simplicissimus*, who lived through the horrors of the Thirty Years' War in Germany.

---

41 Ivan Cankar, *Dream Visions*, trans. Anton Druzina (Willoughby Hill, OH: Slovenia Research Center of America, 1982) 81–4.
42 Ibid., 112–15, here 114–15.
43 Ibid., 115.
44 Ibid., 17–9.
45 Ibid., 65–7.
46 Ibid., 17.
47 Ibid., 67.

When Švejk is asked how long the war will last, he flippantly responds: 'For fifteen years. That is self-evident, for we had already a thirty-year one and we are now twice as smart as earlier.'[48]

Hašek's *The Good Soldier Švejk* is a war novel in which not a single gunshot is fired, and war is not actually portrayed. Luckily, Hašek could not finish it and was unable to send his hero to the front and the Russian side. One may summarize it as millions preparing to kill each other by imposing endless suffering on themselves and others, travelling this way and that, not having an inkling, however, as to why.

The novel begins with Mr Švejk who 'had left military service years before, after having been finally certified by an army medical board as an imbecile, and now lived by selling dogs – ugly, mongrel monstrosities whose pedigrees he forged.'[49] Mrs Müller, his charwoman, tells him that 'they've killed our Ferdinand', but Švejk knows two people named Ferdinand: 'One is a messenger at Průša's, the chemist's, and once by mistake he drank a bottle of hair oil there. The other is Ferdinand Kokoška who collects dog manure.'[50] Once the identity of the murdered Ferdinand is clarified, Švejk goes to his favourite pub, the Chalice, to discuss the chances of a war. Bretschneider, who works for the State Security, takes him to the police headquarters for having offended His Majesty, but the medical committee of the court declares him insane and sends him home.

This opening serves as a microcosm for the novel. Those in power try to suppress those beneath them with the help of rotting institutions, and we see, above all, Švejk's resistance tactics in which each episode tells a story that is even more absurd than the world itself. He plays the imbecile so perfectly that he never slips out of his role, not even when he is alone.

Nevertheless, Švejk is drafted from the reserve contingency when it turns out that the Monarchy is losing. Since he has rheumatic fever, Švejk comes to the draft board in a wheelchair. Accused of malingering, he is put into a hospital and then court-martialed. He then accidentally becomes the batman, or personal servant to the military chaplain, Otto Katz, but the drunken chaplain loses Švejk's services in a game of cards to Senior Lieutenant Lukáš whose batman Švejk then becomes. The Lieutenant is subsequently transferred to a march battalion that is sent to the front. The immediate reason is that Švejk stole the dog of a colonel who was reputed for his imbecility. Unfortunately, the colonel discovers the theft, and this concludes Part I, titled 'Behind the Lines'.

Part II, 'At the Front', describes how Lukáš and Švejk get to their České Budějovice garrison. Švejk misses the train but eventually catches up with his comrades. In the jail carriage he gets to know Marek, a one-year volunteer, who is readily recognized as Hašek himself. Like Švejk, he has a story about everything, though his more general and elevated stories are a bit more didactic and slightly boring.

Part III, 'The Glorious Licking', follows the train of soldiers across Hungary towards the Galician front. At the end of this part, Švejk is mistaken for a Russian and the 'good soldier' becomes an Austrian prisoner of war. The unfinished Part IV, i.e. 'The Glorious Licking Continues', resolves this misunderstanding, and Švejk returns to his unit.

In *The Good Soldier Švejk*, plot – in the traditional sense – is replaced with a series of stories told by Švejk and the other characters. Hašek creates a vast space for storytelling and has Švejk tell more than two hundred exemplary and humorous stories alone. Readers roar with laughter

---

48 Jaroslav Hašek, *The Good Soldier Švejk and his Fortunes in the World War*, trans. Cecil Parrott (Harmondsworth: Penguin, 1973), 739.

49 Ibid., 3.

50 Ibid., 4.

A history of fiction

throughout the entire book despite the fact that the novel is about war time. Hašek employs all kinds of humour, from simple idiocies like, 'The cube is angularity and that's why the cube is angular',[51] to the most vulgar folksy invectives. In the epilogue to Part I, Hašek remarks:

> Those who boggle at strong language are cowards, because it is real life which is shocking them, and weaklings like that are the very people who cause most harm to culture and character. They would like to see the nation grow into a group of over-sensitive little people – masturbators of false culture of the type of St Aloysius, of whom it is said in the book of the monk Eustachius that when he heard a man breaking wind with deafening noise he immediately burst into tears and could only be consoled by prayers.[52]

The basic source of humour for Švejk and his colleagues is that the world itself has become topsy-turvy, absurd and unnatural. Only exaggerated humour can act as a defence against this. The structure of the stories is always the same: Švejk wants something 'good', something that conforms to the ruling norms, but produces something 'bad', which implies that the norms are faulty. Statements that are unnatural and irrational correspond to a reality that contradicts nature and reason. The absurdity of the world becomes visible in statements like the following: 'Sentencing an innocent man to five years, that is something I've heard of, but ten, that's a bit too much';[53] or, 'There is a freedom there [in the lunatic asylum] which not even Socialists have ever dreamed of';[54] and finally, 'There have to be crooks in this world too … If everyone were honest with each other, they'd soon start punching each other's noses.'[55]

It is not only the plot of the novel that is made up of such chatter, but also its characters. Omitting all descriptive and psychological elements, Hašek characterizes his figures via their stories. Precisely for this reason, Švejk has been interpreted in very different ways from the outset. Josef Lada's world-famous illustrations substantially contributed to the most common misinterpretation that Švejk is a 'professional imbecile', for the illustrations portray a true idiot instead of a character who merely mimics one. The 'good soldier' has also been read as embodying both the best and the worst traits of 'a simple son of the folk', 'a cunning servant' or 'a wise clown' type of character. Yet, the text only reveals the following: that he was a soldier dismissed because of his incompetence; that he sells dogs after faking their pedigree; that he does not belong to a church; that he used to work as a chemist's assistant; that he worked in Ostrava; that he was an itinerant journeyman in Bremen; that he is well-read (he can converse as an equal with the university-educated Marek); that his brother is a teacher (although, he may have said this only to annoy Lieutenant Dub who is a teacher in civilian life); and finally, that Mrs. Müller calls him 'sir'.

The novel deviates from traditional psychological-social novels by not offering character portrayals. However, Hašek clearly distinguishes between two types of character. The first and most important is whether the character belongs to the poor and oppressed or to the rich and powerful. All the stories function to reveal this division in the world of the novel, and to indicate which characters are attractive and which are repellent. Every character is clearly placed

---

51 Ibid., 428.
52 Ibid., 214–15.
53 Ibid., 47.
54 Ibid., 31.
55 Ibid., 30.

between the two extremes. Švejk is at one end of this scale, for all his actions are right. The most repellent character, who resides in the opposite camp which includes policemen, officers, judges and the general machinery of the Austro-Hungarian Monarchy, is the idiotic Lieutenant Dub. He is Czech, which shows that the two camps are not separated by nationality. Švejk calms the Hungarian-cursing Private Vodička by claiming that many Hungarians 'can't help being Hungarian'.[56] Švejk, then, has an aversion to all ideologies: 'It's bad … when a chap suddenly starts to get caught up in philosophizing. That always stinks of *delirium tremens*.'[57]

Ivan Olbracht, *Nikola the Outlaw*

Fiction about outlaws became a unique emblem of the war and the post-war confusion with Ivan Olbracht's 1933 novel, *Nikola the Outlaw* (*Nikola Šuhaj loupezník*). The novel is based on the Robin Hood-like legends surrounding a real person: Nikola Šuhaj. The Šuhaj of history was born in the Ruthenian Koločava, then a part of Hungary. After briefly being under Romanian rule, the town became part of Czechoslovakia in 1919, then the Soviet Union in 1945, and finally a part of Ukraine after the disintegration of the Soviet Union. Šuhaj deserted the Monarchy's military twice; the second time, he killed two militia men. He resorted to robbing rich peasants and Jews, but his crimes during monarchic rule were not held against him after the Monarchy disintegrated in 1919. When famine made him resort once more to robbery in 1920, he was arrested; however, he escaped with the help of his wife and subsequently formed a robber band. The Czech authorities expanded the Koločava police force, but the new officers were just as incompetent as the old ones. According to Olbracht in the novel, it was believed that

> the authority of the new state could not be established as long as this bandit was at large, as long as legends should be woven around his person, as long as questioning eyes should follow with secret joy the gendarmes' unsuccessful contest with him, as long as Nikola Šuhaj's name should be on everybody's lips, a synonym for heroism.[58]

In the end, a bounty on Nikola's head did the job: three members of his own gang killed him on 16 August 1921.

The first to write about Šuhaj's life was the Hungarian Béla Illés, who grew up in the Carpathian area and stayed there only briefly after the failure of the Hungarian Soviet Republic, or Commune of 1919 until he was expelled. His Hungarian manuscript was published in German in 1922. He survived his exile in Moscow and became a functionary in the Hungarian communist regime after the war.

Olbracht's novel is not just fictional but it also contains historical facts and reflections on the relationship between fact and fiction. The prologue recounts a legend – told by a cowherd – that Šuhaj was made invulnerable to bullets during the First World War by a witch's brew. In Olbracht's view (found in the epilogue), Šuhaj became immortal through his 'oneness' with the mountains, 'forests and brooks, their bears, herds, and people'.[59] He describes Šuhaj as a pantheistic 'ancient pagan god. God of the earth, master of forests and flocks' who is still alive.[60]

---

56 Ibid., 361.
57 Ibid., 428.
58 Ivan Olbracht, *Nikola the Outlaw*, trans. Marie Holeček (Evanston, IL: Northwestern UP, 2001) 73.
59 Ibid., 215.
60 Ibid., 212.

A history of fiction

In Olbracht's glorified vision, Šuhaj was connected with the people whose fathers, brothers and sons were killed in 'the slaughterhouse of the Austrian Emperor's army'. Since they were tormented by Jewish usurers and new masters, they were all 'outlaws at heart, for living outside the law' was the only way they knew how to defend themselves.[61] Šuhaj became the legendary hero of many folk songs; he became a symbol of the struggle for freedom, 'because he was the friend of the downtrodden and the enemy of the ruling classes'.[62] While the witch's brew could not save Šuhaj, his legend will live on in the traditions of the folk.

Olbracht sympathized with the downtrodden and the 'Robin Hoods' who stole from the rich in order to give to the poor. However, in the novel, Olbracht portrays the poor villagers of Koločava as just as corrupt, cowardly and greedy as the militia and the Jews. Koločava's grotesque little revolution and its aftermath undermine Olbracht's Marxism: while Šuhaj loves the woods, the others usually see the land and the woods as desirable property. Instead of embracing a pantheistic universe, their aim is to own the land. In the village, power belongs to the rich and clever Jews whose ironic and negative portrayal sometimes borders on anti-Semitism.

Dezső Kosztolányi, *Anna Édes*

Representations in fiction of the war and its aftermath may be appropriately concluded with Dezső Kosztolányi's 1926 *Anna Édes* (*Édes Anna*, serialized in *Nyugat*), in which the transition from the 1919 Hungarian Commune to the Horthy regime frames a bizarre murder story. In the novel, the war, which directly motivated the murder in Zsigmond Móricz's abovementioned story 'Poor Folk', is receding into memory and motivates Anna's murder only on the subconscious level. The issue in the novel is not the act of murder itself, but how it is talked about. Language use is also the focus in Kosztolányi's brilliant portrayal of a political turnover. The novel opens with sensationalistic, nasty and ludicrous gossip about the fleeing of Béla Kun, leader of the Commune:

> In the afternoon – at about five o'clock – an aeroplane rose over the Soviet headquarters in the Hotel Hungaria, crossed the Danube and, passing the palace on top of the Várhegy, banked steeply towards the Vérmező Gardens. The pilot of the aircraft was none other than the head of state himself. He flew low, barely sixty feet above ground. His face could be clearly seen. He was pale and unshaven as usual. He grinned at those below and gave an occasional shabby and sardonic wave of farewell. His pockets were stuffed with sweet pastry. He carried jewels, relics of the church and precious stones that had once belonged to well-disposed and generous aristocratic women. As the aeroplane began to climb, and just as it was disappearing from sight, one such gold chain fell right in the middle of the Vérmező.[63]

Since planes do not take off from hotels in the city centre, readers anticipate a fantastical story until the closing words of the first chapter: 'Such at least were the rumours in the Krisztina area.'[64] The narrator has merely adopted, without explicit markers, the chatter of 'well-disposed and generous' aristocratic ladies from Krisztinaváros.

---

61 Ibid., 213.

62 Ibid., 214.

63 Dezső Kosztolányi, *Anna Édes*, trans. by George Szirtes (Budapest: Corvina, 1991), 1.

64 Ibid., 1.

In the chaotic heteroglossia of the subsequent chapter, emblems of the defeated Commune are still visible: the communist newspaper in Kornél Vizy's hands still urges its readers to defend the endangered proletarian fatherland; Róbert Berény's famous communist poster still depicts a 'frenzied sailor' calling its viewers to arms; and young people still sing the communist 'Internationale' in blissful ignorance.[65] At home, 'his excellency' (i.e. Vizy) starts to revert to his old-fashioned authoritarian rhetoric until there is a knock on the door. Frightened, he is ready to take back having just called 'the Reds' 'scoundrels' and he is glad to discover in his pocket the trade-union card he wanted to tear up earlier in the day. The man at the door turns out to be the caretaker who sided with the communists but now hopes to regain Vizy's confidence by offering to fix the broken bell he had long neglected to repair. It is here where heteroglossia reaches its hilarious climax. Unsure of the political situation, both adopt the discourse of the other: Vizy addresses the repentant communist sympathizer as 'comrade', whereas the caretaker, 'crestfallen' about his label, insists on addressing Vizy as 'your excellency'.[66] When Mrs. Vizy returns with the latest gossip, the heteroglossia smoothens into monoglossia.

The rest of *Anna Édes* shows how newsmongering, gossip, chatting at tea parties, fabricating legends, bureaucratic jargon and legalese resuscitate a language that is alien to Anna. She is first identified via an absurd but official 'employment book', in which she must claim, for instance, that she has no beard.[67] Her uncle, the caretaker, proceeds to answer Mrs. Vizy's questions for Anna, not allowing Anna to speak for herself.

As soon as the political situation stabilizes, gossiping shifts to spinning myths about Anna, who becomes the ideal maid at tea parties where the ladies ceaselessly chat about their problems with their own maids. The 'local hub of gossip' is the Viatorisz grocery, but she is also admired at the baker's, the butcher's, the cleaner's and even the undertaker's – though most women had not seen her and only knew her Christian name. The gossipers 'felt like members of a society of the superstitious who had heard of a miraculous cure, some potent religious icon'.[68]

Jancsi, Mrs. Vizy's nephew, prepares to seduce Anna and gets himself fired up with obscene, macho language. Having gone to a boys' school, his only experience of women is through obscene and demeaning 'boys' talk'. Jancsi wants to sweep Anna off her feet, to 'embrace her from behind, and, as was the custom with servant girls, unceremoniously upend her like a sack of flour.'[69] He tries to overcome his timidity by trivializing her with vulgarities:

> One joke, any common joke, some rib-tickling, side-splitting vulgar joke and she'll reel with laughter and fall flat on her back. That's the way with maids. On your back, Susie! … Leap on her, raise her skirt. What can happen? At the worst she'll slap my hand. So what. She is no virgin anyway. You've just got to look at her. Her tits are small and loose. … But she might be a hot little tart. A sweet piece of fluff. A kind of peasant whore.[70]

---

65 Ibid., 4.
66 Ibid., 6.
67 Ibid., 46.
68 Ibid., 94–5.
69 Ibid., 109.
70 Ibid., 113.

A history of fiction

The ensuing love affair entails moments of human communication, yet verbal differences persist. To Anna, Jancsi becomes a 'thou' or 'young master',[71] but Jancsi often has to translate himself into 'maid's language' to make himself understood. The lovers are usually silent together.[72]

One night, to the shock of the town, Anna murders her employers, becoming the Lizzie Borden[73] of Budapest. The official language of Anna's arrest is empty verbiage, while the impersonal and inhuman interrogations of the police and the magistrate lead nowhere. After 'minutely studying the police reports',[74] the magistrate is as ignorant as the gossipers, and Anna cannot help him further.[75] However, the puzzle of the crime creates a momentary human bond between Anna and the presiding judge, who proceeds 'carefully through her testimony, helping the accused, leading her towards the truth'; unfortunately, 'he gets lost in the dark' and she is unable to lead him towards the light. Hence, they stumble together 'like two closely bound blind men'.[76] In the end, he leniently condemns her to 15 years in prison. During her trial, legends about her infernal power are born, but they fade by the time the higher court announces the verdict, and Anna finally ceases to be a conversation topic.

Since Anna does not understand herself, her mind is not transparent, and so even the narrator remains puzzled. However, he becomes a compassionate spokesman for the old, sick and inefficient physician Moviszter who believes that the Vizys turned Anna 'into a machine', treated her 'without humanity' and were outright 'beastly' to her.[77] The jury concludes that Moviszter is deranged, but the narrator holds that without this impairment 'his stature would have shrunk to nothing or been lost in the vast empty spaces of the soul'.[78]

The novel's epilogue shows once more how legends are born, and it serves as Kosztolányi's self-defence against charges that he trimmed his sails according to the changing political winds. In the self-referential epilogue, elections are to be held in 1922, and a lawyer named Druma runs unopposed for a seat in the parliament. Passing Kosztolányi's home with his campaign aids, he claims that Kosztolányi is a communist, but his only evidence is a photo that shows Kosztolányi standing next to commissar József Pogány.[79] When another member of the group cites a Viennese paper that Kosztolányi is a 'devout Christian' now, Druma responds:

> 'He's for everybody and nobody. ... First, he was in the pay of the Jews and took their side, and now he is hired by the Christians. He's a wise man' he winked. 'He knows which side of his bread is buttered.'

Druma calumniates Kosztolányi the way the women of Krisztinaváros slander Kun in the prologue. This puzzles Druma's companions who are used 'to thinking one thing at a time'.[80] Their last thoughts are drowned out by the barking of Kosztolányi's dog. But Hungarian 'barking'

---

71 Ibid., 118–19.
72 Ibid., 119.
73 Editor's note: American Lizzie Borden was the main suspect in the axe murders of her father and stepmother in Fall River, Massachusetts in 1892; she was subsequently tried and acquitted.
74 Ibid., 196.
75 Ibid., 186.
76 Ibid., 203.
77 Ibid., 211.
78 Ibid., 212.
79 Ibid., 219.
80 Ibid., 220.

John Neubauer et al.

about the matter continues when the extreme right-wing newspaper *Harc* ('Struggle') publishes the photo that Druma refers to on 29 July 1944.

The interwar decades

György Lukács coined the term *transzendentale Obdachlosigkeit* ('transcendental homelessness') in an article first published in 1916; by the time the article was published as his book *Die Theorie des Romans* ('Theory of the novel') in 1920, he no longer applied the term to himself for, in exile, he had built a rickety ideological home for himself in the Communist Party of Hungary. For most exiles, though, homelessness remained an existential condition, in a very tangible (acute) sense. The impersonal statistics of the millions who were exiled, expelled, or 'exchanged' later come alive in Joseph Roth's novel *Hotel Savoy* (1924), which portrays life in a Lodz hotel crowded with refugees and soldiers returning home from captivity. Roth's powerful essay 'Juden auf Wanderschaft' ('The Wandering Jews', 1927) also deals with such issues.

We begin and end this section with the waves of exodus that mark the beginning and the end of the interwar years: the first wave of exile consisted mostly of Jewish-Hungarian writers who feared the White Terror that was on the horizon after the collapse of the Hungarian Commune in the fall of 1919; the second wave came with the international exodus of Jewish and left-wing writers from all countries of the region. Between accounts of these two waves, we insert two contrasting sections: first, the history of the PEN International Congresses in the region shows the futile attempts at building a transnational network in defence of individual rights and publication freedom, while the second section shows how dystopian novels about very different futures undermined the optimism of such institutional activities. To show that the 'writing on the wall' was not just announcing Nazi and communist threats from the outside, we include a section on continued ethnic tension in the region.

Fleeing the White Terror in Hungary

The sarcastic fictional gossip of Kun's flight from Budapest in *Anna Édes* was a historical reality for many who participated in Kun's Republic. Lukács, who had been Commissar for Education and Culture, was smuggled out as a chauffeur, while Béla Balázs, who escaped donning fake sideburns and a moustache, saw in the mirror the 'hideous face of a Jewish-broker, with a monocle on my nose'. Balázs's Viennese self-image became maudlin about homelessness. He saw himself as a wandering Jew whose Hungarian strings were nevertheless 'strung over the lyre of his heart' so that he could sing Hungarian songs about his pain.[81] He became a film columnist and later consolidated his views in a pioneering book on silent films, *The Visible Man* (*Der sichtbare Mensch*). He moved to Berlin and he was invited to Moscow when Hitler came to power to put Illés's book *The Tisza River Burns* (*Ég a Tisza*) about the Hungarian Commune on screen. Three years of filming did not produce a film that was permitted to be shown in movie houses, but Balázs earned good money writing children's books. When he reassumed his Hungarian identity in 1945, he discovered with dismay that the new regime also disliked his work.

Ervin Sinkó, who also participated in the short-lived Commune, moved to Serbia from his Vienna exile to write *Optimisták* ('The optimists'), the monumental account of his experiences

---

81 Béla Balázs, *Napló 1914–1922*, Második kötet [Diary 1914–1922, second volume] (Budapest: Magvető, 1982), 361.

A history of fiction

in 1918–19. In 1935, he went to Moscow with the help of Romain Rolland, hoping to find a publisher, but he found only functionaries who reneged on their promises.[82] Sinkó was expelled from the Soviet Union in April 1937 but the long arm of Moscow still reached him in France. After giving a carefully worded lecture about his Moscow experiences, he was baffled to see that his left-wing publication opportunities evaporated. He was discreetly informed that he would find opportunities if he publicly defended the Soviet trials and executions. Poet Louis Aragon transmitted these Moscow directives to Sinkó, but he refused; instead, he fled to Bosnia when the war broke out. His book was finally published in Croatia in the 1950s, as were his much more exciting and revealing Moscow diaries.

PEN Congresses in Budapest, Dubrovnik and Prague

The Trianon Peace Treaty granted political independence to the suppressed Czech, Slovak, Croatian and Romanian nationalities of the Monarchy, but it created new tensions by awarding the newly constituted or enlarged countries two-thirds of Hungary's pre-war territory and half of its former population. The large new Hungarian minorities in these successor states gener-ated a strong irredentist movement in Hungary and became a major obstacle in the attempts to bring about literary and artistic cooperation between the countries of the region. Béla Bartók's folklore research, for instance, was officially unwelcome in Romania, though he worked closely with the Romanian folklorists. Karel Čapek commented on a portrait of Kosztolányi during the 1931 PEN Club Congress held in the Hague, saying that Kosztolányi is smiling in the picture to indicate that he was not angry with the Czech government for denying him entry into the country; Čapek said he even detected a halo around Kosztolányi's head.[83] Kosztolányi, head of the Hungarian PEN Club then, was presumably denied a visa because like Mihály Babits, Attila József, Gyula Juhász and other moderate Hungarian writers, he publicly mourned Hungary's losses.

Among the failed interwar efforts to initiate transnational dialogues on individual rights, artistic freedom and international cooperation, those of the International PEN Club (founded in 1923) were perhaps the most systematic. It must have been no accident that of the last seven pre-war congresses three were held in the region: Budapest (1932), Dubrovnik (1933) and Prague (1938). Kosztolányi prepared the Budapest congress, and though he was scandalously deposed of his position as President of the Hungarian PEN, he remained its key figure and the major editor of the 1932 *Nyugat* double issue (no. 9–10), which celebrated both the congress and the journal's twenty-fifth anniversary. The regional congress participants included Čapek, the Slovak poet Emil Boleslav Lukač and the Romanian writers Victor Eftimiu, Octavian Goga (!) and Liviu Rebreanu, while Čapek, František Langer, Kazimierz Wierzyński and Victor Eftimiu (Isac and Jovan Dučić in the following issue) appeared in the special issue next to such international stars as Thomas Mann, Stefan Zweig, Franz Werfel and Hendrik Pontoppidan.

Čapek's contribution, 'Following the Double-Headed Eagle', extended his remark about Kosztolányi's portrait by urging the Czechs to become more international. The Habsburg double-headed eagles, removed from Czech buildings in 1918, symbolized that the dynasty

---

82 John Neubauer: 'Exile: Home of the Twentieth Century', in *The Exile and Return of Writers from East-Central Europe: A Compendium*, eds John Neubauer and Borbála Zsuzsanna Török (Berlin: de Gruyter, 2009), 4–105. See also: Ervin Sinkó, *Egy regény regénye: Moszkvai naplójegyzetek (1935–1937)* [A novel's novel: Moscow diaries (1935–1937)] (Újvidék: Forum könyvkiadó, 1985), 433.

83 Karel Čapek, *Over Holland* [On the Netherlands] (Amsterdam: van Holkema & Warendorf, 1933), 7.

151

botched the great idea of building a transnational Central Europe; but the Czech tradition not only included a national struggle but also an interest in entering a broader international order. The Czechs were part of the Monarchy's 'League of Nations' but profited little from it. A broader global order could, perhaps, release 'a creative passion, a kermis of spirit, a Dionysian richness'. Čapek naively closed by saying: 'I believe it is the task of politics to break open the road for us, the others'.[84] Alas, the Dubrovnik PEN Congress of 1933 already showed that politics went in the opposite direction. When the international president, H.G. Wells, allowed Ernst Toller to speak out against the recent German book burning, the already Nazified German PEN delegation walked out, followed, somewhat remarkably, by the Austrian and Dutch ones. No Eastern European delegation joined the exodus.

In 1935, Čapek was the leading candidate for the International PEN Presidency, but he withdrew when Jules Romains was also nominated. For the last pre-war congress in Prague, Čapek edited *At the Cross-Roads of Europe*, a volume about the democratic tradition in Czechoslovakia. The pathetic self-praise is a disappointing read, especially since it appeared two months before the Munich agreement and five months before Čapek's death on Christmas day, 1938.

Dystopias in the 1930s

The institutional efforts that writers made in order to prevent the coming disaster inevitably ran them into a dead end. What alternatives were there? Čapek, for one, knew that fiction did not require negotiations, though negotiations could be thematized in fiction. His last great novel, *War with the Newts*, portrays the fight against the oncoming doomsday. Yet, the struggle is in vain because human beings are unable to work together. Published in 1936, the novel makes it clear that nationalism and racism prevent cooperation. Along with Čapek's novel, we will examine works by Arthur Koestler, Stanisław Ignacy Witkiewicz and Sándor Szathmári from the 1930s in order to show both the variety and the common thrust of inverted utopias.

Karel Čapek, *War with the Newts*

In *War with the Newts* (*Válka s mloky*), humans exploit little underwater creatures called Newts: they are ugly salamanders that can only briefly stay out of water. A Dutch sea captain, J. van Toch, accidentally discovers that they can dive for natural pearls, so using the Newts, he puts an impressive collection of pearls together, and ultimately convinces businessman Mr. Gussie H. Bondy to exploit the Newts commercially. The growth of the enterprise accelerates when it turns out that the Newts can also build dams and underwater structures.

However, these champions of productivity, the Newts, are also a great threat to humanity, and Čapek's scenario develops in four steps: 1) the Germans find that northern Newts are racially superior to the others, and Germany, therefore, wants to gain new and longer coastlines in the North; 2) the philosopher Wolf Meynert publishes a book titled, *The Decline of Humanity*; 3) an anonymous character who publishes under the pseudonym 'X' warns against the Newts in a pamphlet titled *X's Warning*; and 4) an international conference at Vaduz seeks an agreement with them. In the closing chapter the author conducts a self-dialogue on whether the destruction of humanity is inevitable.

---

84 Karel Čapek, 'A kétfejű sas nyomában' [Following the double-headed eagle], *Nyugat* 25, no. 9–10 (1932): 522–4.

A history of fiction

Meynert's book coheres with the above-mentioned racist northern-Newt theory. Meynert argues that humanity made a fatal mistake by dividing itself into 'nations, races, faiths, professions, and classes, into rich and poor, into educated and uneducated, into the rulers and the ruled.'[85] 'Stable happiness' can only be achieved by allowing enough 'room only for the few' and by exterminating 'the rest'. But instead of getting rid of 'the rest', man has invented human rights, 'conventions, laws, equality, and humanity' to shield 'the rest'. That is, humans have put 'moral law above the law of Nature' which dictates that only the fit shall survive.[86] In contrast, the Newts discard philosophy, immortality and art; 'they have no conception of fantasy, humour, mysticism, recreation, or dreams; they are absolute realists.'[87] This way, they may build 'racial unity throughout the whole world'.[88] Hence, the Newts will exterminate instead of enslave mankind, their world will be a 'uniform, compact, and so to speak, consistent mass, in all its parts equally primitive', undivided by language, views, necessities, culture or class.[89] All Newts serve one Big Newt Entity, their god, ruler, employer and spiritual leader. The (obviously pre-Nazi) Government bans Meynert's book and he moves to Switzerland.

The avant-garde hopes that the Newts will eliminate traditional culture. For them, the rise of the Newts indicates that there is a cultural revolution on the horizon: 'They may have no art of their own: at least they are not weighed down by idiotic ideals, moribund traditions, and by all that bloated, boring, pedantic trash which was once called poetry, music, architecture, philosophy.'[90] The conservatives, however, support *X's Warning* that the Newts will eliminate everything that is fantastic, ancient and has no purpose. The Newt mentality is practical, technical and utilitarian, which may allow them to build technical marvels, but which only results in mediocrity. X wants a United States of the World against the Newts, but business columnists warn that restricting supplies to the Newts would result in a decrease in production and a serious crisis in many branches of industry.

The Newts revolt against their exploitation which results in war with the humans. They want the *Lebensraum* of inundated continents. They demand that humans evacuate certain coasts so that the continents can be broken down into bays and islands increasing the global coastline five-fold. As a result of these policies, Great Britain loses four-fifths of its shipping within six weeks and declares war on the Newts.[91] In turn, Great Britain increases the production of airplanes to one thousand per day, while its military attempts to poison the Newts with bacteria, petrol and chemicals poured into the Thames. In response, Chief Salamander issues an ultimatum and demands that Great Britian sell the south part of Lincolnshire to the Newts.

The world conference at Vaduz is unable to form a global front against the Newts. None of the nations (except for the inland ones) recognize the Newts as an independent state, but this is mainly in order to 'nationalize' their own Newts. International organizations cannot take diplomatic or military action against all Newts, for every state has jurisdiction over its own Newts. Thus, England's proposal to stop delivering arms and explosives to the Newts is rejected, partly because this would infringe on state rights.[92]

---

85 Karel Čapek, *War with the Newts*, trans. M. & R. Weatherall (Evanston, IL: Northwestern University Press, 1996), 284.
86 Ibid., 285.
87 Ibid., 287.
88 Ibid.
89 Ibid., 286.
90 Ibid., 290.
91 Ibid., 310–12.
92 Ibid., 318–19.

By the time an old man and his son go fishing in Prague's Vltava, most of Germany, Brazil, Egypt, India, Russia and a third of France is already inundated with Newts. Although the Newts had already reached Dresden, Prague seemed safe until they discovered a Newt in the Vltava. The old man, Mr. Povondra, concludes: 'The sea covered everything at one time, and it will do again. That will be the end of the world.'[93]

The last chapter is the author's inner dialogue. Should he not have saved mankind? No, for the logic of the events was irrefutable.[94] The earth will drown as the result of politics and economics, aided by science, industry and public opinion. Commerce, industry and engineering, as well as statesmen and the armies, want the Newts to continue working for the human race.[95] To let the Newts die out through some disease or degeneration would be cheap. But could one not pit Newts against Newts? If left alone, they will surely start fighting each other. It would be most convincing to let the Newts become nationalists. The Lemurian and Atlantis Salamanders speak different English. The Lemurians will claim that all of Africa belongs to them: 'Lemuria for the Lemurians. Out with the foreigners.' This way, they will become permanently hostile nations. They will not be united around a 'True Newtship' but fight for a national glory with the slogan 'Either them or us!'[96] Thus, the Newts can become as self-destructive as human beings. One day they will die out and the surviving human beings may slowly return from the mountains to those shores that remain on the continents.

Arthur Koestler, 'The Good Soldier Schweik Goes to War Again'

In Čapek's novel, humanity is confronted with another species, but, as he remarked, the real threat came from within, not from the outside. He portrays racist and chauvinist theories, but he primarily blames trade and industry rather than ideology for the nationalist positions that prevent human cooperation in the novel. In Arthur Koestler's unpublished manuscript, 'The Good Soldier Schweik Goes to War Again' (*Der gute Soldat Schweik geht wieder in den Krieg*), the threat also comes from within but in the form of an astonishing, if humorous, anticipation of the war and the Holocaust.

The idea of turning Hašek's *Švejk* into an anti-Hitler novel was suggested to Arthur Koestler in 1936 by Willi Münzenberg, a brilliant Moscow-financed leader of anti-fascist propaganda campaigns. Koestler gladly accepted the advance money and moved to the Flemish coastal town of Bredene, where such exiles as Joseph Roth, Hanns Eisler and Egon Erwin Kisch were staying. When the Spanish Civil War broke out, Koestler joined the loyalists and abandoned the unfinished manuscript, surely also because the German Communist Party (KPD) had censured its 'pacifist errors'.[97]

The extant fragmentary manuscript anticipates the Nazi occupation of Czechoslovakia. Švejk, or 'Schweik', since he is now a Czech volunteer in the Wehrmacht, is just released from jail where he sat due to the 'terrible mishap' of having accidentally pissed on the head of an officer. A radio and newspaper blackout allows rumours to run rampant. According to some 'latrine rumours' the anti-Nazi powers unanimously rejected the annexation of Austria and the attack on Bohemia. The French troops are at the Neckar and the Main rivers, while Munich,

---

93 Ibid., 338.
94 Ibid., 340.
95 Ibid., 341.
96 Ibid., 346–7.
97 Koestler, *The Invisible Writing*, 283.

A history of fiction

Leipzig and Dresden have been destroyed from the air. The reborn Spartakists have raised the red flag in Berlin's Olympic Stadium, forcing Hitler, Göring and Göbbels to flee, disguised as rambling journeymen. However, according to the 'latrine opposition', the motorized German troops overran the Netherlands, Belgium and Switzerland. The revolution broke out in Paris, not in Berlin, hoisting the flag of the 1871 Commune. The truly smart ones claim that there is no war at all, for the Western powers gloomily accepted Austria's and Bohemia's annexation. Indeed, according to them, most German troops may already be sent home in the following week.[98]

The efficiency of German radio jamming inspires Schweik to fantasize about other self-destructive technologies. Chemically treated wheat will already rot in the soil, railroad lines will overheat so that the trains will stop in their tracks, car tyres will automatically deflate and coffee beans will get a crust so attractive to birds that no harvest will be needed. Above all, black women will get birth-control pills so that no sons will be killed in wars. As in Hašek, it remains unclear how seriously Schweik means all this.

Schweik becomes an interpreter for the concentration-camp commander Captain Eppert, who is still so fond of the Prussian military that he sends birthday cards to his deposed Emperor. He dislikes the Nazis and he hates the SS. Schweik has to explain to Eppert why a Rabbi is accused of miscegenation with his bride called Löbl. How can sex between two Jews be called miscegenation? The answer is that the Rabbi is a converted Khazar, not a 'real' Jew. Eppert is willing to provide the couple with kosher food, and since he is against making exceptions, he is willing to let everybody eat kosher food. He loves Jewish cooking and his mouth begins to water in anticipation of his first matzo ball. After all, the Führer wants well-treated inmates in his concentration camps!

Disaster strikes when the Nazi *Stürmer* publishes splashy front-page photos about the camp conditions. Eppert is forced to retire and all involved camp personnel are sent to the front. On the way, Schweik and his companions are granted a night in Vienna and Schweik sees the headline 'Germany's Heroic Fight for Peace' in the *Völkischer Beobachter*. His companion is baffled, however, by the report that the Germans did not respond to the provocative French bombing of Nancy. Why should the French bomb their own city? As always, Schweik makes a travesty of Nazi claims:

> You will no doubt admit that Nancy had always been in German hands and is, as they say, an *ur*-German city. It was in Nancy that the battle of Teutoburg was fought during the early Middle Ages; ... Since Goethe was born in Nancy, it is quite natural that we now have re-annexed it to the Reich.[99]

During the night, Schweik is awakened by explosions and finds himself amidst rubble and gaping chasms. Nobody seems alive, and when Schweik tries to open the latrine, he discovers that it is locked from the inside. After desperate cries about his urgent needs he finally hears the whimpering of his former officer Dammert, who often treated Schweik badly. Dammert finally exits and deferentially holds a candle so that Schweik can take care of his 'need'. He thinks that the bombing has swept the Nazis aside and he expects that Schweik will be high up in the new regime. He timidly drops his pants and submits to a thrash that he often used as a verbal threat

---

98 Arthur Koestler, 'Der gute Soldat Schweik geht wieder in den Krieg', unpublished manuscript, catalogued as MS2327/1 in Edinburgh University's Koestler Archives, 61–2.

99 Ibid., 147.

against Schweik. The novel fragment began with 'latrine rumours' and ends in an actual latrine. Could Koestler have continued this humorous dystopia?

Stanisław Ignacy Witkiewicz, *Insatiability*

The avant-garde origins of dystopian fiction are evident in Stanisław Ignacy Witkiewicz's novels. Witkiewicz was a prominent avant-garde artist and is now recognized as the founder of avant-garde theatre. He turned to fiction in the mid-1920s and published *Farewell to Autumn* (*Pożegnanie jesieni*) in 1927 and *Insatiability* (*Nienasycenie*) in 1930. Chaos, decadence, perversion and eroticism became exponentially intensified in the second novel, not only in extensive sex scenes but also in avalanches of verbosity stuffed with interjections, side remarks, bracketed remarks, passages marked 'Information', addresses to the reader and numerous foreign expressions. A Chinese/Japanese invasion finishes this decadent world coupled with the new religiosity that the Malaysian Djevani spreads via Murti-Bing pills. Djevani is considered a mild 'preparation' for socialism in the Chinese version, but in Poland such drivel was only known from hearsay.[100] In the first chapter of *The Captive Mind* (1953) titled 'The Pill of Murti-Bing', Czesław Miłosz writes that the people taking these pills became serene and happy: 'Most affected were all questions pertaining to unsolvable ontological difficulties. A man who swallowed Murti-Bing pills became impervious to any metaphysical concerns.'[101]

Summarizing *Insatiability*'s decadent world is a painful and inadequate exercise. A lengthy 'Information' tells the reader that an 'avalanche of Chinese communism' was 'rolling down from the Altai and Ural mountains onto the Moscow plain.'[102] Since 'none of the bolshevized states in the West relished the thought of becoming fully bolshevized in a pungent Chinese sauce',[103] they pumped piles of money into Poland to build up a bulwark against the Chinese. The Polish dictator Sloboluchovicz (obviously a fictionalized Piłsudski) should stop the 'mobile yellow wall'.[104]

The protagonist Genezyp (Zipcio) Kapen lives through the last days of a 'Western' Poland. After his high school graduation he is promptly sucked off in the woods by a brilliant but lame and hunchback modern composer; he loses his virginity to an ageing but still sex-driven princess; and he listens to philosophical debates between a brilliant logician, her neo-Catholic husband and her son who works for the leftist Syndicate for National Salvation against Sloboluchovicz. A few days later, the princess forces Zipcio to watch her making love to his cousin, which makes him masturbate. His next sexual torturer is the beautiful actress Persy, who teases him naked but forbids him to touch her. He is unaware that she is Sloboluchovicz's mistress. In the end, Zipcio can no longer control himself and kills an unknown man in Persy's house. He seems successful in building up an alibi and falls in love with the sweet and innocent Eliza, who introduces him to the Murti-Bing pills. However, the pill is not yet in full power during their wedding night and the schizophrenic Zipcio strangles Eliza. The next morning, he has to join Sloboluchovicz (and his mistress!) as an adjutant and depart for the decisive battle

---

100 Stanisław Ignacy Witkiewicz, *Insatiability*, trans. Louis Iribarne (Evanston, IL: Northwestern University Press, 1996), 211.
101 Czesław Miłosz, *The Captive Mind*, trans. Jane Zielonko (London: Secker & Warburg, 1953), 4–5.
102 Witkiewicz, *Insatiability*, 107.
103 Ibid., 108.
104 Ibid., 184.

against the Eastern 'hordes'. Everything is lined up to put Sloboluchovicz's brilliant battle plan into action when the dictator suddenly surrenders, and the Chinese politely behead him.

In the new system, art and literary criticism are completely abolished. Zipcio, by now a 'consummate lunatic, a mild catatonic', is forced to marry a Chinese beauty.[105] If the minds in the defeated system sought to satisfy insatiable metaphysical drives, the new system generates insatiable hunger for the de-energizing pills.

Such a summary of events gives a misleading idea of a text in which events are clouded in mist and almost exclusively conveyed in terms of monstrous and shifting psychological and philosophical speculations. As Daniel Gerould writes:

> The Witkacian fictional 'grab bag' eschews any conscious experimentation with narrative technique but stretches the traditional nineteenth-century novel completely out of shape through a monstrous infusion of erotic adventures, philosophical speculations, and apocalyptic predictions of coming disaster, which are sardonically presented by the author's alter ego serving as narrator.[106]

Sándor Szathmári, *Kazohinia*

Schizophrenic madness and disturbing peace are also set against one another in Sándor Szathmári's *Kazohinia* (1941), the final example of dystopian fiction in this section. The novel recasts Gulliver's quadruple shipwrecks (from Jonathan Swift's *Gulliver's Travels*) into the single shipwreck of a modern Gulliver. Nevertheless, the book satirizes three different societies: two societies, the Hins and the Behins, which are found on an imaginary island, and a third society in Gulliver's own England in which Gulliver inadvertently ridicules England by praising its nationalist and social follies.

Szathmári's Gulliver, a medical doctor, volunteers to defend the noble ideals of 'Great Britain and Christian civilization'. His wife, this 'paragon' of a faithful partner and mother,[107] is pleased to send him off to Shanghai in the hopes that the cost of living will be cheaper there so that Gulliver can send more money home. Should he die heroically, life insurance would provide enough for her and the children to cherish his memory in a way befitting of his rank.

When the shipwrecked Gulliver is washed ashore to an island, he is puzzled to see that its inhabitants, the Hins, are not patriots, they have no money or permanent homes of their own, they do not cook and they have no intimate friendships. Poverty, property and class distinctions are unknown. As Gulliver's native informant explains, the island's basic rule is 'kazo', an unconditional acceptance of nature in the service of the common good.[108] In terms of 'kazo', the soul is an unnecessary, even harmful concept, and a source of disharmony with the body. Language, philosophy, history, art, music, morality, law, romantic love and all other mental products are empty, dangerous and wasteful.

In a fleeting affair with a Hin woman, Gulliver discovers that she has no patience with his wasteful romantic drivel and only wants to do 'sexual work' to have two more children.[109]

---

105 Ibid., 524.

106 Daniel Gerould, ed., trans., *The Witkiewicz Reader* (Evanston, IL: Northwestern University Press, 1992), 17.

107 Sándor Szathmári, *Voyage to Kazohinia*, trans. Inez Kemenes (North Adams, IL: New Europe Books, 2012), 3, 9.

108 Szathmári, *Voyage to Kazohinia*, 44–8.

109 Ibid., 126–51, here 129.

Sex with her is sober and mechanical. The Behins, who constitute the island's second society, do hold on to such drivel, therefore, the Hins have placed them into a camp that resembles a lunatic asylum. Frustrated by the equanimity of the Hins and fascinated by the Behin belief in spirituality, Gulliver joins the Behins, but soon discovers that their drivel leads not only to language abuse but also to brutal confrontations between rigid ideologies. One must respond to 'prick-pruck' by putting one's finger on the nose. Should Gulliver fail to do this, he will be condemned; but if he reciprocates, the smiling counterpart will scratch his posterior, which Gulliver must reciprocate in turn.[110]

Gulliver's repeated objections to Behin idiocies ironically echo the Hin criticism. Now he is the one to claim that words and ideas that do not refer to the material world are senseless. Realizing the absurdity of creating words for non-existent things, Gulliver adopts the Hin view that words need to reflect life and must refer to material things, but he fails to recognize that the Behin errors are exaggerated British mistakes. He hopes that telling his story at home will teach his enlightened countrymen to appreciate English manners. Should they not be dismayed to learn that the hungry Behins dizzily stagger around while mountains of food rot away in the warehouses? This could surely not happen at home!

Gulliver's visit to the Behins ends in a bloody dénouement. The Behins want to burn Gulliver at the stake but the Hins rescue him. Subsequently, the Behins attack Gulliver again and the Hins mercilessly spray them with poisonous gas which kills them all. Back with the Hins, Gulliver probes the mentality behind their genocide and is taught a lesson in evolutionary biology. Only those original Behin inhabitants of the island survived whose genes mutated in such a way that made them into lovers of nature. The rest gradually died out, while the new Hin species evolved. In the world of the novel, a Behin is born only when an unfortunate mutation produces a brain without an electric conducting layer, the result of which resembles the primitive mind of the species that died out. Gulliver thinks that Behin mutations are unknown in England, but he is told by Zatamon that he failed to hear the voice of his own culture in the Behin madness: England does indeed have a Behin culture. Gulliver is outraged when he is regretfully informed that the English constitute an 'atavistic, transitional species that must at first drive itself out of the existing world so that the kazo can assume harmonic form'.[111]

Gulliver's pompous national rhetoric and his naïve adulation of his domestic bliss confirm this devastating prediction. This Gulliver remains a brainwashed Englishman. Back home, his wife confesses that she had spent the life insurance for the upkeep of their 'splendid' home, and she encourages him to return to Kazohinia until the thirty-year statute of limitations expires. However, Gulliver reassures her that the royalties of his travel account will compensate for the lost income and he closes his manuscript with the great news that he re-established domestic bliss in his 'cozy English home' after throwing out tactfully, but firmly, a gigolo.[112]

Such a spoof on England was welcome in Hungary, which joined the Axis in 1940. The censor of the first edition of 1941 apparently only demanded that passages relating to Italy's Ethiopian war and to the 'pornographic' love scene be scrapped. For the 1946 edition, Szathmári reinstituted the scrapped passages and added an epilogue in which he regretted that readers did not recognize that he regarded the Hin society as a desirable future. The epilogue has not been reprinted, but its position has been restated in a later postscript by Dezső Keresztury. Critics tend to question Szathmári's re-interpretation but not because the Hins depart from their liberal

---

110 Ibid., 171–5.
111 Ibid., 336.
112 Ibid., 352.

A history of fiction

and rational convictions when they spray the irrational and inhuman Behins to death. It is as if they agreed with Čapek's Wolf Meynert that 'the rest' ought to be eliminated. Szathmári was an engineer by profession. Was he aware of the double bind in the issue?

Contested interwar spaces

The Trianon Peace Treaty inverted rather than resolved the ethnic tension in the region. If earlier the tensions arose largely from struggles of the national minorities to gain cultural and political independence, the conflicts after the war concerned the German and Hungarian minorities in the new, reconstituted or enlarged states. The main sites of tension became then Transylvania, the Vilnius region, Istria, Trieste, as well as former Galicia, Ruthenia and the German-speaking part of Bohemia (called 'Sudetenland' by the Germans). Tragically, none of these sites was able to develop peaceful multilingual and multicultural societies, and by the end of the 1930s, political and military interventions followed. We select trilingual Transylvania as a case study.[113] At the same time, the Stalinist purges in the USSR in the 1930s dramatically reduced the existential space for exiled communists from East Central Europe, a theme that will be discussed using Arthur Koestler's *Darkness at Noon* and Danilo Kiš's *A Tomb for Boris Davidovich*.

Transylvania

The first Transylvanian novel to emerge from the ruins of the Monarchy was Dezső Szabó's *The Swept-Away Village* (*Az elsodort falu*), published on 23 May 1919 shortly after the Hungarian Commune came to power. Szabó was associated with *Nyugat* during the war, and as late as 1915 wrote that instead of killing our enemies we ought to kill the possibility of having enemies at all.[114] But his 1919 novel represented a populist turn, for it chastised his liberal and Western-oriented friends in an expressionistic, emotional, metaphoric-mystic language.

Szabó's novel ends with an apotheosis of its Székely[115] hero, János Böjthe, who returns from the war to his native Transylvanian village in order to start a family and a new life. Böjthe embodies the dormant energies and ethics that Szabó attributed to the Székelys, while the other characters are failures: Miklós Farkas, an Endre Ady-type figure, is driven insane after vacillating between rural values and urban decadence; Judit Farcády, the angelic beauty of the village, loves Miklós but becomes the mistress of Jews and finally a dissolute prostitute in Budapest. The novel's villains are Hungarians who import decadent foreign values into Transylvania: Jews, Western-oriented intellectuals, writers, feminists, aristocrats, clerics and military officers who champion a senseless war. Most lower-class people are overwhelmed by poverty, greed or

---

113 See Cornis-Pope and Neubauer, *History of the Literary Cultures*, vol. 2, particularly the following chapters: Tomas Venclova, 'Vilnius/Wilno/Vilna: The Myth of Division and the Myth of Connection', 11–27; Katarzyna Jerzak, 'The City that is No More, The City that Will Stand Forever: Danzig/Gdańsk as Homeland in the Writings of Günter Grass, Paweł Huelle, and Stefan Chwin', 77–92; Anna Campanile, 'The Torn Soul of a City: Trieste as a Center of Polyphonic Culture and Literature', 145–61; Seth Wolitz, 'Vilna: The Jerusalem of Lithuania', 185–8; Sabina Mihelj, 'Transformations of Imagined Landscapes: Istra and Šavrinija as Intercultural Narratives', 364–73.

114 Dezső Szabó, 'A francia lélek keresztmetszete: Laczkó Géza azonos című cikkéről 1915. I. 24–27' [A cross-section of the French: On Géza Laczkó's article by the same title in 1915, I, pp. 24–27], *Nyugat* 8, no. 3 (1915): 168.

115 Editor's note: 'Székely' refers to the Hungarian community living largely in the Székely Land in Romania.

alcohol. Weak and ugly figures rule over the strong and healthy with the exception of Böjthe who is akin to Władysław Stanisław Reymont's peasants.

Transylvania's transfer to Romania led to widespread irredentism in Hungary and among Transylvanian Hungarians but, surprisingly, during the latter half of the 1920s, it not only allowed a flowering of Transylvania's national literatures but also some short-lived but intense exchanges amongst these literatures. The agents took the form of new journals and artistic organizations. In 1921 Cezar Petrescu launched the substantial Romanian journal *Gândirea* ('Thought') and soon published translations of Ady and Babits. The same year, the poet Sándor Reményik launched the Hungarian journal *Pásztortűz* ('Campfire'). In 1924 a Saxon named Heinrich Zillich launched the journal *Klingsor* in Braşov, while the architect and cultural historian Károly Kós founded the high-quality publishing house Erdélyi Szépmíves Céh ('The Transylvanian fine arts guild') in Cluj. In 1926, the publishing house was taken over by a group called Helikon, a loose association of Hungarian writers in Transylvania who gathered annually between 1926 and 1944 in the Marosvécs castle of János Kemény.

In 1928, the Helikon association launched the journal *Erdélyi Helikon* ('Transylvanian Helicon') under the editorship of Miklós Bánffy, aiming to become an 'observation deck unto the world'.[116] Indeed, over the years the journal published an impressive range of poets from all over the world including several Romanian writers. These Hungarian projects were loosely associated with Kós's theory of Transylvanianism, which belatedly sought coexistence and local autonomy within a federalist structure, expressed by the slogan, 'Transylvania belongs to the Transylvanian nations!' Kós held that the majority of Transylvanians disagreed with the political decisions about Transylvania; Hungary and the other parts of Romania were not aware of its variety. Transylvania's national constituents

> lived their own lives, building their own social and cultural institutions side by side, not mingling with each other but not really bothering each other either. They rarely crossed each other's paths, yet they were in touch with each other, learning from each other, influencing each other.[117]

Between 1926 and 1932, the Saxon journal *Klingsor* and the Hungarian journals *Pásztortűz* and *Erdélyi Helikon* published several special issues including translations from the other journal's language (from German to Hungarian and vice versa), and the writers also spent many evenings together. These promising contacts ended, however, in 1933. That year, Kós translated Adolf Meschendörfer's 1931 novel *Die Stadt im Osten* ('The city in the East'), a book about growing up in Kronstadt/Braşov. When Károly Molter criticized its German orientation,[118] Zillich, who supported the Nazis, responded furiously.[119] Molter then claimed that *Klingsor*'s hitherto hidden German ideology became evident with Hitler's arrival:

---

116 Lajos Áprily, 'Bevezető sorok' [Introductory lines], *Erdélyi Hélikon* 1, no. 1 (1928): 1.

117 Károly Kós, *Transylvania: An Outline of its Cultural History*, trans. Lorna K. Dunbar (Budapest: Szépirodalmi, 1989), 81.

118 Károly Molter, 'A német szellem belháborúja' [The wars of the German spirit] *Erdélyi Helikon*, no. 7 (1933): 459–70.

119 Heinrich Zillich, 'Das Echo der zeitwandelnden Geschehnisse in Deutschland', *Klingsor: siebenbürgische Zeitschrift* 10, no. 4 (1933): 154–5.

A history of fiction

Jews and other minorities Europe-wide have become ever more exposed to the fists of an ever more unrestrained nationalism; suddenly all nationalists become heady with their race and start Jew baiting, start to instil a sense of weakness in all those who are less numerable than the sons of his nation.[120]

In 1936, Zillich published his novel *Zwischen Grenzen und Zeiten* ('Between borders and times'), which portrayed tensions within the Saxon community and conflicts with Transylvania's national groups. Like Szabó, Zillich included war scenes and devoted several chapters to the misery of people fleeing the invading Romanian army in 1916, though he did not portray invader cruelty. The narrator portrays culturally, historically and ethically superior Saxons who resent Magyarization and increasingly identify with their linguistic brothers in Austria and Germany. In the final scene, the protagonist is drafted into the Romanian army to fight the Hungarian Commune. Ferenc Szemlér daringly remarked that Zillich's book was based on the idea that the Germans have a mission both in Europe and the world as a whole. The image that Zillich evoked was 'dangerous and artless' for it arrogated to German culture everything beautiful and good in Europe. No Hungarian writer in Hungary would have dared to write such a review at the time.

The controversy over publishing Mihail Sadoveanu's novel *Baltagul* ('The hatchet') in German is a good example of how the Transylvania Saxons were distrustful of the Romanians as well. Harald Krasser, member of the *Klingsor* circle, translated the novel, but three days before it was due to be published in Munich it was revealed that Sadoveanu had taken over the editorship of two small 'Jewish-Marxist' papers. Krasser was severely reprimanded, and he publicly rejected Sadoveanu's politics in an issue of *Klingsor* in a most cowardly (or ideologically convinced?) manner.[121] Zillich left that year for Germany and became a General Staff officer of the Wehrmacht. He continued publishing after the war and as late as 1968 claimed that the Hungarian writers were afraid to keep contact with the Saxons because of some powerful Jewish donors.

The most impressive figure of the Transylvanian rapprochement was Miklós Bánffy. He represented Kolozsvár in the Hungarian parliament (1910–12), was Director of the Budapest Opera and the National Theatre (1913–18) and was Minister of Foreign Affairs (1921–2). In 1926, he returned to Transylvania and became a Romanian citizen. His *Transylvanian Trilogy* appeared as *Erdélyi történet* in the years 1934–40 but received its deserved international acclaim only when the English translation was published in 1999. The plot, which covers the years 1904–14, shuttles back and forth between aristocratic life in Transylvania, Hungarian politics in Budapest and the private life of Bálint Abády, a young conservative Transylvanian politician. The portrayal of Transylvania is affectionate, the sketches of its declining aristocracy both ironic and sympathetic. The autobiographically coloured Abády admires the leading conservative István Tisza but knows that change is inevitable. Abády is also sensitive to Transylvania's ethnic plurality.

Abády is present when the banner of the real Transylvanian Movement is unfurled on 12 March 1910 in Marosvásárhely. The Movement wanted autonomy for Transylvania but was more modest than Kós's Transylvanianism of the 1920s, which sought a greater amount of independence after Transylvania was already Romanian. The Transylvanian Movement felt

---

120 Károly Molter, 'Az elvarázsolt varázsló: Valami Heinrich Zillingnek' [The spellbound sorcerer: response to Heinrich Zillich], *Erdélyi Helikon*, no. 6 (1934): 459–65, here 461.

121 Harald Krasser, 'Zur deutsch-rumänischen Kulturannäherung', *Klingsor: siebenbürgische Zeitschrift* 13, no. 12 (1936): 472–6.

that the Hungarian government did not respect Transylvania's uniqueness: 'The Transylvanian spirit was slowly being drained away in the maw of Hungarian self-sufficiency and at best was ignored.'[122] Tisza, now in opposition, listens but politely refuses to support a particularistic movement.[123] When Abády promises support 'for a new law governing the rights of minorities' the Székely representatives start 'to demur' and he is forced to table the topic.[124] According to a footnote by the translators, Abády's fictional speech encapsulates Bánffy's maiden speech in the Hungarian Parliament in 1910.[125] Abády maintains, 'we are forced to witness the degradation of our ethnic minorities'. He continues:

> A national policy that is as uncaring as it is ignorant regarding our minority problems is now increasingly provoking dangerous irredentist and seditious tendencies, tendencies which can be justified as provoked by unfair treatment. ... [F]or centuries in Transylvania people have lived happily together regardless of race or creed or language ... Everybody who is or wishes to be at home in this country must be welcomed and made to feel at home with confidence that nowhere will he find any form of discrimination.[126]

Indeed, Abády successfully defends Romanians who are ruthlessly exploited by corrupt, local Hungarian potentates, but this is the only episode in which minorities appear in the novel. Neither Abády nor the narrator proposes concrete steps to grant the Romanians linguistic, political or cultural autonomy.

In 1943, the Hungarian government commissioned Bánffy to negotiate with the Romanian opposition leader Iuliu Maniu about turning jointly against the Nazis, but Maniu insisted on the return of Northern Transylvania to Romania and the attempt failed. Bánffy stayed in Transylvania after the war and moved to Budapest shortly before his death in 1950.

Cosmopolitans in Stalin's prisons

Arthur Koestler, *Darkness at Noon* (1940)

The Hungarian-born Arthur Koestler became a secret member of the German Communist Party in the early 1930s but soon started to question its ideology. He joined the Republican effort in the Spanish Civil War, was captured by the Franquists and put on death row, but an international campaign managed to save him. In 1938, he gave up his Party membership and started to write *Darkness at Noon* in response to his own incarceration and the Moscow trials of the 1930s. The characters are fictitious, but the historical circumstances are real. The protagonist is a synthesis of real victims at the Moscow trials, some of whom Koestler knew personally. The fictional Rubashov, like Koestler, is an internationalist.

---

122 Miklós Bánffy, *They Were Divided (The Writing on the Wall)*, vol. 3, trans. Patrick Thursfield and Katalin Banffy-Jelen (London: Arcadia Books, 2001), 31.
123 Ibid., 31.
124 Ibid., 32.
125 Ibid., 32–6.
126 Ibid., 33, 34.

A history of fiction

Of the epigraphs preceding each Part, the second one is the most revealing. It is a quote by Dietrich von Nieheim, a fifteenth-century Bishop of Verden, Germany:

> When the existence of the Church is threatened, she is released from the command-ments of morality. With unity as the end, the use of every means is sanctified, even cunning, treachery, violence, simony, prison, death. For all order is for the sake of the community, and the individual must be sacrificed to the common good.[127]

The novel's external narrator has no panopticon to survey. His eyes and ears remain all but fixed on Nicholas Salmanovitch Rubashov, a hero of the revolution whose arrest as an alleged conspirator opens the novel.[128] When the cell door slams behind him, he leans against it, lights a cigarette and coolly surveys the site: 'On the bed to his right lay two fairly clean blankets, and the straw mattress looked newly filled. The wash-basin to his left had no plug, but the tap functioned.'[129] Yet, he soon becomes obsessed with his communist experiences, especially with regard to three Party activists he betrayed: the German locksmith Richard, who disagreed with the Party line after the Nazis came to power; Little Loewy, who continued to boycott shipments to Nazi Germany at a Belgian port even after the Moscow Central Committee decided to send shipments to fascist regimes; and Rubashov's own submissive private secretary Arlova from the Belgian Trade Delegation. She became his mistress and expected Rubashov's help when she was accused of conspiracy and put on trial back home, but he only submitted a statement that sharply condemned her opposition. Rubashov disclosed Richard's name to the Nazis to get him arrested; he initiated the expulsion of Little Loewy and his comrades from the Party, which led to Loewy's suicide; and he allowed Arlova's execution.

Rubashov must now undergo the same purges that eliminated these people. He welcomes his first interrogator, Ivanov, an old friend and former battalion commander[130] who admits that their roles could be reversed[131] but regretfully observes that Rubashov consistently refers to the communists as 'you' instead of 'we'. Indeed, Rubashov no longer believes that the Party is infallible and that it serves the interests of the revolution and the future of humanity.[132] He is accused of having participated in a project to kill No. 1 (read: Stalin) and is offered a mild sentence if he confesses but claims that he later withdrew after learning of the criminal plans.[133] Rubashov rejects the lie but is given a fortnight to reconsider. Ivanov conducts his second interrogation in the jail cell and as he enters, Rubashov is irate, telling Ivanov to leave, because of an incident that took place a few days before:[134] Michael Bogrov, a top hero of the revolu-tion, had been led past Rubashov's cell on the way to his execution; he screamed Rubashov's name as he passed, believing that Rubashov had betrayed him. Rubashov assumes that this inci-dent with Bogrov was set up in order to get him to sign the confession. Ivanov tells Rubashov that his brutal subordinate Gletkin staged the scene in order to intimidate Rubashov, and that

---

127 Arthur Koestler, *Darkness at Noon*, trans. Daphne Hardy (New York: Macmillan, 1940), 95.
128 The narrator does not comment and produces only the following passages where Rubashov is absent: Vassilij the porter (7ff and 243–52), Little Loewy (68), Ivanov & Getlin (100–06, 162–3), and Getlin & his secretary (240).
129 Koestler, *Darkness*, 3.
130 Ibid., 78.
131 Ibid., 109.
132 Ibid., 81.
133 Ibid., 91.
134 Ibid., 143–62.

Gletkin did it against his express instructions. He tells Rubashov that he should confess willingly, recognizing its logical necessity:[135] 'one may not regard the world as a sort of metaphysical brothel for emotions. That is the first commandment for us'.[136] Ivanov later tells Gletkin that Rubashov will sign the confession,[137] which he indeed does.

However, the last interrogations are not only delayed, but they are conducted by Gletkin who replaces Ivanov. Gletkin later informs Rubashov that Ivanov was arrested and executed.[138] Gletkin belongs to the new 'Neanderthaler' generation of interrogators who manipulate the body, torture the mind and use false witnesses. In the end, Rubashov consents to signing a confession that burdens him much more than the one he signed for Ivanov.[139] Gletkin responds to his secretary's congratulations by glancing at the blinding lamp that tortured Rubashov and says, this 'plus lack of sleep and physical exhaustion. It is all a matter of constitution'.[140]

The final Part, titled 'The Grammatical Fiction',[141] reflects on the 'I' that the Party's 'We' seeks to suppress. When Rubashov had first hit upon the phrase 'grammatical fiction'[142] for his 'I', he realized that its realm started where rational 'thinking to a conclusion' had stopped. Searching for himself and a proper philosophical perspective, he had to surrender his former logical and even mathematical reasoning. He realized that his declarative utterances had always been accompanied by an internal second voice, which engages him in dialogue.[143] From that point on, Rubashov sympathized with Dostoevsky's Raskolnikov, whereas Ivanov regarded it as 'humanitarian fog-philosophy', for Raskolnikov's case would only be exemplary had he 'bumped off the old woman at the command of the Party'.[144]

Facing death, Rubashov tries to find his Self instead of trying to save his skin. In his diary,[145] he records that the communists follow 'universal reason' down to its final consequence, whatever the costs.[146] But one must have unshakeable faith in the path to follow. No. 1 has this faith, but Rubashov no longer believes in his own infallibility[147] and he is torn, both about the general path and whether to follow his rational thoughts or his new emotional and illogical attitudes. His ideological conviction is further undermined both by his communication with his neighbouring jail-mate who served the Tsarist regime, and by the people he meets while circling around in the jail's courtyard.

Koestler was writing *Darkness at Noon* as Stalin was suppressing communist internationalism and initiating cooperation with the Nazis, the result of which was the Molotov–Ribbentrop Pact of 23 August 1939. In the novel, Little Loewy and his Belgian comrades reject this political shift and Bogrov is executed for opposing No. 1's new policy of building small submarines for 'domestic' purposes instead of large ones for a global revolution.[148] After the war, Stalin's nationalism generated widespread anti-Semitism in the Soviet Union, which left its mark in literature as well.

---

135 Ibid., 148.
136 Ibid., 152.
137 Ibid., 163.
138 Ibid., 219, 227.
139 Ibid., 175, 189–94, 239.
140 Ibid., 240.
141 Ibid., 243–67.
142 Ibid., 111.
143 Ibid., 108–9.
144 Ibid., 155–6.
145 Ibid., 228–9.
146 Ibid., 98.
147 Ibid., 100.
148 Ibid., 150–1.

A history of fiction

Danilo Kiš, 'A Tomb for Boris Davidovich'

Thirty-five years after the publication of *Darkness at Noon*, Kiš tells the story of an old Jewish revolutionary who is tortured into confessing that he was a Western agent in his short story, 'A Tomb for Boris Davidovich' ('Grobnica za Borisa Davidovića', 1975). However, Kiš recounts the story in a manner different from Koestler's claustrophobic style. Central is the issue of identity. Koestler's Rubashov was instrumental in the death of fellow revolutionaries. Only in prison, subjected to the same demands of obedience, does he question his former submissiveness to the ideology of the communal 'we'. While the lie of the forced confession becomes a comparable ethical issue for Boris Davidovich Novsky, the story of his life is presented from the start as a legend or incomplete fiction about multiple identity. In contrast to the cited opening of *Darkness at Noon*, Kiš opens with the 'free-floating' imagination of a narrator:

> History recorded him as Novsky, which is only a pseudonym (or, more precisely, one of his pseudonyms). But what immediately spawns doubt is the question: did history really *record* him? In the index of the *Granat Encyclopedia*, among the 246 authorized biographies and autobiographies of great men and participants in the Revolution, his name is missing.[149]

Kiš's narrator promises to 'try to bring to life the memory of the extraordinary and enigmatic person that was Novsky',[150] however fragmentary and incomplete it will be. He cites a commentator called Haupt who maintains that 'certain omissions' during the revolution and the years immediately following it are due (as in the case of Rubashov) to the fact that Novsky's 'life merges with public life and becomes "a part of history"'.[151] Haupt further points out that the biographies of the *Granat Encyclopedia* were written in the late 1920s with significant omissions and haste ('Haste before death, we might add'[152]) – as if the biographers could anticipate the trials of the 1930s.

After relating a cosmopolitan and adventurous life (with gaps filled by imaginative flights), the second half of the story recounts the confrontations between the arrested communist Novski and his investigator Fedukin.[153] Novsky wants to keep his story as revolutionary leader intact, but he is gradually weakened when each witness is shot on the spot as a result of his refusal to sign the prepared confession. Fedukin and Novsky finally agree on the wording of a confession that would send Novsky into exile. But when he tries to escape from the camp, the guards pursue him, and he jumps into a hot furnace.

Fleeing the Nazis in the 1930s

The trickle of exodus in the latter part of the 1920s dramatically swelled in the second half of the 1930s due to the steadily increasing threat of Hitler's Germany. Witold Gombrowicz's novel *Trans-Atlantyk* raises fundamental issues about writing abroad. Gombrowicz escaped the German invasion of Poland but also kept his distance from post-war communist Poland.

---

149 Danilo Kiš, 'A Tomb for Boris Davidovich', in *A Tomb for Boris Davidovich*, trans. Duška Mikić-Mitchell (New York: Harcourt Brace Jovanovich, 1978), 73–108, here 73.

150 Ibid., 73–4.

151 Ibid., 74.

152 Ibid.

153 Ibid., 89–108.

Gombrowicz's own exit from Poland was unique. He was asked to join and promote the maiden voyage of the Polish transatlantic liner *Chrobry* (named after Bolesław I *Chrobry*, or Bolesław I the Brave, the first King of Poland crowned in 1025), but the war broke out when the boat arrived in Buenos Aires. Gombrowicz decided to stay in Argentina, and his memoirs indicate that he had anticipated the war and took the boat to escape it. He names the protagonist of his novel Witold Gombrowicz and places him in a similar exile situation. The plot, however, deviates from the autobiography, though it revolves around issues of exile. Out of eagerness to secure a living, the fictional namesake must find a place amongst other Poles in Buenos Aires, including the Ambassador, Thomas, a retired Polish army major and his son Ignatius, Gonzalo, a rich and hedonistic homosexual, and three crazy but rich businessmen. Gonzalo is eager to seduce Ignatius. When Thomas is informed of Gonzalo's intentions with his son, he challenges him to a duel. Witold and the Polish industrialists become his seconds for the duel, but they put the bullets in their shirtsleeves instead of in the revolvers. When Witold feels guilty and confesses this to Thomas, things become grotesquely funny: the father now wants to kill his son in order to save his honour; Ignatius plans to commit patricide but bursts out laughing when he approaches his father. In a Carnival, a Brouhaha takes over: 'And on from Laughter to Laughter, Ha-ha with Laughter, ha-ha with Laughter, they ha-ha, ha-ha, they Ha-ha-ha! ...'[154]

Resolving the social and political issues of 1939 in cosmic laughter is itself a political statement. Within the novel, it actually means leaning towards Gonzalo rather than the often pompous, rigid and crazy Poles of Buenos Aires. Gonzalo urges Witold to take sides: 'what is the Land of the Fathers to you? Isn't the Land of the Sons better? Substitute the Land of the Sons for the Land of the Fathers, then you'll see!'[155] When Witold departs, the notion of 'The Land of the Sons' assails him, circling round his nose like an irksome fly, like snuff tickling his nose, until hollow laughter seizes him too: 'The Land of the Sons! The Land of the Sons! Oh, how Stupid this is, how Crazy, insanity pure and simple!'[156] However, he has limited respect for the mentality of the father, and even less for the rest of the Polish community in Buenos Aires. They come out of a Polish cultural and political tradition that he refused to defend by not returning to Europe.

What the 'The Land of the Sons' refers to is more difficult to pinpoint since Ignatius remains in the background. Gonzalo means, of course, his own world, but we should not limit this to his homosexual love for the son. For Witold and some Polish readers this 'Portuguese man born in Libya of a Persian Turkish mother'[157] represents an open world set against the closed Polish tradition. At the end of his account, the fictional Witold is no longer laughing at Gonzalo's world, but rather with it.

During his 18-year stay, the historical Gombrowicz made many attempts to establish himself as a Latin-American writer in this 'Land of the Sons', but publication of *Trans-Atlantyk* by the Instytut Literacki in 1953 (excerpts already appeared in 1951 in the journal *Kultura*) started a European reorientation. The most promising opportunity opened up in 1957 when the briefly liberalized Polish regime permitted the publication of a book that contained a revised (uncensored) version of *Trans-Atlantyk* and Gombrowicz's play *The Marriage* (*Ślub*). Gombrowicz's critique of the pre-war Polish 'Land of the Father' was obviously welcome in a communist

---

154 Witold Gombrowicz, *Trans-Atlantyk: An Alternate Translation*, trans. Danuta Borchardt (New Haven, CT: Yale University Press, 2014), 166, ellipses included in the original.

155 Ibid., 77.

156 Ibid., 79.

157 Ibid., 49.

regime. Speaking to homeland readers as well as those in exile, he took a double track by call-ing the novel grotesque, satirical, fun and absurd, but only referred to himself for he did not feel entitled to write about Poland.[158] And yet, he expected deeper and more comprehensive readings because the novel concerned a view of the nation, about which the exiled Poles and those at home were 'not yet free-minded enough'.[159] He wanted it to be a satire not just of Piłsudski's Poland, but of the 'Poland that has been created by her historical existence and her location in the world'.[160] He wanted people to stop the genuflecting that occurs so often in the novel. Reading it should become a criticism of one's national flaws and make individuals more resistant to the masses. After having set such ambitious goals, Gombrowicz surprisingly ends his preface with a diminuendo: 'Trans-Atlantyk does not have a subject beyond the story that it is telling. It is just a tale, nothing more than just a narrative of a certain world'.[161]

Czesław Miłosz and catastrophism

The catastrophism that appeared in Polish prose and drama of the 1920s and reached its zenith in the lyric poetry of the 1930s can best be described as an opposite pole to the avant-garde. In contrast to the sometimes rather naïve optimism of the latter, the central element of cata-strophism is the grotesque, which portrays the tragic and the comical together in harmony. As opposed to the future-centric world view of the avant-garde, in catastrophism a significant role is given to the past, recalled with the help of various systems of allusion, myth reinterpreta-tions, symbols and archetypes, whereas the future appears only as a period of destruction and catastrophe, as a dystopia. The majority of catastrophists, and this is especially true of the new lyrical generation that entered the scene in the late 1920s, were not interested in the relation-ship between the individual and the community, or the various workings of society, but in the meaning of human existence, the relationship between the individual and authority, and the conflict between man and what transcends, concerns, consumes and haunts him.

The catastrophists had closer links to trends that preceded the avant-garde, such as symbol-ism, art nouveau, neo-romanticism, decadence, etc., although they also took some metaphori-cal and image construction methods from the avant-garde, and especially from expressionism and surrealism. In contrast to avant-garde art, catastrophism returns to set forms; in contrast to the 'incomprehensible' works of the avant-garde, catastrophist literature is 'difficult' and com-plicated in a way that requires a wide knowledge of culture and history.[162]

---

158 Ibid., xviii (Preface to the 1957 edition).
159 Ibid., xv.
160 Ibid., xv–xvi.
161 Ibid., xvii.
162 Jerzy Speina, who has given one of the best descriptions of catastrophism, distinguishes three often interconnected currents within this broad trend. First, technocratic catastrophism, which sees the ex-plosive development of the modern industrial civilization as a mortal danger to humanity. A second major variant of catastrophism may be described as historical philosophy. This kind of catastrophism blames the imbalances of historical development for the future tragedy that will destroy the whole of humanity or turn it into an anthill. The third branch of catastrophism, which expressed the vulner-ability and world alien nature of man, could be referred to as existentialist catastrophism. The genre of catastrophism cannot be clearly assessed: the evaluation of a given work is heavily dependent on whether it came about in the 1920s or 30s, on which branch of catastrophism is dominant in it, on which concrete future the author's fears for humanity are based, on what magnitude of disaster they expect and so on. See Jerzy Speina, *Powieści Stanisława Ignacego Witkiewicza: geneza i struktura* [The novels of Stanisław Ignacy Witkiewicz: genesis and structure] (Toruń: Towarzystwo Naukowe, 1965), 12–15.

Czesław Miłosz is not only one of the greatest poets of the twentieth century, but also one of the leading proponents of catastrophism. Just like the iconic nineteenth-century national poet Adam Mickiewicz, Miłosz was born as a Polish gentleman in Lithuania in 1911, which at the time was part of Russia. He was raised in Vilnius, which according to the 1921 peace treaty had been given to Poland and was half populated by Poles and half populated by Jews. It was here, in an atmosphere of nationalist hatred and disdain for divergence, that Miłosz became a dedicated Europeanist and mixed this commitment with avant-garde leftism and devout Catholicism.

It was from Vilnius in 1939 that he practically had to escape to Warsaw, having been, to all intents and purposes, banished on charges of being left-wing. During the war, Miłosz took part in cultural work for the resistance in Warsaw. Later, as a cultural diplomat in Washington and Paris, he watched from the front row as Central and Eastern Europe became the foreign possession of the Soviet Empire. This is the subject of his novel *Zdobycie władzy* ('The seizure of power'), first published in French in 1953, which is comparable to his book of essays on the same subject, *The Captive Mind* (also published in 1953 as *Zniewolony umysł*). The novel's main protagonist cannot bear the new Soviet reality and defects to the West; the author did the same in 1951. Miłosz first settled in Paris, then he moved to the United States in 1960, where he became professor of Slavic literature at the University of California, Berkeley. Following 1989, he bought an apartment in Cracow and spent most of his time there.

Miłosz's oeuvre is a path along which every single station gets destroyed; they fade into memory one by one and lose their value and reason for existence. It began with the loss of his childhood, which to him meant the loss of nature, as described in his 1955 novel set in the magical landscape of Lithuania, *Dolina Issy* ('The Issa valley'). Miłosz's momentous essay collections are all constructed in a similar manner: as a kind of spiritual autobiography, they begin in Lithuania and Poland in his youth, and through the examination of the philosophical history of the twentieth century, they arrive at the metaphysical questions of humanity in accordance with his belief that the thread of history and its very foundations are themselves metaphysical.

The great question of humanity and the fate of human civilization, and in relation to this, that of Manicheism – why does the evil that was created by God exist in this world and push this civilisation towards destruction? – preoccupied Miłosz throughout his life, even if his poetry changed significantly during the war, becoming – in his own words – more understandable, as normally happens when a poet wants to communicate something important to his readers. The *poeta doctus* who writes classically clear sentences, preserves the cultural heritage of the past, and whose poems are full of references and quotes, becomes increasingly prominent after the life-threatening illegality of the war years.

The development of Miłosz's 'neo-classicism' did not occur without internal struggle. Miłosz resurrects such classical genres as the ode and the poetical treatise – although he infuses them with irony – and the fundamental principle of his whole poetic bearing is metre. It is the poet's task to determine guarantees for his fellow men and this is one of the reasons why, to him, the community of faith and perception embodied by classicism is a positively lost Eden. This is precisely why Miłosz is not a subjective poet and not a lyrical portrayer of experiences; the life of the man named Czesław Miłosz cannot be determined from his poems. His style is the role lyric, an art form that links to the voices of the past while testing the opportunities of the present, which – one can practically sense – was not written by a private individual, but by a 'cultural type'; a historical figure who was born and raised on the border between Roman Catholicism and Orthodoxy; a figure who has survived the depraved, anti-personal teething troubles of enthusiasm for 'social progress'; a figure who, in 1945 and beyond, saw the radical

A history of fiction

change in Polish life and witnessed the ages that attacked Catholic civilization in its most highly developed West European form, and later in an even more highly developed form in America; a figure who, despite all this, has preserved his faith in the value of art and literature, and in the fact that we can distinguish between good and bad literature. The task of the poet is nothing less than to challenge this memory-destroying process and to denote for his fellow man the guarantee of truth and justice.

The Second World War

Fiction about the First World War began to appear as soon as the Monarchy's censorship disappeared; yet fiction about the Second World War remained stunted for a long time because communist censorship was so effective in all countries of the region. Second World War fiction is generally inferior to First World War fiction. Arguably, the best response to the war was Ivo Andrić's *The Bridge on the Drina* (*Na Drini ćuprija*), written during the German occupation of Belgrade and published in 1945. Though the real bridge was the subject of power struggles as well, its complex history interconnects conflicting ethnic groups, traditions, languages and even empires. Thus, even though the novel ends with the destruction of the bridge in the town of Višegrad in 1914, it may be read as an indirect answer to the ferocious violence happening around Andrić as he was writing and can therefore be conceptually linked up with the Second World War.

Fiction glorifying the Slovak National Uprising of 1944 belongs to the region's first pieces of Second World War literature. In Peter Jilemnický's *The Chronicles* (*Kronika*, 1947) Slovak partisans and Soviet parachutists defend a Slovak mountain village against the retreating Germans. The Gypsy thieves join the Uprising when the Germans burn down their settlement. The enemy includes the ethnic Germans and supporters of Jozef Tiso's government. Representing the Uprising as an outstanding mass movement in a Marxist sense became a Slovak narrative pattern. *The Chronicles* was followed by Peter Karvaš's *With Us and Against Us* (*S námi a proti nám*) in 1950, and Vladimír Mináč's trilogy, *Generations* (*Generácia*) published in 1958–61. First to deviate from the heroic style was Ladislav Mňačko, whose *Death Is Called Engelchen* (*Smrť sa volá Engelchen*, 1959) depicts a wounded narrator who tells his story to a nurse, with whom he falls in love, during his post-war convalescence. The post-war love affair, the bourgeois narrator's gradual move towards the Party, the partisan success in killing Nazis and the portrayal of some 'good' German soldiers who join the partisans – all of this is cliché-ridden and predictable. But the novel reveals tensions among the partisans and raises the question whether it was right to kill some high-ranking German officers which resulted in the Germans' retaliation in which they annihilated a Slovak village. The novel's dramatic figure is an enigmatic beautiful Jewess who sleeps with German officers in order to spy on them. After the war, she moves to Canada but is unable to digest her past and commits suicide.

In 1945, Jerzy Andrzejewski, a leading intellectual in the Polish resistance movement, published stories about moral dilemmas in *Night* (*Noc*). In his best-known novel, *Ashes and Diamonds* (*Popiół i diament*, 1948), he towed the Party line by suggesting that the Western-subsidized Home Army engaged in criminal activities against the communists during the post-war years. The young protagonist follows the Home Army, kills a venerable Party secretary and then is himself killed. A sub-plot reveals that a respected judge was a block warden in a concentration camp. The novel's success was enhanced when Andrzej Wajda made a film of it in 1958. It is unclear whether censorship forced Andrzejewski to portray the post-war Home Army as criminal. Like so many others, after the war, he may have believed that the communists were right. The novel fell out of favour after 1989. Andrzejewski was, however, among the first to take a satirical stance against the communist regime with 'The Great Lament of the Paper Head' ('Wielki lament papierowej głowy', 1953).

The Czechoslovak censors prolonged the gestation of Josef Škvorecký's *The Cowards* (*Zbabělci*). Written in 1949, the book follows the last days of Nazi rule through the eyes of a middle-class adolescent who prefers girls and saxophone playing to fighting. Danny's ironic contempt for bourgeois cowardice and his admiration of the communists' courage was apparently not enough for the censors, who prevented the book's publication in the late 1940s. In 1958, the book slipped through censorship but was withdrawn immediately after publication. The publisher's editorial board was subsequently suspended. *The Cowards* was finally published in 1964 but achieved international renown only when Škvorecký went into exile in 1968 and the novel was translated into English.

Bohumil Hrabal's *Closely Watched Trains* (*Ostře sledované vlaky*, 1965) is told by an adolescent boy who is no hero, though he dies while blowing up a German train. Miloš lives in a friendly village where sympathetic women sweeten his bitter experience of sexual maturation. His first sexual experience fails due to premature ejaculation and as a result, he tries to commit suicide. But, his second sexual experience, kindly granted to him by a mature woman from the underground movement, is a success. The gallery of motherly women is completed by the wife of the stationmaster who also advises Miloš about his sexual problems. He dies in the final scene, along with the German he himself shot. When the German cries out '*Mutti! Mutti!*' not for his mother, but for his wife, Miloš remembers his own mother. The female figures bring the warring sides closer to each other. The mood of the tragi-comic story runs from earthy to grotesque, from hilarious to tender. The story represented a breakthrough in fiction about war and resistance, and deservedly received international recognition, especially after Jiří Menzel made an Oscar-winning movie of it.

Hrabal's *I Served the King of England* (*Obsluhoval jsem anglického krále*, 1971) is similarly fantastic and grotesque. It is told by Ditie, a young picaro who never outgrows his adolescence and puny size. Employed in a restaurant/hotel, he serves the elite of the Czechoslovak Republic, the German occupiers and the communists of the post-war era. He seeks power and money but fails to acquire either due to a number of blunders and to his contrary spirit. His war adventures lead him to marry Lise, a German woman who bears him a demented child and dies during an allied bombing. After the war, Ditie is pardoned for his unpatriotic marriage and he builds a fabulous hotel by selling the stamp collection of his former father-in-law. Yet, he voluntarily ends up on a road repair crew. Alternatingly hilarious, erotic, racy and wistful, the novel mocks all forms of patriotism and ideology.

Jerzy Kosinski's *The Painted Bird* (1965) portrays the gruesome experiences of an adolescent narrator in the devastated Polish post-war countryside. Kosinski's claim that these experiences were autobiographical turned out to be untenable. The reason we cite this title here is because the issues concerning authenticity, fiction and facts became important tropes in Holocaust literature and in postmodern fiction. Whether Kosinski deliberately used innovative techniques that continually blur the line between fact and fiction, autobiography and invention, or whether he simply tried to mystify his biography is a matter of continued debate.

Due to censorship, but also to Hungary's political role in the war, very few fictional narratives appeared in the country in the early post-war decades. The most well-known Hungarian text about the war is not fiction, but Sándor Márai's first set of diaries, *Diary 1943–1944* (*Napló*), which he was able to publish in 1945 before the Stalinist regime took over.

A history of fiction

The Holocaust

Personal memories preserved the Holocaust, but its collective memory was belatedly activated. All communist regimes systematically tried to convert accounts of the Holocaust into communist, nationalist and anti-Nazi ideological writings. Since the Holocaust victims were not only Jews but also Romanies, communists and resistance fighters, it is perhaps appropriate to begin with the non-Jewish Polish writer Tadeusz Borowski.

Tadeusz Borowski, *This Way for the Gas, Ladies and Gentlemen*

Borowski, born in Soviet Zhitomir of Polish parents in 1922, wrote about Auschwitz, where he spent two years, soon after he was liberated from Dachau in 1945. His short story collection *This Way for the Gas, Ladies and Gentlemen* (*Pożegnanie z Marią*) was among the very first attempts at Holocaust literature, and its power has not diminished to this day. The narrator of the title story, Tadeusz, is a victim as well as perpetrator for, on the day that the title story begins, he is serving the SS on the loading ramp of the arriving trains. In the opening scene, he is sitting with others in his hot barracks and they are consuming white bread, bacon, tomatoes, sardines and sweets. His French friend hopes to get champagne the next time they go to the platform. The rest of the story recounts gruesome events. He describes the train that arrives from Sosnowiec-Będzin:

> The bolts crack, the doors fall open. A wave of fresh air rushes inside the train. People ... inhumanly crammed, buried under incredible [...] bundles of every description [...] Monstrously squeezed together, they have fainted from heat, suffocated, crushed one another. [...] But before they have a chance to recover [...] bundles are snatched from their hands, coats ripped off their backs, their purses and umbrellas taken away.[163]

The newly arrived ones are sorted out: 'Trucks, loaded with people, start up with a deafening roar and drive off amidst the wailing and screaming of the women separated from their children, and the stupefied silence of the men left behind.'[164] Once everybody got out of the railroad cars, Tadeusz and his colleagues have to clean them: 'We climb inside. In the corners amid human excrement and abandoned wrist-watches lie squashed, trampled infants, naked little monsters with enormous heads and bloated bellies. We carry them out like chickens, holding several in each hand.'[165] After several heart-rending scenes, Tadeusz tells Henri that he has become furious at the arriving people and can no longer feel any pity for them.[166] The gruesome events continue when the second train arrives: 'Big, swollen, puffed-up corpses are being collected from all over the ramp; on top of them are piled the invalids, the smothered, the sick, the unconscious. The heap seethes, howls, groans.'[167] When a little girl falls off the wagon's opened door and starts to run around insanely, an SS man kicks her and shoots her.[168] The 'Canada' men in

---

163 Tadeusz Borowski, 'This Way for the Gas, Ladies and Gentlemen', in *This Way for the Gas, Ladies and Gentlemen*, trans. Barbara Vedder (Harmondsworth: Penguin, 1992 [1967]), 29–49, here 37–8 (first ellipsis appears in the original).
164 Ibid., 38.
165 Ibid., 39.
166 Ibid., 40.
167 Ibid., 45–6.
168 Ibid., 47–8.

the labour gang enrich themselves by robbing food and goods from those that are transported to the gas chambers.

Such stories could not please readers who wanted to sympathize or communists who expected heroic deeds and ideologically useful information about concentration camps. According to Jan Kott, Borowski was accused of amorality, decadence and nihilism.[169] In 1948, he still published *Farewell to Maria* (*Pożegnanie z Marią*) and *Stone World* (*Kamienny świat*) but then turned to journalism, became a political activist and finally committed suicide in 1951. Czesław Miłosz wrote an incisive story about him in the chapter titled 'Beta, the Disappointed Lover' in his *The Captive Mind*.[170]

Imre Kertész, *Fatelessness* (1975)

Why did Imre Kertész title his book *Fatelessness* (*Sorstalanság*) which recounts 15-year-old Gyuri Köves's deportation to Auschwitz and his subsequent survival? A diary entry from 1 May 1965 may suggest an answer: 'What do I call fate? It, in any case, contains the possibility of tragedy.'[171] He goes on to say that 'fatelessness' means being fully determined by an outer, absurd reality, not by a necessity that would flow from our freedom (i.e. as a consequence of our choices). For example, the human beings in Auschwitz are 'fateless' because the inmates are unable to make any choices at all; they are not trapped between equally negative options, for they have no options.

When Gyuri's cattle car arrives at Auschwitz, he describes the sunrise as 'pretty and, on the whole, intriguing'[172] and later, he describes the train station as 'smart'.[173] The deportees are told to get out and the kapos are already entering the wagons to grab their luggage. They urge Gyuri to claim that he is 16. He reluctantly consents, though he sees that older people, children, the infirm, and mothers with children are sent away elsewhere. He is relieved that they are guarded by German soldiers who are neatly dressed and well groomed; it is only the soldiers that radiate solidity and calm in the confusing situation.[174] Accordingly, Gyuri and his friends try to follow the instructions without giving a disorderly impression. Gyuri sees that the soldiers belong to the famous SS but finds them in no sense 'dangerous': 'they were ambling up and down in leisurely fashion … answering questions, nodding, even cordially patting some of us on the back or shoulder.'[175] Gyuri remains calm even when he discovers that they carry whips.[176] The doctor seems satisfied when Gyuri gives his age as 16, but Gyuri himself is slightly concerned when a weak-looking person is included in his group, for this could potentially downgrade the overall health of the group. On the way to the barracks, he is very pleased to discover a neat soccer field and cultivated flower beds.[177]

Gyuri's friendly and pleasant reception in Auschwitz is incompatible with the horrors described by Tadeusz. How can one explain the discrepancy? One factor is the distance from the authors' actual experience: Borowski wrote immediately after the war, while Kertész wrote 15 to 18 years later. The greater temporal distance did not prettify Kertész's memories but allowed him to take

---

169 Jan Kott, 'Introduction', in Borowski, *This Way for the Gas*, 11–26, here 19.
170 Miłosz, *The Captive Mind*, 111–34.
171 Imre Kertész, *Gályanapló* [Galley diary] (Budapest: Magvető, 1992), 19.
172 Imre Kertész, *Fatelessness*, trans. Tim Wilkinson (New York: Vintage, 2004), 75.
173 Ibid., 82.
174 Ibid., 80.
175 Ibid., 83.
176 Ibid., 84.
177 Ibid., 89–90.

a subtler narrative approach. Borowski shows how the autobiographical narrator slides toward a perpetrator mentality in the course of a single corrupting experience. We know virtually nothing about the narrator's background. Since Kertész spends roughly a third of his novel on Gyuri's 1944 experiences in Hungary, readers are already acquainted with his historical, social, and political ignorance, and his submissive disposition. German culture and military order seem to him superior to the Hungarian ones, and he willingly submits to their 'higher order'. When he recognizes the inhumanity of the German order in Auschwitz, Birkenau and Buchenwald, his worldview becomes more sophisticated, but *Fatelessness* does not become a Bildungsroman. Gyuri becomes ill and realizes that logically he should be eliminated like those useless people that were gassed upon their arrival in Auschwitz. It is not this insight that saves him but rather some figures of goodwill that put him into a warm hospital bed. There is no fate at work here.

Once back in Budapest, Gyuri refuses to cooperate with a journalist who wants to publicize his suffering in the hell that was Auschwitz. But Gyuri disagrees also with his former old Jewish neighbours who suggest that he ought to forget his horrible experiences as quickly as possible.[178] He insists that even in the shadow of the gas-chamber smokestacks he had experienced something that resembled happiness:

> Everyone asks only about the hardships and the 'atrocities', whereas for me perhaps it is that experience which will remain the most memorable. Yes, the next time I am asked, I ought to speak about that, the happiness of the concentration camps. If indeed I am asked. And provided I myself don't forget.[179]

Whether wrong or right, he now may become a tragic figure, for fate will allow him to make his own decisions.

Literary fiction as a source for histoire croisée: *Tibor Cseres and Aleksandar Tišma*

Some of the most atrocious massacres during the war did not occur in concentration camps and were not committed by Germans. In January 1942, Hungarian soldiers and gendarmes shot thousands of Serbs and Jews in Novi Sad and dumped their bodies into holes cut in the ice of the frozen Danube as retribution for minor partisan activities in the region. Under pressure, Regent Miklós Horthy initiated an investigation, but Major-General József Grassy and Lieutenant General Ferenc Feketehalmy-Czeydner (and others) fled to Germany. They joined the SS and returned when the German forces entered Hungary in March 1944. Arrested by the Americans after the war, they were executed in Yugoslavia. In June 2013, Hungarian President János Áder publicly apologized in the Serbian Parliament for the massacre. He was following a previous agreement according to which the Serbian Parliament had condemned the post-war massacre against Hungarians in Vojvodina.

There are two novels from the twentieth century that specifically deal with the Novi Sad massacre: Tibor Cseres's *Cold Days* and Aleksandar Tišma's *The Book of Blam* (*Knjiga o Blamu*, 1971). When Cseres wrote *Cold Days* (*Hideg napok*) in 1964, such massacres and the Holocaust were hardly discussed in Europe, especially Eastern Europe. *Cold Days* was an early and particularly courageous attempt to initiate Hungarian self-examination. But Cseres was not in Novi Sad during the razzia and neither was Aleksandar Tišma. Tišma was born to a Serbian father and a

---

178 Ibid., 256.
179 Ibid., 262.

Hungarian-speaking Jewish mother. He studied economics and French language and literature in Budapest during the Second World War, and later graduated with a degree in German Studies from the University of Belgrade. Both men only had access to incomplete documentation of the Novi Sad massacre, but the focus of their novels on the subject is ultimately psychological. Cseres chose dramatic concentration over epic breadth, while Tišma's novel *The Book of Blam* within a broad representation offers a still narrower dramatic focus, the deeply disturbing and moving psychology of Miroslav Blam. We discuss the two novels here as a literary dialogue about an unspeakable event.

Tibor Cseres, *Cold Days*

In *Cold Days*, Cseres puts four Hungarian soldiers of the Novi Sad massacre in a jail cell. A few hints indicate that the war is still going on. The cellmates do not know what they are accused of and why they are jailed together. The narrator is as silent as the narrator in Koestler's *Darkness at Noon* and no outside voices enter the cell. The joint confinement could yield information unavailable to judges and historians. Yet, unlike Akira Kurosawa's film *Rashômon* (1950), the novel does not contrast different perspectives on what happened. The cellmates do not question the truth of the perpetrator stories they hear. Since the recollections reach only the cellmates, the four men seem to speak openly, although they dislike each other and suspect that one of them is a spy. The dynamics of the conversations are shaped by military and social hierarchies. All of them are selfish and obsessed by sexual violence. None of them confesses.[180]

The four cellmates, ensign Pozdor, Lieutenant Tarpataki, Major Büky and Corporal Szabó, downplay their part in the massacre. Büky and Szabó dislike each other. Szabó, who is lowly, poor and unmarried, served under corporal Dorner, who committed shocking murders. Büky is a well-to-do married man, who resented that Major-General Grassy forbade him from bringing his family to Novi Sad. But his love for his family is a sham. Having found comfortable accommodation in the home of a Jewish travelling salesman, he praises his hostess so highly to his anti-Semitic wife in Győr that she becomes jealous, and not without reason. The hostess invites Büky once for dinner; he keeps inviting himself afterwards and then becomes sexually aggressive. 'She pretended she was too afraid to resist'[181] he tells his cellmates, implying that he did not have to rape her, that she consented. Büky hypocritically assures his cellmates that his devotion to his wife and son did not diminish thereby. On the first evening of the razzia the husband was back home. Büky coldheartedly recounts that a Hungarian neighbour was shot dead while taking home a bucket of water because he disobeyed the curfew,[182] but he confides that the following evening there was a *disznótor*, a pig-killing feast, at the house and he began to desire the Serbian wife of the concierge.

According to Büky, the inhabitants regarded him as the guardian angel of the house.[183] But this alleged guardian becomes helpless when a man with a bloody turban is brought to him one morning. His family had been murdered the night before, and, having miraculously survived, he asks that a protocol be taken of the event (which Szabó had already described as Dorner's murder). Büky does not believe the story but prepares a draft report anyway. When Grassy dismissively tears it up, Büky becomes angry, not because he suspected that the man would be murdered (which he was), but because of Grassy's 'unlawful' separation of husbands and wives.

---

180 Tibor Cseres, *Hideg napok* [Cold days] (Budapest: Magvető, 1964).
181 Ibid., 31.
182 Ibid., 34.
183 Ibid., 59–60.

A history of fiction

The gory details of Dorner's atrocious killings ignite the cell. When Szabó relates that he refused to save a boy standing in the row of people about to be executed, Büky prevents him from continuing.[184] Everybody gets fed up with Szabó's story of how Dorner's unit went berserk, and Büky blurts out that during the razzia it suddenly struck him that his wife and son may be in town.[185] He is finally unable to keep his secret and reveals that jealousy did drive his wife and child to Novi Sad just before the start of the razzia. His son became a beloved playmate of the girls in the house, and even his wife found a certain bond with the Jewish and Serbian mothers. Büky instructed them to leave on the next train, but the women and children returned home because trains were no longer leaving from Novi Sad. Returning home later, Büky found his dead host in front of the house, dressed in Büky's own uniform. He was apparently killed while unsuccessfully trying to protect his family with a trick. The women were picked up by Hungarian soldiers, and only the three children were left behind. Büky then started a frantic but unsuccessful search for his wife.[186]

Szabó knows what actually happened, and he recounts the story, not in the name of 'truth' but in order to hurt Büky. There were only 15–20 people left to be murdered at the Danube when a high official arrived with the order to stop the massacre. Dorner protested and was shot dead.[187] The killings were so intensive in the previous hours that the machine guns broke down, and Szabó went to fetch a carriage-pole from a nearby pub which would help keep the hole in the ice open and help push the victims in the icy water. While the machine gunner relaxed in the pub and played with the mostly Jewish children, the adults were lined up outside in their underwear and marched towards the deadly opening in the ice. Three women begged for help, claiming that their husbands were Hungarian officers; one of them could even cite the names of a whole unit, but one of them did not speak Hungarian and she was therefore not trusted. One of Szabó's colleagues dragged the Hungarian-speaking woman to the pub, raped her and forced her back into the row. When one of the other women was shot, the Hungarian woman threw herself unto the rapist's boots, kissing and hugging them while begging for mercy. When Szabó lustfully describes how the iron hook of the carriage-pole tore her underwear, Büky gives a deadly kick to Szabó for he realizes that the infinitely humiliated woman was his wife.[188]

Once Büky and Szabó are removed from the cell, Pozdor and Tarpataki engage in a trivial chat. Pozdor notes that blowing holes in a frozen river was neglected in their military training, while Tarpataki wonders how the authorities knew that so many of the 3,390 victims were old.[189] Pozdor then wonders whether the highest officers are aware that people may want to take revenge on them, and he cynically adds that the Hungarians, after the razzia, will have to face fewer potential revenge-seekers. When new cellmates are added, the massacre becomes a non-topic. After all, their commander stated: 'Gentlemen. Not a word about this!'[190] The razzia remains an *unbewältigte Vergangenheit*, a past that has not been morally worked through.

Cseres avoided a 'black and white' story by not putting the worst criminals in the cell, the real historical perpetrators Sándor Képíró, Grassy and Feketehalmy-Czeydner, or the fictional Dorner. The cellmates share the social prejudices and anti-Semitism of their leaders and merely follow orders. In a very basic way, they reveal the 'banality of evil'. Judging both by what they

---

184 Ibid., 99.
185 Ibid., 100–01.
186 Ibid., 125–6.
187 Ibid., 133–4.
188 Ibid., 138.
189 Ibid., 146.
190 Ibid., 147.

say and do in the cell, their greatest sins were indifference, lack of independence and cowardice. The only important tension between the leaders and the subordinates is Büky's hatred of Grassy for not allowing family members to join the officers. Grassy's apparently capricious deviation from the military rules was obviously part of preparing the razzia, and Büky's fictional family drama paradoxically justifies the decision. The laboratory of the novel's jail cell fails to produce the purging medication that would induce proper healing. The film that András Kovács made of the novel in 1966 diffuses the dramatic confrontations in the cell in order to include many visual scenes. Cseres himself subsequently wrote *Titoist Atrocities in Vojvodina 1944–1945: Serbian Vendetta in Bácska* (originally *Vérbosszú Bácskában*, 1991),[191] a book about the Serbian atrocities against the Hungarians at the end of the war.

Alexandar Tišma, *The Book of Blam*

Tišma ends *The Book of Blam* with a concert in the synagogue of Novi Sad, which, after the war, was converted into a concert hall since the decimated Jewish community could no longer supply a quorum. The protagonist Miroslav Blam encounters Leon Funkenstein during the intermission, who tells him that he survived Bergen-Belsen by following the camp commander's order to play music for those taken to their execution. After the intermission, Blam is unable to listen to Dvořák's 'Serenade for Strings' for he finds the music, the people, the converted synagogue, himself, and everything else, a sham. His entire family was murdered in the massacre of 1942. After the war, Miroslav becomes taciturn, and an omniscient narrator must recount what happened.

While *Cold Days* digs up events from personal memories in an isolated prison cell, Blam's book includes historical, geographical, social and psychological considerations. If the closed space of *Cold Days* goads the characters to speak, Tišma's novel opens with a post-war overview of Novi Sad's centre from the corridor of Blam's building, popularly known as 'Mercurius'. The exchange between perpetrators leaves minimal space for the narrator of *Cold Days*, while the tongue-tied Blam forces the external narrator to speak. Blam lives in the past and is reluctant even to update his address to 'Mercurius'. Vacillating between pleasure and annoyance, 'he dislikes being pigeonholed', and misleadingly uses the outdated 'Old Boulevard 1'.[192] In short, both the victims and the perpetrators are unable to talk about their past.

Why this desire to remain incognito, to live behind a mask, to hide in a mansard apartment that is all but inaccessible? Since Miroslav's family disappeared, one is inclined to ascribe it to the German/Hungarian persecution of Jews in the period 1933–45. However, Blam's timidity and shyness are not simply the result of his Jewish persecution or his sense of guilt that he has unjustifiably survived. Several scenes show that Blam exhibited signs of autism in his pre-persecution childhood. His only sibling, Ester, shows that timid inaction was no inherited family trait. She dies as a resistance fighter, contradicting Hannah Arendt's view that the Jewish East European middle-class failed to resist the aggressors. Miroslav is similarly unable to join his active Serbian friends.

The narrator uses Miroslav's post-war ambling through the former Jewish quarter of Novi Sad to describe the neighbourhood and the history of its former inhabitants, nearly all of whom were murdered on the spot or transported to death camps.[193] Miroslav survived the razzia in

---

191 Tibor Cseres, *Vérbosszú Bácskában* (Budapest: Magvető, 1991); English edition: idem, *Titoist Atrocities in Vojvodina 1944–1945: Serbian Vendetta in Bácska* (Buffalo, NY: Hunyadi, 1993).

192 Aleksandar Tišma, *The Book of Blam*, trans. Michael Henry Heim (New York: Harvest Books, 1998), 2, original publication: idem, *Knjiga o blamu* (Belgrade: Nolit, 1971).

193 Ibid., 22–6.

A history of fiction

relative safety and did not witness the worst atrocities, not due to careful planning but to his ill-considered and malfunctioning marriage to a non-Jewish woman. He got to know Janja at a dance school and she consented to go with him to the movies, as she did every time a boy asked her. The sexual desire that ignited Miroslav when he once saw her in peasant clothes never rekindled later, but he proposed to her and the parents consented because Miroslav had a higher social standing. Once, during the war, Miroslav saw Janja kissing Pedrag Popadić from a tram, but he was unable to talk to her about this.

Since Tišma starts with such a broad background, the razzia only appears in the eleventh chapter, where the narrator adopts perpetrator perspectives that are broader than in *Cold Days*. The chapter opens with an 'objective' topography of the city, described as a kind of horseshoe-shaped spider web,[194] which, in the hands of the Hungarian officers, then becomes the document which helps prepare the house-to-house razzia. The narration follows the combing of particular districts. The first raid on the first day, led by Second Lieutenant Géczy, strictly follows the rules and arrests only two Serb visitors to the city.[195] According to the narrator, Géczy brought his wife to Novi Sad and hurried to the first razzia day from his warm conjugal bed. Whether his wife's presence was authorized remains unclear, but the wife's presence suggests that Tišma was familiar with *Cold Days*. A general (Grassy?) severely reprimands Géczy for the meagre number of arrests and commands him to round up a 'hundred criminals' the next day.[196] To overcome their inhibitions, Géczy and the others are served rum for breakfast. Among the innocent victims he murders that day were Vilim Blam and his wife.[197] Miroslav, who already lives a baptized life with Janja in the Mercurius building, is checked by a police lieutenant who sticks to the rules and gladly accepts Pedrag Popadić's guidance through the building. Miroslav comes through 'clean'.

As in *Cold Days*, the most tragic events in *The Book of Blam* are at the banks of the frozen Danube when the order comes to stop the killing.[198] The gendarmerie officer here is a Magyarized German, who regards the razzia as a 'natural' way to eliminate all non-Hungarian and non-German inhabitants.[199] Though the Krkljuš family has the proper papers, the old couple and their son Slobodan are picked up and delivered at a spot from where they have to walk to their execution on the Danube. On the way, an older man stumbles and falls into the snow; when Slobodan tries to help him to his feet both are shot dead – just minutes before the officer arrives with the orders to stop the killing. All victims are sent home and the Krkljuš parents never get a chance to say goodbye to their son lying dead in the snow. The parallels and contrasts with the murder of Büky's wife in *Cold Days* are striking.

Tišma's narrator moves back and forth between the present as experienced by Blam, fragmentary recollections of Blam's childhood and youth, stories and topographical descriptions supplied by the narrator and scenes imagined by Blam. The temporal and spatial mosaic does not congeal into a consistent image, just like *Cold Days* remains a puzzle of many pieces that readers have to piece together themselves. By portraying some Hungarian perpetrators, Cseres obviously intended to initiate a kind of national self-questioning that could have led to a *Vergangenheitsbewältigung*, or an account of Hungary working through its responsibilities for the

---

194 Ibid., 150–1.
195 Ibid., 152–7.
196 Ibid., 153.
197 Ibid., 156.
198 Ibid., 161–6.
199 Ibid., 161.

past. This did not happen, for the communist regime did not feel responsible for crimes committed under Horthy, and it had no interest in reconciliation with Tito's Yugoslavia. Strikingly, Miroslav in Tišma's novel, a member of the victimized Jewish community, feels as guilty after the war as the perpetrators. For Tišma, Blam's problems were partly autobiographical. On 8 April 1971, he wrote in his diary that *The Book of Blam* threw him into the insecurity of his 'most problematic theme, Jewishness'.[200] Further diary entries from September 1972 indicate that in writing the novel, he felt he was acquiring a new identity (comparable to the new identity that Miroslav acquired in the concert hall, perhaps?): 'Like a hermaphrodite, whose organism took a long time to decide between femininity and masculinity, I became a Jew only now'.[201]

Exile literature, 1945–89

After the war, Nazi supporters from Hungary, Romania and Slovakia fled (often with help from the Vatican) to Franco's Spain and South America, while those who had fled the Nazis in the 1930s started to trickle back home from Paris, London and elsewhere. Some who returned were arrested or even executed by the communist regimes that took over everywhere by 1948. As the Iron Curtain slowly descended, people began to flee westward again. Gyula Schöpflin, Czesław Miłosz and others quit their diplomatic post in the early 1950s to stay in the West. Sławomir Mrożek left Poland in 1963. The suppression of the Prague Spring in 1968 first sent Josef Škvorecký and later Milan Kundera into exile. The last writers to leave in the 1980s were the Banat Swabians in Romania, including Richard Wagner and Herta Müller. The dissolution of Yugoslavia caused a new wave of literary exile as of 1991, with Dubravka Ugrešić, Aleksandar Hemon and Semezdin Mehmedinović as the most important representatives.

Since the newly exiled writers did not know whether they could ever return to their homelands, how they should live and how they should continue their writing became existential questions for them. Should they try reaching the homeland public, the native audience abroad, or rather try to reach an international audience in a foreign language?

Success in the West

Sándor Márai, who left Hungary in 1948 and committed suicide in the US in 1989, exemplifies one extreme. He continued writing in Hungarian and shied away from integrating himself abroad. What he wrote abroad he published himself first; later, minor Hungarian publishers put them out again but with little success. The still untranslated and generally ignored *Ítélet Canudosban* ('Judgment in Canudos') of 1970 may well be the best in his oeuvre. Based on Euclides da Cunha's 1902 Brazilian classic *Os Sertoes* (*Rebellion in the Backlands*), it searchingly re-enacts the confrontations between rebels and state authorities in light of the events in 1968. Like Škvorecký and other exile writers, Márai had little sympathy for the leftist rebels, but the novel went beyond his personal views. Only the future will decide whether this exile novel is not better than *A gyertyák csonkig égnek* (1942), whose first German and French translations in the 1950s were also ignored but new translations in French (*Les Braises*, 1995), in German (*Die Glut*, 1999) and in English (*Embers*, 2001) posthumously canonized Márai.

---

200 Aleksandar Tišma, *Dnevnik 1942–2001* [Diary 1942–2001] (Sremski Karlovci: Izdavačka knjižarnica Zorana Stojanovića, 2001), 535.
201 Ibid., 562.

A history of fiction

The novels of Milan Kundera became canonized when in 2011 their French translations appeared in the prestigious Pléiade collection. Kundera left Czechoslovakia for Paris in 1975 and in 1993, at age 64, began writing in French. He wrote only his first novel, *The Joke* (*Žert*, 1967) while he was still back home. Kundera became internationally famous with *The Unbearable Lightness of Being* (*Nesnesitelná lehkost bytí*, 1984), whose original Czech version Škvorecký's Toronto publishing house released in 1981. As an admirer of Laurence Sterne, Diderot and 'The Depreciated Legacy of Cervantes',[202] Kundera considers himself as a citizen of Europe, and since neither physical phenomena nor unique mental states preoccupy him, the language switch was relatively easy for him. Indeed, no chasm separates his Czech and French texts. He never sought the authenticity of a national language rooted in the nineteenth century.[203]

The Unbearable Lightness of Being opens with reflections on 'eternal recurrence', which Nietzsche originally conceived of as a call to affirm that one would be willing to relive one's life endless times, no matter how miserable it is. Kundera uses the concept as a structural principle. His 'novelistic characters and their destinies gyrate in closed circles, encountering their past, meeting their former acts and mistakes that return to hit them from an unexpected side.'[204] It is not the will of the characters, but rather the rigidity of a system which tends to initiate these repetitions. The plot of Kundera's first novel, *The Joke*, is launched with a postcard that is jokingly signed 'Long live Trotsky!',[205] which the Party takes seriously. Exclusion from the Party is followed by a series of similar treatments by humourless bureaucrats which in turn testifies to this rigidity. *The Unbearable Lightness of Being* is an ironic title, but in this later novel, the protagonist has more space for independent decisions. His insatiable appetite for new sexual affairs leads him through repeated experiences.

To the East Europeans who made their fame with French publications we should mention the two-times Prix-Goncourt winner Romain Gary, who lived in Vilnius until he was 14, and Georges Perec, who was born in Paris but of Yiddish parents who left Poland in the 1920s. Shifting to French was easiest for Romanian writers like Eugène Ionesco, Emil Cioran, Mircea Eliade, Gherasim Luca and Claude Sernet, who became highly regarded French stylists. Vintilă Horia's novel *God is Born in Exile* (*Dieu est né en exil*) about Ovid and Christ in exile even won the Prix Goncourt in 1961, but he was forced to decline the honour when his right-wing past became known.

Ágota Kristóf, who left Hungary in 1956, held lowly industrial jobs for roughly five years before she made extraordinary efforts to learn and write in French. She received international acclaim with *The Notebook* (*Le grand cahier*, 1986), and she added *The Proof* (*La preuve*, 1988) and *The Third Lie* (*Le troisième mensonge*, 1991) to broaden it into a trilogy. She received prizes in France (1986), Switzerland (2001) and Austria (2008).

Journals in the West

Exiles from the region tended to remain divided both within and among national groups. The national groups were usually split internally due to politics and generations. Tensions between the national groups were often about minority issues but could be characterized also as

---

202 Milan Kundera, *The Art of the Novel*, trans. Linda Asher (London: Faber and Faber, 1988), 3–20.

203 Vladimir Papoušek, 'Kundera's Paradise Lost: Paradigm of the Circle', in Neubauer and Török, *Exile and Return of Writers*, 384–93, here 389.

204 Ibid., 385.

205 Milan Kundera, *The Joke*, trans. Michael Henry Heim (London: Penguin Books, 1983), 26.

differences in orientation: the writers looked for international readers or readers in the mother-tongue rather than for exiled readers from other nations in the region. Two exile journals made decisive steps to reach beyond the native audience. The Parisian *Magyar Műhely* ('Hungarian Workshop'), founded in 1962, worked together with French avant-garde writers under the name 'Atelier Hongrois', while in 1971, Romanian Dumitru Țepeneag launched the Parisian journal *Cahiers d'Est* with the explicit goal of building transnational bridges.[206] The journal had an international board and devoted its eighth issue to Hungarian literature.

Kultura was undoubtedly the most important exile journal during the Cold War in terms of contributors, editorial policy, and openness towards the others. Founded in 1946 in Rome by Jerzy Giedroyc, this journal of the Polish Literary Institute (Instytut Literacki) was published just outside of Paris between 1947 and 2000. Giedroyc jealously guarded the independence of his institution, though this was not easy. The Literary Institute had a difficult relationship with the more conservative and militantly anti-communist Polish government-in-exile in London. Giedroyc also cooperated with the Congress for Cultural Freedom until it was disclosed that the CIA subsidized it.

Gustaw Herling-Grudziński, Konstanty Jeleński and Jerzy Stempowski belonged to the circle of editors. The Literary Institute put out such excellent books as Miłosz's *The Captive Mind*, and Gombrowicz's *Trans-Atlantyk* and his diaries. The latter displeased some Polish patriots. *Kultura* welcomed all literary currents and published translations of Russian dissidents as well as of Western writers like Albert Camus and George Orwell.

Kultura tried hard to reach readers in Poland, and it contributed to the cultural life in the homeland in the later phases by promoting samizdat publications and the Solidarity movement. Entering politics was, however, risky. In retrospect, Giedroyc admitted that it was a mistake to support Władysław Gomułka after the events in 1956, and *Kultura*'s turn to the Polish political scene in the second half of the 1970s alienated some of its most prominent contributors. Jeleński and Herling-Grudziński stopped publishing in the journal while Miłosz loosened his ties.

Pavel Tigrid was the editor of the most important Czechoslovak exile journal, *Svědectví* ('Testimony'), which appeared between 1956 and 1992. In contrast to most exile journals, *Svědectví* worked in the spirit of gradualism towards a change in the communist system. Tigrid was often criticized for this and Jan Kolár, a founding member, resigned because of it. Failure to have effects at home, especially in 1968, forced Tigrid to change his strategy, though he held on to the principle that *Svědectví* was no 'émigré journal' but one that sought its audience primarily among readers in Czechoslovakia. Accordingly, Tigrid filled the journal with news from abroad but also with information from the homeland that had been smuggled out and that was otherwise unavailable to readers there. The journal reported extensively about the famous Kafka Conference in 1963 and the 1967 Congress of the Writers' Union that was a stepping-stone towards the Prague Spring in the following year.

The *Irodalmi Újság* ('Literary gazette') was founded in Budapest as the official journal of the Hungarian Writers' Association but was closed down when it sided with the revolution in 1956. After a relaunch in the West in 1957 it ran until 1989, first in London and later in Paris. The first editor, the poet György Faludi, was followed by Tibor Méray in 1962. Its major rival was *Látóhatár* ('Horizon'), founded in 1950 (renamed *Új Látóhatár*, or 'New horizon' in 1958) and published in Munich from 1952 onward. In contrast to *Kultura*, the Hungarian

---

206 John Neubauer, 'Irodalmi Újság in Exile: 1957–1989', in Neubauer and Török, *Exile and Return of Writers*, 204–29, here 224–5; Áron Kibédi Varga, 'The Hungarian *Mikes Kör* and *Magyar Műhely*', in Ibid., 230–41.

A *history of fiction*

journals started to reach readers and writers at home only in the second half of the 1970s. Both had difficulties in recruiting internationally successful Hungarian exile writers like Márai, who jealously guarded his independence and published his exile narratives with minor Hungarian publishers, or Ágota Kristóf, who stopped writing Hungarian poems once she had success with her French prose. Contacts with journals and writers from other countries were sporadic. The *Irodalmi Újság*, for example, published Andrzejewski's 'Great Lament of the Paper Head' with an eight-year delay.

Toward the novel of the 21st century: Péter Nádas

Péter Nádas's body of work and personality represent an unfaltering ethos which, although always changing, is exemplarily consistent. The 'religious muddle'[207] of his life may be summarized by the fact that he was born into a Jewish family in 1942 (he only found out about his untimely religious background at the age of seven), was baptized a Calvinist and then almost automatically became an 'atheist' in lieu of the fact that his parents were communists. However, his first novella, *The Bible* (*A Biblia*, 1965), confronts Christian morality with the 'real socialist world', and as an adult he returned to Protestantism, taking his Calvinist Confirmation and First Communion at the age of 29, although he confessed that he had always been more attracted to Catholicism.[208] In spite of this, or perhaps as a result, he writes:

> It would be misleading if I stated that I had an atheistic upbringing. The possibility of God's existence was not even raised. ... I possess feelings that I am only able to articulate through silence. ... Yet remaining silent could only be meaningful if I managed to formulate the story which allowed me to perceive it [i.e. the snug certainty of the uncertainties of exile]. The story is the shell and God dwells within that shell. ... However, the perception of absence is a form of presence. That is what I am talking about. The unanimity of any creed would deprive me of the certainty of the void.[209]

As an alter ego says in *A Book of Memories* (*Emlékiratok könyve*): 'I wanted something in the here and now, a revelation, a redemption I was waiting for, I can confess this now, but back then I hadn't yet realised that precise knowledge of nothingness should have sufficed.'[210]

Nádas was 16 when his father shot himself and 26 when the 1968 invasion of Czechoslovakia put an end to his youth. He drew the conclusion that history is a disgraceful mass of violent and savage events.[211] He thought that Europe – both Western and Eastern Europe, Paris as well as Prague – had broken with rationality and with a collective future, and had withdrawn into the present, into privacy; had 'escaped into the world of emotions'.[212] Nádas's personal withdrawal was actually a radical change. He gave up journalism and his Budapest flat to move to a reclusive village on a small island on the Danube. There, over the space of four years, he wrote his first

---

207 György Baranyai and Gabriella Pécsi, *Nádas Péter bibliográfia, 1961–1994* [Péter Nádas: a bibliography] (Pécs: Jelenkor, 1994), 16.
208 Ibid.
209 Péter Nádas, 'Burok' in *Esszék* [Essays] (Pécs: Jelenkor, 2001), 5–6.
210 Péter Nádas, *Emlékiratok könyve* [A book of memories] (Budapest: Szépirodalmi, 1986), 1:11.
211 Péter Nádas and Richard Schwartz, *Párbeszéd* [Dialogue] (Pécs: Jelenkor, 1995), 54.
212 Péter Nádas, *Talált cetli* [Notes found] (Pécs: Jelenkor, 1992), 252.

novel, *The End of a Family Novel* (*Egy családregény vége*). The message of his first major work is that the two-thousand-year European narrative is over, history has come to an end, and not at the hands of liberal capitalism, as Francis Fukuyama suggested decades later, but by the crimes of Nazism and Soviet communism. No wonder that it took five years (until 1977) for the book to be published. In the meantime, Nádas began a new novel, *A Book of Memories*, on which he worked for more than ten years. The novel was published uncensored and unexpurgated in 1986, in the final and softer period of János Kádár's dictatorship.

Perhaps the most important characteristic of the changes of 1989 is that literature regained the standing it had lost during the dictatorship; literature became righteous once again. This hardly means the development of some kind of respectable didactic literature, but that morals became directly linked to writing itself. This is what the words of Sándor Márai describe, as popularized by Péter Esterházy: the writer must not think in terms of people and nation, but in terms of subject and predicative,[213] and Nádas also regards it as his most personal literary task to create 'proper sentences'. The grammar was infused with this ethic.

A Book of Memories, Nádas's masterpiece, consists of three first-person narratives. The first is about a young Hungarian writer and his fated love for a German poet in East Berlin (Nádas himself spent more than a year in East Berlin as well as West Berlin). We also find out about the writer's adolescence in Budapest, culminating in the Hungarian revolution of 1956 and about his beloved but repudiated father, a communist state prosecutor. A second memoir, alternating with the first, is a novel the narrator is composing about a German writer at the turn of the century, perhaps an imaginary Thomas Mann. He writes about the Baltic coast, which the Hungarian narrator visited decades later. A third voice belongs to a childhood friend who offers an account not only of their friendship but also of the narrator's murder in the 1970s, in a small village on the Danube.

The book may be read as a historical novel. It is not the gigantic tableau painted by a typical nineteenth-century omniscient storyteller, but rather a synthesis of the East European experience, a mosaic made up of many tragic individual fates told in the first person singular and closely scrutinized. Nádas's *A Book of Memories* is a novel about the body in its preverbal actions and, via these actions, about psychology. It makes you feel that 'no one has really, openly, completely described sex before, or farting, or shitting, or best of all perhaps, kissing (with a whole chapter on that first kiss).'[214] To paraphrase Nádas: it is pornography of a divine origin.[215]

Why then, is the novel so significant, or, as Stanisław Barańczak asks, who needs another 700-page Central-European novel?[216] Nádas says that he begins every novel with his own self, since there are correspondences in his ego, as well as between his experiences and impressions. He first surveys these correspondences and advises others to do the same, thereby offering a method of how to set about writing a book. The survey reveals the identity of a single individual rather than the identity of a nation or a geographical region.[217]

---

213 Péter Esterházy, *Bevezetés a szépirodalomba* [Introduction to literature] (Budapest: Magvető, 1986), 402.

214 Ivan Sanders, 'Az *Emlékiratok könyve* Amerikában és Nagy-Britanniában' [The *Book of Memories* in America and Great Britain], *2000: Irodalmi és társdalmi havilap* 10, no. 9 (1998): 54–8, here 56.

215 Nádas, *Emlékiratok könyve*, 341.

216 Sanders, 'Az Emlékiratok könyve', 55.

217 Baranyai and Pécsi, *Nádas Péter*, 463.

A history of fiction

A father-land hypertext: Franz Kafka, Bruno Schulz, Danilo Kiš and Péter Esterházy

In April 1984, Kundera published 'The Tragedy of Central Europe' in the *New York Review of Books*, a fiery defence of an alleged Central-European culture and a passionate condemnation of a cultural atrophy in the West. György Konrád had a softer 'dream' about it in an article he wrote in 1984–5.

While we disagree with Kundera's view that his region is at the heart of Europe and we do not join those who held on to the concept of Central Europe in the ensuing sharp debates (see the 1990 and 1991 issues of the journal *Cross Currents*), we do perceive a literary hypertext behind some great narratives from the region. At the centre of this hypertext is a father figure which first appeared in Franz Kafka's works and reappeared in the mythologized and poeticized autobiographical narratives of Bruno Schulz, Danilo Kiš and Péter Esterházy. Emperor Francis Joseph, the dying head of a disintegrating empire, looms behind the dying father figures of Joseph Roth's *Radetzky March* and Bruno Schulz's 'Spring'.[218] Kiš recast the Old-Testament dimension of Schulz's father figure, and Esterházy literally plagiarized a story that Kiš wrote about an Esterházy forefather. The hypertext of fathers is a counterpart set against autobiographically documented historical tragedies. Central Europe is no political project here but a mythologized 'father-land'. The imprisoned communists in Koestler's and Kiš's fiction shows that the Central-European hypertext involves more than just father figures.

Bruno Schulz's 'father'

Bruno Schulz lived all his life in Drohobycz, Galicia, not far from Brody, where Joseph Roth was born and raised. At the time, both towns belonged to the Monarchy but are now part of Ukraine. Kafka was Schulz's spiritual-artistic father. In 1936 he translated *The Trial* (*Der Process*) and probably knew the father/son confrontation in Kafka's 'The Judgement' but was unfamiliar with Kafka's non-fictional letter to his actual father, which was first published as late as 1952. Though Kafka may be regarded as the forefather of Schulz and of all the writers discussed in this section, the 'father complex' in his life and his fiction was confrontational, whereas Schulz, Kiš and Esterházy lovingly attempted to understand their mysterious, inexplicable and schizophrenic father characters.

A complex father character (simply called 'Father') is the central figure in both of Schulz's short story collections. The stories under analysis here – surreal in style – are told by a first-person narrator who also happens to be Father's son. Father is introduced in 'Visitation' as the owner of a textile shop in a small town when he becomes bedridden so that a 'bitter smell of illness' settles 'like a rug' in the room.[219] He misses meals, often disappears and starts to shrink. The small shroud of his body 'would finally disappear one day, as unremarked as the grey heap of rubbish swept into a corner, waiting to be taken by Adela [the maid] to the rubbish dump'.[220] The closing story of the second collection, 'Father's Last Escape', fills in the details: Mother happened to catch Father after he metamorphosed into a little crab; by accident, Father ends up boiled on a platter, 'large and swollen from the boiling, pale grey and jellified'.[221] But Schulz's

---

218 Bruno Schulz, 'Spring', in *The Fictions of Bruno Schulz: The Street of Crocodiles & Sanatorium under the Sign of the Hourglass*, trans. Celina Wieniewska (London: Picador, 1988), 150–207.

219 Bruno Schulz, 'Visitation', in Schulz, *Fictions*, 23–9, here 24.

220 Ibid., 29.

221 Schulz, 'Father's Last Escape', in Schulz, *Fictions*, 299–303, here 303.

imagery of Father as dead and unremarked as the rubbish heap in 'Visitation' was merely a simile, for Father is still alive: 'Although boiled and shedding his legs on the way, with his remaining strength he had dragged himself somewhere to begin a homeless wandering, and we never saw him again.'[222] A crabby Wandering Jew, perhaps?

Before his death, Father engages in various mad activities. He would, for instance, run barefoot on the leather sofa to scold Mother for her allegedly sloppy bookkeeping.[223] In contrast, images in the wallpaper would come to life during his own bookkeeping:

> the pullulating jungle of wallpaper, filled with whispers, lisping and hissing, closed in around him. He heard, without looking, a conspiracy of knowingly winking hidden eyes, of alert ears opening up among the flowers on the wall, of dark, smiling mouths.

He is tempted

> to throw himself blindly forwards with a sudden shout to grab fistfuls of those curly arabesques, or of those sheaves of eyes and ears which swarmed out from the night and grew and multiplied, sprouting, with ever-new ghostlike shoots and branches, from the womb of darkness.

He recovers, but his thoughts are 'secretly plumbing the depths of his own entrails. He would hold his breath and listen' during the following weeks.[224] He starts to talk to God, 'as if begging for something or fighting against someone who made insistent claims and issued orders.' One night 'that voice rose threateningly and irresistibly, demanding that he should bear witness to it with his mouth and with his entrails.'[225] The son (and narrator) comes to understand 'the divine anger of saintly men', for he sees 'this man stricken by God's fire, sitting clumsily on an enormous china chamberpot behind a windmill of arms, a screen of desperate wrigglings over which there towered his voice, grown unfamiliar and hard.'[226]

Next, Father invites birds into his room, and they 'perched on the curtain pelmets, on the tops of wardrobes; they nestled in the tangle of tin branches and the metal scrolls of the hanging lamps.'[227] Among them is a condor that uses Father's chamber pot and while it is sleeping, looks like a 'dried-out, shrunken mummy' of the narrator's father.[228] When Father goes even further and begins breeding the birds, the attic became such an appalling mess that Adela 'wrung her hands at the fetid smell that filled the room, the heaps of droppings covering the floor, the tables, and the chairs.'[229] She let the birds fly away. In 'Tailor's Dummies', the narrator claims that this bird affair 'was the last colourful and splendid counter-offensive of fantasy which my father, that incorrigible improviser, that fencing master of imagination, had led against the trenches and defence-works of a sterile and empty winter' and the boredom of the city.[230] He became 'an exiled king who had lost his throne and his kingdom',[231] who in 'Tailor's Dummies'

---

222 Ibid., 303.
223 Schulz, 'Visitation', 24.
224 Ibid., 25.
225 Ibid., 26.
226 Ibid.
227 Schulz, 'Birds', in Schulz, *Fictions*, 30–3, here 32.
228 Ibid., 32.
229 Ibid., 33.
230 Schulz, 'Tailor's Dummies', in Schulz, *Fictions*, 34–48, here 34.
231 Schulz, 'Birds', in Schulz, *Fictions*, 33.

A history of fiction

was 'defending the lost cause of poetry'. Since nobody took his side, 'Father retreated without a fight from the scenes of his recent glory' and took up voluntary exile in an empty room, where everybody forgot about him.[232]

And yet, Father is charmed by the well-shaped bodies of two seamstresses who are taken by the 'magnetism of his strange personality'.[233] The son calls him a 'Heresiarch' as he walks around like a mesmerist, infecting everything with his dangerous charm[234] and with his 'most unusual lectures'.[235] He argues that the 'matchless perfection of the Demiurge' has 'paralysed our own creative instinct',[236] and he asks for a second genesis that will create temporary beings that serve only for a single occasion.[237] Matter is never dead, can always be reshaped;[238] 'we shall give priority to trash. We are simply entranced and enchanted by the cheapness, shabbiness, and inferiority of material'; the new human beings will be 'in the shape and semblance of a tailor's dummy'.[239] He dreams up half organic beings, pseudo fauna and pseudo flora, made via a fantastic fermentation of matter.[240] He gradually becomes more personal while his voice gradually becomes comprehensible.

In retrospect, the son/narrator suspects that his mother had never loved his father. Since his father 'had not been rooted in any woman's heart, he could not merge with any reality and was therefore condemned to float eternally on the periphery of life, in half-real regions, on the margins of existence.'[241] Two contrasting episodes indicate mutability. First, Father copes with his cockroach anxiety by assuming a comparable body. He starts to move 'with the many-limbed, complicated movements of a strange ritual' that imitates 'the ceremonial crawl of a cockroach'. Moving 'on cockroachy paths', he merges 'with that black, uncanny tribe'.[242] With the new inventions of electricity and mechanics, a different demiurgic power comes to fascinate Father. He wants to participate in the 'resourcefulness of human genius'[243] by experimenting with circulations like galvanism, mesmerism and the bicycle that interlinks everything.

Danilo Kiš's 'father' disappears differently

'Schulz is my god', Kiš allegedly told John Updike; hence 'divine inspiration' may have contributed to the making of his family trilogy, which brilliantly fuses first-person autobiographical narration with wildly imaginative third-person excursions. In the trilogy, Kiš unites three existing books: *Early Sorrows* (*Rani jadi*), *Garden, Ashes* (*Bašta pepeo*) and *Hourglass* (*Peščanik* – a title that Schulz had already used). While the father's increasing madness and final disappearance are the family's central problem, life is no 'circus' in this trilogy. We would apply the term 'circus' rather to the trilogy's non-linear narrative pattern, which encircles both real and imaginary motives, just like a circus rider does when going round and round. The resurfacing objects and

---

232 Schulz, 'Tailors's Dummies', in Schulz, *Fictions*, 34.
233 Ibid., 38.
234 Ibid., 39.
235 Ibid., 38–9.
236 Ibid., 40.
237 Ibid., 41.
238 Ibid., 39–40.
239 Ibid., 41.
240 Ibid., 45.
241 Schulz, 'Cockroaches', in Schulz, *Fictions*, 78–81, here 78.
242 Ibid., 81.
243 Schulz, 'The Comet', in Schulz, *Fictions*, 97–111, here 99.

motives always return modified in new contexts without leading, however, to better insights. Just the opposite: things that readers may have understood in a first, realistic presentation often subsequently become foggy – as if the circus horse kicked up clouds of dust. The title *Garden, Ashes* joins, unconnected, the garden of the boy's (or, the protagonist's) childhood and those missing ashes of his father that went up in the Holocaust smokestacks.

The writing of the three volumes was also non-linear. In 1965, Kiš published *Garden, Ashes*; he then collected a series of childhood stories in *Early Sorrows* (1969), and in 1972, he published the final *Hourglass*. The boy assumes his name as Andreas (Andi) Scham in the second volume (*Garden, Ashes*),[244] but then diffuses his identity and actually disappears in the final volume of the trilogy.

The main autobiographical line in *Garden, Ashes* is the boy's growing preoccupation with his father. The book opens with a wonderful description of the tray that the mother brings to the boy's bed in the morning,[245] followed by sharp verbal and even visual depiction of her Singer sewing machine.[246] She anchors him throughout the first two volumes with tangible objects and emotions, and even when she spins verses with him she restrains his 'lyrical excesses'.[247] Nevertheless, the adult Andi-narrator remarks, 'unexpectedly and unpredictably, this account is becoming increasingly the story of my father'.[248]

While both Schulz's fictional and real fathers owned their own businesses, both Kiš's real and fictional fathers were employed by the Hungarian railroads. Kiš's real father did publish a *Bus, Ship, Rail, and Air Travel Guide* in 1930, but the father's project in the novel is to make something poetic out of the dull tables.[249] If Schulz's father character wants a second genesis to create temporary beings for a single occasion, Kiš's Eduard Scham wants 'an apocryphal, sacral bible' in which genesis is repeated but 'all divine injustices and the impotence of man' are rectified.[250] This 'anarchical and esoteric new testament' is meant to contain a theory 'of a universal revolution against God and all His restrictions'.[251] Obsessed with his mad Promethean project, this father also becomes alienated from everybody. Glimpses of his insanity are brilliantly punctuated with the boy's unclear perceptions of the Novi Sad massacre, of a pogrom, of a lynching attempt, and with the exodus of Eduard and the other Jews for the ghetto in Zalaegerszeg.[252] This is where the family sees him for the last time.[253] Schultz's fictional Father and Kiš's real one both disappear, but we know that the latter died in the Holocaust. In Andi's mind, his father lives on as a ghost, as the Holocaust survivor named Eduard Kohn.[254] The insanity of the Nazis and their Hungarian collaborators trumps the father's mad desire to emancipate mankind but not the son's imagination.

Actually, Andi and his mother are the ones who disappear from the text of the *Hourglass*, surviving only in the final 'Letter, or Synopsis', a slightly modified version of an actual letter that Kiš's father wrote to his sister on 5 April 1942.[255] Kiš conceived of the *Hourglass*

---

244 Danilo Kiš, *Garden, Ashes*, trans. William J. Hannaher (New York: Harcourt Brace, 1975), 11.
245 Ibid., 3–15.
246 Ibid., 25–6.
247 Ibid., 150.
248 Ibid., 99.
249 Ibid., 16.
250 Ibid., 34.
251 Ibid., 35.
252 Ibid., 108–15.
253 Ibid., 116–17.
254 Ibid., 118–21.
255 Mark Thompson, *Birth Certificate: The Story of Danilo Kiš* (Ithaca, NY: Cornell University Press, 2013) 150–1.

A history of fiction

when he discovered the letter in 1967: he recast the father in four alternating narratives: the 'Travel Scenes', narrated in the third person, the 'Notes of a Madman' written by an unnamed 'frightened, worried self',[256] the 'Criminal Investigation', which interrogates somebody who knew Eduard Scham, and 'A Witness Interrogated', which asks about the mistreatment of Jews.

Minimal readings can interconnect the themes, events and characters of the four parts. Informed readings should, however, relate the textual elements to three extrinsic frames: the real life of the Kiš family in the 1930s and 40s,[257] the war and the Holocaust – especially the Novi Sad massacre – and the literary connections to Kafka and Schulz.

Péter Esterházy's borrowed and unknown fathers

Eleven years after *Hourglass*, Kiš published a collection of stories titled, *The Encyclopedia of the Dead* (*Enciklopedija Mrtvih*). The story 'To Die for One's Country is Glorious' ('Slavno je za otadžbinu mreti') is about a young character named Esterházy who is on death row for having participated in a peasant uprising against the Habsburgs.[258] In a quaint contribution that commemorated Kiš, Péter Esterházy, the writer, recalls that he first encountered Kiš when reading the story about the condemned fictional Esterházy: 'I knew immediately that this was my text, it was mine, let Kiš have the royalties, the text belonged to me. Me-e. This was a story I had to write, moreover: it was I who had to write it.'[259]

This was no joke. Esterházy first included Endre Bojtár's Hungarian translation of Kiš's 'To Die for One's Country is Glorious' in his *Introduction to Literature* (*Bevezetés a szépirodalomba*), with proper documentation.[260] He not only recycled the text with slight changes in his *Celestial Harmonies* (*Harmonia caelestis*),[261] this time without documentation or referencing Kiš's name, but he even publicly read the plagiarized text to an audience in the family castle of Eisenstadt without identifying Kiš at all. Fearing lawsuits, the publisher of the English edition insisted that the sources be listed at the end of the book.

Arguably, Esterházy appropriated Kiš's story as his own not because it was about his forefather but because he shared the final comments on truth and fiction in Kiš's story. Was the execution of the young Esterházy heroic or staged by his mother? The heroic version was pub-

---

256 Danilo Kiš, *Hourglass*, trans. Ralph Manheim (New York: Farrar Straus Giroux, 1990), 148.

257 Danilo was baptized in the Orthodox faith in Novi Sad in 1939. After the Novi Sad massacre (which his father narrowly escaped) the family moved to his father's native Hungarian village, Kerkabarabás, near Zalaegerszeg. His father was taken to Auschwitz in 1944 and subsequently disappeared. In 1947, he and the rest of his family were repatriated by the Red Cross to his uncle in Cetinje. See Thompson, *Birth Certificate*, 1–2.

258 Guido Snel, 'Gardens of the Mind, Places for Doubt: Fictionalized Autobiography in East-Central Europe', in Cornis-Pope and Neubauer, *History of the Liteary Cultures*, vol. 1, 386–400, here 386–7; Danilo Kiš, *The Encyclopedia of the Dead*, trans. Michael Henry Heim (London: Faber and Faber, 1989), 123–31. Kiš used Roy Medvedev's book on Stalinism and his friend Karl Štajner's book *7000 Days in Siberia*. Although he acknowledged his subtexts, he was accused of plagiarism. To this accusation, he vehemently responded in *The Anatomic Lesson* (*Čas Anatomije*, 1978) and as a result, was then accused of slander; the court, however, overturned the case.

259 Péter Esterházy, 'Der Ich-Erzähler als Provokation des Mimetischen im Diskurs der Phantastik. Péter Esterházy liest Danilo Kiš und Péter Esterházy', *Literaturmagazin* 41 (1998): 170–7, here 172.

260 Péter Esterházy, *Bevezetés a szépirodalomba* [Introduction to literature] (Budapest: Magvető, 1986), 642–5.

261 Péter Esterházy, *Celestial Harmonies*, trans. Judith Sollosy (New York: Ecco, 2004), 23–8 (essay no. 24).

licized by the Sans-culottes and the Jacobins, whereas the version that held that the young man had until the very end hoped for a miraculous reversal, was recorded by the official historians of the Habsburg dynasty in order to prevent the birth of a heroic legend: 'History is written by the victors. Legends are woven by the people. Writers fantasize. Only death is certain.'[262] According to Kiš's biting satire, the issue is not what happened but how stories are hawked by revolutionaries that need ancestors and historians who want to keep the ancient regime alive. Fiction writers make readers aware that history is also invented. This must have encouraged Esterházy to fantasize about fiction and his own ancestors.

The Kafka quotations are conscientiously documented in the 'Suspended' ('Függő') section of Esterházy's *Introduction to Literature*.[263] However, nobody would have noticed Esterházy's most brilliant appropriation in *Hrabal's Book* (*Hrabal könyve*, 1990) had he not given it away himself. This title would usually be understood as a 'book about Hrabal', just as the title *The Book of Blam* signifies in Serbian both the book of and about the main character. This time, however, Hrabal is not only a fictional character but also the co-author, since the text is loaded with unidentified quotations from his writing. Yet, the novel culminates in a conversation between the Lord God and Hrabal, which has additional authors, for it is studded with Czech phrases taken from Kafka's letters to Milena Jesenská, which are, in turn, taken from elsewhere, mostly from Milena's letters to Kafka. The father figure of this book, the Lord, is present through most of the book, but has an uncertain identity and unclear abilities. Towards the end of the novel, the Lord tries to learn to play the saxophone from Charlie Parker, who calls him 'Bruno' (Schulz, perhaps?). Then he addresses Hrabal. Esterházy records the conversation in Czech as well as Hungarian, but the meaning is enigmatic. After the conversation, the Lord makes a clumsy attempt to play the saxophone, but his last attempt on the instrument was 'more of a wheeze and a rattle than music, the admission of its own failure, a choking sob'.[264]

Esterházy's plagiarism of Kafka's letters seems a travesty of Kafka's own obsessive search for an *authentic* style. However, Esterházy's playful inauthenticity also displays Kafka's own appropriations and misappropriations in the ambiguous letters. Who is the father of the Czech words that Esterházy adopted from German letters and inserted into his own Hungarian book? Milena? Kafka? Hrabal? What language can be called authentic or original? Esterházy questions traditional conceptions of authenticity, intellectual property, unadulterated expression, as well as linguistic and ethnic identity. Not unlike Gombrowicz in *Trans-Atlantyk*, he disassembles the Fatherland by bringing together a heterogeneous 'world of the son'.

Esterházy's *bricolage* or 'magpie aesthetics' finds its most powerful expression in *Celestial Harmonies* (2000), whose 'harmony' is a crazy quilt of alien texts, though the title refers back to a musical composition of Count Pál Esterházy I. Part I of the book contains chronologically jumbled anecdotes relating to the family history of the Esterházys, whereas Part II consists of fictional texts relating to the narrator's more immediate family, mostly his father. Though most of these anecdotes are fictional and/or stolen, they offer a rather loving picture of Mátyás Esterházy, Peter's actual father: the communists confiscated his property and later confined him and his family to a village in the countryside. In the novel, the tragic but humorously narrated episodes of the Stalinist years are followed by the less dramatic scenes of the subsequent dec-

---

262 Kiš, *The Encyclopedia of the Dead*, 131.

263 Esterházy, 'Függő' [Suspended], in idem, *Bevezetés a szépirodalomba*, 154–247. Also published separately as *Függő – Bevezetés a szépirodalomba* (Budapest: Ikon, 1993).

264 Péter Esterházy, *The Book of Hrabal*, trans. Judith Sollosy (London: Quartet Books Limited, 1994), 171.

A history of fiction

ades. The family regains its freedom and Mátyás becomes a translator. Nevertheless, the novel concludes with a poignant scene of solitude:

> when we enter the apartment, my father is already sitting by the Hermes Baby which is clattering steadily, like an automatic machine gun, he's pounding it, striking it, and the words come pouring out, going pit-a-pat on the white sheet, one in the wake of the other, words that are not his own, nor were they ever, nor will they ever be.[265]

Like his son later, the father types words of alien texts. However, the father's management of foreign texts acquired a different meaning just before the publication of *Celestial Harmonies*. The son received his father's dossier from the secret police full of his father's informant reports beginning in 1957. Esterházy felt compelled to write his *Javított Kiadás* ('Amended edition', 2002). In addition to refashioning the father image of *Celestial Harmonies* in a painful process of re-examination and mourning, the emendation sheds new light on the fatherland, as well as on various themes and literary techniques that Esterházy had previously employed with playful ease.

The final scene of a typing father now holds a graver meaning, especially the phrase 'words that are not his own'.[266] Once the truth about the father's collaboration is revealed, the final passage about his use of 'borrowed words' can no longer be read innocently, as if the meaning of words does not matter.[267] Surely, Mátyás's reports also contained many invented lies, but the fact remains that he functioned as an informant. The son is now also caught in an epistemological drama. As he remarked on receiving the Peace Prize of the German Book Trade Association in 2004: 'One could say that the game I play in all my novels has caught up with me. I felt this helplessness the whole time I wrote the *Amended Edition*.'[268]

Indeed, in the sequence we have followed, each father is an 'amended edition' of the previous one, and an imaginative fictional amendment of the real ones – except in the case of Esterházy, in which the real father became an amendment of the fictional one. Above all, each fictional father, including Esterházy's, amends notions of the fatherland.

Rejected fatherlands: Herta Müller

Closing this history with the exclusively male construction of an imaginary fatherland would ignore the stylistically and historically unique fiction of Herta Müller, one of the region's recent Nobel-Prize winners. Furthermore, in Müller's fiction we have no amendments, rather a rejection of two different notions of fatherland. She was born in Romania's Banat Swabian community in 1953, after her father served in the SS during the war and her mother was in a Ukrainian forced labour camp for five years after the war. She grew up in the closed German community of her native village that did not reconsider its past, and she studied and worked as a translator in Timişoara under Ceauşescu's dictatorship until she could escape to Germany in 1987. She was active in the literary *Aktionsgruppe Banat* until it had to be disbanded in 1975.

Müller's fiction covers several negative figures of power, each of which is a variant of the father. The negative father figures represent two repressive fatherlands, the native Swabian

---

265 Esterházy, *Celestial Harmonies*, 841.
266 Ibid.
267 Ibid., 843.
268 Marcel Cornis-Pope et al., 'East-Central European Literature after 1989', in Cornis-Pope and Neubauer, *History of the Literary Cultures*, vol. 4, 561–629, here 572.

village and Ceaușescu's communist dictatorship. On the horizon, there looms a third problematic fatherland, Germany, where many readers (and not only those that came from the East) considered Müller's negative image of the Swabian community as a *Nestbeschmutzung*, a befouling of one's own nest. These negative reactions to her work resemble the negative Polish reactions to Gombrowicz's *Trans-Atlantyk*.

Müller's first publication, *Nadirs (Niederungen)*[269] is a collection of short stories, the publication of which was permitted in Bucharest in 1982, surely, on the basis that the stories portray an ugly family and an ugly village in Romania's unwelcome Swabian minority. The uncensored version appeared two years later in Berlin. The autobiographical vignettes that make-up the book are narrated by an unnamed girl in an unnamed Swabian village. The opening story, titled 'The Funeral Sermon', concerns a father character who contains both fictional and autobiographical elements of Müller's actual father. The story is also a good example of Müller's punctuated style: rather than a continuous narrative, the story contains cryptic scenes borne out of reality and nightmares alike. Müller's highly poetic, short sentences do not actually result in a staccato effect because all the words and images they contain demand close scrutiny and reflection on the part of the reader. In the opening lines, the narrator describes a train departing for war; one of the passengers is a young man holding a bouquet of tattered white flowers, while a young hunchbacked woman leads a child out of the station. The story then jumps to the narrator reflecting on family photos which adorn the walls of what might be the narrator's living room. Here, the narrator's mother is pictured on her wedding day without a hump (though she is holding a bouquet of tattered white flowers). Another photo shows the narrator's father in a collar with the 'runes' of the SS on it.[270] The story jumps again to the graveside of the narrator's father, at what seems to be his funeral. Two drunken 'little men' tell the narrator that her father killed a lot of people and that he and four others raped a Russian woman in a turnip field, after which the girl's father 'stuck a turnip' between the Russian woman's legs.[271] One of the drunken little men continues to tell the narrator that a few months after the Russian woman was raped, they attended an opera performance where the shrill voice of the soprano reminded the rapists of the Russian woman's screams. They all decided to leave the opera one by one except for the narrator's father who stayed; after that, he began calling 'all songs turnips and all women turnips'.[272] Having listened to all these horror stories, the girl is unable to give her funeral speech. As a result, she is condemned to death and executed by those who are proud of the community's tradition.[273]

In 'My Family',[274] the girl reports that the father has another child from another woman (the humpbacked one, perhaps?) whom she does not know. Yearly gifts coming and going, as well as comments by the parents and the village people create total confusion about legal and illegal children. Gossip circulates about every father in the village and the identity of the parents remains unclear. Whether blood related or not, the title story ('Nadirs') reveals that the girl's parents are extremely brutal, and the father is routinely intoxicated. The girl is occasionally allowed to tidy his hair, but if she mistakenly touches his face, he angrily shoves her away. The

---

269 Herta Müller, *Nadirs*, trans. Sieglinde Lug (Lincoln, NE: Univ. of Nebraska Press, 1999), originally published in German as *Niederungen* (Berlin: Rotbuch, 1984).
270 Ibid., 1.
271 Ibid., 3.
272 Ibid.
273 Ibid., 4.
274 Ibid., 8–10.

A history of fiction

mother usually shouts at her or hits her with her bony hands. In such moments, she says, 'I would know that I didn't have parents, that these two were nothing at all to me'.[275] Cruelty is everywhere. The father breaks the leg of a calf and then bribes a veterinarian for permission to slaughter it,[276] the mother kills young birds in a nest, while all the villagers mistreat dogs, ducks and other animals.

The 'autofictional' *Herztier* that Müller published in 1994 after her exit from Romania may be read as the second stage in this fictional life. She remembers that the father had died with a swollen liver from drinking, as big as the songs for the Führer he sang to his last days,[277] and she also remembers that he brutally stepped on her hand on purpose,[278] but her references to the father and the Swabian village are sporadic because she now lives in the unnamed city (Timișoara) in the even more oppressive Romanian 'fatherland' of Ceaușescu. Each fatherland gives extra colour to the other. *The Land of Green Plums*, the English title for *Herztier*, actually refers to both fatherlands. The girl associates it with the father's warning that green plums are deadly, but the policemen quickly fill their pockets whenever they can even though it is illegal. 'Plumsucker' becomes a term for corruption and abuse: 'Upstarts, opportunists, sycophants, and people who stepped over dead bodies without remorse were called that. The dictator was called a plumsucker too.'[279]

The girl is constantly spied on by the secret police. Its agent, the vicious Captain Pjele, becomes the new negative father figure, a representative of super-father Ceaușescu. The constant observation creates anxiety, makes everybody and every situation suspicious. One of the narrator's roommates, Lola, hangs herself with the belt that the narrator brought from home. Fear often prevents her from saying and doing dangerous things, and this often instils feelings of guilt in her. She should have helped prevent Lola's suicide; she should not have raised her hand at length in the vote that excluded her from the Party. The girl befriends Tereza but cannot really trust her. She trusts only three Swabian male students (fictional variants of the *Aktionsgruppe Banat*), with whom she can frankly discuss matters of philosophy, politics and poetry.

Did immigrating to Germany, the land of Müller's native language, mean settling in the true fatherland? Not for her. She often speaks of *Aussiedler*, the term that is generally used now for German-speaking people moving from the East to Germany, though it implies 'away' (*aus*). For Müller, language is no home, and the fatherland remains elusive. In a subtle way, she keeps distance from a term that is regaining terrain in Eastern Europe, Europe and much of the world.

Further reading

Andrić, Ivo. *The Bridge on the Drina*, trans. Lovett F. Edwards (New York: Macmillan, 1959).
Andrzejewski, Jerzy. *Ashes and Diamonds*, trans. D.J. Welsh (Harmondsworth: Penguin, 1978).
Bánffy, Miklós. *The Transylvanian Trilogy: Writing on the Wall*, 3 vols, trans. Patrick Thursfield and Katalin Bánffy-Jelen (London: Arcadia Books, 1999).

---

275 Ibid., 52.

276 Ibid., 43–4.

277 Herta Müller, *The Land of Green Plums*, trans. Michael Hoffmann (New York: Granta, 1999), 63.

278 Ibid., 64.

279 Ibid., 50. In the English edition, 'plumsucker' is the translation for the German 'Pflaumenfresser' which is rather closer to 'plum glutton'. 'Bloodsucker' would be more appropriate for the book, for everybody in the slaughterhouse where Kurt works, drinks the blood of the slaughtered animals – a symbol of degradation.

Borowski, Tadeusz. *This Way for the Gas, Ladies and Gentlemen*, trans. Barbara Vedder (Harmondsworth: Penguin, 1992).

Cankar, Ivan. *Dream Visions*, trans. Anton Druzina (Willoughby Hill, OH: Slovenia Research Center of America, 1982).

Čapek, Karel, et al. *At the Cross-roads of Europe: A Historical Outline of the Democratic Idea in Czechoslovakia* (Prague: Pen Club, 1938).

Čapek, Karel. *War with the Newts*, trans. M. & R. Weatherall (Evanston, IL: Northwestern University Press, 1996).

Cornis-Pope, Marcel, and John Neubauer, eds. *History of the Literary Cultures of East-Central Europe: Junctures and Disjunctures in the 19th and 20th Centuries*, 4 vols (Amsterdam: Benjamins, 2004–2010).

Esterházy, Péter. *The Book of Hrabal*, trans. Judith Sollosy (London: Quartet Books Limited, 1994).

Esterházy, Péter. *Celestial Harmonies*, trans. Judith Sollosy (New York: Ecco, 2004).

Faludy, György. *My Happy Days in Hell*, trans. Kathleen Szász (London: André Deutsch, 2002).

Gerould, Daniel, ed., trans. *The Witkiewicz Reader* (Evanston, IL: Northwestern University Press, 1992).

Gombrowicz, Witold. *Trans-Atlantyk: An Alternate Translation*, trans. Danuta Borchardt (New Haven, CT: Yale University Press, 2014).

Hašek, Jaroslav. *The Good Soldier Švejk and His Fortunes in the World War*, trans. Cecil Parrott (Harmondsworth: Penguin, 1973).

Higgonet, Margaret R., ed. *Lines of Fire: Women Writers of World War I* (New York: Penguin Plume, 1999).

Hrabal, Bohumil. *Closely Watched Trains*, trans. Edith Pargeter (Evanston, IL: Northwestern University Press, 1995).

Kafka, Franz. *Letters to Milena*, trans. Philip Boehm (New York: Schocken, 1990).

Kertész, Imre. *Fatelessness*, trans. Tim Wilkinson (New York: Vintage, 2004).

Kiš, Danilo. *Garden, Ashes*, trans. William J. Hannaher (New York: Harcourt Brace, 1975).

Kiš, Danilo. *A Tomb for Boris Davidović*, trans. Duška Mikić-Mitchell (New York: Harcourt Brace Jovanovich, 1978).

Kiš, Danilo. *The Encyclopedia of the Dead*, trans. Michael Henry Heim (London: Faber and Faber, 1989).

Kiš, Danilo. *Hourglass*, trans. Ralph Manheim (New York: Farrar Straus Giroux, 1990).

Koestler, Arthur. *Darkness at Noon*, trans. Daphne Hardy (New York: Macmillan, 1940).

Koestler, Arthur. *The Invisible Writing* (London: Collins, 1954).

Krleža, Miroslav. *On the Edge of Reason*, trans. Zora Depolo (London: Quartet, 1987).

Kundera, Milan. *The Joke*, trans. Michael Henry Heim (London: Penguin Books, 1983).

Kundera, Milan. *The Unbearable Lightness of Being*, trans. Michael Henry Heim (London: Faber and Faber, 1984).

Kundera, Milan. *The Art of the Novel*, trans. Linda Asher (London: Faber and Faber, 1988).

Márai, Sándor. *Memoir of Hungary: 1944–1948*, trans. Albert Tezla (Budapest: Corvina/CEU Press, 1996).

Márai, Sándor. *Embers*, trans. Carol Brown Janeway (New York: Knopf, 2001).

Miłosz, Czesław. *The Captive Mind*, trans. Jane Zielonko (London: Secker & Warburg, 1953).

Miłosz, Czesław. *The History of Polish Literature*, 2nd ed. (Berkeley, CA: University of California Press, 1983).

Molnár, Ferenc. *The Paul Street Boys*, trans. Louis Rittenberg (Budapest: Corvina, 2010).

Müller, Herta. *Nadirs*, trans. Sieglinde Lug (Lincoln: University of Nebraska Press, 1999).

Müller, Herta. *The Land of Green Plums*, trans. Michael Hofmann (New York: Granta, 1999).

Nádas, Péter. *Book of Memories*, trans. Iván Sanders with Imre Goldstein (New York: Farrar, Straus and Giroux, 1997).

Neubauer, John. 'Conflicts and Cooperation between the Romanian, Hungarian, and Saxon Literary Elites in Transylvania, (1850–1945)', in *Cultural Dimensions of Elite Formation in Transylvania (1770–1950)*, eds Victor Karady and Borbála Zsuzsanna Török (Cluj-Napoca: EDRC Foundation, 2008), 159–85.

Neubauer, John. 'Heteroglossia and Revolution: A Bakhtinian Reading of Dezső Kosztolányi´s *Édes Anna*', in *Under Construction: Links for the Site of Literary Theory; Essays in Honour of Hendrik van Gorp*, eds Dirk de Geest, Ortwin de Graef, Dirk Delabastita, Koenraad Geldof, Rita Ghesquière, and José Lambert (Leuven: Leuven University Press, 2000), 69–80.

Neubauer, John, and Borbála Zsuzsanna Török, eds. *The Exile and Return of Writers from East-Central Europe: A Compendium* (Berlin: de Gruyter, 2009).

A history of fiction

Olbracht, Ivan. *Nikola the Outlaw*, trans. Marie Holeček (Evanston, IL: Northwestern University Press, 2001).

Rebreanu, Liviu. *The Forest of the Hanged*, trans. A.V. Wise (London: G. Allen & Unwin, 1930).

Roth, Joseph. *The Radetzky March*, trans. Joachim Neugroschel (New York: Overlook Press, 1995).

Schulz, Bruno. *The Fictions of Bruno Schulz: The Street of Crocodiles & Sanatorium under the Sign of the Hourglass*, trans. Celina Wieniewska (London: Picador, 1988).

Szathmári, Sándor. *Voyage to Kazohinia*, trans. Inez Kemenes (North Adams, IL: New Europe Books, 2012).

Thompson, Mark. *Birth Certificate: The Story of Danilo Kiš* (Ithaca, NY: Cornell UP, 2013).

Tišma, Aleksandar. *The Book of Blam*, trans. Michael Henry Heim (New York: Harvest Books, 1998).

Witkiewicz, Stanisław Ignacy. *Insatiability*, trans. Louis Iribarne (Evanston, IL: Northwestern University Press, 1996).

4

WRITING HISTORY IN TWENTIETH-CENTURY EASTERN EUROPE

Maciej Górny

Introduction

A disclaimer is due from the outset: the twentieth-century historiography of Eastern Europe, a region deemed – if unfairly – 'obsessed with the past', is a topic that far exceeds my own competence and indeed, the confines of this chapter. Speaking more generally, a comparative East Central and Southeastern or Eastern European history of historiography is a rare bird. To my knowledge, only two such attempts have been undertaken. The first, by Josef Macůrek, a Czech historian from Brno, was published in 1946 and thus ends with the Second World War.[1] The second, by Emil Niederhauser, a Hungarian scholar, though published in 1995, only superficially touches upon post-war historiography.[2] If one excludes edited volumes consisting of individual essays rather than forming one coherent narrative, there were also some less ambitious attempts that covered only part of the region[3] or shorter periods of its history.[4]

---

1 Josef Macůrek, *Dějepisectví evropského východu* [Historiography of the European East] (Prague: Historický klub, 1946).
2 Emil Niederhauser, *A történetírás története Kelet-Európában* [A history of historiography in Eastern Europe] (Budapest: História Alapítvány – MTA Történettudományi Intézete, 1995).
3 See Karl Kaser, *Südosteuropäische Geschichte und Geschichtswissenschaft* (Vienna: Böhlau, 2002). After the dissolution of Czechoslovakia, the second edition of František Kutnar's and Jaroslav Marek's *Přehledné dějiny českého a slovenského dějepisectví. Od počátku národní kultury až do sklonku třicátých let 20. století* [The history of Czech and Slovak historiography in outlook: from the beginnings of national culture until the end of the 1930s] (Prague: Lidové Noviny, 1997) ceased to be a 'national' synthesis and became a multinational one, even more so since it was enriched with new sections devoted to the German historiography of Bohemia.
4 Monika Baár, *Historians and Nationalism: East-Central Europe in the Nineteenth Century* (Oxford: Oxford University Press, 2010); Diana Mishkova, Bo Stråth and Balázs Trencsényi, 'Regional History as a "Challenge" to the National Frameworks of Historiography: The Case of Central, Southeastern, and Northern Europe', in *World, Global and European Histories as Challenges to National Representations of the Past*, eds Matthias Middell and Lluis Roura y Aulinas (London: Palgrave Macmillan, 2012), 257–314; Maciej Górny, *The Nation Should Come First: Marxism and Historiography in East Central Europe*, trans. Antoni Górny (Frankfurt a.M.: Lang, 2013).

Writing history in the twentieth-century

There are clearly some technical reasons for this scarcity, linguistic difficulties being one of the most significant. But there are also temporal and structural difficulties resulting both from the nature of intellectual transfers to the region and from its dramatic history. Historiography is not the only field in which East Central and Southeastern Europe offer space for theoretical approaches that might elsewhere succeed or replace each other rather than coexist.[5] At the same time, discontinuity affects intellectual traditions as much as it influences political life, which is particularly true of the twentieth century. In effect, clear temporal divisions between subsequent historiographical 'paradigms' are difficult to draw, and thus, the history of historiography of the region is rather asynchronous. A reader accustomed to a more or less chronological narrative of the 'global' history of historiography may feel inconvenienced when seeing that in East Central and Southeastern Europe, positivism, historicism, Marxism and other methodological currents not only coexisted, but often flourished during the same period. Some other 'schools' were never very present or are missing altogether in Eastern European historiography, while some trends only arrived in parts of the region with considerable delay. To take an example from institutional history: 150 years separate the founding of the Hungarian Academy and the founding of the Albanian Academy of Sciences. There are some disparities in intellectual history too, not dissimilar to the asynchronic development of nationalisms in the region. In a biographical study on Serb historian Slobodan Jovanović, writer Dimitrije Djordjević focused on the personal dimension of these discontinuities:

> When Jovanović went to the *gymnasium*, schoolboys in Beograd were forbidden to carry a stick in the street. Jovanović died in the heyday of rock music and the Beatles. For an old nineteenth-century historian it could be a little too much.[6]

Consequently, while geography and political history offer two ways in which East Central and Southeastern Europe might be treated as a single, if heterogeneous, unit, intellectual history tells a different, more disjointed story. One way to avoid at least some of these problems would be to write a history of historiography in each nation, as Niederhauser did. But doing so would radically restrict the (possible) advantages of *histoire croisée* and, furthermore, it would undermine the cohesiveness of a regional approach. For this reason, the present study takes a problem-oriented approach that is chronologically ordered according to the sequence of the methodological trends that influenced local historians, most of which, though not all, happened to arrive from Western Europe.

Given the asynchronic nature of intellectual transfer, imported theories and methods almost always underwent changes after being adapted to the conditions of the region. The nature of this transfer might be best understood if we shift our focus from more or less 'pure' methodological formulations toward 'trends', from answers given by individual scholars (often representing certain 'historical schools') towards questions deemed meaningful at the time by historians as a group. Seen from this perspective, twentieth-century East Central and Southeastern

---

5 A study on historiographical methods in Eastern Europe can be found in Balázs Trencsényi, 'Conceptual History and Political Languages: On the Central-European Adaptation of the Contextualist-Conceptualist Methodologies of Intellectual History', in *Prague Perspectives I: The History of East Central Europe and Russia*, eds Petr Roubal and Václav Veber (Prague: Národní knihovna ČR, 2004), 142–63, esp. 156–8.

6 Dimitrije Djordjević, 'Historians in Politics: Slobodan Jovanović', *Journal of Contemporary History* 8, no. 1 (1973): 21–40, here 40, italics in the original.

European historiography underwent at least five 'waves' of transfer. The first of these waves echoed a collectivist turn in German and French historiography and coincided most closely with lively and fruitful regional responses to the German *Lamprechtstreit*. The representatives of this 'paradigm' formed the cadres of post-1918 national sciences. In some cases, historians like Mykhailo Hrushevsky and Nicolae Iorga also pursued political careers, a path that had been blazed by nineteenth-century scholar-politicians like František Palacký. The second paradigm, characterized by the influence of German *Volksgeschichte* and the early *Annales* School, shared a devotion to collective and interdisciplinary research, and, more often than not, was wary of what historians saw as the overly hasty generalizations made by some of their older colleagues. The further development of this paradigm was hindered by war and the subsequent rise of Marxism-Leninism. For its part, Marxist-Leninist historiography – the third paradigm in our list – represents by far the most unified methodological tradition in the regional history of historiography. But as early as the late 1950s, another trend came to the fore, and for a time dominated most of the region's historiographies: namely, the influence of the *Annales'* 'second generation', which found its highest expression in the work of Fernand Braudel. Finally, beginning in the 1970s, a turn toward cultural history initiated a period of multiple schools and research directions without any particular set of methodological convictions clearly dominating. Political activism on the part of a rather large number of historians, mostly in the ranks of the democratic opposition, was one of the characteristic traits of this period, and this phenomenon outlived the communist regimes by a decade or so.

Because this study focuses on the intellectual transfer of theories to East Central and Southeastern Europe, it will primarily deal with history as a profession, while also treating other dimensions of historiography. Following Jörn Rüsen, the theories and methods of historiographies will serve as a guide through regional historians' interests and the functions (i.e. political entanglements) of their work.[7] Another consequence is that relatively little attention will be devoted to some specific niches of historical study such as regional history, art history, palaeography, etc.

Students

In 1834, when the young Moldavian aristocrat and Romania's future first prime minister Mihail Kogălniceanu was invited to accompany Prince Mihail Sturdza's sons to France in pursuit of education, it was both an exception and a rule. It was an exception because at the time, there were not many Eastern European students in Western universities. It was a rule, however, in terms of the destination of the future pioneer of Romanian Romantic historiography. But in his last year of life, when asked to characterize his most important experiences, Kogălniceanu referred to another university that he attended, the Friedrich-Wilhelm-Universität in Berlin, calling it his 'second mother'.[8] According to Lucian Nastasă, this seeming paradox was nothing unusual in the whole of East Central Europe up to the late 1930s. Judging from the numbers alone, one might be led to believe that a general Francophilia held the minds of East Central European students for the entire nineteenth century, but

---

7 Jörn Rüsen, *Historische Vernunft: Grundzüge einer Historik I; Die Grundlagen der Geschichtswissenschaft* (Göttingen: Vanderhoeck & Ruprecht, 1983), 24–32.

8 Klaus Heitmann, 'Rumänien und der deutsche Geist – Gestern und Heute', *Revue des Études Sud-Est Européennes* 41, no. 1–4 (2003): 1–14.

Writing history in the twentieth-century

[n]evertheless, the qualitative data indicates the continuation of German intellectual hegemony over Central and Eastern Europe. What cannot be proven statistically becomes more complicated as far as elites are concerned, especially those who exerted essential political influence and who played a major political and cultural role in their times.[9]

Before we turn our attention to the intellectual currents that gained ground in the region, it is worth trying to characterize the preconditions of this transfer. Up to the late 1930s, foreign university education was a decisive factor in the intellectual development of the region's historians.

A number of social and political factors help explain why Germany and Austria played a leading role in the decades preceding 1914. The shift in the European balance of power after Sedan and the unification of Germany was of significance; however, there were also some more practical and less political reasons. Although higher education remained a privilege of the few, it was nevertheless significantly democratized. In contrast to Kogălniceanu's experience, a year or a semester at a foreign university was slowly becoming the norm. As a matter of fact, Eastern European workers, merchants and middle-class citizens were already present in the main centres of the empires, and students simply bolstered the numerous national diasporas in Berlin, Vienna and elsewhere. Simple economic factors also made Germany and Austria-Hungary preferable choices; both had a large number of prestigious universities relatively close to or even within East Central Europe, the easternmost being Alma Mater Francisco Josephina in Czernowitz in Bukovina, and it was much cheaper to study in these universities than in London or Paris. In fact, in the last decades of the nineteenth century, the German-speaking universities attracted growing numbers of Eastern European students, many of them Jewish. Some scientific institutions, most notably the Vienna Institut für Österreichische Geschichtsforschung, had a considerable influence on intellectual life in parts of the region.[10] In the case of stateless nations, an imperial German-language university might not only be the most natural, but simply the only place where students could study.[11] In 1912, 80 per cent of the German Empire's students were foreign, a proportion that would not be reached again in Germany until the 1990s.[12] More than 70 per cent of them came from the Russian Empire, Austria-Hungary and the Balkans. Another incentive was that in most cases their German diplomas were recognized in their countries of origin.[13] The opening of Swiss and then other universities to women further increased the numbers.

---

9 Lucian Nastasă, 'The Education of Romanian University Professors in Western Universities', *Historical Social Research* 33, no. 2 (2008): 221–31, here 224. See also Lucian Nastasă, 'Le role des études à l'étranger dans la carrière des professeurs d'université roumains (1878–1944)', in *L'enseignement des Elites en Europe Centrale (19–20ᵉ siècles)*, eds Victor Karady and Mariusz Kulczykowski (Cracow: Księgarnia Akademicka, 1999), 149–58.

10 Kaser, *Südosteuropäische Geschichte*, 182–4.

11 Slovenian historians studying in Vienna and Graz after the late 1870s are perhaps the best example: Milko Kos, 'Splošna zgodovina', in *Slovenska matica 1864–1964*, ed. France Bernik (Ljubljana: Slovenska Matica, 1964), 168–74.

12 Witold Molik, *Polskie peregrynacje uniwersyteckie do Niemiec 1871–1914* [Polish university peregrinations to Germany, 1871–1914] (Poznań: UAM, 1989), 52–3; Statista, *Anteil ausländischer Studierender an deutschen Hochschulen vom Wintersemester 1998/99 bis 2012/13*, http://de.statista.com/statistik/daten/studie/222/umfrage/anteil-auslaendischer-studenten-an-hochschulen/ (accessed 17 August 2017).

13 Stelian Mândruț, 'Die rumänische Intelligenz und die Wiener Universität, 1867–1918. Allgemeine Betrachtungen', *Revue Roumaine d'Histoire* 34, no. 1–2 (1995): 97–107.

Nastasă's attempt to measure the quantitative and the qualitative impact that international universities had on the Romanian professoriate draws attention to some important trends. Romanian university professors in the humanities who had obtained their doctoral degrees in Germany between 1864 and 1944 outnumbered their colleagues who had graduated from French universities by more than two to one. In medicine, natural science and law, the proportions were exactly the other way around.[14] In other cases, some of these categories diverge: there were more Russian subjects at German medical schools than there were in French faculties of medicine. The humanities, especially the faculty of history, attracted significant numbers of foreign students to Germany. This tendency continued until the late 1930s, despite three factors that might have hemmed it: the establishment of 'national' universities in East Central and Southeastern Europe, the growing chauvinism of German and Austrian students and some professors, and the First World War.

After a series of reforms during the first decade of the twentieth century, the majority of the region's nations established universities that, alongside their practical aims, were seen as symbols of national progress and as remedies for some of their intelligentsia's shortcomings. By 1914, the old universities in Prague (which had been divided along ethnic lines since 1882), Cracow and Budapest had been supplemented by a number of newer universities in Hungary, Galicia, Romania and Bulgaria. All of them took up the German model as a standard not only in respect to scientific rigour, but also, in the words of Bulgarian ethnographer, cultural historian and minister of education Ivan Shishmanov, in order to produce 'a more homogeneous intelligentsia educated within the country'.[15] This did not mean that students were obliged to stay at home for the duration of their studies. Rather, it remained customary to take a semester abroad, and Germany and Austria continued to be the top destinations for historians as much as for anthropologists and geographers.

In the years leading up to the First World War, chauvinists in Berlin and Vienna – in 1904 and 1905 in particular – reacted to the presence of foreign students by rioting. Though anti-Semitism was the main motivation behind the German students' riots, their fury was also directed against the 'overrepresented' Slavic students and professors in some faculties, most notably Slavic philology, one of whose figureheads at the time was Czech Balkanologist Konstantin Jireček.[16] But even though the memoirs of Slavic scholars give some hints about national tensions, these tensions did not deter others from applying. The Slovene ethnographer and historian Niko Županić recalled his Vienna professor Albrecht Penck offending his Slavic students with undiplomatic generalizations almost identical to the sarcastic remarks that his Polish pupil Józef Kostrzewski recalled Berlin's Gustaf Kossinna making.[17] But none of them took these outbursts of chauvinism as a reason to abandon their German professors. In Kostrzewski's words, the reason was that even though Kossinna was a chauvinist, he was also a renowned specialist and brilliant teacher. Personal qualities seemed to have attracted the best of the travelling students, and in most cases, they preferred personal contacts over just reading.

---

14 Nastasă, 'The Education of Romanian University Professors', 228.

15 Marin Pundeff, 'The University of Sofia at Eighty', *Slavic Review* 27, no. 3 (1968): 438–46, here 440.

16 Walter Leitsch, 'Nationalismus in der Wiener Universität zu Beginn des 20. Jahrhunderts: Constantin Jireček und die Beratungen über die Besetzung des Jagić-Lehrstuhls', *Jahrbücher für Geschichte Osteuropas* 30, no. 1 (1982): 100–19.

17 Christian Promitzer, 'Die Kette des Seins und die Konstruktion Jugoslawiens', in *Habsburg Postcolonial. Machtstrukturen und kollektives Gedächtnis*, eds Johannes Feichtinger, Ursula Prutsch and Moritz Csáky (Innsbruck: Studienverlag, 2003), 293; Józef Kostrzewski, *Z mego życia. Pamiętnik* [From my life: a memoir] (Wrocław: Zakład Narodowy im. Ossolińskich, 1970), 74.

Writing history in the twentieth-century

This is well illustrated by one of Karl Lamprecht's Polish students, Wacław Sobieski. In a letter from 1897 to his Cracow colleague Franciszek Bujak, a pioneer of Polish economic history, he expressed his enthusiasm with the way history was taught in Leipzig:

> I will not write much about the Leipzig University, nor about Lamprecht etc., because we will see each other soon anyway, but what I can say in general is that what's going on here is so cool [*bycze*] no Cracow philosopher would ever dream it. Lamprecht, a fantastic chap, storms into the room and stutters under his nose in a hurry – then they project a picture on the wall with the help of some optic machinery – and he stutters again. Listening to him you would say: it's all so commonplace, but after a week, after you go deeper into his two seminars, wow! Then you start to thank your luck to have driven you here. ... I feel at home here, more or less as in Cracow, but the seminar is much cooler – lucky German bastards![18]

The first international historians' congress held in Paris on the occasion of the World Exposition of 1900 marked the symbolic peak of 'Eastern' historians' push to the West. In the absence of many German and British colleagues, representatives of East Central and, even more so, Southeastern Europe made up a large portion of the contributors, with Alexandru D. Xenopol, a Romanian, initiating the congress' central methodological discussion on the question of causality and hypothesis in history.[19] But in the subsequent years, political turmoil reduced exchange between the East and West. In 1903, a bloody coup destabilized Serbia; in 1905, a revolution broke out in the Russian Empire; in 1907, a giant peasant uprising shook Romania. After students protested against Ferdinand I of Coburg's autocratic ambitions in 1907, Bulgaria's Sofia University was temporarily closed. At the same time, radicalized national policy in Germany antagonized Poles. In effect, no Polish (and no Czech) participants took part in the 1908 International Congress of Historical Sciences in Berlin. Perhaps it was the chauvinist atmosphere at the University of Vienna that inspired Oskar Halecki, a son of a general and Viennese resident, to take up his studies in provincial Cracow rather than at home in 1909.[20] In 1912, a series of wars started to torment the region, which would continue for the decade to come. For some younger historians who were called to the front like the Bulgarian Petar Mutafchiev, this meant a break from any intellectual activity. Some of their older colleagues devoted themselves to political activity in favour of the 'national cause', most notably Mykhailo Hrushevsky, the great Ukrainian scholar Nicolae Iorga, who dominated Romanian historiography for several decades, and Serbian anthropologist-geographer Jovan Cvijić, whose expertise proved to be equally important for both the shape of Yugoslavia's borders and its historiography.

Historians' political involvement in the Great War mattered even more for Germany, where overall patriotic enthusiasm later turned into revisionist bitterness for many. This corresponded to the anti-German resentment manifested by some of the alumni, Iorga being one among many. Yet despite nationalist outbursts, the post-1918 educational trajectories of East Central

---

18 Quoted in Andrzej Feliks Grabski, 'Karl Lamprecht i historiografia polska' [Karl Lamprecht and Polish historiography], *Kwartalnik Historii Nauki i Techniki* 26, no. 2 (1981): 315–34, here 320.

19 Karl Dietrich Erdmann, *Toward a Global Community of Historians: The International Committee of Historical Sciences, 1898–2000*, eds Jürgen Kocka, Wolfgang J. Mommsen and Agnes Blänsdorf, trans. Alan Nothnagle (New York: Berghahn, 2005), 13–15.

20 Maciej Salamon, 'Oskar Halecki na Uniwersytecie Jagiellońskim (1909–1918)' [Oskar Halecki on the Jagiellonian University (1909–1918)], in *Oskar Halecki i jego wizja Europy*, ed. Małgorzata Dąbrowska, vol. 1 (Warsaw: IPN, 2012), 16–37.

and Southeastern European historians did not differ much from those before the war. In fact, the numbers of East Central and Southeastern European students in Germany, Austria and France even rose.[21] New opportunities were created by France and Germany's cultural politics[22] and by initiatives within the region, the most impressive of which was Count Kunó Klebelsberg's policy of Hungarian 'cultural superiority'.[23] At the same time, more history students began studying at newly established or 'nationalized' universities and other scientific institutions in the region. Some Hungarian and Russian research institutions were moved to new locations; examples include the universities in Pozsony, Kolozsvár and Warsaw. Others followed a trend exemplified by the University of Dorpat, which underwent a period of rapid de-Russification and a subsequent longer period of de-Germanization to became linguistically Estonian by the 1930s.[24] Nations that had only become autonomous states after the war built new universities and set up ambitious research programmes, most of all in Hungary.[25] What mattered most in the long run seems to have been the decline of linguistic expertise on the part of the new generations of students. It was strengthened by politically motivated decisions, such as in Romania, which eliminated compulsory German lessons in high schools in 1929.[26] A turn towards nationalization in most of the region effectively undermined the liberal character of history education; in the Soviet Union this tendency took a more radical form. The centralist turn of Stalin's policies on academic research in the early 1930s put an abrupt end to the formative period of Ukrainian and Belorussian Soviet historiography. Even before the late 1930s, it was increasingly clear that the pre-1914 tendency toward the internationalization of the region's historical sciences was being reversed. War and the Sovietization of post-war historiography in the Eastern bloc catalyzed this process.

Where to after historicism?

In the first decade of the twentieth century, a small but active group of French, German and American historians recognized a problem within the flourishing historical sciences and formulated a number of solutions to grapple with it. Their concerns were not shared by all their domestic colleagues,[27] but they rhymed well with the striving for modernization and openness of newer European historiographies. Irrespective of the length of the particular tradition of classic historiography in each country, its limits were becoming clear to many scholars. In 1911, Austro-Hungarian Czech Konstantin Jireček published (in German) the first volume of

---

21 Nastasă, 'The Education of Romanian University Professors', 228.

22 On the example of Bulgaria see Elena Boyadijeva, 'Deutschlands kultureller Einfluß auf Bulgarien und die Konkurrenz der anderen Großmächte (1919–1939)', in *Collegium Germania 2. Probleme der Entwicklung Bulgariens in de 20er bis 90er Jahren des 20. Jahrhunderts*, ed. Zwetana Todorova (Sofia: Universitätsverlag Hl. Kliment Ochridski, 1997), 262–72.

23 Steven Bela Vardy, *Modern Hungarian Historiography* (New York: Columbia University Press, 1976), 50–61.

24 Csaba János Kenéz, 'Bildungszentren neuer Staatsvölker nach dem Ersten Weltkrieg – das Beispiel Dorpat', in *Universitäten im östlichen Mitteleuropa: Zwischen Kirche, Staat und Nation – Sozialgeschichtliche und politische Entwicklungen*, eds Peter Wörster and Dorothee M. Goeze (München: Oldenbourg, 2008), 75–83.

25 Ferenc Glatz, 'Historiography, Cultural Policy, and the Organization of Scholarship in Hungary in the 1920s', *Acta Historica Academiae Scientiarum Hungaricae* 17, no. 3–4 (1971): 273–93.

26 Heitmann, 'Rumänien und der deutsche Geist', 257.

27 Lutz Raphael, *Geschichtswissenschaft im Zeitalter der Extreme: Theorien, Methoden, Tendenzen von 1900 bis zur Gegenwart* (München: C.H. Beck, 2003), 73.

Writing history in the twentieth-century

his history of the Serbs. This and subsequent volumes were immediately translated into Serbian. Jireček's narrative was programmatically distanced from any generalizations. He understood the historian's task as 'a modest, source-based, coherent collection of the most important facts from this territory's past'.[28] His book won much praise from specialists in Balkan history, but the positive reviews of Jovan Cvijić, Stojan Novaković and Ljubomir Stojanović valued its practical merits over its theoretical ambitions. *Istorija Srba*, in their view, was a competent compendium of facts that would be of great help to any future synthesis rather than the 'proper' synthesis of national history itself.[29]

Alexandru D. Xenopol's methodological ideas that he presented at the International Congress of Historical Sciences in Paris in 1900 were an answer to the deficiencies of the historicist narrative. Though far from being philosophical speculation or a philosophy of history, Xenopol postulated that historians should use hypotheses in order to connect the verified elements of the past into a coherent story, which he believed would resolve what seemed to have been one of the shortcomings of Jireček's approach. But it did not take long for the limits of the method to come to the surface. To explain his approach, Xenopol chose the continuity between Daco-Romanian antiquity and the first appearance of Wallachians in Romania in the Middle Ages. He was immediately countered by a Hungarian participant, Móricz Darvai, who used Xenopol's method to demonstrate the exact opposite of what Xenopol was trying to prove.[30] In fact, the weakest spot of many of the new methodological trends was the difficulty in applying them to the facts.

The way Karl Lamprecht was received in Germany may be the best illustration of this shortcoming. In his *Deutsche Geschichte* as well as in numerous articles, Lamprecht argued for the universal periodization of world history. He pointed out that his opponents' fixation on politics and the singularity of historical processes made a comparative history inconceivable.[31] His critique was directed against Leopold von Ranke, the godfather of the dominant historiography of the time. *Kulturgeschichte* – Lamprecht's alternative to German historicism – aimed at embracing all spheres of social and individual existence. It was thought of as – anachronistically speaking – an *histoire totale*: 'The period of descriptive historiography has passed away, it is now the time of evolutionary historiography. It is not merely description that is at stake here; we are facing the fundamental shift from one philosophy of history to another.'[32] Though Lamprecht was not ready to call himself a positivist, the positivist inspiration of his theory seems evident. He sought to analyze 'the organism' – either individual, national or that of the whole of Western humanity – in all facets of its existence. To him, history was perfectly materialist, and there was no room for irrational phenomena or God's will. The economy and art were equally representative of a given stage of historical development. One of the most heavily criticized of Lamprecht's ideas was the way in which he periodized history based on the history of art. Lamprecht compared the 'intensity' of artistic styles to the level of economic development of a given epoch. He connected this with a criticism of what

---

28 Constantin Jireček, *Geschichte der Serben*, vol. 1 (Gotha: Perthes, 1911), x; the book appeared in the series on world history edited by Lamprecht.

29 Ivan Dorovský, *Konstantin Jireček. Život a dílo* [Konstantin Jireček: life and work] (Brno: Univerzita J. E. Purkyně, 1983), 189–91.

30 Erdmann, *Toward a Global Community*, 16–17.

31 Roger Chickering, *Karl Lamprecht: A German Academic Life (1856–1915)* (Atlantic Highlands, NJ: Humanities Press International, 1993), 339.

32 Karl Lamprecht, *Alternative zu Ranke: Schriften zur Geschichtstheorie*, ed. Hans Schleier (Leipzig: Reclam, 1988), 137.

he saw as historians' over-reliance on idealist theories of history, charging that idealism was the alibi of lazy historians who wanted to hide behind the 'ideas' and thereby ignore the myriad details that make up social life.[33]

Many have claimed that the extensive criticism of Lamprecht by neo-Rankian German historians during the *Methodenstreit* around 1900 was a bit unfair. Surely, Lamprecht's attempts at translating his own historiographical methodology into practice were rather disappointing. More often than not, the 'universalism' of his approach implied that Germany's history was the standard against which all others were to be measured. This, in turn, fuelled heavy doubts about his knowledge of international history. The final 'victory' of Ranke over Lamprecht saw the latter lose favour in mainstream German historiography; his theories were ultimately relegated to local and regional history and would later play a role in the development of *Volksgeschichte*.[34] At the same time, the main arguments against Ranke were also based on an unfair judgment. Hans Cymorek rightly claims that there was no real contradiction between Leopold von Ranke's theory of history and *Kulturgeschichte*, and that the conservatism of mainstream German historiography was much more developed in Lamprecht's argument than in reality.[35] We could add that when Lamprecht's critique of Ranke began gaining traction, accusing historicism of neglecting social history was also not entirely fair.

East Central and Southeastern European responses to Lamprecht were much more sympathetic than the reception of his work in Germany. As Marja Jalava demonstrates, histories of countries like Finland and Norway invited alternatives to state-centric approaches, thus making Lamprecht's ideas rather fruitful in those places.[36] Aside from Xenopol's comments in *Revue de synthèse historique*, which criticized Lamprecht's alleged overemphasis on the comparative approach and underestimation of the state, and Myron Korduba's similar statements in *Kwartalnik Historyczny* ('Historical quarterly'), most people viewed his ideas favourably.[37] Even Jaroslav Goll, the leader of Czech historicism, advised his favourite student, Josef Pekař, to go to Leipzig, since 'that is now modern and a young man like you should be permitted to follow the latest fashion'.[38] Some of Lamprecht's Finnish, Czech and Polish students worshipped him,[39] but some, like Franciszek Bujak, were less impressed by his seminar. What mattered more than direct references was indirect influence, which manifested itself in the region's historiography.

---

33 Ibid., 189 and 258.

34 Roger Chickering, 'The Lamprecht Controversy', in *Historikerkontroversen*, ed. Hartmut Lehmann (Göttingen: Wallstein, 2000), 15–30, here 26–8.

35 Hans Cymorek, *Georg von Below und die deutsche Geschichtswissenschaft um 1900* (Stuttgart: Steiner, 1998), 215–9.

36 Marja Jalava, 'Kulturgeschichte as a Political Tool: The Finnish Case', in *Historein* 11 (2011): 125–35.

37 Jaroslav Kudrna, 'Zu einigen Fragen des Methodenstreits in der französischen Historiographie um 1900', *Storia della Storiografia* 3 (1983): 62–78. The list of *Deutsche Geschichte*'s international reviews was published in the third edition: Karl Lamprecht, *Deutsche Geschichte, 1. Abt: Urzeit und Mittelalter. Zeitalter des symbolischen, typischen, konventionellen Seelenlebens*, vol. 1 (Berlin: Goertner, 1902).

38 Quoted in Thomas Weiser, 'Josef Pekařs Rezeption Lamprechts Geschichtslehre: Ein Beitrag zur Modernisierung der tschechischen Geschichtswissenschaft', *Storia della Storiografia* 23 (1993): 47–73, here 50. Pekař received similar advice from Antonín Rezek, see Jaroslav Čechura, 'Josef Pekař a Karel Lamprecht', in *K poctě Jaroslava Marka. Sborník prací k 70. narozeninám prof. dr. Jaroslava Marka* [In honor of Jaroslav Marek: collected essays on the occasion of Prof. dr. Jaroslav Marek's 70th birthday], eds Lubomír Slezák and Radomír Vlček (Prague: HÚ AVČR, 1996), 73–85.

39 Matti Viikari, 'Die Tradition der finnischen Geschichtsschreibung und Karl Lamprecht', *Storia della Storiografia* 6 (1984): 33–43.

Writing history in the twentieth-century

The asynchronic nature of transfer turned out to be an advantage for foreign students and historians working in other countries. The very dynamic of the German debate made it difficult for people to see the complementary elements of both positions. German historians simply could not be a neo-Rankian and a 'Lamprechtian' historian at the same time; but things were different for historians from other countries. Foreign scholars worked with historicist craftsmanship while simultaneously drawing freely from new impulses, both enriching the scope of their methods by merging history with neighbouring disciplines (most notably economics and sociology) and deepening their understanding of each theorists' motivations and ways of thinking. While not every front of the German controversy was equally meaningful for their research and their historiographic traditions, such eclecticism was characteristic of some of the most important scholars in the region.

Michał Bobrzyński and Josef Pekař, being mere observers of the *Methodenstreit* around Karl Lamprecht, both combined historicist *Geistesgeschichte* with Lamprecht's periodization and the positivist philosophy of Herbert Spencer and Henry Thomas Buckle. They were 'convinced that art-historical periodization embraces the general cultural orientation of a given generation – an orientation that expresses itself in economic behaviour and political choices no less than in aesthetic taste'.[40] Moreover, as in the most popular of Pekař's publications, *Kniha o Kosti* ('The book on Kost'), they were capable of putting some of Lamprecht's ideas into practice. The first volume of *Kniha o Kosti* was published in 1909 and set out with the intention of studying all levels of social life on a northern Bohemian estate. In the words of Pekař, this was the best way to grasp history's general development between the sixteenth and the nineteenth centuries: 'I think that only such a study of a small territory can lead to the understanding of the whole evolution.'[41] The second volume, published in 1911, seems even closer to the ideals of Lamprecht's *Kulturgeschichte*. Here, Pekař offers a history of the Czech rural population that is rooted in the study of geography and agriculture. High and folk culture of the Bohemian Baroque, another recurrent element of Pekař's understanding of Czech antiquity, added spiritual elements to this largely economic perspective.

There are, however, important differences between the *Kulturgeschichte* as imagined by Lamprecht and the way Pekař practised it. Pekař's favourite pupil, Zdeněk Kalista, said that for the latter, the 'laws of history' were not a necessity but merely a tool of interpretation; they could not help historians make predictions, but they were helpful in explaining the facts. Moreover, Pekař's periodization shared some principal convictions with Ranke's philosophy of history. They both believed that different epochs breathed different air and constituted separate entities and that they should thus be judged according to their own systems of values. The succession of these epochs for them was – again contrary to Lamprecht – a matter of accident rather than historical necessity. Bobrzyński's periodization, on the other hand, was based on legal history and thus came even closer to unifying the ideas of Ranke and Lamprecht.

Bobrzyński and Pekař shared conservative political views and a loyalty to the Habsburgs. Bobrzyński's political career peaked in 1908–13, when he served as the governor of Galicia. Pekař, though also a public intellectual, refused to run for Czechoslovakia's presidency in 1935 (after the resignation of Tomáš G. Masaryk). In their most important works, they challenged

---

40 Maciej Janowski, 'Three Historians', *CEU History Department Yearbook* (2001–02): 199–232, here 203–6.

41 Josef Pekař, 'Předmluva k čtenářům' (1909) [A foreword to the readers], in idem, *Kniha o Kosti*, 2nd ed., vol. 1 (Prague: Melantrich, 1942).

the romantic cliché of a democratic national history: Bobrzyński fervently criticized ancient Poland's political weakness, while Pekař made precise insights into the lives of important individuals. This attitude makes them something of an exception among most of the East Central and Southeastern European historians in the early twentieth century.

Nicolae Iorga's path away from historicism was leading in a slightly different direction. He was much more of a nineteenth-century type of 'political professor' than a public intellectual as Bobrzyński and Pelař. Iorga's political engagement is striking. He had been a socialist before becoming a nationalist. During the First World War, he backed Romania's pro-French politics and in 1919 served as the president to the first national assembly of Romania; in the early 1930s, he even became prime minister. At the same time, he was highly productive as a historian. According to Barbu Theodorescu, Iorga authored approximately 1,200 books and 23,000 articles.[42] His broad interests and knowledge were widely acknowledged, if not without certain irony, his French colleagues calling him 'la bibliotheque d'Alexandrie avant qu'elle ne soit brûlée' ('the library of Alexandia before it burned').[43] Though Iorga contributed to fields as diverse as Byzantine and Ottoman studies, his main focus was on the history of Romania. He authored a concept of the post-Roman quasi-democratic state of free peasantry that, 'embraced by the mountains on every side',[44] preserved ancient Romanian culture after the fall of Constantinople until reunification in the sixteenth century:

> Hence beyond the mountains Michael [the Brave] did not find the amorphous crowd of dirty and ferocious barbarians represented to us by the hatred of their racial opponents, but an indigenous majority of the population with traditions of a very ancient civilization.[45]

Among the many contradictions in the historian's oeuvre, two deserve to be highlighted. First, although Iorga always perceived Romanians as heirs to Mediterranean civilization (hence 'Byzance àpres Byzance') and thus as alien to their Slavic or nomadic neighbours, he was the initiator of the field of Balkan Studies and fostered international cooperation.[46] Second, he combined historicist methods with a firm belief in the mystical force of the people's soul, writing: 'The Folk is not a piece of land, neither a state, nor an economic necessity or a passing deed of the treaties that march through history but a soul ... The people's soul is an almost mystical element.'[47] Most of Iorga's works on the history of Romania are committed to the dogma of Romanian ethnic and territorial continuity, as were the works of Xenopol. Iorga vehemently defended this idea in the volume which appeared in the series that was co-edited by Lamprecht; in it, he attacked the Hungarians, Bulgarians, Greeks and the 'Slavs'. But Iorga's patriotic credo was accompanied by a methodological rigour that was very much in line with Lamprecht's ideas:

---

42 John C. Campbell, 'Nicholas Iorga', in *The Slavonic and East European Review* 26, no. 66 (1947): 44–59, here 46.

43 Dan Berindei, 'Nicolae Iorga à Paris de ses études', *Revue Roumaine d'Histoire* 18, no. 1–4 (2004): 171–5, here 172.

44 Nicolae Iorga, *A History of Roumania: Land, People, Civilisation*, trans. Joseph McCabe (London: Fisher Unwin, 1925), 6.

45 Ibid., 155.

46 See among others Nicolae Iorga, *Histoire des états balcaniques jusqu'a 1924* (Paris: Gamber, 1925).

47 Nicolae Iorga, *Rumänische Seele* (Jena: Gronau, 1933), 3.

Writing history in the twentieth-century

But to write history I do not need love nor hate: what I need are only sources and a modicum of common sense to explain them. What I deliver here is an effect of such an unprejudiced analysis of the authentic sources; through myself the truth hidden in them comes to the surface in an organic shape consolidated within a picture of living culture that shows no lacunae.[48]

A similar mixture of professional scholarship and national mythmaking was typical for early post-war Romanian historiography. In Slavic studies, Ion I. Nistor, rector of the university in newly acquired Cernăuți, denied Ruthenians' influence on Moldavia's culture, claiming them to have been eighteenth-century latecomers to Bucovina: 'Did they fight shoulder to shoulder with the Moldavians to defend this beautiful county? Did they help clear the forests and drain the swamps? … Did they contribute something to its cultural institutions?'[49] For Nistor, the answer was clearly no.

The balance between science and politics was different in the works of 'der kleine Mommsen', historian and archaeologist Vasile Pârvan. Inspired by Wilhelm Dilthey, Lucian Blaga and the concept of *Kulturgeschichte*, he developed ideas of the history of civilization based on the theory of temporal cadences (i.e. distinguishing between stable phenomena, 'vibrations' and 'rhythms').[50] In the heated debates preceding Romania's entrance into the First World War, he opposed the pro-*entente cordiale* stance of Iorga and Xenopol.[51] On the eve of Greater Romanian statehood, he saw the historian's task in educating people to support democracy and non-ethnic state patriotism.[52] And yet, Pârvan also – though less vehemently – contributed to the defensive idea of the ethnic exclusiveness of a 'Latin' Romania among hostile neighbours.[53]

Josef Pekař's rehabilitation of Baroque culture, Catholicism and nobility in Bohemian history coincided with a similar attempt by Gyula Szekfű in Hungary. In 1913, Szekfű published *A száműzött Rákóczi* ('Rákóczi in exile'), a realistic account of Ferenc Rákóczi II's years in exile. At the same time, the book was a criticism of Hungarian historians' lack of professionalism and nationalist bias epitomized in the anti-Catholic 'kuruc' (the name derives from anti-Habsburg insurrectionists from seventeenth and eighteenth centuries) discourse.[54] Szekfű stuck by this conviction even after the dissolution of the monarchy and the rise of nationalism. In the 1930s, Szekfű was still stressing the futility of a politics guaranteed 'only by the Hungarian sword'. He claimed that the rule of the Habsburgs had made it possible 'that Hungary started

---

48 Nicolae Iorga, *Geschichte des rumänischen Volkes im Rahmen seiner Staatsbildungen*, vol. 1 (Gotha: Perthes, 1905), vi–vii.

49 Ion I. Nistor, *Românii și Rutenii în Bucovina. Studiu istoric și statistic* [Romanians and Ruthenians in Bukovina: historical and statistical study] (Bucharest: Socec & Co., 1915), 9, quoted in Radu Mârza, *The History of Romanian Slavic Studies: From the Beginnings until the First World War*, trans. Leonard Ciocan (Cluj-Napoca: Romanian Academy of Sciences, 2008), 184.

50 Alexandru Zub, *Les dilemmes d'un historien. Vasile Pârvan (1882–1927)*, trans. Ileana Cantuniari (Bucharest: Editura Științifică și Enciclopedică, 1985), 96–105.

51 Lucian Boia, *Die Germanophilen: Die rumänische Elite zu Beginn des Ersten Weltkrieges* (Berlin: Frank & Timme, 2014), 104–5.

52 Alexandru Zub, 'Geschichtskultur und Modernisierung Rumäniens im 20. Jahrhundert', in *Revue Roumaine d'Histoire* 43, no. 1–4 (2004): 159–70, esp. 160–61.

53 See Vasile Pârvan, *Dacia: An Outline of the Early Civilizations of the Carpatho-Danubian Countries* (Cambridge: Cambridge University Press, 1928), 201–2.

54 Vardy, *Modern Hungarian Historiography*, 44–7.

towards the longest peaceful period of its modern history'.[55] According to the historian, the particular importance of Habsburg rule was not primarily the economic growth that it brought for Hungary, but the way in which it opened Hungary to the influence of Western, 'Christian-Germanic' culture.

Together with the idea of the convergence of state and nation, this pro-Habsburg bias forms the basis of Szekfű's most successful work, the multivolume *Magyar történet* ('Hungarian history'), co-authored by Bálint Hóman. Following Lamprecht's methodology, the work is broken up into epochs of cultural history. At the same time, Szekfű's and Hóman's narrative was inspired by *Geistesgeschichte* rather than *Kulturgeschichte*, Szekfű himself being an admirer of Friedrich Meinecke, a sentiment visible most of all in his work of 1918, *Der Staat Ungarn: Eine Geschichtsstudie* ('Hungary, the state: a historical study'). It displays an idiosyncratic mixture of historicism and newer historiographical trends; one notable example is when Szekfű identifies foreign policy as one of the 'driving forces' of history.[56] How perplexing this attitude could be might be best illustrated by the introduction to the first volume, which covers early Hungarian history:

> The economic conditions influence the literature, and the great ideological currents, almost on their own, change and form the economic and political conditions. No individual can stand against them, but the moving forces of the history of humanity never work separately; their influence is concurrent, and the primary, steering and decisive forces are the incomprehensible spiritual powers.[57]

This 'spiritual' description did not ignore economic, cultural, judicial, administrative or geographic factors. Scholars have also noted that when Szekfű wrote about 'spirit', he frequently meant 'state'.[58] Hóman, whose volumes on the medieval history of Hungary were published in German translation during the Second World War, wrote a history of the rise and fall of the king's central power. In his words, Carol I's main accomplishment was reducing the power of the aristocracy, which Hóman thought had been engaged in a long-term competition with the state.[59] Even this factually sound and methodologically innovative book could not avoid being

---

55 Gyula Szekfű, 'Abszolutizmus és kiegyezés' [Absolutism and compromise], in *Magyar történet*, vol. 5, eds Bálint Hóman and Gyula Szekfű (Budapest 1936), 466, quoted in Tibor Frank, 'Conflicting Sovereignties: The Habsburg Monarchy in Hungarian Historiography', in *Disputed Territories and Shared Pasts: Overlapping National Histories in Modern Europe*, eds Tibor Frank and Frank Hadler (Basingstoke: Palgrave Macmillan, 2011), 35–65, here 44.

56 Attila Pók, *Klios Schuld, Klios Sühne: Politische Wendepunkte und Historie im Karpatenbecken 1867–2000* (Budapest: MTA Bölcsészettudományi Kutatóközpont, Történettudományi Intézet, 2014), 139–40.

57 Bálint Hóman and Gyula Szekfű, *Magyar történet* [Hungarian history], vol. 1 (Budapest 1928), 5–8, quoted in Ignác Romsics, 'Ungarische Geschichtsschreibung im 20. Jahrhundert – Tendenzen, Autoren, Werke', in *Nationale Geschichtskulturen – Bilanz, Ausstrahlung, Europabezogenheit: Beiträge des internationalen Symposions in der Akademie der Wissenschaften und der Literatur, Mainz, vom 30. September bis 2. Oktober 2004*, ed. Heinz Duchhardt (Mainz: Akademie der Wissenschaften, 2006), 195–220, here 205–6.

58 See Árpád von Klimó, 'Transnationale Perspektiven in der ungarischen Geschichtsschreibung des 20. Jahrhunderts: Von "Hóman-Szekfű" bis "Ránki-Berend"', in Duchhardt, *Nationale Geschichtskulturen*, 221–40.

59 Bálint Hóman, *Geschichte des ungarischen Mittelalters*, vol. 2, *Vom Ende des XII. Jahrhunderts bis zu den Anfängen des Hauses Anjou*, trans. Hildegard von Roose and Max Pfostenkauer (Berlin: Walter de Gruyter, 1943), 397–9.

skewed by a national bias, especially the sections on medieval history penned by Hóman. As in other contemporaneous works of Romanian historiography, his picture of the Slavs (and the Wallachians, too) was overcritical, alleging that their material culture was far less developed than that of the Magyar and Turkic nomads.[60]

The Hungarian audience's reactions to the work of Hóman and Szekfű were more than positive and the book – notwithstanding its length – became a bestseller and the dominant master narrative of Hungarian national history. This was not untypical. In the first decades of the century, quite a few East Central and Southeastern European historians composed large national histories in response to both the self-imposed professional challenge and to the political needs of the state or a stateless nation. One of the most influential historians who wrote on a stateless nation was Mykhailo Hrushevsky. His multivolume *Istoriya Ukrayiny-Rusy, 1898–1936* ('History of Ukraine-Rus') combined a territorial definition of the Ukrainian realm with the idea of historical priority of the Ukrainian people on Ukraine's territory and social progressivism. He 'reclaimed' Kievan Rus' from Russia's history and integrated it into the narrative of a fallen Ukrainian state that was continuously striving for political rebirth. In some respects, closer to the romantic historiography of the nineteenth century, notably in the way it characterized the introduction of feudalism as being the 'fault' of Polish rule over Ukraine, Hrushevsky's oeuvre was inseparably connected to his political activism. For a couple of months in 1918, he served as president of the ephemeral Ukrainian state. Similar to Iorga in his habitus and political ideas, Hrushevsky also enjoyed the professional approval of the Romanian scholar, who reviewed his German publications.[61] Another narrative of a 'stateless nation' was composed by the most prominent Jewish historian of the era and a founder of the Jewish People's Party, Simon Dubnow. Dubnow wrote works on the 'collective soul' of the Jewish diaspora, and, similar to his contemporaries, connected an almost pedantic adherence to sources with a strong political agenda. His criticism was directed at Zionism and assimilationism, whereas he valued movements that strengthened the Jewish community, even at the price of perceived cultural decline as in the case of Hasidism.[62]

Similar to the sociology-inspired work of Bobrzyński, the Croatian historian and politician Ferdo Šišić took a 'genetic' view of history, combining an interdisciplinary approach with the cult of archival study. Consciously avoiding the subordination of history to general rules of development, he stressed the significance of each individual phenomenon. In his view, medieval Croatia was a Croat nation state within a non-national Hungarian kingdom. As Emil Niederhauser has noted, Šišić's work underwent a shift after 1917, when he moved away from the territorial treatment of Croatian history and towards a history based on Croatian ethnicity; this shift developed from the early volumes of *Hrvatska povijest* ('Croatian history') to *Pregled povijesti hrvatskoga naroda* ('History of the Croatian nation in outline') and finally to *Povijest Hrvata* ('History of the Croats').[63] The same tendency was characteristic of the Serb

---

60 Bálint Hóman, *Geschichte des ungarischen Mittelalters*, vol. 1, *Von den ältesten Zeiten bis zum Ende des XII. Jahrhunderts*, trans. Hildegard von Roose and Max Pfostenkauer (Berlin: Walter de Gruyter, 1940), 76–7 and 87–8.

61 Vitalyi Tel'vak, 'Pohl'ady Mykhaila Hrushevskoho v istorychnomu dyskursi zlamu XIX–XX stolittya' [Mykhailo Hrushevsky's opinions within the historical discourse at the turn of the century], in *Historia – mentalność – tożsamość. Miejsce i rola historii oraz historyków w życiu narodu polskiego i ukraińskiego w XIX I XX wieku*, eds Joanna Pisulińska, Paweł Sierżęga and Leonid Zaszkilniak (Rzeszów: Wydawnictwo Uniwersytetu Rzeszowskiego, 2008), 309–19.

62 Viktor E. Kelner, *Simon Dubnow: Eine Biografie*, trans. Martin Arndt (Göttingen: Vanderhoeck & Ruprecht, 2010), 16–21 and 197–223. For Dubnow's interpretation of Hasidism see his *History of the Jews in Russia and Poland*, trans. I. Friedlaender (Bergenfeld, NJ: Avotaynu, 2000), 107–16.

63 Emil Niederhauser, *A történetírás története*, 337–9.

medievalist Stanoje Stanojević, a liberal 'Yugoslavist' who wrote the political *Istorija Srpskoga naroda* ('History of the Serbian nation').[64] Vasil N. Zlatarski, a Bulgarian medievalist, was one of the first professional historians in Bulgaria and founder of the Historical Society in Sofia; in terms of size and dedication to historicist craftmanship, his works might be seen as the Bulgarian counterpart to Šišić and Stanojević.[65] All three historians criticized the nationalist bias of their colleagues while nevertheless subscribing to a nation–centric perspective. This was especially true of Stanojević and Šišić, whose works after 1918 tended to embrace the 'Yugoslav nation' but in reality remained focused on Serbian and Croatian nationality, respectively. Vladimir Ćorović's popular *Istorija Jugoslavije* ('History of Yugoslavia'), published in 1933, was no exception to this rule.[66]

A separate place among these historians was occupied by Zlatarski's most distinguished student, Petar Mutafchiev. Educated in history and geography in Sofia and Munich, he was involved in archaeological and territorial disputes over the rights to Dobruja, which Romanian historians like Iorga claimed was part of Romania.[67] His main historical work is the posthumously edited medieval history of the Bulgarians, but his essays had the greatest impact on Bulgarian historiography.[68] Mutafchiev identified the split between the country's foreign, Byzantine high culture and the masses as the key reason why Bulgaria had experienced failures in the past, claiming that this conflict manifested itself in repeated upsurges of 'nihilism' (one of them being the Bogomils). In a way, his interpretation of the history of the nation echoed much earlier regional debates on 'empty forms' (that is, superficial imports of Western institutions and procedures without a deep reconstruction of the society), but he took it further by making this conservative topos into the main motif of the entirety of Bulgaria's history: 'Everything here is only jumps and turns, quick and violent upsurges, followed by even more shattering downturns and by periods of complete immobility and powerlessness.'[69]

But the composition of new, 'collectivist' syntheses of national pasts was not the only consequence of the methodological turn at the beginning of the twentieth century. *Geistesgeschichte*, or intellectual history, the historiographical use of the concept of civilization, and interdisciplinary approaches that drew on economics and sociology were also important developments in European historiography.

Zdeněk Kalista, a student and follower of Pekař, refined the practice and methodology of *Geistesgeschichte* ('duchovní dějiny' in Czech). At the peak of his career in the late 1930s and

---

64 A review of 1920s Yugoslav historical syntheses can be found in Vladimir Ćorović, 'Histoire Yugoslave', *Revue Historique* 155 (1927): 112–62, esp. 113–19, and Ljubinka Trgovčević, 'South Slav Intellectuals and the Creation of Yugoslavia', in *Yugoslavism: Histories of a Failed Idea 1918–1992*, ed. Dejan Djokić (London: Hurst & Co., 2003), 222–37.

65 A comparison can be found in Josef Matl, 'Zur neueren Historiographie Bulgarien betreffend', *Jahrbücher für Kultur und Geschichte der Slaven* 2, no. 1 (1926): 41–57.

66 Emil Niederhauser, *A történetírás története*, 475–6.

67 Vasil Gyuzelev, 'Zhivot I nauchno tvorchestvo na Petar Mutafchiev' [The life and scientific oeuvre of Petar Mutafchiev], in *Istoriya na blgarskiya narod* [History of the Bulgarian nation], ed. Petar Mutafchiev (Sofia: Izdatelstvo na BAN, 1986), 6–34, here 15; Rumyan Ganchev, 'Zhivot i deloto na prof. Petar Mutafchiev' [Life and work of Prof. Petar Mutafchiev] *Godishnik na Sofiyskiya Universitet sv. Kliment Ohridski* 86 (1993): 95–109.

68 Balázs Trencsényi, *The Politics of 'National Character': A Study in Interwar East European Thought* (London: Routledge, 2012), 145–8.

69 Quoted in Thomas A. Meininger, 'A Troubled Transition: Bulgarian Historiography, 1989–94', *Contemporary European History* 5, no. 1 (1996): 103–18, here 117.

Writing history in the twentieth-century

early 1940s, he formulated what he thought of as a sort of supplement to Jaroslav Goll's work on historicism from the late 1880s. Drawing on Pekař, Kalista understood the historian's task as analyzing psychological changes effected by temporal, social, economic and geographic factors, claiming that the 'rhythm' of an epoch could be read from cultural products like neo-Gothic churches and English landscape parks.[70] The Sovietization of Czechoslovak historiography contributed to the petrification of his methodological credo: imprisoned, silenced and marginalized at home, he remained faithful to his ideas, continuing to publish in exile all the way up to his 1982 work, *Tvář baroka* ('The face of baroque'), an impressive piece of *Geistesgeschichte* that undertakes an analysis of the Baroque state of mind.

A second major product of the international historians' debates around 1900 was the historiographical utilization of the concept of civilization(s), which ultimately contributed to the development of geopolitics and the field of anthropogeography. Various versions of the political division of Europe into East and West typically informed such concepts. Milan Šufflay saw the division in the Balkans that separated 'occidental' Croats and 'oriental' Serbs.[71] Oskar Halecki and some other Polish authors, most notably Feliks Koneczny, adopted similar styles of thinking.[72] At the International Congress of Historical Sciences in 1923, Halecki presented a concept of the division between East Central and Southeastern European civilization on the one hand and Russian-dominated Eurasian civilization on the other. Halecki's later publications garnered considerable interest, especially in the United States, where they had been originally published, and in Germany (in translation).[73] Ironically, the tendency to exclude Russia from European civilization was equally present in the Russian historiography of the period. In the decade after 1917, 'Eurasianism' flourished, particularly among Russian émigrés in Western Europe. In their view, the Asiatic component of Russian culture played a substantial role in the country's past and would continue to be important in its future.[74] During the First World War, many authors in East Central and Southeastern Europe subscribed to this view, even though they typically remained attached to it only so long as it served their wartime political agenda.[75] What makes these theories relevant for historians of historiography is the way in which they relied on historical research: Šufflay based his generalizations on his own works on Balkan history, predominantly that of Albania; Halecki was a renowned medievalist. Thus, their theories of the cultural divisions of Europe and Asia remained closer to historiography than did post-1945 political science-oriented research. They also utilized works of their fellow historians, sometimes to the embarrassment of the latter. Such was the case with Šufflay's interpretation of

---

70 Zdeněk Kalista, *Cesty historikova myšlení. Prameny k moderní české historiografii* [The ways of historian's thinking: sources for modern Czech historiography], vol. 1, ed. Zdeněk Beneš (Prague: Garamond, 2002), 238.

71 Milan Šufflay, 'The Depths of National Consciousness', in *Discourses of Collective Identity in Central and Southeast Europe (1770–1945)*, vol. 4, *Anti-Modernism: Radical Revisions of Collective Identity*, eds Diana Mishkova, Balázs Trencsényi and Marius Turda (Budapest: CEU Press, 2014), 273–81, here 274–7.

72 Feliks Koneczny, *O wielości cywilizacyj* [On the plurality of civilizations] (Cracow: Gebethner i Wolff, 1935); Mirosław Filipowicz, *Wobec Rosji. Studia z dziejów historiografii polskiej od końca XIX wieku po II wojnę światową* [Facing Russia: studies from the Polish history of historiography from the 19th century until the Second World War] (Lublin: Instytut Europy Środkowej, 2000).

73 Hans-Jürgen Bömelburg, 'Oskar Halecki i historiografia niemieckojęzyczna' [Oskar Halecki and German historiography], in Dąbrowska, *Oskar Halecki i jego wizja*, vol. 1, 208–22.

74 Stefan Wiederkehr, *Die eurasische Bewegung: Wissenschaft und Politik in der russischen Emigration der Zwischenkriegszeit und in postsowjetischen Russland* (Köln: Böhlau, 2007).

75 Such was the case of Hrushevsky's wartime publications and Ivo Pilar's historical-political study. See L. v. Südland, *Die südslawische Frage und der Weltkrieg* (Vienna: Manz, 1918).

Šišić's *Hrvatska povijest*, which Šufflay understood as a factual argument in favour of his theory, despite the author's mild protests.[76]

Vyacheslav Lypynsky's interpretation of Ukraine's history was also informed by his interpretation of civilization discourse. Inspired by Eurasianists, he believed that both state and territory shaped its inhabitants. Though born to a Polish family, Lypynsky himself felt Ukrainian and expected other representatives of the Polish-speaking Ukrainian gentry to feel the same way. Contrary to Hrushevsky's democratic view, Lypynsky saw Ukraine as a more or less 'normal' European nation that had, unfortunately, gotten lost on its way to statehood. Consequently, he interpreted some crucial elements of Ukrainian history not as social, but as purely national events. Most notable is his reading of Khmelnytsky's uprising of 1648. He claimed that in order to create a Ukrainian state, it would be necessary to 'repeat' the uprising, this time directed against Russia. What makes his state-centric (*derzhavnyc'kyj*) view of history particularly interesting is his idea that Ukraine's national development was belated because it lacked the elite and the state, which he thought were the only powers capable of turning a nationality into a nation.

The third new direction in methodology birthed by the international historians' debates in the early 1900s were approaches that bridged economics, sociology and history. Of course, in some respects, all three disciplines reveal striking similarities. In Leipzig, economics students from East Central and Southeastern Europe attended lectures by Lujo Brentano, Lamprecht, Friedrich Ratzel and Wilhelm Roscher no less frequently than history students. And some of them also made political careers, notably Aleksandar Tsankov, prime minister of Bulgaria from 1923 to 1926.[77] Marxist sociology developed independently with its most powerful expressions in Hungary and Romania.[78] In Daniel Chirot's view, the debate between Ștefan Zeletin and Șerban Voinea (the latter drawing on the work of Constantin Dobrogeanu-Gherea) on regional backwardness in the early twentieth century can even be seen as a prelude to international historians' interest in the topic in the second half of the twentieth century.[79] Thus, the interrelations between the disciplines during this period can be viewed from at least three different perspectives: that of a historian, a sociologist or an economist. This becomes quite clear when we compare the German historians' criticism of Lamprecht with the reaction of his early Polish reviewer Zofia Daszyńska-Golińska. In contrast to most of his critics, she did not try to defend history from Lamprecht's speculative theorizing, but instead claimed that an economist or a sociologist are better equipped to deal with it and, hence, it is history, not sociology, in Lamprecht's model that leads one astray.[80] Within this chapter, however, the focus will be on historians rather than on economists or sociologists addressing historical topics.

---

76 Milan Šufflay's review of Šišić's works and response in *Starohrvatska prosvijeta* 1, no. 1–2 (1927): 118–25.

77 Nikolay Nenovsky and Pencho Penchev, 'The Evolution of German Historical School in Bulgaria (1878–1944)', *ICER Working Papers* no. 8 (2013): www.bemservizi.unito.it/repec/icr/wp2013/ICERwp08-13.pdf.

78 See Emilia Mineva, 'On the Reception of Marxism in Bulgaria,' *Studies in East European Thought* 53 (2001): 61–74; Olga Zobel, 'Ungarns Gesellschaft und Staat bei Oszkár Jászi', *Ungarn-Jahrbuch* 3 (1971): 135–74.

79 Daniel Chirot, 'A Romanian Prelude to Contemporary Debates about Development', *Review: A Journal of the Fernand Braudel Center for the Study of Economics, Historical Systems, and Civilizations* 2, no. 1 (1978): 115–23. On Gherea see Constantin Dobrogeanu-Gherea, 'Neo-Serfdom', in *Discourses of Collective Identity*, vol. 3/1, *Modernism: The Creation of Nation-States*, eds Ahmet Ersoy, Maciej Górny and Vangelis Kechriotis (Budapest: CEU Press, 2010), 419–25.

80 Grabski, 'Karl Lamprecht', 323–5.

Writing history in the twentieth-century

The challenge of interdisciplinarity

In 1967, speaking to professors and students of Warsaw University, Fernand Braudel claimed that:

> Social and economic history was, of course, born in Poland, in the midst of that group which gathered around that most extraordinary historian, Franciszek Bujak ... anticipating in this the work done only later by the English, the French and the Germans.[81]

Though Braudel was surely paying lip service to the hospitality of the Poles, his statement was not totally exaggerated. In fact, in the period before the First World War, some of the most inspiring historians in East Central Europe were interested in economic history. Bujak figured prominently among them, including others such as Jan Rutkowski, Sándor Domanovszky and Bedřich Mendl. All four made the case for an interdisciplinary approach to historiography and believed that historians should use new types of sources like inventories, customs documents, tariff records and cadastres. Such an approach required a collective effort; thus, both Bujak and Domanovszky encouraged students and teachers to do research within their local institutions.[82] The outcome of such collective effort was an economic and social model rather than a synthesis of national history, even though Bujak and Domanovszky appreciated the role of collective (national) psychology.[83] Among Bujak's most interesting works are his studies of Polish rural settlements and the economic condition of the peasantry. But he also pioneered sociological research on the political identities of the peasantry, notably in his study on the Galician village Żmiąca (1903). Rutkowski, co-editor of the socio-economic *Roczniki Dziejów Społecznych i Gospodarczych* ('Social and economic history yearbook') with Bujak, was led by his studies on tariffs and prices to the more general question of the genesis of Europe's economic dualism between the capitalist West and feudal, or semi-feudal, East.[84] Setting forth the stereotyped, though largely true vision of Bohemian history as being characterized by regionally unparalleled urbanization, Mendl concentrated on the economic history of cities, predominantly Prague. He introduced the concept of social crisis into Czech historiography.[85] Domanovszky also encouraged his students at the University of Budapest to study the history of Hungarian agriculture.[86] Summarizing their efforts, he concentrated on what he saw as the short-lived economic prosperity of great Hungarian estates.[87] The quality of these historians' social and economic research significantly improved scholarship on regional history, even though some of

---

81 Fernand Braudel, 'Historia i badanie teraźniejszości' [History and the study of the present], *Historia i trwanie* [History and duration], trans. Bronisław Geremek (Warsaw: Czytelnik, 1971), 337.

82 Anita Shelton, 'Franciszek Bujak (1875–1953)', in *Nation and History: Polish Historians from the Enlightenment to the Second World War*, eds Peter Brock, John D. Stanley and Piotr J. Wróbel (Toronto: University of Toronto Press, 2006), 280–96.

83 Andrzej Feliks Grabski, *Kształty historii* [Shapes of history] (Lodz: Wydawnictwo Łódzkie, 1985), 323–4.

84 Jerzy Topolski, *O nowy model historii. Jan Rutkowski (1886–1949)* [For a new model of history: Jan Rutkowski (1886–1949)] (Warsaw: PWN, 1986), 264–8.

85 Jan Horský, 'Die "Idealtypen" Max Webers und die tschechische Geschichtsschreibung', *Österreichische Zeitschrift für Geschichtswissenschaften* 4, no. 4 (1993): 642–50.

86 Vardy, *Modern Hungarian Historiography*, 165–8.

87 Alexander Domanovszky, 'Zur Geschichte der Gutsherrschaft in Ungarn', in *Wirtschaft und Kultur: Festschrift zum 70. Geburtstag von Alfons Dopsch* (Baden bei Wien: Rohrer, 1938), 441–69.

them were occasionally tempted to return to the older style of national history à la Iorga. This is best illustrated by Domanovszky's disappointing synthesis of Hungary's history, *Die Geschichte Ungarns* ('The history of Hungary'). Published in German right after the Treaty of Trianon, it contained surprisingly few economic and cultural insights. Instead, it included revisionist and anti-Semitic tones to come to the apocalyptic conclusion that Europe was being threatened by 'Bolshevism's muzzle'.[88]

Yet, in general terms, economic and social history has widened the perspective of more traditional historians winning a permanent place within their research scope. Two of the most important platforms for regional historians interested in new interdisciplinary trends were Alfons Dopsch's *Seminar für Wirtschafts- und Kulturgeschichte* ('Seminar for economic and cultural history') and Marceli Handelsman's seminars. One of the central figures of interwar historiography and esteemed by his students, many of whom also attended Alfons Dopsch's lectures, Handelsman wanted to write 'integral' history that brought together a series of different fields. Inspired by Gabriel Monod, his works range from the history of early medieval France to contemporary history (then the nineteenth century). He contributed to the lively historical debates on the comparative method, feudalism, the birth of national consciousness in Europe, mentalities and – in a long-lasting controversy with the Czech Slavist and historian Jaroslav Bidlo – the definition of East Central, Eastern or 'Slavic' Europe. His ambition was

> to connect the development of Poland with the simultaneously unfolding developments of the great nations of Western Europe as well as educing the connection and influence of Polish life on the developments of its neighbouring peoples of Central and Eastern, and Southeastern Europe. I devote my attention to social collectivities trying to discern changes in the moods, attitudes, intellectual dispositions of the whole of the nation, not just certain outstanding elements. However, I do not neglect these elements; rather I see in them the leaders, often the exponents, of the psychology of the collective. In comparison to the biographical method I should describe my method as socio-psychological.[89]

At times, Handelsman's understanding of history came very close to what would come to dominate the field in the second half of the twentieth century. As early as 1924, he concluded that 'a subtle critique by "a Febvre"' brings old historiographical formulas to an end proposing instead an attempt at unifying heterogeneous material that would result in 'an idea, not accomplished yet, but highly suggestive, rather a thought-provoking concept than a system that would require official acceptance'.[90]

The variety of his students' research attests to Handelsman's openness to new methods and topics.[91] For instance, Marxism inspired their work on social history. Some of them, notably

---

88 Alexander Domanovszky, *Die Geschichte Ungarns* (München: Rösl & Cie, 1923), 377–9.

89 Marceli Handelsman, *Kwartalnik Historyczny* [Historical quarterly] (1937), quoted in Marian B. Biskupski, 'Marceli Handelsman (1882–1945)', in Brock, Stanley and Wróbel, *Nation and History*, 352–85, here 372.

90 Marceli Handelsman, 'Najnowsze tendencje nauki historycznej' [Newest tendencies in historical science], *Przegląd Warszawski* 40 (1924): 27–35, here 32.

91 See *Księga pamiątkowa ku uczczeniu dwudziestopięcioletniej działalności naukowej prof. Marcelego Handelsmana, wydana staraniem i nakładem uczniów* [Memory book for the 25th anniversary of Marceli Handelsman's academic work published with and by his students] (Warsaw, 1929).

Writing history in the twentieth-century

Stanisław Arnold and Marian Henryk Serejski, belonged to the group that introduced historical materialism to post-war Poland.

In Czechoslovakia, a much more decisively Marxian view was represented by Jan Slavík, who was known as a critic of Pekař's interpretation of the Hussite revolution.[92] Ironically, though not exceptionally, the Czech 'hard' Marxist was to become a victim of Stalinism. Less ideological social historians were more likely to stay free but were not always able to keep their posts under the new order. For instance, István Hajnal, whose interests in technical progress, literacy and methodological independence secured him a special place within the circle of Sándor Domanovszky, was forced into retirement in 1950.[93]

The rise and international impact of East Central European economic and social history owed much to the new state structures, an example being the cultural and scientific politics of Count Klebelsberg in Hungary discussed above. More importantly, the development of new universities, institutes and journals devoted specifically to economic and social history encouraged the development of further research. Many of the prominent historians in the field had a good number of students and were willing to introduce them to their respective disciplines' international community. The appearances of both the historians and their students at three interwar congresses demonstrated freshly acquired self-confidence. Handelsman's role during all three of them (1923, 1928 and 1933) provides particularly striking evidence of such confidence in the discipline. A Czech participant of the Brussels congress (1923), Jan Bedřich Novák, impressed by the theoretical level of the dispute between Handelsman and Marc Bloch on the origins of feudalism, stressed the visibility of East Central and Southeastern European historians: 'I remember that ten years ago there was a similar Czech–Polish–South-Slavic group in London, but, contrary to the present, it hid somewhere in the corner of the world's congress.'[94]

Five years later in Oslo, Czech participant (and elected head of the Comité International des Sciences Historiques, CISH) Josef Šusta divided his time between Handelsman's and Jan Dembiński's presentations on the origins of national consciousness in the Middle Ages, Nicolae Iorga's lecture on the unity between Europe's East and West in the same epoch, and Marc Bloch's analysis of medieval social history.[95] A look at the minutes of the congress shows that Marc Bloch's presentation was preceded by Kazimierz Tymieniecki's paper on Eastern Europe's social history and followed by Jan Rutkowski's paper on Europe's dualism of agrarian development.[96] After the congress, Handelsman advocated applying Bloch's perspective to the comparative study of Eastern Europe's history, which he thought would serve to balance out the heretofore one-sided focus on institutions rather than societies.[97] Finally, in 1933, the international historians' congress took place within East Central Europe, in Warsaw. Thanks to the efforts of Handelsman, a separate Jewish contingent presented its work, and there was a record-high number of participants from Poland, Czechoslovakia, Romania and Hungary. There were also a considerable number of German historians, including some from Danzig. Many of them

---

92 On the polemics with Pekař see Jaroslav Bouček, *Jan Slavík. Příběh zakázaného historika* [Jan Slavík: the story of a forbidden historian] (Prague: H & H, 2002), 78–99.

93 Vardy, *Modern Hungarian Historiography*, 200–04.

94 Jan Bedřich Novák, 'O mezinárodním kongresu věd historických v Bruselu' [On the international congress of historical sciences in Brussels], *Český Časopis Historický* 29 (1923): 183–8, here 184.

95 Josef Šusta, 'O mezinárodním kongresu věd historických v Oslo' [On the international congress of historical sciences in Oslo], *Český Časopis Historický* 34 (1928): 613–20.

96 *VIe Congrès International des Sciences Historiques: Résumés des communications présentées au congrès* (Oslo: Le Comité Organisateur du Congrès, 1928), 262–7.

97 Marceli Handelsman, *Monde Slave ou Europe Orientale* (Warsaw: Hoesick, 1930), 125.

were proponents of so-called *Volksgeschichte*, a strain of historiography that was developing in parallel to the economic-social approach.[98]

The question as to whether the *Annales* School can be compared to German *Volksgeschichte* has been extensively treated by Peter Schöttler, who concluded that they had no significant exchange.[99] Moreover, there was a basic difference in the philosophy of history on both banks of the Rhine. Whereas the holistic approach of Febvre and Bloch aimed at analyzing the existing social and spatial structures, proponents of *Volksgeschichte* like Hermann Aubin sought to describe the *Volk* as a national utopia that would be realized in the future; thus, their project was normative.[100] Nevertheless, there were many similarities between these two parallel historical schools, first and foremost being their modern, interdisciplinary approach. In 1938, it was precisely this aspect of *Volksgeschichte* that Karel Stloukal identified as the most promising; he saw potential in *Volksgeschichte*'s interest in the history of peasantry (understood as the best representative of the nation), in settlement history, and in the history of Germans living abroad (i.e., *Auslandsdeutschtum*). The negative aspects of *Volksgeschichte* were, to his mind, its romantic concept of the nation, its biologistic conception of ethnicity, its politicization of history and its 'openly stated desire to write history with a hammer'.[101] Still, he believed that historians could benefit from the new 'turn'.

In Germany, *Kulturgeschichte* in many ways preceded *Volksgeschichte*. In Hungary, Domanovszky's counter-narrative to Hóman-Szekfű's nationalistic approach was titled *Magyar Művelődéstörténet* ('Hungarian cultural history'), while Elemér Mályusz baptized his methodological school *népiségtörténet* (evoking the notion of the Volk – *nép* and *történet* refer to something like 'national' or 'people's' history). Neither the nation's soul, nor the judicial tradition and its state structures were essential for this type of historiography which placed the Magyar people, the folk, at its centre in the same way that German *Volksgeschichte* placed the German people at its centre. It was rather the folk – in Mályusz's case the Magyar folk – that was at its centre. Like its German counterpart, Mályusz's historiography was interdisciplinary, deploying methods drawn from geography, linguistics, ethnography, archaelogy and statistics. Although Mályusz was forced into retirement by the post-1945 communist government and banned from teaching, the cultural nationalism characteristic of his work and that of his students continued to exert an influence on Hungarian historiography. In a characteristic article on the Order of Saint Paul published in 1960, Mályusz concentrated on the national, or rather ethnic Magyar character of some of the Order's reformers in order to draw conclusions about Hungary's contribution to *Devotio Moderna* and 'the human personality'.[102] The same sense of

---

98 *VII* Congrès International des Sciences Historiques. Résumés des communications présentées au congrès* (Warsaw: Comité Organisateur du Congrès, 1933).

99 Peter Schöttler, 'Die intellektuelle Rheingrenze: Wie lassen sich die französischen Annales und die NS-Volksgeschichte vergleichen?', in *Die Nation schreiben: Geschichtswissenschaft im internationalen Vergleich*, eds Christoph Conrad and Sebastian Conrad (Göttingen: Vanderhoeck & Ruprecht, 2002), 271–94.

100 Ibid., 288. On the methodological debates on *Volksgeschichte*, see Willi Oberkrome, 'Aspekte der deutschsprachigen "Volksgeschichte"', in *Zwischen Konfrontation und Kompromiss: Oldenburger Symposium: 'Interethnische Beziehungen in Ostmitteleuropa als historiographisches Problem der 1930er/1940er Jahre'*, ed. Michael Garleff (München: Oldenbourg, 1995), 37–46.

101 Karel Stloukal, *Hlavní proudy v současné historiografii* [Main trends in contemporary historiography] (Prague: self-published, 1938), 14–15.

102 Elemér Mályusz, 'Zakon paulinów i devotio moderna' [Pauline fathers and devotion moderna], in *Mediaevalia. W 50 rocznicę pracy naukowej Jana Dąbrowskiego*, eds Józef Garbacik, et al.(Warsaw: Państwowe Wydawnictwo Naukowe, 1960), 263–83.

Writing history in the twentieth-century

continuity of the interwar paradigm is conveyed by the 1970s and 80s Slovak polemics (primarily penned by Branislav Varsik) against Mályusz's interwar theses on the ethnic composition of medieval Hungary.[103]

This transfer leading to many German-Hungarian parallels (including references to the notions of *Volksboden* and *Kulturboden*) evoking the 'national' territory in terms of biology and culture[104] may seem rather atypical in its directness. It is little wonder that the school of Hungarian ethnohistory led by Mályusz clashed with its German counterpart over the territory and ethnicity of German inhabitants of pre-Trianon Hungary and over German claims to cultural superiority in the region.[105] To some extent, similar historical experiences might help explain these parallels between German and Hungarian historiography. In both countries, the humiliation of the Paris treaties motivated many historians to shift their attention to structures and institutions that were seemingly older, stronger and more durable than the state. It is both inspiring and frightening to observe the intellectual quality and interdisciplinarity of the German and Hungarian revisionist movements. It is noteworthy that the Hungarian campaign for the unity of Saint Stephen's Crown started before the German revisionist campaign. The perceived urgency of the question of nationalities stimulated the prominent geographer and politician Count Pál Teleki to undertake geographical studies on the 'racial' composition of the country as early as the first decade of the century.[106] Thanks to his work prior to November 1918, it was already an organized enterprise to which many geographers, ethnographers, historians and statisticians were committed. At the beginning of the revisionist campaign, historians sought to prove the invalidity of Trianon by arguing that Hungarian culture was superior to all other nationalities of Saint Stephen's Crown. Although usually combined with the promise of the equal political status of minorities in the future restored Hungary, such a picture would hardly be acceptable to the minorities.[107] Soon, more sophisticated works followed the first wave of revisionist propaganda, this time directed towards the foreign elites rather than the native nationalists. The integrity of the state was based on its nationality structure, the economic unity of the Carpathian Basin and the 'natural' status of its borders along with the arguments based on legal history.[108] Teleki argued that such 'objective' data mattered more than linguistic differences.[109]

History alone would have been insufficient to support an argument for the unity of the territory of pre-Trianon Hungary, and the same can be said of ethnography. The most glaring contradiction lies in the way in which the historians making these arguments also claimed that Magyar culture was superior to the cultures of the minorities, which would have had

---

103 Armin Höller, 'Die tschechoslowakische Historiographie der siebziger und achtziger Jahre: Ihre Auseinandersetzung mit der ungarischen Geschichtsforschung', *Ungarn-Jahrbuch* (1989): 211–26.

104 See Romsics, 'Ungarische Geschichtsschreibung im 20. Jahrhundert', 209–11.

105 Vardy, *Modern Hungarian Historiography*, 105.

106 Teleki's *Ethnographical Map of Hungary Based on Density of Population* (based on the 1910 census) significantly minimized the ethnic territories of Romanians and Slovaks by excluding sparsely inhabited mountainous areas and is probably the best example of a piece of pre-war research that was employed in the post-war revisionist campaign.

107 Anikó Kovács-Bertrand, *Der ungarische Revisionismus nach dem Ersten Weltkrieg: Der publizistische Kampf gegen den Friedensvertrag von Trianon (1918–1931)* (München: Oldenbourg, 1997), 45–49.

108 Marián Hronský, *Boj o Slovensko a Trianon 1918–1920* [The struggle for Slovakia and Trianon 1918–1920] (Bratislava: Národné literárne centrum, 1998), 239–52.

109 Ignác Romsics, 'The Trianon Peace Treaty in Hungarian Historiography and Political Thinking', in *Hungary's Historical Legacies: Studies in Honor of Steven Béla Várdy*, eds Dennis P. Hupchick and R. William Weisberger (Boulder, CO: Columbia University Press, 2000), 89–104.

serious consequences for the cultural status of minorities in Hungary.[110] Thus, historians used more 'objective' evidence drawn from hydrography, climatology and geomorphology.[111] The ethnographic maps created under the tutorship of Teleki, even prior to the First World War, sought to point out the differences between the ethnic make-up of communities in the 'Romanian' mountains and in the centre of Transylvania, going so far as to analyze differences in housing and population density.[112] But even in geographical or economic analyses, history always remained at hand. Teleki's claim was that the ethnic composition of medieval Hungary included a greater proportion of Magyars than it did in later eras, which he used to support the argument that Magyars thus had a historically justified right to the territory where they were living. However, his thesis on the organic nature of Hungary's borders seems most significant: 'Whereas the whole country – a well combined synthetic region – possesses frontiers of the greatest geographical weight and strength, it is not possible to distinctly separate the different natural regions inside the country from each other.'[113] As Péter Treitz and Károly Papp tried to argue, it was nature itself that predetermined the unity of Hungary:

> The geographical unity of Hungary awakens a feeling of unity among all those peo-
> ple living within the frontiers. An excellent example of this is the fact that nearly all
> the Slovaks and Ruthenians living in the mountainous districts still desire to remain
> Hungarian subjects.[114]

When it became clear that they were not convincing their English or French readers, the revisionist authors moved the Cassandric strain: 'States are not rootless things, but are rooted in the surface of the earth … The wise men of the Peace Conference did not reckon with these relations, and ignored them when drawing the Trianon frontiers.'[115]

It is within this political and intellectual context that the 'first spatial turn' of Hungarian historiography took place. It had some interesting parallels in the region. In Holm Sundhaussen's view, not all of them coincided with explicit territorial revisionism. Typically, they sought to draw a distinction between ethnic and state structures. In the Balkans and in the Baltic states, *Volksgeschichte* helped to fill the 'a-historic' gap between these nations' first appearance in the Middle Ages and their 'national awakenings' in the nineteenth century.[116] In the case of Latvia and Estonia, another stimulus was the evolution of local German historiography. One of the most esteemed representatives of the latter, Reinhard Wittram, announced the new paradigm of the 1930s in which 'the racial-biological, spiritual-intellectual processes are to be seen as the

---

110 See Miklós Zeidler, *Ideas on Territorial Revision in Hungary 1920–1945*, trans. Thomas J. DeKornfeld and Helen DeKornfeld (Wayne, NJ: Center for Hungarian Studies, 2007), 72–3.

111 Anikó Kovács-Bertrand, *Der ungarische Revisionismus*, 61.

112 Leon Dominian, *The Frontiers of Language and Nationality in Europe* (New York: American Geographical Society, 1917), 339.

113 Pál Teleki, *Short Notes on the Economical and Political Geography of Hungary* (Budapest: Hornyánszky, 1919), 4.

114 Peter Treitz and Charles de Papp, *Geographical Unity of Hungary* (Budapest: Pfeifer, 1920), 4.

115 Francis Fodor, 'The Treaty of Trianon in the Light of Geography', in *Justice for Hungary: Review and Criticism of the Effect of the Treaty of Trianon*, ed. Albert Apponyi (London: Longmans Green & Co. Ltd., 1928), 327–41, here 330.

116 Holm Sundhaussen, 'Serbische Volksgeschichte. Historiker und Ethnologen im Kampf um Volk und Raum vom Ende des 19. bis zum Ende des 20. Jahrhunderts', in *Volksgeschichten im Europa der Zwischenkriegszeit*, ed. Manfred Hettling (Göttingen: Vanderhoeck & Ruprecht, 2003), 301–24.

Writing history in the twentieth-century

most important part of Volksgeschichte, and we will be never able to ignore the mother-classes [*Mutterschichten*] of our people, and first and foremost the peasantry'.[117]

Given the fact that the first Latvian- and Estonian-language universities opened in 1919 and there had been virtually no professional historiography in either country prior to that, one might say that *Volksgeschichte* was the first historiographical theory propagated and further developed in the Baltics. In the end, the fact that it could rise to such a dominant position might have had something to do with the small number of students and professors of history. In Estonia, for example, only sixteen students completed undergraduate studies in history between 1919 and 1934, and only five students completed their doctorate in the same period.[118] In Latvia, the native term for folk (*tauta*) was widely used to 'domesticate' the new trend. In the first issue of *Latvijas Vēstures Institūta Žurnāls* ('Journal of the Latvian History Institute'), the journal's editor, Augusts Tentelis, characterized the turn towards *Volksgeschichte* in Latvia as follows:

> the biggest task still lies ahead: to find new, heretofore unrecognized historical sources about Latvians, to use them and to publish them. We will study our past in the spirit of nationalism, looking at it with the eyes of Latvian historians. There is no antagonism between the spirit of nationalism and the truth of history. It seems to us that the history of a particular *tauta* can be understood best and most fundamentally only by a person who belongs to that *tauta*.[119]

Hans Kruus and Arveds Švābe were the most prominent representatives of this Baltic historical school. The former edited a collective national history of Estonia that foregrounded the ethnic unity of the Estonian people. This interpretive framework might have forced the contributors to the volume to negatively assess Estonian history between the thirteenth century and the nineteenth century, but Kruus' left-wing politics and attachment to the peasantry allowed him to shine a positive light on the popular unrest of the seventeenth, eighteenth and nineteenth centuries.[120] The historians' evaluation of the role of Russia was ambivalent, claiming that although Russia never did anything to facilitate the Estonian national awakening, it 'objectively' contributed to the cultural renaissance of the Baltic peoples by challenging German dominance in the region. Kruus' interest in the history of peasants along with his critical view of Baltic Germans helped him adapt to the reality of Soviet Estonia. Though shortly arrested in the early 1950s, he was soon released and continued doing research on the agrarian history of the Baltic region. In his case, the transition from *Volk* to the 'masses' proved relatively easy.

This was not the case for his Latvian colleague, Švābe. In many respects a member of the same cohort of Baltic nationalists as Kruus, Švābe was politically on the right. Like Kruus, he studied at a Russian university and based his interpretation of Latvia's past on the elevated status of the 'history-less' peasantry. Contrary to Kruus, but in concord with many practitioners of

---

117 Reinhard Wittram, 'Die Wendung zur Volksgeschichte', *Baltische Monatshefte* (1936): 566–77, here 570, quoted in Jörg Hackmann, 'Ethnos oder Region? Probleme der Baltischen Historiographie im 20. Jahrhundert', *Zeitschrift für Ostmitteleuropa-Forschung* 50, no. 4 (2001): 531–56, here 538–9.

118 Toivo U. Raun, 'The Image of the Baltic German Elites in Twentieth-Century Estonian Historiography: The 1930s vs. the 1970s', *Journal of Baltic Studies* 30, no. 4 (1999): 338–51.

119 Augusts Tentelis, 'Lastītājiem' [To the reader], *Latvijas Vēstures Institūta Žurnāls* 1, no. 1 (1937): 3–7, quoted in Andrejs Plakans, 'Looking Backward: The Eighteenth and Nineteenth Centuries in Inter-War Latvian Historiography', *Journal of Baltic Studies* 30, no. 4 (1999): 293–306, here 298–9.

120 Sirje Kivimäe and Jüri Kivimäe, 'Hans Kruus und die deutsch-estnische Kontroverse', in Garleff, *Zwischen Konfrontation und Kompromiss*, 155–70.

Volksgeschichte, he did research on both history and ethnography in the belief that he would be able to fill in the gaps of his nation's history with elements of its unwritten culture.[121] In an attempt to counter the Baltic-German historical narrative, Švābe postulated the existence of medieval Latvian statehood in the twelfth and thirteenth centuries.[122] Deported to Germany in 1944, he never returned to Latvia, choosing to stay in exile.

The territorial focus of the Hungarian *népiségtörténet* had some interesting parallels in the new Yugoslavia. Before the First World War, a Serbian student of Albrecht Penck, Jovan Cvijić, composed an ethno-psychological account of the people of the Balkans. Inspired by early German geopolitics, he developed a theory that, being in accordance with the norms of science, identified Serbia as the natural 'centre' of the peninsula and marginalized its local rival, Bulgaria.[123] His scientific successes, strengthened by the international political position he acquired during the First World War, culminated in the paradigm shift of the neighbouring discipline: historiography thus giving more space to ethnology-inspired research on rural cultures.[124] This becomes even more evident in the light of Nikola Radojčić's summary of the state of Yugoslav historiography in the 1920s:

> The modern Serb historiography of today is like this: there are very few source editions and the existing ones are not critical enough. One branch of source editing, the publication of old Serb sources, has been utterly neglected. The old Serbian and foreign dictionaries do not suffice in helping to understand Serb sources. Historical biographies and bibliographies do not exist. Source analysis and monographic research of individual questions, until recently the strongest and, largely, the only segment of Serbian historiography, are in a sufficient state but the future prospects are very weak in the face of declining knowledge of ancient languages. Attempts at a national synthesis do show up, but due to the lack of published sources and other support, their prospects are limited.[125]

According to the authors informed by ethnography and anthropology, such as Cvijić or Jovan Erdeljanović, Serbs represented the purest of the Dinaric race possessing the following characteristics: energetic, intelligent, riotous, moral, impulsive and creative.[126] Cvijić's characterological and territorial claims still influence Serbian historiography to this day. In the interwar period, some of Cvijić's students published groundbreaking works that fused ethnology with political history and geography. In the words of Serbian ethnographer Tihomir Georgević, a contemporary of Cvijić, ethnographic evidence could fill the gaps in the region's historical past just as it did for Latvia and Estonia:

---

121 Edgar Anderson, 'Arveds Švabe (1888–1959)', *Journal of Central European Affairs* 20, no. 1 (1960): 84–91.

122 Inesis Feldmanis, 'Die lettische Historiographie', in Garleff, *Zwischen Konfrontation und Kompromiss*, 133–8.

123 Snezhana Dimitrova, 'Jovan Cvijić on the Periphery and the Centre', *Études balkaniques*, 3–4 (1996): 82–91.

124 Jovan Cvijić, *La Péninsule balkanique, géographie humaine* (Paris: Colin, 1918).

125 Nikola Radojčić, 'Krátký přehed moderní srbské historiografie' [A short overview of modern Serbian historiography], *Český Časopis Historický* 31 (1925): 357–68, here 367–8.

126 Jovan Cvijić, *Psihičke osnove južnih Slovena* [The psychological profile of south Slavs] (Belgrade: SKZ, 2006), 28–48.

Writing history in the twentieth-century

It is a mine of information on the subject of Serbian national customs, culture, and national self-revelation; it is also full of references to historic events in Serbia's past, her historic sites and personages. If anyone were to conceive of the idea of delimiting the frontiers of the Serbian nation on the basis of the area over which Serbian popular and national tradition extends, he would be well on the side of truth. Serbian national ballads from the Serbian lands outside Macedonia always refer to the latter as a Serbian land.[127]

Jovan Erdeljanović's substantial study on Montenegro focused on the ethnic Serbian character of the province, its folk culture, and ethnic migrations throughout its history.[128] Jevto Dedijer, who died in 1918 shortly after having returned from wartime exile in France, analyzed another aspect of the ethnic history of the Western Balkans. Dedijer sought not only to conduct research on the material and intellectual culture of the Serbs, but also to understand what he saw as the loss of Serbian national identity either through conversion to Islam or 'Bulgarisation'. Serbian national-ism rooted in notions of a unified Serbian ethnicity in the contested provinces of Kosovo and Bosnia and Herzegovina survived in post-1945 Yugoslavia and continues to this day.[129]

A somewhat different, though equally durable and perhaps even more inspiring, impact of the new paradigm can be observed within Slovenian historiography. Like in Serbia, it was inspired by geographical research, most of all by the works of Anton Melik.[130] And similar to Cvijić's conception of the Balkans, it was politically motivated. Surely, it is no accident that Slovenian historians' attention was especially directed to their border with Italy seen in the light of corresponding disciplines of history, ethnography and geography with an aesthetic touch:

> Trieste and Gorica, to judge from their origin, urbanistic development and prevailing type in art up to the most recent times, clearly belong to the ambient of the Karst and Littoral, an ambient bitterly realistic and strange to the Italian mildness.[131]

Ljudmil Hauptmann was one of the first Ljubljana-based historians to focus on geography. In the 1920s and 1930s, he published extensively on the arrival of Slavs in the Balkans and their later conflicts with the Germans.[132] Milko Kos and some of his students analyzed medieval set-tlements and medieval colonization with a special focus on the city of Ljubljana;[133] prominent among them were Fran Zwitter and Bogo Grafenauer. Zwitter worked with historical statistics

---

127 Tihomir Georgevitch, *Macedonia* (London: Allen & Unwin, 1918), 211, quoted in Joel M. Halpern and Eugene A. Hammel, 'Observations on the Intellectual History of Ethnology and Other Social Sciences in Yugoslavia', *Comparative Studies in Society and History* 11, no. 1 (1969): 17–26, here 20.

128 Jovan Erdeljanović, *Stara Crna Gora. Etnička prošlost i formiranje crnogorskih plemena* [The old Montene-gro: the ethnic past and the forming of Montenegrin tribes] (Belgrade: Slovo Ljubve, 1978).

129 See Atanasije Urošević, *Kosovo* (Belgrade: Naučno delo, 1965); Milovan Radovanović, *Etnicki i de-mografski procesi na Kosovu i Metohiji* [Ethnic and demographic processes in Kosovo and Metohija] (Belgrade: Liber Press, 2004).

130 On the personality of Melik and a comparison between his influence on Slovenian culture and that of Jovan Cvijić see Anton Melik, 'A Nation in the Making', in Ersoy, Górny and Kechriotis, *Discourses of Collective Identity*, vol. 3/1, 351–6.

131 Fran Rumovš and France Kidrič, Introduction to *The Julian March: Studies on its History and Civiliza-tion*, eds Milko Kos, et al. (Ljubljana: Academy of Sciences & Arts, 1946), 7–10, here 8–9.

132 Josef Žontar, 'Hauptprobleme der jugoslavischen Sozial- und Wirtschaftsgeschichte', *Vierteljahrschrift für Sozial- und Wirtschaftsgeschichte*, 27, no. 4 (1934): 347–73, here 350–54.

133 Milko Kos, *Srednjeveška Ljubljana. Topografski opis mesta in okolice* [Medieval Ljubljana: the topography of the town and its surroundings] (Ljubljana: Kronika, 1955).

and demography before he moved to the study of nationality in Austria-Hungary.[134] After 1945, Grafenauer combined these elements with Marxism, shifting his attention from peasant settlements to peasant culture, social riots and economic history.[135] While interdisciplinarity remained a key element of his approach, his methodological studies from the 1960s show that he subscribed to Fernand Braudel's understanding of total history. Interestingly enough, he criticized the newest developments in French historiography. For the Slovene historian, both microhistory and an all too excessive attachment to statistics seemed contrary to the principles of Marc Bloch and Lucien Febvre, which he saw more or less fulfilled by his own work.[136] At the same time, the question of ethnic and geographical borders, so important to interwar Slovenian historiography, remained vital for him. As late as 1992, he still engaged in debates with other historians over the history of Slovenia's northern border and Slovene ethnic groups living outside the national territory.[137]

Slavic colonization of the Balkans and ethnic borders attracted the attention of many other historians in Yugoslavia. Ironically, this group consisted both of scholars who identified with the new state as well as its detractors. Niko Župani was perhaps the most visible representative of the first group. A Slovene by birth, he gained recognition as a 'racial anthropologist' after he conducted measurements of Turkish and Bulgarian prisoners of war in Serbian custody in 1912 and 1913. In Yugoslavia, he became the first director of the Slovene Ethnographic Museum, and in 1940, he became head of the ethnology seminar at the university in Ljubljana.[138] For Župani , the 'racial' unity of Serbs and Croats was a fact attested to not only by history and linguistics, but first and foremost by anthropology. That gave the impulse to a long-lasting debate on the timing and nature of the arrival of Slavs in the Balkans. Contrary to Šišić and Hauptmann, Županić drew on Ludwik Gumplowicz's theory of conquest to conclude that there was 'an invasion by Serbs and Croats', thus describing them in a way that paralleled 1930s German historiographers' descriptions of medieval German colonization and Hóman's treatment of the Magyar conquest of the Slavs:

> From the political and psychological point of view we must believe that these Serbs and Croats felt themselves legally and morally superior, not only to the Avars and Vlachs, but also to the 'Slavs' liberated from the Avars. The Serbs and Croats must

---

134 Pavle Blaznik, Bogo Grafenauer and Sergij Vilfan, *Gospodarka in družebna zgodovina Slovencev. Zgodovina agrarnih panog, I zvezek: Agrarno gospodarstvo* [The economic and social history of the Slovenes: the history of agrarian relations, part I; agrarian economy] (Ljubljana: SAVU, 1970), iii–xi; Fran Zwitter, Jaroslav Šidak and Vaso Bogdanov, *Les problemes nationaux dans la monarchie des Habsbourg* (Belgrade: Comité National Yougoslave des Sciences Historiques, 1960).

135 Bogo Grafenauer, *Zgodovina slovenskega naroda, III, zvezek: Doba prve krize fevdalne družbe na Slovenskem od začetka kmečkih uporov do viška protestantskega gibanja* [History of the Slovene nation, vol. III: the crisis period of the feudal order in Slovenia from early peasant uprisings to the height of the protestant movement] (Ljubljana: Kmečka knjiga, 1956), esp. 173–6.

136 Bogo Grafenauer, 'Problemi metodologije istorijskih nauka u svetlu nekoliko novih radova o metodologiji istorije' [Methodology problems in historical science in the light of some newer works on the methodology of history], *Jugoslavski Istorijski Časopis* 1 (1965): 41–68.

137 Dušan Nećak, 'Bogo Grafenauer in koroški Slovenci po drugi svetovni vojni' [Bogo Grafenauer and Carinthian Slovenes after the Second World War], in *Grafenauerjev zbornik*, eds Vicenc Rajšp, et al. (Ljubljana: Znanstvenoraziskovalni Center SAZU, 1996), 119–23.

138 Rajko Muršič, 'Forefathers and Successors at the Department of Ethnology and Cultural Anthropology, University of Ljubljana: Paths in the Development of Slovene Ethnology/Cultural Anthropology', *Studia Ethnologica Croatica* 20 (2008): 107–25.

Writing history in the twentieth-century

have occupied higher social positions in the administration and the army. They became a privileged class in the state.[139]

While Županić's settlement studies (and his racial theories) aimed at forging unity between the Serbs and Croats, similar reasoning could lead to somewhat different conclusions. Ivo Pilar's interpretation of Bosnian Bogomilism, for example, postulated the ethnically Croatian character of Bosnia, which had, in his view, unfortunately been split by the fact that both the Orthodox and Catholic Churches viewed the Bosnian Church as heretical; he believed this was one of the factors that stood in the way of long-term Croatian sovereignty.[140] Both the pro-Serb Županić and the more critical Croats, most notably Ivo Pilar and Milan Šufflay, eagerly used the language and concepts of racial anthropology. In Pilar and Šufflay's view, however, these concepts served to illustrate the racial distinction between whiter, taller, and more frequently blue-eyed Croats and their 'Mongolized' Balkan neighbours. The wartime Independent State of Croatia promoted this part of the Croatian historians' works to its official ideology.[141]

Understanding their nation's history through the concept of *Volk* and the concomitant focus on population and territorial issues proved to be, surprisingly, less attractive to scholars of the two countries directly affected by the original German *Volksgeschichte*. Neither in Poland nor in Czechoslovakia did this line of historical reasoning ever transform into a proper school. Maciej Janowski hypothesizes that this may be due to the weakness of the revisionist agenda in both countries.[142] Nevertheless, some individuals and institutions entered into (politically motivated) debate with individuals and institutions of German *Ostforschung*, and in doing so, often adapted the same ways of thinking. For example, a Polish medievalist from Poznań, Kazimierz Tymieniecki, consequently criticized Hermann Aubin's publications on German colonization by using his own research on the native origins of Poland's medieval towns. In Poznań, Toruń, Gdynia and Katowice, i.e. along the Polish–German border, interdisciplinary institutes devoted to *badania zachodnie* ('Western research'), a parallel to *Ostforschung*, were created; some of them still exist today, most prominent among them being the Instytut Zachodni in Poznań. Marian Wojciechowski, a Poznań medievalist, was by far the most active academic manager (i.e. a skilful player, politician and historian) in the vein of Aubin or Albert Brackmann. But prior to 1945, he could only dream of the kind of financial means that they had access to.[143]

---

139 Niko Županić, 'The Serb Settlement in the Macedonian Town of Srbčište in the VIIth Century and the Ethnological and Sociological Moment in the Report of Constantinus Porphyrogenetes Concerning the Advent of Serbs and Croats', *Etnolog* 2 (1928): 26–35, here 30.

140 Zlatko Matijević, 'Dr. Ivo Pilar i problem Crkve bosanske ("bogumilstvo")' [Dr. Ivo Pilar and the question of the Bosnian church ('Bogomilism')], *PILAR – Časopis za društvene I humanističke studije*, 1, no. 1 (2006): 69–81.

141 Nevenko Bartulin, 'The Ideal Nordic-Dinaric Racial Type: Racial Anthropology in the Independent State of Croatia', *Review of Croatian History* 5, no. 1 (2009): 189–219; see also Rory Yeomans, *Visions of Annihilation: The Ustasha Regime and the Cultural Politics of Fascism, 1941–1945* (Pittsburgh, PA: University of Pittsburgh Press, 2012).

142 Maciej Janowski, 'Mirrors for the Nation: Imagining the National Past among the Poles and Czechs in the Nineteenth and Twentieth Centuries', in *The Contested Nation: Ethnicity, Class, Religion and Gender in National Histories*, eds Stefan Berger and Chris Lorenz (Basingstoke: Palgrave Macmillan, 2008), 442–62.

143 Rudolf Jaworski, 'Deutsche Ostforschung und polnische Westforschung in ihren historisch-politischen Bezügen', in *Deutsche Ostforschung und polnische Westforschung im Spannungsfeld von Wissenschaft und Politik. Disziplinen im Vergleich*, eds Jan M. Piskorski, Jörg Hackmann and Rudolf Jaworski (Osnabrück: Fibre, 2002), 16–18.

In Czechoslovakia, similar clashes were an internal affair, since the local German historians (and until 1938, Czechoslovak citizens) more or less completely subscribed to the new paradigm. Josef Pfitzner's *Sudeten German History* (1935) was a typical application of the new school. Similar to Pilar, he stressed that the Germans in Bohemia were autochthonic, but he supported, at least in words, the peaceful coexistence of the largest ethnic groups in the Czechoslovak state.[144] The outbreak of the controversy over the cultural and historical priority of the Bohemian Germans came with a delay and was fuelled by Pfitzner's publication of two pro-German letters written by the senile Josef Pekař in Konrad Henlein's journal *Die Zeit* in 1936. Josef Šusta, Jaroslav Werstadt and Jan Slavík's criticism inspired by this publication embraced Pfitzner's general concept of Bohemian history, notably the politicization of the *Volksgeschichte*.[145] These reactions were caused by disappointment with the nationalist turn of the promising Bohemian historian.

In the 1920s and 1930s, a marginal though interesting offshoot of historical geography developed in the form of transnational settlement studies centred upon the Carpathians. Polish, Hungarian, Czechoslovak and Ukrainian historians and geographers such as Volodymyr Kubyjovych, Elemér Mályusz, Václav Chaloupecký, Alexander Húščava, Ludomir Sawicki, Jiří Král, Jozef Martinka and many others contributed to the historiography of the shepherd economy and land ownership structure.[146] This special interest in the specificity of the Carpathians' settlement history, property structure, and social and economic development in some cases corresponded with the more scientific concerns of historical geography as a genuinely non-national discipline. Perhaps, some historians have claimed, Carpathians were an extreme case of a space that makes national history nearly impossible. In the words of Tadeusz Manteuffel, another participant in these debates, borders needed to be historicized, which meant that their shifts over time made any attempt at drawing straight lines an exercise in futility.[147]

Perhaps the most thought-provoking challenge to the collectivist historiography inspired by Lamprecht came in 1931 when a group of young, French-educated Romanian scholars challenged Iorga and founded a new historical journal, *Revista istorică română* ('Romanian historical review'). In the words of one of them, Petre P. Panaitescu:

> The 'youth's' programme calls for the detailed scientific critique and review of historical publications, declares war on dilettantism, breaks away from romanticism, concentrates, especially, on cultural history and on Eastern Europe as well as on the methodology of history. The success of the first volumes of the new journal proves the correctness of such a programme, which enjoys a favourable reception among Romanian historians.[148]

---

144 Josef Pfitzner, 'Sudeten German History', in *Discourses of Collective Identity in Central and Southeast Europe 1770–1945*, vol. 3/2, *Modernism: Representations of National Culture*, eds Ahmet Ersoy, Maciej Górny and Vangelis Kechriotis (Budapest: CEU Press, 2010), 379–86.

145 Frank Hadler and Vojtěch Šustek, 'Josef Pfitzner (1901–1945). Historiker, Geschichtsprofessor und Geschichtspolitiker', in *Prager Professoren 1938–1948 zwischen Wissenschaft und Politik*, ed. Monika Glettler and Alena Míšková (Essen: Klartext, 2001), 105–36.

146 Jiří Král, *Die anthropogeographische Durchforschung der Slowakei und Karpathorusslands in den Jahren 1919–1934* (Bratislava: self-published, 1935), 5–30; Ladislav Tajták, 'Prínos profesora Jozefa Martinku do historickej geografie na Slovensku' [The contribution of Prof. Josef Martinka to historical geography in Slovakia], *Geographia Cassoviensis* 5, no. 1 (2011): 7–11.

147 Tadeusz Manteuffel, 'Metoda oznaczania granic w geografii historycznej' [The method of border-marking in historical geography], in *Księga pamiątkowa*, no page.

148 Petre P. Panaitescu, 'Historiografja rumuńska w latach 1930–1933' [Romanian historiography in the years 1930–1933], *Kwartalnik Historyczny* 48, no. 1 (1934): 47–56, here 48.

Writing history in the twentieth-century

At first, Panaitescu, Constantin C. Giurescu and Georghe I. Brătianu, the leaders of the 'new school', rejected the nationalist pathos of Romanian historiography, and, even more so, the use of speculation to fill in the gaps in the sources. The most radical among them, Panaitescu, undermined the heroic myth of Wallachia's and Moldavia's struggle against the Ottoman Empire by suggesting that the principalities' autonomy was a side-effect of their marginality rather than heroic resistance.[149] Moreover, in Panaitescu's view, the role of the Slavs in Romania's history no longer occupied a place in the shameful margins but rather moved to the centre of the narrative. But the young historians' enthusiasm for objective research dissipated after they overthrew Iorga's dominance. Their central position within national historiography led them to ask the same internationally contested questions that had bothered their older colleagues.

Brătianu's 1937 book *Une énigme et un miracle historique: le peuple roumain* ('An enigma and a miracle of history: the Romanian nation') offered a recapitulation of Romanian continuity theory and suggested that there was territorial congruence between ancient Dacia and modern Greater Romania. He criticized neighbours who questioned the authenticity of Romania's national mythology (notably, Petar Mutafchiev). His book proposed that the unity of the Romanian provinces was a 'historic law' and a materialization of a national instinct.[150] Giurescu, who out of the three had the longest career, repeatedly confirmed the continuity theory in his post-war publications.[151] Additionally, he claimed that the 'Romanian–Bulgarian' tsardom of the twelfth century was ethnically and culturally Romanian.[152] The conclusions of these works could have equally stemmed from Iorga's or Xenopol's pen: 'Throughout the centuries, close economic, political and cultural relations were maintained between the three countries of Wallachia, Moldavia and Transylvania, inhabited by one and the same native Romanian population.'[153] All three very actively participated in the extreme-right Romanian political movements of the interwar period.

At the same time, there can be no doubt that Giurescu, Brătianu and Panaitescu were formidable historians, modern in their methodological ideas and, as will be shown in one of the subsequent chapters, fully in line with the French socio-economic historiography of their time. *Revista istorică romănă* devoted considerable space to cultural, social and economic history while gradually shifting its focus from the regional to the national past. Logically, the new school aimed at challenging the dominance of Iorga's synthetic approach. Giurescu's 1935 *Istoria romănilor* ('The history of the Romanians') was a decisive step on the way. In the foreword, the young historian proposed a new approach to history writing, distinct from both idealism and Marxist materialism:

> I do not think the development of a nation's life ... can be understood through material or economic facts alone, as is claimed by the adherents of historical materialism. Nor do I agree with the other theory according to which everything may be explained by ideas and culture. To understand the complex development of humanity

---

149 Lucian Boia, *History and Myth in Romanian Consciousness* (Budapest: CEU Press, 2001), 69.

150 Georghe I. Brătianu, *Une énigme et un miracle historique: le peuple roumain. A propos du livre de M. Ferdinand Lot sur les invasions barbares et de quelques ouvrages récents sur les origines du peuple roumain* (Bucharest: Imprimerie National, 1937), esp. 121–4.

151 See Constantin C. Giurescu, *The Making of the Romanian National Unitary State* (Bucharest: Meridiane, 1980) and Constantin C. Giurescu and Dinu C. Giurescu, *Geschichte der Rumänen*, trans. Adolf Armbruster (Bucharest: Wissenschaftlicher und Enzyklopädischer Verlag, 1980).

152 Giurescu and Giurescu, *Geschichte der Rumänen*, 96.

153 Giurescu, *The Making of*, 8.

or a part of it, one needs to focus on both factors, spirit and matter. They coexist in every moment of history; they only change their intensity.[154]

Giurescu was the one representative of the new school who moved closest to the paradigm of *Volksgeschichte*. In the late 1930s and early 1940s, he concentrated on Romanian settlement studies both within the country's borders and in what was then Soviet Ukraine.[155] Perhaps the most striking example of the persistent influence of this paradigm on his work was composed in the 1970s. In his history of the Romanian forest, Giurescu combined aestheticized, romantic claims about the forest as the nation's natural refuge with a detailed study of economic, settlement and environmental history informed by cartography, anthropology, linguistics, heraldry and ecology.[156]

The history of *Volksgeschichte* outlined here attests to the truth of Manfred Hettling's view that it had an international character. Centred upon notions of statehood, territory and culture, *Volksgeschichte* sought to heal the wounds of the defeated and give historical legitimacy to the nations that were not autonomous states before the end of the First World War. All three key terms – statehood, territory and culture – were not only intercheangable, but more importantly, interwar historians used them in a radical way, thus giving the whole methodology a political slant.[157]

In conclusion, East Central and Southeastern European responses to the challenge of interdisciplinary research either centred upon the notions of ethnically defined territory or on social and economic history. These two trends represented the last wave of methodological innovation before the Sovietization of the regional historiographies. But even before the political suppression of non-Marxist methodologies, most of the region's countries experienced heavy blows. Both Poland and Yugoslavia were greatly affected by the war and occupation, and even in less traumatized Romania and Czechoslovakia, the two decades between 1930 and 1950 were marked by the death, imprisonment or exile of many leading scholars. The list is impressive: in Czechoslovakia, Josef Pekař died in 1937, Bedřich Mendl killed himself in 1940 to avoid German persecution; Josef Šusta, accused of collaborating with the Nazis, committed suicide in 1945; Kamil Krofta died after being released from a Nazi concentration camp; Zdeněk Kalista was sent to prison in 1951, where he would spend the next 15 years; Jan Slavík left the country for good, and Josef Pfitzner was executed in 1945. Simon Dubnow was murdered by the Germans in the Riga Ghetto in 1941. In Yugoslavia, Milan Šufflay was murdered in 1931, apparently by secret police agents; Ivo Pilar suffered the same fate in 1933. Jovan Erdeljanović died in 1944, Ferdo Šišić in 1940; Vladimir Ćorović escaped the occupied country and died in a plane crash in 1941. Slobodan Jovanović, a 'historicist' specialist of the nineteenth-century history of Serbia and later head of the exile government in London, emigrated in 1941 never to return. In Bulgaria, Vasil Zlatarski passed away in 1935, followed by Petar Mutafchiev in 1943. Franciszek Bujak abandoned his scientific activity in 1949, Jan Rutkowski died in 1949 and Marceli Handelsman fell victim to the German concentration camps (first Gross-Rosen, and finally Mittelbau-Dora) in 1945. Oskar Halecki never returned from wartime exile. Bálint Hóman died in prison in 1951 after being sentenced as a member of the Hungarian fascist government. Vyacheslav Lypynsky died in exile in 1931, Mykhailo Hrushevsky in 1934. Nicolae

---

154 Quoted in Alexandru Zub, 'Constantin C. Giurescu und der Ursprung seiner Synthese der rumänischen Geschichte', *Südost-Forschungen* 38 (1979): 191–205, here 201.

155 Ibid., 196–8.

156 Constantin C. Giurescu, *A History of the Romanian Forest*, trans. Eugenia Farca (Bucharest: Editura ARSR, 1980).

157 Manfred Hettling, 'Volk und Volksgeschichten in Europa', in Hettling, *Volksgeschichten*, 7–37, esp. 34–6.

Writing history in the twentieth-century

Iorga was murdered by the Romanian fascists in 1940, Gheorghe I. Brătianu was arrested by the communist regime in 1950 and died in prison three years later. The war put an end to whole branches of historiography, such as Jewish historiography in Poland.[158] Such a dramatic change could not leave the region's historiographies unaffected. In many ways, it made the task of Sovietization easier than it would otherwise have been.

The frost comes from the Kremlin

A few sentences in Josef Šusta's report on the 1928 historical congress in Oslo were devoted to the Soviet delegation under Mikhail Pokrovskij. According to Šusta, the most striking element of the Soviet historian's presentation was his conviction that historical materialism was the correct method and that all other methodologies were mere intellectual errors. This line of reasoning, the Czech observer stated, seemed odd and exotic for most of those present.[159] However, some Eastern European historians had already had encounters with Soviet Marxism prior to 1945.

This applies most of all to Belarus and Ukraine. Here, the consolidation of Soviet power was followed by several years of more or less peaceful work with the 'bourgeois' historians. The situation changed in the late 1920s with the first wave of purges directed against 'nationalists', typically established non-Marxists.[160] In both westernmost Soviet republics, the purges were even more thorough, consequent and repetitious than in the Russian centre, which was partly due to the party's paranoid fear of the alleged Polish secret agents. The purges began in 1929/30 with the arrest of the 'monarchists'; in Belarus, this category covered an entire generation of scholars born in the 1870s and 1880s, which included Uadzimir Picheta, among others.[161] Another purge followed Pokrovskij's death in the early 1930s. This time, the historians at the Belarussian Academy of Sciences suffered the most loss, 33 of them having been arrested. Subsequently, smaller scale purges occurred in 1933 and 1936, which were then followed by a larger wave in 1937 (45 scholars arrested) and 1938 (27 arrested, almost all of whom were immediately executed). The later purges mostly affected Pokrovskij's students. Consequently, in practice the only established professionals who remained after the war were the rehabilitated victims of the first wave of purges, notably Picheta.[162]

The same sequence of disastrous persecutions decimated Soviet Ukrainian historiography. Here, the purges were first directed against the adherents of Hrushevsky's national-democratic interpretation of national history. His main rival, nicknamed the 'Ukrainian Pokrovskij', Matvij Iavorskyi, launched a campaign against the old historian in the late 1920s.[163] However, irrespective of whether they were 'nationalists' or 'internationalists', Ukrainian historians could not

---

158 Philip Friedman, 'Polish Jewish Historiography between the Two Wars (1918–1939)', *Jewish Social Studies* 11, no. 4 (1949): 373–408.

159 Šusta, 'O mezinárodním', 617.

160 M. P Mokhnacheva, 'Sovetskaya istoricheskaya nauka na mezhdynarodnykh forumakh: istoki nesostoyavshegosya dialoga' [Soviet historical science in international forums: the origins of the failed dialogue], in *Sovetskaya istoriografiya*, ed. Yu. N. Afanas'ev (Moskva: Rossiyskij gosudarstvennyj gumanitnyj universitet, 1996), 81–98.

161 Rainer Lindner, 'Nationalhistoriker im Stalinismus: zum Profil der akademischen Intelligenz in Weißrußland, 1921–1946', *Jahrbücher für Geschichte Osteuropas* 47, no. 2 (1999): 187–209.

162 Rainer Lindner, 'Geschichte und Geschichtsbetrieb im Weißrußland der Stalinzeit', *Zeitschrift für Ostmitteleuropa-Forschung* 50, no. 2 (2001): 198–213.

163 Serhii Plokhy, *Ukraine and Russia: Representations of the Past* (Toronto: University of Toronto Press, 2008), 102–5.

escape the same fate. While Hrushevsky died early enough to avoid arrest, Iavorskyi ended up in the Gulag.[164]

The near-collapse of Stalin's empire during the war paved the way for the return of some older historians and their perspectives on history. The national perspective ceased being viewed as suspect. As Moscow historian Nikolai Druzhinin, a member of the Soviet Academy, claimed in *Voprosy istorii* ('Questions of history') in 1949: 'starting from the concept of class struggle as the basic criterion we should, however, keep in mind that the general regularities of the historical process do not exclude its national particularities'.[165] Some of the leading East Central European intellectuals of conservative leaning took this phase in Stalin's policy for the new permanent norm and hoped to avoid clashes between their national traditions and Sovietization. Some of them seemed to believe it to be the new raison d'état. This was the conviction of Gyula Szekfű, who became the first post-war Hungarian ambassador to the Soviet Union.[166] But for non-Russian nationalities of the Soviet Union, this return to national history was less of a revolution than for Russia proper. Until the death of Stalin in 1953, accusations of 'nationalism' were used to defame Ukrainian and Belarusian scholars; in fact, it often simply meant that they did not show sufficient enthusiasm for Russian nationalism.[167] Throughout the whole communist period, the axiom of ancient Rus' unity, restored in 1654, remained the dominant position.[168] This mechanism was quickly recognized by some open-minded, critical Russian Soviet scholars, notably Anna Pankratova, who denounced the Russian nationalism of the Stalinist narrative and cautiously searched for ways to reconcile the dominant Russian narrative with that of the Soviet nationalities and bourgeois Western European historiographies.[169] At the twentieth congress of the Communist Party of the Soviet Union in 1956, she boldly stated:

> The Soviet state broke off with the tsarist politics of robbery and exploitation, beginning a new era in international relations. For that reason, all those who perceive the tsarist expansive wars, contrary to the opinion of Marx and Engels, as fair, those who idealize the Franco-Russian alliance in the late nineteenth century or the tsarist politics in China, are utterly wrong.[170]

The same tension between 'national values' and Soviet Marxism characterized post-1945 historiographies of East Central and Southeastern Europe. The Soviet Union's dominant position

---

164 Serhy Yekelchyk, *Stalin's Empire of Memory: Russian-Ukrainian Relations in the Soviet Historical Imagination* (Toronto: University of Toronto Press, 2004), 15–22.

165 Quoted in Bogdan Iacob, 'Paradigm Dynamics of Historiography in the Soviet Union (1931–1953)', *Historical Yearbook* 4 (2007): 15–28, here 23.

166 Irene Raab Epstein, *Gyula Szekfű: A Study in the Political Basis of Hungarian Historiography* (New York: Garland Publishers, 1987), 301–5.

167 See Yekelchyk, *Stalin's Empire of Memory*, 24–57.

168 Roman Serbyn, 'Rus' in the Soviet Scheme of East Slavic History', in *Eastern Europe: Historical Essays Presented to Professor Milos Mladenovic on His Sixty-Fifth Birthday by His Students*, ed. H. C. Schlieper (Toronto: New Review Books, 1969), 169–82; Stephan M. Horak, 'Ukrainian Historiography 1953–1963', *Slavic Review* 24, no. 2 (1965): 258–72. On a similar interpretation of Belarus' history see Oswald P. Backus III, 'The History of Belorussia in Recent Soviet Historiography', *Jahrbücher für Geschichte Osteuropas* 11, no. 1 (1963): 79–96.

169 Alexander Kan, 'Anna Pankratova and Voprosy Istorii: An Innovatory and Critical Historical Journal of the Soviet 1950s', *Storia della Storiografia* 29 (1996): 71–97.

170 Anna M. Pankratowa, 'Unsere ruhmvolle Geschichte – wichtige Quelle des Studiums', *Wissenschaftliche Beilage der FORUM* 3, no. 3 (1956): 10–16, here 15.

Writing history in the twentieth-century

made things more complex for Polish, Hungarian, Czech, Bulgarian and other historians, who had to take into account not merely the national history of their own state, but also that of Russia. Though this remained valid in most of the region's countries throughout most of the period under scrutiny, it never even came close to the situation of the Soviet nations.

The 1950s are commonly perceived as the most disastrous period in the post-war history of the region, a conviction attributable in large measure to the cultural policies of Stalinism. 'Historical science' underwent serious institutional changes. A major Stalinist goal was to transform the social and political character of the educated classes of society while imposing party control over the academic community and creating a socially acceptable narrative of national history.

Soviet apparatchiks hoped to realize the first of these aims by reshaping university admissions policy. As György Péteri claims: 'From this point, "class affiliation" became a legitimate criterion for selecting students and faculty, and fields of scholarship of high ideological significance were purged and populated with new, politically reliable, but often intellectually inferior personnel.'[171] In order to make it possible for students from workers' and peasants' families to reach the introductory university level, certain preparatory courses were created that would enable participants to matriculate after one to three years and then enter their chosen course of study without having to take a formal examination.[172]

Despite local differences, there were some general features common to the organization of all universities in the socialist states. From the late 1940s, research was subjected to central planning. Although continuously criticized and even ridiculed, this practice has survived in Eastern European academies to the present day. The separation of research and teaching became one of the main tenets of the new historiography. Historical research was to be concentrated in the elite institutes of history within the respective academies of science, which began being opened outside the Soviet Union in 1948. The principal aim of the institutes' staff was to prepare Marxist university handbooks on national history that could be used in schools and lower-level universities. But several of the institutes also helped revive appreciation for the local history of places like the federal or autonomous republics in Yugoslavia and Czechoslovakia and peripheral cities in Poland.[173] Thus, although the institutes were the direct effect of centralization, they sometimes were able to work as agents of decentralization. The initial organization of the institutes reflected this fact rather mechanically: the research units were typically divided by time periods in accordance with the chronological divisions of the textbooks. The institutes also hosted editorial committees of the newly established or 'reformed' central historical journals, which included *Századok* ('Centuries'), *Kwartalnik Historyczny* ('Historical quarterly'), *Československý Časopis Historický* ('Czechoslovak historical journal'), *Historický Časopis Slovenskej Akadémie Vied* ('Historical journal of the Slovak Academy of Sciences'), *Istoricheski Pregled* ('History review') and *Istoriski Zapisi* ('Historical records'). There was an inherent contradiction in the conception of the new institutes: on the one hand, they were supposed to generate exclusively Marxist historiographical knowledge, but on the other hand, they served as a

---

171 György Péteri, 'The Communist Idea of the University: An Essay Inspired by the Hungarian Experience', in *Universities under Dictatorship*, eds John Connelly and Michale Grüttner (University Park, PA: Penn State University Press, 2005), 153.

172 For an overview of communist university policy, see John Connelly, *Captive University: The Sovietization of East German, Czech and Polish Higher Education 1945–1956* (Chapel Hill, NC: University of North Carolina Press, 2000).

173 Viktor Novak, 'Outline of Yugoslav Historiography', in *Dix années d'historiographie yougoslave 1945–1955*, ed. Jorjo Tadić (Belgrade: Jugoslavija, 1959), 11–25.

haven for numerous non-Marxist scholars. In effect, some of the institutes, notably in Poland and Hungary, put convinced Marxists and young researchers into the same buildings as older 'bourgeois' academics.

The determination to achieve substantial change in historiography was motivated by the desire to replace older historical narratives with a new Marxist interpretation of history. On the other hand, the same goal served to moderate the scientific policies of the communist parties: it turned out that the supply of quality, professional historians was not limitless. To produce historiography of some quality – be it Marxist or non-Marxist – professionals were badly needed. Even in Hungary, which had a relatively strong group of communist intellectuals (including György Lukács), the revolutionary fervour was exhausted within months rather than years. As Erzsébet Andics, one of the 'Stalinist' leaders of Hungarian historiography, predicted in 1949, without the assistance of some 'bourgeois' colleagues, 'the battle for the 5-year plan will be lost'.[174] Thus, the official policy towards the historiographical establishment sought to create new, Marxist elites while at the same time trying to attract the prominent 'progressives' who were not party members.

The implementation of policy guidelines handed down from Moscow was, however, different in each country. Bulgaria and Romania, both Axis states during the war, exerted the tightest control on academics. In Sofia, for instance, the first wave of 'antifascist action' came as early as 1944, resulting not only in the ritual condemnation of the deceased Mutafchiev, but also in the arrest of fellow professors like Nikolay Stanishev, Mikhail Arnaudov and Ivan Duichev, and, perhaps more importantly, over 3,000 students. Soviet intervention ultimately tempered the local communists' radicalism (launched by the Soviet Academic Nikolai Derzhavin who personally protested against Arnaudov's persecution). Indeed, the purges affected a broad spectrum of people, some of them simply for not being communists. After 1946, a new wave of purges hit Bulgarian scientific institutions.[175] Things cooled off after the Bulgarians realized that they could not conduct serious research on national history without the help of 'bourgeois' colleagues, as the Hungarians had learned shortly before. The president of the Bulgarian Academy of Sciences, Todor Pavlov, admitted this in 1954, claiming that it was necessary 'to utilize the knowledge and experience of all specialists whether or not they are party members'.[176] In Romania, the 1947 party programme announced 'that Romanian history would have to be written all over again, for its bourgeois form was unscientific and lacked the necessary materialist underpinnings'.[177] In a country which, in contrast to Bulgaria, had had a strong native fascist movement, almost 80 per cent of the professoriate had to leave their positions while the old academy was dissolved completely before being recreated.[178]

Large-scale purges occurred in the Czech lands in 1948. Their allegedly 'democratic' character (students and professors were expelled not by the authorities but by special committees composed of their colleagues) strengthened their impact on the academic environment,

---

174 Quoted in Balázs Németh, 'Nationalism and Socialist Patriotism in the Hungarian Historiography between 1948 and 1956, and its Influence on the Post-1956 Era' (M.A. thesis, Budapest College, 1995), 8.

175 Nada Zhivkova, 'Chistka v bolgarskoj akademii nauk, 9 Sept. 1944–1949' [Cleaning at the Bulgarian academy of sciences, 9 Sept. 1944–1949], *Bulgarian Historical Review* 32, no. 3–4 (2004): 168–92.

176 Quoted in Marin Pundeff, 'Bulgarian Historiography, 1942–1958', *The American Historical Review* 66, no. 3 (1961): 682–93, here 683.

177 Katharine Verdery, *National Ideology under Socialism: Identity and Cultural Politics in Ceauşescu's Romania* (Berkeley, CA: University of California Press, 1991), 111.

178 Ibid., 106–10.

Writing history in the twentieth-century

although the percentage of dismissed professors was far smaller than that of the expelled students. At the same time, the Czech purges terrorized the professoriate. Interestingly, the Slovak part of the common state did not witness such a severe 'cultural revolution'; however, in a symbolic act, Daniel Rapant was dismissed, a historian of the national movement who had had an extraordinary impact on contemporaneous Slovak historiography.[179] Similarly, no such extensive campaign against the professoriate was launched in either Poland or Hungary. There, formal acknowledgement of the superiority of Marxist-Leninist methodology was usually sufficient to secure one's academic career, though central posts were often monopolized by party intellectuals. The 'bourgeois' remainder simply adapted to its new circumstances.[180]

In the end, however, similar attempts at reproducing the model of Soviet science and the equally similar opportunism of most East Central and Southeastern European historians failed to impose uniformity on historiography in all of the Eastern bloc states. Throughout the region, however, some party functionaries were perceived as the new 'natural' leaders of the historical profession. Dozens of people were referred to as the 'tsar (or tsarina) of Marxist historiography'. Interestingly, this seems to be the first moment in the history of the region's historical writing when women figured prominently in the discipline's landscape. In quantitative terms, women's share among historians grew considerably throughout the communist period. In Bulgaria, over 40 per cent of historians were women by the mid-1980s; most of them, however, held lower academic positions.[181] Some individuals, such as Żanna Kormanowa and Celina Bobińska in Poland or Erzsbét Andics in Hungary more or less aptly aspired to the position of Anna Pankratova. A special place in the history of Bulgarian historiography was occupied by Lyudmila Zhivkova, the daughter of the Party and State leader. Under her guidance, Bulgaria undertook efforts to liberalize and professionalize historical and archaeological research, which was received positively by otherwise sceptical Western observers.[182]

There is some evidence for the fact that the directors' positions at the history institutes were initially reserved for the prominent members of the privileged communist elite, the *nomenklatura* (though, typically, not for women). This was the case in Bulgaria, where Dimitar Kosev ran the Bulgarian Academy of Science's History Institute and was in charge of the publication of a Marxist synthesis of the history of Bulgaria.[183] Yet, the actual developments were mostly not according to the plan. More often than not the leadership of the centralized historiographies was entrusted to individuals of strong and independent character. But sometimes, other party members got a chance at higher positions, too. In Czechoslovakia, three young scholars and party members were given the three most prestigious posts: Josef Macek, the first director of the Institute of History of the Czechoslovak Academy of Sciences; František Graus, the editor-in-chief of the newly created *Československý Časopis Historický*; and Ľudovít Holotík, director of the Institute of History of the Slovak Academy of Sciences. The appointments of these three young men, each around the age of thirty, obviously interfered with the hopes and aspirations of their elder colleagues. In Hungary, Erik Molnár, a Marxist jurist and historian held in high esteem far beyond the communist core, assumed the directorship of the Institute of History of

---

179 M. Mark Stolárik, 'The Painful Birth of Slovak Historiography in the 20th Century', *Zeitschrift für Ostmitteleuropa-Forschung* 50 (2001), 161–87.

180 István Deák, 'Hungary', *The American Historical Review* 97, no. 4 (1992): 1041–63, here 1055.

181 Krassimira Daskalova, 'The Politics of a Discipline: Women Historians in Twentieth Century Bulgaria', *Storia della Storiografia* 46 (2004): 171–87.

182 Hans-Joachim Hoppe, 'Politik und Geschichtswissenschaft in Bulgarien 1968–1978', *Jahrbücher für Geschichte Osteuropas* 28, no. 2 (1980): 243–86, here 254–5.

183 Ibid., 253–4.

the Hungarian Academy of Sciences. In Croatia, Jaroslav Šidak, a professor of the University of Zagreb, president of the historians' association and editor-in-chief of the *Historijski zbornik* ('Historical proceedings'), proved capable of challenging the privileged position of the academy by taking control over central projects: in particular, the handbook in national history and the main historical journal.[184] The most interesting deviation from the initial 'revolutionary' agenda was the nomination of Tadeusz Manteuffel to the directorship of the Institute of History of the Polish Academy in 1952, because Manteuffel was neither a Marxist nor a party member. Manteuffel had been the main organizer of the 1933 International Congress of Historical Sciences in Warsaw. Such choices reflect the differences between East Central and Southeastern European policies towards the academic historical establishment. In Bulgaria and Romania, the 'fascist' past of some scholars facilitated the purges. In Czechoslovakia, party functionaries followed the anti-intellectual traditions of the Czech left, even at the expense of the quality of research. Many young, ideologically driven functionaries provided visible evidence that a new Czech and Slovak historiography was being created. This was not the case in Hungary and Poland, where scholarly excellence was largely preserved and broader cooperation between Marxist and 'bourgeois' historians was fostered.

The different national responses to Sovietization and Stalinization should be viewed in the proper historical context. The early 1950s were marked by political purges from which no Soviet-bloc country's historical profession escaped untouched. Dozens of historians were imprisoned on various charges, and some of them were expelled from their faculties and forbidden to teach, as was the case with Slovak historian Daniel Rapant and Polish historian Henryk Wereszycki. The progress of the Marxist coup in historiography is easy to follow in the pages of the official periodicals. Within a relatively short period of time, most connections to Western scholarship were cut, while conversely, the reception of Soviet historiography far exceeded the limits of 'normal' scientific exchange. Newspeak infected the language of the historical publications (and, for that matter, of almost all professional vocabularies). The leaders of local communist parties were honoured as prominent philosophers of history following in the footsteps of Joseph Stalin. Many young historians conducted Marxist-inspired research on social and economic history. But the majority of historical publications in the 1950s, ironically, consisted not of modern, methodologically advanced studies, but of rather traditional narratives dominated by old conceptions of the nation. The key intellectual tool of these narratives was the 'progressive tradition', which indicated the permanent assessment of historical figures and phenomena. Such figures were divided into 'progressive' and 'reactionary' categories, a procedure which handicapped the analytical potential of Marxism. Thus, the main task of Marxist historians was to collect the comprehensive catalogue of historical facts and personalities that preceded the teleologically understood 'end of history'. At the same time, it was important to identify the 'reactionary' forces within any nation's history.

The outcome of these efforts differed from case to case. With reference to the scheme formulated by Lutz Raphael, two main models dominated.[185] The first could be characterized as more 'national' or 'rightist', the second as 'a-national' or 'leftist'. In general, some of the Marxist-Leninist interpretations were simply at odds with the national master narrative, while others merely employed a new Marxist vocabulary to retell an old story of the nation. In every

---

184 Magdalena Najbar-Agičić, *U skladu s marksizmom ili činjenicama? Hrvatska historiografija 1945–1960* [According to Marxism or to the facts? Croatian historiography 1945–1960] (Zagreb: Ibis Grafika, 2013), esp. 184–9.

185 Raphael, *Geschichtswissenschaft*, 58–89.

Writing history in the twentieth-century

case, the nation and the state overshadowed class. The method by which Marxist narratives were formulated was far removed from accepted scholarly standards. Instead of free competition among various interpretations, a unified, clearly Marxist interpretation, which covered all important historical phenomena, was the rule.

However, while methodological discussions were silenced, debate did not disappear completely. Within the Marxist-Leninist historical sciences, there was space for the exchange of views *before* the canonization of a single interpretation. In some cases, more or less 'national' interpretations struggled to achieve the status of being the sole Marxist interpretation of a given phenomenon. Such discussion was often accompanied by harsh polemics, threats and political accusations; though more or less masked, it did indeed constitute scholarly discussion and was all a part of the process of creating a unified historical narrative. The main aim of historians was to push through 'their' interpretation and to incorporate it into the official historical narrative. And in fact, most of the Marxist historiographies of the 1950s succeeded in creating a coherent 'progressive' national history, though rarely in the previously planned form of a swiftly published multivolume collective synthesis. Analyzing all of these narratives would exceed the limits of this chapter, so I will simply touch on some representative examples and controversies.

In the Slovak part of Czechoslovakia, Marxist historians reproduced many of the traditional interpretations of Slovak history that were rooted in the pro-Czech nineteenth-century national movement. The Slovak historical narrative began with the establishment of Great Moravia, 'the first common Czechoslovak state', as it was often called.[186] In fact, the symbolic sharing of this early state structure between Slovaks and Czechs would provide the main historical support for the unity of Czechoslovakia, because older Slovak interpretations tended to preserve the Great Moravian heritage for Slovaks only.[187] Later on, Marxist researchers searched for arguments supporting the thesis that Slavic inhabitants exerted a decisive impact on the medieval Hungarian kingdom. The next turning point of Slovak history was defined as the uprising of miners in Banská Bistrica in 1525–6, which, as it turns out, was probably the most creative Marxist contribution to Slovak history. An invention of historian Peter Ratkoš, the uprising was interpreted as a native Slovak 'early bourgeois revolution', a domestic counterpart to the German Peasants' War of the 1520s and the Bohemian Hussite movement of a century earlier. Even before 1989, it was clear to professionals that the author of this 'discovery' had played freely with the facts.

Apart from this notable exception, the early modern era did not hold much interest for Marxist historians, most of whom spent their time researching the period when the Slovak 'national awakening' began. Marxist historiography provided new contributions and approaches to the historiography of the 'national awakening', including a reinterpretation of the first codification of the Slovak language by the Catholic priest Anton Bernolák. In the interwar period, Bernolák had been perceived as a *Magyarón*, a de-nationalized Slovak, and it fell to the Marxists to secure his place as an important historical figure. Subsequent developments in the nineteenth-century Slovak national movement provided by far the most important material for the new narrative, and Marxist historians depicted Ľudovít Štúr as the 'personification' of the national movement. Subsequent Marxist research concentrated on the development of this movement in the second half of the nineteenth century as well as on the origins of the Slovak working class. Finally, Slovak Marxist interpretations of the Czechoslovak state mostly reproduced the position of

---

186 Ľudovít Holotík, ed., *Dejiny Slovenska (tézy)* [History of Slovakia (theses)] (Bratislava: Historický ústav SAV, 1955), 22.

187 Stolárik, 'The Painful Birth', 161–5.

Soviet researchers, who were critical of both the Slovak nationalist camp and the policies of the Czechoslovak state. The short-lived Slovak Soviet Republic created during the invasion of the Hungarian Red Army in 1919 was counted among the last 'positive' phenomena of Slovakia's pre-1945 history.[188]

As mentioned above, many historians were focused on striking a methodological balance between nationalism and Marxism, and even politicians became interested in the issue. Historiography in the Balkans provides some rich examples. The first half of the 1950s saw burning historical controversies in Yugoslavia over the nature of 'Ottoman feudalism' and the status of sixteenth- and seventeenth-century Montenegro within the Ottoman Empire. Branislav Djurdjev, a Bosnian orientalist and at that time the director of the Museum of Bosnia-Herzegovina, claimed that the introduction of Ottoman rule that replaced the feudalism of the Serbian state was, in fact, reactionary. Criticizing the 'nihilist' positions of Serbian economic historian Sergije Dimitrijević, Djurdjev insisted on a 'dialectical' interpretation that deemed the less oppressive Ottoman system responsible for delaying the peasant revolution, which is to say, hemming historical progress. In other words, Djurdjev claimed that the relatively progressive nature of Serbian feudalism relied precisely on its backwardness and harshness.[189] Shortly afterwards, another controversy saw Djurdjev in a less favourable position. Traditionally, historians had viewed Montenegro as being nearly politically independent under the Ottomans. Djurdjev questioned this view in 1953, insisting that the province acquired political autonomy no sooner than the end of the seventeenth century. His findings were, in part, supported by a Montenegrin scholar, Gligor Stanojević and − more importantly − by Milovan Djilas, who celebrated Djurdjev as a 'de-mythologizer' of the national past. Soon thereafter, Djilas' fall and subsequent imprisonment released a wave of criticism that ultimately reached Djurdjev, putting brakes on his career for a couple of years.[190]

Another long-contested issue was the interpretation of the social and economic character of Ottoman rule in the Balkans and, consequently, of the attempts at emancipation from it. The issue provides a pointed lens for viewing the methodological shifts in Balkan historiography, which moved from purely socio-economic readings to nation-biased narratives to first attempts at structuralist 'revisionism' in the 1960s, which again questioned the nationalist interpretations. In Bulgaria, the *haiduks* were characterized as fighters for social and national liberation from the Ottoman yoke and were seen as providing a link between medieval statehood and national revival, neither of which were necessarily new interpretations.[191] According to Roumen Daskalov, the topic of Bulgaria's national revival

> became the terrain of a kind of scholarly dissent in the form of the affirmation of the 'national' against the 'national nihilism' of the early Stalinist years. As an epoch of national formation, the Revival seems naturally designated to that purpose. But one can note the growing comfort of the regime with a broader Revival legacy … that

---

188 For a comprehensive overview of Slovak Marxist historiography see Adam Hudek, *Najpolitickejšia veda. Slovenská historiografia v rokoch 1948–1968* [The most political science: Slovak historiography 1948–1968] (Bratislava: Historický ústav SAV, 2010), esp. 170–84.

189 Wayne S. Vucinich, 'The Yugoslav Lands in the Ottoman Period: Postwar Marxist Interpretations of Indigenous and Ottoman Institutions', *The Journal of Modern History* 27, no. 3 (1955): 287–305.

190 Wayne S. Vucinich, 'The Montenegrin Istoriski Zapisi (1948–1953)', *Journal of Central European Affairs* 15, no. 4 (1956): 395–400.

191 Yannis Sygkelos, *Nationalism from the Left: The Bulgarian Communist Party during the Second World War and the Early Post-War Years* (Leiden: Brill, 2011), 193.

Writing history in the twentieth-century

went parallel with its claim for the extension of its social basis ... Besides, the practical merger of the party with the state made the Communist regime increasingly into a bearer of the 'state idea' (in contrast to the subversive identification of the earlier socialists with the revolutionaries of the Revival). The shift of the Communist regime ... toward nationalism also worked to increase the range of acceptable figures and political trends. Ironically, the 'revisionist' efforts of many historians in fact brought new assets into the patrimony of the regime.[192]

A comparable shift occurred in Romania, but ultimately played out more dramatically. A comparable shift took place in Romania, but ultimately played out more dramatically. Post-war changes not only saw some historians lose their jobs and others rise to prominence; as elsewhere, they also had an impact on the national narrative.

Firstly, the role of Russia was massively reinterpreted, notably in the works of Mihail Roller. In Roller's view, Russia had always been on the side of Romania's progress and national interest. Secondly, the Slavic elements in Romania's history were elevated to the position previously held by 'Romanity'. In Roller's case, this even extended to the Slavicization of the language, that is, the replacement of some Latin-based words with their equivalents of Slavic origin.[193] In the first half of the 1960s, Nicolae Ceaușescu's rise to the head of state was accompanied by a paradigm shift in historiography (Roller did not live to see this as he died in 1958). The publication of Marx's caustic remarks on the role of Russia in the Danubian Principalities in 1964 marked the beginning of the rapid de-Sovietization. However, the liberalization was short-lived. Romanian historiography of the 1970s in many respects resembled that of the 1950s, but without the latter's Russophilia. Instead, historians returned to topics that had interested Iorga and before him Xenopol, and, like their predecessors, they took a very dogmatic approach.[194]

Scholars focused on the ethnic continuity of the Romanian lands from pre-Roman times up to the country's unification in 1918. At the 1965 Vienna CISH congress, Ion Nestor, an academic historian and archaeologist, argued that the continuity was an indisputable truth.[195] Throughout the 1970s and 1980s, some minor controversies between Romanian historians and their Bulgarian colleagues arose over the question of the ethnic character of the medieval Bulgarian state: was it Bulgarian, Bulgaro-Romanian or – as some Romanian scholars wanted (notably Giurescu and Brătianu's ex-collaborator Mihai Berza) – Romano-Bulgarian. With time, the official interpretation solidified into an act of nationalist faith. In the early 1980s, Viorica Moisuc (who, interestingly enough, became an extreme right-wing member of the European Parliament in 2007) viewed the nation's history as a heroic act of endurance:

The defence of this territory from encroaching attempts represents an old form of patriotism. In Central and Southeast Europe, this phenomenon existed since remote times. The civilization of the Romanians, the state of which is two millennia old, had

---

192 Roumen Daskalov, *The Making of a Nation in the Balkans: Historiography of the Bulgarian Revival* (Budapest: CEU Press, 2004), 245–6.

193 Florian Kührer, "'Vom avea grijă de voi": Russland und Sowjetunion in der stalinistischen rumänischen Historiographie', *Transylvanian Review* 18, no. 3 (2009): 133–46.

194 Ulf Brunnbauer, 'Historical Writing in the Balkans', in *The Oxford History of Historical Writing*, vol. 5, *Historical Writing since 1945*, eds Axel Schneider and Daniel Woolf (Oxford: Oxford University Press, 2011), 353–74, here 360–62.

195 Ion Nestor in *CISH XXIIe Congrès International des Sciences Historiques, Vienne, 29 aout – 5 septembre 1965*, vol. 5, *Actes* (Vienna: Berger & Söhne, 1965), 381.

steadily developed on the selfsame territory, and the defence of the homeland was the task of each generation.[196]

A similar combination of an oppressive regime, autarchic ideology and nationalist historiography developed in Albania. Historical discontinuities not unfamiliar to the other countries of the region led Albanian historians to attempt to 'defragment' national history. They focused on the history of the native ancient Illyrians before the acts of the fifteenth-century national hero Skanderbeg, or George Castriot.[197] Though Skanderbeg had already played an important role in the interwar politics of history, with King Zogu claiming to be his descendant, he took on cult status in the second half of the 1960s. As in Romania in the 1980s, the sheer endurance of the brave leader and his heroic people were celebrated, notably during the 500th anniversary of Skanderbeg's death in 1968.[198] Prime Minister Mehmet Shehu, the second person in state after Enver Hoxha, claimed that the acts of Skanderbeg formed the core of Albania's national past:

> Many historians ask and still do not understand how it was possible for the small Albanian nation under the leadership of George Kastrioti Skanderbeg to defend itself against the biggest and most powerful empire of these times, to keep on fighting a titanic fight for 25 years, and to achieve brilliant victories that astonished the world. We Marxists-Leninists understand well the reasons of our forefathers' 'miracle', the Albanian nation under Skanderbeg's leadership. The decisive factor and the only source of this heroic resistance and victories in the long and unequal fight were the people's masses, in the first place the peasantry ... Everyone took part in the fight against the Ottomans' power under Skanderbeg's leadership: men, women and children.[199]

The decline of Marxist-Leninist historiography after the post-1956 thaw differed in speed from country to country. In Hungary, despite (or, in part, because of) the tragic outcome of the 1956 uprising, the late 1950s saw an important debate on aristocratic resistance to Habsburg rule in the seventeenth and eighteenth centuries. The initiator of this debate, Erik Molnár, insisted on the modernizing character of the central monarchic power, questioning the progressive credentials of the Hungarian noblemen and thus, in a way, following in Szekfű's footsteps.[200] On the local level, some elements of the 'progressive' tradition proved more durable. This can be

---

196 Viorica Moisuc, Foreword to *Assertion of Unitary, Independent National States in Central and Southeast Europe (1821–1923)*, eds Viorica Moisuc and Ion Calafeteanu, trans. Mary Lăzărescu, Adriana Ionescu-Pârâu and Alexandru Alkalay (Bucharest: Editura Academiei RSR, 1980), 7–14, here 7.

197 Stefanaq Pollo and Arben Puto, *The History of Albania from Its Origins to the Present Day*, trans. Carol Wiseman and Ginnie Hole (London: Routledge & Kegan Paul, 1981), 3–4.

198 Oliver Jens Schmitt, 'Skanderbeg reitet weiter: Wiederfindung und Erfindung eines (National-)Helden im balkanischen und gesamteuropäischen Kontext (15.–21. Jahrhundert)', in *Schnittstellen: Gesellschaft, Nation, Konflikt und Erinnerung in Südosteuropa; Festschrift für Holm Sundhausen zum 65. Geburtstag*, eds Ulf Brunnbauer, Andreas Helmedach and Stefan Troebst (München: Oldenbourg, 2007), 401–20.

199 Oliver Jens Schmitt, *Skanderbeg: Der neue Alexander auf dem Balkan* (Regensburg: Friedrich Pustet, 2009), 313.

200 Pók, *Klios Schuld*, 16–17; Michal Kopeček, *Hledání ztraceného smyslu revoluce. Zrod a počátky marxistického revizionismu ve Střední Evropě 1953–1960* [In search of the lost meaning of the revolution: the birth and early years of Marxist revisionism in Central Europe 1953–1960] (Prague: Argo, 2009), 128–30.

Writing history in the twentieth-century

illustrated by writings on one of the communist historians' main topics of interest, fascism. In Georgi Dimitrov's classic definition, fascism represented a stage in the development of capitalism. His definition, like the positions of the interwar communist parties on this issue, facilitated for the identification of native 'fascisms'.

In the early 1950s, interwar autocratic regimes were typically called fascist. In the most significant case, Hungary, historians even claimed that the native Hungarian version of fascism predated both the Italian and the German forms, 'showing – for the first time – what fascism, which would wildly ravage Europe two decades later and drive millions of people to war, looked like'.[201] Things changed, however, with the liberalization of some of the communist regimes. As early as the 1960s, East German members of the joint Polish-GDR historians' commission were astonished by the vehemence with which their Polish colleagues refused to call Józef Piłsudski's dictatorship fascist.[202] Almost a decade later, a Hungarian researcher, Miklós Lackó, insisted on the authoritarian character of interwar dictatorships. In 1972, this position was also supported by Polish social historian Janusz Żarnowski at a meeting between Polish and Bulgarian historians in Sofia. Despite initial shock among the Bulgarian historians, they adopted similar interpretations of interwar Bulgarian authoritarianism a few years later.[203]

Viewed from the perspective of the professional development of the region's historiographies, the Marxism–Leninism of the 1950s (and its remnants) represents a rupture rather than another phase of their evolution. In fact, valuable research in social and economic history, though *per se* Marxist, occupied a marginal position. Instead, political history dominated the historical field, which was for its part dominated by two main narratives. The first represented what could be called the *historia sacra* of the communist state: it covered the history of the worker's movement, of socialist and communist parties, and recent history, with a prominent role played by the local repercussions of the Great October Socialist Revolution.[204] The second was national history. Here, paradoxically, continuities prevailed over discontinuities. Despite seasonal departures from ethno-nationalist ideologies, in the long run Marxist-Leninist historiography ended up adopting much of it. In the early 1990s, one of the first analysts of this phenomenon, Ľubomír Lipták, viewed historians' laziness as the cause of the durability and strength of the nation-centred perspective, especially among 'smaller' (i.e. those perceived as genuinely democratic and egalitarian) nations.[205] Fortunately, not all East Central and Southeastern European historians took this convenient path.

---

201 Elek Karsai and Ervin Pamlényi, *Fehérterror* [White Terror] (Budapest: Művelt Nép, 1951), 71, quoted in Péter Apor, *Fabricating Authenticity in Soviet Hungary: The Afterlife of the First Hungarian Soviet Republic in the Age of State Socialism* (London: Anthem Press, 2014), 101.

202 Maciej Górny, 'Polsko-enerdowskie spotkania historyków: granice porozumienia' [Polish-GDR historians' cooperation: the limits of understanding], in *Interakcje. Leksykon komunikowania polsko-niemieckiego*, eds Alfred Gall, Jacek Grębowiec, Justyna Kalicińska, Kornelia Kończal, Izabella Surynt, vol. 2 (Wrocław: Atut, 2015), 495–504.

203 Roumen Daskalov, *Debating the Past: Modern Bulgarian History: From Stambolov to Zhivkov* (Budapest: CEU Press, 2011), 155–62.

204 Ferenc Mucsi, 'K vengerskoj istoriografii Velikoj Oktyabrskoj socialisticheskoj revolyucii (istorichno-tematicheskij obzor)' [On Hungarian historiography of the great October Socialist Revolution (historical and thematic review)], *Acta Historica Academiae Scientarum Hungaricae* 33, no. 1 (1987): 67–75; Górny, *The Nation*, 178–88.

205 See Ľubomír Lipták, *Storočie dlhšie ako sto rokov. O dejinách a historiografii* [A century longer than a hundred years: history and historiography] (Bratislava: Kalligram, 1999), 46.

Maciej Górny

Social and economic history: the influence of the *Annales* School

The close personal and scientific ties between social and economic historians from Poland and Hungary and the so-called second generation of the *Annales* School seems to have become a cliché and, hence, it has repeatedly been put into question. This happens not only in view of the local reception of British working-class history or personal ties with the Bielefeld School and other West German academic milieus.[206] In a sarcastic comment about the local impact of the *Annales*, Patryk Pleskot, a Polish researcher, claimed that even though everyone knows that they had an enormous influence, nobody knows exactly what it was.[207] The fact is that in the 1960s and 1970s, Polish and Hungarian scholars entered into dialogue with the most influential and promising French historical school. Supported by personal ties, Polish authors like Witold Kula, Tadeusz Manteuffel, Aleksander Gieysztor, Andrzej Wyczański, Bronisław Geremek and Marian Małowist were not only inspired by Fernand Braudel and his colleagues and students, but also started to pay off this intellectual debt by undertaking a comprehensive analysis of the development of capitalism in East Central Europe. Kula's work is the most exemplary in this regard, and his theses on Eastern Europe were included in Braudel's panoramic history of capitalism. A similar thing may be said about some of Sándor Domanovszky's students, most notably István Hajnal and István Szabó; it could also be said of scholars influenced by Hajnal such as László Makkai,[208] and László Vekerdi. In the late 1960s and early 1970s, Polish historians, being perhaps the most mobile nation of the Eastern bloc, went to France to visit French research institutions more often than they entered all the other socialist states combined (except for the Soviet Union).[209] Research stipends financed by the French together with bilateral conferences strengthened these ties.

Organized jointly by Fernand Braudel and Zsigmond Pál Pach, the Hungarian-French conference on economic history in Budapest in 1968 played a similar role for Hungarian historians.[210] Another Franco-Hungarian meeting in Tihany that took place in 1977 was attended by Béla Köpeczi, Kálmán Benda, Éva H. Balázs, Domokos Kosáry, Miklós Lackó, György Ránki and Emil Niederhauser.[211] In both Hungary and Poland, many translations of the *Annales* historians' works appeared on the book market; in one particular case, the Polish translation even

---

206 Rudolf Kučera, 'Facing Marxist Orthodoxy: Western Marxism, The Making, and the Communist Historiographies of Czechoslovakia and Poland, 1948–1990', *International Review of Social History* 61, no. 1 (2016): 35–50.

207 Patryk Pleskot, *Intelektualni sąsiedzi. Kontakty historyków polskich ze środowiskiem 'Annales' 1945–1989* [Intellectual neighbors: Polish historians' contacts to the 'Annales'-milieu] (Warsaw: IPN, 2010), 690.

208 Together with Zsigmond Pál Pach, Makkai contributed to the 1974 volume dedicated to Marian Małowist; they were the only authors in the volume from the Eastern bloc: László Makkai, 'La structure et la productivité de l'économie agraire de la Hongrie aus milieu du XVIIe siècle', in *Społeczeństwo, gospodarka, kultura. Studia ofiarowane Marianowi Małowistowi w czterdziestolecie pracy naukowej*, eds Stanisław Herbst, et al. (Warsaw: PWN, 1974), 197–210.

209 Krzysztof Pomian, 'Impact of the Annales School in Eastern Europe', *Review: A Journal of the Fernand Braudel Center for the Study of Economics, Historical Systems, and Civilizations* 1, no. 3–4 (1978): 101–18, here 118. See also Patryk Pleskot, 'Niecodzienne życie polskich uczonych podczas wizyt w krajach Zachodu w latach pięćdziesiątych i sześćdziesiątych XX wieku' [The extraordinary adventures of Polish scholars visiting the West in the 1950s and 1960s], *Przegląd Historyczny* 98, no. 2 (2007): 197–214.

210 László Makkai, V. Zimányi and László Katus, 'Une conference franco-hongroise d'histoire économique à Budapest', *Acta Historica Academiae Scientiarum Hungaricae* 15, no. 3–4 (1969): 335–65.

211 Gábor Klaniczay, 'Le Goff and Medieval History in Central and Eastern Europe', in *The Work of Jacques Le Goff and the Challenges of Medieval History*, ed. Miri Rubin (Woodbridge: The Boydell Press, 1997), 223–37, here 224–5.

Writing history in the twentieth-century

preceded the French edition.[212] Major historical publications were reviewed and discussed on both sides of the Iron Curtain. More importantly, perhaps, books by Polish and Hungarian authors quite regularly appeared in French translation. The connection between some Eastern European historiographies and France after 1956 was doubtless a side-effect of political liberalization. This fact is confirmed by the apparent absence of Czechoslovak historians from the intellectual transfer of the late 1960s and 1970s, when the process of normalization was having a stifling effect on methodological debates. Martin Nodl claimed that Czechoslovak historians were forced to engage in a 'discourse in their heads' because they were prohibited from putting their unorthodox ideas on paper.[213]

Because contact was limited to certain regions and certain times, to what extent can one talk about regional, East Central and Southeastern European versions of the ideas of the *Annales* School? To answer this question, one has to take into account two things that facilitated cooperation with French historians while simultaneously strengthening some distinctive features of East Central and Southeastern European social and economic history. First, as we already know, historians from the region were present at the birth of the new school: they attended the same interwar conferences and congresses, and they discussed and often disagreed with the founding fathers of the *Annales*. In the first phase of the *Annales* journal's history, Lucien Febvre began cooperating with Lucie Varga and Franz Borkenau, Jewish immigrants from Vienna who sustained interest in East Central European issues (and contemporary German-language historiography).[214] This interwar phase of cooperation with Eastern European colleagues mostly involved local research institutes that specialized in economic and social history. Though Poles and Hungarians cooperated with their French counterparts more than any other historians in East Central Europe, there were some individual contacts elsewhere too, notably in Romania. Apart from economic historians like Bujak, Rutkowski and Domanovszky, Marc Bloch and Gheorghe I. Brătianu were friends, and the latter's publications on Genovese trade and the medieval history of the Black Sea region were reviewed by the *Annales* in the 1930s.[215] In 1946, Brătianu wrote an extremely lengthy obituary for Bloch claiming that he was 'the pioneer of the study of the economic conditions in the Middle Ages' and a 'maverick'.[216] The most striking example of Brătianu's engagement with the French historical school is his *La Mer Noire, dès origins à la conquête ottoman* ('The Black Sea, from the origins to the Ottoman conquest'), which was published posthumously in 1968. In a two-volume essay reminiscent of Braudel's *La Méditerranée et le monde méditerranéen à l'époque de Philippe II* ('The Mediterranean and the Mediterranean world in the age of Philip II'), Brătianu describes the region's geography, ethnography and history from prehistoric times up to the 'Ottoman monopoly' in the fifteenth century.

The second element that contributed to the spread of social and economic research in the region was Marxism. Although in its most dogmatic versions Marxism petrified into nation-

---

212 Braudel's *Historia i trwanie* was selected and prepared by Bronisław Geremek and Witold Kula prior to the French edition of 1969, but it first appeared in 1971 after a delay.

213 Nodl, 'Otázky', 168–9.

214 Peter Schöttler, 'Die Annales und Österreich in den zwanziger und dreißiger Jahren', *Österreichische Zeitschrift für Geschichtswissenschaften* 4, no. 1 (1993): 74–99.

215 Lucian Boia, 'L'Historiographie roumaine et l'école des "Annales". Quelques interferences', *Analele Universitatii Bucureşti* 28 (1979): 31–40, esp. 36–8.

216 Gheorghe I. Brătianu, 'Un savant et un soldat: Marc Bloch', *Revue des Études Sud-Est Européennes* 23 (1946): 5–20, here 19.

237

centred political history, it also opened space for economic research and the study of the 'oppressed classes'. Some of the Marxists of East Central and Southeastern Europe attracted the interest of members of the *Annales* School, who were, in principle, open to methodological pluralism. The answer to the question as to what made Eastern European Marxists so interested in French historiography seems quite easy. For their part, tt was the Eastern European Marxists' flexible attitude toward the dominant methodology. It has become customary to stress their supposed distance from Marxism. One of the experts in this field gives a good example of this kind of interpretation:

> It was probably this openness that underlay the interest of the *Annales* group, especially in the 1950s and 1960s, in the historical achievements of Eastern Europe, especially Poland, where attempts were made to give a more 'human', unorthodox face to materialism imposed from above. Only in the latter version was 'Marxism-non-Marxism' digestible for Western scholars, who because of their leftist views needed some Marxist dressing, under which the ideas were hiding that had no connection with Marx.[217]

Nevertheless, 'Marxism-non-Marxism' was still Marxism. None of the East Central and Southeastern European historians who collaborated with the *Annales* group ever declared himself an anti-Marxist. To the contrary, many of them stressed their devotion to the ideas of Marx. They were surely unorthodox, just as Pekař or Szekfű were unorthodox several decades before them. But in the context of twentieth-century Eastern European historiography, their methodological unorthodoxy adheres to the rule.

Henri H. Stahl worked closely with Dimitrie Gusti on sociological and ethnological research in Romanian villages in the 1920s and 1930s. The empirical knowledge of traditional rural life and close observation of market transformations informed Stahl's research on a crucial problem of East Central and Southeastern European economic history – the region's place within the development of capitalism. Stahl claimed that the transition from the feudal order (or, in his words, 'tributary states') to capitalism in the region was accompanied by phenomena that distinguished it from Western Europe, the 'second serfdom' being the most important. For Stahl, however, the durability of traditional economic patterns in the village meant that the 'first serfdom' never actually took place.[218] Research on this local deviation from the general trend of economic development in Europe was one of the main contributions of Eastern European scholars to Fernand Braudel's project of writing an all-encompassing history of capitalism. David Prodan's studies on the agrarian history of Transylvania were also important. His general observation echoed the debates of historians from other countries of the region:

> But the potential progress of agriculture [from the sixteenth century onwards] would encounter a powerful impediment in the fact that labour was enserfed and displaced toward cultivation on the manor. Grave obstacles would now impede the progress

---

217 Patryk Pleskot, 'Marxism in the Historiography of "Annales" in the Opinion of its Creators and Critics', *Acta Poloniae Historica* 96 (2007): 182–205, here 205.

218 Henri H. Stahl, *Traditional Romanian Village Communities: The Transition from the Communal to the Capitalist Mode of Production in the Danube Region*, trans. Daniel Chirot and Holley Coulter Chirot (Cambridge: Cambridge University Press, 1980).

Writing history in the twentieth-century

of agriculture in general. The intensification of feudal relations would retard urban development, further reduce industrial production, and block any economic invigoration … The forces of production would cease to develop, with the result that feudal relations would be excessively prolonged, as was true of Central and Eastern Europe more broadly.[219]

For some historiographies in Eastern Europe, this development had an immense impact. For the first time, historical research broke out of the constraints of strictly national history and expanded its scope by looking at the whole region and sometimes even beyond it. And in contrast to the national bias of interwar *Volksgeschichte*, the new historiography broadened not only the choice of research topics and tools of historical interpretation, but also historians' intellectual perspective, opening their eyes to historical comparison and transfer. The latter change in turn proved to be instrumental in influencing new research that was national in factual content but truly open-minded in the art of dealing with historical processes in Eastern Europe.

Apart from the direct collaborations discussed above, many historians were inspired by the French historical school, some of whom conducted original research that enriched their fields of study, which is particularly true of the medievalists. Research into the social margins and oppressed proved to be the most fertile ground on which Marxism, some elements of the older historiographical traditions and French inspiration could meet. František Graus, and later Bronisław Geremek, contributed to research on the lowest social strata of medieval towns.[220] Particularly interesting is the way in which Geremek was also able to establish himself as a prominent specialist in the field in French historiography. In Czechoslovakia, the Hussites and other heretics had always been popular topics of historical research. František Šmahel's books published in the late 1960s and – after being 'exiled' to the museum in Tábor – in the 1990s interpreted their history anew by conducting structural analyses and drawing on the history of mentalities. Josef Petráň and Václav Husa studied the Czech peasantry, and Jerzy Kłoczowski analyzed Church structures and Church geography with the aim of doing a comparative analysis of the introduction of Christianity to East Central Europe.

In the 1960s, Byzantine and Ottoman studies thrived in Romania and Bulgaria.[221] In 1966, the First International Congress of Balkan and Southeastern European Studies was held in Sofia, bringing together scholars from fields as diverse as ethnography and linguistics.[222] Nikolai Todorov's study on the 'Balkan type' of urbanism is among the most prominent effects of this

---

219 David Prodan, 'Serfdom in Sixteenth-Century Transylvania', *Review: A Journal of the Fernand Braudel Center for the Study of Economics, Historical Systems, and Civilizations* 9, no. 4 (1986): 649–78, here 677.

220 Martin Nodl, 'Otázky recepce francouzské historiografie v Českém prostředí: totální dějiny, dlouhé trvání a mentality' [The reception of the French historiography in the Czech environment: *histoire totale, longue durée* and mentalities], in *Dějepisectví mezi vědou a politikou. Úvahy o historiografii 19. a 20. Století*, idem (Brno: CDK, 2007), 139–69, here 149–52.

221 Bogdan Murgescu, 'Byzantine and Ottoman Studies in the Romanian Historiography: A Brief Overview', in *Clio in the Balkans: The Politics of History Education*, ed. Christina Koulouri (Thessaloniki: Center for Democracy and Reconciliation in Southeast Europe, 2002), 148–62, here 150.

222 Jacob M. Landau, 'Bulgarian Studies on the Ottoman Empire and Turkey', *Middle Eastern Studies* 19, no. 1 (1983): 119–25; for an overview of Bulgarian Balkan studies see Nikolai Todorov, *Razvitie, postizheniya i zadachi na balkanistikata v Bylgariya* [Development, achievements and objectives of Bulgarian Balkan studies] (Sophia: BAN, 1977).

development, as are his studies on Balkan demography.[223] Other researchers working on the economic and settlement history of the Balkans included Bistra Cvetkova also from Bulgaria, Metodi Sokoloski from Macedonia, Vuk Vinaver from Serbia, Ljuben Berov, a prominent Bulgarian economist and historian, and Skendër Rizaj from Kosovo.[224] In Romania in the late 1960s, Mihai Berza's seminar hosted some representatives of the *Annales* 'second generation', including Georges Duby and Pierre Chaunu, and in 1969 a joint workshop was organized in Bucharest.[225] In the field of cultural studies, Alexandru Duțu applied Lucien Febvre's ideas to the interpretation of 'late' Romanian humanism in the seventeenth century.[226]

Hungary and Poland formed a core for pathbreaking social and economic research. A whole generation of researchers arrived on the scene, bringing with them new topics and interpretations. Under the influence of Witold Kula, a research centre for Polish social history was founded at the Institute of History of the Polish Academy of Sciences. It was later supplemented by the Historical Institute of Warsaw University, which focused on international (often non-European) economic history and was directed by Marian Małowist. In both Poland and Hungary, the liberal directors of the institutes (Zsigmond Pál Pach and Tadeusz Manteuffel) personally contributed to and supported new, ambitious research programmes. It is not without a certain irony that the scientific structures created in the early 1950s with the aim of accelerating the Sovietization of local historiographies ended up contributing to the development of new research trends. Ironic too is the fact that work conducted to support the Stalinist narrative of progress in East Central Europe ultimately came to be replaced by research on the region's backwardness. Marxist historians from both Poland and Hungary cooperated on a number of bilateral joint conferences on problems of regional backwardness from a historical perspective, sometimes concealing the notion of 'backwardness' under euphemistic descriptions like the 'Prussian course of agricultural development', a concept that East German economic historian Jürgen Kuczynski and Kula extensively debated.[227] In many respects, their findings were as similar to Stahl's as was the economic development of various countries in the region.[228] Social inequality was a prominent topic of their research, which was probably a choice influenced by Marxism.[229]

---

223 Nikolai Todorov, *Balkanskiyat grad XV-XIX vek. Socialno-ikonomichesko i demografsko razvitie* [The Balkan city between the 15th and 19th centuries: socio-economic and demographic developments] (Sophia: Nauka i izkustvo, 1972); idem, 'La situation démographique de la péninsule balcanique au cours des XVe et XVIe siècles', *Annuaire de l'Université de Sofia, Faculté de Philosophie et d'Histoire* 53, no. 2 (1969): 193–226.

224 Halil İnalcık, 'Impact of the "Annales" School on Ottoman Studies and New Findings', *A Journal of the Fernand Braudel Center for the Study of Economics, Historical Systems, and Civilizations* 1, no. 3–4 (1978): 69–96.

225 Boia, 'L'historiographie', 38–40.

226 See Alexandru Duțu, *Romanian Humanists and European Culture: A Contribution to Comparative Cultural History* (Bucharest: Editura ARSR, 1977).

227 Emil Niederhauser, *Eastern Europe in Recent Hungarian Historiography* (Budapest: Akadémiai Kiadó, 1975); Witold Kula, 'Uwagi o przewrocie przemysłowym w krajach Europy Wschodniej (1958)' [Remarks on the intellectual turn in Eastern Europe], in *Historia, zacofanie, rozwój*, idem (Warsaw: Czytelnik, 1983), 64–76.

228 See for example Zsigmond Pál Pach, *Die ungarische Agrarentwicklung im 16.–17. Jahrhundert: Abbiegung vom westeuropäischen Entwicklungsgang* (Budapest: Akadémiai Kiadó, 1964).

229 On Kálmán Benda, László Katus, Ilona Bolla, Jenő Szűcs and Imre Wellmann, see Holger Fischer, 'Neuere Entwicklungen in der ungarischen Sozialgeschichtsforschung', *Archiv für Sozialgeschichte* 34 (1994): 131–56, esp. 143–5.

Writing history in the twentieth-century

In the long run, it was precisely this combination of 'progressive' methodology and 'backward' historical realities that was essential for the international impact of this research. The tools for analyzing the world's peripheries and inequalities were scarce. Eastern European historians were able to deliver their own interpretations that were compatible with the influential work of people like Immanuel Wallerstein (a self-proclaimed student of Marian Małowist).[230] Some of them, notably Iván Berend and György Ránki, offered alternative models.[231] They placed their country within a region spread between Bulgaria and Romania on the one side and Great Britain, France and Germany on the other side. At the same time, even in their early writings they had sought to describe the general pattern of underdevelopment in Hungary:

> Like other countries, Hungary was caught up in the surging tide of capitalist development which – half a century later – raised her from the level of a purely agricultural country to the higher status of an agricultural-industrial one; yet, even at the peak of capitalist development, right up to the end of World War II, she remained a country with a moderately developed industry and belonged to the economically backward areas of Europe.[232]

A common feature of studies on the economic history of East Central and Southeastern Europe between the fifteenth and twentieth century has been to situate the region's backwardness within the context of a world-systems analysis. Thus, Małowist, Kula, Pach and, in the case of nineteenth-century Bulgaria, Konstantin Kosev,[233] all view the economic development of Western Europe as having conditioned the specific path taken by the continent's East. In Ránki's words, the consequence was that the industrial revolution 'was in Eastern Europe not only delayed by 50 to 100 years, but in fact never took place there in the Western sense'.[234] This perspective helped further the comparative work of scholars like Małowist and Antoni Mączak, who looked beyond Europe for other examples of 'economic colonialism'.[235]

New trends in the region's historiographies were repetitively and predictably announced as logical enrichments of Marxism. In Péter Hanák's understanding of the problem, which was

---

230 Immanuel Wallerstein, 'Preface: Marian Małowist: An Appreciation', in Marian Małowist, *Western Europe, Eastern Europe and World Development, 13th–18th Centuries*, eds Jean Batou and Henryk Szlajfer (Leiden: Brill, 2010), vii–ix.

231 Anna Sosnowska, *Zrozumieć zacofanie. Spory historyków o Europę Wschodnią (1947–1994)* [Understanding backwardness: historians' disputes about Eastern Europe] (Warsaw: Trio, 2004), 45–55. See also Zsigmond Pál Pach, 'Colony or Periphery? The Position of East-Central Europe at the Dawn of Modern Times', *Aula* 13, no. 2 (1991): 191–8.

232 Iván T. Berend and György Ránki, 'The Hungarian Manufacturing Industry, its Place in Europe (1900–1938)', in *Etudes historiques publieés par la Commission Nationale des Historiens Hongrois*, ed. Iván T. Berend (Budapest: Akadémiai Kiadó, 1960), 421–57, here 456. See also Iván T. Berend, 'Contribution to the History of Hungarian Economic Policy in the Two Decades Following the Second World War', *Acta Historica Academiae Scientarum Hungaricae* 13, no. 1–2 (1967): 3–47.

233 Konstantin Kosev, *Za kapitisticheskoto razvitie na Bylgarskite zemi prez 60-te I 70-te godini na XIX vek* [On the development of capitalism in Bulgarian lands in the 1860s and 1870s] (Sophia: BAH, 1968).

234 Quoted in Péter Hanák, '"Range" and "Constraint". Scope of Action and Fixed Course in György Ránki's Historical Approach', *Acta Historica Academiae Scientarum Hungaricae* 34, no. 4 (1988): 359–73, here 364.

235 Antoni Mączak, 'Marian Małowist 1909–1988', in *Europa i jej ekspansja XIV-XVII w.*, ed. Marian Małowist (Warsaw: Wydawnictwo Naukowe PWN, 1993), 5–12.

almost identical with the view Jerzy Topolski expressed three years later,[236] there simply could not be a conflict between Marxism and the *Annales* School:

> Since change in the immanent dimension of history and even *longue durée* structures, are only of relative validity, the structural and functional models employed by economics and sociology are more suitable for a precise description of processes and states of affairs at any given time … The usefulness of quantification, and the question whether history can be an exact science, has been debated frequently by Hungarian historians. Recently, economic historians in particular have proved more receptive to the social sciences … The Marxist view of history, which rests on a materialistic basis, and which recognizes objective laws and regularities, is particularly open and suitable for achieving such standards.[237]

Yet, such reconciliation was not an uncontroversial issue. For some Marxists, the introduction of the *Annales* School into the curricula of the newly created seminars in the history of historiography was a step too far. At first, there was no significant resistance to Jerzy Topolski's 1973 *Metodologia historii* ('Methodology of history') and, likewise, no general discussion followed the publication of a collection of Marxist and non-Marxist (including Braudel and Reinhart Koselleck, among others) theoretical articles in 1977.[238] But in 1977, when Mirjana Gross, a Croat historian of historiography, published a synthesis of international historical scholarship that strongly emphasized the French school's affinity with Marxism and even proposed that the latter be replaced by the former altogether, one of the few methodological controversies in the history of Eastern bloc's historiography broke out.[239] Branislav Djurdjev, perhaps also stirred by Gross' ostentatious appreciation of 'progressive' Slovenian historians, criticized her work, writing that the *Annales* School and Marxism were not just two branches of structuralism, because, according to him, Marx's philosophy had an individual, 'humanistic' dimension that the French school lacked.[240] The debate between the two Yugoslav scholars did not recall the political and ideological conflicts of the 1950s; rather, it was professional and substantial. And it soon proved to be outdated, because a process of methodological and political differentiation began in the 1970s with various speeds in different countries that more or less smoothly passed through the revolutions and turmoil of 1989–90 and persists to this day.

This Marxist criticism of the local adherents of the *Annales* School did not necessarily signal the decrease of the *Annales* School's influence, which continued to manifest itself in at least two ways. First, all the way into the 1990s, original research in Romania and Bulgaria continued to draw on the structural approach of the second generation of the *Annales* School. Published in

---

236 Pomian, 'Impact', 113.

237 Péter Hanák, 'Short Survey of Recent Literature on Hungarian Economic History', *The Economic History Review* 24, no. 4 (1971): 667–81, here 673.

238 Ferenc Glatz and Emil Niederhauser, eds, *Történetelméleti és módszertani tanulmányok* [Studies in the theory of history and methodology] (Budapest: Gondolat, 1977).

239 Mirjana Gross, *Historijska znanost. Razvoj, oblik, smjerovi* [Historical science: development, current shape, directions] (Zagreb: Sveučilište u Zagrebu, Institut za Hrvatsku Povijest, 1976).

240 Michael B. Petrovich, 'Structural History and Yugoslav Marxism', *Slavic Review* 39, no. 2 (1980): 292–6. Gross stresses the avant-garde role of Slovenian historians within Yugoslavia, particularly Fran Zwitter and Bogo Grafenauer, or 'Cvit and Bogo', as she calls them in a memorial volume for Grafenauer: Mirjana Gross, 'Kako pisati o povijesti historiografije?' [How to write on the history of historiography], in Rajšp, et al., *Grafenauerjev zbornik*, 161–8.

Writing history in the twentieth-century

1999, Bogdan Murgescu's synthesis of Romanian history's connection to universal history is a prominent example.[241] Such 'Braudelian' historical sources like fiscal and customs documents informed Tsvetana Georgieva's book on the social history of the Balkans between the fifteenth and seventeenth centuries.[242] In many countries of East Central and Southeastern Europe, a certain editorial belatedness saw Braudel, Bloch, Duby and Le Goff rising in popularity at the moment when their ideas had already been subject to criticism and revision by the subsequent 'generation' of the *Annales* School. Most Czech, Bulgarian and Romanian editions of their basic publications appeared after 1989. Prior to that, their books had spread partly through existing translations in other Slavic languages, the most important channels being the movement of Polish books to Czechoslovakia and the Soviet Union.

The methodological and generational changes experienced by the French historians from the late 1960s to the 1990s marked a second wave of *Annales* influence on East Central and Southeastern European historiography. In 1988, the editors of the *Annales ESC*[243] distanced themselves from the extensive use of statistics, marking the final phase of the shift from macro-structures and demography to historical anthropology and psychology.[244] With a slight delay, a similar tendency could be seen behind the Iron Curtain too, its first manifestation being the study of mentalities. Interestingly, in most cases this 'paradigm shift' occurred within the works of individual scholars rather than between generational groups. Bronisław Geremek and František Šmahel may serve as examples. In the 1960s, Geremek conducted research on the mentalities of medieval Polish society,[245] while in the early 1970s, Šmahel began studying the problem of national consciousness in Bohemia between the thirteenth and fifteenth century.[246] The history of the nationality of Polish lands, Bohemia and Western Europe in the Middle Ages was analyzed by Benedykt Zientara, František Graus and Šmahel leading to the formulation of a variety of pre-nineteenth-century forms of nationality.[247] Jenő Szűcs also did work on this topic, both in dedicated studies and in his widely known essay 'The Three Historical Regions of Europe' (1983), in which he discusses 'regional structures' and problems of identity.[248]

---

241 Bogdan Murgescu, *Istorie românească – istorie universală* [Romanian history – universal history] (Bucharest: Teora, 1999); see Cristina Petrescu and Dragoş Petrescu, 'Mastering vs. Coming to Terms with the Past: A Critical Analysis of Post-Communist Romanian Historiography', in *Narratives Unbound: Historical Studies in Post-Communist Eastern Europe*, eds Sorin Antohi, Balázs Trencsényi and Péter Apor (Budapest: CEU Press, 2007), 311–408, here 332–5.

242 Cvetana Georgieva, *Prostranstvo i prostranstva na Bylgarite XV–XVII vek* [Space and spaces in Bulgaria, 15th–17th cent.] (Sofia: Lik, 1999); see Ivan Elenkov and Daniela Koleva, 'Historical Studies in Post-Communist Bulgaria: Between Academic Standards and Political Agendas', in Antohi, Trencsényi and Apor, *Narratives Unbound*, 409–86, here 429–31.

243 ESC – *Economies, sociétés, civilisations* – was added to the journal's title in 1946.

244 Tomasz Wiślicz, *Krótkie trwanie. Problemy historiografii francuskiej lat dziewięćdziesiątych XX wieku* [Short duration: questions of French historiography of the 1990s] (Warsaw: PAN, 2004), 8–14.

245 Hanna Zaremska, 'Bronisław Geremek – zawód historyk' [Bronisław Geremek – the profession of a historian], in Bronisław Geremek, *O średniowieczu*, eds Hanna Zaremska and Agnieszka Niegowska (Warsaw: IH PAN, 2012), 7–33, here 24–6.

246 František Šmahel, *Idea národa v husitských Čechách* [The national idea in Hussite Bohemia] (Prague: Argo, 2000).

247 Šmahel, *Idea*, 12–21; Benedykt Zientara, 'Nationale Strukturen des Mittelalters: Ein Versuch zur Kritik der Terminologie des Nationalbewußtseins unter besonderer Berücksichtigung osteuropäischer Literatur', *Saeculum* 32 (1981): 301–16.

248 Jenő Szűcs, 'The Three Historical Regions of Europe: An Outline', *Acta Historica Academiae Scientiarum Hungaricae* 29, no. 2–4 (1983): 131–84.

Beliefs, religious representations, superstitions and sensual perceptions belonged to the popular topics of the early 1990s, with Gábor Klaniczay's works being perhaps the most significant example.[249] Similar topics were studied by historians of early modern East Central Europe like István György Tóth, Janusz Tazbir and Josef Macek, whose late *Jagellonský věk v českých zemích (1471–1526)* ('The Jagiellonian age in Bohemia'), published in three volumes between 1992 and 1999, aimed at providing an all-encompassing account of the epoch. As Macek himself put it, there were

> deeper historical forces operating in the Jagellonian age and shaping the overall structure of society, manifesting themselves not only in political activity and religious movements, but also in the mentality and culture of each social stratum and class, especially in everyday life.[250]

The 'Macedonian salad' method

The historical studies influenced by the *Annales* School formed the only post-Marxist methodological current that virtually dominated at least a considerable part of the region's historiographies up to the 1990s. Since then, the sheer plurality of methods and topics evades attempts at even an approximate generalization. Some of them, however, have made particularly noteworthy findings and/or influenced wider audiences' visions of the past. These will be briefly discussed in the following pages. Interestingly, most of the trends in East Central and Southeastern European historiographies developed independently of the major political changes brought on by the 1989 'revolutions'. Though crucial for the reappraisal of some of the traditions, topics and personalities that had been silenced under state socialism, the political transformation did not have any direct causal effect on the development of new methods.

While the influence of the *Annales* School continued to dominate in medieval and early modern studies, some other theories were instrumental for the further development of modern social history. For instance, in the 1970s and 1980s, Polish historians developed a strong interest for the social history of Hans-Ulrich Wehler and Jürgen Kocka. They sought to compose a thorough synthesis of Poland's social history, a task realized in the mid–1980s by a group of authors that included Andrzej Wyczański and Janusz Żarnowski.[251] An important aspect of 1980s studies on the social history of East Central Europe after the eighteenth century was the gradual widening of the 'class base'. Initial Marxist interest in the history of the working class had fallen into a largely political history of the 'organized representation' of workers, which is to say socialist and communist parties.[252] On the other hand, as early as the 1960s, it was gradually enriched by interest in other social groups, such as the intelligentsia and the bourgeoisie.

---

249 Gábor Klaniczay, *Holy Rulers and Blessed Princesses* (Cambridge: Cambridge University Press, 2002).

250 Quoted in Pavel Kolář and Michal Kopeček, 'A Difficult Quest for New Paradigms: Czech Historiography after 1989', in Antohi, Trencsényi and Apor, *Narratives Unbound*, 173–247, here 185.

251 Wacław Długoborski, 'Die sozialgeschichtliche Forschung in Polen', *Jahrbücher für Geschichte Osteuropas* 37, no. 1 (1989): 81–115.

252 Jiří Matejček, 'Die Arbeiterbewegung in den böhmischen Ländern bis zum Jahre 1914: Emanzipation der Arbeiterschaft oder eine Proletariathegemonie?', *Mitteilungsblatt des Instituts für Soziale Bewegungen* 23 (2003): 26–35; see also Fischer, 'Neuere Entwicklungen', 133–4.

Writing history in the twentieth-century

Though present almost everywhere[253] social history was particularly well-received in Poland. Like the *Annales'* shift from quantitative to qualitative research discussed above, Ryszarda Czepulis-Rastenis' initial insistence on continuing to use statistical data was gradually abandoned as the shift toward cultural history led social historians closer to the history of ideas.[254] At the same time, the so-called Warsaw School of the history of ideas, which included Jerzy Jedlicki, Andrzej Walicki, Jerzy Szacki, Bronisław Baczko, and Leszek Kołakowski, sprang from the intellectual soil of non-orthodox Polish Marxism. Jedlicki's work best exemplifies the continuity between the economic and social research of the 1960s and the history of ideas. In one of his early Marxist texts, he discussed the influence of 'national' culture on the content of 'national' politics. In a manner later adapted in literary history by Maria Janion and Maria Żmigrodzka, he analyzed Romantic poetry and music and their impact on the psychology of historical actors. Jedlicki's research on the Polish intelligentsia also connects social and intellectual perspectives. He described the nineteenth-century discourse of backwardness and intellectual responses to it by drawing on modernization theory, which in Eastern Europe was often used to analyze the region's backwardness and its 'progress' towards what was long perceived as the Western norm. At the same time, he studied the social and economic realities 'behind' the history of ideas. This aspect of his work on the history of the intelligentsia also played a guiding role in the three-volume study of intellectual history in Poland edited by Jedlicki and written by himself and his students (2008). In the first part of the book, Maciej Janowski poses 'social' and 'spatial' questions: what was the social basis of the emerging class of intellectuals and what were its points of crystallization? He answers by looking at cultural life in Warsaw, with its libraries, bookshops, theatres, salons, offices, coffee shops and parks.[255]

In Hungary, a similar path was taken by a group of scholars dealing with nineteenth-century social history, which was the era most studied by social historians between the 1970s and the early 1990s.[256] In contrast to Poland, urban studies was the most popular topic there: Vera Bácskai, Károly Vörös and, most of all, Péter Hanák were leading specialists in the field. Starting, as many others, from Marxist social history Hanák analyzed further the phenomenon of embourgeoisement before turning to cultural history. Like Jürgen Kocka, Hanák took a comparative perspective on cultural history and placed an emphasis on social norms:

> One looks beyond the peaks of high culture and its achievements, to embrace urban mass culture and the cultural products of peasants, traditionally relegated to folklore. I see as relevant to cultural history, instead of aesthetic worth or artistic excellence, the representative values and forces that shape the lifestyle and ideas of a community – in short, its normative behavior.[257]

Another relatively well-represented field of research was Czech social history of the nineteenth century. Otto Urban's early synthesis of the 'short' nineteenth century (between the

---

253 For Slovak and Czech studies see Dušan Kováč, 'Probleme der sozialhistorischen Forschung zum 19. und 20. Jahrhundert in der slowakischen Historiographie', *Archiv für Sozialgeschichte* 34 (1994): 111–30.

254 Nora Koestler, 'Polnische Intelligenz als sozialgeschichtliches Problem', *Jahrbücher für Geschichte Osteuropas* 31, no. 4 (1983): 543–62.

255 Maciej Janowski, *Narodziny inteligencji 1750–1831* [The birth of the intelligentsia 1750–1831] (Warsaw: IH PAN, Neriton, 2008), 37–42.

256 Fischer, 'Neuere Entwicklungen', 142.

257 Péter Hanák, *The Garden and the Workshop: Essays on the Cultural History of Vienna and Budapest* (Princeton, NJ: Princeton University Press, 1988), 28.

Bach regime and 1914) in Bohemian history remains a seminal work;[258] Jiří Kořalka, who was strongly influenced by German social history, and Jiří Malíř did similar research on Moravian history.[259]

These new directions in social history ultimately ended up pushing its practitioners towards a seemingly very different field of research, namely conceptual and intellectual history, where they drew influence from a variety of sources, including *Begriffsgeschichte* and the 'Cambridge School'.[260] Interestingly, some East Central European specialists in this field like László Kontler studied Western European history rather than that of their own regions. Works of conceptual history on the regional 'versions' of important European intellectual and political currents demonstrate how newer research trends have been 'domesticized' in various ways: Key works include Diana Mishkova's study of Balkan liberalism, Iván Zoltán Dénes' study of Hungarian conservatism, and Maciej Janowski's study of Polish liberalism. The topics of these studies are typically local versions of political ideologies that, though known from the Western European context, work very differently in Eastern Europe. The difference between the political language and practical content has been aptly illustrated by Dubravka Stojanović in the case of the highly problematic 'democratization' in early twentieth-century Serbia.[261]

The move away from the materialistic and general towards the cultural and particular deserves attention, particularly because it had unintended effects on the region's historiography. One of them is the flourishing of nationality studies. Though deeply rooted in the kind of self-interest of young national cultures characteristic of the nineteenth century, this discipline, too, paved the way for theoretical innovations that had an impact beyond the region. The number of historians of nationalisms is large and still growing. Some of them, however, deserve special mention due to their methodological output. In the 1960s, in both Czechoslovakia and in Poland, Miroslav Hroch and Józef Chlebowczyk developed models for the national awakenings of 'small and young' nations. Both strived for a formula – occasionally even a quasi-mathematical formula – that would explain how identities moved from an early phase of 'ourness' towards a nation, placing special focus on questions of assimilation and acculturation.[262] Partly inspired by them, nationalism has become one of the main, if not the central topic of regional historical research in Poland and Czechoslovakia since the 1970s.

Among the studies that applied Hroch's model to a specific national case, those by by Canadian-Ukrainian historian Orest Subtelny and US-Ukrainian historian Roman Szporluk deserve special mention, as do Jaroslav Hrytsak's history of Ukraine. Other foundational studies

---

258 Otto Urban, *Česká společnost 1848–1914* [Czech society 1848–1914] (Prague: Svoboda, 1982).

259 Kolář and Kopeček, 'A Difficult Quest', 194–5.

260 On the productivity of different approaches to the history of East Central Europe see Trencsényi, 'Conceptual History'.

261 Diana Mishkova, 'The Interesting Anomaly of Balkan Liberalism', in *Liberty and the Search for Identity: Imperial Heritages and Liberal Nationalisms in a Comparative Perspective*, ed. Iván Zoltán Dénes (Budapest: CEU Press, 2006), 399–456; Maciej Janowski, *Polska myśl liberalna do 1918 roku* [Polish liberal thought until 1918] (Cracow: Znak, 1998); Dubravka Stojanović, *Srbija i demokratija 1904–1914. Istorijska studija o 'zlatnom dobu' srpske demokratije* [Serbia and democracy 1904–1914: a historical study of the 'Golden Age' of Serbian democracy] (Belgrade: Udruženje za društvenu istoriju, 2004); Iván Zoltán Dénes, *Conservative Ideology in the Making* (Budapest: CEU Press, 2009).

262 Hans-Jürgen Puhle, 'Miroslav Hroch im Kontext der Theorien über den Nationalismus', in *Historische Nationsforschung im geteilten Europa 1945–1989*, eds Pavel Kolář and Miloš Řezník (Köln: SH-Verlag, 2012), 73–85; Józef Chlebowczyk, 'Some Issues of National Assimilation and Linguistic-Ethnic Borderland (in the Area of Former Austro-Hungarian Monarchy)', *Acta Poloniae Historica* 108 (2013): 149–95.

Writing history in the twentieth-century

on national culture and history include Dessislava Lilova's book on the Bulgarian ethnonym and education in the nineteenth century, Tomasz Kizwalter's Gellnerist interpretation of the Polish national idea, and Nikša Stančić's studies on nineteenth-century Croatia.[263] These later historians were particularly interested in the works of past historians who had done comparative analyses of nation-building processes. Henryk Wereszycki and Emil Niederhauser (the latter largely ignoring methodological questions) convincingly proved Austria-Hungary to represent a particularly fruitful example of intertwined 'national awakenings'.[264] All of the studies mentioned insisted on the discursive regularity identified by Chlebowczyk:

> What is more, under the banner of reinstatement of the assets (no matter whether factual or phantasmal) lost once in the past, national camps representing minority communities put forth desiderata concerning re-assimilation, or claim-based, policies. This, logically enough, leads to a nationalistic expansionism also on the part of those national camps which in the period of their formation initially assumed a purely defensive position.[265]

National myths being part of national ideologies, they became the subject of historical analysis. Throughout East Central and Southeastern Europe, beginning in the 1970s and continuing up to this day, 'national myths' and 'stereotypes' are among the most popular research topics. While this field has uncovered interesting findings, it has rarely been the site of methodological innovation or broad comparison. More often than not, both the concepts of 'myths' and 'stereotypes' seem to imply a rather straightforward, mostly anti-nationalist and 'progressivist' perspective that seeks to demystify myths and reject prejudices. As a whole, this strain of East Central and Southeastern European historiography thus cannot be treated as constituting a methodological trend or school in and of itself.

However, there have been some attempts to change the state of things and propose alternative ways of analyzing similar phenomena. The semiotic interpretation of nineteenth-century national movements is noteworthy here. Inspired by the Tartu–Moscow Semiotic School, some Czech literary scientists and historians, most notably Vladimír Macura, analyzed the structures of the popular genre of 'national myths', treating them as systems of signs that generate symbolic meanings. The process of the Czech national revival with its potent organizational

---

263 Jarosław Hrycak, *Historia Ukrainy 1772–1999. Narodziny nowoczesnego narodu* [The history of Ukraine 1772–1999: the birth of the modern nation], trans. Katarzyna Kotyńska (Lublin: Instytut Europy Środkowo-Wschodniej, 2000); Orest Subtelny, *Ukraine: A History* (Toronto: University of Toronto Press, 1988); Desislava Lilova, *Vyzrozhdenskite znacheniya na nacionalnoto ime* [The meaning of national names in the national awakening] (Sofia: Prosveta, 2003); Tomasz Kizwalter, *O nowoczesności narodu. Przypadek polski* [On the modernity of the nation: the Polish case] (Warsaw: Semper, 1999). Interestingly enough, the first prime minister of Estonia, Mart Laar, authored a PhD dissertation that applied Hroch's model to the Estonian 'national awakening': see Jörg Hackmann, 'Das Paradigma der "kleinen Nation" in der historischen Nationalismusforschung Miroslav Hroch und die historische Nationalismusforschung in Nordosteuropa', in Kolář and Řezník, *Historische Nationsforschung*, 87–101; Nikša Stančić, *Hrvatska nacionalna ideologija preporodnog pokreta u Dalmaciji: Mihovil Pavlinović i njegov krug do 1869* [Croatian national ideology of the awakening movement] (Zagreb: Sveučilište u Zagrebu Centar za povijesne znanosti, 1980).

264 Emil Niederhauser, *The Rise of Nationality in Eastern Europe* (Budapest: Corvina, 1981); Henryk Wereszycki, *Pod berłem Habsburgów* [Under the scepter of the Habsburgs] (Cracow: Wydawnictwo Literackie, 1975).

265 Chlebowczyk, 'Some Issues', 193.

and intellectual energy was a more than fruitful object to such an analysis. Macura's book *Český sen* ('Czech dreams') viewed the Czech 'national awakening' as a series of interrelated 'dreams' about the future of the Czech nation rather than as a response to the reality of nineteenth-century Bohemia. Macura's reference to the 'discursiveness' of national culture goes so far as to inquire into the role of the literary historian in shaping his object of study.

Another research field that repeatedly revisits national myths and stereotypes is the history of historiography. Its most prominent representatives are from Poland, Romania and Ukraine, but in the 1980s and 1990s, this discipline was developing in almost all countries of the region, and some scholars undertook comparative studies on historians from different countries. A student of Marceli Handelsman and a Marxist, Marian Henryk Serejski played a key role in the development of the Polish history of historiography, expanding the scope of this, by nature, rather narrow topic. Serejski's student Andrzej Feliks Grabski defined the history of historiography as

> an analysis of various forms of thinking about the past, not restricted to those that are part of the so-called scientific reflection on history and refer to the modern concept of science; secondly, it places a strong accent on the holistic view of historiography, equally treating the organizational structures, theoretical fundaments, and interpretations of the past.[266]

One of the most hotly debated Romanian authors of the latest decades, Lucian Boia, has taken a similar path.[267]

Although the 'cultural turn' of the historiographies in East Central and Southeastern Europe can be seen as an argument in favour of their strong connection to the main trends of international historical science, the side effects have been controversial. While the turn has produced innovative studies, the new fields of research it uncovered had the odd effect of pushing researchers back towards national history rather than encouraging them to work on regional or global history. And in contrast to Kula, Ránki or Berend, Macura and Grabski do not offer a general scheme, an analysis that, while skilfully adjusted, might be useful anytime and anywhere. Miroslav Hroch's theory of the development of national movements was probably the last such general theory from East Central Europe to enjoy international acclaim. Though it drew from the history of the Czech national revival, Hroch was able to develop a universal model that was applicable to other times and places and inspired just as many studies as works on Eastern European backwardness. Unsurprisingly, the persuasive power of the 'national' topics proved to be strongest on a national level. Jerzy Jedlicki's most important book is an interesting example of this. The English translation of the book – *Jakiej cywilizacji Polacy potrzebują* (literally: 'What kind of civilization do the Poles need?') – gave it a new title that might better reflect its 'general' value for the interpretation of any debate on national or regional backwardness: *The Suburb of Europe*.

When viewed in the context of the resurgence of topics and narratives that had been banned under communist rule, the amount of research being done on national mythologies and nation-building processes is less surprising. Beginning in the late 1970s, nationalism, which was tolerated and then finally accepted, increasingly permeated official historical production. Fuelled by political tensions between Hungary and Romania and Bulgaria and Yugoslavia, these works

---

266 Rafał Stobiecki, 'Wprowadzenie' [Introduction], in Andrzej F. Grabski, *Dzieje historiografii* (Poznań: Wydawnictwo Poznańskie, 2003), xiii.

267 Boia, *History*.

Writing history in the twentieth-century

were limited mostly by geopolitical concerns, which is to say fear of strong neighbours or ethnic conflict. The conflicts between historians from Bulgaria and Yugoslavia intensified in 1978 after negotiations over the settlement of the Macedonian Question broke down; they flared up again in 1989 for the same reason.[268] Prior to that, the disintegration of Yugoslavia's historiography resulted in the increasing separation of national narratives. In the 1980s, previously critical interpretations of Greater Serbian politics were abandoned.[269] In Poland and Hungary, historians like Ignác Romsics and Andrzej Garlicki undertook a partial 'rehabilitation' of interwar history, giving special attention to non-communist and anti-communist politicians like József Piłsudski, Roman Dmowski, István Tisza, István Bethlen and Count Klebelsberg.[270] Thus, the barrier between the official historiography, samizdat editions and exile occasionally blurred with authors present in all three distribution channels roughly at the same time.

In the late 1980s, even such inconvenient truths as the Molotov–Ribbentrop Pact and the deportations of Lithuanians, Latvians, Poles, Estonians, Jews, Ukrainians, Belorussians, Moldovans and others to the Soviet Union gradually entered public discourse after perestroika. The absence of censorship and political dictates in the 1990s meant that former Marxist-Leninists or even – as in the case of Milan Ďurica's revival in Slovakia – former right-wing political emigrants had the freedom to espouse ethnocentric narratives.[271] Typically, such narratives operate with the vision of a separate and monolithic national body that is victimized by equally monolithic hostile neighbours, as has been shown with the example of Croatia by Maja Brkljačić.[272] Because they give fuel to the radical right, such narratives have had a particularly strong impact in de facto multinational states like the former Yugoslavia and post-Soviet Estonia and Latvia, which both have sizeable Russian minorities.

> By asserting that the state that came into existence in 1990 is in effect the legal restoration of the historic homeland, such radical nationalists can claim that only citizens of that inter-war state and their descendants should form the legal foundation of the restored citizen-polity … Those who settled in the homeland during the Soviet period are therefore represented as 'the colonizing other', a remnant of 'a civil garrison of the empire' and potential 'fifth columnists' who threaten the stability if not territorial integrity of the political homeland.[273]

Two more emotionally laden topics have come to set the tone of the region's historiographical debates in the 1990s and after. Though temporally apart, they seem to be discursively connected. The first is the study of the communist period. With its own prehistory dating back to the very beginnings of the system, this field of research has generated an extensive body of studies devoted mostly to the repressive state apparatuses and the brutal way in which the new authorities were installed in East Central and Southeastern Europe after the war. Its strongest

---

268 Hoppe, 'Politik', 280; Meininger, 'A Troubled Transition', 113–14.

269 Brunnbauer, 'Historical Writing', 363–4.

270 Péter Apor and Balázs Trencsényi, 'Fine-Tuning the Polyphonic Past: Hungarian Historical Writing in the 1990s' in Antohi, Trencsényi and Apor, *Narratives Unbound*, 1–100, here 39–40.

271 Zora Hlavičková, 'Wedged Between National and Trans-National History: Slovak Historiography in the 1990s', in Antohi, Trencsényi and Apor, *Narratives Unbound*, 249–310, here 259.

272 Maja Brkljačić, 'What Past Is Present?', *International Journal of Politics, Culture and Society* 17, no. 1 (2003): 41–52.

273 Graham Smith, et al., *Nation-Building in the Post-Soviet Borderlands: The Politics of National Identities* (Cambridge: Cambridge University Press, 1998), 96.

regional varieties developed in the countries especially affected by regime brutality, chiefly Albania and Romania, with less spectacular representations in the former Yugoslavia. Studies on the history of communism also thrived in Poland and Hungary. Initially, historians chose to focus on the early years of the dictatorship, the period of Stalinization being the second choice.[274] Most of the studies published in the 1990s subscribed to the totalitarian paradigm, albeit in slightly different ways in each country. In Czechoslovakia (after 1993: the Czech Republic and Slovakia), the suppression of the Prague Spring played a central role in research on the history of communism, as did studies on popular non-violent resistance; in Hungary, the suppression of the 1956 uprising received much attention; and in Poland, authors focused on the critical turns in 1956, 1968 and 1980. Also notable is the fact that Romanian, Ukrainian and Polish historiography reintroduced post-war armed anti-communist resistance to collective memory after 1989.

It took until about the second half of the 1990s before historical research into the communist past made its way into the various fields and sub-fields of social, cultural and intellectual history. At about the same time, as Michal Kopeček argues,

> with the legitimacy of the political system basically stabilized, the communist past increasingly became a field of political struggle with distinct variants of politics of memory being used as expedient political tools. The most visible of these was the activist anti-communist memory politics, which strove to repair and recreate the 'memory of the nation'.[275]

The institutional representation of such memory wars can be found in the variously named institutes for national remembrance. The (then) Gauck Institute (Die Behörde des Bundesbeauftragten für die Unterlagen des Staatssicherheitsdienstes der ehemaligen Deutschen Demokratischen Republik, or, the Federal Commissioner for the Records of the State Security Service of the former German Democratic Republic) was long seen as setting the standard in Central and Eastern Europe. Romania constituted the lone exception: prior to the establishment of the National Council for the Study of the Archives of Securitate (CNSAS) in 1999, the National Institute for the Study of Totalitarianism, created by the post-communist president Ion Iliescu, was less devoted to the study of communism and more to the study of the stigmatization of ethnic minorities.[276]

The second heavily debated topic of the region's post-1989 historiographies is the Holocaust and wartime relations between ethnic majorities and Jewish minorities. In Poland, meticulous research has been accompanied by fervent public debates initiated by Polish editions of Jan Tomasz Gross' and Irena Grudzińska-Gross' books on the massacres of Jews at the hands of their Polish neighbours and on wartime and post-war 'gold fever', or the blackmail and robbery of the Jews in hiding, the denouncement of those who hid them, and also the theft of

---

274 Ulf Brunnbauer, 'Ein neuer weißer Fleck? Der Realsozialismus in der aktuellen Geschichtsschreibung in Südosteuropa', in *Zwischen Amnesie und Nostalgie. Die Erinnerung an den Kommunismus in Südosteuropa*, eds Ulf Brunnbauer and Stefan Troebst (Köln: Böhlau, 2007), 87–111.

275 Michal Kopeček, 'From the Politics of History to Memory as Political Language: Czech Dealings with the Communist Past after 1989', *Forum Geschichtskulturen, Czechia*, Version: 1.0, 16 December 2013, https://www.cultures-of-history.uni-jena.de/debates/czech/czech-republic-from-the-politics-of-history-to-memory-as-political-language/ (accessed 21 April 2020).

276 Brunnbauer, 'Ein neuer weißer Fleck?', 102–4.

Writing history in the twentieth-century

the property of those who were murdered.[277] Though the Polish debate was singular in this regard, the problems it uncovered seem to be a rule rather than the Polish 'exception'. In his comparison of historians' and laypeoples' views of the history of the persecution of Jews in their respective countries, from Latvia to Romania, John-Paul Himka rightly underscores 'the relation between the recollection of communist atrocities and the resistance to consciousness of the Holocaust' as being the main barrier standing in the way of these countries coming to terms with this chapter in their common past.[278] This process is complicated by new forms of anti-Semitism that harp on the myth that Jews played a special role in the establishment of the Soviet and national communist regimes. This is particularly pronounced in countries like Lithuania, where local complicity in the Holocaust is intertwined with the history of national anti-Soviet resistance. The national uprising in the wake of the German invasion of the Soviet Union in June 1941 was accompanied by large-scale pogroms of Lithuania's Jews accused of Bolshevik sympathies.[279] Furthermore, Lithuanian auxiliary units in the German military massacred thousands of Jews in Lithuania and Belarus.[280]

Although prior to 1990 it only received sporadic treatment in the samizdat and exile editions in Poland, Czechoslovakia and Hungary, with the fall of the communist states, historical research on the Holocaust, pogroms and Jewish history has produced a number of strong works, including some detailed studies on various aspects of Jewish strategies of survival and the death camps. In most countries, there are journals and research institutes dedicated to the study of Jewish history, and there have been some systematic studies of neighbourhoods and towns that had large Jewish populations before the Holocaust.[281] Another strain of research on the Holocaust has focused on the anthropology of anti-Semitism and anti-Semitic violence. In Hungary, Tamás Kende has done work in this field.[282] In the Czech Republic, a pathbreaking study was published by Michal Frankl,[283] and Joanna Tokarska-Bakir has done important work in Poland.[284] Additionally, some scholars have conducted research on the persecution and murder of other ethnic groups during the Holocaust; works like those of Lithuanian historians

---

277 Jan Tomasz Gross, *Neighbors: The Destruction of the Jewish Community in Jedwabne, Poland* (Princeton, NJ: Princeton University Press, 2001); Jan Tomasz Gross, *Fear: Anti-Semitism in Poland after Auschwitz; An Essay in Historical Interpretation* (Princeton, NJ: Princeton University Press, 2006); Jan Tomasz Gross and Irena Grudzińska-Gross, *Złote żniwa. Rzecz o tym, co się działo na obrzeżach zagłady Żydów* [Golden harvest: what happened on the margins of the Holocaust] (Cracow: Znak, 2011).

278 John-Paul Himka, 'Obstacles to the Integration of the Holocaust into Post-Communist East European Historical Narratives', *Canadian Slavonic Papers* 50, no. 3–4 (2008): 359–72.

279 Liudas Truska, 'The Crisis of Lithuanian and Jewish Relations (June 1940–June 1941)', in *Holokausto prielaidos. Antisemitizmas Lietuvoje XIX a. antroji pusė – 1941 m. birželis*, eds Liudas Truska and Vygautas Vareilus (Vilnius: Margi Raštai, 2004), 173–208.

280 Arūnas Bubnys, 'Die litauischen Hilfspolizeibataillone und der Holocaust', in *Holocaust in Litauen: Krieg, Judenmorde und Kollaboration im Jahre 1941*, eds Vincas Bartusevičius, Joachim Tauber and Wolfram Welte (Köln: Böhlau, 2003), 117–31.

281 This seems to represent the typical approach in Croatia with publications by Zvonko Marčić, Tome Šalić and Vjekoslav Žugaj. See Ivo Goldstein, 'Historiografija o Židovima u Hrvatskoj' [Historiography on Jews in Croatia], *Radovi – Zavod na hrvatsku povijest*, 34–6 (2004): 285–90.

282 Apor and Trencsényi, 'Fine-Tuning', 46–8.

283 Michal Frankl, *Emancipace od Židů. Český antisemitismus na konci 19. století* [Emancipation from the Jews: Czech anti-Semitism in late 19th century] (Prague: Paseka, 2008).

284 Most of all Joanna Tokarska-Bakir, *Legendy o krwi. Antropologia przesądu* [Blood legends: the anthropology of prejudice] (Warsaw: WAB, 2008) and idem, *Okrzyki pogromowe. Szkice z antropologii historycznej Polski lat 1939–1946* [Pogrom screams: sketches in anthropology of the history of Poland 1939–1946] (Wołowiec: Czarne, 2012).

Liudas Truska and Leonidas Donskis and Polish historians Barbara Engelking and Monika Polit caused considerable public debate in their home countries.[285]

Both communism and the Holocaust are far more than 'mere history'. Their social and cultural impact situates them in the realm of collective memory and gives them the power to shape collective identities. Thus, it is not a matter of chance that memory research is one the newest, most popular trends in countries all over East Central and Southeastern Europe. Fields from sociology through anthropology to oral history have engaged in memory research, which fits well with the region's tradition of historical research on myth- and nation-building. At the same time, the reception of memory studies provides another example of a 'distorted' application of Western European ideas to East Central and Southeastern European subject matter and research traditions.

It would be an oversimplification to claim that the 'memory turn' in France and other Western European countries has passed unnoticed in the former Eastern bloc. Even if it only played a marginal role, historians in almost every East Central and Southeastern European country made reference to it throughout the 1990s. Pierre Nora is one of the most important figures in this strain of historiography, and it was during this decade that the first translations of parts of Nora's works started to appear in Hungary and Russia.[286] In the 2000s, parts of *Les lieux de mémoire* ('Realms of memory') as well as short programmatic essays were published in Poland, Romania and Bulgaria.[287] Pierre Nora's work also appeared in translation in other countries of the region, mostly in conference volumes.[288] Finally, over a decade after the Hungarian translation, the introductory essay to the French volume appeared in Czech and Polish.[289] But as of today, few authors in East Central or Southeastern Europe have applied Nora's ideas in a

---

285 Klaus Richter, 'Der Holocaust in der litauischen Historiographie seit 1991', *Zeitschrift für Ostmitteleuropa-Forschung* 56, no. 3 (2007): 389–415; Barbara Engelking, '*Szanowny panie Gistapo'. Donosy do władz niemieckich w Warszawie i okolicach w latach 1940–1941* ['Dear Mr. Gestapo': denunciations to the German authorities in and around Warsaw 1940–1941] (Warsaw: Stowarzyszenie Centrum Badań nad Zagładą Żydów, 2003); Monika Polit, '*Moja żydowska dusza nie obawia się dnia sądu'. Mordechaj Chaim Rumkowski. Prawda i zmyślenie* ['My Jewish soul is not afraid of Judgment Day': Mordechaj Chaim Rumkowski; truth and fiction] (Warsaw: Stowarzyszenie Centrum Badań nad Zagładą Żydów, 2012).

286 Ferenc Laczó and Máté Zombory, 'Between Transnational Embeddedness and Relative Isolation: The Moderate Rise of Memory Studies in Hungary', *Acta Poloniae Historica* 106 (2012): 99–126; Kornelia Kończal, 'Les lieux de mémoire: The Unparalleled Career of a Research Concept', *Acta Poloniae Historica* 106 (2012): 5–31.

287 Pierre Nora, 'Czas pamięci' [The memory time], trans. Wiktor Dłuski, *Res Publica Nowa* 7 15, no. 153 (2001): 37–43; idem, 'Czy Europa istnieje?' [Does Europe exist?], trans. Kornelia Kończal, *Gazeta Wyborcza* from 11./12.08.2007; idem, 'Wolność dla historii' [Freedom for history], trans. Jolanta Kurska, *Gazeta Wyborcza*, 24 October 2008; idem, 'Excedentul de memorie' [Memory surplus], trans. Marina Vazaca, *Lettre internationale* 41/42 (2002): 123–26; idem, 'Întronarea mondială a istoriei' [The global entanglement of history], trans. Mihai Luca, *Observator Cultural* 5, no. 238 (2004): 9–11; idem, 'Naţiunea – sălaş al memoriei?' [The nation – a shelter of memory?], trans. Magda Ispas, *Luceafărul*, 23 May 2001, 23; idem, ed., *Mesta na pamet i konstruirane na nastoyashcheto* [Realms of memory and constructing authenticity], trans. Vesela Genova et al. (Sofia: Dom-na-naukite-za-choveka-i-obshtestvoto, 2004).

288 Pierre Nora, 'Pasaulinė atminties viešpatija' [The realm of global history], in *Europos kultūros profiliai: atmintis, tapatumas, religija*, ed. Almantas Samalavičius (Vilnius: Kulturos Barai, 2007), 9–24.

289 See Kornelia Kończal and Maciej Górny, 'Miejsca pamięci w Europie Środkowo-Wschodniej, czyli o regionalnej (anty)recepcji wędrującego pojęcia lieu de memoire' [Realms of memory in East Central Europe or a regional (anti) reception of a travelling concept of lieu de memoire], in *Historie wzajemnych oddziaływań*, ed. Robert Traba (Warsaw: Narodowe Centrum Kultury, Centrum Badań Historycznych PAN w Berlinie, 2014), 363–86.

Writing history in the twentieth-century

consequent manner in a historical study. This is surprising if one considers the numerous studies on realms of memory in the 1990s in Western Europe.

The immediate reception of the concept remains limited. More importantly (and paradoxically), the application of methodological innovations like Pierre Nora's concept of the realms of memory seem to be hindered by the persistence of the native scientific traditions that preceded it. The intense preoccupation of East Central and Southeastern European historians with the discursiveness of national history, the formation of collective identities and shared interpretations of the past in the form of myths has shaped the region's approach to issues treated in France and other Western European countries under the label of *lieux de mémoire*. Over the last few years, however, the region's scholars have shown an increasing interest in the concept of *lieu de mémoire* which can be observed in some local attempts on the national or even bilateral level.

Furthermore, a few monographs written by Central and Eastern European researchers have been inspired by Nora's approach. Interestingly enough, all of them share certain features that were less visible in Nora's project and in most of the Western European projects that draw on his approach to the history of memory. Mostly due to the complex relations between different ethnicities in the region and the weak central power of the states, Central and Eastern European *lieux de mémoire* divide communities more often than they unite them. The points of crystallization of collective identities are therefore filled with contradictory meanings. Gabriela Kiliánová's study on the history of Slovak, Magyar and German appropriations of the symbolic space of Mount Devín is a direct application of the concept of *lieu de mémoire* (translated as *pamätne mesto*, i.e. 'memorable place' rather than 'place of memory').[290] The most recent large-scale collaborative project between Polish and German historians analyzed common and divided realms of memory.[291] Perhaps this sensitivity to the multiple codes that are combined in geographical sites, historical personalities or ethnic groups represents one of the ways in which East Central and Southeastern Europe has sought to pay its debts to international historical scholarship incurred over the long twentieth century.

Conclusion

Seen through the prism of intellectual transfers, the history of the historical profession and historical narratives in East Central and Southeastern Europe offers a vibrant picture. The transfers' timing and subsequent paths differ significantly: some methodological currents were hardly present at all in East Central and Southeastern Europe, while others were more dominant in the region than they were in France or Germany. Some of the Western inspirations were turned into something new or even – as one can argue in the case of Pekař's creative adaptation of Lamprecht's ideas – something equally elaborate and thought-provoking as the original. Perhaps even the latest trend, regional memory studies, bears signs of reciprocal influence: while the method has inspired local research, this research on local specificities might in turn lead historians to rethink some parts of the method. The quality of a region's scholarship might be judged according to its ability to develop such new perspectives. If this is true, East Central

---

290 Gabriela Kiliánová, *Identita a pamäť. Devín/Theben/Devény ako pamätné miesto* [Identity and memory: Devín/Theben/Devény as a realm of memory] (Bratislava: Ústav etnológie SAV, 2005).

291 Robert Traba, Hans Henning Hahn, Maciej Górny and Kornelia Kończal, eds, *Polsko-niemieckie miejsca pamięci* [Polish-German realms of memory], vols. 1–4 (Warsaw: 2011–2015) [=*Deutsch-polnische Erinnerungsorte*, vols. 1–4 (Paderborn: Schöningh, 2011–2015)].

and Southeastern Europe in the twentieth century form a unit, or perhaps better, a space of similar experience.

The practical conditions of this transfer offer an interesting case study. Looking back on a century of historiography, the history of the region's international ties might be better viewed as a circle rather than as a straight line. In the beginning of this chapter, we considered local historians' close connections to the discipline's leaders, most of them either French or German, and their personal accounts of these relationships. The latest developments seem to have restored the personal contacts that were loosened in the 1950s and 1960s, with rising numbers of East Central and Southeastern European scholars studying and working abroad, now in countries like the United States and Great Britain. To say that this repetition is an example of Friedrich Engels' theory of spiral development, in which phenomena reappear on a higher level, would be, perhaps, too bold. But it certainly is an expression of life.

Further reading

Antohi, Sorin, Balázs Trencsényi, and Péter Apor, eds. *Narratives Unbound: Historical Studies in Post-Communist Eastern Europe* (Budapest: CEU Press, 2007).

Apor, Péter. *Fabricating Authenticity in Soviet Hungary: The Afterlife of the First Hungarian Soviet Republic in the Age of State Socialism* (London: Anthem Press, 2014).

Baár, Monika. *Historians and Nationalism: East-Central Europe in the Nineteenth Century* (Oxford: Oxford University Press, 2010).

Berger, Stefan, and Chris Lorenz, eds. *The Contested Nation: Ethnicity, Class, Religion and Gender in National Histories* (Basingstoke: Palgrave Macmillan, 2008).

Boia, Lucian. *History and Myth in Romanian Consciousness* (Budapest: CEU Press, 2001).

Brock, Peter, John D. Stanley, and Piotr J. Wróbel, eds. *Nation and History: Polish Historians from the Enlightenment to the Second World War* (Toronto: University of Toronto Press, 2006).

Chickering, Roger. *Karl Lamprecht: A German Academic Life (1856–1915)* (Atlantic Highlands, NJ: Humanities Press International, 1993).

Connelly, John. *Captive University: The Sovietization of East German, Czech and Polish Higher Education 1945–1956* (Chapel Hill, NC: University of North Carolina Press, 2000).

Connelly, John, and Michale Grüttner, eds. *Universities under Dictatorship* (University Park, PA: Penn State University Press, 2005).

Daskalov, Roumen. *Debating the Past: Modern Bulgarian History: From Stambolov to Zhivkov* (Budapest: CEU Press, 2011).

Daskalov, Roumen. *The Making of a Nation in the Balkans: Historiography of the Bulgarian Revival* (Budapest: CEU Press, 2004).

Dénes, Iván Zoltán. *Conservative Ideology in the Making* (Budapest: CEU Press, 2009).

Dénes, Iván Zoltán, ed. *Liberty and the Search for Identity: Imperial Heritages and Liberal Nationalisms in a Comparative Perspective* (Budapest: CEU Press, 2006).

Djokić, Dejan, ed. *Yugoslavism: Histories of a Failed Idea 1918–1992* (London: Hurst & Co., 2003).

Dominian, Leon. *The Frontiers of Language and Nationality in Europe* (New York: American Geographical Society, 1917).

Duțu, Alexandru. *Romanian Humanists and European Culture: A Contribution to Comparative Cultural History* (Bucharest: Editura ARSR, 1977).

Epstein, Irene Raab. *Gyula Szekfű: A Study in the Political Basis of Hungarian Historiography* (New York: Garland Publishers, 1987).

Erdmann, Karl Dietrich. *Toward a Global Community of Historians: The International Committee of Historical Sciences, 1898–2000*, eds Jürgen Kocka, Wolfgang J. Mommsen, and Agnes Blänsdorf, trans. Alan Nothnagle (New York: Berghahn, 2005).

Ersoy, Ahmet, Maciej Górny, and Vangelis Kechriotis, eds. *Discourses of Collective Identity*, vol. 3/1, *Modernism: The Creation of Nation-States* (Budapest: CEU Press, 2010).

Ersoy, Ahmet, Maciej Górny, and Vangelis Kechriotis, eds. *Discourses of Collective Identity in Central and Southeast Europe 1770–1945*, vol. 3/2, *Modernism: Representations of National Culture* (Budapest: CEU Press, 2010).

Writing history in the twentieth-century

Frank, Tibor, Frank Hadler, eds. *Disputed Territories and Shared Pasts: Overlapping National Histories in Modern Europe* (Basingstoke: Palgrave Macmillan, 2011).

Górny, Maciej. *The Nation Should Come First: Marxism and Historiography in East Central Europe*, trans. Antoni Górny (Frankfurt a.M.: Lang, 2013).

Gross, Jan Tomasz. *Fear: Anti-Semitism in Poland after Auschwitz; An Essay in Historical Interpretation* (Princeton, NJ: Princeton University Press, 2006).

Gross, Jan Tomasz. *Neighbors: The Destruction of the Jewish Community in Jedwabne, Poland* (Princeton, NJ: Princeton University Press, 2001).

Hanák, Péter. *The Garden and the Workshop: Essays on the Cultural History of Vienna and Budapest* (Princeton, NJ: Princeton University Press, 1988).

Hupchick, Dennis P., and R. William Weisberger, eds. *Hungary's Historical Legacies: Studies in Honor of Steven Béla Várdy* (Boulder, CO: Columbia University Press, 2000).

Klaniczay, Gábor. *Holy Rulers and Blessed Princesses* (Cambridge: Cambridge University Press, 2002).

Kos, Milko, France Stele, Antun Barac, Franc Kidrič, and France Marolt. *The Julian March: Studies on Its History and Civilization* (Ljubljana: Academy of Sciences & Arts, 1946).

Małowist, Marian. *Western Europe, Eastern Europe and World Development, 13th–18th Centuries*, eds Jean Batou, and Henryk Szlajfer (Leiden: Brill, 2010).

Mârza, Radu. *The History of Romanian Slavic Studies: From the Beginnings until the First World War*, trans. Leonard Ciocan (Cluj-Napoca: Romanian Academy of Sciences, 2008).

Middell, Matthias, and Lluis Roura y Aulinas, eds. *World, Global and European Histories as Challenges to National Representations of the Past* (London: Palgrave Macmillan, 2012).

Mishkova, Diana, Balázs Trencsényi, and Marius Turda, eds. *Anti-Modernism: Radical Revisions of Collective Identity* (Budapest: CEU Press, 2014).

Niederhauser, Emil. *Eastern Europe in Recent Hungarian Historiography* (Budapest: Akadémiai Kiadó, 1975).

Niederhauser, Emil. *The Rise of Nationality in Eastern Europe* (Budapest: Corvina, 1981).

Plokhy, Serhii. *Ukraine and Russia: Representations of the Past* (Toronto: University of Toronto Press, 2008).

Pollo, Stefanaq, and Arben Puto. *The History of Albania from Its Origins to the Present Day*, trans. Carol Wiseman, and Ginnie Hole (London: Routledge & Kegan Paul, 1981).

Roubal, Petr, and Václav Veber, eds. *Prague Perspectives I: The History of East Central Europe and Russia* (Prague: Národní knihovna ČR, 2004).

Rubin, Miri, ed. *The Work of Jacques Le Goff and the Challenges of Medieval History* (Woodbridge: The Boydell Press, 1997).

Schlieper, H.C., ed. *Eastern Europe: Historical Essays Presented to Professor Milos Mladenovic on His Sixty-Fifth Birthday by His Students* (Toronto: New Review Books, 1969).

Schneider, Axel, and Daniel Woolf, eds. *The Oxford History of Historical Writing*, vol. 5, *Historical Writing since 1945* (Oxford: Oxford University Press, 2011).

Smith, Graham, Vivien Law, Andrew Wilson, Annette Bohr, and Edward Allworth. *Nation-Building in the Post-Soviet Borderlands: The Politics of National Identities* (Cambridge: Cambridge University Press, 1998).

Subtelny, Orest. *Ukraine: A History* (Toronto: University of Toronto Press, 1988).

Sygkelos, Yannis. *Nationalism from the Left: The Bulgarian Communist Party during the Second World War and the Early Post-War Years* (Leiden: Brill, 2011).

Trencsényi, Balázs. *The Politics of 'National Character': A Study in Interwar East European Thought* (London: Routledge, 2012).

Vardy, Steven Bela. *Modern Hungarian Historiography* (New York: Columbia University Press, 1976).

Verdery, Katharine. *National Ideology under Socialism: Identity and Cultural Politics in Ceauşescu's Romania* (Berkeley, CA: University of California Press, 1991).

Yekelchyk, Serhy. *Stalin's Empire of Memory: Russian-Ukrainian Relations in the Soviet Historical Imagination* (Toronto: University of Toronto Press, 2004).

Yeomans, Rory. *Visions of Annihilation: The Ustasha Regime and the Cultural Politics of Fascism, 1941–1945* (Pittsburgh, PA: University of Pittsburgh Press, 2012).

Zeidler, Miklós. *Ideas on Territorial Revision in Hungary 1920–1945*, trans. Thomas J. DeKornfeld, and Helen DeKornfeld (Wayne, NJ: Center for Hungarian Studies, 2007).

5

NATIONALIZATION VS. SECULARIZATION

The Christian churches in East Central Europe

John Connelly

As societies become modern, people stop going to church. Until recently this seemed a generally valid statement about what happens when populations become urban, educated and wealthy. In fact, this idea relied upon studies of Western Europe, places where Christian churches are churches of state, as in Sweden, England and Scotland. In these countries, the church became so bound to establishment interests as to appear venal and partisan rather than religious and universal; first it lost favour with the middle classes, then the urban working classes, and then it sacrificed its social importance, as witnessed in declines in religious practice as well as belief in a personal God.[1]

Recent studies have cast doubt upon the general validity of these findings. The United States, for example, is unquestionably modern and secularized, but features a buoyant religious life, reflected in church attendance that seems shockingly high by European

---

1 Hugh McLeod, *Secularisation in Western Europe, 1848–1914* (New York: St. Martin's Press, 2000), 4; Steve Bruce, *God is Dead: Secularization in the West* (Oxford: Blackwell, 2002). This article uses the understanding of secularization prominent among American sociologists of religion: it denotes the 'decline of religious beliefs and practices among individuals'. See José Casanova, 'Rethinking Secularization: A Global Comparative Perspective', *The Hedgehog Review* 8, nos. 1–2 (2006): 9. For overviews of the literature see David Martin, *On Secularization: Towards a Revised General Theory* (Farnham: Ashgate, 2005); Detlef Pollack, Olaf Müller and Gert Pickel, introduction to *The Social Significance of Religion in the Enlarged Europe*, eds Detlef Pollack, Olaf Müller and Gert Pickel (Farnham: Ashgate, 2012), 1–26; Brian Porter-Szűcs, 'Christianity, Christians, and the Story of Modernity in Eastern Europe', in *Christianity and Modernity in Eastern Europe*, eds Brian Porter-Szűcs and Bruce Berglund (Budapest: CEU Press, 2010), 1–34. On the erosion and differentiation of secularization theory even among its proponents in the past two decades see Detlef Pollack, 'Varieties of Secularization Theory and their Indispensable Core', *Germanic Review* 90 (2015): 60–79. Further complications arise from the question of whether religious traditions themselves do not undergo self-secularization, for example during the Protestant Reformation, and the degree to which churches manage to 'collude' with secular institutions, for example in science or politics. See Casanova, 'Rethinking Secularization', 10–11.

Nationalization vs. secularization

standards.[2] It is not an exception. The economist L. R. Iannaccone has found that countries with competing churches feature higher percentages of populations believing in God, Heaven and Hell. In multi-religious societies like the United States, 'markets' for religions, with little state regulation, stimulate demand by catering to personal 'spiritual' needs.[3] By contrast, official state churches seem to suffocate religiosity.[4] The question is whether Western Europe and North America constitute models or whether these are but two constellations among multiple modernities.[5]

Because it lay beyond the Iron Curtain, and because of the multiplicity of languages spoken there, East Central Europe – the nation states between Russia and Germany – remains mostly uncovered territory in studies of secularization, an unperceived and thus unlamented victim of (West)Euro-centrism.[6] But a superficial glance shows that this region does not conform to patterns that have emerged in North America or Western Europe.

In the Christian Orthodox east, historical churches remain popular and vibrant, even if church attendance is low. Numbers of Romanians or Serbs fulfilling the most basic requirements of belief, saying they believe in God and belong to their religious communities, are far higher than in Western Europe. Yet in contrast to the United States, these societies do not present long lists of 'consumer' choices for religion that might fit individual tastes, and despite the influx of Western cults after 1989, they remain largely mono-religious. Why has religion weathered the challenges of modernization in these places? Indeed: how has it withstood several generations of atheist states bent upon driving religion out of the public sphere altogether?

One response would point to Christianity's ability to lay claims to personal and group identity; for many, being Serb or Bulgarian or Romanian implies being Serb or Bulgarian or

---

2 This is the paradox noted by Tocqueville of the co-existence and mutual reinforcement of the religious and secular or 'worldly': 'not only do the Americans practice their religion out of self-interest, but they often even place in this world the interest which they have in practicing it'. They approached religion, in John Diggins' formulation, as a proposition that could 'well pay off'. Tocqueville quoted in John Diggins, *The Lost Soul of American Politics* (Chicago, IL: University of Chicago Press, 1984), 252.

3 Studies emphasizing the role of individual choice in multi-religious societies as bolstering each 'option' are sometimes called 'supply side', featuring competitive and open markets for religion. See for instance Rodney Stark and Laurence R. Iannoccone, 'A Supply-Side Reinterpretation of the "Secularization" of Europe', *Journal for the Scientific Study of Religion* 33 (1992): 230–52; Steve Bruce, 'The Supply-Side Model of Religion: The Nordic and Baltic States', *Journal for the Scientific Study of Religion* 39, no. 1 (2000): 32–46. See also the discussion with sources in Pollack, Müller and Pickel, introduction to *The Social Significance of Religion*.

4 Anca Cojoc, 'After the Fall: The Impact of Government Regulation on Church Attendance in Eastern Europe, 1990–2004', *Public Choice* 142 (2010): 485–96.

5 The idea of multiple modernities goes back to S.N. Eisenstadt, who noted that Max Weber equated modernity with the decline of the unquestioned legitimacy of a divinely ordained social order. That idea was based on Western experience; contemporary religious movements 'seek to engage in a selective denial' of some premises of Western modernity and celebrate their own traditions, denying a Western monopoly on modernity. See S.N. Eisenstadt, 'Multiple Modernities', *Daedalus* 29, no. 1 (2000): 1–29, here 22. In José Casanova's productive formulation, this idea draws attention to the ways in which 'all traditions and civilizations are radically transformed in the processes of modernization, but they also have the possibility of shaping in particular ways the institutionalization of modern traits. Traditions are forced to respond and adjust to modern conditions, but in the process of reformulating their traditions for modern contexts, they also help to shape the particular forms of modernity.' Casanova, 'Rethinking Secularization', 12–14.

6 We see this, for example, when Casanova discusses 'European secularization' and 'the exceptional character of European religious developments' and has in mind Western Europe only; more accurately: he permits Western Europe to speak for all of Europe. See Casanova, 'Rethinking Secularization', 14–15.

257

Romanian Orthodox. In much of the region, religion intersects with nationalism and the two become coterminous, evidently strengthening both sides of the equation. According to Rogers Brubaker, religious and national cults constitute sources 'of identifying oneself and others, of construing sameness and difference, and of situating and placing oneself in relation to others' as well as 'powerful frameworks of imagining community'.[7] The trend extends to Poland, Croatia, Slovenia and Slovakia, traditionally Roman Catholic societies where adherence to the norms and rituals of an institutional Christian church is strong because they have become entwined with national identity.

But that is only the beginning of the story. Though the Czech lands and Hungary have been historically mostly Roman Catholic – which they share with Poland and Croatia – they conform more to the trends witnessed in Northern and Western Europe. Church congregations are tiny, institutional affiliation is exceptional, and remarkably, numbers of atheists are high by international standards at 61 and 46 per cent in the Czech lands and Hungary respectively. Yet we know that national sentiment is no less strong in these places and that the history of the 'nation' in these places has been – arguably – bound tightly to that of the local church. In most of the region, the medieval foundations of statehood coincided with the entry of Christianity, and in all cases major saints are also national heroes, for example St Stephan, St Hedwig and St Wenceslas.[8]

The question follows as to why some nationalisms find Christianity a hospitable space to grow and prosper and others do not. How is it that some local nationalisms failed to enter into the Christian churches? Why are Czechs and Hungarians, though they live in similarly modern environments, more likely to reject Christianity than Poles and Serbs? Until recently, students of nationalism like Ernest Gellner or Eric Hobsbawm – themselves native to Central Europe – assumed that nationalism as a modern ideology had to displace religion.[9] That has not happened. But when there is a contradiction between church and nation, which side prevails and why?

A comparative study of religion in Eastern Europe can sharpen our understanding of both secularization and nationalization and the relation between the two. It also adds a historical dimension that has been absent in studies of secularization, which tend to register differences between countries, but not explain them historically. It also helps us break the blinkered perspective of studies that portray the West as the entire continent, a perspective exemplified by José Casanova's astonishment at the 'exceptional character of *European* secularization' and his question as to why

> national churches, once they ceded to the secular nation-state their traditional histori-cal function as community cults – that is, as collective representations of the imagined national communities and carriers of the collective memory – also lost in the process their ability to function as religions of individual salvation.[10]

---

7 They provide a 'set of schemas, templates and metaphors for making sense of the social world as well as supramundane worlds'. Rogers Brubaker, 'Religion and Nationalism: Four Approaches', *Nations and Nationalism* 18, no. 1 (2012): 4.

8 Exceptions: Romania, Slovakia, Slovenia, Macedonia, so-called non-historic nations (Friedrich Engels). Historic eastern Hungarian regions, Transylvania in particular, were home to vibrant Protestant churches.

9 Eric J. Hobsbawm, *Nations and Nationalism since 1780* (Cambridge: Cambridge University Press, 1992); Ernest Gellner, *Nations and Nationalism* (Ithaca, NY: Cornell University Press, 1983).

10 Casanova, 'Rethinking Secularization', 15 (emphasis added).

A look beyond the Elbe and Leitha rivers shows this is not *the* European story.

Adding to the puzzle is that just prior to the foundation of national states, the supposed leaders of national movements – intellectuals – were hostile to religion, including in Poland and Serbia. Just the same, some organized churches fully reciprocated the suspicion. The Catholic Church, for example, considered nationalism a modern heresy. Religion and nationalism seemed to repel each other, and symbiosis was hardly imaginable. An exception was the Czech Tomáš G. Masaryk, ethnic nationalist extraordinaire, but also a devout if unorthodox Christian. Yet the nation state he helped craft, today's Czech Republic, is perhaps the most atheistic on the continent.

The religious origins of East Central Europe's nationalism

For answers, we have to look to the time when the region's idea of nationhood came into being, namely the late eighteenth century. The story is not so much 'Eastern European' as 'East Rhenish'. As proposed in the early work of Rogers Brubaker, European understandings of the nation were divided between 'Western' and 'Eastern European' by the western boundaries of Germany.[11] The former, comprising citizens possessing equal rights, was 'civic', and the latter, a community sharing language and culture and a common myth of origin, 'ethnic'. The two overlap in certain ways but are also distinct.[12] Interesting for historians of nationalism and religion are two things: that the primogenitors of the Central and Eastern European ideas of the nation were Protestant theologians; and that, like nationalists everywhere, they formed their ideas out of a sense of humiliation: they were Germans of lower social background humiliated by leading French Enlightenment thinkers who were counts, barons and high clergy.[13] From the start, this kind of nationalism detested ethnic others: both who they were and what they thought.[14]

A good person to start with is Johann Georg Hamann, a now obscure Pietistic Protestant who had close ties to Immanuel Kant. What bothered him was the alienation of French thinkers from actual human history. In his view, their ideas abstracted life, missing the essence that lay in the particular. Hamann was especially troubled by the French idea that language was replicable and not unique. Attacking the rationalism of the enlightenment in favour of individual self-expression, he rejected the tendency to raise reason above all modes of human perception. He believed it was neither the only mode of thinking nor the most revealing.[15]

These ideas structured the thought of Hamann's influential pupil, Johann Gottfried Herder, a student of theology who became an admired preacher at the cathedral in Riga and the court in

---

11 Rogers Brubaker, *Citizenship and Nationhood in France and Germany* (Cambridge, MA: Harvard University Press, 1992). Earlier students of nationhood had popularized the division of Western and Eastern nationalism. For a critical discussion, see Krzysztof Jakułowski, 'Western (Civic) "versus" Eastern (Ethnic) Nationalism: The Origins and Critique of the Dichotomy', *Polish Sociological Review* 3, no. 171 (2010): 289–303.

12 Ethnic nationalism was an addition to the civic models coming from France, mediated via the influence of German Enlightenment and Romantic philosophy.

13 Isaiah Berlin wrote: 'Lessing, Kant, Herder, Fichte were all very humbly born. Hegel, Schelling, Schiller, Hölderlin were lower middle-class.' *The Roots of Romanticism* (Princeton, NJ: Princeton University Press, 1999), 38.

14 This contrasts with Brian Porter-Szűcs' idea that nationalism 'began to hate' in the late nineteenth century. I argue it was in the DNA of east Rhenish ethnic nationalism. See Brian Porter-Szűcs, *When Nationalism Began to Hate* (Oxford: Oxford University Press, 2000).

15 Berlin, *The Roots of Romanticism*, 40–6.

Weimar. In fact, he was so impressive on a visit to Rome that the Vatican Propaganda Secretary Stefano Borgia humorously introduced him to fellow cardinals in 1788 as the 'Archbishop of Saxony Weimar'.[16] After his death in 1803, Herder became the source of inspiration for nationalists throughout Central and Eastern Europe all the way to the Russian border.

Herder taught that God carried out his will through many peoples with their specific cultures. Their languages were not secondary by-products of historical development, let alone jargons spoken by illiterate peasants, but holy repositories 'of tradition, history, religion, and principles of life'.[17] Like Hamann, he insisted on the unique, untranslatable quality of each people's tongue. This gave a basis for Herder's idea that every culture was the 'authentic expression of its speakers'. According to Anthony D. Smith, 'this idea of uniqueness, along with a certain emotionalism, was the legacy of pietism to nationalism'.[18]

In Herder's view, states existed for 'the sake of peoples – nations – and not the other way around'. 'Just as God tolerates all the languages of the world', he wrote, 'so should a ruler not only tolerate, but also honour the different languages of his people.'[19] Extraordinary is how one man's ideas could influence the thinking of the intellectual classes of half a continent.[20] In 1830, the German poet Johann Wolfgang von Goethe said that 'Herder's ideas have gone so deeply into mass consciousness that few who read them in our day will find them enlightening.' His thoughts 'had been borrowed so extensively by many thousands of others that they seemed commonsensical.'[21] Goethe meant Europe east of the Rhine: amazingly, Herder's history was just then being translated into French.

In the lands with Slavic-speaking populations, intellectuals seemed to plagiarize Herder's ideas because they served as a useful ideology for nation-building.[22] The sense of belonging they propagated, Anthony D. Smith tells us, relied upon the religious mythology of chosen nations,

---

16 Technically he was Protestant superintendent; this according to Friedrich Schiller. Martin Kessler, 'Herders Kirchenamt in Sachsen-Weimar', in *Johann Gottfried Herder: Aspekte eines Lebenswerkes*, eds Martin Kessler and Volker Leppin (Berlin: de Gruyter, 2005), 327–51.

17 Anthony D. Smith, *Chosen Peoples: Sacred Sources of National Identity* (Oxford: Oxford University Press, 2003), 45.

18 Ibid.

19 Cited in Hugh LeCaine Agnew, *Origins of the Czech National Renascence* (Pittsburgh, PA: University of Pittsburgh Press, 1993), 64.

20 Maria Ciesla-Korytowska claims that Herder 'himself constituted a turning point in the history of cognition, introducing feelings into the "philosophical field as a gnosiological category"'. She continues: 'Undoubtedly, already in Rousseau's writings and novels we find certain elements of future Romantic theory of cognition based on feelings and intuition.' 'On Romantic Cognition', in *Romantic Poetry*, ed. Angela Esterhammer (Amsterdam: John Benjamins, 2002), 39–54, here 40–1.

21 J.W. Goethe, introduction to Thomas Carlyle, *Leben Schillers* (Frankfurt a.M.: Heinrich Wilmans, 1830), ix. Goethe is referring specifically to Herder's *Ideen zur Philosophie der Geschichte der Menschheit*.

22 Enthusiasts included Slovaks Pavel Josef Šafárik and Jan Kollár, Slovene and Czech linguists Jernej Kopitar and Joseph Dobrovský, and leading Polish awakeners like Wawrzyniec Surowiecki or Kazimierz Brodziński. T.G. Masaryk called Herder *Praeceptor Slavorum*. He also deeply influenced leading Romantic figures in Poland like the historian Joachim Lelewel. Tadeusz Namowicz, *Johann Gottfried Herder: z zagadnień przełomu oświecenia w Niemczech w drugiej połowie XVIII wieku* [Johann Gottfried Herder: the Enlightenment in Germany in the second half of the eighteenth century] (Olsztyn: Ośrodek Badań Nauk. im. Wojciecha Kętrzyńskiego, 1995); Monika Baár, *Historians and Nationalism: East-Central Europe in the Nineteenth Century* (Oxford: Oxford University Press, 2010), 111; Alice Gérard, 'M. Serejski, Joachim Lelewel, traduction française', *Annales. Économies, Sociétés, Civilisations* 20, no. 6 (1965): 1288–91. On Mickiewicz and Herder see Vejas Liulevicius, *The German Myth of the East* (Oxford: Oxford University Press, 2009), 59.

Nationalization vs. secularization

which is bound up with claims to particular terrains and urges to recover lost 'communal heroism and creativity, and to pave the way to fulfilment of higher destinies, through the regenerative power of mass and individual sacrifice.'[23]

Thus, unlike French nationalism, the Central and Eastern European variety emerged not among enlightened doubters, atheists, or deists, but among fervent Christians. The national awakeners in the Czecho-Slavic or Southern Slavic lands shared Herder's priestly personality and the desire to preach to others, to guard what was holy and to redeem souls as well as peoples. Czech linguist Josef Jungmann had wanted to be a priest but became an academic instead, and his friend Dobrovský was a priest who had wanted to be a missionary. The Slovak poet Ján Kollár acted as minister to a Protestant congregation at Pest and his friend, the South Slav patriot Josip Juraj Strossmayer, was a bishop in Đakovo. Ante Starčević, the founder of modern Croatian nationalism, had studied theology in preparation for the priesthood.[24] The fathers of the Czech nation, historian František Palacký and sociologist Tomáš G. Masaryk, were devout Protestants, and the national movements in Croatia, Slovenia and Slovakia were led by priests.

These early patriots did not think that national communities of feeling would replace religious communities of belief. Reminiscent of the ancient doctrine of two realms, they thought the religious legitimated the secular and that without the religious, the secular had no legitimacy.[25] As it began to enter into the Orthodox world, Eastern European nationalism was never separate from religion. It underwent a period of dynamic growth at German universities shortly after Herder's death and was then spread to every corner of East Central Europe by his Slavic disciples. And here the exception proves the rule. Hungarians were not 'Slavic', but became obsessed with Herder because he had predicted Hungary would be devoured by a Slavic and Germanic onslaught and disappear without a trace.[26] This horror scenario gave even greater impetus to Magyar patriots in their famous nation-creating activities – writing dictionaries, translating dramas, producing historical narratives and building schools in the vast non-Hungarian-speaking areas of the Hungarian Kingdom.

This common background casts the differences in Eastern Europeans' nationhood and religiosity in bold relief. Although the thought of Herder was constitutive and vital everywhere in various ways, the nexus of religion and nation remained strong in some places, weak in others.

The older scholarship tends to speak of nationalism as a 'replacement religion'. However, it did not replace religion as an institution. Scholars now invoke various kinds of symbiosis: interpenetration, overlapping, ways in which two systems of belief strengthen each other. There is no general theory that says that they tend to weaken each other, but there are times when the national appears to supersede or displace religion.[27] In some places, Christianity withered while nationalism remained strong. The following section seeks to analyze cases in which religion as part of the symbiosis declined and ceased to be relevant, as in the Czech lands, leaving in its wake impressive populations of non-believers.

---

23 Smith, *Chosen Peoples*, 254–5.

24 Milan Šarić, 'Život i rad dra Ante Starčevića' [Life and work of Dr Ante Starčević], *Hrvatska misao: smotra za narodno gospodarstvo, knjizevnost* 1 (1902): 133.

25 Martin Schulze Wessel, introduction to *Die Nationalisierung der Religion und der Sakralisierung der Nation im östlichen Europa*, ed. Martin Schulze Wessel (Stuttgart: Steiner Verlag, 2006), 7–14, here 9.

26 Iván Zoltán Dénes, 'Political Vocabularies of the Hungarian Liberals and Conservatives', in *Liberty and the Search for Identity*, ed. Iván Zoltán Dénes (Budapest: CEU Press, 2006), 155–96, here 173.

27 Martin Schulze Wessel, 'Religion und Nationalismus in der Geschichte Tschechiens und der Slowakei', in *Religion und Nation: Tschechen, Deutsche, und Slowaken im 20. Jahrhundert*, eds Kristina Kaiserova, Eduard Niznansky and Martin Schulze Wessel (Essen: Klartext, 2015), 8–9.

John Connelly

Religion in national movements

Symbiosis is too weak a word. Christian narratives and institutions provided a structure that could sustain and nourish national identities. Some historians have even written that Eastern Europeans did not need Herder to tell them 'who they were', highlighting the significance of the Serbian national movement (and also of early nineteenth-century Polish elites, whose traditions of statehood were within living memory).[28] The Serb national movement, like all others, depended on the efforts of linguists and historians to give it form, but it inherited a national mythology buttressed on Christianity from a much earlier time.

First was the Kosovo myth, a set of ideas kept alive in folk poetry and sung over centuries among mostly illiterate peasants. According to the myth, the Serb prince Lazar had preferred to die for a 'heavenly kingdom' in the struggle with the Ottomans at Kosovo Polje in 1389 rather than live for earthly riches. This myth clearly defined the identity and cohesiveness of the Serb people, even if the geographic boundaries of a future state were not yet evident.[29] In the seventeenth century, Ottoman rule seemed unending, but tradition assured Serbs it was temporary. The epic poems, sung in the intimacy of long winter evenings, told them they were Christian and 'virtuous' while the occupiers and local Muslims – called 'Turks' though Slavic speaking – lived from others' labour and practised deceit.

Second was the institution that gave visible form to Serbian nationhood, namely the Serbian Orthodox Church, which persisted through centuries of Ottoman rule and kept the idea of a glorious past alive. The Patriarchate of Peć, a self-governing (autocephalous) branch of the Orthodox Church under the Patriarch of Constantinople, referred to the territory under its ecclesiastical jurisdiction as the 'Serbian lands'. Like the Patriarchate of Constantinople, it held to the idea that Ottoman rule was temporary.[30] Some of the church's 58 saints, depicted in icons, had been kings and queens and princes and lords, and they were never forgotten by Serbian peasants.

Thanks to Serbian Orthodoxy and epic tales, literacy, normally a breakthrough point for national consciousness, was less important in Serbia. Regardless of whether they could read or write, Serbs knew they were Serbs, and they expected a large state in the event of independence.[31] In 1809, the revolutionary Karađorđe Petrović said:

> Twice the hopes of Kosovo Christians were dashed that they would once again govern their own lands. But now that almost all Slavic lands of the Turkish empire have been liberated, we hope that the hour of freedom will dawn for Kosovo as well. And there will perhaps still be bloody wars for the sake of this important piece of land. For whoever has Kosovo, that one will be lord of the Balkan peninsula.[32]

In Slovakia (North Hungary), Slovenia (Carynthia, Carniola) and Croatia with its Dalmatian lands, the nationalist movements forged bonds with Roman Catholicism, though in the Slovak case the core of the national awakeners consisted of Protestants like Jan Kollár and Pavel Josef

---

28 Michael Boro Petrovich, 'Karadzic and Nationalism', *Serbian Studies* 4, no. 3 (1988): 41–57, here 42.

29 The Serb national movement attempted to recreate the largest Serb state that had existed in the middle ages while claiming as members everyone who spoke the Stokavian dialect, Orthodox or not.

30 Barbara Jelavich, *History of the Balkans*, vol. 1 (Cambridge: Cambridge University Press, 1983), 91–2.

31 Petrovich, 'Karadzic and Nationalism', 42.

32 Quoted in Thomas Emmert, *Serbian Golgotha: Kosovo, 1389* (New York: Columbia University Press, 1990), 207.

Nationalization vs. secularization

Šafárik. There was a Croat nobility with rights and limited self-rule dating back centuries, but what Slovakia, Slovenia and Croatia had in common were illiterate and rural Slavic populations. The vernacular used in Roman Catholic sermons (if not the liturgy) formed the basis of their identity against efforts of Magyar and German states and religious hierarchies to make them Hungarian and German.

By the 1890s, the overlap of religious and national identity was so strong that the major nationalist parties in Slovenia and Slovakia, called 'people's parties', could draw upon the large base of the church to become vehicles for national self-assertion, and they began establishing social programmes as well. They fostered the creation of language schools, but also sought to pool 'Slavic' capital in order to enable the local ethnic element to prosper. This took place against the background of struggles for national independence in Cisleithenia, pushed on by growing literacy and expanded franchise.[33] The Slavic priest, in touch with and dependent upon the vernacular of peasants and their local piety, was set against liberal German and Hungarian-speaking teachers motivated by the aims of their own majority state nationalism. In addition, priests had to contend with the rise of social democracy, which was itself becoming nationalized.[34]

The relation of the Croat peasant movement to Catholicism was more ambivalent. The leaders were largely secular, but like their counterparts in other national movements – including Giuseppe Mazzini in Italy, and later Roman Dmowski in Poland – they recognized the usefulness of Catholic symbolism and rituals for their version of politics. Religion originally had the function of helping peoples resist assimilation by alien powers, but it gained new strength in the fight against secularization and aggressive de-nationalization. Writing about a later period, Stella Alexander claims:

> It is nationalism that feeds religious feeling while the churches cling desperately to their role as guardians of the soul of the nation. This has recently been vividly illustrated in Croatia where the Catholic Church has been celebrating thirteen hundred years of Catholicism ... with processions and pilgrimages. It is difficult to see how these two historical events [first bishopric at Niš in the seventh century; Croatian link to Rome from 879] are linked in any except a romantic sense to the more recent history of the Croats but the church has attempted to transform them into a symbol of the identity of Catholicism with the Croatian people.[35]

The Slovak and South Slav movements were inspired by the Czech national movement, which became a model for unifying ethnic groups lacking nationally conscious elites and native

---

33 In Hungary, the franchise remained limited, partly in concern over the ethnically foreign element. Thus, in 1910 only 6.4 per cent of the population in Hungary could vote. See Tibor Frank, 'Hungary and the Dual Monarchy', in *A History of Hungary*, eds Peter F. Sugar, Péter Hanák and Tibor Frank (Bloomington, IN: Indiana University Press, 1990), 252–66, here 263.

34 Ulfried Burz, 'Die katholische Kirche in der Habsburgermonarchie und die südslawische Frage: Vom Völkerfrühling zum Völkerwinter (1848–1914)', in *Cirkvi a narody strednej Europy (1800–1950)*, eds Peter Švorc, Ľubica Harbuľová and Karl Schwarz (Prešov: Universum, 2008), 271–80, here 277–9. Of the Slovak national intelligentsia active between 1780 and 1848, well over half were either Catholic priests or Protestant pastors. See Roman Holec, 'Problémy vzťahu' cirkev – národ – štat v dlhom 19. storočí a rok 1918' [Problems of the relationship between church, people, and state in the long nineteenth century and 1918], in Švorc, Harbuľová and Schwarz, *Cirkvi a narody strednej Europyi*, 36–56.

35 Stella Alexander, 'Religion and National Identity in Yugoslavia', *Studies in Church History* 18 (1983): 591–607.

cultural institutions. Over the course of the nineteenth century, Czech national awakeners had made Czech-speakers strong enough – in terms of education, self-assertiveness, administrative expertise and economic wealth – to form a full range of political parties and ultimately build a Czech state. Leaders of the Slovene, Croat and Slovak movements studied in Prague after Czech faculties opened at the university there in 1882.

The relation of the Czech movement to Christian cults was necessary but ambivalent. Both qualities are visible in the writings of the historian František Palacký, whose family had retained its Protestant beliefs over generations of suppression to such an extent that after Joseph II's Tolerance Edict, it unearthed holy books that had been kept buried on family property. In Palacký's interpretation, the greatest achievement of the Czech nation had been the work of the fifteenth-century Hussites, a founding movement of Protestantism unjustly ignored by German historians like Leopold von Ranke. Jan Hus was executed as a heretic, but it was the 'fall of a hero who dies for right and truth'. The Hussites disappeared in time but not in eternity, where they will 'always gleam as a model and mirror as long as humanity exists'.[36] Thus, in keeping with Herder's intuitions, Palacký propagated a quasi-religious mission for his nation, justifying it before God and history.

Yet Palacký's own Protestant family's past as a persecuted minority testified to ambivalence: because of a counter-reformation carried out after the defeat of the mostly Protestant Czech nobility at White Mountain in 1620, Roman Catholicism was the dominant faith in the Czech lands. Part of this counter-reformation was the destruction of thousands of 'heretical' books, which is to say books written in Czech. In 1803, the Bohemian patriot Karel Tham said that a Jesuit missionary had boasted of burning 60,000 Czech language books.[37] To burn books was to kill a people.

Though many early patriots were priests, the Czech movement became not just non-Catholic, but anti-Catholic. As such, it was directed against the existing religious cult practices in the great majority of churches in Bohemia and Moravia. Czech Catholicism tested the patriotism of many Czechs in a way that became unsustainable. Jan Hus, still considered a heretic by the Church four centuries later, was for Czechs both a religious and national patriot. He had even invented the haček diacritical mark. If nationalism east of the Rhine generally arose from a sense of humiliation, here it stood in the oppressive shadow not only of a 'foreign' (though native) people – the Germans – but also of the Roman Catholic Church. The Czech national movement portrayed Catholicism as serving a foreign state.[38] The closest approximation may have been the presence of Islam in Serbia or Orthodoxy in Russian Poland, but there the local population had not been forced to practise those religions.

On top of this came a ferocious battle among the Czech political elite of the 1870s between liberal secularism and political Catholicism.[39] Tomáš G. Masaryk, the later first Republic's founder and 'symbol' who was born Catholic, had been critical of the Church for neglecting

---

36 Joseph Zacek, *Palacký: The Historian as Scholar and Nationalist* (The Hague: Mouton, 1970), 87.

37 This was Antonín Koniáš, himself a Bohemian. Karel Ignaz Tham, *Über den Charakter der Slawen, dann über den Ursprung, die Schicksale, Vollkommenheiten, und die Nützlichkeit und Wichtigkeit der böhmische Sprache* (Prague, 1803), 13.

38 Jiří Hanuš, *Tradice českého katolicismu ve 20. století* [Traditions of Czech Catholicism] (Brno: Center for the Study of Democracy and Culture, 2005), 54.

39 Yet as a result the anti-clericals did not leave the Church; instead, they became nominal Catholics who no longer practised the faith. See Martin Schulze Wessel, 'Konfessionelle Konflikte in der Ersten Tschechoslowakischen Republik: Zum Problem des Status von Konfessionen im Nationalstaat', in *Religion im Nationalstaat zwischen den Weltkriegen 1918–1939: Polen – Tschechoslowakei – Ungarn – Rumänien*, eds Hans-Christian Maner and Martin Schulze Wessel (Stuttgart: Steiner, 2002), 73–102, here 77.

the ethical functions of religion and praised the heroes of the Czech national movement – Kollár, Palacký and Havlíček – for their idea that religion was the core of the Czech national character. He claimed that the Czech question itself was a 'religious' question, raised against the theocratic absolutism of the Habsburgs.[40] Thus, if the movement was anti-clerical, it was not anti-religious: indeed, it became a kind of religion itself, with cults, saints, symbols and rituals; Palacký and Masaryk became more revered than any Catholic prelate.

When Masaryk's state was founded in 1918, the result was a numerically strong Catholicism as a 'cultural minority' in a largely secular Czech society.[41] Attendance at Mass varied by region: high in cities and small towns, moderate in bourgeois neighbourhoods of cities but approaching non-existence in industrial areas.[42] Cities were places where socialist and other anti-clerical messages were widely and freely propagated.

The question for the new state was whether people would follow Masaryk's lead and not simply reject Catholicism, but also become worshippers in a Czechoslovak national church created by renegade Catholic priests. Among the first acts of the patriots was to knock down a pillar topped by the Virgin Mary in Prague's Old Town Square in October 1918 while singing patriotic songs and shouting, 'down with tyranny'. Masaryk said the column symbolized 'political humiliation' and the destruction of the democratic Czech nation.[43] Since its unveiling in 1915, a modernist sculpture of Jan Hus has dominated Prague's Old Town Square.

In Poland, just hours by train to the northeast, destroying a statue of Mary would have seemed blasphemy, not just against the Church, but against the nation. On 1 April 1656, after defeating the Swedes in battle, King Jan Kazimierz, in the company of Poland's bishops and in the presence of the Papal legate, declared Mary 'Queen of Poland' in the Cathedral at Lviv. The Virgin was taken to have assured a miraculous victory against the Swedes at Częstochowa the previous year. The papacy permitted this cult to flourish because Poland promoted the Counter-Reformation, in this case against Protestant Scandinavia. Roman Catholicism could unite Poles against neighbours to the south and east as well, who were Muslim and Orthodox (until the Second Partition of 1772, Poland bordered the Ottoman Empire).

But Catholicism's relation to Polish nationalism was ambivalent. The Church did not endorse reforms of the Polish state in the late eighteenth century or the independence movements of the nineteenth. Tsar Alexander I supported Catholicism in the Polish lands he controlled after the Congress of Vienna in 1815 as part of his idea of creating a Third Rome, a place of cross-denominational Christian rebirth after the French Revolution. If anything, it was enlightened Polish elites who wanted to place the Church under closer state supervision when they drew up a constitution for the Kingdom of Warsaw.[44] Up through the 1820s, the Church hierarchy

---

40 Czechs were natural democrats. See Schulze Wessel, 'Konfessionelle Konflikte', 82. As late as 1934, Masaryk described Catholicism as the 'worst enemy of our dear people'. Ibid., 83.

41 Ibid., 80.

42 Church attendance broke down almost completely in Plzeň during the First World War, while maintaining about 50 per cent in bourgeois areas (Vinohrady) of Prague. Schulze Wessel, 'Konfessionelle Konflikte', 78.

43 Nancy M. Wingfield, *Flag Wars and Stone Saints: How the Bohemian Lands Became Czech* (Cambridge, MA: Harvard University Press, 2007), 147. The monuments were of figures like John Nepomuk and Joseph II. In all, 273 cases of monument destruction were recorded by January 1921. See also Schulze Wessel, 'Konfessionelle Konflikte', 86.

44 This was a liberal programme inherited from Jansenism. Hanna Kowalska-Stus, 'Polskaya katolicheskaya Tserkov' v politicheskich planach Aleksandra I' [The Polish Catholic Church in the political plans of Alexander I], *Roczniki humanistyczne* 7 (2013): 149–60.

enjoyed the favour of the monarchy, but matters worsened under Nicholas I, especially after the 1830–31 uprising. Nicholas was determined to Russify the Poles for their own good and made his Polish lands an indivisible part of the Russian Empire. Polish institutions of higher learning were closed, church lands were secularized and the clergy given fixed salaries.[45] In 1839, he did away with the Uniate Church (an Eastern rite church in Union with Rome) and began limiting the numbers of Catholic churches allowed while promoting Orthodoxy. After the failed uprising of 1863, most religious orders were closed, and hundreds of priests sent to Siberia. Similarly, the Prussian state attempted to limit the role of Polish Catholicism. The trajectory was the opposite in the Austrian partition, where Catholicism suffered Josephinian restrictions in the late eighteenth century but settled into a position of privilege after the mid-1800s.

In most of the Polish lands, the Church thus came to be seen as a persecuted Polish institution, and patriotic literature took on religious themes as well. In the villages where the great majority of Polish-speakers lived, priests were the source of authority, and in contrast to the population at large tended to be educated.[46] Within the independence movement, even those who opposed clericalism 'connected progressive and patriotic thought with Catholicism'. And even those who resented the conservative papacy for its failure to support the Polish cause still insisted that religion should serve as the foundation of all values of the nation.[47]

Catholicism was considered an important part of Polish tradition, with the Polish nation understood in 'primordial' terms. But Polish Catholicism was of a very 'special kind': it was generally tolerant, respected freedom and did not persecute people of other faiths. This was how Poles during the Partitions defended their claim to stand among the nations of Europe. A symbiosis was imagined. Writing in the 1840s, the Republican patriot Józef Ordęga repeated Herder's idea that even before Christianity was established, Poles had been a Slavic civilization based on love of justice and love of one's neighbour, but that only with the coming of Christianity had Poland become a nation. In the 1870s, the writer and painter Józef Ignacy Kraszewski claimed that over its thousand-year history, Poland had always been Catholic and that it owed its very civilization to Catholicism, but also that tolerance was part of the national character: It was 'never fanatical', he claimed. He thought Austrian Catholicism was corrupted by materialism, while the more genuine Polish version had managed to maintain faith in its pure form.[48]

But Catholicism was not simply a force for repelling challenges from the outside: it also promoted European unity. Through Catholic ideas and culture the peoples of Europe could be united, some patriots argued, leaving Poland the mission of keeping peace.[49] In contrast to other European nations that remained passive, patriots claimed that Poland's willingness to sacrifice in armed uprisings was evidence of its Christian heroism and martyrdom.

Catholicism's usefulness extended across different social groups and different types of patriotism. The poet Adam Mickiewicz combined messianic and democratic ideas in his notion of patriotism. After the end of the Polish Commonwealth, freemasonry had a large following

---

45 Nicholas V. Riasanovsky, *Nicholas I and Official Nationality in Russia* (Berkeley, CA: University of California Press, 1959), 229.

46 Tadeusz Łepkowski, *Polska: narodziny nowoczesnego narodu, 1764–1870* [Poland: the birth of a modern nation 1764–1870] (Poznań: Wydawnictwo Poznańskiego Towarzystwa Przyjaciół Nauk, 2003), 473–81.

47 Alix Landgrebe, *Wenn es Polen nicht gäbe, dann müsste es erfunden werden: Die Entwicklung des polnischen Nationalbewusstseins im europäischen Kontext* (Wiesbaden: Harrassowitz, 2003), 241.

48 Ibid., 238–9, 242.

49 Ibid., 243.

Nationalization vs. secularization

among Polish elites. And even though they were anathema for the Church hierarchy, the masons found the Church a useful institution.[50] In the late nineteenth century, Poland's intelligentsia, though largely secular, was still more 'Catholic' than elsewhere, especially due to the fact that the Polish Church had been persecuted by foreign occupiers. Intellectuals recognized and praised the common people for their piety. Whatever special gifts lay in the Polish national spirit, they were inseparable from Catholicism. In the end, it became impossible to say whether religious faith determined ideas about the nation or vice versa.

There were regional variations. The Warsaw intelligentsia of the 1880s proved receptive to the western cult of positivism, with science as the 'guarantor of civilizational development, but also the key to satisfying all metaphysical longings and fears of human individuals'.[51] Intellectuals who remained religious were nevertheless critical of both the Church hierarchy and Poland's 'backward' religiosity, which they thought was just one reflection of the societal backwardness they detested. The positivist author Bolesław Prus wrote that people went to church as if to a show, happy that the sacrament of confession took care of all life's difficulties.[52] He thought people were too invested in the idea that God had the 'task' of giving Poles health and riches and of returning freedom to the 'chosen people'. The Church, for its part, looked upon positivist and liberal ideas with deep scepticism. But in Austrian-controlled Cracow, the intelligentsia was more conservative and closer to the Church, and the clergy itself was generally more intellectual.[53]

Hungary shows how a secularizing state and liberal establishment could drive the Church to a position of relative social irrelevance, just as leading sociologists of religion once predicted. Similar to France, Christianity in Hungary was divided between the official Catholic Church majority and a small but vitally important Protestant – mostly Calvinist – minority who were more nationalist than Hungary's Catholics. Since the sixteenth century they claimed to stand against Catholic Vienna and appealed to the lower gentry, making the Hungarian-speaking gentry of Transylvania a self-conscious nation. But similar to Poland, Catholicism was tied to the state's medieval foundation. The country's first king, King Stephen I (1001–38), had personally established the dioceses, and from then up until the nineteenth century, the Catholic Church in Hungary was a pillar of Hungarian statehood and culture that enjoyed special privileges.[54]

But with the reign of Habsburg enlightened despot Joseph II, the Hungarian Church took its first blows: the state reduced the clergy to state servants, and the Catholic Church receded as the state took charge of religious education, guaranteed the equality of all Christian faiths and

---

50 Paul Zawadzki, 'Nationalism, Democracy, and Religion', in *Revisiting Nationalism: Theories and Practices*, eds Alain Dieckhoff and Christophe Jaffrelot (London: Hurst, 2005), 165–90, here 171.

51 Magdalena Micińska, *Inteligencja na rozdrożach 1864–1918* [Intelligentsia at the crossroads] (Warsaw: Instytut Historii PAN, 2008), 94–6.

52 Bohdan Cywiński, *Korzenie tożsamości* [The roots of identity] (Rome: Papieski Instytut Studiów Kościelnych, 1982), 63.

53 Micińska, *Inteligencja na rozdrożach*, 94–6.

54 Similar to Croatia and Poland, a view emerged of the Church as a bulwark of Christendom against challenges from the East. See Norbert Spannenberger, 'Die katholische Kirche in Ungarn in ihren nationalen und gesellschaftlichen Bedeutungen 1919–1939', in Maner and Wessel, *Religion im Nationalstaat*, 157–76. On the power of the Reformation to create a sense of early modern nationhood among Transylvania's Hungarian speakers, see Louis J. Elteto, 'Reformation Literature and National Consciousness', in *Transylvania: The Roots of Ethnic Conflict*, eds John F. Cadzow, Andrew Ludanyi and Louis J. Elteto (Kent, OH: The Kent State University Press, 1983), 61–70, here 65.

made it easier to leave Catholicism and marry outside it.[55] Within the German and Hungarian lands, the Catholic Church supported the dominant regime while keeping away from nationalist politics, while Hungarian and German-speaking Protestants became staunch nationalists.

The Catholic Church's agnosticism towards the national question combined with the support of the old land-holding elites to help erode popular religiosity. Beyond a few brave priests, Catholic prelates mostly stood on the side-lines during the democratic ferment of 1848–9. But after the Compromise of 1867 that divided the Monarchy, giving the Hungarian gentry control of the eastern half, the Catholic hierarchy was happy to become a pillar of the liberal establishment. Bishops, often of noble background, lived like magnates and lost contact with priests and parishioners, acting to protect the institution's power and wealth. The comfortable clergy also tended to neglect tasks of pastoral work and kept catechesis to an absolute minimum, while colluding in the official policies of Magyarizing Slovak Catholics in seminaries.

There were sumptuously observed feast days, but the population drifted away from church practice: with the end of their formal education, people's contact with the churches withered; participation in the sacraments became a rarity; and often communion taken at holy matrimony was the last sacrament taken before extreme unction. The Hungarian intelligentsia frowned upon public displays of piety as redolent of clericalism, ultramontanism and bigotry, and High Mass was at best an occasion to hear good music and observe fine dress (called 'perfumed mass' – *szagos mise*).[56]

In the reading of one missionary Jesuit who tried to revive Christian practice in interwar Hungary – among other things with appeals to nationalism and anti-Semitism – liberal society had succumbed to practices of freemasonry while dedicating itself to a quest for material affluence. Supposedly, the traumas of the First World War and Hungary's loss of two-thirds of its territory at Trianon again opened hearts for the Church's message, and a symbiosis between nation and Christianity recommenced in earnest on the basis of modern chauvinist ideas.

In national terms, the Calvinist church, strongest in eastern Hungary, was thought to represent the more 'Magyar' church (*confessio Hungarica*); all Calvinists in Hungarian lands were Magyar, in contrast to Catholics, some of whom were Croat, German or Slovak. In 1910, Calvinists made up a quarter of all Magyars.[57] Protestant churches, including Lutherans (about 4 per cent) took an active role in liberal politics, but like Catholics, Protestant pastors neglected to do pastoral work, and impoverished peasants sought solace from the preaching of 'peasant prophets' of various sects (Baptists, Adventists, Jehovah's Witnesses). As in Catholicism, a renewal movement took off in the early twentieth century.[58]

Magyars were dispersed among Christian confessions more than any other Eastern European people, and this fact was recognized as dividing the national movement, making it difficult to identify any particular religion with the nation as such. In the words of the poet Ferenc Kölcsey, this meant that 'inhabitants of the same clod of earth hated each other because they worshiped at different altars'.[59] Hungarian Protestants felt warmer acceptance in Germany and Holland than from Catholics in their own country. Thus, as national feeling burgeoned, pressures grew

---

55 Adriányi believes that such 'liberal' measures weakened the church. Gabriel Adriányi, *Beiträge zur Kirchengeschichte Ungarns* (Munich: Rudolf Trofenik, 1986), 117.

56 Ibid., 123–5.

57 The number had dropped from just over 30 per cent in 1880. Laszlo Katus, 'Die Magyaren', in *Die Habsburgermonarchie*, vol. 3, *Die Völker des Reiches*, eds Adam Wandruszka and Peter Urbanitsch (Vienna: Verlag der österreichischen Akademie der Wissenschaften, 1980), 410–88, here 441.

58 Ibid., 443.

59 Julius von Farkas, *Die ungarische Romantik* (Berlin: de Gruyter, 1931), 93–4.

Nationalization vs. secularization

to reduce these contrasts of culture.[60] In the meantime, liberals and Transylvanian Calvinists were the unquestioned nationalists, and Catholicism suffered.[61]

Despite reform efforts of the interwar years, neither Catholic nor Protestant churches recovered the sympathies of believers. Hungarian Christian churches grew so close to the state that they lacked the resources that might have enabled them to take a critical perspective on Hungarian nationalism.[62] So in the end, here too the powerful and wealthy institution – under conditions of unchallenged hegemony – seemed a servant of establishment interests, which robbed it of opportunities to establish an independent profile.

As we go further south-east, we see Christianity uniting and dividing in different ways. For centuries, Orthodoxy had been one faith under mostly Greek cultural dominance. But after the late eighteenth century, as Ottoman power waned, Romanian, Bulgarian and Serb clergy sought to free themselves from Greek control.[63] This movement from within the churches coincided with the growth of national movements that recreated vernaculars. Serb and Bulgarian Orthodoxy became prime markers of national identity. In Serbia, Orthodoxy had the function of reinforcing claims on territory for a future state that would extend from Kosovo through old Serbia and into Bosnia and Croatia, though as in other places, the national elite was secular and the rare churchgoers among them seemed exotic.

Nikola Pašić, Prime Minister of Serbia and Yugoslavia off and on from 1891 to 1926, prevailed over other progressives who found the village to be a 'relic of barbarism', and argued instead that the Serb people needed institutions to safeguard them against the 'pressure of the West and to bring vitality and advancement to them'. Like Polish liberals, he went on to emphasize the unique virtues of local national Christianity, saying that the Eastern Church, unlike the absolutist Latin one, was a 'democratic and people's church' that brought peace and love, and as such was better able to 'accommodate development, human improvement, innovation and scientific progress'.[64]

In Romania, the Christian confessions were split between the principalities of Moldavia and Wallachia, where the Romanian church had achieved ecclesiastical independence (autocephaly) against the Greek church by the 1870s, and Transylvania, which had both Uniate and Orthodox hierarchies. They did not compete in the way that Catholicism and Protestantism did in the Hungarian lands because both were national churches, even though the Orthodox claimed to be the more original branch, and over time many parishes reverted back to the supposedly pure faith. Still, both constituted backbones of Romanian ethnic identity in Transylvania and continued to do so after the First World War, especially against Catholic and Protestant Germans and Magyars.[65]

---

60 Ibid.

61 Liberalism and Protestantism were mutually reinforcing: 'Calvinist and Lutheran churches in Hungary had enthusiastically embraced nineteenth century liberalism as a guarantor of tolerance.' Paul Hanebrink, 'Christianity, Nation, State: The Case of Christian Hungary', in Berglund and Porter, *Christianity and Modernity in Eastern Europe*, 61–84, here 72.

62 Andreas Nix, *Zivilreligion und Aufklärung: Der zivilreligiöse Strang der Aufklärung* (Berlin: LIT, 2012), 308.

63 Emanuel Turczynski, *Konfession und Nation: Zur Frühgeschichte der serbischen und rumänischen Nationsbildung* (Düsseldorf: Cornelsen, 1976), 135.

64 Diana Mishkova and Roumen Daskalov, '"Forms without Substance": Debates on the Transfer of Western Models to the Balkans', in *Entangled Histories of the Balkans*, vol. 2, eds Diana Mishkova and Roumen Daskalov (Leiden: Brill, 2013), 1–97, here 61.

65 Until the Uniate Church was suppressed. See below.

By the late nineteenth century, patterns in the relationship between religion and nation began to develop across East Central Europe. The most striking aspects are the symbiosis between the two realms, the opportunism that drove the relationship on, and the ways in which nationalism took advantage of elements of religious heritage. But the relationship also could not ignore the deeper history. A number of early Czech patriots like Gelasius Dobner, Bernard Bolzano and Jan Arnold were Roman Catholic priests, yet the emerging movement also took account of a history that included as a hero Jan Hus, a man Rome considered a heretic.[66] And when the historian František Palacký uncovered chapters of counter-reformation history in which native Czech religiosity and the vernacular had been suppressed, the conclusion was that Catholicism was anti-Czech. The movement's response was to connect the national narrative to the very deep history of Hussitism and represent it as embodying something essentially Czech but on the verge of complete eradication.

In the Polish or Serb cases, church institutions had supported elements of a national narrative for centuries. Serb church liturgy spoke of Serb kings. Nevertheless, there were still obstacles. Across the European continent, liberals were devoted to scientific thinking, and the Roman Catholic Church declared nationalism anathema. In all cases, nationalists had what Pieter Judson called 'hard ideological work' in front of them when specifying how nation and religion would relate.[67]

The Hungarian case demonstrates how a Christian institution with significant resources could nevertheless atrophy because it was seen as irrelevant for the national cause, and more particularly because it failed to address social questions. The political success of the 1867 Compromise, guaranteeing Hungary's elite control of the vast Hungarian Kingdom, placed the Church in clear alignment with the powerful and it lost a vital role in a narrative of 'national struggle', which was crucial to Slovene, Croatian, Slovak and Polish Catholicism.

State and religion in the new national states

As an international institution, the Catholic Church tried to stand above competing national ideologies in the cataclysm of the First World War, posing as an impartial mediator among the warring parties. More importantly, it did nothing to alienate one 'Catholic nation' from any other in order not to risk a schism and a weakening of the universal church. These policies continued into the interwar years, when Pope Pius XI (1922–39) knew of the injustice of the French occupation of the German Ruhr (1923), or of Italian aggression in North Africa (1935) but failed to condemn them. The pope worried that open censure of Nazism might cause Hitler to take the Church out of Germany as Henry VIII had taken it out of England.[68]

This supranational policy was not a celebration of any one nation's claims but was a recognition that flawed human nature made conflict and violence inevitable, and that the Church had to be protected across borders as a universal repository of grace. In order not to endanger its

---

66 Franz Leander Fillafer, 'Das Elend der Kategorien: Aufklärung und Josephinismus in der zentraleuropäischen Historiographie, 1918–1945', in *Josephenismus zwischen den Regimen: Eduard Winter, Fritz Valjavec und die zentraleuropäischen Historiographien im 20. Jahrhundert*, eds Franz Leander Fillafer and Thomas Wallnig (Vienna: Böhlau, 2016), 51–101, here 71–4.

67 Pieter Judson, *Guardians of the Nation: Activists on the Language Frontiers of Imperial Austria* (Cambridge, MA: Harvard University Press, 2006), 6.

68 Jacques Kornberg, *The Pope's Dilemma: Pius XII Faces Atrocities and Genocide in the Second World War* (Toronto: University of Toronto Press, 2015), 245.

Nationalization vs. secularization

position in any one nation, it therefore tolerated nationalist readings of Christianity according to which 'clergy everywhere made God a steadfast ally of their own nation at war'.[69]

Thus, we see ambivalence and opportunism in the church hierarchies operating in the nation states created in 1918/19 across East Central Europe, a region that until recently had been governed by divine right monarchies and now stood under unmediated rule of threatening ideologies like republicanism, liberalism and socialism. Socialism roused special fears due to its rooting in atheistic Marxist thought, but liberalism also seemed ill-suited to providing sound order and was reviled for holding doors open to communism.[70] The Catholic Church was less concerned with the fact that liberalism in Germany and Italy had ushered in fascism, yet it stopped short of endorsing 'totalitarianism', a form of government realized in the Soviet Union, but increasingly it seemed, in Nazi Germany as well.[71]

But the new Polish state, though a republic, was also not anti-Catholic or anti-Christian. The state's March 1921 constitution was modelled on the French one but rejected the idea of a complete separation of church and state. It granted religious freedoms, and though not establishing Catholicism as a state religion, did bestow upon the Church the status of *primus inter pares* among organized religions and implied that the church should influence public and private morality. The state agreed not to intervene in matters of church governance or canon law.[72]

Both major political movements, The Polish Socialist Party (and Marshal Piłsudski's *Sanacja*) and Roman Dmowski's National Democracy (*Endecja*), were secular, and both thus stood at some distance from Christianity. Still, both came to an arrangement with the Church. Dmowski, though a natural scientist, recognized that Catholicism constituted the dominant religion and was 'executor of the religious aspects of state life'.[73] And after leading a coup d'état in 1926, former socialist Piłsudski produced a constitution that made the president responsible only to 'God and history' while retaining the leading role of the Catholic Church.[74]

Church leaders warned Piłsudski's successors not to risk a 'struggle' with the Church when the Marshal died in 1935: the prelates worried that the constitution he promulgated shortly before dying, with its strong executive powers and anti-democratic tenor, might endanger the freedom of manoeuvre of the Church and related organizations. Interestingly, it was a right-wing newspaper that instructed the political class that not only the state, but also religion formed the life of the nation; indeed, religion stood above the state.[75] This was not simply a form of recognizing or praising Christianity but was also a latent threat to politicize the Church.

---

69 Ibid., 272, 277.

70 *Mały Dziennik*, 21 March 1937, cited in Edward Wynot, 'The Catholic Church and the Polish State, 1935–1939', *Journal of Church and State* 15, no. 2 (1973): 223–40, here 224.

71 For example: Józef Kobyliński, *Totalizm państwowy ze stanowiska katolickiego. Istota i geneza państwa totalnego* [State totalism from a Catholic standpoint: the essence and genesis of the total state] (Poznań, 1936), cited in Wynot, 'The Catholic Church', 224. On the uncertainty among Polish Catholics about how to respond to the totalitarian challenge see Ronald Modras, *The Catholic Church and Anti-Semitism: Poland 1933–39* (Chur, Switzerland: Harwood Academic Publishers, 1994), 79–87.

72 The church was governed by its own laws. 'Ustawa z dnia 17. Marca 1921' [Law of 21 March 1921], *Dziennik Ustaw*, Poz. 267, Artykułu 114, 654; Wynot, 'The Catholic Church', 225; Neal Pease, *Rome's Most Faithful Daughter* (Athens, OH: Ohio University Press, 2009), 60.

73 Peter D. Stachura, *Poland, 1918–1945: An Interpretative and Documentary History of the Second Republic* (London: Routledge, 2004), 108.

74 Ivan T. Berend, *Decades of Crisis: Central and Eastern Europe before World War II* (Berkeley, CA: University of California Press, 1998), 316.

75 *Mały Dziennik* 1 (1935), cited in Wynot, 'The Catholic Church', 227.

However, the top Church hierarchy was guarded in its criticism for two reasons: first, it welcomed the strengthening of state authority under Piłsudski's Sanacja, and second, it looked forward to steps aimed at creating a corporatist socio-economic-political order in Poland, which seemed in keeping with the Church's social teachings.[76]

Though cognizant of the dangers of excessive dependence upon the political realm, church leaders wanted more state support. In 1936, Catholic spokesmen demanded a constitutional change that would make Catholicism Poland's ruling religion, essentially the status guaranteed to Orthodoxy in Romania. In 1937, the mass political formation supposed to organize active support for the government in a semi-fascist manner – OZON (Camp of National Unity) – adopted an 'Ideological-Political Declaration' stating that the Catholic Church should be treated 'with solicitous care'. Yet the Church leadership received news of this support with 'considerable restraint'.[77] Clearly it was concerned about creating an appearance of ideological alignment with secular, right-wing forces. Unlike their Hungarian or Romanian counterparts, Polish Church officials were instructed to remain aloof from political parties or controversies. Particularly frustrating for OZON was its failure to gain support of Catholic Action, a movement of lay Catholics founded in nineteenth-century Italy that aimed at filling public life with Christian values and countering liberal trends. Though it encouraged lay activism, Catholic Action was not meant to free the laity from hierarchical control. It was given special encouragement in the papal encyclical *Ubi arcano* (1922).[78]

For its part, OZON continued reaffirming its 'deep ties with the Catholic church' and attempted to drum up support through shared anti-communism and its own supposed 'Christian ethic'. If there was discord, it does not appear to have been serious. In the vital sphere of education, the government issued an order that required all teachers to familiarize themselves with the programme of Catholic religious instruction. And while the Church's plan to have a 5 per cent 'church duty' levied on all state income and fees received from Catholics passed as a bill in the Sejm in 1932, it was not implemented before the war broke out.[79]

There was good reason for the state to be attracted to Catholic organizations: they were pervasive and strong. The Church's strategy was to occupy social and cultural space with a Catholic presence in order to displace other, competing forces – above all those of the 'secular' world.[80] Beginning in the 1920s, there were dozens of organizations that had the goal of knitting together elements of the Catholic world, and after 1930, the Catholic Action became strong in Poland.[81] Catholic newspapers had print runs of 800,000 and periodicals of 600,000. Beginning in 1937 there were Institutes of Advanced Religious Culture in 13 cities.[82] No won-

---

76 Wynot, 'The Catholic Church', 228.

77 Ibid., 231; Pease, *Rome's Daughter*, 191.

78 Stella Alexander, 'Croatia: The Catholic Church and Clergy, 1919–1945', in *Catholics, the State, and the European Radical Right 1919–1945*, eds Richard J. Wolff and Jörg K. Hoensch (New York: Columbia University Press, 1987), 31–66, here 44; Pius XI, *Ubi Arcano Dei Consilio*, Encyclical letter, 23 December 1922, http://www.vatican.va/content/pius-xi/en/encyclicals/documents/hf_p-xi_enc_19221223_ubi-arcano-dei-consilio.html (accessed 16 February 2017).

79 No executive order was issued. Wynot, 'The Catholic Church', 235.

80 Leon Dyczewski, 'Religijność społeczeństwa polskiego' [The religiosity of Polish society], *Collectanea theologica* 42 (1972): 27–43.

81 The centre was in Poznań. See Pius XI, *Ubi Arcano*.

82 There were 916 students in the Warsaw school in 1938. Bohdan Cywiński, *Ogniem próbowane: Z dziejów najnowszych Kościoła katolickiego w Europie Środkowo-Wschodniej* [Tested by fire: from the most recent history of the Catholic Church in East Central Europe] (Warsaw: Wydawnictwa Szkolne i Pedagogiczne, 1993), 64–5.

Nationalization vs. secularization

der the state wanted to siphon cultural and political legitimacy from the Church. Its statistical office did not even register non-believers.[83]

Yet despite this evident strength, the Church felt besieged by forces that threatened its hold on the lives of believers. Take the issue of marriage. Catholicism considered all sexual relations outside the sacrament of matrimony sinful, imperilling a person's immortal soul. The idea that Poles might have only a civil marriage was unthinkable for the Church. Education was another sphere of contention. Because their eternal salvation was at stake, it was crucial for young people to learn the basic teachings of Catholic ethics. Thus, all talk of removing or reducing Church presence in educational institutions was not only unacceptable – it was considered deeply hostile. The historian Bohdan Cywiński writes that even decades after the fact, the 'postulate of secularism in all these matters was formulated extremely sharply and aggressively toward the church'. The socialist left and minority groups wanted to 'eliminate totally' the Church's presence in public life.[84] No matter how meekly the secular side formulated its demands, they appeared extreme in the eyes of the Church and its supporters.

The sense of threat became acute when it seemed to enter the church itself. For example, in the 'modernist crisis' before the First World War, a relatively small group of Catholic intellectuals advocating modern readings of scripture and active participation of the faithful in Mass triggered a furious reaction from the Vatican, leading to interrogations, purging and an 'anti-modernist' oath that was required of all priests until the Second Vatican Council.[85]

But if the defensive reaction was vigorous, it was not hysterical or reactionary. The Polish Church, from bishops to parish priests and laity, engaged the modern world, not only in the economy but also culturally and in social, political and philosophical thought, deep into the spectrum of the radical right. The Church's anti-modernism and its sense of pervasive conspiracies threatening the Church made some Catholics into natural allies of Polish anti-Semites, who were likewise determined to defend the ethnic people. In this case, the border between Church and society blurred entirely.[86]

In Romania, the Orthodox Church remained relatively dominant in state and society through the interwar years (72.6 per cent of the population was Orthodox). But as in Poland, church institutions had to 'share' the new national territory with other faiths: Uniate (7.9 per cent), Protestant (6.5 per cent) and Roman Catholic (6.8 per cent).[87] This was a departure from the smaller pre-war Romania (The Regat), which was overwhelmingly Orthodox.

---

83 The number of 'other' (besides Roman Catholics, Jews, Protestants, Orthodox and E. Rite Catholics) went from 0.3 per cent of the population to 0.6 per cent from 1920 to 1930. *Historia Polski w liczbach* [Polish history in numbers] (Warsaw: Central Statistical Office, 2003), 382–3, 385–6, cited in Brian Porter-Szűcs, *Poland in the Modern World: Beyond Martyrdom* (Chichester: Wiley-Blackwell, 2014), 127. In 1931 the statistical office registered 45,700 of 31,915,800 citizens who had not indicated confession or whose confession was 'undefined'. *Główny urząd statystyczny Rzeczypospolitej Polskiej, Mały rocznik statystyczny* [Polish statistical yearbook] (Warsaw: Central Statistical Office, 1938), 24.

84 Cywiński, *Ogniem próbowane*, 66.

85 The oath was titled *Sacrorum antistitum* and was over 6,000 words long. Brian Porter, 'Antisemitism and the Search for a Catholic Identity', in *Antisemitism and its Opponents in Modern Poland*, ed. Robert Blobaum (Ithaca, NY: Cornell University Press, 2005), 103–23, here 120.

86 Porter shows that racist and racialist attitudes permeated deep into Catholic thought. Porter, 'Antisemitism', 110–11.

87 Hans-Christian Maner, 'Kirchen in Rumänien: Faktoren demokratischer Stabilität in der Zwischenkriegszeit? Zum Verhältnis von orthodoxer, römisch-katholischer und griechisch-katholischer Kirche', in *Religion und Nationalstaat zwischen den Weltkriegen 1918–1939*, eds Hans-Christian Maner and Martin Schulze Wessel (Stuttgart: Steiner, 2002), 104.

Despite the new complexity, the 1923 constitution, just like that of 1866, identified Orthodoxy as the 'dominant' religion of state.[88] Like Poland, Romania understood itself as a national state, treating the Orthodox and Uniate churches as 'national churches'.[89] The other churches received no special mention in the constitution, a fact that led to bitter protests. The contrast to Czechoslovakia, Germany and Yugoslavia was clear: in none of these states did the constitution favour a particular religion.[90]

Protestants and Catholics lived in former Habsburg areas of Romania: Transylvania, Maramureş, the Banat and Bukovina, but these areas were also populated by significant numbers of Orthodox and Uniate citizens. The Uniate as well as Orthodox and other churches in Transylvania harshly criticized political life in the interwar years, claiming that the political parties demonstrated little concern or knowledge of basic notions of law and justice.[91] The Uniates were particularly fierce in their criticism of the dominant National Liberal Party of Ion I. C. Brătianu.[92]

The problems of inter-confessionality were aggravated by the expectations of the Romanian Orthodox Church (ROC) that members of the Uniate Church would 'return' to Orthodoxy. It misunderstood the Czech case, where a tiny national 'Czechoslovak' church was created among Catholic dissenters but failed to achieve broader resonance. In the eyes of the Orthodox Church, the Uniates faced a decision: whether to side with 'the true law' or with the 'anti-Romanian' dissenters in the Catholic Church, who were agents of 'papism'. Uniates refused compromise.[93] The aggressive approach of the Orthodox Church seemed threatening even in areas where the Uniates were numerically superior.[94] In some cases, the Orthodox seized Uniate churches and Uniates complained of a shift that had taken place with the creation of the new state: from Hungarian chauvinism to Orthodox fanaticism. Many Catholics refused to recognize the new state and imagined its presence in Transylvania as temporary. Religion had raised the national conflicts to a level of drama that, at least according to some, involved a clash between Eastern and Western culture.[95]

In Hungary, the searing violence of the Béla Kun Soviet Republic (1919), combined with the humiliating loss of territory at Trianon (1920), left the Church traumatized and supportive of the irredentist, conservative regime of Admiral Miklós Horthy (served as Regent, 1920–44). The short-lived 133-day Hungarian Soviet Republic had closed some 3,000 Catholic schools, launched terror against priests, and plundered and confiscated church property, while Trianon had left only one of Hungary's three archdioceses and three of its sixteen dioceses intact.[96] Like the state, the Church lost land to foreign powers – Czechoslovakia, Romania and Yugoslavia –

---

88 'Article 21, Constitutiunea din 1866', *Monitorul Oficial* 142 (1/13 June 1866); 'Article 22, Constitutiunea din 1923', *Monitorul Oficial* 282 (29 March 1923). The 1923 constitution also placed the Uniate Church ahead of the other faiths. Dietmar Müller, *Staatsbürger auf Widerruf: Juden und Muslime als Alteritätspartner im rumänischen und serbischen Nationscode: Ethnonationale Staatsbürgerschaftskonzepte 1878–1941* (Wiesbaden: Harrassowitz, 2005).

89 Müller, *Staatsbürger*, 256.

90 Maner, 'Kirchen', 109. Despite protests, the Uniates accepted the constitution and their favoured status.

91 Ibid., 107. They also complained of problems in education and financial policy.

92 The Uniate Church supported the Romanian National Party of Transylvania. Ibid., 108.

93 Ibid., 110–11.

94 In Maramureş (county) there were 8,489 Orthodox and 104,132 Uniates in 1930. Ibid., 114.

95 Ibid., 112–13. The Hungarian Catholic Church was not a 'centre' of irredentism, but untactful and provocative statements by the clergy had the effect of poisoning the situation.

96 This does not include Croatia. Spannenberger, 'Katholische Kirche', 161.

Nationalization vs. secularization

none of which was well-disposed to Catholicism. The new Hungary was, in contrast to pre-war multi-ethnic Hungary, majority Roman Catholic (62.8 per cent).[97]

Catholic commentators claimed they could adjust to different political forms, but in fact they preferred the re-established kingdom to a Republic.[98] The Church supported the state's main agenda of restoring Hungary to its pre-Trianon borders. It rejected liberalism as being incapable of solving Hungary's problems and as promoting secularization, and with that, an anti-patriotic, immoral and anti-Christian way of life. The government of Béla Kun had been internationalist and atheist, and so the new government had to be national and Christian.[99] The connection of church and nation was reflected in the prayer Hungarian school children said every morning: 'I believe in one God, I believe in one fatherland, I believe in one eternal godly justice, I believe in the resurrection of Hungary.'[100]

From the Church's perspective, a positive side of this development was the impressive growth of institutional Catholicism, inspired in part by the Vatican's support for lay activities through the Catholic Action. In 1937 there were 16,474 Catholic associations in Hungary, and the youth organizations like the working youth (30,000 members) and scouts (170,000 members) were particularly impressive. Priests acted as chaplains for the paramilitary Levente youth association, meant to train young people outside the restrictions imposed at Trianon. Catholic schooling also thrived, with 2,835 primary schools, 14 preparatory high schools and 13 theological colleges.[101] Hungary's largest university student organization was the Foederatio Emericana, run by the Cistercian Order.

Technically, this and other organizations were not supposed to be involved in political life, but in fact they supported the official Christian-national state policy. Church leaders saw themselves as partners of the state and not society: their mission was to conduct moral education and maintain social and political stability. Clergy served as government ministers, for example, of education and of work, and bishops sat in the upper house of Parliament. The Church hierarchy showed little concern about problems of poverty, or the fact that Hungarian peasants had too little land, and the Church remained an institution of great wealth, dominated by socially conservative, aristocratically minded elites.[102] At the same time, contemporary sources speak of a deepening religiosity in the population, with the lower clergy enjoying respect and influence in village life. At the level of the state, more than half of the intellectual elite had attended Catholic educational institutions.[103]

The new Czechoslovakia was a comparatively secular state, and no single religion could claim to represent the 'Czechoslovak nation' which, as time would tell, was a fictional product

---

97 Ibid., 159, 162. In 1910, Catholics had been a minority in Hungary, constituting 49.3 per cent of the population. Antal Aldásy, 'Hungary', in *The Catholic Encyclopedia*, vol. 7, eds Charles George Herbermann, Edward A. Pace, Condé B. Pallen, Thomas J. Shahan and John J. Wayne (New York: Robert Appleton Company, 1913), 547–62, here 559.

98 Hungary was a kingdom under regency from 1920 to 1946. Later, bishop (of Veszprém) Tihamér Tóth wrote in 1921 that the 'republic means anarchy, the expulsion of the king, the death of law'. See Spannenberger, 'Katholische Kirche', 163.

99 Ibid., 165–7.

100 Peter Hanák, 'Hungary: 1918–1945', in *The Columbia History of Eastern Europe in the Twentieth Century*, ed. Joseph Held (New York: Columbia University Press, 1992), 175.

101 All of these enjoyed some state support and taught a relatively high number of students. The Piarists had 5,047 students in 10 high schools in 1931. See Spannenberger, 'Katholische Kirche', 171.

102 Ibid., 175.

103 Ibid., 170–1. This supposedly reflected a success in balancing traditionally strong Protestant influence.

of the Czech national movement. Czechs and Slovaks were overwhelmingly Catholic, even though the Czechs were so mostly in name. Nevertheless, the Catholic Church felt itself to be a minority church. Czechoslovakia's constitution did not identify any confession as dominant, and the large German and Hungarian ethnic minorities were religiously mixed.[104] In contrast to citizens of Hungary, Poland or Romania, a large number of Czechoslovaks (7.8 per cent) indicated they had no confession, and a further 7.3 per cent left the traditional Christian churches to join a new Czechoslovak church, whose clergy was chiefly made up of Catholic priests with modernist leanings.[105] This institution's central symbol became Jan Hus, the early Protestant reformer burned at the stake in 1415.[106]

Throughout the interwar period, conflicts flared between an outsider Roman Catholic discourse that considered Hus a traitor, heretic and 'bad preacher' and the popular and 'progressive' language of Czech nationalism. For example, in 1923 a number of Czech town councils formulated resolutions against Catholic reactionaries who questioned the 'most holy and valuable things for every honest and progressive Czech', namely 'spiritual and intellectual freedom and unadulterated memory of the bearer of and warrior for truth, Jan Hus'.[107] They claimed that only the memory of Hus had permitted the 'Czechoslovak' people to carry through their national revolution. The resolution was supported by the Czechoslovak Hussite Church, the Protestant Evangelical Church, the Sokol gymnastic movement, as well as some associations and mainstream government parties: the Agrarians, Social Democrats and National Democrats.[108]

Even though they were largely secular, it would have been impossible to imagine Poland's Socialists or National Democrats supporting an anti-Catholic cause in a similar way, because any challenges in religious terms – Orthodoxy or Protestantism – would have been portrayed as anti-Polish.

But for all the monument smashing, the Czechoslovak state proved to be relatively tolerant. Unlike Western European states that required civil marriage, it permitted citizens to choose civil or church ceremonies.[109] Though the Czechoslovak Church seized and used Catholic Church structures in the early years of the Republic, almost all were returned by 1924, and four years later, the state signed a concordat with the Vatican.[110]

There were pockets of pious Catholics, especially in Moravia, and they staged 'resistance' via associations: strong in middle class milieus, poorly organized in the countryside, almost non-existent in industrial areas. These included Catholic schools, savings banks and sports clubs, all aimed at maintaining a Catholic monopoly on forming worldviews. On the eve of the First World War, the modernist Czech (Catholic) clergy had opposed this segregationist approach and rejected the idea that Christianity had to stand against modern society and with the dynasty. The United States, they claimed, demonstrated that a worker could be a 'social and political democrat' as well as a good Christian.[111]

---

104 Schulze Wessel, 'Konfessionelle Konflikte', 73.
105 And that number was growing. See ibid., 99.
106 It modernized the liturgy (using Czech instead of Latin) and integrated cultic figures from Czech history into religious life, hoping to reduce the gap between life and faith. See ibid., 84.
107 Ibid., 88.
108 Including the Reading Association, the Association of Friends of Theater, etc. Ibid.
109 Ibid., 75.
110 In the years 1920–22, 86 churches were taken or shared. By 1924, 82 had been returned. See ibid., 89; Frank J. Coppa, *Politics and Papacy in the Modern World* (Westport, CT: Praeger, 2008), 102.
111 Schulze Wessel, 'Konfessionelle Konflikte', 78–9.

Nationalization vs. secularization

If Czechoslovak identity failed, it was due in large part to how Catholicism divided Czechs from Slovaks. Slovaks did not view attacks on monuments dedicated to the Virgin as iconoclastic, let alone patriotic, but rather as sacrilegious. All secularization measures undertaken by the new state in Slovakia were projected as being the fault of the 'godless Czechs' who were robbing Slovaks and Hungarians of their faith. Not coincidentally, Catholic priests led the Slovak national movement of the interwar years, first Andrej Hlinka and then Jozef Tiso.[112]

Like Czechoslovakia, Yugoslavia was the state of a supposed nation – the Yugoslavs – that had grown out of the ideas of romantic nationalists in the early nineteenth century but had little institutional form, let alone social constituency. In fact, the peoples of the state were divided by historical experience and religion. The major marker for Croat identity was Roman Catholicism, while Serbs, Montenegrins and Macedonians were Orthodox, and Slovenes, who speak their own South Slav language, were Roman Catholic. The Bosnian population was about 33 per cent Muslim, 44 per cent Serb and 23 per cent Croat (in the 1920s there was some openness as to whether Muslims might be Serb or Croat nationals).

According to the Serb constitutions of 1880, 1901 and 1903, the Serb Orthodox Church was the religion of state.[113] The 1921 Vidovdan Constitution of the Kingdom of Serbs, Croats and Slovenes (officially Yugoslavia after 1929) made all religions equal, but the Catholic Church viewed the liberal character of the new state with suspicion. It retained the Serb School Law of 1904, which did not recognize confessional schools. As a result, the Catholic Church lost its elementary and middle schools and a number of Church devotional associations were closed. School-aged children were forced to join the secular state organization, and at times Catholic youth organizations were harassed and shut down.[114] A land reform of 1919 cost the Church 20 convents and monasteries.[115] And to make matters worse for Catholics as well as Protestants, the state was not entirely true to liberal principles. For example, it proclaimed a celebration of Orthodox feasts, like St Sava's day, which the Catholic hierarchy rejected as a threat to faith. Catholics further accused the state of tolerating disturbances of their religious processions.[116] Even events that might seem petty were not. For example, Catholics discerned a threat to the faith when children purchased icons to St Sava to display in classrooms. This was an effort by the 'schismatics' to steal adherents and endanger their eternal souls.[117]

The extremely nationalist, if tiny and illegal Croat Ustasha organization, as well as the illegal and popular Communist Party drew strength from state policies that repressed the religious Croat student organizations, because these policies led alienated young men to turn to

---

112 Their party gained 6.9 per cent of the ballots to the Chamber of Deputies in the 1925 and 1935 national elections. Ibid., 76; Roman Holec, 'Die slowakische politische Elite vor 1918', in Kaiserova, Niznansky and Schulze Wessel, *Religion und Nation*, 35; Joseph Rothschild, *East Central Europe between the Two World Wars* (Seattle, WA: University of Washington Press, 1974), 110, 126; on the perception of the 'godless Czechs', see Hugh Seton-Watson, *Eastern Europe between the World Wars* (Cambridge: Cambridge University Press, 1945), 176.

113 Tvrtko P. Sojčić, *Die 'Lösung' der kroatischen Frage zwischen 1939 und 1945: Kalküle und Illusionen* (Stuttgart: Steiner, 2008), 277.

114 The 'Eagles' [Orlovi] were founded in 1920 but shut down in 1929; they re-emerged as the 'Crusaders' [Križari] in the 1930s. See Jozo Tomasevich, *War and Revolution in Yugoslavia, 1941–1945* (Stanford, CA: Stanford University Press, 2001), 526.

115 Gabriel Adriányi, *Geschichte der Kirche Osteuropas im 20. Jahrhundert* (Paderborn: Schöningh, 1992), 145.

116 Tomasevich, *War and Revolution*, 525.

117 Christian Axboe Nielsen, *Making Yugoslavs: Identity in King Alexander's Yugoslavia* (Toronto: University of Toronto Press, 2014), 302.

radicalism.[118] Still, Croat Peasant Party leader Vladko Maček drew a distinction: even if there was discrimination against Catholics, there was no persecution of the Catholic Church.[119] For example, there were a dozen organizations in the 1930s for young Catholic men and women within Catholic Action, and the Church retained a powerful press organ.[120]

In one important sense, the new state was less 'secularizing' than its counterparts in the west (or the Czechoslovak state): in all of Yugoslavia, excepting Vojvodina, couples had to be married in a religious ceremony.[121] The state gave churches subsidies for keeping records of births, marriages and deaths, and in effect they acted as an arm of public administration.[122] In 1936, Yugoslav authorities counted only 12 children among 435,600 live births to parents who indicated they were 'without confession'.[123] Even though it lost schools, the Church's orders maintained high schools in areas with Catholic populations and continued to influence education in primary schools because religious education was mandatory.[124] And if the Church lost property, it also retained much urban and agricultural real estate from which it derived income.[125]

For all its talk of alienation, the Catholic Church, like the other Christian churches, was an implicit ally in the regime's fight against freemasonry and communism. This agenda also coincided with Christian support for anti-Semitism, because communists were routinely identified as Jews. The Croat *Katolički List*, for example, claimed that 'Jew-Marxists' were undermining the Slav spirit in Russian culture and society: 'Jew-Marxists are aliens', one author wrote in January 1934, 'the land is alien to them ... they ruin the country with great facility, they lightheartedly undertake scientific experiments on peoples, no misfortune which befalls Russia, neither famine nor death, touches them.'[126] At the same time, this paper condemned Nazism as the 'worst heresy ... a falling away from Christianity'.[127]

The Vatican had opposed the creation of a Serb-dominated Yugoslavia because of the dangers it saw to the Catholic Church, which had enjoyed a dominant role in the Habsburg lands. It would have preferred a Danube federation or independent Croatian and Slovene states.[128] However, the Catholic clergy in Croatia and Bosnia-Herzegovina tended at first to support Yugoslavia, largely due to Italy's interest in seizing Dalmatia.[129] So here too, religion was bound up with the national cause, albeit in a different way. There was also an older 'Cyril-Methodius'

---

118 Alexander, 'Croatia', 42.

119 Tomasevich, *War and Revolution*, 526.

120 The Catholic press 'promoted its spiritual and secular objectives in institutions of higher learning, the arts and the professions'. Ibid., 526. The Catholic Action in Croatia was founded in late 1934. See Alexander, 'Croatia', 44.

121 Church courts took care of divorce. Tomasevich, *War and Revolution*, 526.

122 Ibid.

123 The other categories were: Orthodox, Roman Catholic, Greek Catholic, Old Catholic, Protestant, Muslim, Jewish and other confessions. *Royaume de Yougoslavie, Annuaire statistique* (Belgrade: Opšta državna statistika, 1938), 81.

124 Tomasevich, *War and Revolution*, 526.

125 It also ran charitable organizations. See ibid., 526.

126 Cited in Alexander, 'Croatia', 43. Jews tore 'everything to bits' and were described as 'cosmopolitans without patriotism ... without national roots, without principles ... they sell everything and ruin everything ...' Ibid.

127 Ibid., 43.

128 Klaus Buchenau, 'Katholizismus und Jugoslawismus: Zur Nationalisierung der Religion bei den Kroaten', in *Religion und Nation–Nation und Religion: Beiträge zu einer unbewältigten Geschichte*, eds Michael Geyer and Hartmut Lehmann (Göttingen: Wallstein, 2004), 225–54, here 230.

129 Ibid., 231.

Nationalization vs. secularization

idea propagated in the nineteenth century by Bishop Josip Juraj Strossmayer – a Croat critic of the Vatican centralism – that emphasized cooperation and was popular with the Zagreb archbishop Antun Bauer and his successor Alojzije Stepinac.

The Serb-dominated state administration saw a rival in the Catholic Church, a perspective that was also coloured by the recent past: Serb nationalists claimed the Catholic Habsburg Monarchy had tried to 'exterminate' them.[130] And in contrast to the Serb Orthodox Church, whose leadership was within the country, the Catholic leadership exercised authority from Rome, which also happened to be the capital of a state that had irredentist claims on Yugoslav Dalmatia.[131]

The Serb and Croat nationalist elites, much like their Polish and Czech counterparts, tended to be nominal adherents of their people's brand of Christianity (the Muslims were not yet considered a nationality), and were careful not to grow close to the institutional churches in a way that would imply dependence. Slovenia was more like Slovakia, where the clergy was formative of the national movement, including its upper cadres: the Slovene leader Anton Korošec was, like his Slovak counterpart, a Prelate (Monsignor) of the Catholic Church. In both cases, as noted above, the Catholic political party was known as a 'people's party', signalling the usefulness to the universal church in elevating a national cause, with the assumption that the national enemy was a confessional foreigner.[132]

The major political movement in Croatia, and also the main vehicle for Croat nationalism, the Croatian Peasant Party, was wary of dependence on the Catholic Church and endeavoured to keep its distance. In 1923, recognizing the dangers of competition from an institution with international networks of power, its leader, Stjepan Radić, even considered forming a Croatian Catholic Church separate from Rome.[133] He was known for his folk piety and liked to open meetings in rural areas with the greeting: 'Praise be to Jesus and Mary, down with the priests!' Yet he also enjoyed the support of many Catholic clerics.[134]

Radić the secular nationalist was more eager to reject the Yugoslav state than was the Croatian Catholic church hierarchy, which sought accommodation.[135] The Church on Croatian territory to the west, in the Zagreb diocese, was especially moderate, and its leadership was attuned to Strossmayer's Cyril and Methodius ideas of South Slav unity. In general, however, the Croatian church was traditional, and though deeply anti-communist it did not become involved in party politics before or during the war.[136]

---

130 Ante Tresic-Pavičić, *In Darkest Europe: Austria-Hungary's Effort to Exterminate her Jugoslav Subjects; Speeches and Questions in the Parliaments of Vienna and Budapest and in the Croatian Sabor (Diet) in Zagreb* (London: The Near East, 1917).

131 Buchenau, 'Katholizismus und Jugoslawismus', 230.

132 The Slovene was created in the 1890s; the Slovak in 1905, as a splinter from the Hungarian People's Party, both in reaction to liberalism and socialism. An Italian People's Party, predecessor to Christian Democracy, existed from 1919 to 1926; in 1945 an equivalent was created in Austria as the Austrian People's Party. Its predecessor, the Christian Social Party of Austria, existed from 1891 to 1934. The Weimar People's Party was not Catholic, but liberal. However, a Bavarian People's Party was a regional offshoot of the Centre Party until 1933.

133 Stella Alexander writes: 'In Croatia the church follows the people, it does not lead them.' Alexander, 'Croatia', 33.

134 Tomasevich, *War and Revolution*, 526.

135 Buchenau, 'Katholizismus', 233.

136 Stella Alexander writes that the Croatian church was not 'pro-fascist', though many individual priests supported the Ustasha regime, and indeed, the hierarchy welcomed independence under its auspices in 1941. See Alexander, 'Croatia', 34.

By the 1930s, most Catholic parishioners were finding Yugoslav national integration an evident failure and by the end of the decade, even the hierarchy saw its pledges of loyalty to the Yugoslav state as being formal in nature, not reflecting any deeper affective or moral attachment.[137] Thus, even before the Yugoslav army had capitulated in 1941, Zagreb Archbishop Stepinac extended his congratulations to the Ustasha leadership for forming an independent Croatian state.[138]

But the Ustasha viewed Catholicism as representing a foreign, non-Croatian power, and its leaders, like their nineteenth-century inspiration Ante Starčević, looked with some admiration upon Orthodoxy as a force that had helped unite the Serb people. They of course resented the 'fact' that Serb Orthodoxy had extended its influence westward and 'Serbianized' a supposedly Croat population in parts of Bosnia and Croatia, and if Ante Pavelić called Catholicism a pillar of Croatian identity during his reign as *poglavnik* (leader) of the Ustasha state, it was for political reasons.[139]

Bosnia, a land between in the lands between, was considered for centuries 'mission territory' by the Catholic Church and entrusted to the Franciscans. Aided partly by the favouritism of the Habsburgs and partly by immigration, Catholicism grew. The Catholic leader, ultra-nationalist Sarajevo archbishop Ivan Šarić, sought contact with the Ustasha even when it was a tiny movement in exile before the Second World War. He established 17 new parishes in the interwar years, accompanied by Catholic centres, causing Bosnian Serbs to worry that Catholicism would overwhelm them. At the same time, the Serbian Orthodox Church grew assertive about the Serb character of the province.[140]

After the Second World War, the Serb side, supported by the communist regime, portrayed Catholic complicity with the Ustasha as extreme in order to de-legitimize Catholicism and thus nationalism within Croatia. For its part, the Croat side complained of attempts at national and religious extermination at the hands of the Serb-communist and thus anti-Catholic regime.

Though religion tacked its way toward the national cause in the interwar period, the relations varied in interesting ways. Everywhere we see a balancing act. If in Yugoslavia the Church was at pains not to identify closely with a national movement or drift too far from the state, in Poland the authoritarian Sanacja regime and the Church were both careful not to go too far in criticism of the other, despite their different attitudes towards civil marriage. Both had much to lose from alienation. Even if weaker than their counterparts in Poland or Romania, Hungarian churches still showed vibrancy and maintained an important institutional presence, reflecting the contours of a society still largely agrarian and traditional, at the gates of secularization.

The radical right, anti-Semitism, fascism, collaboration

The competition between Orthodoxy and Western Christianity in Greater Romania gave anti-Semites a chance to promote their agenda as fascist Christians. From the early 1920s, out of the radical-right student milieus of Moldavia, came the closest symbiosis of a modern total ideology and Christianity ever seen. The leader was the Messiah-like Corneliu Zelea Codreanu, a law student who, with other toughs, liked to assault Jews and Communists in the university town

---

137 Archbishop Stepinac of Zagreb thus gave quiet support to activists for the Croatian cause, though he did not support the Ustashe as such. See Buchenau, 'Katholizismus', 237–8.

138 Ibid.

139 Ibid., 239.

140 Tomasevich, *War and Revolution*, 527.

Nationalization vs. secularization

Iaşi. In 1923, authorities arrested him for conspiracy to murder those responsible in Romania's government for extending citizenship to Jews, and while in prison, he experienced a 'vision' of the Archangel Michael, urging him to dedicate his life to God. Four years later, Codreanu formed the Legion of St. Michael – also known as the Iron Guard – which preached national cleansing and the liberation of peasants.

Unlike in fascist Italy or Germany, the presence of religion in rural and small-town Romania was very strong, and to this day, outright atheism remains marginal. But Codreanu's followers in the Iron Guard were not ordinary believers or ordinary fascists: they were fanatical about their Christianity and operated in Christian terms with constant references to tropes of suffering and redemption. Because of the overt and sincere religiosity of Legion members, Roger Eatwell has called the Legion clerical fascist, but the Guard was not clerical in the sense of being carried by the clergy.[141] Its practices and beliefs diverged from those of the Orthodox Church, and the most prominent Guardist priest was forced to leave the church when forced to choose one belief over the other.

Still, the two sides of the relationship found it difficult to let go because both came to depend upon it. By the 1930s, Orthodox prelates knew that the Legion was competing with them for the same flock, but also that Legion activists enlivened Christian devotion, protecting the flock from creeping secularization and the dangers of socialism.

Take the legionary leaders Ion Moţa and Vasile Marin, who were killed in Spain in 1937: the Legion leadership had the bodies paraded around Romania by railway in order to show that the Legion was willing to make blood sacrifice. Cluj's Bishop Nicolae Colan praised their fight against 'the red madness' and stated that 'treasuring their supreme sacrifice, God did not leave them prisoners to the enemies, and their souls made their way to the Heavens'.[142] Guard leader Codreanu recited an oath at the funeral of the martyred leaders:

> I swear before God, before your holy sacrifice, for Christ and the Legion, to tear from me the earthly happiness, to render myself from humanly love and, for the resurrection of my People, to be ready for death at any time!

After the oath, a procession formed taking the two bodies to the 'Sfântul Ilie Gorgani' Church, where they were kept until burial. A legionary squad formed a cross with their own bodies, and the procession carried the crosses of Moţa and Marin as well as flowers sent by Hitler, Mussolini and Franco.[143]

This synthesis of Legionary and Christian ritual produced frenzy among the crowds, causing many to genuflect and swear oaths who previously had had no intention of doing so.[144] Thousands of peasants greeted the train on their knees, but there were also many priests, including high clergy, who joined in the rituals, celebrating services for the slain legionaries, whose

---

141 Roger Eatwell, 'Reflection on Fascism and Religion', *Totalitarian Movements and Political Religion* 4 (2003): 145–66, here 146.

142 Moţa's father was an Orthodox priest. Valentin Săndulescu, 'Sacralised Politics in Action: The February 1937 Burial of the Romanian Legionary Leaders Ion Moţa and Vasile Marin', *Totalitarian Movements and Political Religions* 8, no. 2 (2007): 259–69, here 264.

143 Ibid., 265.

144 One police report read as follows: 'the intensity of those moments/everything taking place in front of the coffins draped with Romanian colours/generated within the audience a sense of mysticism that deeply impressed even those that were not members of the "All for the Fatherland" party, and a part of them also took the oath.' Quoted ibid., 266.

deeds they praised. Some 400 priests were counted at the funeral in Bucharest. The Legion's ranks swelled, from 96,000 in January 1937 to 272,000 by the end of the year.[145]

At no time did Orthodox leaders take a stand against the Legion; instead, the clergy supported the Legion's nationalism, including its doctrine that Jews were the source of all evils confronting Romanian society, whether in the city or the countryside.[146] Patriarchs Miron Cristea and Nicodim (Nicolae Munteanu), both outspoken anti-Semites, confirmed this stance.[147] In August 1937, Cristea asked in an article reprinted throughout the nationalist press: 'Why should the Jews enjoy the privilege of living like parasites upon our backs? ... It is logical and holy to react to them.'[148]

Legionaries worked within the church and the movement without sensing a contradiction. One rank and file member said they were 'lunatics for Christ'. Though many Christians in Germany supported Hitler's regime, fanaticism for Christ was not a prominent characteristic of Nazi party members.[149] Similarly in Poland, right-wing Christians never so closely coupled devotion to their political cause with Christianity. The real deity for German Christians or Falanga faithful was the nation, and they did not need scripture to make their case. As in Nazi Germany, Christian theologians were willing to portray the Christian bible as anti-Judaic, to cut off its connection to Hebrew sources, and to claim that Jesus was not Jewish.[150]

After 1943, Germany's Nazi Party adopted rhetoric in favour of Western civilization (against Bolshevism), but not of Christianity (against atheism). By contrast, the Legion's writings were suffused with Christian 'content',[151] and its leader Codreanu spoke of fulfilling the will of Christ. 'The final aim is not life', he wrote in 1936, but '*the Resurrection. The resurrection of the nations in the name of Jesus Christ the Saviour.*'[152]

Although thousands of clergymen carried out mixed Guardist and Christian rituals and shared the movement's nationalist sentiments, the high church leadership took efforts to maintain distance, sensing the movement's revolutionary impetus. Ultimately, the Church was a pillar of the regime of Carol II, which in 1938 arrested the Legionary leadership and executed

---

145 Ibid., 262–4, 267.

146 See Cristian Romocea, *Church and State: Religious Nationalism and State Identification in Post-Communist Romania* (London: Continuum, 2011).

147 In 1940, Nicodim blamed the loss of Bukovina and Bessarabia on the Jews, saying: 'God has shown to the leader of our country the path toward a sacred and redeeming alliance with the German nation and sent the armies to the Divine Crusade against destructive Bolshevism ... which has found here villainous souls ready to serve him. These companions of Satan have been found mostly among the nation that had brought damnation upon itself and its sons, since it had crucified the Son of God.' Of course, it was really the alliance with Nazi Germany (and its alliance with the Soviet Union) that caused the loss of those territories. Ibid., 135.

148 'Rumanian Church Leader Prints Attack on Jews', *Jewish Telegraph Agency*, 20 August 1937; 'Logical and Holy', *Time*, 28 March 1938, 137.

149 According to Ilie Imbrescu, Legionaries 'subjugated the political to the spiritual and transformed into a religious faith their fight and sacrifice for a Christian "Romania of the Romanians"'. Constantin Iordachi, *Charisma, Politics and Violence: The Legion of the 'Archangel Michael' in Inter-War Romania* (Trondheim: Trondheim Studies on East European Cultures and Societies, 2004), 116.

150 The prominent Iron Guard intellectual and theology professor Nichifor Crainic did just this.

151 A statement from the Legion journal *Axa* from 1933: 'Between the heavenly army of Saint Michael and the innocent souls of the Legionaries sacrificed for the national idea, a new pact has been established in a miraculous way, a new agreement between the sky and the earth which will bring, as in other times, Salvation.' Quoted in Iordachi, *Charisma, Politics and Violence*, 116.

152 Quoted in Săndulescu, 'Sacralised Politics', 261.

Nationalization vs. secularization

its top leaders, including Codreanu. At that time, Orthodox priests who supported the Legion were interned at a camp in Sadaclia.[153]

Similar to their Romanian counterparts, Christian leaders in Hungary were not attached to democratic models of government. Leading priests had registered doubts about republicanism even before the socialist revolution of Béla Kun in 1919. Also similar to Romania, the churches lent ideological support to anti-democratic impulses, for example by sanctioning the discrimination of Jews, while nevertheless stopping short of endorsing full-scale violence. Christian leaders also tended to be uncomfortable when the radical right claimed to be defending Christianity, as in the notion of 'Christian Hungary'. That was a job for the churches. They knew, as Paul Hanebrink writes, that a 'Christian moral order as it was embraced by the extreme right served nationalist politics above all else.'[154]

The Catholic Church also had problems with the revolutionary agenda of the radical right. Premier Gyula Gömbös (who served from 1932 to 1936) wanted to promote a unified corporatist state and desired agricultural reforms that would have threatened the church's land holdings.[155] The Christian Economic and Social Party, the second largest party in Hungary after the 1932 elections, supported land reform that would not have affected Church holdings, and Catholic Action said land reform was justified and did not imply an alliance with liberalism. Progressive Catholics went further, insisting the Church distribute sizeable holdings to landless peasants.[156] Some young Catholic leaders – whose spokesman would later change his name to Mindszenty – asserted their anti-Semitic credentials: they had 'fought against Jews for decades ... even when practically everyone in the country was a friend of the Jews.'[157] They hoped to convince readers that they could represent the nation better than the fascist Arrow Cross.

But the Church was not radical enough to siphon off support from the far right. On the one hand, the Arrow Cross employed Christian ideas and symbols, and held St László – opponent of Rome and conqueror of Croatia, who forbade marriage between Christians and Jews – higher than St István (St Stephan), Hungary's Patron. But they merged Christian thought with racism claiming that Jesus was not Jewish but a member of the 'Godvanian race'. Prominent Catholics and Protestants pushed back and said that Hungarian identity could not be based on racial purity. In contrast to the Arrow Cross, Christian nationalism seemed 'weak indeed', falling behind in modern nationalism as well as social reform.[158] As Europe descended into war, the competitive relation continued, with the Church supporting restrictions against Jews in two of three anti-Jewish laws as well as popular irredentism, but ultimately standing with conservative

---

153 Iordachi, *Charisma, Politics and Violence*, 117.

154 Paul Hanebrink, *In Defense of Christian Hungary: Religion, Nationalism, and Anti-Semitism, 1890–1944* (Ithaca, NY: Cornell University Press, 2006), 141.

155 Ultimately, he did not succeed with radical social policy. He died in 1936. See Spannenberger, 'Katholische Kirche', 173.

156 In 1929, 30 Catholic intellectuals from within the Wesselényi Reform Club (closely related to the Miklós Bartha Society) in Budapest wrote a letter to the Primate demanding the church divest itself of latifundia and distribute the land to landless peasants. The government dissolved the group the following year. Progressive Catholics also founded so-called Prohászka working communities devoted to social reform. See Gyula Borbándi, 'Geistige Bewegungen in Ungarn zwischen den beiden Weltkriegen', *Ungarn Jahrbuch* 6 (1974/75): 143–4.

157 Hanebrink, *In Defense of Christian Hungary*, 156–7.

158 Ibid., 143–4.

forces close to Horthy, holding back the brown tide. In 1944, members of the Church hierarchy helped shield Jews in Budapest from deportation.[159]

According to the historian Brian Porter-Szűcs, collusion of the church in anti-Semitism is a relatively recent phenomenon, dating to the decades preceding the First World War. Prior to that, prominent Church writers were at pains to distance themselves from racially based hatred. In 1885, a leading Warsaw Catholic periodical remonstrated against the prominent anti-Semite Jan Jeleński for 'descending from the position of Christian love' and 'soaking his pen in hatred'. 'The German, the Jews, and every human being', wrote the anonymous author, 'is a brother to the Pole, if the Pole recognizes God as his father.'[160]

But then influential modern Catholics adapted themselves to both anti-Semitic thought and practice, so that by the 1930s, a 'great deal of undisguised anti-Semitism had penetrated the Church in Poland'.[161] What distinguished the newer trend were generalizations about Jews as an ethnic or even racial entity. In a 1936 pastoral letter, August Cardinal Hlond wrote that Jews 'fight against the Catholic Church, they are free-thinkers and constitute the vanguard of atheism, of the Bolshevik movement, and of revolutionary activity'. But he tried to separate himself from the 'unconditional anti-Jewish principle' imported from Nazi Germany. While it was 'permissible to love one's own nation more', he cautioned, it was 'not permissible to hate anyone. Not even Jews.'[162]

During the war, the Church in Poland had a mixed record just like churches in other countries, although the circumstances differed. It opposed a fascism imported from abroad and directed against Catholics as well as Jews, but it failed to overcome traditional Christian anti-Judaism and take a firm stance against anti-Semitism. Many priests died for siding with the anti-Nazi Home Army, but generally failed to support the tens of thousands of Jews who sought shelter after escape from ghettos and transports to the death camps.[163] At the same time, individual Christians, including some former anti-Semites, organized shelter for Jewish children, saving thousands of lives. The ambivalent posture continued into the post-war period, when the Church hierarchy failed to condemn the pogrom Kielce of July 1946, in which 42 Jews lost their lives.[164]

---

159 The laws circumscribed Jewish participation in public life, for example setting quotas for percentages of Jews allowed in certain professions or in higher education. The Church objected to the third law of 1941 because it affected Jewish converts and some people born as Christians who were considered Jewish for racial reasons. See Randolph L. Braham, 'The Christian Churches of Hungary and the Holocaust', *Yad Vashem Studies* 29 (2001): 241–80.

160 Porter writes that the reluctance on the part of Catholic authors to embrace modern anti-Semitism extended to Galicia, and its echoes could be heard into the 1920s. Brian Porter, 'Antisemitism and Catholic Identity', in Blobaum, *Antisemitism and its Opponents*, 105–6.

161 Ibid., 106.

162 He continued: 'One does well to prefer one's own kind in commercial dealings and to avoid Jewish stores and Jewish stalls in the markets, but it is not permissible to demolish Jewish businesses, destroy their merchandise, break windows, torpedo houses. One ought to fence oneself off against the harmful moral influences of Jewry, to separate oneself against its anti-Christian culture, and especially to boycott the Jewish press and the demoralizing Jewish publications. But it is not permissible to assault Jews, to hit, maim or blacken them … When divine mercy enlightens a Jew, and he accepts sincerely his and our Messiah, let us greet him with joy in the Christian midst.' Celia Stopnicka Heller, *On the Edge of Destruction: Jews of Poland between the Two World Wars* (Detroit, MI: Wayne State University Press, 1994), 113.

163 Jan Grabowski, *Hunt for the Jews* (Bloomington, IN: Indiana University Press, 2013).

164 Jan Gross, *Fear: Anti-Semitism in Poland after Auschwitz* (Princeton, NJ: Princeton University Press, 2006), 134–53.

Poland during the Second World War is often taken to stand for the Eastern European region as a whole, but it poses unusual challenges to historical memory because popular resistance to Nazism co-existed with widespread indifference toward the mass murder of Jews. Across the region, the borders between collusion and cooperation are difficult to discern. In Romania, we saw a close unity of Christian cult and fascism, involving not only priests in the Iron Guard or the toleration of right-radicalism by clergy – both present in clerical fascism in Croatia and Slovakia – but the inextricable intertwining of national extremist and Christian messages, making both seem necessary for the other.

For the most part, the Christian clergy had emerged from deeply nationalist populations and reflected their values. In Croatia, the upper clergy could not ignore the sentiments of the lower clergy and adapted to popular nationalism, though the ultra-nationalist movement was tiny. The Polish Catholic hierarchy issued statements denouncing racism but called discrimination against Jews acceptable. National Democracy in Poland may have seemed proto-fascist, but ultimately it upheld the status quo against revolutionary forces of right and left. With the exception of some radical Franciscans in Croatia, only in Romania did Christians participate as co-revolutionaries in the racial war.

Hungary provided a counterpoint, with the church hierarchy ultimately forced to disavow racism when it infringed on deep, implicit principles of orthodox belief: Christ, after all, was a Jew. But the whirlwind of the Nazi revolution levelled distinctions, and ultimately even Romania began sheltering Jews: after it became clear that Nazi Germany was losing the war in early 1943, Romania began denying German demands to hand over Jews for deportation in the hope of a post-war settlement that would favour Romania's national ambitions, especially in Transylvania. Hungary would have liked to have wrested itself from collusion with Nazi Germany, but after the Wehrmacht occupied the country in March 1944, a right-wing government formed that colluded with German forces in deporting 437,000 Jews to Auschwitz. This was the last significant Eastern European Jewish community surviving at that point.

The post-war period: religion and people's democracy

Authors disagree on the war's impact on the strength of the post-war Church. Its mixed record in Germany was said to have weakened Christianity permanently, but disentangling its moral failings from other secularizing forces is difficult. While in post-war Poland and Croatia Catholicism was criticized for collusion with the occupier and churchmen were put on trial, it remained the one institution that stood between the ethnic nation and state.[165] In Poland, the Church paradoxically seemed to gain strength despite the huge losses of life during the war, and in Croatia, the fact that some members of the clergy had collaborated with the Nazis did not weaken the Church's position in the national narrative. For deeper historical reasons, Catholicism did not play similar roles in the Czech lands or in Hungary, although

---

165 On the trial of Archbishop Stepinac and other Catholic priests in post-war Yugoslavia, see Stella Alexander, *Church and State in Yugoslavia since 1945* (Cambridge: Cambridge University Press, 1979), 95–120. On the major Polish defendant, Kielce bishop Czesław Kaczmarek, and other accused priests see Anna Bikont and Joanna Szczęsna, 'Biskup Kaczmarek, skazazany, wymazany' [Bishop Kaczmarek: condemned, obliterated], *Gazeta Wyborcza*, 26 September 2003. In both cases, the priests placed on trial during the Stalinist period had cozied up to fascist authorities and left themselves open to attack. For instance, Kaczmarek had published a pastoral letter in 1942 warning of the dangers Jewish children posed for Christian children. See Dariusz Libionka, 'Anti-Semitism, Anti-Judaism and the Polish Catholic Clergy', in Blobaum, *Anti-Semitism and its Opponents*, 233–64, here 243.

church attendance in Hungary rose under Stalinism as a form of protest.[166] The story of Eastern Orthodoxy, because of the intertwining of church narratives with those of nation, differs somewhat, and the population's nominal adherence to Christianity was little affected by the tides of total rule.

As interesting as the churches' ambiguous record during the war, is how this record was instrumentalized through memory politics after the war. Thus, in Germany, though bishops failed to take a strong stance against the Nazi regime, the Church portrayed itself as having stood in quiet but firm resistance. Communists portrayed the churches as having curried favour with fascism and supported collaborationist regimes, especially in France, Croatia and Slovakia.[167] Each view had elements of truth, but each was portrayed in its respective context – East and West – as representing a complete truth. The polarized perception was present from 1945 onward, before anyone anticipated the division of Europe.

But when the Cold War descended in 1947, the Eastern European regimes began working actively to make religion irrelevant, and that remained policy for decades. The director of Hungary's State Office for Church Affairs declared as late as 1979 – during détente! – that the construction of the communist social order involved the elimination of all religions.[168] And the relatively moderate Yugoslav regime preached that Marxism 'views all religions and churches, all religious organizations whatsoever, as organs of bourgeois reaction, which serve to buttress the exploitation and stultification of the working class.' This meant 'religious institutions and organizations endeavour to hold people in subjection … Marxism, whose main task is the development of class struggle cannot be neutral vis-à-vis religion, just as religion is not neutral in that struggle …'[169]

Whatever authorities meant by exploitation and subjection, it was clear that for them the Church's activities were never entirely religious, that is 'other-worldly', because it represented an order that was supposed to disappear. As workers' power increased religion *had to* fade. Thus, when the Church succeeded in pastoral work it was criticized for unfair tactics, proselytization and the revival of forgotten and harmful rituals. If religion persisted in any form, this was a sign that hostile ideas and interests persisted as well. Thus, when 'bourgeois' nationalism emerged as a force in Croatia in the 1970s, the Catholic Church quickly became a target, castigated for being a 'prime mover behind the hostility toward our social communities, behind the sowing of hatred between nations, clericalism and fascist obscurantism'.[170]

---

166 See Miklós Tomka, 'Ungarn: Kirchen als Faktoren des revolutionären Umbruchs', in *Kirche und Revolution: Das Christentum in Ostmitteleuropa vor und nach 1989*, eds Hans-Joachim Veen, Peter März and Franz-Josef Schlichting (Köln: Böhlau, 2009), 101–10, here 106. See also Gergely Rosta, 'Church and Religion in Hungary: Between Religious Individualization and Secularization', in Pollack, Müller and Pickel, *The Social Significance of Religion*, 187–205, here 189: 'During the first decade of the Communist dictatorship, the sacramental statistics of the Catholic Church report an intensification of religious life.'

167 In a meeting with the Croatian Catholic clergy of 2 June 1945, Josip Broz Tito expressed disappointment at the Catholic clergy's wartime behaviour, though in fact it was quite mixed. See Mateja Režek, 'Cuius Regio Eius Religio: The Relationship of Communist Authorities with the Catholic Church in Slovenia and Yugoslavia after 1945', in *The Sovietization of Eastern Europe: New Perspectives on the Postwar Period*, eds Balázs Apor, Peter Apor and Edward Arfon Rees (Washington, DC: New Academia Publishing, 2008), 213–33, here 215.

168 Adriányi, *Geschichte der Kirche*, 105.

169 Cited in Sabrina P. Ramet, *Cross and Commissar: The Politics of Religion in Eastern Europe and the USSR* (Bloomington, IN: Indiana University Press, 1987), 101.

170 The statement was made in 1981 to a Bosnian audience by the orthodox Croatian Marxist and 'Hero of the Yugoslav Nation' Milutin Baltić. Ibid., 102.

Nationalization vs. secularization

But the battle lines were not drawn as simply as the Marxist state claimed. Obscurantism involves the 'opposition to the increase and spread of knowledge', and thus the speaker was simply repeating the tired idea that religion and science stand in necessary contradiction. Beginning in the nineteenth century, however, Catholic leaders pronounced religion and science as separate spheres that did not stand in conflict. They built upon warnings against ignorance of science stretching back to St Augustine, who told Christians of his time that those who disdained science made their faith ridiculous.[171] Theories of evolution made Catholics of the modern age deeply uneasy, yet the Vatican was prudent and said nothing that science might prove false, and the Church's teaching authority did not contradict evolutionary science.[172]

And not all Marxists were as doctrinaire as the Yugoslav communist cited above. More liberal elements believed that religion was destined to fade but were willing to view it as a private affair. Religion's energies might even be useful for building socialism.[173] Thus, tensions persisted between tolerating religion and 'encouraging' its decline, between actively persecuting it while imposing atheist views. In Yugoslavia, the tensions produced stalemate: on the one hand, the state recognized that the working class had an ideology that was atheism, but on the other hand, that atheist views should not be forced on the populace.[174]

Because Marxist regimes could not deny their anti-religious heritage, many religious believers did not trust compromise. In the early 1980s, leading figures in the Zagreb Cathedral chapter rejected Christian-Marxist dialogue out of hand. 'The Marxists are bent on atheizing society', one said. 'The reason that the Marxists make concessions to the church is not any sort of mellowing, but simply that the Church is a fact. What we must do is make the Church a bigger fact.'[175] One movement grew at the expense of the other.

But if there was scepticism, there was also ample room for clerical collaboration which began as pragmatism but ended up as an unstable syncretism. For example, Split's Archbishop Frane Franić portrayed self-managing socialism as the 'best' of all systems, going so far as to claim that Marxism was useful because dialectical-historical materialism made Christianity 'purify itself and renew itself spiritually'.[176] At the same time, Franić was a man of dialogue who led efforts to repair divisions between Eastern and Western Christianity, and in 1966, he held a groundbreaking ecumenical meeting in the Split cathedral with the Serb Orthodox priest Marko Plavša – an event viewed with suspicion in both the Orthodox and Catholic hierarchies. There had been nothing like it in a thousand years.[177]

---

171 St. Augustine, 'The Literal Meaning of Genesis', in *Ancient Christian Writers*, no. 41, ed. J.H. Taylor (New York: Paulist Press, 1982).

172 From an address to the Pontifical Academy of Sciences, 30 November 1941. Don O'Leary, *Roman Catholicism and Modern Science* (New York: Bloomsbury, 2006), 142. In 1931, the Catholic Encyclopaedic Dictionary called the kind of evolution Catholics could accept 'moderate evolution', which permitted belief in 'natural development of all the species of the animal and vegetable world from a few primitive types created by God.' See R. Scott Appleby, 'Exposing Darwin's "Hidden Agenda": Roman Catholic Responses to Evolution, 1875–1925', in Disseminating Darwinism: The Role of Place, Race, Religion and Gender, eds Ronald L. Numbers and John Stenhouse (Cambridge: Cambridge University Press, 1999), 173–208, here 185–93.

173 Ramet, *Cross and Commissar*, 101.

174 Atheist views were, however, reflected in schoolbooks. See ibid., 104.

175 Ibid., from an interview conducted by Ramet herself.

176 Ibid., 108–10. However, Franić was not a 'collaborator' and was deeply critical of the 'progressive' theological society Christianity Today, though the issue seems to have been one of authority rather than any kind of theological dispute.

177 Vjekoslav Perica, *Balkan Idols: Religion and Nationalism in Yugoslav States* (Oxford: Oxford University Press, 2002), 32.

Marxism was to the Christian faiths as they were to each other, at least before the ecumenical revolution described by Franić. They were parallel. Pre-Vatican II Catholicism, like Marxism, demanded complete surrender at the level of belief.[178] The Church did not ask if believers were partly literate and therefore experienced faith in folk terms, or whether they were intellectuals who comprehended the finer points of theology. Rather, it demanded adherence to basic tenets of dogma because otherwise believers opened themselves to the perils of damnation.[179]

That made the situation after 1945 different from any previously known. People's democracy was not non-religious but was rather a different kind of religious state: it sought to foster a kind of faithfulness, and it was more religious than any of its predecessors, whether they be the Catholic Habsburgs or secular nationalists like Tomáš G. Masaryk. Marxism demanded loyalty extending into realms that had not previously concerned conventional states and made itself a competitor to the churches.[180] Like Christianity, Marxism did not make allowances for the sophistication of the believer and required adherence to basic teachings, above all, the eschatology of socialism's victory.

But this zero-sum ideological struggle is only the most sensational challenge state socialism brought to religious faith. More than previous regimes, people's democracy wanted to make societies modern, and that meant transforming the lived environment in ways that weakened religious adherence. By forcing rates of economic growth unprecedented in the region and making societies urban and mobile, the new regimes accelerated processes of secularization, which, according to Sabrina Ramet, displaced 'a system of values based on divine law, honour, and custom by a system of values based on civil law, self-interest, fashion and monetary terms of exchange.'[181] Whatever the doubts about the impact of modernity on religion, the new order was about making concrete and steel, industry, mass society, secular education, secular marriage, nuclear families – all through processes of rationalization.[182] It was about upending the village and small-town environments in which religion as 'community cult' has thrived.[183]

For these reasons, the Stalin years in East Central Europe (1948–55) concentrated the challenges both of state-led modernization and the ideological clash of Marxism with religion. Stalinism brought not only the forced construction of new industries and the expansion of cities, but also the closing of seminaries, arrest of priests and the suppression of religion from public life, whether in the form of healthcare, education, land-tenure or national feast days and pilgrimages. Laws were passed to separate church from state, and though technically they guaranteed freedom of conscience and religious practice, their implementation was often arbitrary. The church's press disappeared, its property was seized and nationalized, religious holidays were abolished and thousands of religious men and women harassed and put on trial. The state

---

178 The Second Vatican Council was a meeting of Roman Catholic bishops from 1962 to 1965 meant to bring the Church up to date, and produced important changes in liturgy, church governance, freedom of conscience, teaching on the Church's role in the world and its attitude towards other faiths. See John O'Malley, *What Happened at Vatican II* (Cambridge, MA: Harvard University Press, 2008).

179 Peter F. Sugar, 'The Historical Role of Religious Institutions in Eastern Europe and their Place in the Communist Party-State', in *Religion and Nationalism in Soviet and East European Politics*, ed. Sabrina P. Ramet (Durham, NC: Duke University Press, 1989), 42–58, here 45.

180 Ibid., 45.

181 Ramet, *Cross and Commissar*, 7.

182 See the description of Stalinism as civilization in Stephen Kotkin, *Magnetic Mountain* (Berkeley, CA: University of California Press, 1995).

183 Casanova, 'Rethinking Secularization', 15.

Nationalization vs. secularization

disseminated aggressive atheistic propaganda through public media and schooling.[184] Despite the 1948 break with Stalin and the inflow of considerable Western aid, the Yugoslav case differed only slightly, as discussed in greater detail below. There were new accents after 1951, but the harassment of clergy continued, as did pressures to join official associations meant to harness their energies for the state.[185]

In contrast to the Soviet state, the Eastern European regimes had to confront an international organization with vast material and moral resources outside the region in the form of the Roman Catholic Church. All tried to create their own national Catholic churches, but all failed, most grievously in Poland, where Catholicism was more implicated in the national narrative and where attacking the Church was viewed as attacking the nation.[186]

Still, even in Poland, the repressive measures began early on. In September 1945, Poland's new rulers tore up the Concordat of 20 years earlier. The following year, Church printing houses were nationalized and censorship introduced. In 1948, the state dissolved Catholic youth groups and created a 'Catholic' movement meant to subvert the Church that was called the PAX Association and was led by the former fascist Bolesław Piasecki, who had been turned by the NKVD (the People's Commissariat for Internal Affairs). Within a year, PAX had enrolled 200 priests ('peace priests'). Poland's government confiscated baptismal records and expropriated church hospitals, children's homes, kindergartens and schools. Church charitable organizations were closed, and their belongings confiscated.[187]

In order to sustain pastoral care, Poland's Primate Cardinal Stefan Wyszyński reached an agreement with the state on 14 April 1950, the first such accord between a Catholic national hierarchy and a communist regime.[188] The former recognized the state's economic and 'peace' policy, and the latter acknowledged the Church's right to carry out religious instruction in schools, to maintain the Catholic University in Lublin and the religious press, to carry out religious services and to continue pastoral care in hospitals, prisons and the army.

But the government kept only part of the bargain. It arrested and tried clergymen in show trials, the most sensational involving Kielce Bishop Czesław Kaczmarek, accused of wartime collaboration and disseminating propaganda in favour of his 'bosses' in Washington and the Vatican. It closed down seminaries, took religious education out of public schools and purged the Catholic weekly *Tygodnik Powszechny* ('Catholic weekly'), installing its own editorial team. At the same time, the regime bolstered the 'loyal' Catholic publishing enterprise of PAX.

The government claimed such measures were a response to the Vatican's refusal to appoint bishops in Poland's western territories. In 1951, Polish authorities removed the 'apostolic administrators' the Pope had appointed in the five western dioceses (still considered German), and replaced them with loyal chapter vicars, mostly from the PAX movement. In order to avoid a schism, Wyszyński recognized them as legitimate, but in September 1953, he was placed under arrest for refusing to take an oath of loyalty.[189]

Three years later, Władysław Gomułka freed Wyszyński as part of de-Stalinization, and other arrested clergymen followed. An agreement followed that accorded the Church fewer

---

184 Režek, 'Cuius Regio', 213.
185 Alexander, *Church and State*, 226–35.
186 Režek, 'Cuius Regio', 214.
187 Adriányi, *Geschichte der Kirche*, 71.
188 Mikołaj Stanisław Kunicki, *Between the Brown and the Red: Nationalism, Catholicism and Communism in Twentieth-Century Poland; The Politics of Bolesław Piasecki* (Athens, OH: Ohio University Press, 2012), 96.
189 Adriányi, *Geschichte der Kirche*, 72; Kunicki, *Between the Brown and the Red*, 97–8.

rights, but restored religious education, property to religious orders and the freedom to select bishops. Now the Church hierarchy removed the 'peace priests' from their offices, replaced the capital vicars and took stricter control of seminaries. In the 1960s, the government removed religious instruction from schools once more, but the Church set up extracurricular instruction, so that in 1966 some 80 per cent of elementary school students were taking catechism lessons.[190]

A pattern soon developed: by responding to increasing state repression, the Church grew stronger. It held its ground and began to occupy new spaces in the national narrative. Its most charismatic bishop was the young Karol Wojtyła, a stirring orator with a doctorate in philosophy who spoke numerous foreign languages, but also commanded the popular vernacular after having worked at a quarry and a factory during Nazi occupation. He and Wyszyński placed religious imagery in opposition to state nationalism, but they were responding to opportunities as much as creating them.

A moment of truth occurred in 1960 in the steel town of Nowa Huta, where the government had retracted permission to build a church on the grounds that socialist workers did not need religion. Authorities moved to reclaim the site by clearing away a large wooden cross the faithful had planted there. When workmen with shovels and picks arrived on 27 April 1960, women passers-by put their arms around the cross, while others pelted the workers with clumps of earth, forcing them to retreat. People from surrounding apartment buildings then gathered and re-anchored the cross in the earth. The crowd burgeoned as shifts emptied from the steel works, and, after hours of rioting, 181 police were injured and almost 500 demonstrators arrested. Yet the cross remained.[191] On his first visit to Poland as Pope John Paul II in 1979, Wojtyła said that this act had signalled new possibilities for Christian resistance to secularization.

But this was only the best-known clash.[192] Even more dramatic was the preparation for the 1,000-year anniversary of the Polish state, which also signified a millennium of Polish Catholicism. In 1957, Wyszyński had a duplicate of the 'Black Madonna' of Częstochowa painted and took it to Rome to be blessed by Pope Pius XII (1939–58). Polish troops had carried the original during a 'miraculous' victory over the Swedes in 1652, after which King Jan Sobieski had declared Mary 'Queen of Poland'. Wyszyński ordered the copy to be carried in pilgrimages around Poland and displayed in every parish. By June 1966, state officials grew tired of the spectacle and had the picture packed off to Częstochowa. People joked that the Virgin had been kidnapped. The processions continued with an *empty frame* where the picture had been, and everyone knew what it signified.[193]

Gomułka staged a final assault after Poland's bishops turned to their German counterparts in 1965, 'forgiving and asking for forgiveness'.[194] They knew that re-connecting Poland to the West depended on reconciliation with West Germany. Party agitators blew this into an act of 'treason' and asked in countless meetings if the bishops even remembered who started the war. Poles had nothing to apologize for. In 1966, authorities staged events to eclipse those planned by the Church and sent riot police to rough up people leaving celebratory masses in Warsaw.

---

190 There were 10,000 religious teachers, including 1,785 nuns. Adriányi, *Geschichte der Kirche*, 72–3.
191 Paweł Machcewicz, *Władysław Gomułka* (Warsaw: Wydawnictwa Szkolne i Pedagogiczne, 1995), 59.
192 Others occurred in Zielona Góra and Przemysl.
193 Karol Sauerland, 'Die Verhaftung der Schwarzen Madonna', *Frankfurter Allgemeine Zeitung*, 17 August 2010; Zygmunt Zielinski, *Kościół w Polsce: 1944–2002* [The church in Poland: 1944–2002] (Radom: Polskie Wydawnictwo Encyklopedyczne, 2003).
194 Hansjakob Stehle, 'Wir vergeben und bitten um Vergebung', *Die Zeit*, 29 September 1978, edition on the estate of Cardinal Kominek.

Nationalization vs. secularization

Provocateurs chanted: 'Down with Wyszyński! Traitor!' Fighting also broke out in Cracow, Gdansk and Lublin, and hundreds were taken into custody.[195]

Yet in autumn 1967, the anti-Church campaign fell silent. Cardinal Wojtyła learned that a church could be built in Nowa Huta after all. By that point the Polish economy was sputtering and Gomułka faced challenges from intellectuals and industrial labour, among whom sympathies had grown for the victimized Church. He could not afford to antagonize the Church any longer. Within a few years, four million children were attending instruction at 20,000 'catechetical stations [*punkty*]' that had gone up like 'mushrooms after the rain'.[196] In 1974, 4,200 candidates entered the priesthood.[197] When Wojtyła became pope in 1978, the linking of milieus – church, workers, intellectuals and peasants – to contest the party's narrative about Poland was complete. The result was the Polish trade union, Solidarność ('Solidarity').

Because of Catholicism's different place in their country's national imagination, Czechoslovak communists took measures unimaginable in Poland and came close to destroying the Church as a public presence. After February 1948, the state shut down Catholic schools, facilities, all but two seminaries, religious orders (including 226 monasteries and 720 convents), associations and the Catholic press, and then proceeded to seize their property.[198] In October 1949, the State Office for Church Affairs assumed control of church affairs, in a sense taking it into receivership, making it financially dependent upon the state.[199] Authorities vetted candidates for priestly duties and demanded they take oaths of loyalty to the 'people's democratic order'.[200] In language echoing enlightened despotism, the law on 'economically securing the church by the state' portrayed the state as being guided by a concern for proper religious practice.[201]

The state also interned nuns and monks for 're-education' and then conducted show trials of church leaders.[202] In 1950, the Greek Catholic Church was dissolved – a pattern followed throughout the bloc – and its property taken over by the Orthodox Church, which was obedient to Moscow's Patriarch. As in Poland, the government created a pro-communist 'peace priest' movement whose members assumed important church offices.[203] By 1955, 13 bishops had been removed from their offices and over 500 priests arrested, with another 1,500 forbidden

---

195 Sauerland, 'Die Verhaftung'.

196 Andrzej Paczkowski, *Pół wieku Dziejów Polski* [A half-century of Polish history] (Warsaw: Wydawnictwo Naukowe PWN, 1996), 343.

197 In 1965 there were 14,420 diocesan priests and 3,408 priests in religious orders; the number of Catholics was 27.1 million. In 1978, 569 new priests were ordained. At that time, there were 19,923 active priests. Adriányi, *Geschichte der Kirche*, 73–5.

198 For *likvidaci klášterů*, or 'the liquidation of cloisters'.

199 Zákon ze dne 14. října 1949, kterým se zřizuje Státní úřad pro věci církevní. 217/1949 Sbírka zákonů republiky Československé, Ročník 1949, 639 [The law of 14 October 1949 creating the state office for church matters]. The minister was Alexej Čepička, Klement Gottwald's son-in-law, a former inmate of Auschwitz.

200 Quoted in Hanuš, *Tradice*, 139.

201 Regulated by Zákon ze dne 14. října 1949, o hospodářském zabezpečení církví a náboženských společností státem. 218/1949 Sbírka zákonů republiky Československé, Ročník 1949, 640–1 [The law of 14 October 1949 on measures by the state to secure churches and religious communities economically].

202 The internment took place in the monasteries at Zeliv and Bec. See Milan J. Reban, 'The Catholic Church in Czechoslovakia', in *Catholicism and Politics in Communist Societies*, ed. Sabrina P. Ramet (Durham, NC: Duke University Press, 1990), 142–58, here 149.

203 Including, according to Karel Kaplan, the posts of canon, vicar-capitular, and vicar general in most diocesan organizations, thus the key administrative positions. Reban, 'The Catholic Church', 149–50.

to carry out their duties. Some 1,163 priests belonging to religious orders were forbidden from carrying out any pastoral function. Though the state claimed to care about properly staffing church offices, by 1979, of 4,436 Catholic parishes, 3,175 did not have their own pastor (in 1949 there had been 7,330 priests).[204] Priests driven from office were obliged to pursue other professions. Thus, in the 1960s, one bishop had a day job as a construction worker, another as a glass grinder, still another as a clerk in Prague's city administration.[205]

More important than seizing buildings or land was taking control of the terms of mutual understanding and making priests admit that 'socialism' was the basic reality of life.[206] Thus, beyond requiring loyalty oaths, communal authorities 'invited' priests to public discussions on topics such as building socialism or convincing parishioners to join voluntary work brigades. Rather than simply destroy religion, the state encouraged a syncretism that made the Christian religion part of a faith that supported state programmes.[207] The state benefitted from pre-Vatican II attitudes towards the state that were grounded in Paul's letter to the Romans (13:1): 'There is no authority except from God, and the authorities that exist are appointed by God.'[208] In addition, loyalty to the state had been well rooted in the Habsburg times, when it was seen as requisite for maintaining 'social order'.[209]

The Czechoslovak media portrayed the majority of priests, young and old, as eager to serve the people's democratic regime, and indeed some clerics of working class background claimed to be delighted to help build socialism, while others used Sunday sermons to urge farmers to make compulsory deliveries.[210] Masses, but also pilgrimages to sites devoted to the Blessed Mother, now became part of the state's 'peace' offensive. One festive Mass combining a pilgrimage with a 'peace manifestation' culminated in thanks for Generalissimus Joseph Stalin and 'our people's democratic government, because it has finally realized that which Christians have been praying for for centuries: our daily bread.' Christ's teachings about peace among nations meant that Christians should help unmask all 'enemies of peace'.[211]

This humiliating course was modified during the Prague Spring of 1968, but with the 'normalization' that followed the Warsaw Pact invasion, anti-Church policies returned with a vigour, making Czechoslovakia a place where priests had to prepare for ordination in secret and then travel to a foreign country – sometimes the GDR – to receive Holy Orders.[212] Though also secretly ordained, Czech bishops were soon identified by the secret police and carefully watched.[213] Even Czechs wanting to baptize their children often did so in secret. A 'peace priest' movement ('Pacem in terris') was revived in 1971, but a decade later the Vatican forbade priests from belonging to it.[214] Some 10–20 per cent of the clergy remained members neverthe-

---

204 Adriányi, *Geschichte der Kirche*, 87–8.

205 Hansjakob Stehle, *Eastern Politics of the Vatican 1917–1979* (Athens, OH: Ohio University Press, 1981), 274.

206 Hanuš, *Tradice*, 138.

207 Ibid., 136–8.

208 NKJV. The next line (Romans 13:2) is even more compelling: 'Therefore whoever resists the authority resists the ordinance of God, and those who resist will bring judgment on themselves.'

209 Hanuš, *Tradice*, 140.

210 Examples in: Hanuš, *Tradice*, 137, 40.

211 From Moravia in 1950. Ibid., 145.

212 For the reminiscence of a priest who went to Erfurt for ordination see Tomáš Halík, *Ptal jsem se cest* [I asked the way] (Prague: Portál, 1997)

213 Adriányi, *Geschichte der Kirche*, 88.

214 As part of a ban on belonging to political movements. Papal decree *Quidam episcopi* (1982).

Nationalization vs. secularization

less, protected by Josef Vrána, titular bishop of Olomouc as well as a secret police informer. The Vatican had acceded to his appointment in 1973 in order to secure three other nominations.[215]

Communists in Hungary were similarly uncompromising at first. They arrested and tried priests and bishops, dissolved 705 monasteries and convents, created a state office to control church affairs and confiscated 460,000 hectares of land, along with schools, clubs, organizations, printing presses and old age homes. Pastoral activities were restricted to the realm of worship and religious instruction ceased. State authorities monitored admission to seminaries, and within a few years the number of candidates for priesthood dropped from 1,779 to 300.[216] Here too there was a peace priest organization whose agents were smuggled into leading positions. Priests who remained at liberty were expected to spout propaganda for communist policies – like Soviet peace initiatives, collectivization and five-year plans – while praising the regime's devotion to religious freedom.[217]

Interestingly, this persecution, combined with the generally dire circumstances of Stalinism, had the effect of stimulating demand for the sacraments. The number of attendants at Sunday church services increased from the late 1940s to the early 1950s to over 70 per cent of adults, much higher than in the periods before or after. The churches became the 'most important institutions of quiet opposition'.[218]

A semblance of normalcy took hold in the Kádár years thanks to policies of pragmatic integration. In September 1964, the government signed an accord with the Vatican recognizing the Church's right to name bishops. Still, repression did not cease, and the state perfected networks of informers, especially in the Protestant churches that had no advocate like the Vatican beyond Hungary's borders. It persecuted priests who worked with young people and forced clergy to appear in person for regular interrogations.[219] Nothing, not even the production of a stamp with the parish insignia, could happen without state approval. Alongside the official apparatus a special section of state security was devoted to church surveillance and not only collected information, but also applied pressure on clergy, often of a psychological nature. In response, John Paul II directed his first letter to a national episcopate to Hungary, reminding bishops of their duty to serve only God.[220]

Some observers spoke of the churches as 'double decker buses', claiming that because the hierarchy was concerned with maintaining a modus vivendi, it opened itself to 'collaboration' by speaking out in support of socialism. For all the talk of opposition between Rome and communism, the Vatican was willing to sign an agreement with János Kádár as early as 1964, when other Western states would have little to do with him.[221] At that point, Kádár was not yet seen

---

215 Adriányi, *Geschichte der Kirche*, 88–9. Vrána agreed to work for the secret police on 20 November 1964: Archiv Bezpečnostních Složek, www.abscr.cz/data/knihy/OST/9/OST_9_5.jpg (accessed 16 February 2017). See Tomáš Benedikt Zbranek, 'Životní příběh kontroverzního biskupa' [The life story of a controversial bishop], *Historický obzor* 19, no. 1/2 (2008): 32–4.

216 Adriányi, *Geschichte der Kirche*, 104–5.

217 Ibid.

218 Tomka, 'Ungarn', 106.

219 Trials of priests took place in 1965, 1966, 1967, 1970 and 1972.

220 Adriányi, *Geschichte der Kirche*, 106.

221 Tomka, 'Ungarn', 106. The United States did not exchange ambassadors until 1967, despite recognition that Kádár had accomplished more effective liberalization than any other communist bloc country, for example by permitting travel to the West. On the depth of the bitterness over the crushing of the 1956 revolt, see David Halberstam, 'U.S. and Hungary Now Wider Apart', *New York Times*, 27 August 1965. On the appointment of a US Ambassador see CIA, *World Factbook* (Washington, DC: Directorate of Intelligence, 1970), 301.

as the pragmatic steward of goulash communism, but was still the bloody suppressor of 1956 who had ordered the hanging of Imre Nagy and other freedom fighters. But basic pastoral care was a paramount need for the Church hierarchy. The less fortunate result of this approach was that by the 1980s, when communism was failing and opposition groups rising, the hierarchy was more interested in preserving arrangements with the state than giving support to those struggling for greater freedoms. It was falling back upon patterns of the establishment Church dating back to the Habsburg days.

This syndrome was by no means limited to Hungary: we see it among bishops of all Christian denominations, for example Lutherans in the GDR or Orthodox in Romania, and even among the supposedly uncompromising figures. In Poland, Cardinal Wyszyński did not openly endorse the strikes that broke out in 1980 and led to Solidarność. But the issue goes beyond religion. We also see the stance of compromise in the behaviour of Western Social Democrats in the 1980s, who were more interested in protecting spaces for 'dialogue' with Moscow or East Berlin than establishing lines of communication to workers in Poland or underground intellectuals in Bohemia.[222] Any modus vivendi tended to legitimate the other contracting party and gradually stabilize relations of dependence. In the words of sociologist Miklós Tomka, it made the churches seem like a 'conformist prop' of the party state.[223]

In a trend that also played out in Romania and the GDR, priests and other religious persons at the grassroots level, disgusted by policies of accommodation among the bishops, insisted on conducting religious lives with approval neither from the state nor from the bishops. This seemingly apolitical behaviour was in fact deeply political, because Church and state colluded.[224] In one famous case, efforts at achieving political and theological independence exposed the Piarist priest György Bulányi to disciplinary measures from both state and Church hierarchy. Bulányi, who preached humility and non-violence in the Franciscan style, had set up grassroots groups that were critical of the accommodationist stance of the official church, favoured the independent peace movement and 'human dignity', and also sought 'radical change in the structure of the church, involving a redefinition of the roles of laity, the priesthood, and the bishops'.[225] What the state-church condominium had done was to provoke calls for restoration of authentic Christianity.[226]

Bulányi's bishop ordered him to cease and was supported by the Vatican of John Paul II. In September 1986, Bulányi received a detailed letter from Cardinal Joseph Ratzinger, Prefect of the Sacred Congregation for the Doctrine of the Faith, charging him with errors in four areas.[227] Bulányi's case was sensational but not unique. By the late 1980s there were some 5,000 grass-roots communities or 'basis groups' in Hungary with 70,000–100,000 members. In contrast to Bulányi, they were overwhelmingly loyal to their bishops.[228]

---

222 Timothy Garton Ash, *In Europe's Name: Germany and the Divided Continent* (New York: Random House, 1993).

223 Tomka, 'Ungarn', 107.

224 Adriányi, *Geschichte der Kirche*, 107.

225 Barbara J. Falk, *The Dilemmas of Dissidence in East-Central Europe: Citizen Intellectuals and Philosopher Kings* (Budapest: CEU Press, 2003), 144.

226 Sabrina P. Ramet, *Social Currents in Eastern Europe: The Sources and Consequences of the Great Transformation* (Durham, NC: Duke University Press, 1995), 161.

227 These were: rejection of the doctrine of apostolic continuity; failure to maintain a clear distinction between clergy and laity (by, for example, letting lay persons act as spiritual leaders); the idea that private conscience may override church authority; and support for ordination of women. See Ramet, *Catholicism and Politics*, 21.

228 Ibid., 20. Ramet identifies five kinds of basis communities in Hungary, of which only the last, the 'bush' communities, were severe and uncompromising in their opposition to church authority.

Nationalization vs. secularization

Miklós Tomka, though critical of the church hierarchy, reminds us that there was no way to separate the upper and lower floors of the double decker church. On the one hand, activist priests used facilities provided by the institution, and on the other, top church officials, while acting as though they knew nothing about basis group activities, did what they could to protect them beneath the radar. In the late 1980s, as the prestige of the party state crumbled, public opinion held that the churches possessed an exalted legitimacy, higher than all secular institutions.[229] At the same time, church institutions, even the basis groups, had no direct role in the processes in which power was transformed in the late 1980s, though members of those groups were among the first put up for election in communes.[230]

One explanation provided by sociologists for the attractiveness of basis groups was the atomization of Hungarian society after the 1956 Revolution and *accelerating modernization*. The official census gives the basic picture. The number of workers active in agriculture fell from 53.8 per cent in 1949 to 18.6 per cent in 1980, a process that continued, leading to the 'uprooting' of half the population. The spread of television and automobile culture helped 'cover' the consequences of atomization, but not completely: consumption of alcohol doubled, the number of deaths by cirrhosis of the liver tripled and the already high suicide rate increased 165 per cent over two decades.[231] The church basis groups paralleled other efforts by Hungarians to organize life for themselves: in private enterprise, in the grey economy, in clubs, circles of friends, hobby groups. The state tolerated such activity but did not encourage it. The underground churches were part of this second society, a place where independent thought was encouraged.

The movement was perhaps all the more important in a country where only 20 per cent of believers went to Mass, recruitment to priesthood had reached catastrophic lows and voluntary religious instruction in schools attracted few students.[232] By the end of the Kádár-era, the Church had shrunk to the dimensions of counterparts in Western Europe.[233] The category 'non-religious', which did not exist in 1949, amounted to 14.5 per cent in 2001 (an additional 10.8 per cent were of 'unknown' religion, also a category not counted before 1949). In 1980, some 60.7 per cent of Hungarians described themselves as non-religious in a poll conducted by the communist regime.[234]

Though Yugoslavia had a reputation for being a more liberal, 'maverick' Marxist regime, its history maps easily onto the more general one of repression we witness elsewhere, both in the early 'Stalinist' years (1945–8) and thereafter. Right after the war, the militant Partisan leadership self-confidently regarded religion as an 'unscientific illusion that reflected the alienation of man'. The church was a class enemy to be subdued, and Catholicism was seen as a particular problem because of its relations to Rome and supposed failure to side with the antifascist resistance.[235] Moreover, as mentioned above, the Vatican figured as a national enemy because it was reputed to side with Italy, against which Yugoslavia had perennial territorial conflicts.[236]

---

229 Tomka, 'Ungarn', 108.

230 The negotiations for transition were left to the reform communists and the actors of the new opposition groups. Ibid., 108–9.

231 Ibid., 103.

232 The number of pupils taking part in religious instruction decreased from 40 to 6 per cent from 1955 to 1975. Károly Kocsis, 'Spatial and Temporal changes in the Relationship between Church and State in Hungary', *GeoJournal* 67, no. 4 (2006): 357–71, here 364, 366.

233 Adriányi, *Geschichte der Kirche*, 107–8.

234 The number of Catholics went from 67.8 per cent (1949) to 51.9 per cent (2001), Calvinists from 21.9 to 15.9 per cent. Kocsis, 'Spatial and Temporal', 66.

235 Režek, 'Cuius Regio', 214–15.

236 In his meeting with Croatian church dignitaries in June 1945, Tito said precisely that the Vatican sided with Italy. Ibid., 215.

Catholicism had been unreserved in its hostility towards communism, and that stance continued in a letter addressed by Croatian bishops to believers on the eve of elections in September 1945, a letter Josip Broz Tito called a 'declaration of war'. In it, the bishops condemned the government's materialist philosophy along with other ideologies and social systems not based upon Christianity. They accused the government of pursuing an anti-church policy and demanded the return of all assets and freedom for the Catholic press, religious education and charitable work. They also drew attention to the Church's own record of suffering: 243 priests had been killed and 169 arrested since 1941.[237]

Because the Partisans had come to power mostly on their own, they could ignore calls for restraint coming from Moscow in the early post-war years and began building socialism. That meant seizing Church lands and closing religious schools other than seminaries. Priests could give religious instruction in state schools, but children attended only when their parents approved. Initially dozens, then hundreds of priests were arrested and placed on trial. In January 1952, the bishop of Ljubljana was attacked by a mob at the central train station: one man poured gasoline on the bishop then set him on fire. Though badly burned, the bishop survived while the attacker got off with a nominal punishment.[238]

The break with Stalin in 1948 and the advent of self-managing socialism did nothing to dampen convictions among Partisan leaders that the churches were an enemy. Edvard Kardelj, the leading voice on ideology, wrote in January 1952 that 'the enemy's power today rises, above all, from the Church and the peasants' backward religiosity.' 'We do not persecute religion and indeed we leave this matter to each individual person', Tito added in April.

> We cannot allow children to be educated according to the desires of those who have taken a very different path than the one we would like to take. The state has the right and the duty to educate its children. In this regard, we will never bend to outside pressure.[239]

In the spring of 1952, a law was passed abolishing catechism in schools.[240]

That same year, the state made priests join a patriotic association in order to foster the 'internal disintegration of the Church and its hierarchy'.[241] The Vatican's response was to excommunicate the society's founders and forbid participation.[242] The following year, Yugoslavia broke relations with Rome. The most visible object of dispute was Archbishop Stepinac, whom the Vatican had made a cardinal without consulting Belgrade. A rift persisted through the 1950s, a time of confrontation and increasing persecution, which included further attacks on priests. The West, despite providing Yugoslavia with millions of dollars in aid and loans, had little to no influence on this process.[243]

---

237 A further 89 were missing. Ibid., 216.

238 Ibid., 221.

239 Ibid., 220.

240 Ibid., 219–22.

241 Its purpose was identified by a leading Slovene communist in a January 1952 meeting of the Slovene Politburo. Ibid., 222.

242 About half of all Slovene priests joined the 'Cyril and Methodius Association of Catholic Priests' in Slovenia between 1949 and 1952. Similar organizations were created in Bosnia and Croatia; due to opposition, only about one-tenth of Croatia's priests joined. All attempts by the regime to reverse the Vatican's *non expedit* (non-cooperation) order as well as the excommunications failed. In December 1953, the highest church dignitary to join, Gorica's bishop Mihael Toros, resigned. Ibid., 223–4.

243 The West, for example, demanded that Stepinac be released. Ibid., 224

Nationalization vs. secularization

The situation normalized under Pope John XXIII (1958–63). In a protocol signed in 1966, the Yugoslav government recognized the Vatican's jurisdiction over the Church in spiritual matters, and the Holy See confirmed that the Church would not intervene in politics. Full diplomatic relations resumed four years later.[244] The state seemed willing to take these steps because secularization had left Catholicism less of a threat. According to Mateja Režek, by this point the Church in Yugoslavia 'no longer figured as a significant social force capable of guiding or noticeably affecting the development of society'.[245]

The arrangement also reflected a lessening of Cold War tensions, something that also had an influence on the Vatican: it was no longer crucial to emphasize hostility toward 'socialism'. But the exact relationship was unclear. No Catholic Church went as far as Lutheran churches in the GDR, which called themselves 'church in socialism'.[246] Still, as we have seen, some form of collaboration was unavoidable, and it even had a certain usefulness. Despite criticisms of Protestant accommodation, the cooperative stance of East German churches permitted them to harbour civil society groups that took a prominent role in the events of 1989.[247]

Romania seems to have been the polar opposite of the relatively moderate regimes in Hungary or Yugoslavia, but the basic constellation of murky battle lines and mutual accommodation was visible here as well. Even during the worst period of persecution, the regime's strategy was compromise. There was no other choice. The tiny communist movement of the mid-1940s faced a mostly rural population whose universe revolved around the church: its conservatism and traditionalism 'prevented the new regime from enforcing its authority on the religious denominations'.[248]

Policies of compromise predated the formation of Greater Romania in 1918 and went back to modi vivendi found by the churches and diverse groups of rulers: Ottoman, Habsburg and Hungarian. Rather than complete destruction, the Party oversaw the construction, as Anca Maria Şincan states, of a 'paradoxical hybrid regime in which the state allowed the functioning of religious denominations and their access to the public sphere in order to use them for its own purposes'.[249] They appear to have had common enemies and common agendas.

Take Archbishop Nicolae Bălan, Metropolitan of Transylvania, an early voice of opposition in the Orthodox Church after the Second World War. He proved willing to tone down his criticism, in part because he was compromised by his support of the Iron Guard.[250] Rather than arrest him, authorities entrusted him with administering 'Greek Catholic unification', a programme on the Soviet model of destroying the Greek Catholic (Uniate) Church by forcibly uniting it with the Orthodox Church. The policy commenced in October 1948 with a 'congress' in Cluj featuring 38 Uniate priests who requested reunion with the Orthodox Church. The Romanian Patriarch cooperated, and on 21 October, a 'unification celebration' took place,

---

244 Ibid., 232.
245 Ibid.
246 At their Synod of 1971, East German Evangelical Lutheran churches declared that they did not want to be a church 'next to, or against, but a Church within socialism'. Quoted in Otto Luchterhandt, 'Zur Situation und Position der Evangelischen Kirche', in *Die Innere und äußere Lage der DDR*, ed. Georg Brunner (Berlin: Duncker & Humblot, 1982), 141–83, here 157.
247 For a comparative study, see Herbert Heinecke, *Konfession und Politik in der DDR: Das Wechselverhältnis von Kirche und Staat im Vergleich zwischen evangelischer und katholischer Kirche* (Leipzig: Evangelische Verlagsanstalt, 2002).
248 Anca Maria Şincan, 'Mechanisms of State Control over Religious Denominations in Romania in the Late 1940s and Early 1950s', in Apor, Apor and Rees, *The Sovietization of Eastern Europe*, 201–12.
249 Ibid., 202.
250 Ibid., 205; Anca Maria Şincan, 'Of Middlemen and Intermediaries: Negotiating the State-Church Relationship in Communist Romania' (PhD diss., Central European University, Budapest, 2011), 92.

after which the Uniate Church ceased to exist.[251] A total of 2,536 churches and 1,794 parishes in 5 dioceses fell to the state, which 'redistributed' them to the Orthodox Church. All 6 Uniate bishops and hundreds of priests disappeared behind bars.[252] The Vatican responded by supporting an underground church, but bishops ordained in secret were soon arrested by the secret police.

The state also made use of functionaries inherited from the Ministry of Religious Denominations. The functionaries infiltrated churches, where they learned details of internal power struggles. Valerian Zaharia, for example, became bishop of Oradea in 1952 when his predecessor was forced to resign. He then became a party 'mole' in the Holy Synod of the Romanian Orthodox Church.[253] Over the decades, a cosy intimacy formed between church and state, and it did not wane with the Nicolae Ceauşescu regime's radical turn to chauvinist nationalism in the late 1960s. The story was not limited to the Orthodox hierarchy. László Tőkés, the Hungarian reformed pastor whose looming transfer ignited protests in Timişoara in December 1989, found that his own church's leaders had also settled into a comfortable arrangement with the powerful, and indeed constituted a front line for its defence.[254]

State socialism exposed East Central Europe to the assumption that religion was hostile to the interests of the working class and bound to fade, and everywhere measures were taken to make this happen according to the dialectic once described by Czesław Miłosz: 'I predict the house will burn; then I pour gasoline over the stove. The house burns; my prediction is fulfilled.'[255] The 'worker's state' seized property, closed instruction, placed nuns and priests on trial and created new organizations with the goal of compromising the clergy. Yet the outcomes differed by national tradition and according to how useful Christianity seemed to the rulers, especially in the post-Stalin age when the Stalinist-era dialectic weakened, becoming more prognostication than short-term prediction, more inspiration than prescription. With the receding of utopia, the post-Stalin period also falls under the heading 'national communism', once a heresy associated with Tito, now a fall-back position reminiscent of the early church adjusting to the failure of eschatological promises to be fulfilled in a single generation.[256]

Poland stands out for how state and Church vied to embody the nation's narrative; and it was the only place where Church and society formed a 'front' against state power. Not all Poles were Catholic, especially among the intelligentsia, but few felt alienated when crosses and other religious imagery crept into anti-state manifestations. A victory for 'religion' – the building of a church, the consecration of a new plaque for the martyred priest Jerzy Popiełuszko or today's saint 'John Paul the Great' – was a victory for society, for 'Poland'.[257] Even an apparently empty

---

251 Adriányi, *Geschichte der Kirche*, 132–3. The official decree stating this was issued on 1 December 1948.

252 By 1953, 53 priests had been killed, 250 had died or were expelled and about 200 were doing forced labour. By the late 1950s, of some 3,331 Roman and Greek Catholic priests 1,405 had lost their lives. Ibid., 132.

253 Further cases included the theologian Liviu Stan, who worked in the Department of Religious Denominations, but also kept a position in the Theology Institute, and the Patriarch Iustin Moisescu, who worked for the Department as inspector. There were also cases of Catholics and Protestants who similarly worked for the state within their respective hierarchies. See Şincan, 'Mechanisms', 205–6.

254 See László Tőkés, *The Fall of Tyrants* (Wheaton, IL: Crossway, 1991).

255 Czesław Miłosz, *The Captive Mind*, trans. Jane Zielonko (New York: Secker & Warburg, 1953), 15.

256 See Zbigniew Brzezinski, *The Soviet Bloc: Unity and Conflict* (Cambridge, MA: Harvard University Press, 1967).

257 Popiełuszko was a popular opposition priest in Warsaw. He was abducted and murdered by the secret police in 1983.

Nationalization vs. secularization

religious signifier – the blank frame that had held the painting of the Virgin – represented something Poles understood as vital for their national past and present.

No other place could compete with Poland for the drama of the church-state contest, but the state and churches became involved throughout the bloc in unlikely compromises by the 1960s. In 1964, the Vatican came to terms with a Hungarian regime widely seen as murderous, and everywhere questions have emerged of whether churches colluded with communist power and helped solidify it. The bishops tended to advise the faithful against open protests. At the same time, in no place could Christianity be practised without restrictions, and so the question after 1989 was what difference communism made for religious life in general.

Post-socialism

To this question there is no uniform answer. If one measures religiosity by weekly attendance at Catholic Mass, then some of the highest figures in the economically developed world are found in Poland and Romania, the latter a place which had a hard-line communist regime.[258] In both countries, over 55 per cent of Catholics attend, as compared with 22 per cent among Catholics in Germany and 12 per cent in France. For Catholics, Mass attendance is a requirement of the faith; according to the Catholic catechism, to fail to participate in the Eucharist on Sunday, short of a 'serious reason', is a grave sin.[259] These two places also stand ahead of Catholic communities in numerous developing countries like Mexico, Argentina and Brazil, and are bettered only by Ghana, Burkina Faso, Zimbabwe, Nigeria and Rwanda.[260]

By contrast, consider the Czech lands, where in 1950, just after the communist seizure of power, 93.9 per cent declared themselves believers.[261] Presently, just under a third of Czechs call themselves 'believing', while 61 per cent are 'atheist'.[262] In equally modern and secular West Germany, only about 8 per cent of the population are willing to declare themselves atheist, while in former East Germany the number is about 20 per cent.[263] For whatever reason, Czech atheists not only do not believe in God, but are eager to confess this fact to census takers.[264]

---

258 In 2002, Roman Catholics made up 4.7 per cent of the Romanian population and were overwhelmingly concentrated in Transylvania. See Secretariatul de Stat Pentru Culte, 'Biserica Romano-Catolică' [The Roman Catholic Church], http://culte.gov.ro/?page_id=695 (accessed 21 April 2020); https://commons.wikimedia.org/wiki/Category:2002_Romanian_census#/media/File:Romano-catolici_Romania_(2002).png (accessed 13 December 2016).

259 59.8% in Poland, 57.4% in Romania. From: World Values Survey, reprinted by the Center for Applied Research in the Apostolate (CARA) at Georgetown University, http://cara.georgetown.edu/CARA-Services/intmassattendance.html (accessed 28 January 2020).

260 Ibid.

261 Of these 81.3 per cent were Roman Catholic, 4.8 per cent Czech brethren, and 11 per cent members of the Czechoslovak Hussite Church. See Církev, 'Náboženské vyznání obyvatelstva ČR podle posledních výsledků sčítání lidu' [The religious confessions of the population of the Czech Republic by the most recent census data], http://tisk.cirkev.cz/z-domova/nabo-enske-vyznani-obyvatelstva-cr-podle-poslednich-vysledku-scitani-lidu/[Czech bishops' conference] (accessed 8 February 2017).

262 A further 8.9 per cent are not recorded. From the 2001 Czech census. Ibid.

263 In both places, far more people in fact 'practise' atheism. A 2005 EU study determined that for about one quarter of Germans, 'neither spirit, nor God, nor a higher power exist'. See Stefan Schmitt, 'Erlösung unerwünscht', *Die Zeit*, 9 September 2010.

264 Numbers of Czech believers dropped from 43.9 per cent in 1991 to 32.1 per cent in 2001. The number of male believers was 28.6 per cent and female 35.5 per cent. From the 2001 Czech census: Církev, 'Náboženské vyznání obyvatelstva ČR' [Religious confession of the population of the Czech Republic].

Table 5.1 Percentage of people who declare themselves Atheist or Agnostic

Czech lands	61
Hungary	35–46
Bulgaria	34–40
Slovakia	10–28
Croatia	7
Poland	3–6
Romania	4
Serbia	3

Notes: surveys taken in the late 1990s and early 2000s, with the exception of Serbia which was taken in 2014.

Sources: Phil Zuckerman, 'Atheism: Contemporary Rates and Patterns', in *Cambridge Companion to Atheism*, ed. Michael Martin (Cambridge: Cambridge University Press, 2007), 49–52. The Serb figure was taken from Gallup International, *Voice of the People, 2015: What the World Thinks; Global and Regional Issues* (Zurich: WIN/Gallup International, 2015), 135, www.gallup-international.com/wp-content/uploads/2017/10/GIA-Book-2015.pdf (accessed 30 January 2020).

As this is part of a larger data set, social scientists Ronald Inglehart and Pippa Norris offer an explanation embracing the globe: in 'societies characterized by plentiful food distribution, excellent public healthcare, and widely accessible housing, religiosity wanes. Conversely, in societies where food and shelter are scarce, and life is generally less secure, religious belief is strong.' 'The levels of societal and individual security in any society', they continue, 'seem to provide the most persuasive and parsimonious explanation.'[265] But they cannot account for variations within East Central Europe: living standards and social security do not explain threefold and sixfold differences in the index of religiosity between Czechs, Croats or Slovaks. Likewise, José Casanova's explanations based on the persistence of traditional milieus or American-style 'marketplaces' for religion cannot account for the differences. The erosion of traditional communities that tend to support religiosity was similar throughout the former Soviet bloc, and largely mono-religious places like Serbia show measures of religiosity similar to the USA.

The narrative of nationalization and secularization offered above has greater explanatory power: when forces of secularization and modernization are unleashed upon a country where religion is hostile or irrelevant to the national narrative, religion suffers. The Battle of White Mountain (1620) and forced re-Catholicization by a national enemy in the following centuries explain the disdain Czechs have for their 'nominal' Catholic faith. The fact that the Czech Catholic Church has had to call in over 200 Polish priests to staff parish churches does not suggest any improvement is in sight.[266]

The Czech case suggests that religiosity declines when it seems not only irrelevant to national identity, but opposed to it: for specific reasons of historical development, to be Christian seems to be in tension with what it means to be Czech. Contempt for Christianity became 'socially sanctioned' in the Czech lands; otherwise, Czech communist functionaries

265 This is partly their wording, partly a summary of their views in Zuckerman, 'Atheism', 57.
266 Ian Willoughby, 'With Few Czechs Getting Ordained Czech Catholic Church Turns to Polish Priests', Radio Praha, www.radio.cz/en/section/ice_special/with-few-czechs-getting-ordained-czech-catholic-church-turns-to-polish-priests (accessed 8 February 2017).

Nationalization vs. secularization

could not have subjected priests and other religious persons to degrading humiliation, even after Stalinism.[267]

The more moderate data on religious decline registered in Bulgaria or Slovakia are in keeping with mainstream European figures. They are also perhaps more in line with the findings of comparative sociology, though figures from the latter might be broken down by ethnicity: only some 80 per cent of the Slovak Republic's population is ethnically Slovak, while 8.5 per cent is Hungarian, and numbers of believers are lower in the southern regions where ethnic Hungarians reside, as well as in cities like Košice and Prešov.[268]

In Hungary, the higher level of a-religiosity reflects the weakness of churches associated with powerful political establishments in a context where Christianity was not vital to the national movement. As in Germany, the 'nation' was split among competing Christian confessions, but unlike the German variant, Hungarian Catholicism did not benefit from persecution like the Kulturkampf of Bismarck's Germany, which caused German Catholics to form quasi-ethnic milieus of self-defence against the secular and Protestant governing order, helping preserve Catholicism over several generations.[269] The upper hierarchy of the Hungarian Catholic Church was more reminiscent of parts of Central and South America (Honduras, Cuba) where the bishops were not only pro-establishment, but reactionary, in league with forces opposed to basic tasks of social justice like land reform.

The case of Hungary also reveals the analytical limits of a strict division between atheist/agnostic and 'believer'. Faith does not simply become unfaith, but rather transforms into a mixed form: no longer orthodox, but not fully God-denying either. Among many Hungarians, religion continues as an 'individual' experience. When researchers conducting a survey in 2000 asked respondents whether they were religious according to church teaching or religious 'in his/her own way', the results were 13.5 and 56.9 per cent respectively, and in 2008 17.9 and 48.3 per cent, respectively. From 1990 to 2008, the number of those answering positively the question of whether they are believers increased, from 47.5 to 63.5 per cent; but within that figure, belief in a personal God went from 38.6 to 40.9, while belief in a 'supernatural entity' went from 8.9 to 22.6 per cent.[270] We can connect this development to an international trend of decreasing 'religious literacy' and the persistence of certain religious practices with little to no relation to any church whatsoever.[271] What people along the continuum have in common is prayer: in 2008, almost two thirds of Hungarians confessed to taking some moments for prayer and meditation every now and then.[272]

---

267 'Social sanction' was the term used by Jan T. Gross to depict the passive to supportive behaviour of the residents of Kielce during the 1946 pogrom. See Gross, *Fear*, 159.

268 In those regions, numbers of Reformed Church adherents are higher. René Matlovič, Viera Vlčkov and Kvetoslava Matlovičov, 'Religiosity in Slovakia after the Social Change in 1989', in *The Changing World Religion Map*, ed. Stanley D. Brunn (Heidelberg: Springer, 2015), 1031–45, here 1036–9.

269 The milieu consisted of a 'multitude of associations and organizations, which pervaded all areas of life and held them together through a Catholic interpretation of reality.' These included sporting clubs, workers' associations, schools, press and, of course, a political party, the Centre Party. Also aiding Catholicism was the Church's more exclusive claim to offer salvation as well as more 'miraculous' methods of conferring sacrality and thus mediating salvation, especially the seven sacraments. See Detlef Pollack and Gergely Rosta, *Religion in der Moderne: Ein internationaler Vergleich* (Frankfurt: Campus, 2015), 168–9.

270 Rosta, 'Church and Religion', 200.

271 Stephen Prothero, *Religious Literacy: What Every American Needs to Know – and Doesn't* (New York: HarperCollins, 2008).

272 Rosta, 'Church and Religion', 198–9.

If the Czech lands represented an extreme in one direction, Poland, Romania and Serbia were an extreme in the other. In Serbia, a nation for which many Czechs feel deep sympathy and which seemed a smaller twin version of the Czech lands in the nineteenth century, the number of people describing themselves as 'atheist' to state census officials has declined since the collapse of communism: from 890,031 in 1953 to 159,642 in 1991 then to 40,068 in 2002.[273] But these are insignificant numbers in the population in general. At all times during and after communism, the overwhelming majority of Serbs told census takers that they were Orthodox. For example, the 2002 census recorded 6,620,669 Serbs and 6,371,584 Orthodox believers in Serbia.[274] According to data from the 1980s, religious practice had an insignificant place in Serb lives, with about 3 per cent of young people calling themselves religious.[275] Yet by the late 1990s, the number of avowed believers in the general population had risen to 60 per cent.

In Serbia, Christianity seems to be a vestige of national identity, never completely discarded, even among the decidedly anti- and a-religious. It seems that people are ready to summon it during periods of national calamity, such as during the 1990s, with the understanding that the saints and the Church hierarchy have always stood on the side of the Serb people. The Norwegian journalist Åsne Seierstad wrote that in Belgrade around the turn of the millennium it had become 'modern' to

> go to church, especially in large cities. Every Sunday, the houses of the Lord are filled with urban, often highly educated people. Baptism is nowadays 'in', and atheism for the old-fashioned. Young people, even the educated, go to monasteries in search of something to believe in.[276]

At the same time, the Serb Orthodox hierarchy carried the banner for the Serb national narrative, and leading figures blessed the activities of people subsequently tried as war criminals, even providing them shelter.[277] And under Vojislav Koštunica, Serb Orthodox religion returned to schools in full force in a condominium that seemed mutually beneficial.[278]

Across the battle lines to the north, the Croatian church hierarchy supported the nationalist regime of Franjo Tudjman. Yet given the close relation of Catholicism and the Croatian national narrative, even the 1994 visit of John Paul II to Zagreb, where he preached tolerance

---

273 The number spiked a bit to 80,053 in 2011.

274 Statistical Office of the Republic of Serbia, *Census of Population, Households and Dwellings in the Republic of Serbia* (Belgrade: 2011), 13, 16. Some of these may have been of other nationalities: there were 16,459 Bulgarians, 14,355 Macedonians, 34,515 Romanians and 2,199 Russians.

275 The numbers of believers in Serbia proper were much lower than those in Catholic areas (among youth about 30 per cent in Catholic areas, 3 per cent in Orthodox areas). Not only that, but some 90 per cent of young people in traditionally Serb Orthodox regions said they felt a 'positive aversion' toward religion. Regional surveys in the 1970s showed that 30 per cent of young people in Split and 70 per cent in Vojvodina called themselves atheist. Cited in Ramet, *Cross and Commissar*, 99.

276 Srđan M. Jovanović, 'Orthodoxy in Serbia: A Newfound Religiosity', *Humanicus* 8 (2013), www. humanicus.org/global/issues/humanicus-8-2013/humanicus-8-2013-6.pdf (accessed 16 February 2017).

277 Perica, *Balkan Idols*, 173: 'The Greece-based Hilandar monastery offered Karadžić monastic life as protection from the prosecution.' Åsne Seierstad, *With their Backs to the Wall*, trans. Sindre Kartvel (New York: Virago, 2006), 118; Mitja Velikonja, *Religious Separation and Political Intolerance in Bosnia-Herzegovina* (College Station, TX: Texas A&M University Press, 2003).

278 Jovanović, 'Orthodoxy in Serbia'.

Nationalization vs. secularization

and peace, seemed to support the Croat cause.[279] There was something ancient, but also fresh and revolutionary about its role here. Since the 1970s, the Catholic Church has taken on the semi-official title of 'Church of the Croats' (*Crkva u Hrvata*), emphasizing its role in creating a new nation state.[280] In contrast to trends in Eastern Christianity, the point here was to position Croatia securely in 'Western' civilization. Politicians from the Croatian Democratic Union (HDZ), but also their Social Democratic rivals, hardly missed a chance to appear in Zagreb's cathedral on Sundays, and Croatia was one of few places in Europe where church-going increased, though there were distinctions among the faithful. In a 2004 survey, 78 per cent of Zagreb residents said they were religious, but only 40 per cent accepted everything that the faith teaches.[281]

In contrast to the Eastern churches, the Catholic Church in Croatia occasionally took a firm stance against the governing power. In 1998, the new head of the Croat church, Josip Bozanić, made headlines by defying the Tudjman regime, preaching ethnic tolerance and castigating the state's 'sinful structure'. The new appointee owed loyalty first and foremost to Rome, not Zagreb.[282] The priests Zvonimir Bono Šagi and Ivan Grubišić, among others, called Tudjman's privatization immoral as well as harmful to ideals of *national* integration. In an interesting mélange of socialist and nationalist argumentation, the former said that what had been called 'social property' under communism should be distributed among its creators: the working people.[283] At the same time, the Church has done well in material terms, and in 2005 it figured among the five wealthiest corporations in Croatia. Perhaps presaging a fate similar to the Church in Hungary, this evidently close relation to power and wealth has damaged the Church's moral authority.[284]

Romanian Orthodoxy (ROC) is even more noteworthy when considered against the background of secularization narratives. Despite decades of communist rule, those among the Orthodox population describing themselves as religious reached 97 per cent in 2004 (the highest in Europe). The 2002 census showed that 99.6 per cent of the Romanian population claimed to belong to an officially recognized religious denomination.[285] The ROC leadership

---

279 It was seen less as 'a pilgrimage of peace and more a signal of support for a new Catholic state'. Timothy Byrnes, *Transnational Catholicism in Postcommunist Europe* (Lanham, MD: Rowman & Littlefield, 2001), 99.

280 Vjekoslav Perica, 'The Most Catholic Country in Europe? Church, State, and Society in Contemporary Croatia', *Religion, State and Society* 34, no. 4 (2006): 312.

281 See Ibid., 321. The number of non-religious dropped from 34 per cent in 1989 to 8 per cent in 2004. The number of churchgoers was around 30 per cent, higher than all Western European countries save Ireland and Portugal (37 per cent), than all Eastern European countries save Poland (59 per cent) and Slovakia (40 per cent), and similar to Italy (31 per cent) and Romania (27 per cent). GESIS, *European Values Survey 2008*, European Values Study, https://www.gesis.org/en/services/data-analysis/international-survey-programs/european-values-study/4th-wave-2008 (accessed 21 April 2020).

282 This was an about-face from policy of previous leadership. See Tracy Wilkinson, 'In an About-Face for Croatian Church, Archbishop Talks Up Tolerance', *Los Angeles Times*, 26 April 1998: 'A few weeks after he was chosen to head the Roman Catholic Church in Croatia, Msgr. Josip Bozanić invited a fledgling association of dissident television journalists to a personal audience … He urges tolerance for ethnic enemies, pledges to fight for democracy and human rights, and tells priests to work on behalf of the poor and not the privileged … The appointment of Bozanić signals a remarkable shift in a country where Catholic leaders, since Croatia declared its independence in 1991, too often joined in lock step with politicians to promote xenophobic nationalism over brotherhood and reconciliation.'

283 Perica, 'Most Catholic', 313.

284 Ibid., 313–14.

285 Romocea, *Church and State*, 5.

is split on European identity, with those educated in Western Europe, especially in the cultural 'ally' France, more positively disposed.[286]

More is at work here than the simple cohabitation of religious and national narratives. As the historian Zoe Knox has written, in the uncertainty of the post-communist era, churches throughout Eastern Europe have worked to achieve the cultural status of a national church and to 'foster links with post-communist political elites, reduce the influence (and sometimes the actions) of religious minorities, and promote the synonymy between religious and national identity.'[287] The success of this approach is most evident in Russia, perhaps because the atheist regime lasted longer than in East Central Europe. Russia's post-communist rulers have absorbed the legitimacy provided by the religious institution, and in 2016 the symbiosis went so far that the state forbade all religious activity outside of officially recognized church structures.[288] This is an extreme not seen further west, though it is impossible to say what steps rising illiberal democracies might take as they seek new forms of legitimation.

In Russia, we also see the importance of how questions of religious belief are posed. When a 1996 survey asked people whether they were members of a particular confession, 38 per cent answered yes and 58 per cent no. But when the question was changed to read: 'do you consider yourself Orthodox, Catholic, Muslim, or Jewish or a non-religious person?', the answer was: 75 per cent Orthodox, 4 per cent Muslim, 1 per cent Catholic, 1 per cent Protestant. Only 4 per cent called themselves non-religious.[289] A stigma has become attached to being a-religious; according to an influential narrative, one strong point of being Russian is to stand in opposition to the decadent, 'secular' West.

But that tells us little about how religious values filter into everyday life. In Russia too, the largely 'unchurched' yet church-identified population takes a highly individualized approach. In a survey taken in March 2006, over 70 per cent of Russians called themselves 'religious', but only 20.9 per cent said they were religious according to the teachings of their church and about half a per cent said they were religious in their own way. Only 14.4 per cent went to church once or several times a month, but 45.4 per cent reported praying at least several times a month. The connection with the sacred was strongly, if not fully, Orthodox: two-thirds of Russians claim that holy objects from Russian Orthodox culture had some power, such as icons and crucifixes.[290] In Russia, but also Romania and Serbia, Euroscepticism regarding Europe's

---

286 Lavinia Stan and Lucian Turcescu, 'Orthodoxy and EU Integration: Opportunity or Stumbling Block?' *Sphere of Politics* 146, www.sferapoliticii.ro/sfera/146/art02-stan_turcescu.html (accessed 8 February 2017).

287 Cited in: Jerry G. Pankhurst and Alar Kilp, 'Religion, the Russian Nation and the State: Domestic and International Dimensions: An Introduction', *Religion, State & Society* 41, no. 3 (2013): 226–43, here 229. An additional factor was the fact that the churches came back into possession of significant real estate and regained the ability to distribute resources, including jobs.

288 Especially affected are minority churches like Baptists and Jehovah's Witnesses. See Marc Bennetts, 'A New Russian Law Targets Evangelicals', *Newsweek*, 30 September 2016.

289 Fifteen per cent said they were unsure of their religious identity. Detlef Pollack, 'Wiederkehr der Religionen? Beschreibung und Erklärung des religiösen Wandels in den postkommunistischen Staaten Ost- und Ostmitteleuropas', in Veen, März and Schlichting, *Kirche und Revolution*, 133–56, here 139.

290 Marat Shterin, 'Secularization or De-secularization? The Challenges of and from the Post-Soviet Experience', in Pollack, Müller and Pickel, *The Social Significance of Religion*, 143–67, here 147–50.

Nationalization vs. secularization

supposed materialism or 'satisfaction of the belly' helps bolster both regional and Orthodox religious identity.[291]

Thus, East Central Europe is characterized by multiple places that have modernized and secularized, but where organized religion seems to benefit from opposition to precisely these phenomena. This is the opposite of what old secularization theory led one to expect but makes sense if one considers religion an element of group identity. In these cases, the 'group' clings to religion as a response to foreign (Western) influence. This also applies to Poland, where the conservative hierarchy both brandishes the John Paul II legacy as a key to Polish identity, while benefitting from the sort of anti-European scepticism reflected in institutions like Radio Maria. The paradox involves a universal church's structures being used not only in favour of a particular national narrative, but against a European one.

What about belief in a country that exports priests near and far? Poland conforms more to European trends than one might suspect. In 2006, 95 per cent of Poles claimed to be Catholic, but far fewer live their lives according to the teachings of the Catholic Church strictly speaking; 38.7 per cent say they are religious 'in their own way', and only slightly more than half share the orthodox Catholic view on the nature of God as personal (56.4 per cent), while 31.5 per cent believe in a spirit or 'life force'. Since the fall of communism, confidence in the institutional church has declined by more than 30 per cent, and the close symbolic unity of church and nation forged under communism has frayed.[292]

Like other Europeans, Poles have experienced a considerable 'secularization of the mind', that is, an ability to think in terms of separation between religious and other spheres.[293] This is a process that began generations ago. It originated in a time when confessional scepticism dominated in the educated classes and has advanced in other sectors at differing rates since then. But the nature of this separating and weighing of spheres differs by context. Living faith one's 'own way' might be technically more orthodox in Poland because knowledge of church teachings is stronger there than in places where religious instruction was subject to greater state control, like Slovakia or Hungary. But in Eastern Europe, the orthodoxy may be more familiar than in Western Europe because the Iron Curtain kept out more 'liberal' currents of thought. In contrast to what the Archbishop of Częstochowa Stanisław Nowak recently preached, the Church no longer teaches that there is no salvation outside it.[294]

Christianity has produced different kinds of practice depending on national narrative, yet the story is not so much one of political religions intertwining with 'real religions', but of different kinds of syntheses and syncretisms emerging over many generations, Christian nationalisms and national Christianities. Christianity has produced real religions in the standard definition given by Clifford Geertz:

---

291 Stan and Turcescu, 'Orthodoxy'.

292 Dorota Hall, 'Questioning Secularization: Church and Religion in Poland', in Pollack, Müller and Pickel, *The Social Significance of Religion*, 121–41, here 122 and 129.

293 The scientific, the political, the medical, family, the educational, etc. See Karel Dobbelaere, *Secularization: An Analysis at Three Levels* (Brussels: Peter Lang, 2002), 169.

294 See the report of his sermon of 29 October 2016 at http://czestochowskie24.pl/kosciol/poza-kosciolem-nie-ma-zbawienia/. On actual church teaching in this regard see Francis A. Sullivan, 'Vatican II and the Postconciliar Magisterium on the Salvation of Adherents of Other Religions', in *After Vatican II: Trajectories and Hermeneutics*, eds James Heft and John O'Malley (Grand Rapids, MI: Wm. B. Eerdmans Publishing, 2012), 68–95.

A system of symbols which acts to establish powerful, pervasive, and long-lasting moods and motivations in men by formulating conceptions of a general order of existence and clothing these conceptions with such an aura of factuality that the moods and motivations seem uniquely realistic.[295]

Or, alternatively, according to the pithier definition given by Sabrina Ramet, for whom religion is 'an interrelated set of assumptions about the nature and meaning of human existence, which are thought to have absolute validity and which are actively propagated by an institution or organized sect.' For Ramet, the ability of Christianity to mix with nationalism is obvious: religion can spiritualize the concept of national destiny and 'infuse the preservation of ethnic culture with intrinsic value'.[296] So a religious leader will claim that God sides with a particular faith and also against other faiths/peoples.[297]

How far can religion and nationalism 'travel' with each other before one side begins to lose energy or legitimacy? Religion thrives through nationalism when the nation seems challenged, questioned, and indeed when the existential circumstances suddenly appear gravely uncertain. This explains the resurrection from near death of religious ritual in Russia or Serbia and the sudden eagerness of communist functionaries like Vladimir Putin or Slobodan Milošević to make the sign of the cross. Perhaps it explains the distinction between Romania and Bulgaria: in the former case, the Romanian Orthodox and Uniate faiths serve as clear markers for Romanians against Calvinism, Islam and Roman Catholicism, other brands of Orthodoxy and Uniate faith. In Bulgaria, no such urgency attaches to the local Christian cult.

The religion–nation symbiosis seems to prosper when the two elements need each other. When the nation is proud and successful and prosperous and even confidently ecumenical and international (as in Scandinavia), then Christian religions can seem dispensable, weak precisely because they need the state for simple survival. While most Swedes are part of the Swedish (Lutheran) Church, that church's visible structures are all but empty, its basic teachings of justice or love so deeply absorbed into the civil society narrative that the church is irrelevant for the present, a living relic. To put it differently: without a need for the transcendent – to account for a nation's supposed worthiness before history – the church in the embrace of the nation state withers.

What of the region discussed in this chapter? In some ways, the history, even recent, confirms its distinctiveness. The high value attached to national identity and reflected in religious adherence among Serbs or Poles is related to a still recent history of foreign subjugation. The Czech case proves the point in the opposite direction: this modern nation continues to defy 'general European' trends through a highly distinct hostility toward organized Christianity. But to understand this one has to look at a national history stretching back centuries. The countries further west and south appear by contrast more moderate when it comes to the relation between religion and national (and thus personal) identity.

---

295 Clifford Geertz, 'Religion as a Cultural System', in *Anthropological Approaches to the Study of Religion*, ed. Michael Banton (London: Tavistock Publications, 1966), 1–46, here 3. Geertz has the advantage of being very inclusive and seems to include all known phenomena called 'religious'. See also Stanisław Obirek, *Umysł wyzwolony: w poszukiwaniu dojrzałego katolicyzmu* [The liberated mind: in search of a mature Catholicism] (Warsaw: W.A.B., 2011), 25.

296 Sabrina P. Ramet, 'The Interplay of Religious Policy and Nationalities Policy in the Soviet Union and Eastern Europe', in *Religions and Nationalism in Soviet and East European Politics*, ed. Sabrina P. Ramet (Durham, NC: Duke University Press, 1989), 3–41, here 7.

297 Ibid.

Nationalization vs. secularization

Older ideas of correlations between secularization and modernization retain some purchase. The Czech lands and East Germany were the most industrially developed, highly educated and urbanized areas of the former Eastern bloc, and their measurements of a-religiosity are similar. However, Poland, Hungary and Slovakia have similar levels of wealth, but radically different numbers of strongly religious, on the one hand, and strongly a-religious, on the other.

To speak of countries to the east *and* west points to the fact that the region is not cut off from global history: it both interacts with broader trends and exemplifies them. Some trends and divisions predate the time of this study, and the emergence of its subject, East Central Europe. The most striking finding on a background of two centuries is the persistence of Orthodoxy with little regard to political regime.

Will the Western churches of Eastern Europe share the fate of France, England and Bohemia? We have said little about the content of Christian belief, about what Western and Eastern Christians mean when they address God in their various rites, how they experience the transcendent through liturgy, why the cult that is 'meaning-giving' for one generation loses credibility for the next. The cultural critic Leszek Kołakowski worried that with advancing secularization, Europe might lose its connection to its mythic origins of religion, to sources of criteria of good and evil: 'Christianity was the place in our culture from which such differentiations derived', he said in 1993.[298]

But at the same time, one of contemporary Europe's most popular Catholic intellectuals, the Czech priest Tomáš Halík, is not worried. To the contrary, Halík, a papal prelate and one-time adviser to Václav Havel, ordained in secret in the GDR in 1978 because persecution made it impossible at home, believes that secularization gives Christianity a fresh chance to recover the mysterious God that the Apostle Paul spoke about to the Athenians, lost in the course of history 'to the temptation to exchange the paradoxical God of Christ's Easter story for a "familiar god" conforming to the human notions and expectations.'[299] Halík explained why he is happy not only to be a Catholic, but to minister in a largely atheist environment: 'In Poland, it is so normal to be Catholic. But here, it is something of a provocation. And you know, I think it is good to provoke people sometimes.'[300] His books are translated into Western languages in a way that is not paralleled by other religious thinkers from the 'East'. For him, secularization provides a 'great opportunity to clean and open up a space in which we may hear anew Paul's message', precisely because 'for a large proportion of Europeans, God is an unknown and alien god'.[301]

---

298 Leszek Kołakowski, *Kościół w krainie wolności* [The church in the land of freedom] (Krakow: Znak, 2011), 23: 'There is a danger that traditional belief will die out.' See also Siegfried Lenz, *Gespräche mit Manes Sperber und Leszek Kołakowski* (Munich: DTV, 1980), 111.

299 Tomáš Halík, *Patience with God: The Story of Zacchaeus Continuing in Us* (New York: Crown, 2009), 113–21.

300 Rick Lyman, 'Not All Will Follow This Star in the East: The Rev. Tomas Halik Castigates Putin for Russia's Seizure of Crimea', *New York Times*, 4 July 2014.

301 See for example his *Donner du temps à l'éternité, la patience envers Dieu* (Paris: Editions du Cerf, 2014); *Geduld mit Gott: Leiden und Geduld in Zeiten des Glaubens* (Freiburg: Herder, 2010); *Night of the Confessor: Christian Faith in an Age of Uncertainty* (New York: Image, 2012). The citation is from his *Patience with God: The Story of Zacchaeus Continuing in Us* (New York, 2009), 116.

Further reading

Agnew, Hugh LeCaine. *Origins of the Czech National Renascence* (Pittsburgh, PA: University of Pittsburgh Press, 1993).

Alexander, Stella. *Church and State in Yugoslavia since 1945* (Cambridge: Cambridge University Press, 1979).

Apor, Balázs, Peter Apor and Edward Arfon Rees, eds. *The Sovietization of Eastern Europe: New Perspectives on the Postwar Period* (Washington, DC: New Academia Publishing, 2008).

Ash, Timothy Garton. *In Europe's Name: Germany and the Divided Continent* (New York: Random House, 1993).

Baár, Monika. *Historians and Nationalism: East-Central Europe in the Nineteenth Century* (Oxford: Oxford University Press, 2010).

Berend, Ivan T. *Decades of Crisis: Central and Eastern Europe before World War II* (Berkeley, CA: University of California Press, 1998).

Berglund, Bruce R. and Brian A. Porter, eds. *Christianity and Modernity in Eastern Europe* (Budapest: CEU Press, 2010).

Berlin, Isaiah. *The Roots of Romanticism* (Princeton, NJ: Princeton University Press, 1999).

Blobaum, Robert, ed. *Antisemitism and Its Opponents in Modern Poland* (Ithaca, NY: Cornell University Press, 2005).

Brubaker, Rogers. *Citizenship and Nationhood in France and Germany* (Cambridge, MA: Harvard University Press, 1992).

Bruce, Steve. *God is Dead: Secularization in the West* (Oxford: Blackwell, 2002).

Brunn, Stanley D., ed. *The Changing World Religion Map* (Heidelberg: Springer, 2015).

Brzezinski, Zbigniew. *The Soviet Bloc: Unity and Conflict* (Cambridge, MA: Harvard University Press, 1967).

Byrnes, Timothy. *Transnational Catholicism in Postcommunist Europe* (Lanham, MD: Rowman & Littlefield, 2001).

Cadzow, John F., Andrew Ludanyi and Louis J. Elteto, eds. *Transylvania: The Roots of Ethnic Conflict* (Kent, OH: The Kent State University Press, 1983).

Coppa, Frank J. *Politics and Papacy in the Modern World* (Westport, CT: Praeger, 2008).

Dénes, Iván Zoltán. *Liberty and the Search for Identity*, ed. Iván Zoltán Dénes (Budapest: CEU Press, 2006).

Dieckhoff, Alain and Christophe Jaffrelot, eds. *Revisiting Nationalism: Theories and Practices* (London: Hurst, 2005).

Diggins, John. *The Lost Soul of American Politics* (Chicago, IL: University of Chicago Press, 1984).

Dobbelaere, Karel. *Secularization: An Analysis at Three Levels* (Brussels: Peter Lang, 2002).

Emmert, Thomas. *Serbian Golgotha: Kosovo, 1389* (New York: Columbia University Press, 1990).

Esterhammer, Angela, ed. *Romantic Poetry* (Amsterdam: John Benjamins, 2002).

Falk, Barbara J. *The Dilemmas of Dissidence in East-Central Europe: Citizen Intellectuals and Philosopher Kings* (Budapest: CEU Press, 2003).

Gellner, Ernest. *Nations and Nationalism* (Ithaca, NY: Cornell University Press, 1983).

Grabowski, Jan. *Hunt for the Jews* (Bloomington, IN: Indiana University Press, 2013).

Gross, Jan. *Fear: Anti-Semitism in Poland after Auschwitz* (Princeton, NJ: Princeton University Press, 2006).

Halík, Tomáš. *Night of the Confessor: Christian Faith in an Age of Uncertainty* (New York: Image, 2012).

Halík, Tomáš. *Patience with God: The Story of Zacchaeus Continuing in Us* (New York: Crown, 2009).

Hanebrink, Paul. *In Defense of Christian Hungary: Religion, Nationalism, and Anti-Semitism, 1890–1944* (Ithaca, NY: Cornell University Press, 2006).

Heft, James and John O'Malley, eds. *After Vatican II: Trajectories and Hermeneutics* (Grand Rapids, MI: Wm. B. Eerdmans Publishing, 2012).

Held, Joseph, ed. *The Columbia History of Eastern Europe in the Twentieth Century* (New York: Columbia University Press, 1992).

Heller, Celia Stopnicka. *On the Edge of Destruction: Jews of Poland between the Two World Wars* (Detroit, MI: Wayne State University Press, 1994).

Herbermann, Charles George, et al., eds. *The Catholic Encyclopedia*, vol. 7 (New York: Robert Appleton Company, 1913).

Hobsbawm, Eric J. *Nations and Nationalism since 1780* (Cambridge: Cambridge University Press, 1992).

Iordachi, Constantin. *Charisma, Politics and Violence: The Legion of the 'Archangel Michael' in Inter-War Romania* (Trondheim: Trondheim Studies on East European Cultures and Societies, 2004).

Nationalization vs. secularization

Jelavich, Barbara. *History of the Balkans*, vol. 1 (Cambridge: Cambridge University Press, 1983).

Judson, Pieter. *Guardians of the Nation: Activists on the Language Frontiers of Imperial Austria* (Cambridge, MA: Harvard University Press, 2006).

Kornberg, Jacques. *The Pope's Dilemma: Pius XII Faces Atrocities and Genocide in the Second World War* (Toronto: University of Toronto Press, 2015).

Kotkin, Stephen. *Magnetic Mountain* (Berkeley, CA: University of California Press, 1995).

Kunicki, Mikołaj Stanisław. *Between the Brown and the Red: Nationalism, Catholicism and Communism in Twentieth-Century Poland; The Politics of Bolesław Piasecki* (Athens, OH: Ohio University Press, 2012).

Liulevicius, Vejas. *The German Myth of the East* (Oxford: Oxford University Press, 2009).

Martin, David. *On Secularization: Towards a Revised General Theory* (Farnham: Ashgate, 2005).

McLeod, Hugh. *Secularisation in Western Europe, 1848–1914* (New York: St. Martin's Press, 2000).

Michael, Banton, ed. *Anthropological Approaches to the Study of Religion* (London: Tavistock Publications, 1966).

Michael, Martin, ed. *Cambridge Companion to Atheism* (Cambridge: Cambridge University Press, 2007).

Miłosz, Czesław. *The Captive Mind*, trans. Jane Zielonko (New York: Secker & Warburg, 1953).

Mishkova, Diana and Roumen Daskalov, eds. *Entangled Histories of the Balkans*, vol. 2 (Leiden: Brill, 2013).

Modras, Ronald. *The Catholic Church and Anti-Semitism: Poland 1933–39* (Chur, Switzerland: Harwood Academic Publishers, 1994).

Nielsen, Christian Axboe. *Making Yugoslavs: Identity in King Alexander's Yugoslavia* (Toronto: University of Toronto Press, 2014).

Numbers, Ronald L. and John Stenhouse, eds. *Disseminating Darwinism: The Role of Place, Race, Religion and Gender* (Cambridge: Cambridge University Press, 1999).

O'Leary, Don. *Roman Catholicism and Modern Science* (New York: Bloomsbury, 2006).

O'Malley, John. *What Happened at Vatican II* (Cambridge, MA: Harvard University Press, 2008).

Pease, Neal. *Rome's Most Faithful Daughter* (Athens, OH: Ohio University Press, 2009).

Perica, Vjekoslav. *Balkan Idols: Religion and Nationalism in Yugoslav States* (Oxford: Oxford University Press, 2002).

Pollack, Detlef, Olaf Müller and Gert Pickel, eds. *The Social Significance of Religion in the Enlarged Europe* (Farnham: Ashgate, 2012).

Porter-Szűcs, Brian. *Poland in the Modern World: Beyond Martyrdom* (Chichester: Wiley-Blackwell, 2014).

Porter-Szűcs, Brian. *When Nationalism Began to Hate* (Oxford: Oxford University Press, 2000).

Prothero, Stephen. *Religious Literacy: What Every American Needs to Know – And Doesn't* (New York: HarperCollins, 2008).

Ramet, Sabrina P., ed. *Catholicism and Politics in Communist Societies* (Durham, NC: Duke University Press, 1990).

Ramet, Sabrina P. *Cross and Commissar: The Politics of Religion in Eastern Europe and the USSR* (Bloomington, IN: Indiana University Press, 1987).

Ramet, Sabrina P., ed. *Religion and Nationalism in Soviet and East European Politics* (Durham, NC: Duke University Press, 1989).

Ramet, Sabrina P. *Social Currents in Eastern Europe: The Sources and Consequences of the Great Transformation* (Durham, NC: Duke University Press, 1995).

Riasanovsky, Nicholas V. *Nicholas I and Official Nationality in Russia* (Berkeley, CA: University of California Press, 1959).

Romocea, Cristian. *Church and State: Religious Nationalism and State Identification in Post-Communist Romania* (London: Continuum, 2011).

Rothschild, Joseph. *East Central Europe between the Two World Wars* (Seattle, WA: University of Washington Press, 1974).

Seierstad, Åsne. *With Their Backs to the Wall*, trans. Sindre Kartvel (New York: Virago, 2006).

Seton-Watson, Hugh. *Eastern Europe between the World Wars* (Cambridge: Cambridge University Press, 1945).

Șincan, Anca Maria. 'Of Middlemen and Intermediaries: Negotiating the State-Church Relationship in Communist Romania' (PhD diss., Central European University, Budapest, 2011).

Smith, Anthony D. *Chosen Peoples: Sacred Sources of National Identity* (Oxford: Oxford University Press, 2003).

Stachura, Peter D. *Poland, 1918–1945: An Interpretative and Documentary History of the Second Republic* (London: Routledge, 2004).

Stehle, Hansjakob. *Eastern Politics of the Vatican 1917–1979* (Athens, OH: Ohio University Press, 1981).

John Connelly

Sugar, Peter F., Péter Hanák and Tibor Frank, eds. *A History of Hungary* (Bloomington, IN: Indiana University Press, 1990).

Taylor, J.H., ed. *Ancient Christian Writers*, no. 41 (New York: Paulist Press, 1982).

Tőkés, László. *The Fall of Tyrants* (Wheaton, IL: Crossway, 1991).

Tomasevich, Jozo. *War and Revolution in Yugoslavia, 1941–1945* (Stanford, CA: Stanford University Press, 2001).

Tresic-Pavičić, Ante. *In Darkest Europe: Austria-Hungary's Effort to Exterminate Her Jugoslav Subjects; Speeches and Questions in the Parliaments of Vienna and Budapest and in the Croatian Sabor (Diet) in Zagreb* (London: The Near East, 1917).

Velikonja, Mitja. *Religious Separation and Political Intolerance in Bosnia-Herzegovina* (College Station, TX: Texas A&M University Press, 2003).

Wingfield, Nancy M. *Flag Wars and Stone Saints: How the Bohemian Lands Became Czech* (Cambridge, MA: Harvard University Press, 2007).

Wolff, Richard J. and Jörg K. Hoensch, eds. *Catholics, the State, and the European Radical Right 1919–1945* (New York: Columbia University Press, 1987).

Zacek, Joseph. *Palacký: The Historian as Scholar and Nationalist* (The Hague: Mouton, 1970).

6

VISUAL CULTURES
Tele-visions

Anikó Imre

Introduction

Histories of visual culture in twentieth-century Eastern Europe evoke forms of high art: cinema, painting, photography etc. Histories of television in the region are very recent and, for the most part, nation-based.[1] This scarcity is somewhat surprising since television has been a crucial barometer of the political, economic and cultural life of Eastern European societies. In the most obvious sense, it is an institution that lives in the intersection of the public and domestic spheres, between top-down attempts at influencing viewers and bottom-up demands for entertainment. Art films and literature have been the preferred and often the only available sources that informed the world beyond the Iron Curtain about life in really existing socialism. But these high cultural accounts were produced by and for the most part also *for* intellectuals and artists who were already part of a cosmopolitan circulation of talent.[2] Whereas much of art and literature informs us of the relationship between the party leadership and the intellectual elite, TV grants us a sense of the real complexity of the relationship between the party leadership and the public. Recovering television's history throws into question the enduring and near-exclusive attention to (dissident) literature, film and journalism that has defined academic approaches to socialist cultures. It offers an alternative view, from the vantage point of everyday practices of socialism. These practices were motivated by discourses and desires that considerably muddy the entrenched idea of a binary opposition between official party-led cultures and dissident intellectual cultures.

By virtue of its cross-border production, circulation and consumption, television also challenges the national containment of these relationships. Socialist television's geographical

---

1 Paulina Bren, *The Greengrocer and His TV: The Culture of Communism after the 1968 Prague Spring* (Ithaca, NY: Cornell University Press, 2010); Kristin Roth-Ey, *Moscow Prime Time: How the Soviet Union Built the Media Empire that Lost the Cultural Cold War* (Ithaca, NY: Cornell University Press, 2011); Christine E. Evans, *Between Truth and Time: A History of Soviet Central Television* (New Haven, CT: Yale University Press, 2016); Heather Gumbert, *Envisioning Socialism Television and the Cold War in the German Democratic Republic* (Ann Arbor, MI: University of Michigan Press, 2014).

2 Anikó Imre, 'Postcolonial Media Studies in Postsocialist Europe', *boundary 2* 41, no. 1 (Spring 2014): 113–34.

boundaries stretch beyond the Soviet Empire. Its histories are both anchored in pre-socialist cultures and continue into post-socialism, never in isolation from the world of liberal capitalism even in the most isolated places and times. Television industries under Soviet influence developed in simultaneity and interaction with those in Western Europe and beyond. Sylwia Szostak shows that socialist TV has followed John Ellis's three-stage chronology: beginning with the post-war era of scarcity, then moving to the 1960s–1970s era of availability, and then into the era of plenty since the 1980s, with the exception of a slight delay in the most recent phase.[3] Charlotte Brunsdon's application of Raymond Williams' concept of emergent, dominant and residual cultures to European broadcast television is also relevant to an examination of television in the East.[4]

As Heather Gumbert writes in her account of early East German TV, the historical experiment of socialism is so profoundly rooted in the history of modernity that socialism and liberal capitalism cannot be disentangled.[5] But the goal of this chapter is not to assimilate the history of Eastern European socialist TV into that of Western European social democracies. It is, to borrow Sabina Mihelj's words, to think of socialist television 'as a specific subtype of modern television, designed to promote an alternative vision of modernity, modern belonging, economics and culture'.[6]

Writing a history of socialist television histories is therefore a large and necessarily collective project only recently begun by scholars in research centres in Europe and scattered across the globe.[7] There is a reason why, as Dana Mustata writes, 'there is a momentum for television histories from Eastern Europe'.[8] Revisiting socialist television also inevitably rewrites European and global TV histories by virtue of questioning television's reigning national logic, as well as the Cold War divisions between East and West and between socialism and post-socialism. The particular hybridities developed by socialist and post-socialist television outline, above all, a regional pattern, which is itself rooted in the shared imperial histories on which the region's

---

3 Sylwia Szostak, 'Poland's Return to Europe: Polish Terrestrial Broadcasters and TV Fiction', *Journal of European Television History and Culture* 1, no. 2 (2012): 80.

4 Charlotte Brunsdon, 'Is Television Studies History?', *Cinema Journal* 47, no. 3 (Spring 2008): 129.

5 Heather Gumbert, *Envisioning Socialism: Television and the Cold War in the German Democratic Republic* (Ann Arbor: University of Michigan Press, 2014), 4.

6 Sabina Mihelj, 'Understanding Socialist Television: Concepts, Objects, Methods', *VIEW: Journal of European Television History and Culture* 3, no. 5 (2014): 16.

7 See: Anikó Imre, Timothy Havens and Katalin Lustyik, eds, *Popular Television in Eastern Europe During and Since Socialism* (New York: Routledge, 2013). The European (Post)Socialist Television History Network and its accompanying project 'Television Histories in (Post)Socialist Europe' were launched in September 2013 in order to offer an international collaborative platform for scholars working on television histories in Eastern Europe. The network was founded by Dana Mustata along with Anikó Imre, Ferenc Hammer, Irena Reifová and Lars Lundgren. Other recent initiatives include Sabina Mihelj's project 'Screening Socialism' and the 'Television in Europe beyond the Iron Curtain' conference organized by Friedrich-Alexander-Universität Erlangen-Nürnberg in December 2013. Other influential volumes, used as crucial reference points throughout this book, are: on late socialist Czech television fiction, Paulina Bren, *The Greengrocer and His TV*; Kristin Roth-Ey, *Moscow Prime Time*; Christine E. Evans, *Between Truth and Time*; Jan Culik, *National Mythologies in Central European TV Series: How J.R. Won the Cold War* (Eastbourne: Sussex Academic Press, 2013); and a special issue of the *Historical Journal of Film, Radio and Television* (Vol. 24, Nr. 3, 2014) dedicated to television in the former GDR.

8 See Dana Mustata, 'Editorial', *VIEW Journal of European Television History & Culture* 3, no. 5 (2014): 1–6.

Visual cultures

television infrastructures were built as well as which programming trends, distribution patterns and reception practices have continued into the present day.

Broadcast television around the world has enjoyed an unparalleled capacity to gather the nation-family around the proverbial fireplace. Television under state socialism was no exception. There is no doubt that the only way to do justice to its history is by understanding the intimate cultural clues and affective bonds it wove among national citizens over time. At the same time, it is important to resist the power of nationalism which has the ability to monopolize emerging histories; it is also important to refuse to yield these emerging histories entirely to the institutional influence of nation states.[9] The momentum around studying television as a way of accessing real-life socialism provides an opportunity to reconsider the Cold War as more than the binary struggle between the two superpowers and the nation states in their respective satellite systems. Socialist elite cultures formed around literature, theatre and film have been almost exclusively wrapped up in the bipolar model and have adopted its dominant nation-based worldview. This approach internalizes and confirms the assumptions of marginal nationalisms: intellectual leaders rightly speak for and unite the population in strict opposition to the oppressive political regime. Such a model leaves unrepresentable subnational and transnational affiliations that would disrupt this alignment.

Television gives us access to subtle but all the more significant subnational divisions within the 'public' that both socialist ideology itself and Cold War discourses about socialism have envisioned as homogeneous. Instead of confirming the blanket oppression of the people by authoritarian or dictatorial leaders, the history of television highlights the more fluid workings of micro-oppressions and exclusions: of women, of non-normative sexualities, of foreigners, of the Roma and other non-white populations. These exclusions were and continue to be embedded in the very structure of nationalism which socialist TV adopted from Western public broadcasters. However, they failed to be enforced in a straightforward fashion thanks to the unpredictable, pleasure-based, entertainment-focused workings of television. Determining what TV viewers wanted or even watched is crucial to understanding socialist television and socialism through the lens of television; it is not an easy task, however. The scarcity and unreliability of both viewing data and viewer memories are obvious obstacles. Most socialist television industries established more or less developed audience-research branches by the late 1960s. This was a vast improvement from counting the number of viewer letters, let alone weighing the mailbag, which was the preferred method of measuring audience interest in early Soviet television.[10] But even empirical, survey-based audience research remained somewhat unreliable. In the Soviet Union, the surveys were often face-to-face rather than anonymous and contained leading questions.[11] This was not a Soviet specificity: while Western European public broadcasters were more invested in audience research since they had to justify their public support, their surveys often produced the impression of an aspirational, static and passive national audience.[12]

---

9 See also Sabina Mihelj's argument against 'methodological nationalism' in her 'Understanding Socialist Television'.

10 Roth-Ey, *Moscow Prime Time*, 268.

11 Ibid.

12 Mats Björkin and Juan Francisco Gutierrez Lozano, 'European Television Audiences: Localising the Viewers', in *A European Television History*, eds Jonathan Bignell and Andreas Fickers (New York: Blackwell, 2008), 215.

Anikó Imre

The emergence of TV in Eastern Europe: a European perspective

Television was first introduced in most countries of the region during the pre-war period, in step with the United States and Western Europe. Small-scale state television broadcasting began in the interwar years.[13] The first experiments with television viewing were collective experiences before corporations began to push for standardized domestic viewing in the 1930s. In Nazi Germany, television was crucial to the National Socialists' cultural policy after they came to power in 1933.[14] The 1936 Berlin Olympics stimulated further interest in television as a technology of mass persuasion. Viewing rooms were established in cities to hold audiences as large as 400 viewers. And even after the war, when interest in television technology picked up again all over Europe, domestic viewing remained a collective experience organized around the first, scattered TV sets.[15]

The Second World War and its aftermath interrupted the development of television infrastructures. State broadcasting did not start up again until the 1950s, beginning, for the most part, with sporadic broadcasts received by a few thousand subscribers in each country. Regional cooperation began almost immediately. The first programme exchange, a 1957 Hungarian initiative titled Intervision, included Czechoslovakia, Poland, the German Democratic Republic and Hungary.[16] In comparison, post-war British and French television continued pre-war experiments and began limited service in 1945. Radiotelevisione Italiana (RAI) began service in 1952; Danish and Belgian broadcasting began in 1953, Spain in 1956, Sweden and Portugal in 1957, Finland in 1958, Norway in 1960, Switzerland in 1958, Ireland in 1961, Gibraltar and Malta in 1962 and Greece in 1966.[17]

Much like elsewhere in Europe, by the 1960s the proliferation of television sets in the home and the quality and quantity of programming transformed socialist television into a truly national form of entertainment. In Hungary, where regular broadcasting began in 1957, the number of programming hours per week jumped from 22 to 40 between 1960 and 1965.[18] The Slovenian broadcaster, Television Ljubljana, started transmitting its own television programming in 1958, with 700–800 television sets in Slovenia and about 4,000 in all of Yugoslavia (compared to 90 per cent of all homes in the US at that time).[19] In Czechoslovakia, where the war also interrupted pre-war experimental broadcasts, trial public broadcasts began in 1953. The rapid increase in television access in the 1960s played a central role in the liberalization of the country's political climate. This liberalization came to a halt following the Prague Spring of 1968, which was brutally crushed by the Soviet Union.[20] Television Romania was established in 1956 and added a second channel in 1968. This was then suspended from 1985 to 1989 due to dictator Nicolae Ceaușescu's energy-

---

13 1936 in Hungary and 1937 in Poland.

14 Gumbert, *Envisioning Socialism*, 16.

15 Jonathan Bignell and Andreas Fickers, 'Introduction: Comparative European Perspectives on Television History', in Bignell and Fickers, *A European Television History*, 24.

16 Péter Dunavölgyi, 'A magyar televíziózás története' [The history of Hungarian television I (1957)], http://dunavolgyipeter.hu/televizio_tortenet/a_magyar_televiziozas_tortenete_az_1950-as_evekben/1957 (accessed 8 October 2018).

17 Knut Hickethier, 'Early TV: Imagining and Realising Television', in Bignell and Fickers, *A European Television History*, 55–78.

18 Péter Dunavölgyi, 'A magyar televíziózás története a hatvanas években, 1965' [The history of Hungarian television in the sixties, 1965], http://dunavolgyipeter.hu/televizio_tortenet/a_magyar_televiziozas_az_1960-as_evekben/1965 (accessed 8 October 2018).

19 Maruša Pušnik and Gregor Starc, 'An Entertaining (R)evolution: The Rise of Television in Socialist Slovenia', *Media Culture and Society* 30, no. 6 (2008): 777–93.

20 Horace Newcomb, ed., *Encyclopedia of Television* (London: Routledge, 2004), 640.

Visual cultures

saving programme.[21] In most countries, however, the mid-1960s saw the launch of a second channel and the extension of broadcast time to five, then six, and eventually seven days a week.

By the mid-1960s, all Soviet satellite governments faced pressure to revise their ideological positions and programming policies in order to adjust to the opportunities and challenges presented by the new home-based mass medium. The launch of communication satellites – beginning with Sputnik-1 in 1957, the first Earth-orbiting artificial satellite and a key component of the Soviet space and communication strategy – increased the regimes' fear over their populations' access to Western programming. This challenge could only be minimized by re-channelling the desires for a capitalist lifestyle by fostering national cohesion on the party leadership's own terms. Socialist governments therefore began a strategic domestic production of scripted programming in the 1960s. Much like in Western Europe, the first post-war broadcasts produced in socialist Eastern Europe were of live theatrical and sporting events, as well as news programming, feature films and a range of educational cultural programming. Similar to Western European public broadcasting, television's shift to the centre of public culture in the 1960s allowed socialist governments to expand and solidify their educational-propaganda directives by packaging them in increasingly entertaining forms.

The ideological goals behind the new programming policy had to be carefully formulated lest they undermine a regionally coordinated vision of socialist utopia. Media and communication reforms in the 1960s therefore focused on television as the main institution for implanting socialist democratic values within entertainment. Television had to provide carefully selected information. It also had to shape citizens' tastes so that they might understand and value Eurocentric art and culture and resist what were widely perceived as the detrimental effects of television: reducing faculties of appreciation for cultural quality as well as a general mental and physical laziness.[22]

The greatest political risk involved in the expansion of television broadcasting was that, unlike feature films or print publications, broadcast signals could not simply be confined to state borders. Inhabitants of large regions in Yugoslavia, East Germany, Czechoslovakia, Hungary and Albania received either Austrian, Italian or West German programming. Shared TV signals had the most profound effect in East Germany, where most viewers (with the exception of the 'Valley of the Clueless' near Dresden, where signals didn't reach) were able to view West German broadcasting, often especially directed at East German viewers, in a shared language. But border-crossing signals literally disrupted communism even in the most isolated corners of the communist empire. In Enver Hoxha's Albania, while the communist elite retained the

---

21 Dana Mustata, 'Television in the Age of (Post)Communism', in *Popular Television in Eastern Europe During and since Socialism*, eds Anikó Imre, Timothy Havens and Katalin Lustyik (New York: Routledge, 2013), 47–64.

22 For instance, to conform to these directives, Hungarian Television (MTV) divided its programming in 1968 among different departments in the following manner: art films and programmes that promoted cultural appreciation made up 30 per cent of all programmes; 9 per cent of broadcast time went to literary and dramatic programming; news programmes, responsible for political agitation, consisted of 29 per cent; youth and children's programming made up 11.5 per cent; and informational programming such as nature documentaries took up 2.5 per cent. In addition, a daily morning programme called *Iskolatévé* [School television] where experts gave lectures on a broad range of academic subjects to viewers invested in supplementary education, made up 11 per cent. With the addition of Friday, a sixth day of weekly programming, that year (Monday remained a non-broadcast day devoted to work), programmes were reorganized so that each weekday had a distinct educational profile. Entertainment programmes were reserved for the weekend. See Edina Horváth, 'A magyar televízió müsorpolitikája – 1968' [Hungarian Television's programme policy], in Hungarian Television (MTV) Archives, www.tvarchivum.hu/?id=279930.

privilege of watching foreign broadcasts in the 1960s, restrictions placed on the rest of the population were removed during the brief liberal period of the early 1970s. By 1973, the party leadership realized that the pleasures of Italian programmes enchanted its populations rather than demonizing capitalism, so they launched a campaign against foreign liberalism. However, much like everywhere else, the signal jammers installed were ineffective, especially in border areas where one did not need antennae to receive signals.[23]

In a similar vein, TV-deprived Romanians took advantage of the overspill of terrestrial broadcast signals to watch more liberalized Hungarian, Bulgarian and Yugoslav programming in the 1970s and 1980s[24] as a means of escaping the isolation and deprivation imposed by the Ceauşescu regime. Annemarie Marinescu's ethnographic research conducted in the Romanian part of the Banat region (bordering Yugoslavia and Hungary) shows that it was not only the significant bilingual and trilingual populations who watched foreign TV: Romanian viewers actually went to the trouble of learning foreign languages just to access a slice of the outside world. Ironically, the nationalistic restriction on bodily mobility across borders motivated a TV-mediated flow of exchange that recreated, at least virtually, the multilingual, multi-ethnic culture of the region before and during the Habsburg Empire.[25]

Romanian viewers' reactions to Yugoslav and Hungarian TV echo Annika Lepp and Mervi Pantti's interviews with Estonian viewers, who were fixated on Finnish programming in the 1970s and 80s, after the Finnish Broadcasting Company (YLE) built a new TV broadcast transmitter in Espoo, which brought Finnish TV to viewers in northern Estonia. Even though only two Finnish public broadcast channels existed during this period, these carried both American and Western European series. This opportunity even created a weekend 'TV tourism' from other parts of Estonia to the northern areas, which allowed Estonians to follow their favourite serials. Many people who lived in the north were also able to learn Finnish from TV, which immediately conferred cultural capital that could be converted into economic capital as trade with Finland expanded in the 1980s and 90s.[26] Television thus facilitated cultural identification with Nordic Europe, re-establishing the Baltic region's older imperial ties with Scandinavia in a quest for independence from the Soviet Empire.

The interconnectedness of television systems across the Iron Curtain was not limited to simultaneous development but was ensured by ongoing exchanges from the start.[27] As

---

23 Idrit Idrizi, 'Das magische Gerät: Die Bedeutung des Fernsehers im isolierten Albanien und für die Erforschung des albanischen Kommunismus' (paper presented at the conference 'Television in Europe beyond the Iron Curtain – National and Transnational Perspectives since the 1950s,' Friedrich-Alexander-Universität Erlangen-Nürnberg, December 5–7, 2013); see also, Paolo Carelli, 'Italianization Accomplished: Forms and Structures of Albanian Television's Dependency on Italian Media and Culture', *VIEW: Journal of European Television History and Culture* 3, no. 5 (2014): 68–78.

24 Mustata, 'Television in the Age of (Post)Communism', 47–64.

25 Annemarie Sorescu-Marinkovic, 'We Didn't Have Anything, They Had It All: Watching Yugoslav Television in Communist Romania' (paper presented at the conference 'Television in Europe beyond the Iron Curtain – National and Transnational Perspectives since the 1950s', Friedrich-Alexander-Universität Erlangen-Nürnberg, December 5–7, 2013).

26 Annika Lepp and Mervi Pantti, 'Window to the West: Memories of Watching Finnish Television in Estonia During the Soviet Period', *VIEW: Journal of European Television History and Culture* 3, no. 2 (2012): 76–86.

27 See: Heather Gumbert, 'Exploring Transnational Media Exchange in the 1960s', *VIEW: Journal of European Television History and Culture* 3, no. 5 (2014): 50–59; Thomas Beutelschmidt and Richard Oehmig, 'Connected Enemies? Programming Transfer between East and West during the Cold War and the Example of East German Television', *VIEW: Journal of European Television History and Culture* 3, no. 5 (2014): 60–67.

Visual cultures

Jonathan Bignell and Andreas Fickers write in the introduction to their important edited collection, *A European Television History*, international cooperation, while more densely woven among Western countries, also included the East. The cross-border nature of radio waves resulted in international, non-governmental broadcasting institutions such as the International Broadcasting Union (IBU, founded in 1925), the European Broadcasting Union (EBU, 1950) and the Organisation Internationale de Radiodiffusion et de Télévision (OIRT, 1946), which became the dedicated 'eastern' network.[28]

European cooperation was initially made necessary because of technical issues: before the Second World War, there were different technical standards for the number of lines and images per second as a way of protecting the national industries of TV set makers.[29] The IBU was created to regulate international broadcasting but was broken up after the war partly due to the German army's abuse of its technical facilities, and partly due to competition with the OIRT, which was founded by Soviet proposition. The EBU was established in reaction to the OIRT in an effort led by the BBC to form a union for Western European broadcasters. The EBU initially included 23 broadcasters, but soon expanded to include some Mediterranean and Middle Eastern companies. The OIRT and the EBU finally merged in 1993 with the idea of developing a shared European consciousness.[30]

While the Cold War did split the continent's television industries into two networks, television diplomacy conducted by executives and creatives helped keep channels between them open. Finland, balanced between Eastern and Western interests, was a member of both the EBU and the OIRT.[31] After Finland (1965), Mongolia joined the OIRT in 1972, Cuba in 1979 and Afghanistan and Vietnam in 1982. Collaboration between the two networks became increasingly active as the Cold War thawed: the first discussion of exchanges happened in 1956, while the first Eurovision-Intervision transmission, coverage of the Rome Olympics, was broadcast in 1960.[32] Programme exchanges were particularly extensive in children's television programming,[33] where Eastern European broadcasters made a very significant, though rarely acknowledged, contribution. The programme exchanges ensured that most of Europe was watching many of the same programmes, often simultaneously. The dual system of broadcasting was adopted in most EBU countries by the 1980s. This was not the case for all capitalist countries. For example, Greece allowed private television to exist only in 1989, the year the Cold War officially ended.[34]

A shared socialist ethos of Public Service Broadcasting (PSB) permeated these exchanges and was based on a common European ethical and ideological ground that leads us back to the pre-Cold War era. The main features, successes and difficulties of PSB have been a common denominator across all of these television cultures: the government-led mission to inform and educate while promoting nationalism, which has always been challenged by both the

---

28 Jonathan Bignell and Andreas Fickers, 'Introduction: Comparative European Perspectives on Television History', in Bignell and Fickers, *A European Television History*, 27.

29 Christina Adamou, Isabelle Gaillard and Dana Mustata, 'Institutionalizing European Television: The Shaping of European Television Institutions and Infrastructures', in Bignell and Fickers, *A European Television History*, 91.

30 Ibid., 78–100.

31 Heidi Keinonen, 'Early Commercial Television in Finland: Balancing between East and West', *Media History* 18, no. 2 (2012): 177–89.

32 Andreas Fickers and Jonathan Bignell, 'Conclusion: Reflections on Doing European Television History', in Bignell and Fickers, *A European Television History*, 229–56.

33 Adamou, Gaillard and Mustata, 'Institutionalizing European Television', 94.

34 Fickers and Bignell, 'Conclusion', 235.

Anikó Imre

imperative to entertain[35] and the nationalistic cultural hierarchy that assigned a low value to television.[36]

Bignell and Fickers argue that the identity of TV was already defined by the 1930s and crystallized around what was to become a shared European public broadcasting mission at the broadcasting technology exhibits of the 1937 Paris World Fair. A clear difference emerged in how American and European television broadcasters marked out their future ethos. In the European version, spearheaded by German discourse, nation and education already appeared as key terms, in clear distinction with commercialization and entertainment, which characterized US discourses around television.[37] As Bignell and Fickers conclude,

> The dominance of the public service concept of broadcasting in the European context and the commercial patterns in the US shaped hegemonic narrations of television on each side of the Atlantic. The World's Fairs in Paris and New York both created and represented alternative symbolic frameworks in which television as a revolutionary technology and a new mass medium was presented. They were two windows giving a slightly different view of the new electronic 'window on the world.'[38]

Bignell and Fickers offer a valuable model and methodology to write European TV history comparatively. Yet, even they treat the other Europe as a mere addition, confirming its status as the Cold War mystery land out of sync with European history. Their otherwise very thorough introduction only includes a few paragraphs about Eastern Europe. These reiterate blanket assumptions about the region: TV and other media institutions were closely controlled by Soviet-influenced governments until 1989; regional programme exchange remained within and restricted to the COMECON countries; and the function of television was to publicize decisions made by the ruling party, to educate the population and to establish a channel of communication between the party and the people.[39] They do include a disclaimer for reducing Europe to Western Europe, blaming this on the scarcity of TV historians in Eastern Europe. Indeed, of the 29 contributing authors, only 2 are from and write about the former East.[40]

Not only did television under socialism generally operate in a liberalized fashion, with little or no censorship – apart from extreme cases and periods of dictatorship, as in Ceauşescu's Romania – tight state control and censorship also characterized periods of Western European broadcasting. As Bignell and Fickers argue, the Nazi government in Germany was interested in the propaganda value of television, partly in order to compete with large US corporations. Television was formed under military dictatorship in Greece in 1967, and the second channel remained under direct army control until 1982. Throughout this period, the government censored all programmes, particularly the news. Key TV personnel were selected based on their ideological conformity. Even the French government monitored and censored television programmes from the 1950s onwards. Under Charles de Gaulle, this was direct political control, impacting every type of programme, which also provoked direct resistance during the

---

35 Keinonen, 'Early Commercial Television in Finland', 177–89; Hickethier, 'Early TV', 55–78.
36 See: Adamou, Gaillard and Mustata, 'Institutionalizing European Television', 94; Jérôme Bourdon, Juan Carlos Ibanez, Catherine Johnson and Eggo Mueller, 'Searching for an Identity for Television: Programmes, Genres, Formats', in Bignell and Fickers, *A European Television History*, 101–26.
37 Fickers and Bignell, 'Conclusion', 233.
38 Ibid., 234.
39 Bignell and Fickers, 'Introduction', 5.
40 Fickers and Bignell, 'Conclusion', 235.

1968 strikes, when some TV personnel resigned rather than submitting scripts ahead of time. At the same time, commercial radio and the press were free to criticize the government, which ensured some pluralism of opinion.[41]

Using television as an instrument of positive propaganda also united Eastern and Western broadcasters around educational initiatives – first to promote literacy in rural regions and then to educate the population about a wide range of subjects. Most often, propaganda took on very subtle forms in the East, not unlike it did in the West. By the 1970s, dramatic programming was recognized as much more hospitable and effective for affirming the regimes' cultural and political directives than news and other factual programming, which were hardly taken seriously by the public. Even humour and comedy shows, which were ostensibly charged with anti-regime criticism, can be seen as a strategically tolerated form that co-opted both artists and audiences and served the parties' interests.

Whose television?

Rather than an instrument of propaganda, television was an ambivalent medium in the hands of party authorities. Sabina Mihelj explains that, through the 1960s, mass, private television viewing was a new phenomenon in Yugoslavia, which neither broadcasters nor politicians had yet learned to master. More centralized attempts at political control over television increased only in the 1970s.[42] Kristin Roth-Ey describes the post-war development of Soviet television as a messy process that resisted straightforward historical periodization and silver-bullet explanations. It proceeded by trial and error and was in no way determined by technological innovation. Its relationship to Soviet political tradition, to other arts and to modern Soviet life in general remained unsettled until the 1970s: 'Television was in the paradoxical position of being celebrated and denigrated, pampered and ignored in its first formative post-war decades'.[43]

Television caused a great deal of confusion to authorities, professionals and viewers throughout its socialist history. This was particularly true in its early era. After experimental broadcasts during the interwar period, television was re-launched in most countries after the war in the mid-1950s, in synchronicity with similar developments in Western Europe. While communist parties in the 1950s technically owned the new institution, its purpose and potential remained something of a mystery to them. Television's technological base as well as its programming were a mixture of ideas imported and borrowed from Western European broadcasters filtered through Soviet ideological directives. Communist parties tried to mould the new medium to their own purposes: they developed centralized programming to standardize citizens' everyday domestic life rhythms. But they were also compelled to sever content from the actual experience of socialism, which invariably fell short of the idealistic image depicted by party propaganda. In the early decades, this contradictory goal yielded boosterish docu-fictions, educational programming, uplifting entertainment such as theatrical coverage of Russian and European classics, doctored news and domestically produced dramatic serials focused firmly on the romanticized historical past, rather than the present.[44]

---

41 Adamou, Gaillard and Mustata, 'Institutionalizing European Television', 78–100.

42 Sabina Mihelj, 'The Politics of Privatization: Television Entertainment and the Yugoslav Sixties', in *The Socialist Sixties: Crossing Borders in the Second World*, eds Anne Gorsuch and Diane Koenker (Bloomington, IN: Indiana University Press, 2013), 251–67.

43 Roth-Ey, *Moscow Prime Time*, 179.

44 Anikó Imre, 'National History and Cross-National Television Edutainment', *Journal of Popular Film and Television* 40, no. 3 (Fall 2012): 119–30.

By the late 1960s, when TV sets became the norm in households, socialist authorities had to reckon with television's power as a mass medium. But party officials were never quite sure how to control or appropriate television and were thus relegated to playing catch-up. By the end of its first decade, television had already become identified by viewers as a medium of leisure. It had irrevocably absorbed elements from radio, which had incorporated the earlier legacy of 'bourgeois' stage variety entertainment. This 'bourgeois' element, most visible in television comedy, only became more pronounced during the 1970s and 1980s as socialism thawed. The gap between the projective ideals and the actual experiential realities of socialism sustained a layer of ironic distance between television and its viewers. This was exacerbated by the increasing leakage of information about capitalist lifestyles and consumer products despite even the most repressive states' efforts to keep it out.

Television's lower cultural status often allowed it to pass under the radar of censorship. It also kept away writers and actors who were reluctant to be associated with such a frivolous medium, and who preferred to work in film and literature – something constantly bemoaned by party executives and television's leadership. Despite its nominal centralization, television operated through a range of alternative approaches that were often ad hoc and subject to party functionaries' own idiosyncrasies and preferences. Long-time party leaders' attitudes towards television best illustrate this pattern.

Leonid Brezhnev had programmes made for him and his family by his appointed head of Soviet television, Sergey Lapin. Roth-Ey characterizes television in the Lapin era as a kind of court TV to the Kremlin, with Lapin as chief courtier.[45] Lapin's TV programmes issued a special address to politically important viewers in their homes. Brezhnev's house had two TV sets: a Soviet model for Brezhnev and his wife and a Japanese model with a VCR for the younger generations.[46] By contrast, it was common knowledge in Hungarian Television that Party Secretary János Kádár did not watch television at all.[47] Given his enormous political power, Kádár's own cultural snobbery had a trickle-down effect, which allowed the head of television, almost invariably a sophisticated professional rather than an apparatchik, to make important programming and personnel decisions without party involvement.

In yet another telling case, in the 1970s, Romanian dictator Nicolae Ceauşescu created a hospitable environment in Romania for importing entertaining US series in order to demonstrate his independence from the Soviet Union and to curry favour with the West. In the 1980s, however, as his reign turned increasingly megalomaniacal, he reduced television broadcasting to a few hours a week, dictating that content be mostly about him and his family. This version of court TV was not simply made *for* the royal family: the family was virtually its only content.[48] Erich Honecker, Secretary of the East German Socialist Unity Party (SED), also single-handedly redefined television and redirected its history when he famously diagnosed 'a certain boredom' around television and urged it to create 'good entertainment' at the Eighth Congress of the SED in 1971. As a result, the SED folded entertainment into its ideology as an important condition for reproducing labour and raising intellectually active individuals.[49]

---

45 Roth-Ey, *Moscow Prime Time*, 220.

46 Ibid., 279.

47 István Vágó, Endre Aczél, Katalin Szegvári, László Szabó and Péter Dunavölgyi, interviewed by Anikó Imre (Budapest, December 2012 and December 2013).

48 Ib Bondebjerg, et al., 'American Television: Point of Reference or European Nightmare?', in Bignell and Fickers, *A European Television History*, 154–83, 177–81.

49 Rüdiger Steinmetz and Reinhold Viehoff, 'The Program History of Genres of Entertainment on GDR Television', *Historical Journal of Film, Radio and Television* 24, no. 3 (2004): 320.

Visual cultures

Far from being simply amusing anecdotes, these stories demonstrate the confusion television caused in the attitudes of the highest-ranking decision-makers. They had to reconcile the political role as a potential instrument of centralized control with the private and emotional relationship they themselves had with television. This dual function had a direct effect on how television operated in socialist countries. Part of the political establishments' and more prestigious cultural institutions' hostility was fear of competition. As early as 1951, the Soviet Ministry of Cinematography lobbied the communist party to ban feature films on television to prevent the loss of ticket sales at the movies. Theatres also tried to limit broadcast access to performances. Both efforts were unsuccessful, but the hierarchy remained in place.[50]

At the same time, top-down hostility and confusion actually sustained television's bottom-up momentum throughout the socialist period, giving viewers some leverage in defining the medium's development. Television's cultural stigma and subsequent low pay also allowed for laboratories of innovation to be formed, where the first creative professionals could invent television programmes in a trial and error process of mixing roles, technologies and genres. This environment attracted young people who cared less about prestige than about new challenges.[51] Television was an exciting place to work, fuelled by camaraderie, enthusiasm and a sense of genuine collaboration, which spilled out into lasting friendships outside of work.

Socialist TV's favoured mode: educational realism

Television under Soviet-style socialism followed Western European broadcasters' commitment to realism and an ethos of public service. In addition, Soviet and Western European versions of socialism both drew on the values of cultural nationalism, which involved a preference for educating and enlightening all social classes. The differences between East and West were less evident in the principles than in the degree of dogmatism with which they were put into televisual practice. More precisely, while the letter of Marxist-Leninist imperatives continued to be repeated in the public discourses of Soviet-controlled countries well into the 1980s, its spirit operated much more closely to the ideological principles of Western European social democracies. This discrepancy between letter and spirit enacted an ongoing performative repetition of the socialist order in the East. In and on television, the discrepancy was particularly striking. The more elitist, austere, realistic and educational television attempted to be, the more it was mocked and abandoned by viewers who wanted fiction, humour and entertainment. In essence, Eastern European socialist TV reproduced in more pure form, and preserved well into the 1980s, the educational principles and realistic aesthetic that Western European public broadcasters gradually abandoned under pressure from competition with commercial broadcasters.

The genres most closely associated with public service were also at the centre of socialist programming. These are genres that valued politically committed documentary realism above fictional representations. The aesthetic of socialist realism they adopted was supposed to support an overarching educational mandate to teach viewers how to be good socialist citizens. Much of post-war European public television was meant to teach its viewers how to read and write, to understand maths, physics and geography, to appreciate fine national and European literature, film and music and to adhere to Marxist-Leninist philosophical principles. But it also offered a broader educational programme on how to raise children and navigate legal issues. It offered

---

50 Roth-Ey, *Moscow Prime Time*, 196.

51 Ibid., 225.

lessons on cooking, sewing, gardening, agricultural work, mining and operating heavy machinery. Television was anything but cheap in its intentions. It was driven by noble initiatives to democratize access to education, to create a level playing field among people of different class and educational backgrounds, and to socialize the individual as always primarily a community member.

The prevalence of such programmes on socialist TV is unsurprising: realism was the preferred aesthetic delivery channel of Marxist-Leninist ideologies in Soviet-controlled regions. However, to dismiss socialist TV's realist genres as mere propaganda devices not worthy of serious analysis would be hasty. First of all, as a mass medium charged with fostering national cohesion, much of television is didactic. What distinguished socialist television's approach was that it did not make any secret of its didactic intentions. It was supervised by government departments that had 'agitation' and 'propaganda' in their names after all, even if these terms did not quite carry the nefarious connotations they have taken on in English.

But television, perhaps more than any other socialist institution, fell short of controlling the relay between the leadership and the citizenry. This was partly because it entered the scene in the late 1950s and only rose to mass medium status in the 1960s. By then the post-war Stalinist purges were over and communism had begun to soften into centralized socialism in most countries. While the party leadership had made TV an increasingly crucial element in its cultural policy by the 1970s, once such policies were translated into TV programmes that became embedded in the daily lives of the citizens, the effects and interpretations of these policies proved elusive and difficult to control. Instead, television turned its antennae towards hybrid influences, including foreign ones, and foregrounded the very internal contradictions of official ideology and rhetoric.

One of the most confusing points was socialist realism itself. Realism was both an essential principle and a stumbling block for television. The official Marxist-Leninist worldview presumed and prescribed a clear-cut relationship between what John Corner distinguishes as 'thematic realism' and 'formal realism'. Thematic realism is the relationship between a programme's content and reality. Marxist materialism declared reality to be objectively pre-existent. Formal realism is the programme's way of achieving 'real-seemingness' through representation.[52] This mediation is something socialist ideology had to downplay. Corner introduces this distinction because, in British television studies, while realism had come to be regarded as television's central aesthetic and social project, its use has also remained ungrounded and confusing. This is because any notion of realism, whether a project of verisimilitude or a reference to the real, is based on a normative construction of 'the real' whose existence is 'disputable independently of any media representation'.[53]

Marxism presumed the existence of material reality and assigned representation a mirroring, rather than a reconstructing, re-presenting role. Idealist philosophies, while not banned, were simply taught to be wrong. The system's great seduction lay precisely in holding out the promise that it possessed historical truth and placed everyone on the road to its fulfilment, the perfect society. However, life under socialism was a far cry from this eventual good life. By the 1960s, as the grand promise appeared to be further and further delayed and as communist parties redirected and adjusted their truth-seeking ideologies to match the reality of economic lag and the deficit of political trust, the gap between public Marxist rhetoric and its translation into the

---

52 John Corner, 'Presumption as Theory: "Realism" in Television Studies', in idem, *Studying Media: Problems of Theory and Method* (Edinburgh: Edinburgh University Press, 1998), 68.

53 Ibid., 70.

Visual cultures

private sector became increasingly wide. This is the gap in which television quietly performed its work of ideological fermentation. By the mid-1960s, socialist parties began to grab onto the new mass medium as a vehicle around which to consolidate their dwindling legitimacy. Because of its ability to link the private and the public spheres, television became a laboratory in which to adjust the recipe for making an ideal, then a merely adequate, and finally just a liveable socialist society. The economic contours of this society resembled capitalism more and more with each reform, particularly in the most Western-leaning countries, while holding on to the social protections and nationalistic cultural leanings typical of Western European social democracies.

Realism became a flexible ideological and aesthetic instrument throughout the course of these adjustments. While factual programming that 'mirrored' reality, such as news shows and documentary programmes, was given greater priority and higher cultural value than fiction, most TV programming also contained an element of utopianism. Instead of depicting life as it was, it shifted the emphasis to teaching citizens how to behave in an ideal socialist society. 'Reality' thus functioned in two inseparable dimensions: the present as it looked now and how it *should* look in the future. The two dimensions were inextricably linked by television's educational mission.

A survey of the rhetoric of periodical assessments of Hungarian television by party officials and television professionals alike foregrounds a common script in these decades. The authors of these assessments issue the same wishful-thinking reports year after year, driven by principles that drifted further and further into the past of nostalgia as the future drifted into the future of utopia: they take a self-boosting count of the many hours of broadcasting devoted to news, education, factual and current affairs programming, documentaries, theatre broadcasts, historical teleplays, adaptations of literary classics and programme exchanges with other Soviet countries. They express some carefully worded reservations about the 'tentative' approach to teaching the social sciences on TV caused by the many 'unresolved' historical questions and the 'inadequate courage' of some of the professionals. They also note 'divided opinions' about popular entertainment programmes, whether imported crime series or home-produced pop music talent shows or humorous shows, which are often 'in bad taste'. Then they propose plans for the future: to increase the level of political awareness and expand political education.[54] For instance, after the Tenth Annual Congress of the Hungarian Socialist Worker's Party, an article in the party newspaper states: 'The hardest task for the leaders of our television is to find the right balance between providing cultural service and guiding the audience. Because this right balance has not yet emerged with reassuring certainty'.[55] Likewise, according to a prominent critic writing in the journal *Rádió és TV Szemle* ('Radio and TV guide'): 'Society does not yet prescribe the mandatory behavioural models and achievement levels in the sphere of entertainment as it does in the sphere of education and the acquisition of higher culture'.[56]

The audience imagined by such assessments was always a bit disappointing: always falling behind the desirable curve, never quite sophisticated or enlightened enough; always falling

---

54 See the report 'Television's Broadcasting Policy' by Pécsi Ferenc, the vice president of Hungarian Television, report for the Hungarian Socialist Workers' Party (MSZMP)'s Agitation and Propaganda Division, from 08.10.1969, MSZMP APO 288f.22/1969/19.öe. Ag.350, Hungarian National Manuscript Archive.

55 Miklós Jovánovics, 'Pro and Contra Television', *Népszabadság* (27 September 1970).

56 Tamás Szecskő, 'Szórakoztatás – Műsorpolitika' [Entertainment – programming policy], *Rádió és TV Szemle* 71, no. 3 (1971): 9.

slightly short of the standards marked out by high literature and art films, the true vehicles of aspirational Eastern European cultural nationalisms. The 'not yet' thinking forcefully ignored the fact that the majority of viewers preferred fictional and entertaining programming to tele-education according to viewer surveys and letters.

By the late 1960s, Eastern European socialist television broadcasters were fairly well-established, provided at least six days of programming per week, in some countries introduced a second channel, and began to experiment with colour. Socialist authorities tried to assert more control over television the more it was slipping away. This control manifested itself in the centralized planning of programming structures, directives for scientific research on television's effects and efforts to integrate television into the foundational mechanisms of a socialist society. One of the main strategies utilized by socialist authorities employed for message control was to insist on a line of separation between fictional and factual programming. While genres in both categories were designed to model socialist citizenship, there was a strict hierarchy between the two. The only exception to the low value assigned to TV fiction was art. But what qualified as art was also determined by ideological principles: although it did not have to be realistic, it was assumed to be educational, contributing to the central mission of 'taste training'. It had to demonstrate a social commitment to the cause of the nation, to European high culture and to the future of socialism – for instance, in the form of moralistic historical teleplays and theatrical broadcasts of European classics. As the vice president of Magyar Rádió és Televízió ('Hungarian Radio and Television'), Ferenc Pécsi, put it in 1969, 'Television is a journalistic institution, film, theatre and even school'.[57]

This phrase captures the spirit of 'education dictatorship' – a term that Heather Gumbert applies to the German Democratic Republic, which can be safely generalized across the socialist region.[58] Indeed, in the GDR, feature films and TV films made up 22.4 per cent of broadcasting time in 1968; news programmes accounted for 16.9 per cent and sports 14.8 per cent. By 1970, the proportion of sports was reduced to 6.6 per cent while feature films increased to 26.3 per cent, educational programming to 10.2 per cent and informational, news and current affairs to 17.7 per cent. In the early 1970s, the proportion of political documentaries and current affairs continued to increase.[59] A large part of the schedule was taken up by reality-based programmes that were only indirectly educational in intention. This was a varied category, which ranged from historical teleplays through various public affairs formats to variety and quiz shows. In 1968, TV separated from radio, which brought more independence to the former. As a result of General Secretary Erich Honecker's famous critique of television in 1971, reforms were introduced to improve the programming structure and offer better entertainment and more effective journalism.[60]

In 1959, Polish broadcaster TVP allocated 45 per cent of TV's airtime to current affairs and news programmes.[61] In Hungary, in the 1970s, 25 per cent of programming was political and economic in theme, 50 per cent was classified as cultural, art and entertainment and

---

57 Ferenc Pécsi, 'Heti ötven órában' [Fifty hours a week], *Film Színház Muzsika* (4 January 1969): 1.

58 Heather Gumbert, *Envisioning Socialism: Television and the Cold War in the German Democratic Republic* (Ann Arbor, MI: University of Michigan Press, 2014), 2.

59 Markus Schubert and Hans-Joerg Stiehler, 'A Program Structure Analysis of East German Television, 1968–74', *Historical Journal of Film, Radio and Television* 24, no. 2 (2004): 347.

60 Ibid., 345.

61 Tadeusz Pikulski, *Prywatna historia telewizji publicznej* [The private history of public television] (Warsaw: Muza 2002), 41.

Visual cultures

25 per cent was dedicated to education, children and youth programming and school TV.[62] In 1972, Hungarian TV's total annual programming time (close to 170,000 minutes) was distributed between the various programming desks in the following manner: 22.9 per cent for the political division, 15.1 per cent for school TV, 14.9 per cent for the international exchange and film division, 10.4 per cent for the youth and educational division, 9.4 per cent for the entertainment and music division, 6.9 per cent for the literature and drama division, 8.1 per cent for the evening news and 4.2 per cent for the public cultural division.[63] It is obvious that the educational intent crossed the divisions and left very little, if any, broadcast time untouched.

TV as school

The most direct result of imagining TV as a massive school house was School TV. School TV's antecedents can be found in the French tele-clubs, which are perhaps the most influential examples of education in the context of collective viewing. They began in 1951 and mostly operated in rural primary schools, where people could attend TV transmissions by the state broadcaster RTF (*Radiodiffusion-Télévision Française*) once or twice a week. Screenings were followed by public discussions about the programmes. The initiative gained support from UNESCO in 1953, which helped produce a series of theme-based programmes. Tele-clubs expanded beyond France to Italy and Japan and later to India, Senegal and Cote d'Ivoire in the 1960s and 1970s.[64] They drew on antecedents in radio such as the BBC's Listening Groups (1927–47), which provided early adult education; farm radio programming based in Canada for adult education produced by the Canadian Broadcasting Corporation (CBC), and farm radio produced in cooperation between UNESCO and All India Radio in Poona, which was followed by similar radio experiments in the developing world. Educational radio broadcasting aimed at school children also preceded public service educational television in Belgium, Switzerland, Germany, Portugal and other countries throughout the 1920s, 30s and 40s.[65]

In the socialist region, School TV was launched in the 1960s. In most countries, it complemented and then replaced School Radio. In Hungary, for instance, School Radio was introduced in 1962 but began to decline as television rose in popularity.[66] Hungarian TV offered its first explicitly educational programme as early as 1959. The programme, titled *Gyermekeinkről* ('About our children'), featured an educational expert giving lectures on issues of child-rearing, illustrated by didactic docu-fictional scenes the expert wrote himself, which were performed by professional actors.[67] The programme presumably targeted women, who were understood to be in charge of parenting. Actual School TV began in 1961 with experimental courses in the Russian language.[68] These were soon followed by lectures in physics, chemistry, literature and history, planned in coordination with centralized school curricula. The broadcasts were first

---

62 Árpád Thiery, 'Interview with Ferenc Pécsi, Vice President of Hungarian Radio and Television', *Népszava* (3 January 1972).

63 Péter Dunavölgyi, 'A magyar televíziózás története a hetvenes években: 1972' [The history of Hungarian television in the seventies: 1972], http://dunavolgyipeter.hu/televizio_tortenet/a_magyar_televiziozas_tortenete_az_1970-as_evekben/1972 (accessed 8 October 2018).

64 Ira Wagman, 'Tele-Clubs and European Television History beyond the Screen', *VIEW: Journal of European Television History and Culture* 1, no. 2 (2012): 118.

65 Ibid., 123.

66 Huszár, Tiborné, '10 éves az iskolarádió' [School radio is 10-years-old], *Rádió és TV Szemle* 2 (1973).

67 Dunavölgyi, '1959'.

68 'A TV-ben hallottuk' [We heard it on TV], *Rádió és Televízió Újság* 33 (1961).

shown in 50–100 selected elementary and high schools and continuing education night courses for working adults.[69]

School TV expanded on a national scale in 1964, along with a campaign to put TV sets into every school. In 1964, there were a total of 700–800 TV sets in schools; by 1965, there were 2,122.[70] In 1970, a newspaper report proudly announced that the 'Television for Every School' campaign had been a success: every school that had electricity now had at least one TV set. As elsewhere in Europe, the movement had initially focused on small, sparsely inhabited, farmland places. It moved gradually into smaller towns and cities. In 1970, there were still about 400 schools left without electricity; but in approximately 100 of these they had installed a generator just so they could turn on the TV set donated to the school.[71] According to a survey in 1974, by then 60 per cent of all elementary schools were incorporating School TV into instruction.[72] Authorities had hoped television would effect a breakthrough in adult education as well. As late as 1962, almost one third of Hungary's population had not completed eighth grade.[73]

The Polish story was similar: *Szkoła telewizyjna* ('School TV') made its first appearance in 1960, first as an experiment, but with the ultimate purpose of complementing the school curriculum in a visually appealing way. Initially, 900 schools subscribed, since not many more owned a TV set. The curriculum was divided into thematic blocks, which were hosted by scientists and other academics.[74] As elsewhere, School TV found its real mission outside of the centralized curriculum: in rural areas, in adult and continuing education and in lifestyle education. In 1970, TVP1 aired 718 hours of educational programming, including 500 hours of 'School TV' and 'TV Polytechnic' lectures.[75]

Romania's 'School TV', *Telescoala*, was launched in 1968 as a joint effort between Romanian Radio and Television and the Ministry of Education. As elsewhere, it delivered lessons that complemented classroom instruction in particular subjects. Initially, these were constructed as televised lectures for students of all ages. They included *Consultatii pentru elevi* ('Tutorials for students'), *Telescoala, Universitatea TV* ('The TV university') and in an initiative unique to Romania, foreign language courses in French, English, Spanish, German and Russian. Within a few years, as in other countries of the region, school TV grew to offer educational programmes that taught technical and practical skills, such as *Consultatii tehnice* ('Technical consultations') or the children's competition programme *Ex-Terra*. These were typically scheduled on the weekends or in the evening broadcast block that began at 6 p.m., following a daily break in broad-

---

69 Proposal prepared on 28 June 1962, by István Tömpe and Jenő Lugossy for the Agitation and Propaganda Division of the Hungarian Socialist Workers' Party's Central Committee titled, '*A televízió és rádió rendszeres bevezetése az altalános és középoktatásba*' [The systematic introduction of television and radio into primary and secondary education], MOL- 288f22/10 öe. MSZMP KB Agit. prop. Oszt., Hungarian National Document Archives.

70 Endre Kelemen, 'Mozaikok az Iskolatelevízió történetéből' [Mosaics from the history of school TV], *Rádió és TV Szemle* 2 (1974): 18–31.

71 See: Gábor Szenes's article on School TV, *Népszabadság* (6 March 1970).

72 György Csepeli, 'Rádiónk és televíziónk közművelődési szemlélete és gyakorlata' [Our radio and television's theory and practice of mass education], *Rádió és TV Szemle* 6, no. 3 (1973): 5–16. This is an interview with MTV Programming Director, György Sándor.

73 Proposal by István Tömpe and Jenő Lugossy. MOL- 288f22/10 öe. MSZMP KB Agit. prop. Oszt., Hungarian National Document Archives.

74 Pikulski, *Prywatna historia telewizji publicznej*, 95. Thanks to Maria Zalewska for the translation.

75 Andrzej Kozieł, *Za chwilę dalszy ciąg programu: Telewizja Polska czterech dekad 1952–1989* [In a moment the programme will continue: Polish television for four decades 1952–1989] (Warsaw: Oficyna Wydawnicza Aspra-Jr, 2003), 162–3.

Visual cultures

casting in the afternoon. As elsewhere, weekend children's magazines combined educational, instructional and entertaining programmes. Romanian television also offered educational programmes focusing on general knowledge (e.g. *Universal Sotron* – 'Universal hopscotch') and civic issues (e.g. *Bratara de aur* – 'The golden profession').[76]

As in Romania, School TV gradually expanded in socialist countries to include all grade levels and learning areas, and to address everyone from those enrolled in formal education to those who just wanted to pick up a bit of quantum physics on a Saturday morning.[77] Much like the BBC, it developed into a 'free university' by 1975. The curriculum heavily targeted the natural sciences, where unmediated 'truth' could be delivered by academic experts. Socialist School TV was also linked up with similar TV and radio initiatives across Europe. This tele-educational network was featured at international television festivals and an annual international meeting in Paris.[78]

It is important to note that, even in the Eastern bloc, School TV was not seen as simply, or even primarily, a propaganda instrument. Rather, it was considered a tool of social transformation that could bring knowledge and cultural sophistication to the masses by opening a window to the world in tiny schoolhouses, community centres and eventually family homes. The knowledge disseminated was to be a grand equalizer among different social classes, professions and educational levels. There was a great deal of enthusiasm about tele-education in the early years. In a speech given in 1966 in the Hungarian Parliament, a representative called *School TV*, then broadcasting four days a week, a key element of the cultural revolution brought about by television.[79]

School TV was by no means a universal success, however. By the 1970s, more and more questions arose as to how far it really enhanced public education when it was directly interwoven into the centralized curriculum. The problem was not just the fact that scientific experts were rarely the most charismatic television personalities, but also the technical conditions of transmission and reception: small black-and-white sets with frequent signal problems. The initiative to bring television into the classrooms largely ignored the fact that 1970s TV sets were not suitable for classroom viewing. Small village and farm schools were the exception: here school TV was often the primary source of learning given the shortage of educators trained in specialized subjects, and where students were truly cut off from modern technological developments, including electricity in some cases.[80]

The two most targeted areas remained science and art. Both were conceived in a top-down fashion as fields where one should aim to find truth – either scientific truth based in the objectively existing material world or the Kantian aesthetic truth revealed by the canonized creations

---

76 Dana Mustata, 'The Power of Television: Including the Historicizing of the Live Romanian Revolution' (PhD diss., Utrecht University, 2011).

77 On the history of educational broadcasting in Bulgaria, see Martin Marinos, 'New Media, New Habits: Socialist Television and the Struggle for "Harmonious Consumption" in 1960s Bulgaria', *Digital Icons: Studies in Russian, Eurasian and Central European New Media* 15 (2016): 37–55.

78 The 1970 'Prix Jeunesse International 1970,' held in Munich, awarded the main prize in the 'Youth' category to an episode called '*Szerelem*' ('Love') in Hungarian School TV's *Szülők, gyerekek, együtt* ('Parents, children together') series (script Katalin Benedek, director Ilona Katkics). See: Péter Dunavölgyi, 'A magyar televíziózás története a hetvenes években: 1970' [The history of Hungarian television in the seventies: 1970]. http://dunavolgyipeter.hu/televizio_tortenet/a_magyar_televiziozas_tortenete_az_1970-as_evekben/1970 (accessed 8 October 2018); Árpád Halasi, 'Iskolatelevízió', *Magyar Ifjúság* (18 March 1967).

79 Representative Ernő Mihályfi's speech. See: *Országgyűlési Napló* [Parliamentary minutes], Session 21 (27 January 1966).

80 Kelemen, 'Mozaikok az Iskolatelevízió történetéből', 20.

of the truly talented. In this teleological journey, only expert guidance would suffice. There were countless programmes focused on popular science education. Romanian science programmes included *Romania la ora atomului* ('Romania at the time of the atom'), *Panoramic stiintific* ('Scientific panoramic') and *Univers XX*.[81] In 1960, Polish TV launched *Wszechnica telewizyjna* ('The TV academy'), a block of programmes dedicated to science education. Some of the popular shows this included were *Eureka*, *Spotkania z przyrodą* ('Rendezvous with nature'), *Magazyn postępu technicznego* ('Magazine of technical progress'), *Klinika Zdrowego Czlowieka* ('The healthy man's clinic'), *Klub opowieści z myszką* ('The little mouse story club') and, perhaps most popular of all, *Piórkiem i węglem* ('With pen and charcoal'), hosted by the beloved Professor Wiktor Zin.[82]

The 1966 Hungarian series *A fény természete* ('The nature of light') had two academic experts discuss the science of light, which they illustrated with drawings.[83] A more promising approach was taken by *Kronovízió* ('Chronovision') in 1970, which adopted the model of a time machine to track the history of research on nuclear energy, a theme central to Cold War geopolitics. Even this more creative framework could not overcome the difficulty of teaching a specialized topic to a broad audience, however. Things were not helped by the fact that the series was hosted by a handful of, by definition, male physicists, who could only hope to appeal to a handful of teenagers dedicated to physics.

Tele-education found more success with viewers when it moved from teaching school subjects to areas of self-improvement. In the Hungary of the 1960s and 70s, there was a programme for just about anything that could or should be learned, from algebra to ballroom dancing. In the least formalized, lifestyle programmes, television personalities were recruited to replace professors. Youth were especially treasured as an audience to educate.

Socialist TV also developed an educational version of niche programming, addressing targeted social classes and groups such as factory workers, agricultural professionals, women and youth. Some courses offered specialized instruction for young people going into trades or farming rather than university studies. Agricultural programmes were in particular abundance.

In 1959, Polish TV's rural agricultural programme *Niedzielna biesiada* ('Sunday feast') was launched. It was a two-hour show that offered practical tips to farmers. The year 1962 saw the beginning of the educational series *Telewizyjny Kurs Rolniczy* ('TV course in agriculture').[84] That same year, Hungarian TV aired a series of 17 one-hour educational lectures on farming, broadcast every Wednesday.[85] In 1965, it created a programme called *Figyelem, mérnökök, technikusok!* ('Attention engineers, technicians!'). The first episode was a programme about 'moving material'.[86] Many of these experiments stretched the limits of televisuality. Another set of specialized offerings prepared the children of workers and peasants for university studies. The Hungarian *Irány az egyetem!* ('Off to university') in 1969 was a 24-lecture, open-access course in physics and maths.[87]

---

81 Mustata, 'The Power of Television'.

82 Pikulski, *Prywatna historia telewizji publicznej*, 95–96.

83 The discussion featured professors Elemér Sas, Lajos Jánossy and Péter Varga. See: Péter Dunavölgyi, 'A magyar televíziózás története a hatvanas években: 1966' [The history of Hungarian television in the sixties: 1966], http://dunavolgyipeter.hu/televizio_tortenet/a_magyar_televiziozas_tortenete_az_1960-as_evekben/1966 (accessed 8 October 2018).

84 Pikulski, *Prywatna historia telewizji publicznej*, 96–7.

85 Dunavölgyi, '1962'.

86 Dunavölgyi, '1965'.

87 Its closest contemporary version is probably something like Khan Academy on YouTube. The major difference is that it was taught by the most distinguished university professors. See: Dunavölgyi, '1969'.

Visual cultures

The default national viewer addressed by socialist television was a white, heterosexual male citizen, whether a young boy, a teenager or a grown man. This, again, was not a particularly eastern, Soviet socialist feature. Western European PSBs also favoured the male citizen in their address; and they also idealized the worker, who needed to be shown the way to enlightenment. Indeed, the figure of the worker – disciplined, eager to be educated even after a full day's work – seemed best to fit the ideal target of public broadcasters.

The few programmes with a female audience explicitly signalled their invitation to a special demographic, which existed somewhere on the margins of citizenship, imagined to be dedicated to gendered duties such as mothering and cooking. These were also the only programmes with a majority of female creative personnel.[88] The Hungarian programme *Nők fóruma* ('The women's forum'), for instance, offered an episode on children of divorced parents, assuming, of course, that it was the mother who kept custody of her children after divorce. *Anita, a 'tévé-bébi'* ('Anita, the "TV baby"') made her first appearance in Hungary in 1965 as the star of a proto-reality series that followed Anita and her family from the moment of her birth with the intention of teaching mothers useful skills when caring for an infant and a small child. It was one of many semi-educational programmes that discussed and illustrated recurring family issues, similar to *Csak felnőtteknek* ('Only for adults') and later, the very popular and long-running *Családi kör* ('Family circle').

Political education

The category of education most favoured by party authorities, but least successful with audiences, was overtly ideological, agitational-propaganda (agitprop) programming about Marxism, socialism and the workings of a socialist society. In Romania, the genre included *Cadran: Emisiune de actualitate internationala* ('Dial: a programme of international current affairs'); economic current affairs programmes such as *Cabinetul economic TV* ('The economic TV cabinet'), *Revista economica TV* ('The economic TV magazine') and *Actualitatea in economie* ('The economic actuality'); and political programmes such as *Agenda politica* ('The political agenda') and *Cincinalul 1966–1970 in cifre si imagini* ('The five-year plan in figures and images').[89]

In Hungary, the unimaginatively named seven-part series *Politikai tanfolyam a televízióban* ('Political course on TV') launched in 1965 on a fortnightly basis. It featured TV education on subjects such as current issues in world politics, the development of the socialist world system, the world economy and the meaning of work in socialism. As the *Radio and TV Guide* optimistically wrote, it was meant to be watched collectively in offices, factory clubs and cultural centres.[90] To show how out of touch the socialist party was with television as a medium, in 1969 the Central Committee's Agitation and Propaganda Division decided to broaden the range of themes to be covered by the course to include cultural revolution, contemporary issues in science and the decisions of the Central Committee. They also increased broadcast time from 30 to 40 minutes to include illustrations in addition to the 20–25-minute lectures.[91]

There were exceptions even within this driest and most shunned tele-educational genre. Socialist parties made more concerted efforts to catch up with television's development by

---

88 I expand on programmes addressing a female audience in the sub-chapter *Women and the late socialist domestic drama*.
89 Mustata, 'The Power of Television'.
90 R.J., 'Politikai tanfolyam a televízióban' [Political course on TV], *Rádió és Televízió Újság* 48 (1965).
91 Document MSZMP APO 288f.22/1969, Hungarian National Document Archive.

the end of the 1960s. By then it was obvious in much of the region that economic and political thaw had to be accelerated. Television could be used as a forum to inform citizens about these new developments and revise the party's original goals in a careful manner that made the introduction of free-market mechanisms and the expansion of consumerism appear to be an organic stage of socialism's progress. In Hungary, one of the first programmes designed to ease the transition to what the Kádár regime named the 'New Economic Mechanism' was the 1969 *Ruble, Forint, Dollar* (~Rubel, Forint, Dollar). This was an entirely party-controlled, didactic show whose mission was to inform the public about and popularize the Economic Committee's decision to expand the range of products on the domestic market and improve relations with the world market. By contrast, in the same year, television produced an altogether novel animated propaganda series called *Magyarázom a mechanizmust* ('I explain the mechanism') whose episodes illustrated specific aspects of the new economic policy. The series came to be known as 'Dr Brain' after its host: a bespectacled, by definition male, cartoon professor figure with an oversized head, who faced the TV classroom from behind his desk. The public recognized him as someone modelled after Professor Öveges, the most popular tele-scientist of the socialist period, who was lively enough to host his own show.[92] The counter-intuitive idea to explain economic policy through animation, however simple in style, was a breakthrough in educational-propaganda programming, due to the tight, humorous format and the character, whose name also evoked associations of science fiction. The series literally animated the robotic party representatives who usually populated propaganda programmes.

The series was so successful that it continued throughout the seventies in subsequent *I Explain ...* series: *I Explain the Future, I Explain Ourselves, I Explain the Explanation*, etc. The animated teaching format inspired a similar series in 1988: *Párbeszéd* ('Dialogue') featuring the popular actor Péter Haumann and a devilish cartoon figure discussing a planned tax reform during the twilight of socialism. It was later resurrected as part of the post-socialist *Modern Képmesék* ('Modern picture stories') series produced by the public broadcaster.

Taste education

When it came to the other major area of tele-education, art and culture, countless programmes took on the cause of 'taste education' by introducing citizens to classical music, art, literature and cinema. Theatrical broadcasts and concerts remained on the agenda throughout the period along with art films and quality serials exchanged among socialist countries and imported from Western Europe. A long-running programme on Polish television, *Słuchamy i patrzymy* ('We listen and we watch'), specialized in popularizing classical music. The programme ran during primetime and featured an orchestra performing live in the studio.[93] The 20 episodes of *Po prostu muzyka* ('Simply the music') created by Polish television's 'school department' in 1982–83, were meant to educate first and second graders about music. *Pegaz* ('Pegasus'), Polish TV's high-profile magazine for cultural and art education, first aired in 1959 and continued to earn its primetime 8 pm slot on Saturdays. It consisted of film, book and art reviews, which were taken

---

92 He was similar to the Polish Professor Zin, host of the show *Piorkiem i węglem* [By powder and coal]. Prof. Zin would use a piece of charcoal to draw building constructions on a big white piece of paper, while discussing the history of art and architecture. His talent for vivid narration made his programme an instant classic and he became one of the most revered TV personalities of the era. His show remained on the air for 30 years. Thanks to Maria Zalewska for this information.

93 Pikulski, *Prywatna historia telewizji publicznej*, 70.

Visual cultures

very seriously by the audience and culture critics. Its creators came up with a clever solution to attract a younger audience as well: the last few minutes of the show were devoted to Western media stars who were visiting Poland. In this way, younger members of the audience while waiting to hear a few words about the Rolling Stones or Marlene Dietrich learned a great deal about sculpture, architecture or cinema.[94] One peculiarity of socialist art-educational broadcasting was the abundant airtime allotted to reciting poetry. Polish television regularly included actors reading out poems for the TV audience. It also offered a programme, *Baj Baj* ('Bye bye'), that introduced children to the world of art history through using puppets as early as 1958.[95]

Hungarian TV had its own classical music department, which, just in the year 1969, offered four educational series aimed at 'the broadest audiences': one programme featuring Leonard Bernstein; another named *Legyen a zene mindenkié* ('Music should belong to everyone'); *TV Season's Ticket*, a concert series that had been put together based on viewer requests; and *A szereposztástól a premierig* ('From casting to premier'), which offered a behind-the-scenes look at opera productions, hosted by famous conductors.[96]

Clearly, the normative moral universe and condescending address of some of these programmes was at odds with the overall goal of democratizing education. One tell-tale sign of this friction is how many of these shows were actually titled 'club' of some kind or another. Even Soviet television's most watched programme contained the word club in the title, a quiz and game show called *The Club of the Merry and Quick-Witted* known as 'KVN', for short. The Soviet series *The Film and Travel Club* educated viewers about film and travel. As Kristin Roth-Ey dryly notes, it was host Vladimir Schneiderov's own club, and he was the only traveller. Other programmes also issued a selective address to a supposedly undifferentiated national audience. Even more lively variety shows, such as the Soviet *Stories of Heroism*, about the heroes of the Second World War, which were conversational and introduced interesting individuals to the audience, featured carefully selected role models: usually young, well-spoken men. They functioned like clubs driven by leading personalities.[97]

Educational TV as a democratic forum

By the 1970s, more and more educational programmes began to solicit viewers' emotional engagement and participation, hitting playful and humorous characters like Dr Brain and employing well-liked, entertaining personalities as guides instead of scholars. In the long run, these proved to be the most enduring shows; many of them even survived socialism.

Such was the case with Romanian *Teleenciclopedia* ('Tele-Encyclopaedia'), a general interest magazine, which mixed fiction films with short documentaries featuring the voices of popular actors, singers and other celebrities as narrators. It took a thematic approach to topics of general knowledge. Since it was neither elitist nor exclusivist, *Tele-Encyclopaedia* actually popularized scientific knowledge in Romania. The balance it struck between informative, educational programming and popular, general topics of interest guaranteed its survival through the 1980s, when programming was reduced to two hours a day.[98]

---

94 Ibid., 92.
95 Ibid., 95.
96 János Vesernyés, 'Komolyzenei rovat' [Column on classical music], *Film Színház Muzsika* 5 (1969).
97 Roth-Ey, *Moscow Prime Time*, 73.
98 Mustata, 'The Power of Television'.

The Hungarian programme most similar to *Tele-Encyclopaedia* was called *Delta*. It was a long-running popular TV show launched in 1964 that covered mostly scientific and technological topics of common interest. One key to its success was its charming host Júlia Kudlik, one of the most universally liked announcers and celebrities of the entire period. While viewers responded very positively to *Delta*, critics voiced what was an evident conflict between the serious, masculine nature of positivist science espoused by the programme's short documentary segments and the blond female host associated with the maternal, decorative position of the programme announcer. One critic wrote a thinly veiled condescending assessment in a national newspaper in 1972:

> Júlia Kudlik's lovely smile is legendary among the audience and in the press. Her charming personality seduces even those who are less interested in the programme. However, she's entrapped by *Delta*, which is on every Sunday. She is expected to make science popular; she is expected to talk about subjects she obviously doesn't know much about. So, she has no choice but to stick to the script. This script is nothing more than the routine text that accompanies short science-news documentaries. Therefore, she and *Delta* are not in harmony. She should save that lovely smile for topics closer to her personality.[99]

Polish TV launched its first current affairs programme, *Tele-Echo*, in 1956. It was broadcast until 1981. Like *Delta*, it featured a charming hostess, Irena Dziedzic, who was also the creator and writer of the programme. It covered current affairs, art and culture in an interview format. During its 25-year history, *Tele-Echo* hosted over 12,000 guests. While Dziedzic was often – and rightly so – accused of political conformism, Tadeusz Pikulski calls her a phenomenal example of a TV personality, who was able to stir intense emotions.[100] Her role was somewhat similar to that of legendary Soviet Central Television hostess Valentina Leonteva, who hosted the melodramatic talk show *Ot vsei dushi* ('From the bottom of my heart') between 1972 and 1987, a programme that, as Christine Evans argues, played a central role in visualizing the 'Soviet way of life' through the emotional display of a Soviet way of feeling.[101]

Programmes dispensing legal advice formed a separate subgenre. The East German series *Das Fernsehgericht tagt* ('The TV court meets') was launched in 1961 on ARD (Consortium of public broadcasters in the Federal Republic of Germany) and ran for 74 episodes until 1978. It featured trial scenes dramatized by actors playing plaintiffs and defendants. The judges and state attorneys who appeared on the show were actual professionals. The format drew on American legal television shows, which had been on the air since the 1950s. Each trial lasted two days, broadcast as 90-minute episodes in primetime, on consecutive weekdays. This was followed by a hiatus of several weeks. The sitting judge, Dr August Detleve Sommerkamp, affectionately nicknamed *Papa Gnädig* ('Merciful papa') by the audience, had been an active trial judge for 36 years before he began his television career. During breaks in the trial, reporter Giselher Schaar asked people in the studio audience about their opinions on the case. In its first nine years, the programme worked exclusively with professional actors. In 1970 they began to involve

---

99 András Lukácsy's critique of the 'Delta' broadcast from 9 April 1972, *Magyar Hírlap* (9 April 1972).
100 Pikulski, *Prywatna historia telewizji publicznej*, 54.
101 Christine Evans, 'The "Soviet Way of Life" as a Way of Feeling: Emotion and Influence on Soviet Central Television in the Brezhnev Era', *Cahiers du Monde Russe* 56, no. 2 (Spring 2015): 543–70.

Visual cultures

non-professionals.[102] Other courtroom shows followed, including one about marriage problems, one that allowed the audience to act as judges, and one about traffic cases. Greta Olson argues that the post-unification German reality show *Richterin Barbara Salesch* ('Judge Barbara Salesch'), 1999–2012, allegedly modelled after *Judge Judy* (1996–present), also draws on the rich legacy of Cold War courtroom shows, particularly *Das Fernsehgericht tagt*.[103]

The most memorable Polish educational courtroom shows were *16-tu przekupnych* ('The corruptible sixteen') and *Wszyscy jestesmy sedziami* ('We are all judges'), the latter of which was an educational programme about the judiciary system, which involved prosecutors, judges, witnesses and public. The Hungarian socialist proto-reality programme *Jogi esetek* ('Legal cases') also featured common legal cases for the purpose of education. It employed actors who dramatized these cases, and a beloved legal expert, attorney Pál Erőss, who had a flair for translating legal quandaries into simple, but lively, language.

Many of these programmes increasingly mixed documentary realism and fiction and also reached into viewers' actual lives, making television a more vivid, organic and lively platform for public engagement. Once again, the same programme types could be found throughout the region, many of them also variants of Western European PSB programmes. While the resistance to finding any redeeming value to television remained steadfast throughout the period, it was also increasingly recognized among TV professionals and critics that television viewing was not simply a passive state unworthy of the active socialist citizen. Rather, it was interwoven with other activities socialist ideology deemed educational, such as reading, listening to classical music or learning about the natural world. Thus, television's function was seen as a spark button that would ignite further inquiries, preferably pursued in a collective framework and enhanced by playful engagement. Self-directed, lifelong learning is a very contemporary idea, as is the notion that competitive play enhances interest and participation. György Sándor, programming director of Hungarian Television from 1958 to 1985, in an interview in the journal *Radio and Television Review*, said that television was a central 'force of organization'. Hundreds of groups were formed to create local versions of the popular quiz show *Ki Mit Tud* ('Who knows what') and organize folk music circles inspired by the popular competition show *Felszállott a páva* ('Fly peacock').[104] By the 1970s, television functioned not only as a schoolhouse but also as a public forum.

The 1969 tellingly titled Hungarian programme *Fórum* ('Forum') bypassed lectures and propaganda and invited artists, intellectuals and politicians to live town hall meetings in changing locations. It put party leaders in front of the cameras and connected them with actual viewers, who asked questions about the economy and its reforms, political issues and foreign relations. On the 15 September 1972 broadcast, for instance, Péter Vályi, Vice President of the Council of Ministers,[105] answered questions about foreign economic relations from the workers in the meeting room of the electric factory Egyesült Izzó and from viewers who called in.

---

102 Michael Reufsteck and Stefan Niggemeier, *Das Fernsehlexikon: Alles über 7000 Sendungen von Ally McBeal bis zur ZDF-Hitparade* (München: Goldmann Verlag, 2005). My thanks to Greta Olson for helping me locate this source and assisting me with the translation.

103 Greta Olson, 'Intersections of Gender and Legal Culture in Two Women Judge Shows: Judge Judy and Richterin Barbara Salesch', in *Contemporary Gender Relations and Changes in Legal Cultures*, eds Hanne Petersen, José María Lorenzo Villaverde and Ingrid Lund-Andersen (Copenhagen: DJOF, 2013), 29–58.

104 Csepeli, 'Rádiónk és televíziónk közművelődési', 5.

105 Vályi was invited on only after a long exchange with other party officials had approved his participation. See Dunavölgyi, '1972'.

In this experimental format, 'forum' meant an actual public forum, where party officials took a considerable risk: they realized they could not hide behind official releases any more in the age of television; but once on TV, they were unprepared for the visibility it afforded. In the 1972 edition mentioned above, Vályi is obviously uncomfortable. If anything, his answers foreground the effort with which he is trying to avoid straight answers, falling back on clichéd phrases that evidently fail to convince the audience. The camera intentionally pans around the room to show knowing smirks and even explicit scepticism. Faced with actual questions from real citizens on live television, Vályi's canned phrases widen the gap between the leaders' performance of the principles of socialism and the actual direction socialism was taking. In 1969, in the daily newspaper *Népszabadság* ('Free nation'), one critic wrote in reference to the programme's increasing reliance on viewer questions commenting thus: 'What we saw on Thursday night's edition of *Forum* was superior to the usual public affairs programmes ... There is more at stake here than discussing economic matters in a popular format. If we consider antecedents such as the interview János Kádár gave last summer, or the conversation with Jenő Fock, or the television interview given by Zoltán Komócsin about foreign affairs or the answers leaders in the capital gave to viewers' questions, we see a definite effort to make matters of governance more public'.[106]

Another commentator even went so far as to sneak some criticism of the programme's transparency within the requisite praise. In the party's print organ *Free Nation*, he commented on a 1969 *Forum* edition that dealt with socialist law and legislature:

> The legal edition of *Forum* was the most exciting public affairs programme of the week and perhaps the most successful edition of this question-and-answer programme so far. Gradually, everyone is beginning to figure out how the programme works – viewers and participants alike. The questions are direct; the answers are open. It'll bring further progress if we hear less of the phrase 'we'll examine the question', and if the respondent offers his personal opinion about the problem at hand. Statesmen are allowed to indicate if the opinion is theirs alone and not an official statement.[107]

The desire to use television as a public forum brought forth a region-wide format. The Yugoslav programme *Current Debates*, which aired on TV Belgrade from 1965 to 1969, was very similar to *Forum*. It was a participatory discussion programme that revolved around current issues, selected based on audience suggestions, including unemployment, living standards and political reforms. The East German *Prisma* ('Prism') ran from 1963 to 1991. As Heather Gumbert explains, it was one of the most tangible outcomes of the Agitation Commission's appeal to television producers to create popular programming that would uncover and find solutions to the contradictions of socialism.[108] The ultimate goal, of course, was to teach viewers to see themselves as part of a functioning socialist collective. Gerhard Scheumann, creator and first host of the show, modelled *Prism* after the West German current affairs magazine *Panorama*. Unlike *Panorama*, however, which focused on large-scale political issues, *Prism* was positioned as a liaison between the party leadership and ordinary citizens, inviting viewers to contribute questions, comments and complaints about a variety of issues that affected everyday socialist

---

106 László Rózsa's critique of *Fórum*, *Népszabadság* (18 January 1969).
107 Tibor Hegedűs, '*Fórum* – belpolitikai téma: a szocialista jogalkotás, jogalkalmazás' [Forum – issues of domestic politics: socialist law and legislation], *Népszabadság* (14 May 1969).
108 Gumbert, *Envisioning Socialism*, 146.

Visual cultures

lives.[109] Like *Forum, Prism* performed a delicate dance. On the one hand, it offered critical, participatory journalism that invited viewers to feel like they had a voice in shaping the system – and that the SED was on their side. On the other hand, *Prism* embraced the leeway to be critical of the party and did offer a variety of previously unheard voices to be part of the national conversation, which could not be contained within the message of a triumphant socialism. In one of the most memorable cases, *Prism* successfully intervened on behalf of a young woman who was disqualified from attending teachers' training college because she refused to swim and failed gym class due to an earlier water-related trauma.[110]

Programmes like *Prism* opened the door to welcome audiences wider than ever before. Television had begun to take advantage of its unique ability to let people watch and vicariously participate in the lives of others. Propelled by the socialist ethos of collectivity, such programmes shifted the attention to collective memory and systemic inequality rather than displaying others' misery in a voyeuristic fashion. For instance, the popular Hungarian series *Ebédszünet* ('Lunch break'), launched in 1971 and hosted by Mária Balogh, followed up on viewer letters that called attention to such systemic problems. One of the broadcasts in 1971 explored the inhumane conditions of a provincial industrial area, where factory leaders had refused to make even the slightest improvements over the previous 20 years. *Lunch Break*'s crew travelled to the location and interviewed the workers. According to one commentator: 'Television's principle on *Lunch Break* is not cheap sensationalism. Rather, it uses the force of the public forum to press those in charge to make progressive decisions.'[111] The same year also saw the beginning of another long-running programme *Nyitott boríték* ('Open envelope'), in which hostess Margit Molnár tried to solve problems raised by viewer letters. As the *Radio and TV Guide* explained, the programme was prompted by the fact that viewers saw television as an institution that could bring remote locations and issues into public visibility. It is this collective responsibility that the programme's creators took up and put into practice.[112]

Some programmes incorporated playful and entertaining elements that successfully tapped into the intimacy created by television at the intersection of private and public lives and anticipated reality programmes. The 1963 Hungarian *Belépés csak tévénézőknek!* ('Entry only to TV viewers!') invited viewers to behind-the-scenes locations of institutions such as the police department, the state water company, Hunnia Film Studio, the National Manuscript Archive and television itself. Another participatory programme that directly anticipated reality subgenres, *Ki tud róla?* ('Who knows about them?' in 1970) published photographs in the *Radio and TV Guide* taken in the immediate post-war years of 1945–9, soliciting responses from people who recognized themselves or others. One hundred applicants were then selected for interviews and the post-war lives of 20 of those in the images were portrayed in the series. Co-creator Dezső Radványi said in an interview that '[We wanted to] meet the generation who undertook the socialist revolution for whom the issue of our nation and people was a personal issue.'[113]

---

109 Ibid., 145.

110 Ibid., 145–46.

111 Anonymous article about *Lunch Break* in *Film Színház Muzsika* 6 (1971). See Dunavölgyi, '1971'.

112 The *Radio and TV Guide* introduced the new programme this way: 'TV receives countless letters in which viewers ask for advice to solve various problems. Of course, television employees aren't able to respond to every request, but they try to help with those that have broader public implications and concern the common good. This new programme deals with these common issues raised by viewer letters. It also emphasizes responsibility to one another.' See: Dunavölgyi, '1971'. My translation.

113 Interview with Dezső Radványi, *Radio and TV Guide* 45 (1970).

This opening towards socially committed participatory TV was accompanied by television's experiments with mixing realist and fictional genres as a way of reaching viewers and loosening the definition of tele-education. It deserves more than a note here that socialist television was always a welcoming home for prolific documentary productions and exhibitions. In Hungary alone, a separate documentary department was set up in 1972, born out of the realization that television was well-suited to ethnographic portraits that are also critical analyses of social problems. They produced 40 films a year in a studio that operated separately from Mafilm, the state film production company where most documentary productions had previously been developed, although collaborations continued.[114]

Documentary work also involved contributions by amateur filmmakers, a tradition that goes back to the very beginnings of television. In 1972, a new series titled *Pergő képek* ('Spinning images') was dedicated to such work as a complement to the amateur documentary film festival. Some of the most outstanding and enduring achievements of the documentary genre were created by women who thus expanded their reach into television beyond the pretty faces and reassuring voices of the programme continuity announcers. It is also likely that television provided more space for female directors since male filmmakers were disdainful of television and reluctant to associate with it, with few exceptions. In Hungary, women reinvigorated television documentaries in the 1960s, and brought home international prizes at film festivals.

Television and national entertainment

Historical drama

Most state socialist regimes recognized early on that in order to capitalize on the propaganda potential of television, they had to do more than prohibit and censor foreign programme flows. To retain some control over the medium that John Ellis has called 'the private life of the nation state',[115] they had to get in on the game and provide their populations with domestic, party-approved entertainment. Nationalism became the cornerstone and mediating terrain of socialist governments' media policies across the region, and television was the key instrument of nationalistic edutainment. By the 1960s, Stalinist principles of forced Marxist-Leninist internationalism had lost their credibility in most countries along with the idea of a communist utopia of a classless, egalitarian international brotherhood. This created an opening for national regimes to adjust the central Soviet rhetoric in order to consolidate their own domestic powers. The dispersion of television broadcasting allowed for the subtle and measured deployment of entertainment in the domestic sphere in order to both alleviate widespread disappointment with the realities of socialism and to strengthen patriotic identification with the cause of the nation.

The quintessential genre of popular fictional television during its first two formative decades was the historical adventure series. Socialist historical drama serials participated in a European circulation that reached across the Iron Curtain. From the beginning, most East European viewers were exposed to a number of successful Western historical European serials, which were safe to import for socialist TV, including the German *Heimat* series (1984–2000), and Britain's *The Forsyte Saga* (1967–69), *The Onedin Line* (1971–80) and *Brideshead*

---

114 Mariann Ember, 'Hakni vagy újfajta filmezés' [A gig or a new kind of film], *Filmkultúra* 3 (1972). Interview with Radványi Dezső.

115 John Ellis, *Visible Fictions* (London: Routledge, 1982), 5.

Revisited (1981). Many were literary adaptations with strong cultural pedigree that narrated stories about the nation, often dealing with cultural roots and formative moments in history. They tended to have high production values to match their cultural quality.[116] The profile of historical dramas in smaller Western European countries with less abundant resources for television production is quite similar to that of the Eastern European historical serials. For instance, the majority of Flemish TV's output in the 1960s was driven by the cultural nationalism of the Flemish community in Belgium and consisted of literary and theatrical adaptations. These serials followed the same script: they drew on literary sources and recreated rural life in Flanders in the first half of the twentieth century. They became known as the 'peasant drama'.[117] The prototypical Flemish period-serial *Wij, heren van Zichem* ('We, the lords of Zichem', 1969), was set in the 1920s. It was adapted from the novels of Ernest Claes, which were part of the broader *Heimatkunst* ('regional art') that inspired much TV and film drama from the 1960s to 80s in Belgium and Germany. It had a popular cast, a light tone accessible to everyone and everyday situations that crystallized around conflicts between the village people and the francophone village baron, and between Catholics and the freethinking blacksmith. The show was set against the rise of socialism and liberalism and the struggle for the emancipation of the Flemish language against French. It built on the mythology of suppressed and resistant Flemish folk culture and took a nostalgic look at the harsh but pure life in the idyllic countryside.[118]

Alexander Dhoest writes that the show reached 78 per cent of the Flemish viewership in March 1969 and remains one of the most popular Flemish serials. Flemish resistance to the French influence within Belgium also found an outlet in a popular drama that incorporated both high literary and popular folk culture. Similar to Eastern European historical serials of the period, it was a vehicle of cultural nationalism, representing 'the endeavour to culturally emancipate the nation as opposed to political nationalism striving for independence'.[119] The structure of this cultural nationalism betrays an inferiority complex similar to what motivated Hungarian, Polish or Czechoslovak serials of the time, a complex offset by the cultural credit drawn from literary classics on the one hand and the mythology of an authentic, idealized folk culture on the other.[120]

Sitcoms, soap operas and dramatic serials produced in the United States during the postwar years became synonymous with commercial, scripted TV entertainment worldwide. In contrast, when television became a household fixture in socialist countries in the 1960s, national broadcasters modelled their first domestically produced serials after a narrow selection of foreign entertainment fictions focused on the past and turned sharply away from the present. This generic preference had several advantages. Importing historical drama serials reduced the likelihood that Western products and lifestyles, and with them, the contagious 'ideology of consumer capitalism' would spread. Furthermore, from the late 1960s through the 1970s, during their heyday, domestically produced historical adventure serials allowed socialist regimes to teach selective history lessons and foster national identifications that also

---

116 Sonja De Leeuw et al., 'TV Nations or Global Medium? European Television between National Institution and Window on the World', in Bignell and Fickers, *A European Television History*, 127–53, here 134.

117 Ibid., 139.

118 Ibid., 141.

119 Alexander Dhoest, 'Quality and/as National Identity: Press Discourse on Flemish Period TV Drama', *European Journal of Cultural Studies* 7, no. 3 (2004): 311.

120 Ibid., 318.

appeared to conform to ideological prescriptions demanded by the Soviet occupiers. These serials often ostentatiously demonstrated adherence to Soviet socialist dogma in formal matters such as the glorification of folk culture or plotlines that rewarded peasant characters at the expense of the wealthy and powerful. Although such elements appear campy today, they were subtle enough to avoid undermining the shows' power of identification with the real emotional draw, the nationalistic narratives and spectacle. In the most liberal socialist countries, the programmes' propagandistic excess was released in another register of entertainment, political cabaret, inspiring hilarious, ironic send-ups. The nationalistic lessons of these programmes were born out of the powerful convergence between folk mythology and high cultural legitimation. Historical adventure serials glorified masculine national heroism in the face of political oppression, a travelling metaphor that could be applied to any threat to national sovereignty with little regard for historical accuracy of such depictions. The serials situated these heroic struggles in the national past, but the dominant allegorical framework remained: national resistance against Soviet domination.

Two popular serials, the Hungarian *A Tenkes kapitánya* ('The captain of the Tenkes', 1964), and the Polish *Janosik* (1974), are exemplary of the broader aesthetic, social and media policy trends of the 1960s and 70s. Their success with audiences and the effectiveness of their political messages are rooted in three interrelated factors, all of which identify television entertainment as a key terrain for sustaining nationalisms and for visualizing the contradictions at the core of these nationalisms at the same time.

The first aspect is the socialist historical adventure series' loose treatment of historical facts, places and people. Paradoxically, this mythical quality proved essential to consolidating a spatio-temporally bound, linear national history around prominent historical actors. Both shows featured semi-fictional characters against a vague historical backdrop. As I show, the genealogy of the Janosik story that informed the TV series is particularly informative since the historical Janosik actually lived and moved across multilingual and multicultural territories well before the nineteenth-century struggles for national sovereignty began and before twentieth-century national borders were drawn.

Second, the nationalistic projects at the heart of these adventure series were supported by a contradictory double cultural legitimation. They borrowed from the alleged authenticity of folk culture while also fulfilling Marxist-Leninist expectations. However, this folk authenticity was invariably established through the mediation of national poets and writers, who have assumed ideological leadership roles in the cause of national independence since the late eighteenth century. The Janosik myth illustrates well how transnational figures became appropriated from folk mythology to spearhead singular national narratives in nineteenth-century literature. This, in turn, legitimized their re-adaptation into nationalistic popular cultures in film and television in the twentieth century. Regional and continental programme exchanges and shared broadcast signals then released these figures into international television flows again. However, the fact that their narrative patterns were recognizable across national borders, thanks to shared regional histories and patterns of nationalism, has not deprived these serials of their primary function as anchors of popular nationalisms.

Third, the historical figures after whom the protagonists were modelled were far from heroic. They were social bandits – local Robin Hood figures – who embodied a wish-fulfilling, contradictory collective that belonged to a European cultural sphere and voluntarily submitted to a Western European exoticization of the periphery. The prevalence of such outlaw heroes lent a regional specificity to the development of nationalisms and nation states in Eastern and Southern Europe.

Comedy, cabaret and political humour

After television established itself as a mass institution in the 1950s and 60s, every country developed similar comedy genres, which necessarily drew on pre-socialist forms of humour. In the Central and Eastern European countries, these pre-socialist forms derived from the tradition of stage cabaret and, when adapted to TV, continued to carry the generic label of 'cabaret' as a fairly specific socialist TV genre.

The most influential European traditions were the French cabaret and the German *Kabarett*. While the English equivalent of the word refers to musical entertainment featuring humour, comedy, song, dance and theatre, the original European phenomenon also implied political satire. The lighter, more entertaining elements and the satirical, more politicized elements coexisted in a fairly liberal environment until the Second World War. This peaceful combination was the key to the popularity of cabaret during the Weimar Republic: cabaret was both a medium for political expression and critique, and an outlet for much-needed distraction and amusement during the years of economic crisis and war preparation. Political cabaret flourished in Germany in the Weimar period – employing serious writers such as Klaus Mann and Erich Kästner – only to be repressed by the Nazi regime in 1933, when German-speaking cabaret artists fled to Switzerland, Scandinavia, France or the United States.[121]

Polish stage cabaret originated in Cracow: the first Polish cabaret, *Zielony Balonik* ('Green balloon') was founded there in 1905. One of its creators, Tadeusz Boy-Żeleński, was an *enfant terrible* of the Polish literary scene and an important figure in the 'Young Poland' movement. Much of cabaret took the form of satirical short plays, which, similar to Germany, included some of the leaders of Cracow's political and cultural circles. It was sophisticated entertainment that addressed literary and cultural elites rather than broad audiences.[122]

In the Austro-Hungarian Monarchy, Budapest was a most hospitable city for cabaret: the first Hungarian-language cabaret, *Bonbonnière Kabaré* ('The Bonbonier'), opened there in 1907.[123] Like elsewhere in the region, cabaret was a progressive space, where comedians directly responded to current political events with wit and courage. The best writers of the time wrote and performed on stage, many of them former journalists for whom journalism and political satire were two sides of the same coin. At the end of the First World War there were about 30 cabarets in Budapest. By the end of the Second World War, there were about 50 despite increasing anti-Semitism and, after 1939, mass deportations, which devastated the cabaret since most comedians were Jewish.[124] It was during these years that performers assembled a rhetorical toolkit that bypassed the attention of the pro-German police and was to be deployed successfully during socialism. These performative strategies included slips of the tongue, playing dumb, ambiguity, double meaning and overidentification.

After the war, stage cabarets reopened just before TV cabaret began in the 1950s. In the GDR, the first post-war stage cabaret, *Die Distel* ('The thistle'), opened in 1953 in East Berlin,

---

121 Genevieve Judson-Jourdain, 'Cultures of Drink: Song, Dance, Alcohol and Politics in 20th Century German Cabarets', https://courses.cit.cornell.edu/his452/Alcohol/germancabaret.html (accessed 8 October 2018).

122 Thanks to Maria Zalewska for the research.

123 G. Apats, 'Szeszélyes évadok' [Capricious seasons], 2007, www.origo.hu/teve/20071130-100-eves-a-magyar-kabare-szeszelyes-evszakok-tortenete.html (accessed 8 October 2018).

124 Z. Rick, 'A pesti kabarék a II. világháború idején' [Budapest cabarets during the Second World War], 2008, www.mazsike.hu/pesti+kabarek+a+ii+vilaghaboru+idejen.html (accessed 8 October 2018).

while West German cabaret was concentrated around Düsseldorf, Munich and West Berlin. Stage and TV cabaret developed hand in hand and often exchanged talent, personnel and entire shows during socialism. In Budapest, after the devastation of the war, theatres needed to be rebuilt. The first cabaret reopened there as early as 1945. For a few years, until communist dictatorship took over, there seemed to be a true opportunity to deploy political humour as the language of a broad public sphere, widening cabaret's niche, cosmopolitan appeal beyond the capital. The forced communist takeover in 1949 squashed such hopes and planted mistrust of the government again. Censorship became dogmatic: it struck down on political satire and briefly banned political cabaret. Cabaret was considered by the party leadership a self-serving, cynical bourgeois pastime that had no place in a communist society of the future.[125] In response, cabaret performers adopted forms of ironic overidentification with the regime's own rhetoric and rituals in these early years – forms that Soviet political humour was to take only in the 1970s and 80s. Hungarian comedians of the 1950s and early 60s, first on stage and radio and increasingly on television, demonstrated excessive rhetorical loyalty to party requirements of behaviour and thought. They memorized revolutionary slogans and songs, pointed out the moral corruption of capitalism with zeal, and celebrated factory workers for their productivity. They did so while winking at the audience, who fully understood the parodic intent of these extreme performances.[126]

In socialist Hungary, the political thaw began relatively early, shortly after the failed 1956 anti-Soviet revolution, when János Kádár began his long authoritarian reign as Secretary General of the Socialist Party. Television, which became a mass medium around this time, almost immediately adapted political humour from Hungarian Radio, which had itself incorporated forms of stage cabaret. The post-1956 thaw re-established the Budapest petit-bourgeoisie of the original political cabaret as its comedic inspiration, with unspoken party approval. Television thus played a crucial role in shoring up bourgeois humour and values. In 1957, just a year after television's post-war relaunch and the crushed revolt against Soviet occupation, television broadcast a live memorial show from the theatre Literary Stage dedicated to the legacy of Endre Nagy, the godfather of pre-war political cabaret.[127] The same year saw the first New Year's cabaret, another live theatrical broadcast, which was hosted by some of the most popular comedians.[128]

In a parallel development in Poland, the first political TV cabaret was broadcast on New Year's Eve, 1960. It was so popular that people stopped dancing at parties that night to watch it. It was followed in the 1960s by new live entertainment shows. As in Budapest, many of the political cabaret programmes drew on the interwar Polish cabaret tradition. *Kabaret Starszych Panów* ('Cabaret of two old men'), which ran from 1958 to 1966, displayed nostalgia for the bygone era of pre-war elegance and the sophistication of the urban intelligentsia. The programme reached cult status over the years and still elicits immediate recognition among all Poles.[129] It featured two performers, Jeremi Przybora, who wrote the script, and Jerzy

---

125 Á. Alpár, 'A pesti kabaré' [The Budapest cabaret], 2011, http://tbeck.beckground.hu/szinhaz/htm/25. htm (accessed 8 October 2018).

126 Vilmos Faragó, 'Magyar Általános Szórakoztató' [Hungarian general entertainment], *Filmvilág* 1 (1984): 59–60.

127 Péter Dunavölgyi, 'A magyar televíziózás története az 1950-es években: 1957' [The history of Hungarian television in the fifties: 1957], http://dunavolgyipeter.hu/televizio_tortenet/a_magyar_televiziozas_tortenete_az_1950-as_evekben/1957 (accessed 8 October 2018).

128 Ibid.

129 Pikulski, *Prywatna historia telewizji publicznej*, 74.

Visual cultures

Wasowski, who wrote the music. The two met while working for Polish radio. Their sense of humour was 'absurdist, sophisticated, and elegant'.[130] Przybora and Wasowski played two bourgeois characters, Pan (Mr) A and Pan B, who were dressed in dinner jackets and bowler hats and discussed the events of the day. Direct political references were uncommon; jokes were usually camouflaged to pass censorship.[131] True to the cabaret format, their act included a great deal of musical elements. The show also had a range of celebrity guests – mostly actors. There were two new editions per year, each followed by multiple reruns. Tadeusz Pikulski recalls that the authors' guiding idea was to 'provide entertainment, to amuse themselves and their audiences by detaching them from the grey, boring and ugly everyday life and rampant vulgarity'.[132] In its heyday, the programme was criticized for romanticizing the outdated style and sensibilities of the pre-war era. The socialist youth organization rejected the programme for being insufficiently progressive and direct.[133]

The thaw era lightened TV cabaret even further. Several of the most memorable and popular programmes in Poland were associated with Olga Lipińska, a theatre and TV director and satirical artist, and one of the few women in the world of socialist comedy. She directed and produced *Kabaret Olgi Lipinskiej* ('The Olga Lipińska cabaret'), a 50-minute programme that premiered in 1974 (under a different title), ran until 2005 and was resurrected in 2010. Lipińska was also involved in the creation of a New Year's Eve special edition cabaret called *Szopka noworoczna* ('New Year's crib'), that summarized the past year's events in comic style. Lipińska's other TV cabaret productions include *Głupia sprawa* ('Stupid thing'), 1968–70, *Gallux Show*, 1970–74, *Właśnie leci kabarecik* ('The cabaret is on'), 1975–7, and *Kurtyna w górę* ('Curtain up'), 1977–81. Her cabaret was infused with the regional tradition of the absurd and surreal, particularly with the humour of the pre-war Warsaw poet Konstanty Ildefons Gałczyński. Like *Cabaret of Two Old Men*, Lipińska's cabaret included celebrity guests as well as musical numbers and offered cultural and social commentary that carefully evaded direct politicizing and branded itself as 'pure entertainment'. In turn, it was accused of promoting bourgeois kitsch and undermining the wholesome, realistic and educational ethos of socialism.

In the Romania of the 1960s, the programme *Varietati* ('Varieties') was broadcast every Sunday afternoon. It featured political satire and comedy skits sandwiched between dance and musical numbers.[134] Other humorous and satirical variety programmes included *Intalnire cu umorul si satira* ('Date with humour and satire'), *Umor si satira* ('Humour and satire'), and *Intalnirea de la ora 10* ('The 10 o'clock meeting'), all shown on Saturday evenings; and *Varietati musical-coreografice* ('Musical and choreographic varieties') and *Studioul muzicii usoare* ('The studio of pop music') aired on Sunday evenings.[135] In the GDR, the values and tastes of the Weimar period reigned supreme despite the party's concerted efforts to create more revolutionary television programming and to overcome the distinction between bourgeois and working-class tastes.[136] Viewers' rejection of political-artistic experiments and their demand for light entertainment

---

130 Marek Haltof, *Polish National Cinema* (Oxford: Berghahn Books, 2002), 140.

131 Pikulski, *Prywatna historia telewizji publicznej*, 75.

132 Ibid., 74.

133 Ibid., 75.

134 Silviu Brucan, 'Idila mea cu televiziunea' [My idyll with the television], in *Viziune-Tele* (Bucharest: TVR Directia de Logistica si Memorie, 1996), 41.

135 Dana Mustata, 'Reassembling a History of Romanian Television Programmes', in *The Power of Television: Including the Historicizing of the Live Romanian Revolution* (PhD diss., Utrecht University, 2011).

136 Gumbert, *Envisioning Socialism*, 156.

forced the SED to shift direction in the early 1960s from 'the revolutionary, grassroots transformation of popular culture' to the nationalistic embrace of 'warmed-over bourgeois values'.[137]

Nevertheless, throughout the region, party leaders continued to express consternation about the TV boom of pre-war forms of light entertainment. One typical summary prepared by a party official for the Hungarian Socialist Party Committee in the spring of 1959 speculated that there were 'many reasons' for bourgeois cabaret's return. 'Television, even when its editors know exactly what they want, has difficulties doing something radically different in the genre of entertainment than in other media. One can only change this with collective effort', she proposed with mandatory optimism.[138] The 1966 report of the Hungarian National Council of Trade Unions also zeroed in on political cabaret in its annual assessment of TV programming: 'Certain political cabaret programmes are tasteless; their political content is ambiguous, and they often cause outrage among groups of more politically evolved workers'.[139] Even the president of Hungarian Television at the time, István Tömpe, felt compelled to express moral caution about TV cabaret in his 1966 annual report: 'We need to reduce the number of political cabaret programmes. We need to ensure that political jokes elevate, rather than disrupt, the spirit of public political exchange'.[140]

But such caution was increasingly reduced to empty rhetoric. Pre-war forms of variety entertainment not only survived into socialism but became progressively more frequent on TV. One obvious reason for this was that TV comedy was fed by and inherited its talent from stage comedy and then radio. The three institutions existed in symbiosis throughout the socialist decades. As elsewhere, cabaret performers were predominantly Jewish. While their community had been devastated by the Holocaust and subsequent emigration, most Jewish comedians also deemphasized their ethnic heritage, as the entire Jewish question became taboo during socialism. But what helped 'bourgeois' comedy thrive in the first place was that its occasional use of political satire was overshadowed by an array of light cabaret acts, including many musical numbers. The latter remained safely disconnected from the turbulent world of the 1960s, 70s and 80s and adopted the depoliticized, nostalgic tone often deployed in the service of the nationalistic cultural policies of socialist governments.

Foreign observers of socialism would have been shocked by the number of these depoliticized comedy–variety entertainment programmes. In Hungary alone, TV offerings included shows such as *Nemcsak a tükör görbe* ('It's not just the mirror that's crooked', 1965), based on humorous skits written by classical and contemporary comic writers; *Pesti kabaré* ('The cabaret of Budapest', 1969–70), a four-part series that reinvigorated the bourgeois heritage of comic writing with adaptations of early-twentieth-century writers Ferenc Molnár, Gáspár Heltai and Frigyes Karinthy; the two-part *Kabaré utca* ('Cabaret street', 1971), and the 1970 news-satire series *Sajtókabaré* ('Press cabaret'); *Csak férfiaknak* ('Only for men', 1968), which featured a retrograde, patriarchal take on gender roles within marriage; the similar *Kriminális* ('Criminal', 1972) and *Mondom a magamét* ('Saying what I'm saying', 1975), both broadcast from the *Mikroszkóp Színpad*

---

137 Ibid., 157.

138 In the summer of 1959, Mrs K.I., Party Secretary for the TV Union, prepared a report for the Central Committee. See: Dunavölgyi, '1959'.

139 Report from the National Council of Labor Unions, 'Vélemények a Televízió munkájáról' [Assessment of television's work], March 29, 1966. 288f 22/1966/288f 22/1966/agit/73/3. Hungarian National Document Archives.

140 Report about the Work of Television prepared by the President of Hungarian Television, 'Jelentés a Televízió munkájáról', March 31, 1966. 288f 22/1966/11 ö.e, agit/375. Hungarian National Document Archives.

('Microscope stage'), one of several Budapest theatres devoted to comedy; and a number of one-man shows that typically featured older comedians. In 1969, the series *Pesti cabaret – vagy amin a nagyapáink szórakoztak* ('Pest cabaret – or what amused our grandfathers') was broadcast, with the explicit intention of evoking the satirical cabaret scene of early-twentieth-century Budapest.[141] A critic dubbed the programme a 'cabaret museum' because of its intention to reproduce the authentic feel of the interwar context along with its original jokes.[142]

The abundance of lewd songs, dance numbers and vaudeville acts on TV was a strange phenomenon within the regimented, centrally controlled routine and material scarcity of everyday socialism. Bourgeois cabaret was not simply in conflict with a socialist-realist aesthetic and the mission to educate the public; it was outdated and out of place because it obviously belonged to a different, more decadent era. While there must have been a demographic of older viewers who remembered the interwar and war periods and shared a taste for these acts, these programmes had little to do with the everyday life of much of the population, especially younger people. They were the odd packaging one had to unwrap to get to the occasional more contemporary, edgy, satirical cabaret.

TV, game shows and competition

The fact that game and quiz shows were present and popular throughout the history of socialist TV is at least somewhat counter-intuitive. After all, game shows were one of the popular genres that Jérôme Bourdon calls the 'ghosts' of public service broadcasting even in Western Europe, where it was no less popular. It was often considered a 'bad genre' or 'a damning synecdoche for the whole of the medium'.[143] Game shows were repeatedly accused of turning knowledge into trivia; its history is blemished by cases of corruption; it pitted participants against one another for financial or other material gain; it created television celebrities; and it thrived on humiliating candidates for viewers' voyeuristic pleasure. In this regard, it built a slippery historical slope towards the murky flood of reality programming.[144]

In Eastern Europe, these formats bring up even more fundamental contradictions embedded in the structure of socialism. In the first place, since they were not domestically developed for the most part, they once again reveal socialism's intricate international connections with capitalism. They were often formats more or less directly borrowed from Western European public service broadcasters and, like those broadcasters, also incorporated elements of American commercial variants. The generic boundaries between game, quiz and variety shows tended to be unclear everywhere. While they changed over the decades to register the political and economic shifts in national or regional socialist cultures, we can also see the same types crop up everywhere. Some were coordinated with the help of Intervision. Such was the case of a 1963 quiz show about space travel that included local broadcasts from member countries; or *Fly By*, the 1967 international competition among flight attendants organized by 11 international airlines, which also included live local broadcasts from socialist capitals.[145] Other programmes,

---

141 Dunavölgyi, '1969'.

142 Anna Vilcsek, 'Critique', *Magyar Nemzet* (30 April 1969).

143 Jérôme Bourdon, 'Old and New Ghosts: Public Service Television and the Popular – A History', *European Journal of Cultural Studies* 7, no. 3 (2004): 283–304, here 287.

144 Ibid.

145 Péter Dunavölgyi, 'A magyar televíziózás története a hatvanas években: 1967' [The history of Hungarian television in the sixties: 1967], http://dunavolgyipeter.hu/televizio_tortenet/a_magyar_televiziozas_tortenete_az_1960-as_evekben/1967 (accessed 8 October 2018).

Anikó Imre

such as musical talent shows, were seen by governments as prime export products. Despite their ambiguous moral status, game and quiz shows remained staples of socialist programming. They contribute to an alternative prehistory of reality-based programmes and of the entire bipolar Cold War world order.

Furthermore, while socialist television programmes participated in the circulation of European and American game show formats, for the most part they adapted these formats to the stricter moral codes of socialist citizen training. With the genre, socialist TV found a balance between educational content and an entertaining format. As I show, this balance was elusive to begin with. But when commercial television broke up Western European public broadcasters' monopoly in the 1970s, the ensuing dual-system broadcasting also pushed socialist game shows to become less educational, more commercialized, and even more popular than before. The 1970s and 80s brought about the golden age of the genre. The golden age issued a threat to the equilibrium between the official ideologies of state socialism and the 'capitalist' properties of most game show formats. These programmes, after all, whipped up competition, fostered a desire for consumer goods and revolved around individual talent rather than democratic participation.

At first sight, the role of competition appears to be one of the clearest divides between the two world systems. At the heart of socialism is a collaborative, collective ethos, routinely set in contrast with the competitive and individualistic forces that drive capitalism. How is it that the competitive nature of these programmes was embraced by socialist populations and authorities alike without causing significant ideological friction? Does the popularity of televisual competition undermine our received notions about socialism? Or, to take the implications a step further, what does the popularity of game shows explain to us about the fact that socialism produced several individualistic, ambitious and competitive generations? This is evident not only in socialist countries' achievements in sports, the arts and the sciences but also in the ease with which a large number of citizens and institutions adjusted to the demands of cut-throat individual competition in the early 1990s.

An obvious answer would be that socialist ideals of collectivity and democratic collaboration fizzled out by the ideological thaw of the late 1960s. Game shows, which became staples of socialist entertainment by this time, nurtured cynicism towards socialist ideals and a corresponding longing for the consumer comforts of capitalism. While there is certainly some truth to this, the situation is far more complicated. What the seamless embrace of the genre reveals is the existence of an inherently competitive structure within everyday socialist societies. This is a historically layered framework whose roots reach back to pre-Cold War Europe and whose traces show their most visible patterns in popular culture. In other words, quiz and game shows are much more than instruments of entertainment and education; they represent sedimented historical and ideological practices. What follows is an examination of the layers of competition as they crystallize within game and quiz show formats in relation to Cold War international relations and nationalism, consumption and a romanticized notion of talent. I conclude this section with a brief look at post-Cold War changes in quiz and game shows following the arrival of codified formats.

The German Democratic Republic was another major laboratory of socialist competition. The entire history of GDR television can be seen in terms of increasing competition for its own audiences against the lure of West German TV.[146] This is why TV historians have argued

---

146 Claudia Dittmar, 'GDR Television in Competition with West German Programming', *Historical Journal of Film, Radio and Television* 24, no. 3 (2004): 327–43, here 328.

Visual cultures

that German TV history can only be written as a combined and comparative account of Eastern and Western developments.[147] The demand for entertaining television content presented itself earlier and more urgently in the GDR than elsewhere in the Soviet camp. In 1967, the GDR's department of entertainment issued guidelines dictating that aesthetic experiments that were too intellectually demanding were to be avoided.[148] At the SED's eighth congress in 1971, Party Secretary Erich Honecker famously diagnosed 'a certain boredom' around television and urged that TV should create 'good entertainment'. The SED thus folded entertainment into its ideology as an important condition for reproducing labour and raising intellectually active individuals. This form of entertainment was still to be distinctly socialist, unlike the 'pseudo-entertaining measures' employed by capitalist media, which lacked a 'positive, character-forming and culturally educating component'.[149] GDR television chairman Heinz Adameck put these new guidelines into practice, phrasing the initiative in the language of competition and even war: the task was to keep people in the line of fire in order to increase their socialist awareness and prevent them from turning to West German channels.[150]

The most notorious results of ongoing competition were news programmes that took clips from the other side and rebroadcast them out of context with leading commentary. The GDR's *Der schwarze Kanal* ('The black channel', 1960–89) was modelled on the West German *Die rote Optik* ('The red optics', 1958–60), which used East German clips for its own anti-Soviet agitation.[151] The Federal Republic of Germany (FRG) hit hardest by showing off its superior lifestyle, implying that the GDR was economically lagging behind. East German propaganda zeroed in on the misled, isolated individual of capitalism and the FRG's lenience towards Nazi ideology.[152] FRG broadcast signals reached all territories in the GDR except for the so-called 'Valley of the Clueless', near Dresden, whereas on the Western side only between four and five per cent of viewers could receive GDR programming. East German viewers living close to FRG transmitters had the most variety: even back in the late 1960s they had at least five channels to choose from, including ZDF, the regional affiliates of ARD and the second GDR network. The ZDF magazine show *Drüben* ('Over there') was produced in 1966 specifically for East German audiences. Morning programming on ARD was scheduled to compete with the GDR morning show. Rather than opting to watch only the Western broadcast, however, evidence shows that GDR viewers watched both in parallel fashion, making constant choices.[153]

The GDR tried to incorporate West German TV into its own programming and pitted popular Western shows against its own most successful products. This was especially important at crucial weekly viewing times.[154] In Friday primetime, the beginning of the weekend, East German TV showed thrillers, as well as popular clips from old movies, as part of the variety show *Rumpelkammer* ('Junk room', 1955–90). Saturday night was reserved for variety shows such as *Ein Kessel Buntes* ('A colourful kettle'), which competed with ZDF's and ARD's programming. Sunday night was important in influencing the following week's mood, so they

---

147 Ibid., 317.
148 Uwe Breitenborn, '"Memphis Tennessee" in Borstendorf: Boundaries Set and Transcended in East German Television Entertainment', *Historical Journal of Film, Radio and Television* 24, no. 3 (2004): 392.
149 Ruediger Steinmetz and Reinhold Viehoff, 'The Program History of Genres of Entertainment on GDR Television', *Historical Journal of Film, Radio and Television* 24, no. 3 (2004): 320.
150 Dittmar, 'GDR Television', 322.
151 Ibid., 329.
152 Ibid., 334–5.
153 Ibid., 327.
154 Ibid., 337.

broadcast the thriller serial *Polizeiruf 110* ('Police call 110'), dramas and feature films, variety shows and game shows such as *Schätzen Sie mal* ('Take a guess').[155]

East German quiz and game shows were strategically important in this relationship of competitive co-dependence. East German TV began broadcasting game shows within the first years of its existence, which often served as travelling formats that inspired similar programmes in other countries. Much like on Western European public service television, quiz shows were an early genre of socialist TV everywhere, introduced as part of live broadcasting in the late 1950s. If we trace their history, we see a transformation from the early, open-ended formats of the 1950s to more or less centralized attempts at instituting more rules and controls so that the genre would better serve the mass educational policies of the 1960s. The earliest formats arose in an era of fairly low regulation and high confusion among socialist parties as to the purposes, potentials and dangers of the new medium. This uncertainty gave TV professionals some leeway to experiment with the genre, which was inexpensive to produce. Similar to Western European public service television,[156] the distinction between variety and game shows remained unclear. As entertainment increasingly came to define television during the 1970s and 80s, quiz and game show formats bore more and more of the pressure from capitalist competition and viewer demand. Direct, codified format-borrowing began on a large scale in the 1990s.[157] By the 1980s, the switch to dual (public and commercial) broadcasting in Western Europe had further diluted the public service content within game, quiz and variety shows.[158] In anticipation of the advent of commercial networks – first allowed in West Germany in 1984 – ARD and ZDF reformed their programming to include even more entertainment. This was the beginning of the end for East German TV, which lost its identity amidst increasing competition.[159]

At the other end of the spectrum, we find Romanian television, where the oppressive Ceauşescu regime reversed 1960s policies of relative openness and eliminated most programming in the 1970s and 80s that was not direct propaganda. This is why the two most popular new genres of post-Ceauşescu Romanian television were quiz shows and political talk shows, created as a sort of belated public service forum to make up for their absence during communism. As Dana Mustata writes, the quiz show *Robingo*, a Sunday primetime programme under a UK licence, was the first general knowledge quiz show in Romania.[160]

Most other socialist television programming was situated in between the two poles of the openly competitive GDR and the isolated, entertainment-deprived Romania. The latter's programming and operations display constant awareness of competition with the West, even if in a less pressing race for viewership than was the case in the GDR. But the comparisons with the West were so common in the print and electronic media that Cold War competition registered as a neutral state of affairs rather than a constitutive condition of everyday socialism. A closer look at the main types of quiz and game shows throughout the region helps to make visible the historical layers and political structures of the underlying competitive fabric of socialism.

---

155 Ibid., 336.

156 With the exception of the BBC; see Bourdon, 'Old and New Ghosts', 288.

157 Noémi Dóra Dankovics, 'Játékmesterek és vetélkedőműsorok a magyar televíziózás történetében' [Quiz show hosts and game shows in the history of Hungarian television], (PhD diss., Budapest College of Communication and Business, 2012).

158 Bourdon, 'Old and New Ghosts', 288.

159 Dittmar, 'GDR Television', 339.

160 Dana Mustata, 'The Power of Television: Including the Historicizing of the Live Romanian Revolution', (PhD diss., Utrecht University, 2011), see chapter 4: 'Reassembling a History of Romanian Television Programmes'.

Visual cultures

Popular music competitions – predecessors of the 'Idol' format – were especially dangerous terrain for socialist parties. In Hungary, the first *Táncdalfesztivál* ('Pop music festival') held in the summer of 1966, had 464 entries written by 300 composers. The work of 52 songwriters was selected into the three televised preliminaries that preceded the primetime finale. The normative value system of such programmes is revealed by the fact that, while technically a competition for songwriters, all eyes and emotions were trained on the performers themselves, whose careers were boosted by their televised exposure as they helped popularize and legitimate contemporary Western musical styles.[161]

Despite its capitalistic characteristics, the programme was accepted by party authorities not only because of its enormous success with audiences but also because it made pop music television an exportable product that created a good reputation for Hungarian culture. The presence of Western experts in the festival's international jury also helped facilitate international exchanges.[162] In addition, party leaders argued that popularizing local pop music made it less likely that younger people would be seduced by Western music which thus reduces the dangerous attractiveness of capitalist lifestyles in general. Despite the official endorsement, *Pop Music Festival* was such a radical departure from the demure, educational tone of Hungarian TV that it provoked letters of protest from die-hard socialist viewers, especially those from rural areas. János Gulyás, party secretary for the Red Star Tractor Factory Brigade in the city of Eger, objected to the long hair, clothing and Western musical style of one of the festival winners, and the British performing contracts earned by others, which he thought was an altogether dangerous thing to allow.[163] Ferenc Gódor from the Party's Agitational and Propaganda Division responded:

> The letter writer only sees the negative aspects of the festival. He ignores the fact that, with the creation of a new type of native music, Hungarian beat, we have managed to shut out Western songs and have satisfied young people prone to admiring the West by offering them the work of Hungarian songwriters, which have become professional hits. The fact that we even manage to export some of these songs is evidence of Hungarian artists' talent.[164]

These calculations proved correct since the second round of the *Pop Music Festival* in 1967 garnered 1,378 entries. The three preliminaries alone attracted 649,008 audience votes, as opposed to the first year's 140,000. Eleven foreign stations ordered the finale's broadcast's copy, which aired live from a Budapest theatre.[165]

In Romania, the five-day televised *Cerbul de Aur* ('Golden stag festival') ran annually between 1968 and 1971, during Romania's brief period of opening towards the West while simultaneously distancing itself from the Soviet Union. The show invited major European stars and awarded

---

161 Dunavölgyi, '1966'.
162 András Budai, 'A Magyar Rádió és Televízió nemzetközi kapcsolatai' [Hungarian radio and television's international connections], in *Tanfolyamok, Előadások a Televízióról* (MRT Tömegkommunikációs Kutatóközpont, 1970).
163 János Gulyás, Secretary of Vörös Csillag [Red Star] Tractor Factory's Eger division. Document MSZMP APO 288f.22./1968/15.ö.e. AG 10/120, Hungarian Document Archives. No exact date indicated.
164 Response to Gulyás by Jenő Gerencsér from the Hungarian Socialist Workers' Party's Agitation and Propaganda Division. Document MSZMP APO 88f.22./1968/15.ö.e. AG 10/120/3 from 04.16.1968, Hungarian Document Archives.
165 Dunavölgyi, '1967'.

significant cash prizes. In the 1969 edition of the festival, about 20 national television companies announced their participation. The festival's broadcast included advertisements for consumer products and was accompanied by televised foreign language lessons. The National Lottery offered prizes in the form of trips to Paris and Rome. Ceaușescu put a stop to the festival in 1971 in the name of a cultural nationalization programme under the leadership of the newly appointed National Council for Radio and Television headed by Secretary of Culture Dumitru Popescu.

Advertising and consumerism

All socialist countries engaged in some form of television advertising. This in itself is not that surprising given that, as Gumbert succinctly put it, 'the entire system was geared towards advertising itself'.[166] As I discussed earlier, competition was inherent to the structure of Soviet-type socialism since the system was built on utopian principles that needed constant fortification, justification and adjustment on the domestic front, particularly in light of ongoing competition and comparisons with Western European socialist democracies.

Commercials bore the traces of these ideological negotiations in a range of aesthetic forms that would be characterized as awkward, funny or campy today. Much of early television advertising resembled public service announcements. These were often fairly lengthy and tedious short films about products or services or informational videos about the dangers of smoking or littering. The East German film studio DEFA began to make TV commercials in the 1960s but cancelled production in the 1970s because there simply were not enough products to advertise. Like other socialist countries, the GDR continued to produce informational public service announcements. Television also assisted in inserting overt product placement that helped manage the inadequacies of socialist economic planning. For instance, they would feature herring recipes on cooking shows in order to move excess herring out of warehouses.[167]

The largest supplier of ads for Soviet TV was Eesti Reklaamfilm (Estonian Commercial Film Company), which began making TV commercials in 1967 and continued to produce over 5,000 TV commercials advertising a variety of organizations, services and products over the company's 24-year run. It was headed by Eedu Ojamaa, a documentary filmmaker.[168] Soviet ads were broadcast in five-minute advertising blocks that aired three times a day in order to minimize interruption. They became one of the highlights of daily television programming, televisual events that gathered a massive cult following. As elsewhere, they displayed symptoms of central economic planning's weaknesses. They often advertised products that were in short supply or even non-existent by the time the ad aired; or they were aired pre-emptively, in the hope that the product would be available in time. In a way that was common all throughout the region, what these ads lacked in production value and marketing savvy they often made up for in creativity.[169]

---

166 Heather Gumbert, paper presented at the conference 'Television in Europe beyond the Iron Curtain – National and Transnational Perspectives since the 1950s', Friedrich-Alexander-Universität Erlangen-Nürnberg, 5–7 December 2013.

167 Ibid.; Thomas Beutelschmidt, 'East German TV and Global Transfers' (paper presented at the conference 'Television in Europe beyond the Iron Curtain – National and Transnational Perspectives since the 1950s', Friedrich-Alexander-Universität Erlangen-Nürnberg, 5–7 December 2013).

168 Cory Doctorow, 'Soviet TV Advertisements from the 1970s and 1980s', 17 February 2013, http://boingboing.net/2013/02/17/soviet-tv-advertisements-from.html (accessed 10 October 2018).

169 'The Only Anthology of Retro Soviet TV Commercials', www.retrosovietads.com/ (accessed 10 October 2018).

Visual cultures

Polish ads in particular were often abstract and even absurd, especially when they promoted products that were not yet available in stores. In Poland, TV advertising began as early as 1956. At first, it was limited to only 15 minutes per week. The first ads were modelled after promotional segments developed for Polish Radio.

TV advertising in the most liberalized socialist economies was embedded in an extensive set of commercial features. In fact, Sabina Mihelj has argued that, in some ways, television networks of the Yugoslav member states were more commercially oriented than some Western European public broadcasters. Yugoslavia's relative ideological independence from the Warsaw Pact under Josip Broz Tito's leadership also opened up greater financial independence for media elites in exchange for supplementing decreasing state revenue. Advertising on Yugoslav TV grew from 4.2 per cent to 6.2 per cent between 1968 and 1971. First this meant advertising blocks; later, commercials eventually began to interrupt programmes, which provoked some backlash from viewers. Commercially funded programming also existed in Yugoslavia in the form of sports and entertainment sponsorship. As early as 1968, 20.8 per cent of Ljubljana TV's revenue came from advertising. One Slovenian radio station even advertised in Italian to Italian audiences across the border in order to attract major revenue.

Typical products advertised were food, cosmetics, chemical products and services. In 1968/9, the Yugoslav Telecommunications Commission approved and gave frequency to a fully commercial music radio station that would broadcast to Italian audiences. The plan was only cancelled because the army raised alarm over security issues. There was also some concern about the probable loss of revenue for Yugoslav broadcasters. These objections were couched in ideological terms. In Yugoslavia, we see the most developed form of consumer culture under state socialism. The appearance of advertising to harness market competition went hand in hand with the emergence of niche markets and audience research. The first studies of commercials' audience ratings were conducted in the 1960s with the purpose of making commercials more effective.[170]

The situation was similar in Hungary. Hungarian Radio and Television established its marketing department in 1968. This created an institutional framework around the commercial activities that had been features of Hungarian broadcasting from the start, what the institution's long-time commercial director Ilona Pócsik calls a 'manager' type of thinking. The first advertisements appeared in the late 1950s, just a few years after television's launch in 1956. These first ads came out of an agreement between Hungarian Television and the advertising agency Magyar Hirdető ('Hungarian advertiser'), which had been in the business of movie advertising since the 1940s. In the beginning, TV ads were run as text columns interspersed with pictures. Television's marketing arm also produced ads for a set of other large state institutions, such as unions. The foreign trade agency Hungexpo advertised products for foreign trade exhibitions.[171]

Television's own marketing activities went well beyond the production of commercials. They encompassed a wide range of activities that yielded commercial profit: concert organization, film, video and record production and distribution, book publishing, and trading film rights. As in the case of Yugoslav TV, Pócsik and her team placed significant emphasis on contact with viewers. They established a public information department for this purpose in the 1970s, which was in charge of organizing public access across the country and responding

---

170 Sabina Mihelj, keynote address (paper presented at the symposium 'Television Histories in (Post)Socialist Europe', Stockholm, November 2013).

171 Ilona Pócsik, interview by Anikó Imre, December 2013.

to viewer letters and calls. Even though such outreach continued to run under the label of 'propaganda', it more closely resembled public relations. Such activities required the creation of hybrid categories such as 'socially oriented propaganda', which referred to providing free or inexpensive informational outlets for socialist institutions that catered to public health or education. From the 1970s onwards, programme sponsorship was allowed, although it remained wrapped in ideological discomfort for the regime.[172]

The marketing department had its own separate budget, which was independent from Radio and Television's central budget. While the department paid taxes on its profits, the majority of the money it made from commercial activities was reinvested back into television. As was true for the rest of Hungarian Television's operations, party authorities rarely interfered. When they did, they often did so mistakenly, hearing political resonances where there were none. Pócsik's example is the advertising slogan for the coffee brand Idea: 'Over there and over here, Idea is liked everywhere' ('*Odaát és ideát kedvelik az Ideát*'). A party apparatchik was convinced that 'over there' referred to the West and had the ad cancelled. Other former TV professionals I have interviewed also frequently recall such misunderstandings. These illustrate well the ideological confusions in which the system increasingly entangled itself, and which wove a particularly dense web around television.

While its extensive marketing activity sat uncomfortably within socialist ideology, it was also clear that Radio and Television was greatly invested in the profits thus produced. As Pócsik put it, 'We looked for every possible commercial revenue. We took advantage of every opportunity that produced profits'. According to a summary of Hungarian Radio and Television's marketing activities, produced in 1988 for the twentieth anniversary of the marketing department's existence, in 20 years, they increased their annual revenue 40-fold, from 3.9 million to 200 million; and their staff from 5 to 80 people.[173]

Television and radio marketing was modelled after foreign – mostly Western European – examples and continued to function as a bloodline between Hungarian socialism and market-oriented European social democracies. In the early 1980s, Hungary was the first socialist country to join the European Group of Television Advertising (EGTA). Founded in 1974, EGTA was a non-profit group that included virtually all Western European broadcasters. This opened the door to more frequent East–West professional exchanges. In the 1980s, Hungarian TV's marketing department rapidly built up an institutional infrastructure using ethical codes, contract conditions, research frameworks and other elements adapted from Western examples. As a result, by 1989 'everything already existed on a small scale', as Pócsik put it, which prepared the ground for a smooth transition to television's post-socialist, market-based operations. Professional travel and exchanges also meant that marketing professionals such as Pócsik lived schizophrenic lives. Their actual daily jobs, while creative and essential to the socialist economy, were looked down upon and officially only 'tolerated'. Pócsik says she was occasionally handed lists of actors who were not allowed to appear in commercials for fear that it would compromise their cultural capital.

The rules of EGTA membership also meant that Hungarian TV was not allowed to deny the advertising of foreign products. Since most of these were not actually available or permitted in Hungary, the marketing department had to find bogus reasons for refusing these ads. Through

---

172 'Az RTV Belkereskedelmi Igazgatóság tevékenysége 1968–88 között' [Report on the activities of Hungarian Television and Radio's commercial department 1968–88], internal departmental correspondence, courtesy of Ilona Pócsik.

173 Ibid.

Visual cultures

the mid-1980s, most television advertising revolved around domestic or Warsaw Pact agencies or services including appliance repair, dry-cleaning, car insurance or various department stores. Most ads were rather general since the ordering agencies did not have long-term marketing plans. Therefore, their commercials served as templates that could be repurposed with minor editing. There were no lavish ads for cars, which were an item of scarcity on the socialist common market, and for which people had to wait for years. Ads for medications were also prohibited, as was political advertising.

'The weak economy was mirrored in the quality of commercials', says Pócsik. In fact, the broadcasting fee was higher than the cost of production – a proportion that was flipped after 1989. The exceptions to the poor quality were ads made by Mafilm, the state film studios, rather than by Radio and Television. These had higher production budgets and more professional production facilities and more commonly advertised products and brands. These late socialist, shinier commercials tend to stand for all socialist commercials in nostalgic remembrances. Late socialist commercials thus constitute a genre of continuity between late socialism and post-socialist capitalism. For viewers who remember late socialism, they represent an anchor in the sea of commercials that flooded the region after socialism officially ended. Their awkwardness and imperfection is a platform for bonding, which is manifest in the ironic winks over the low-quality products that the commercials advertised, and which everyone shared and used. Compared to the perfect veneer of contemporary commercials and the terror of endless choices provided by corporations, state socialism seems like a navigable, manageable state of affairs.

TV, family and gender

The feminist context in which television studies is embedded has been largely absent in research about socialist and post-socialist television cultures. Any serious attention to television already needs justification in and of itself against the dismissal of television as a low-quality medium within cultures of a defensive patriarchal bent that have long nurtured a hostility towards feminism. Television has been neglected by academic fields focused on studies of Soviet and Eastern European cultures as well. Slavic Studies has traditionally been anchored in the study of literature and other more established art forms, while history and the social sciences have concerned themselves with large-scale issues of socio-political change. One branch of anthropological research has recently begun to incorporate cultural studies in its inquiries and explore aspects of everyday life under and after socialism.[174] However, even such work has stayed clear of television's dangerously feminizing vortex.

Even more recently, the first extensive studies of socialist television have been produced by pioneering historians such as Paulina Bren, Kristin Roth-Ey and Heather Gumbert.[175] These otherwise pathbreaking, meticulously researched and lively books still tread cautiously around issues of gender. When they do engage with such issues, they tend to adopt a sociological lens to look at the ways in which changing political–economic circumstances forced socialist regimes to adjust their policy and attitudes towards women and how these changes were

---

174 See: Hana Cervinkova, 'Postcolonialism, Postsocialism and the Anthropology of East-Central Europe', *Journal of Postcolonial Writing* 48, no. 2 (2012): 155–63, here 156; Narcis Tulbure, 'Introduction to Special Issue: Global Socialisms and Postsocialisms', *Anthropology of Eastern Europe Review* 27, no. 2 (2009): 2–18, here 4.

175 See: Gumbert, *Envisioning Socialism*; Bren, *The Greengrocer and His TV*; Roth-Ey, *Moscow Prime Time*.

reflected by the institution of television. While these studies at least acknowledge the elephant in the room, they remain within the confines of liberal feminism, assuming an essentialist division between the sexes, which is determined by specific national contexts. This is also the direction pursued by gender studies that focuses on this region. Gender studies scholars, however, tend to omit television from their concerns altogether.[176] Finally, media and communication studies have largely limited their attention to issues of policy and regulation in the course of the post-socialist transition, and have had very little interest in either television or its history.[177]

I consider Eastern European television's gendered address in terms of scheduling and content, and in terms of women's participation as TV professionals and viewers. I linger on the late socialist domestic drama serial, a regionally specific formation most comparable to the 'soap opera', which manifested itself across national varieties. I then follow the story of this transitional genre into post-socialism, when foreign drama inundated the market along with feminist ideas, which have hindered as much as stimulated gender politics in the region.

The socialist period interrupted the pre-war trajectory of academic and activist feminism and filtered most gender-related politics and research through the communist concern with the so-called 'woman question' as defined by Friedrich Engels, August Bebel, Vladimir Ilyich Lenin, Rosa Luxemburg, Joseph Stalin and other major ideologues.[178] In effect, socialist state feminism was comprised of policies that segregated women into a homogenized social group identified with special needs and tasks – reproduction, family care and emotional labour – and with inferior skills for political participation – excessive emotional identification and an insufficient ability to reason. The flipside of this homogenization included policies of 'positive discrimination' in the form of generous maternity leave, free childcare centres and reduced-cost meals. Following the end of state socialism in the 1990s, such policies were radically reduced if not entirely removed.[179]

Socialist TV issued a decidedly masculine address to its citizens, especially compared to US post-war programming. After the first years of scrambling, while it was maturing technologically, television became a medium dedicated to education in the broadest sense, working

---

176 On representative writings in (post)socialist studies of women and gender see: Zillah Eisenstein, 'Eastern European Male Democracies: A Problem of Unequal Equality', in *Gender Politics and Post-Communism*, eds Nanette Funk and Magda Mueller (New York: Routledge, 1993), 303–30; Agnieszka Graff, 'The Return of the Real Man: Gender and E.U. Accession in Three Polish Weeklies', 2005, www.indiana.edu/~reeiweb/newsEvents/pre2006/graffpaper.pdf (accessed 18 October 2018); Djurdja Knezevic, 'Affective Nationalism', in *Transitions, Environments, Translations: Feminism in International Politics*, eds Joan Wallach Scott, Cora Kaplan and Debra Keates (London: Routledge, 2004), 65–71; Anikó Imre, 'Lesbian Nationalism', *Signs* 33, no. 2 (2007): 255–82; Laurie Occhipinti, 'Two Steps Back? Anti-Feminism in Eastern Europe', *Anthropology Today* 12, no. 6 (1996): 13–18; Barbara Einhorn, *Cinderella Goes to the Market: Citizenship, Gender and Women's Movements in East Central Europe* (London: Verso, 1993); Susan Gal and Gail Kligman, *Reproducing Gender: Politics, Publics and Everyday Life After Socialism* (Princeton, NJ: Princeton University Press, 2000); Shana Penn and Jill Massino, eds, *Gender Politics and Everyday Life in State Socialist East and Central Europe* (New York: Palgrave Macmillan, 2009); Éva Fodor, 'Smiling Women and Fighting Men: The Gender of the Communist Subject in State Socialist Hungary', *Gender and Society* 16, no. 2 (2002): 240–63; Susan Zimmermann, 'Gender Regime and Gender Struggle in Hungarian State Socialism', *Aspasia* 4, no. 1 (2010): 1–24.
177 The exceptions are equally significant here: see the work of Zala Volcic, Karmen Erjavec, Nadia Kaneva, Elza Ibroscheva and a handful of others.
178 See Fodor, 'Smiling Women and Fighting Men', 240–63.
179 Ibid.; Zimmermann, 'Gender Regime', 1–24.

Visual cultures

in a socialist-realist mode, as I discuss in the first part of this chapter. Women were not absent as TV professionals, screen characters or consumers; nevertheless, all these positions were configured as masculine, were dominated by men and assigned specialized, narrow roles to women.

By the mid-1960s, socialist parties had caught up with the ideological potential of television and were busy shaping its profile as a public institution. Unlike TV in the US, which explicitly favoured the housewife in the post-war home who may be receptive to advertising, socialist TV targeted the man who plops down on the sofa after a long day at the factory. Surveys in the Soviet Union and Eastern Europe consistently showed that men spent more time watching TV than women.[180] Roth-Ey notes that cartoonists in Soviet magazines and newspapers often made fun of the isolated and obsessed TV viewer – who was almost always a man.[181] In 1976, Hungarian men spent 95 minutes a day watching TV while women spent only 84 minutes. This difference persisted into the 1980s. A 1986 analysis explains 'there is no doubt that one of the reasons for this difference is that the world of Hungarian telecommunications is populated by educated men over 30 in leadership positions'.[182]

When women were addressed by television as an audience at all, they were considered a special demographic who needed targeted political-educational programmes, much like factory workers, university students or the elderly. This niche address invariably revolved around the family and the household and focused on issues of caretaking, lifestyle and education. In Romania, public service TV magazines for women bore titles such as *Emisiune pentru femei* ('Programme for women') and *Caminul* ('The home') in the 1960s, *Clubul Femina* ('Feminine club') in the 1970s, *Noi, femeile* ('Us, women') and *Universul Femeilor* (Women's universe') in the 1980s. The Romanian *TV Guide* previewed the following segments to be covered in the 21 October 1967 edition of *Programme for Women*: a women's clothing department; a leather trench coat; a leather clothing factory; an exhibition of culinary products; master chefs; the woman at home and at work; a fashion show; dining at the Dunarea restaurant; painting and sculpture; practical tips; and cosmetic treatments with modern technology. In the 1980s, such programmes developed a stronger propagandistic agenda to promote the ideal socialist woman, modelled by Elena Ceauşescu. *Us, Women* and *Women's Universe* discussed agricultural work, the working woman, female leaders in different professions, the revolutionary woman and the many virtues of Elena. The 27 May 1984 broadcast of *Almanahul familiei* ('Family almanac') included the following topics, according to the *TV Guide*: school for mothers; food for newborns; how to harvest bee venom in your own garden; how to raise silkworms; quitting work for pregnant women or stay-at-home mothers; the home pharmacy; culinary recipes and healthy lifestyles.[183]

A similar shift towards more explicit propagandistic content occurred in Hungarian so-called 'women's programmes' of the 1960s. The Hungarian Central Committee's Agitation and Propaganda Division's evaluation of public interest magazine programmes for women, such as *Lányok, asszonyok* ('Girls and women') reads:

> [Such programmes] help the educational work of the Youth Communist Organization, schools and the family in diverse ways. It is commendable that television offers

---

180 Roth-Ey, *Moscow Prime Time*, 202. This was reinforced in a 1970s survey conducted by Polish Radio and Television. See: Dunavölgyi, '1970'.
181 Roth-Ey, *Moscow Prime Time*, 203.
182 Margit Benkő, 'Életmód és Tévénézés' [The way of life and television watching], *Kultúra és közösség* 3 (1986): 32–3.
183 Dana Mustata, e-mail message to Anikó Imre, 13 September 2013.

353

specialized programmes to address women. These kinds of programmes were rather apolitical at first; today, however, they are more politicized and pay more attention to the problems of working women and girls.[184]

Women in TV production

Women in TV typically worked behind the scenes, except as actresses and programme announcers. Most announcers were women. Their job was to let viewers know about upcoming programmes on the broadcast menu in a pleasant monotone, with a reassuring smile. And reassure they did. They were a reliable, attractive presence; operating in a modest, non-flirtatious socialist mode, mothers of the national family that television recreated every night. Their role reflected and reinforced women's social roles in general: to look good, follow instructions without having an opinion and occasionally model a fashionable hairstyle or blouse. Above all, their presence ensured an intimacy between the home and the nation by marking the dependable, repetitive rhythm of the socialist day, week and year in a pleasant manner. Viewers referred to announcers by first names as if they were family members. According to Russian critic Anri Vartanov, announcers were custodians of the TV hearth and priestesses of the cathedral of television, embraced by viewers as representatives of ideal womanhood.[185]

At the same time, the overwhelming majority of above-the-line personnel, including most of the creatives – writers, directors and reporters – were men. The memorable exceptions only proved the rule. In the first part, I mention Valentina Leontyeva, the long-time hostess of the Soviet programme *From the Bottom of My Heart*, launched in 1972. As Christine Evans argues, it was crucial to have a woman host a programme charged with giving an emotional boost to the party's emphasis on socialist lifestyle and nationalist mythology.[186]

Leontyeva's legacy is similar to that of Irena Dziedzic, the hostess of the first Polish cultural current-affairs magazine *Tele-Echo* (1956–81). While Dziedzic's TV presence was much less sentimental than Leontyeva's, both were accused of political conformism, particularly after 1989. Polish sociologist Paweł Śpiewak writes that Dziedzic tried very hard to 'create an atmosphere of charming conversation, during which no one said anything interesting or important. As if it were embarrassing to mention important or – God forbid – painful things in such good company.'[187] Others call Dziedzic a phenomenal TV personality because of her ability to stir up intense emotions.[188] Also relevant here is Olga Lipińska who, as we have seen, was a legendary Polish satirical artist, talk show host, writer and director and key figure of TV cabaret in Poland.

However, for the most part, when women received a creative assignment, this was typically bracketed as women's issues and social issues – a nice addition, but marginal to the concerns of national citizenship. The occasional powerful woman on television often did everything possible to efface herself and masquerade as one of the boys. When Hungarian director of

---

184 Hungarian Socialist Workers' Party Central Committee, MOL – 288f 22/1959 6.öe./23. MSZMP KP, Agitációs és Propaganda Osztály [Department of Agitation and Propaganda files], Hungarian National Document Archives.

185 Roth-Ey, *Moscow Prime Time*, 243.

186 Evans, 'The "Soviet Way of Life" as Way of Feeling'.

187 Pikulski, *Prywatna historia telewizji publicznej*, 54.

188 Ibid.

Visual cultures

photography (DP) Marietta Vecsei, who worked for the nightly TV news programme, received a festival award in 1969, she was reluctant to be interviewed on TV. In the print interview published with her in *TV Guide*, most questions revolved around what it is like to be such a curiosity – a female DP. How can a woman perform such a physically demanding job? To the question whether she had met other female DPs, Vecsei responded: 'Here in Hungary I'm the only one. But once in a Moscow newsreel I saw another girl. It would be nice to find out who she is and meet her'.[189]

To take an even more illustrative example, virtually the entire socialist history of Hungarian TV news centred around the work of one woman. Matúz Józsefné (also known as, Mrs Joseph Matúz, Mrs Matúz, or simply Matúzné) was tasked with creating the first independent news programme during the institution's first year – 1957 – and she remained news director in charge of successive versions of the primetime news broadcast *Hiradó* ('News') throughout the socialist period, for an unprecedented 29 years.

Television compelled, but also allowed, women to assert themselves in the available forms of masquerade – genres whose formal conformity to the regime's ideological preferences was beyond question. In Hungary, documentary or docu-fictional forms that foregrounded a social-ist-realist aesthetic and social commitment experienced a golden age beginning in the 1960s, thanks to the work of some outstanding female directors. The 1962 teleplay *Menekülés a börtönbe* ('Escape to prison'), written by the female duo Ágnes Fedor and Judit Kovács, takes place in 1944 and revolves around a woman who is hiding out with fake papers. It received an award at the 1962 Cannes Film Festival. Another realistic teleplay set during the War, *Nő a barakkban*, ('Woman in the barracks'), was also created by two women, director Éva Zsurzs and writer Boris Palotai. It won a series of surprise international recognitions for Hungarian television in the early 1960s, including the Golden Nymph Award at the second annual Monte Carlo TV Festival in 1962. In an interview with director Zsurzs in the *Radio and TV Guide* which fol-lowed the story for three consecutive weeks, it turned out that the members of the festival jury could not believe that the teleplay was written by a woman since there was not a single female character in it. The play was about an international group of prisoners in a Nazi concentration camp towards the end of the war; its title character was an imaginary woman.

Stories that related to the Second World War and the Holocaust were a fairly safe shield for female writers and directors to contribute to television as they were favoured by the ruling party that had built its legitimacy on post-war regime change, liberation and peace. They also came with an instant interpretive fodder that related their significance to universal, human issues. These factors muted the gendered undertones of the production and reception no matter how significant these were.

Nevertheless, women in the forefront of television documentary production often came out with highly gendered topics and treatments. But instead of taking on politics directly, women did better with the politics of empathy, calling public attention to the plight of neglected groups who needed care, such as children, the elderly, ethnic minorities, isolated rural populations and the ill. On Hungarian TV, these productions included *Bognár Anna világa* ('The world of Anna Bognár', 1963), directed by Márta Kende, a moving documentary that had a decisive impact on the emerging genre of TV sociography. The film portrayed a 52-year-old blind woman living on a farm, who gets her vision back after a successful eye surgery. Margit Molnár's documentary *Leányanyák* ('Teen mothers', 1970), created a stir when it explored the plight of pregnant teen-agers. In the same year, Molnár also hosted the public affairs programme called *The Women's*

---

189 See: Dunavölgyi, '1969'.

Forum. Unlike the previous socialist educational niche programme, *Girls and Women* (1964), each episode of Molnár's show was dedicated to specific areas where public culture blatantly discriminated against women and families: how children of divorced parents coped; or the effects of inflexible work schedules on the lives of mothers who had to get their children to childcare at dawn to make it to work.

Women and late socialist lifestyle TV

Of course, no matter how incisive TV sociographies were, their audiences remained limited mostly to urban, educated viewers. Programmes that blurred the boundaries between fiction and documentary fared better. The thaw period, beginning in the late 1960s, brought political and economic changes that required socialist parties to readjust their gender policies. As Soviet-controlled countries fell behind in production and imported more and more Western programming, competition with the West shifted to the sphere of consumer ideology and leisure, bundled under the term 'socialist lifestyle'. By the 1970s, the penetration of TV sets in most countries of the region caught up with Western levels.[190] At the same time, most domestic programmes were too didactic and tedious, while Western programming could not be shut out thanks to shared broadcast signals along borders and the appearance of recording technologies, cable and satellite in the 1980s.

The shift in competition with the West from production to consumption and 'lifestyle' in the late 1960s redirected the spotlight onto women as key agents of socialist citizenship. Éva Fodor writes that, in Hungary, the 'woman question' had been considered 'resolved' by the end of the 1960s but was reopened following a 1970 party decree that put women's role in society back on the agenda. In the decade that followed, 110 reports were produced on women's roles in society by a variety of state institutions.[191] The single party-controlled women's organization called the Women's Council published about 40 books that mostly focused on lifestyle and consumption, such as skin care, self-help, child-rearing, divorce and cooking.[192]

Historian Susan Zimmermann captures the peculiarity of socialist gender policies in the following contradiction: socialist states made extraordinary efforts to include women in the workforce and to ensure (heterosexual, white) women's equality with men in terms of civil and family rights. These efforts 'constituted a spectacular intervention into the traditional relationship between the sexes and hierarchical family structures'.[193] They questioned women's dependence on men and the family. At the same time, socialist governments consistently and anxiously limited women's equality by maintaining a wage gap between the sexes, ignoring or minimizing women's unpaid domestic labour and insisting on women's biological roles as mothers and caretakers. This contradiction resulted in 'practices and attitudes that conflicted directly with official policy and efforts at creating equality, or activities that undermined official policy at unnoticed, disregarded or hard-to-influence levels'.[194]

While sociologists and historians have adequately explored both official and unofficial policies towards women, the crucial role that socialist, particularly late socialist, popular media culture played in processing these contradictory attitudes has escaped the attention it deserves. In

---

190 Bren, *The Greengrocer and His TV*, 112.
191 Fodor, 'Smiling Women and Fighting Men', 251.
192 Ibid., 249.
193 Zimmermann, 'Gender Regime', 11.
194 Ibid.

the next part, I will focus on the late socialist dramatic serial as a juncture where official policy and everyday attitudes inevitably met, clashed and ultimately compromised, paving the way for a post-socialist version of post-feminism.

Women and the late socialist domestic drama

Late socialist, Eastern European domestic drama serials were developed in an atmosphere of increased attention to women, consumerism and the ideological power of emotional engagement. They continued the earlier project of political education in less didactic, more entertaining ways.[195] They also took for granted viewers' familiarity with and yearning for imported dramatic serials. While most domestic scripted dramas of the early socialist period revolved around men doing manly things in the public sphere, from war and adventure dramas to historical mini-series, the post-1960s period variously called the 'thaw', 'consolidation' or 'normalization' era, turned the spotlight on the family as the microcosm of the socialist nation.

In some ways, the 'socialist soap opera' returned television to its gendered roots. Much like Western soap opera, it showcased communities that were metaphors for modern society, offering fictional 'feminine' pleasures of identification.[196] In other ways, however, the socialist soap was a peculiar hybrid specific to the conditions of late socialism. Rather than addressing women only as consumers, it addressed them first and foremost as citizens whose biological features simply assigned them to unique roles within the socialist collective. It was also distinct in tone and aesthetic as it absorbed the influence of other socialist TV genres, most prominently the didacticism of public affairs programmes and the satirical tone of comedy shows.

While socialist soaps were not overtly politicized, they all modelled ideal socialist lifestyles in ensemble dramas that encompassed the workplace and the family. Unlike historical dramas whose narratives occurred in the past and revolved around heroic male figures in the public arena, these domestic serials took place in the present and featured central female characters who acted as problem-solvers and linchpins between the public and the private spheres. I am most interested in how this regional genre placed women centre stage in order to emphasize the shift from production to consumption and lifestyle in competition with the West. I conclude that these serials prepared a smooth transition to a post-feminist, post-socialist landscape where feminism ostensibly never existed and is, presumably, unnecessary.

The TV world of the 1970s and 80s probably would not have resembled anything one would expect from a socialist country. In essence, it was no different from the transitional terrain of Western European broadcasters. In fact, much of Europe enjoyed the same types of popular programmes in the 1980s. These ranged from German crime dramas such as *Tatort* ('Crime scene') to popular American drama and soap serials such as *Colombo*, *Star Trek*, *The Fugitive*, *Kojak*, *Charlie's Angels*, *Starsky and Hutch*, *Roots*, *Dynasty* and *Dallas*, or the Brazilian *Isaura*, to more high-brow fictions such as the German *Heimat* and the US series *Holocaust*. In most Eastern and Western European countries, the gap between domestic supply and audience demand for American-style drama caused a great deal of consternation about US media

---

195 As Paulina Bren points out, this was not an isolated strategy. Under Brazil's military rule, Globo television network teamed up with the government to showcase upscale lifestyles in telenovelas as a sign of modernization and upward mobility. See Paulina Bren, *The Greengrocer and His TV*, 125.

196 Ien Ang and Jon Stratton, 'The End of Civilization as We Knew It: *Chances* and the Postrealist Soap Opera', in *To Be Continued ... Soap Operas Around the World*, ed. Robert C. Allen (London: Routledge, 1995), 122–44.

imperialism as a threat to national cultures and to public broadcasting. The exception was Britain, where a cross-pollination of imports and format exchanges with the US had been ingrained in television from the very beginning.[197]

As Sabina Mihelj shows, as early as the 1960s, the percentage of foreign programmes in Eastern Europe (excluding the Soviet Union) ranged from 17 per cent in Poland to 45 per cent in Bulgaria. In the early 1970s, 12 per cent of all imported programming on Hungarian television came from the UK, 10 per cent from France and 10 per cent from West Germany. In non-aligned Yugoslavia, a full 80 per cent of all imported programmes came from outside of the socialist bloc and 40 per cent from the US alone. In the early 1980s, an average of 43 per cent of imported programming in Eastern Europe came from Western Europe, almost equalling the 45 per cent that came from the Soviet Union and other Eastern European countries.[198] As I have already noted, even in Albania, perhaps the most isolated country during the Cold War, a period of relative liberalization began in the 1970s. While Enver Hoxha's dictatorship tried to keep the consumption of foreign media under control, broadcast signals from Italy could not be successfully blocked.[199] In Romania, where television experienced a regression under dictatorial control, selected US content and genre models were nevertheless welcome – not the least due to Ceaușescu's attempt to demonstrate his Western orientation and independence from Russia.[200] It was only in the mid-1980s, as the regime became especially isolated and paranoid, that the temporary second channel set up in 1968 ceased to operate (in 1985), and broadcasting hours were reduced from 10–11 to 4–5 hours per day on weekends and to 2 hours on weekdays. *Dallas* was one of the last programmes to go. It was broadcast on Saturdays until the early 1980s but was severely censored and abridged.[201]

In Hungary, the rate of imported programmes in 1985 was 40 per cent, 80 per cent of which came from the US. A 60-minute imported drama episode cost an average of 1,000 US dollars or 60,000 Hungarian forint, while it would have cost 4 to 5 million forint to produce domestically. About a quarter of the population had a choice of programming beyond Hungarian TV's offerings through access either to a VCR or to foreign channels. By the mid-80s, the estimated number of VHS machines was 100,000 – that is, roughly one attached to every fifth TV set.[202] When browsing the Hungarian popular press and specialized media journals in the 1980s, one can immediately see an obsession with the idea of entertainment, the realization that television is inevitably transforming into a mass medium devoted to relaxation and fun. The debates are routinely configured in terms of the choice, or rather the clash, between the 'value-transmitting' and 'audience-focused' functions of television, with a clear transition from the former to the

---

197 Ib Bondebjerg et al., 'American Television: Point of Reference or European Nightmare?', in Bignell and Fickers, *A European Television History*, 154–83.

198 See Sabina Mihelj, 'Television Entertainment in Socialist Eastern Europe: Between Cold War Politics and Global Developments', in *Popular Television in Eastern Europe During and Since Socialism*, eds Anikó Imre, Timothy Havens and Katalin Lustyik (London: Routledge, 2012), 13–29.

199 Idrit Idrizi, 'Das magische Gerät: Die Bedeutung des Fernsehers im isolierten Albanien und für die Erforschung des albanischen Kommunismus' (paper presented at the conference 'Television in Europe beyond the Iron Curtain – National and Transnational Perspectives since the 1950s', Friedrich-Alexander-Universität Erlangen-Nürnberg, December 5–7, 2013).

200 As is widely known, Ceaușescu built his legitimacy on currying favour with Western countries. He visited Nixon and even gained 'most favoured nation' status in the US in 1975.

201 Bondebjerg et al., 'American Television', 177–8.

202 János Horvát, 'Külföldi műsorok a magyar képernyőn' [Foreign programmes on Hungarian screens], *Pártélet* (August–September 1986): 89–93.

Visual cultures

latter.[203] Surveys show, as elsewhere in the Soviet camp, that people rejected the educational programmes that had overwhelmed socialist television.[204] They chose foreign drama series, talent shows and sports programmes or tuned in to better programming from neighbouring countries. In the late 1980s, Hungarian TV was woefully unequipped to meet the demand for television entertainment. Its technical facilities did not allow for more than 95 to 100 hours of programming per week between the two channels.[205] In 1986, the first satellite channel, Sky Channel, launched in 1982 as a holding of Rupert Murdoch's News International, premiered at the Budapest Hilton before it was made available to households. Just over 7 million Western European households were able to access Sky Channel at this time.[206]

Print publications about television's transformation repeatedly struck a resigned tone about the force of the market, which small media economies were powerless to resist. They noted that television was in a bind between its commitment to national programming and viewers' increasingly diverse needs. One compromise was to give primetime slots to imported drama serials that cut across various niche desires, such as the West German crime series *Derrick*, the British family saga *The Onedin Line* or the Czech soap opera *Žena za pultem* ('Women behind the counter').[207]

Popular socialist serials presented far less ideological risk on primetime than the ever-popular American serials, which were feared to provoke ambiguous or subversive interpretations.[208] The East German broadcaster DFF (Deutscher Fernsehfunk) was never able to fill its schedule with original programming from the beginning.[209] In the GDR, competition was especially intense because of the ready availability of West German programmes.[210] In 1968, a new cultural policy was launched under the name 'Range and Diversity'.[211] The new policy pushed television drama to the forefront as the privileged vehicle for reaching viewers, replacing more didactic genres that had failed to create a socialist consciousness. The newly favoured genres included live studio films, made-for-TV movies and dramatic series. Ratings became a much more important indicator than before in deciding which shows should be kept on the air – although, much like elsewhere in the bloc, domestic production still lagged behind the increasing broadcast time.[212]

---

203 'Közönségtisztelő televízió' [An audience-friendly television], *Magyar Hírlap* (20 August 1986).

204 Horvát, 'Külföldi műsorok', 89–93.

205 L.G., 'Másfélből kettő' [Two out of one and a half], *Magyar Nemzet* (20 September 1988).

206 'Beszélgetés a műholdas televíziózásról. Megnyíló égi csatorna' [Celestials channel opens], *HVG* (8 November 1986).

207 Horvát, 'Külföldi műsorok', 90.

208 Such was the case with the 1977 mini-series *Washington: Behind Closed Doors*, a historical drama about the Nixon administration. On the one hand, it was aired in most socialist countries because it contained internal criticism of the capitalist system. On the other hand, however, it demonstrated that the ability to elect or impeach a president was subject to the will of the people. See Horvát, 'Külföldi műsorok', 91.

209 Heather Gumbert, 'Shoring Up Socialism: Transnational Media Exchange and Cultural Sovereignty in the GDR' (paper presented at the conference 'Television in Europe beyond the Iron Curtain – National and Transnational Perspectives since the 1950s', Friedrich-Alexander-Universität Erlangen-Nürnberg, December 5–7, 2013).

210 Stewart Anderson, 'Modern Viewers, Feudal Television Archives: How to Study German Fernsehspiele of the 1960s from a National Perspective', *Critical Studies in Television* 5, no. 2 (2010): 92–104.

211 Thomas Beutelschmidt and Henning Frage, '"Range and Diversity" in the GDR? Television Drama in the Early 1970s', *Historical Journal of Film, Radio and Television* 24, no. 3 (2004): 441–54.

212 Beutelschmidt and Frage, 'Range and Diversity', 443.

The turn towards entertainment gained momentum after Head of State Erich Honecker famously declared at the eighth SED Party Conference in 1972 that television needed to 'overcome a certain type of tedium' and 'take the desire for good entertainment into account'.[213] The programming reform in the wake of this criticism brought an increase in programming hours. As for content, while news and current affairs remained privileged on both channels, on DFF 2 the proportion of feature films, TV films (*Fernsehspiele*) and dramatic series rose by almost 10 per cent to a total of 38.2 per cent – as opposed to the 20.3 per cent of news and information programmes and 10.9 per cent of musical programmes, 6.3 per cent of airtime was dedicated to special events designated as 'ceremonies and parades' and 6.4 per cent to news programmes.[214] As elsewhere, the new direction manifested itself in a more humorous tone, an increased concern with contemporary topics rather than classical stage plays or historical drama, and featured reasonably well-rounded characters who also carried the collective mission of modelling the 'socialist lifestyle'.[215] In other words, the protagonists still needed to be exemplary socialist workers, but their breadth and depth increased. As Thomas Beutelschmidt and Henning Frage argue, 'The inclusion of psychological, social and even gender-specific conflicts can be considered the most important reform in this time period.'[216]

A closer look at some of the most popular late socialist domestic serials highlights the narrative and ideological features that constitute a historically and geopolitically specific cycle that resembles the soap opera. At the same time, the case studies allow for identifying local differences within the cycle. While Czech soaps were the most successful in terms of ratings and geographical reach, the genre was also popular in Poland, Hungary, Bulgaria and the GDR. Soap opera-type dramas were also produced in the Baltic republics of the Soviet Union while Soviet Central Television refused to adopt the genre.[217]

Socialist domestic serials were character-driven dramas with basic plotlines. It was the characters who carried didactic messages in a more or less successfully fictionalized form. The protagonists were ordinary people in situations recognizable to viewers – a winning strategy to create the appearance of bottom-up design and thus inspire trust and loyalty. It clearly worked. Unlike the majority of programming in earlier decades, these serials consolidated national audiences. According to a 1988 Czechoslovak TV survey, 82 per cent of viewers watched domestic serials; and some episodes reached over 90 per cent of viewers.[218] Even in the era of broadcast monopoly, this is an impressive feat.

Such serials were carefully planned so that they would strike a desirable balance between demonstrating political conformity to socialist ideals and gently mocking the realities of those ideals. They relied on the fictionalized, serialized format to influence public opinion and model proper socialist behaviour. However, this residue of propaganda was balanced by social satire and humour. The serials were set in the present and wove together family and public dynamics. The conduits were almost invariably women, who were able to navigate both spheres with

---

213 Ibid., 445.

214 Markus Schubert and Hans-Jeorg Stiehler, 'A Program Structure Analysis of East German Television, 1968–1974', *Historical Journal of Film, Radio and Television* 24, no. 4 (2004): 345–53.

215 Beutelschmidt and Frage, 'Range and Diversity', 446.

216 Ibid., 448.

217 This was not the case in the Soviet Union: following some experiments with the genre, Central Television returned to the historical serial formula. See Simon Huxtable's presentation at the workshop 'Rethinking Socialist TV: Viewers, Genres, Messages', Association for Slavic and East European Studies annual convention, November 2014.

218 Bren, *The Greengrocer and His TV*, 130.

Visual cultures

success. Children were also often smarter than the parents and served as mouthpieces to state evident truths. Many of the shows were set in housing blocks or workplaces, where a cross-section of society could be displayed and a desirable balance between critique and conformity could be demonstrated. Despite their evident mass appeal, political value to the party and enduring popularity, they were shunned by national critics and have just recently been discovered by cultural and media studies scholars.

Perhaps the most beloved Polish serial of all time, *Czterdziestolatek* ('Being forty') was created by prolific writer-director Jerzy Gurza and aired from 1974 to 1978. The serial revolves around a 'typical' Polish middle-class family ensconced in their housing development and workplace environments. The title character is engineer Stefan Karwowski, married to wife Magda, who works for the city's waterworks. They are parents to two school-aged children, Jagoda and Marek, who regularly prove to be much more insightful than their parents. While the serial was meant to foreground the security and comfort of Edward Gierek's socialism,[219] there is also a satirical subterfuge about living conditions in housing blocks and other absurdities of the era.[220] A typical product of Poland's economic and political thaw, *Being Forty* was one of several comic versions of the socialist 'neighbour' programmes produced around the region, set in a panel dwelling of interconnected families, whose class and professional diversity was meant to represent socialist society. The extreme popularity of the show has to do with the fact that it only brushes with political issues superficially and humorously. Instead, the main storylines concern personal problems viewers could identify with – midlife crises, extramarital affairs, quitting smoking, hair loss, fitness, professional life, social activities and so on.[221]

Television in Yugoslavia produced remarkably similar serials in the same period. Both *Spavajte mirno* ('Sleep peacefully'), produced by TV Belgrade in Serbia in 1968, and *Naše malo misto* ('Our small town'), made by TV Zagreb in Croatia from 1970 to 1971, used humour as a means of eliciting identification with socialist ideological principles. The eight episodes of *Sleep Peacefully* address major social problems including unemployment, income disparity, social solidarity and corruption in a way that lays blame at the feet of bad, corrupt individuals who try to undermine an otherwise perfectly good system that is always open to improvement. *Our Small Town* is even more depoliticized. It is set in a picturesque little town on the Adriatic coast and follows the lives of local inhabitants from 1936 to 1970. The socio-political context is reduced to a backdrop of important narrative events, which have to do with personal relationships, leisure activities and shopping trips to Trieste. Such events demonstrate the safety and security of the late socialist lifestyle, deemed superior to the hectic Western pace. Mihelj explains that the humorous treatment, combined with the migration of important issues from the public to the private sphere, made these programmes particularly popular – a tendency already visible in *Our*

---

219 During the decade he spent in office (1970–80), First Secretary Edward Gierek had an ambitious plan to raise living standards. Unfortunately, it was financed by massive borrowing, largely responsible for Poland's economic collapse in the 1980s. 'Edward Gierek Obituary', *The Telegraph*, 31 July 2001, www.telegraph.co.uk/news/obituaries/1335845/Edward-Gierek.html (accessed 21 October 2018). Thanks to Maria Zalewska for research and translation.

220 It is part of a cycle of Polish satirical soaps produced in the 1970s and 1980s, including *Alternatywy 4*, 1986 ('4 Alternative Street'); *Wojna Domowa*, 1965–6 '(Civil War'), *Daleko od Szosy*, 1976 ('Far from the highway') and *Jan Serce*, 1982 ('John Heart'), see Kinga Bloch, 'The Life and Afterlife of a Socialist Media Friend: On the Long-Term Cultural Relevance of the Polish TV Series *Czterdziestolatek*', *VIEW Journal* 2, no. 3 (2013): 88–98.

221 Bloch, 'The Life and Afterlife of a Socialist Media Friend'.

Small Town and most clearly exemplified in TV Belgrade's popular comedic serial *Pozorište u kući* ('Theatre in the home', 1973–84).[222]

The comic soap opera *Theatre in the Home* ran for four non-consecutive seasons in 1972, 1973, 1975 and 1984. It was also remade in 2007, adapted to a post-socialist context. A comedy soap based around a family who lived in a housing development, it belongs to the cycle of 'housing block' drama serials along with the Polish *The 40-Year-Old*, the Hungarian *District 78* and *Neighbours*. During its long span, the serial chronicled the expansion of consumer society in Yugoslavia. Products such as the Yugoslav car Zastava 750 and fashion items are frequently foregrounded in the episodes; comic situations often arise from the systemic deficiencies of socialism, which are treated with light satire.[223]

The Hungarian comical-satirical serial *A 78-as körzet* ('District 78', 1982) offers few surprises after even this brief introduction to similar Polish and Yugoslav programmes. One difference is that, instead of the multi-storey housing development, the narrative setting is a district of Budapest that consists mostly of single-family homes. Although most of the episodes revolve around the dilapidated conditions of the district (unpaved roads, outdoor toilets, a divorced couple having to share a divided space), this is still a fairly idealized setting in itself given severe housing shortages under socialism.

Nowhere was socialist soap production as prolific and profitable as in Czechoslovakia. Dramatic serials date back to 1959 when *Rodina Blahova* ('Family Blahova') began broadcasting live once a month. There were 280 more serial broadcasts that followed during the socialist period. The most popular of these were created by the writer-director duo Jaroslav Dietl and Jaroslav Dudek during the thaw period and circulated within and beyond the region. By the 1970s, the genre settled into a one-hour format, with four 12–13-episode serials covering the entire year.[224] Dietl was a veteran of Czechoslovak television, but was an open-minded writer well ahead of his time who was little appreciated by the critical establishment despite the massive national and international success of his serials. He was keen to learn and adapt from foreign models throughout his career.[225]

His most popular soap opera *Nemocnice na kraji města* ('Hospital at the edge of town', 1977), drew an average viewership of 88 per cent and was also roaringly successful in many other Soviet bloc countries as well as West Germany,[226] the Soviet Union, Poland, Romania, Hungary, Bulgaria, Yugoslavia and Cuba. It was also broadcast in Austria, Switzerland, Finland, Cyprus, Australia, China and Afghanistan.[227] *Hospital at the Edge of Town* was bought by Norddeutscher Rundfunk (NDR), who kept the East German dubbing but re-edited the serial into nine 58-minute episodes rather than keeping the 13 episodes of varying lengths. Ratings proved

---

222 Mihelj, 'The Politics of Privatization', 251–67.

223 Nevena Dakovic and Aleksandra Milanovic, 'Socialist Family Sitcom: Bridging the East-West Divide in the 1970s' (paper presented at the conference 'Television in Europe beyond the Iron Curtain – National and Transnational Perspectives since the 1950s', Friedrich-Alexander-Universität Erlangen-Nürnberg, December 5–7, 2013).

224 Bren, *The Greengrocer and His TV*, 126.

225 Dietl's serials clearly forced the party to reassess its relationship to viewers. Dietl placed great emphasis on success measured by ratings: he aimed to have at least 9 million viewers out of a population of 15 million. Paulina Bren gives a detailed account of his trajectory, from the 1975 *Hamr Dynasty*, about forced agricultural collectivization, through his prolific annual output of new soaps. See: Bren, *The Greengrocer and His TV*, 133.

226 Ibid., 144.

227 Petr Bednařík, 'The Production of Czechoslovakia's Most Popular Television Serial "The Hospital on the Outskirts" and Its Post-1989 Repeats', *VIEW Journal* 2, no. 3 (2013): 27–36.

Visual cultures

the international appeal of the programme: when the station ARD broadcast it in prime time weekly in April 1980, the show reached 19–20 million viewers.[228] In a major marketing coup, Czechoslovak TV co-produced a second season for West German audiences in 1981, with an investment of 2 million West German Deutschmarks. While the programme's original purpose was to promote socialist healthcare, its popularity and translatability is ironically due to its utopian depiction of the socialist hospital. The well-equipped hospital with kind doctors who care about their patients more closely resembled American medical soaps.

The soap opera genre has been called escapist or at least utopian, depicting a universe of privileged consumption.[229] The Dietl serial with the most direct gendered address, *Women Behind the Counter* (1977), fully indulges in this utopianism. The protagonist, Anna Holubova, works in the delicatessen section of a grocery store behind a stack of canned caviar; her daily interactions take place among heaps of tropical fruits and an extravagant array of cheeses, which do not accurately reflect the much more austere shopping conditions of the 1970s. But the show stands out in the first place because it was designed to demonstrate the success of state feminism.[230] The feminized workplace setting allowed the 12-episode programme to focus on a female collective and thus model women's desirable roles in socialist society. Characters and narrative arcs were determined by an ideological framework: the morally superior, helpful characters were all party members while the anti-social, selfish characters were not – although, unlike in the earlier period of strict socialist realism, these 'bad' characters were gently mocked for their consumer greed or bourgeois manners rather than punished.[231]

As elsewhere in the region, the post-1968 period of normalization had brought about a crisis of masculinity and foregrounded the woman's role as a major anchoring power for nationalism in Czechoslovakia.[232] The female proportion of the workforce was 47 per cent in 1971 compared to 30–40 per cent in Austria and Germany. The socialist state invested in the idealized image of the socialist woman as independent, desirable and capable but who does not need help from men. While *Women Behind the Counter* depicted women doing it all with heroism and success, like other socialist drama serials, it also endorsed men's leadership positions in the public sphere and their minimal obligations in the domestic sphere. Serials like *Women Behind the Counter* were surrounded by other, less popular Czechoslovak programmes that demonstrated men's superior decision-making and leadership abilities in public life, such as ('Man at the town hall', 1976) and ('The northern district', 1980).[233] One would not see men cleaning or taking care of children in such serials: rather, one would see them bumbling around and in constant need of female help. The socialist soap confirmed the gendered status quo of state feminism, which further naturalized the traditional division of roles while vastly expanding women's workload. Women tended to blame their burden on the system and its failed feminism, rather than men and nationalism[234] in a tragic twist that helped demonize feminism as a whole and prepared the ground for the post-feminist turn.

---

228 Ibid.
229 Christine Geraghty, 'Soap Opera and Utopia', in *Cultural Theory and Popular Culture: A Reader*, ed. John Storey (Harlow: Pearson Press, 1993), 246–54.
230 Jakub Machek, '"Women behind the Counter" As a Female Prototype: Prime Time Popular Culture in 1970s and 1980s Czechoslovakia', *Media Research* 16, no. 1 (2010): 31–52, here 44.
231 Ibid.
232 Ibid., 169.
233 Machek, 'The Counter Lady', 48.
234 Ibid., 47.

Late socialist serials give us a retrospective glimpse into a gradual economic and cultural transformation that prepared for a transition to capitalism, rather than the sudden and spectacular implosion that came to define the narrative of socialism's demise. They show that this transformation had a gendered infrastructure carefully cultivated by party policy towards women and deployed in popular genres that hid didactic messages in realistic-utopian fictional plots that also opened the door to unpredictable practices of reception. These shows were often experimental mixes of old and new, of American commercial quality and European PSB quality – made to answer, in varying degrees, to state socialist educational propaganda. They were the unique products of an industry that was open to novelty but had not yet yielded the primacy of domestic production to a ratings and advertising-driven market. The genre proved flexible enough for the purposes of socialist states looking for ways to accommodate their disillusioned audiences' escape from vacuous public rituals into home-based entertainment and an emerging second economy. It also provided a surprising aesthetic continuity with the socialist-realist requirements of an earlier, post-war communism, given the reliance of both socialist realism and soap opera on stock characters. The socialist soap made for a tenuous compromise with entertainment and consumerism since too much explicit propaganda risked alienating the audience while too much realism risked releasing affective discontent and ambivalence about the regime.

Paulina Bren writes that late socialist culture resembled American culture in the 1980s, establishing a significant similarity between East and West after 1968. Bren references Lauren Berlant's characterization of a shrinking public realm and slipping government control in the US, balanced by a growing and increasingly fragmented set of private worlds. Bren notes that this realization undermines the 'existing historiography of binaries' between official versus unofficial cultures, the first and second economy, party elite versus dissident elite and a politicized public sphere versus a depoliticized private sphere. Television consistently directs us to the grey in-between zones.[235]

Conclusion

Thankfully, work on Soviet and Eastern European TV histories is no longer in short supply. In fact, those of us researching socialism and television now face the opposite problem: there is too much new material to process and incorporate into any single project. This is a delightful problem to have. Instead of gatekeeping and competition, it has given rise to some extremely productive collaborations that unapologetically criss-cross Eastern and Western Europe, North America and other post-socialist locations in an expanding network dedicated to mapping the global history of socialist TV.[236] The emerging work on the history of socialist TV has effectively removed the Cold War lens that has occluded alternative histories of European television. Instead of a clear-cut East–West divide, we see various local and regional patterns defined by cultural and political-economic similarities and differences. A much more essential difference emerges between what Bourdon et al. call the 'courteous' European model that reigned through the 1980s and the 'competitive' Americanized model that challenged European broadcasters to shift to a dual broadcasting mode in a commercial, multi-channel and deregulated global environment.[237] In this alternative historical view, Eastern European broadcasters were simply a little slower to join the competitive model. But competition always underscored their

---

235 Bren, *The Greengrocer and His TV*, 7–9.
236 See: footnote 6.
237 Bourdon, Ibanez, Johnson and Mueller, 'Searching for an Identity for Television', 101–26.

Visual cultures

operation, as I explain above. During times of nominal state monopoly, states always had to vie for the attention of viewers distracted by foreign broadcasts and, from the late 1980s, satellite programming. In addition, state broadcasters were continually compelled to increase the volume of imports needed to fill schedules on state channels.[238]

As I emphasized throughout this chapter, no technical innovation, programme or policy can be isolated from its regional, European and global contexts. While national histories do need to be written and remain crucial resources, I have focused attention on patterns that stretched across national borders and defied common assumptions about the story and the potential of both socialism and television. This work can only be accomplished collectively. The conclusion that jumps out from virtually all of this recent work is that the story of blind adherence to ideological dogma has been a Cold War construction from the very beginning. Through the window that television opens, we see more or less desperate, often belated, attempts at top-down control, constantly tempered by other, often officially unspoken, imperatives that these societies absorbed and negotiated, such as the actual needs of viewers to be entertained, educated and invited to consume, the power of competition and experiments with various realist aesthetics in order to construct and convey authenticity. We must also remember that Eastern Europe is just one piece of the Soviet Empire and a fraction of the world system that embraced socialist ideologies during the Cold War. Research on the history of television under global socialism would have to enact a truly global collaboration. When this work materializes, it will have an enormous impact on our understanding of socialism, television, the Cold War and its aftermath.

Further reading

Allen, Robert C., ed. *To Be Continued ... Soap Operas around the World* (London: Routledge, 1995).

Bignell, Jonathan, and Andreas Fickers, eds. *A European Television History* (New York: Blackwell, 2008).

Bren, Paulina. *The Greengrocer and His TV: The Culture of Communism after the 1968 Prague Spring* (Ithaca, NY: Cornell University Press, 2010).

Corner, John. *Studying Media: Problems of Theory and Method* (Edinburgh: Edinburgh University Press, 1998).

Culik, Jan. *National Mythologies in Central European TV Series: How J.R. Won the Cold War* (Eastbourne: Sussex Academic Press, 2013).

Einhorn, Barbara. *Cinderella Goes to the Market: Citizenship, Gender and Women's Movements in East Central Europe* (London: Verso, 1993).

Ellis, John. *Visible Fictions* (London: Routledge, 1982).

Evans, Christine E. *Between Truth and Time: A History of Soviet Central Television* (New Haven, CT: Yale University Press, 2016).

Funk, Nanette, and Magda Mueller, eds. *Gender Politics and Post-Communism* (New York: Routledge, 1993).

Gal, Susan, and Gail Kligman. *Reproducing Gender: Politics, Publics and Everyday Life after Socialism* (Princeton, NJ: Princeton University Press, 2000).

Gorsuch, Anne, and Diane Koenker, eds. *The Socialist Sixties: Crossing Borders in the Second World* (Bloomington, IN: Indiana University Press, 2013).

Gumbert, Heather. *Envisioning Socialism Television and the Cold War in the German Democratic Republic* (Ann Arbor, MI: University of Michigan Press, 2014).

Haltof, Marek. *Polish National Cinema* (Oxford: Berghahn Books, 2002).

Imre, Anikó, Timothy Havens, and Katalin Lustyik, eds. *Popular Television in Eastern Europe during and since Socialism* (New York: Routledge, 2013).

Mustata, Dana. 'The Power of Television: Including the Historicizing of the Live Romanian Revolution' (PhD diss., Utrecht University, 2011).

---

238 See Mihelj, 'Understanding Socialist Television'.

Newcomb, Horace, ed. *Encyclopedia of Television* (London: Routledge, 2004).

Penn, Shana, and Jill Massino, eds. *Gender Politics and Everyday Life in State Socialist East and Central Europe* (New York: Palgrave Macmillan, 2009).

Petersen, Hanne, José María Lorenzo Villaverde, and Ingrid Lund-Andersen, eds. *Contemporary Gender Relations and Changes in Legal Cultures* (Copenhagen: DJOF, 2013).

Reufsteck, Michael, and Stefan Niggemeier. *Das Fernsehlexikon: Alles über 7000 Sendungen von Ally McBeal bis zur ZDF-Hitparade* (München: Goldmann Verlag, 2005).

Roth-Ey, Kristin. *Moscow Prime Time: How the Soviet Union Built the Media Empire that Lost the Cultural Cold War* (Ithaca, NY: Cornell University Press, 2011).

Scott, Joan Wallach, Cora Kaplan, and Debra Keates, eds. *Transitions, Environments, Translations: Feminism in International Politics* (London: Routledge, 2004).

Storey, John, ed. *Cultural Theory and Popular Culture: A Reader* (Harlow: Pearson Press, 1993).

INDEX

Adameck, Heinz 345
Adenauer, Konrad 43
Ady, Endre 134, 137–8, 140, 159, 160
Aksakov, Ivan 36
Alexander I, Emperor of Russia 265
Alexander, Stella 263, 279n133, 279n136
Anderson, Benedict 80
Andics, Erzsébet 228–9
Andrić, Ivo 133, 139, 169
Andrzejewski, Jerzy 169–70, 181
Antohi, Sorin 6, 62–3
Antonescu, Ion 102, 110
Aragon, Louis 151
Arany, János 138
Arnaudov, Mikhail 228
Arnold, Jan 270
Arnold, Stanisław 213
Atatürk, Mustafa Kemal 120
Aubin, Hermann 214

Babits, Mihály 135, 137, 140, 151, 160
Bachynsky, Iulian 73
Bácskai, Vera 245
Baczko, Bronisław 112, 245
Bahr, Hermann 133
Bălan, Nicolae 297
Balázs, Béla 139, 150
Balázs, Éva H. 236
Balogh, Mária 335
Balzer, Oswald 4
Bánffy, Miklós 160–2
Barańczak, Stanisław 182
Bartók, Béla 138, 151
Baťa, Jan Antonín 95
Baudouin de Courtenay, Jan Niecisław Ignacy 29
Bauer, Antun 279
Bauer, Otto 74, 121

Bebel, August 352
Beck, Józef 36n156
Benda, Kálmán 236
Beneš, Edvard 19–21, 20n74, 26–7, 38–9, 45, 83
Benko, Artur Grado 134
Beöthy, Zsolt 135
Berend, Iván 48–9, 241, 248
Bergson, Henri 21, 23
Berlant, Lauren 364
Berlin, Isaiah 70, 259n13
Bernolák, Anton 231
Bernstein, Leonard 331
Berza, Mihai 233, 240
Bethlen, István 249
Bibó, István 47, 70, 76, 79, 122–4, 127
Bićanić, Rudolf 92
Bidlo, Jaroslav 26, 28, 29n121, 31–6, 45, 47, 55, 212
Bignell, Jonathan 317–18
Biskupski, Mieczysław B. 5, 29, 36
Blackbourn, David 70
Blaga, Lucian 205
Blagoev, Dimitar 90
Bloch, Marc 213–14, 220, 237, 243
Bobchev, Stefan 8, 27–8
Bobińska, Celina 229
Bobrownicka, Maria 61
Bobrzyński, Michał 203–4, 207
Bogdan, Ioan 11
Boia, Lucian 126, 248
Bojtár, Endre 49, 52, 187
Bolzano, Bernard 123, 270
Bono Šagi, Zvonimir 303
Borgia, Stefano 260
Boris III, King of Bulgaria 102
Borkenau, Franz 237
Borowski, Tadeusz 171–3

Index

Bourdon, Jérôme 343, 364
Boy-Żeleński, Tadeusz 339
Bozanić, Josip 303, 303n282
Brackmann, Albert 221
Brăncuşi, Constantin 125
Brătianu, Georghe I. 223, 225, 233, 237
Brătianu, Ion I. C. 274
Braudel, Fernand 48, 64, 196, 211, 220, 236–8, 242–3
Brezhnev, Leonid 320
Brkljačić, Maja 249
Brodziński, Kazimierz 260n22
Brubaker, Rogers 258–9
Brunsdon, Charlotte 312
Brzozowski, Stanisław 5n16, 89
Buber, Martin 103
Buckle, Henry Thomas 203
Buelens, Geert 139
Bujak, Franciszek 199, 202, 211, 224, 237
Bulányi, György 294
Busek, Erhard 53

Camus, Albert 180
Canetti, Elias 133
Cankar, Ivan 133, 139, 142–3
Čapek, Josef 134
Čapek, Karel 20, 108, 151–4, 159
Carol I, King of Romania 206
Carol II, King of Romania 85, 282
Casanova, José 257n5, 257n6, 258, 300
Castriot, George (a.k.a. Skanderberg) 234
Čaušević, Džemaludin 103
Ceauşescu, Elena 353
Ceauşescu, Nicolae 125, 189–91, 233, 298, 314, 316, 318, 320, 346, 348, 358
Cecil, Svatopluk 8
Čepička, Alexej 291n199
Čerina, Vladimir 73
Černý, Václav 45
Cesarec, August 76
Chaloupecký, Václav 222
Chaplin, Charlie 109
Chaunu, Pierre 240
Chirot, Daniel 210
Chlebowczyk, Józef 51, 80, 246–7
Cioran, Emil 109–11, 124, 179
Civ'jan, Tat'jana 64
Čivraný, Lumír 44
Claes, Ernest 337
Codreanu, Corneliu Zelea 110, 280–3
Colan, Nicolae 281
Ćorović, Vladimir 208, 224
Count Pál Esterházy I 188
Crainic, Nichifor 101–2, 104, 282n150
Cristea, Miron 282
Crnjanski, Miloš 139, 142
Cseres, Tibor 173–7

da Cunha, Euclides 178
Cvetkova, Bistra 240
Cvijić, Jovan 11–12, 12n40, 16, 25, 199, 201, 218–19
Cymorek, Hans 202
Cywiński, Bohdan 273
Czepulis-Rastenis, Ryszarda 245

Darvai, Móricz 201
Daskalov, Roumen 232
Daszyńska-Golińska, Zofia 210
Dedijer, Jevto 219
Dembiński, Jan 213
Dénes, Iván Zoltán 246
Derzhavin, Nikolai 228
Deutsch, Karl 78
Dhoest, Alexander 337
Dietl, Jaroslav 362–3
Dietrich, Marlene 331
Dilthey, Wilhelm 205
Dimitrijević, Sergije 232
Dimitrov, Georgi 235
Djilas, Milovan 77, 87, 98, 232
Djordjević, Dimitrije 195
Djurdjev, Branislav 232, 242
Dmowski, Roman 5, 17, 28, 72, 84, 249, 263, 271
Dobner, Gelasius 270
Dobrogeanu-Gherea, Alexandru 90
Dobrogeanu-Gherea, Constantin 90, 121, 210
Dobrovský, Joseph 260n22, 261
Domanovszky, Sándor (Alexander) 211–14, 236–7
Donáth, Ferenc 76
Donskis, Leonidas 252
Dopsch, Alfons 212
Dostál, Josef 20
Drăghicescu, Dumitru 119
Druzhinin, Nikolai 226
Dubnow, Simon 207, 224
Duby, Georges 240, 243
Duchiński, Franciszek 5
Dučić, Isac 151
Dučić, Jovan 151
Dudek, Jaroslav 362
Duichev, Ivan 228
Đurić, Miloš 23–4
Đurica, Milan 249
Durych, Jaroslav 102
Duţu, Alexandru 240
Dvorník, František (Francis) 45
Dvorniković, Vladimir 15, 25, 42
Dziedzic, Irena 332, 354

Eatwell, Roger 281
Eftimiu, Victor 151
Eisler, Hanns 154
Eley, Geoff 70
Eliade, Mircea 10, 111, 119–20, 124, 126, 179

Index

Ellis, John 312, 336
Eminescu, Mihai 125
Engelking, Barbara 252
Engels, Friedrich 45, 48, 112, 226, 254, 258n8, 352
Erdei, Ferenc 76, 92–3, 122
Erdeljanović, Jovan 218–19, 224
Erőss, Pál 333
Esterházy, Mátyás 188
Esterházy, Péter 182–3, 187–9
Evans, Christine 332, 354

Faludi, György 180
Farkas, Miklós 159
Fedor, Ágnes 355
Fehér, Ferenc 50, 112
Feketehalmy-Czeydner, Ferenc 173, 175
Fenyő, Miksa 135
Ferdinand I, King of Bulgaria 199
Ferrero, Guglielmo 122
Fickers, Andreas 317–18
Fierlinger, Zdeněk 108
Fock, Jenő 334
Fodor, Éva 356
Fondane (or, Fundoianu), Benjamin 110
Francis Joseph I, Emperor of Austria, King of
    Hungary 141, 183
Franić, Frane 287–8
Frankl, Michal 251
Franz Ferdinand, Archduke of Austria 73, 141
Freud, Sigmund 133
Friedman, Victor 64

Galabov, Konstantin 14
Gałczyński, Konstanty Ildefons 341
Garlicki, Andrzej 249
Gary, Romain 179
Gaulle, Charles de 318
Geertz, Clifford 305, 306n295
Gellner, Ernest 80, 247, 258
Georgescu, Vlad 80
Georgević, Tihomir 218
Geremek, Bronisław 236, 237n212, 239, 243
Gerould, Daniel 157
Gesemann, Gerhard 16, 43n185
Gide, André 109
Giedroyc, Jerzy 125, 180
Gierek, Edward 361
Gieysztor, Aleksander 51, 51n217, 236
Giurescu, Constantin C. 223–4, 233
Glemp, Cardinal Józef 104
Gódor, Ferenc 347
Goethe, Johann Wolfgang von 155, 260
Goga, Octavian 138, 151
Goll, Jaroslav 202, 209
Gömbös, Gyula 283
Gombrowicz, Witold 165–7, 180, 188, 190
Gomułka, Władysław 180, 289–91

Górski, Artur 134
Gottwald, Klement 291n199
Grabski, Andrzej Feliks 248
Grafenauer, Bogo 219–20, 242n240
Gramsci, Antonio 93
Grass, Günter 133
Grassy, József 173–7
Graus, František 229, 239, 243
Gross, Jan Tomasz 125, 250, 301n267
Gross, Mirjana 242
Grubišić, Ivan 303
Grudzińska-Gross, Irena 250
Gulyás, János 347
Gumbert, Heather 312, 324, 334, 348, 351
Gumplowicz, Ludwik 220
Gurza, Jerzy 361
Gusti, Dimitrie 92, 238
Gyulai, Pál 135

Hadzhiyski, Ivan 94, 98
Hajnal, István 40, 213, 236
Halecki, Oskar 29–36, 36n155, 39, 48, 50–1, 199,
    209, 224
Halík, Tomáš 105, 307
Hamann, Johann Georg 259–60
Hanák, Péter 52–3, 241, 245
Handelsman, Marceli 28–31, 33–6, 79, 212–13,
    224, 248
Handžić, Mehmed 103
Hašek, Jaroslav 132n1, 136, 139, 143–45, 154–5
Haumann, Péter 330
Hauptman, Ljudmil 219–20
Havel, Václav 36, 55n238, 56–7, 62, 70,
    113–14, 307
Hayek, Friedrich August von 95
Hebbel, Friedrich 106
Heller, Ágnes 112
Heltai, Gáspár 342
Hemingway, Ernest 139
Hemon, Aleksandar 178
Henlein, Konrad 222
Henry VIII, King of England 270
Herder, Johann Gottfried 259–62, 264, 266
Herling-Grudziński, Gustaw 180
Herriot, Édouard 108
Hettling Manfred 224
Higonnet, Margaret 139
Himka, John-Paul 251
Hlaváček, Karel 134–5
Hlinka, Andrej 277
Hlond, Cardinal August 284
Hobsbawm, Eric 80, 258
Hodža, Milan 27, 39, 74
Hofmannsthal, Hugo von 133
Holotík, Ľudovít 229
Hóman, Bálint 206–7, 214, 220, 224
Honecker, Erich 320, 324, 345, 360

Index

Horia, Vintilă 179
Horthy, Miklós 173, 178, 274, 284
Horváth, János 135
Hoxha, Enver 234, 315, 358
Hrabal, Bohumil 170, 188
Hroch, Miroslav 6, 246, 247n263, 248, 55n238, 80
Hromádka, Josef L. 104
Hrushevsky, Mykhailo 9, 196, 199, 207, 209n75, 210, 224–6
Hrytsak, Jaroslav 246
Hus, Jan 264–5, 270, 276
Husa, Václav 239
Húščava, Alexander 222

Iannaccone, L. R. 257
Iavorskyi, Matvij 225–6
Ignotus (Hugo Veigelsberg) 135, 139
Illyés, Gyula 76
Imbrescu, Ilie 282n149
Inglehart, Ronald 300
Ionesco, Eugène 52, 58, 179
Iorga, Nicolae 11, 42, 196, 199, 204–5, 207–8, 212–13, 222–3, 225, 233
Isac, Emil 135
Ishirkov, Anastas 12
Istrati, Panait 109
Izetbegović, Alija 105

Jalava, Marja 202
Janáček, Leoš 138
Janev, Sotir 108
Janion, Maria 245
Janowski, Maciej 221, 245–6
Jasinowski, Bogumił 5
Jászi, Oszkár 74
Jaworski, Władysław Leopold 17
Jedlicki, Jerzy 245, 248
Jeleński, Jan 284
Jeleński, Konstanty 180
Jesenký, Janko 139
Jesenská, Milena 188
Jilemnický, Peter 169
Jireček, Konstantin 198, 200–1
John XXIII, Pope (1958–1963) 297
Joseph II, Holy Roman Emperor 264, 265n43, 267
Jovanović, Dragoljub 111
Jovanović, Slobodan 84–5, 224, 195
József, Attila 151
Juhász, Gyula 151
Jünger, Ernst 139
Jungmann, Josef 261

Kaczmarek, Czesław 285n165, 289
Kádár, János 182, 293, 320, 334, 340
Kaffka, Margit 140
Kafka, Franz 183, 187–8
Kalinka, Walerian 4

Kalista, Zdeněk 203, 208–9, 210
Kangrgra, Milan 112
Kant, Immanuel 259
Karásek, Jiří 134–5
Kardelj, Edvard 77, 87, 296
Karinthy, Frigyes 342
Karvaš, Peter 169
Kaser, Karl 64–5
Kassák, Lajos 134
Kästner, Erich 339
Kazimierz, Jan 265
Kemény, István 98
Kemény, János 160
Kende, Márta 355
Kende, Tamás 251
Képíró, Sándor 175
Keresztury, Dezső 158
Kertész, Imre 133, 172–3
Keyserling, Hermann 21
Kiliánová, Gabriela 253
Kiš, Danilo 124, 127, 159, 165, 183, 185–8
Kisch, Egon Erwin 136, 154
Kiss, Csaba 54
Kizwalter, Tomasz 247
Klages, Ludwig 109
Klaniczay, Gábor 244
Klebelsberg, Kunó von 200, 213, 249
Kłoczowski, Jerzy 51, 239
Knox, Zoe 304
Kochanowski, Jan Karol 17
Kocka, Jürgen 70, 244–5
Kodály, Zoltán 138
Koestler, Arthur 136, 152, 154–6, 159, 162–5, 174, 183
Kogălniceanu, Mihail 196–7
Kohák, Erazim 123
Kohn, Hans 78, 80
Kołakowski, Leszek 105, 112–13, 245, 307
Kolár, Jan 180
Kölcsey, Ferenc 268
Kollár, Jan 260n22, 261–2, 265
Komócsin, Zoltán 334
Koneczny, Feliks 14, 17–18, 209
Koniáš, Antonín 264n37
Konica, Faik 81
Konrád, György 54–5, 55n238, 56–8, 98, 183
Konstantin, Pável 135
Kontler, László 246
Kopeček, Michal 250
Köpeczi, Béla 236
Kopitar, Jernej 260n22
Korduba, Myron 202
Kormanowa, Żanna 229
Korošec, Anton 279
Kós, Károly 160–1
Kos, Milko 219
Kosáry, Domokos 236

Index

Koselleck, Reinhart xvi, 116, 242
Kosev, Dimitar 229
Kosev, Konstantin 241
Kosík, Karel 77, 112–13, 127
Kosinski, Jerzy 170
Kossinna, Gustaf 198
Kostrzewski, Józef 198
Koštunica, Vojislav 302
Kosztolányi, Dezső 136–7, 147–9, 151
Kott, Jan 172
Kovács, András 176
Kovács, Imre 76
Kovács, Judit 355
Koyré, Alexandre 70
Král, Jiří 222
Kramář, Karel 8, 26–8, 83
Krasser, Harald 161
Kraszewski, Józef Ignacy 266
Kratochvíl, Zdeněk 136
Krejčí, František Václav 20–1, 40
Krek, Janez E. 100
Křen, Jan 44, 57
Krishnamurti, Jiddu 109
Kristóf, Ágota 179, 181
Krleža, Miroslav 76, 139, 142
Krofta, Kamil 224
Kroutvor, Josef 57–8
Krúdy, Gyula 137
Kruus, Hans 217
Kubyjovych, Volodymyr 222
Kucharzewski, Jan 5
Kuczynski, Jürgen 240
Kudlik, Júlia 332
Kula, Witold 48–9, 236, 237n212, 240–1, 248
Kun, Béla 107, 147, 149–50, 274–5, 283
Kundera, Milan 36, 50, 54–8, 178–9, 183
Kurosawa, Akira 174
Kusý, Miroslav 47
Kutnar, František 79, 83, 194n3

Lackó, Miklós 235–6
Lada, Josef 145
Lamprecht, Karl 199, 201–4, 206, 210, 222, 253
Langer, František 136, 151
Lapin, Sergey 320
Lednicki, Wenceslas (Wacław) 29, 46
Lelewel, Joachim 260n22
Lemberg, Eugen 78
Lenin, Vladimir Ilyich 109, 352
Leo XIII, Pope (1878–1903) 99
Leontyeva, Valentina 354
Lepp, Annika 316
Lilova, Dessislava 247
Lipińska, Olga 341, 354
Lipski, Jan Józef 125
Lipták, Ľubomír 235
Ljotić, Dimitrije 101–2

Longen, Emil Artur 136
Losonczy, Géza 76
Lotman, Yurii 123
Luca, Gherasim 179
Lueger, Karl 100
Lukač, Emil Boleslav 151
Lukács, György (Georg) 69n3, 106–7, 150, 228
Lukinich, Imre 33
Lutosławski, Wincenty 5
Luxemburg, Rosa 352
Lypynsky, Vyacheslav 82–3, 210, 224

Macek, Josef 229, 244
Maček, Vladko 278
Macura, Josef 36
Macura, Vladimír 7, 37, 55, 123–4, 247–8
Macůrek, Josef 47–8, 194
Mączak, Antoni 241
Madgearu, Virgil 91
Magris, Claudio 52
de Maistre, Joseph 111
Makkai, László 236
Małowist, Marian 48–9, 236, 240–1
Mályusz, Elemér 214–15, 222
Maniu, Iuliu 162
Mann, Klaus 339
Mann, Thomas 106, 151, 182
Mannheim, Karl 90
Manoilescu, Mihail 85–6
Manteuffel, Tadeusz 222, 230, 236, 240
Márai, Sándor 170, 178, 181–2
Marin, Vasile 281
Marinescu, Annemarie 316
Marković, Mihailo 112
Márkus, György 112
Martinka, Jozef 222
Masaryk, Tomáš G. 7, 18–21, 26, 37–9, 74, 78, 83, 108, 121, 127, 203, 259, 260n22, 261, 264–5, 288
Massis, Henri 119
Matolcsy, Mátyás 96
Matúz Józsefné, Rózsa 355
Mazzini, Giuseppe 72, 263
Mehmedinović, Semezdin 178
Meinecke, Friedrich 80, 128, 206
Melik, Anton 219
Mendl, Bedřich 211, 224
Menzel, Jiří 170
Méray, Tibor 180
Merxhani, Branko 120
Meschendörfer, Adolf 160
Metropolitan Cyril of Plovdiv 102
Metropolitan Mihailo of Belgrade 99
Michalik, Jan 136
Michnik, Adam 70, 114–15
Mičić, Ljubomir 15–16
Mickiewicz, Adam 168, 266

Index

Mieroszewski, Juliusz 125
Mihelj, Sabina 312, 313n9, 319, 349, 358, 361
Milošević, Miloš 22
Milošević, Slobodan 306
Miłosz, Czesław 54, 55n238, 132n1, 133, 138, 156, 167–8, 172, 178, 180, 298
Milutinović, Zoran 23
Mináč, Vladimír 169
Mindszenty, Cardinal József 104, 283
Minulescu, Ion 134, 136
Mises, Ludwig von 95
Mishkova, Diana 246
Miszlivetz, Ferenc 59
Mitrany, David 79
Mňačko, Ladislav 169
Moisuc, Viorica 233
Moisescu, Iustin 298n253
Möller van den Bruck, Arthur 21
Molnár, Erik 229, 234
Molnár, Ferenc 136–7, 139, 342
Molnár, Margit 335, 355–6
Molter, Károly 160
Monod, Gabriel 212
Mónus, Illés 93
Móricz, Zsigmond 140, 147
Moța, Ion 281
Mrożek, Sławomir 178
Müller, Herta 133, 178, 189–91
Munteanu, Nicolae (Nicodim) 282
Münzenberg, Willi 154
Murgescu, Bogdan 243
Mussolini, Benito 73, 109, 281
Mustata, Dana 312, 346
Mutafchiev, Petar 199, 208, 223–4, 228

Nádas, Péter 132n1, 181–2
Nagy, Endre 137, 340
Nagy, Imre 107, 294
Nagy, Töhötöm 104
Nastasă, Lucian 196, 198
Naumann, Friedrich 31, 38
Nejedlý, Zdeněk 44
Nestor, Ion 233
Nicholas I, Emperor of Russia 266
Niederhauser, Emil 47, 80, 194–5, 207, 236, 247
Nieheim, Dietrich von 163
Nietzsche, Friedrich 133, 179
Nistor, Ion I. 205
Nodl, Martin 237
Noica, Constantin 124–5
Noli, Fan 81–2
Nora, Pierre 252–3
Norris, Pippa 300
Novák, Jan Bedřich 213
Novaković, Stojan 201
Nowaczyński, Adolf 136
Nowak, Stanisław 305

Ojamaa, Eedu 348
Olbracht, Ivan 146–7
Olson, Greta 333
Ordęga, Józef 266
Ortega y Gasset, José 13
Orwell, George 180
Osvát, Ernő 135

Pach, Zsigmond Pál 48, 236, 240–1
Palacký, František 7, 37, 78, 113, 123, 196, 261, 264–5, 270
Palotai, Boris 355
Panaitescu, Petre P. 222–3
Pankratova, Anna 226, 229
Pantti, Mervi 316
Papacostea, Victor 41
Papanastasiou, Alexandros 82
Papp, Károly 216
Pârvan, Vasile 205
Pašić, Nikola 269
Patočka, Jan 70, 113, 123–4
Pauker, Ana 97
Paulová, Milada 35
Pavlov, Todor 228
Pécsi, Ferenc 324
Pekař, Josef 202–5, 208–9, 213, 222, 224, 238, 253
Penck, Albrecht 198, 218
Penev, Boyan 12
Perec, Georges 179
Perényi, József 48
Peroutka, Ferdinand 20, 39, 83–4, 121
Péteri, György 227
Petőfi, Sándor 138
Petráň, Josef 239
Petrescu, Cezar 160
Petrović, Gajo 112
Petrović, Karađorđe 262
Petrović, Rastko 13
Pfitzner, Josef 222, 224
Piasecki, Bolesław 102, 104, 289
Picheta, Uadzimir 225
Pikulski, Tadeusz 332, 341
Pilar, Ivo 209n75, 221–2, 224
Piłsudski, Józef 84, 156, 167, 235, 249, 271, 272
Pinochet, Augusto 88
Pius XI, Pope (1922–1939) 270
Pius XII, Pope (1939–1958) 290
Plavša, Marko 287
Pleskot, Patryk 236
Pócsik, Ilona 349–51
Pokrovskij, Mikhail 225
Polakovič, Štefan 86
Polit, Monika 252
Pontoppidan, Hendrik 151
Popescu, Dumitru 348
Popiełuszko, Jerzy 298
Popović, Justin 16

Index

Popovici, Aurel C. 74
Procházka, Arnošt 134–5
Prodan, David 238
Prohászka, Ottokár 100–1
Prus, Bolesław 267
Przybora, Jeremi 340–1
Przybyszewski, Stanisław 133, 135
Putin, Vladimir 306

Radić, Stjepan 279
Radica, Bogdan 122–3
Rádl, Emanuel 79, 123
Radojčić, Nikola 218
Rădulescu-Motru, Constantin 117–18
Radványi, Dezső 335
Rákóczi, Ferenc II 205
Rakovski, Krastyu (Christian) 74–5, 109
Ranke, Leopold von 7, 201–3, 264
Ránki, György 48–9, 236, 241, 248
Rapacka, Joanna 61
Rapant, Daniel 229–30
Raphael, Lutz 230
Ratkoš, Peter 231
Ratzel, Friedrich 12, 210
Ratzinger, Cardinal Joseph (later Pope Benedict XVI) 294
Rebreanu, Liviu 139–42, 151
Remarque, Erich Maria 139
Reményik, Sándor 160
Renan, Ernest 8
Reymont, Władysław Stanisław 133, 138, 160
Režek, Mateja 286n167, 297
Rizaj, Skendër 240
Rolland, Romain 109, 151
Roller, Mihail 233
Romains, Jules 152
Romsics, Ignác 249
Roth, Joseph 52, 141–2, 150, 154, 183
Roth, Klaus 64
Roth-Ey, Kristin 319–20, 331, 351, 353
Rutkowski, Jan 211, 213, 224, 237

Sadoveanu, Mihail 161
Šafárik, Pavel Josef 260n22, 262–3
Šalda, František Xaver 39–40
Šalkaus, Stasys 119
Sándor, György 326n72, 333
Šarić, Ivan 280
Sawicki, Ludomir 222
Schaar, Giselher 332
Schaff, Adam 112
Scheumann, Gerhard 334
Schiemann, Paul 74
Schlögel, Karl 53, 57
Schmitt, Carl 116
Schneiderov, Vladimir 331
Schöpflin, Gyula 178

Schulz, Bruno 141, 183–8
Schulze Wessel, Martin 56n241, 58
Seierstad, Åsne 302
Seifert, Jaroslav 133
Serejski, Marian Henryk 213, 248
Serge, Victor 109
Sernet, Claude 179
Seton-Watson, Hugh 46
Shehu, Mehmet 234
Sheytanov, Nayden 24
Shishmanov, Ivan 11, 198
Šidak, Jaroslav 230
Sienkiewicz, Henryk 133
Sima, Horia 110
Šimečka, Milan 56, 58
Simmel, Georg 106
Şincan, Anca Maria 297
Singer, Isaac Bashevis 133
Sinkó, Ervin 150–1
Šišić, Ferdo 207–8, 210, 220, 224
Skerlić, Jovan 3–4
Skoropadsky, Pavlo 82
Škvorecký, Josef 170, 178–9
Skwarczyński, Adam 84
Slavík, Jan 213, 222, 224
Šmahel, František 239, 243
Smith, Anthony D. 80, 260
Smoleński, Władysław 5
Sobieski, Jan, King of Poland 290
Sobieski, Wacław 5, 199
Sombart, Werner 94
Sommerkamp, August Detleve 332
Souvarine, Boris 109
Spencer, Herbert 203
Spengler, Oswald 13, 18, 21–2, 24, 30, 109
Śpiewak, Paweł 354
Stahl, Henri H. 92, 238, 240
Stalin, Joseph 75–6, 111, 162–4, 200, 226, 230, 288, 292, 296, 352
Stamboliyski, Aleksandar 91
Stan, Liviu 298n253
Stančić, Nikša 247
Stăniloae, Dumitru 104
Stanishev, Nikolay 228
Stanojević, Gligor 232
Stanojević, Stanoje 208
Starčević, Ante 261, 280
Stefanović, Svetislav 23
Stelescu, Mihail 109
Stempowski, Jerzy 17, 180
Stephen I, King of Hungary 267
Stepinac, Alojzije 279–80, 285n165, 296
Stere, Constantin 91
Stloukal, Karel 214
Stoianovich, Traian 64
Stojadinović, Milan 85
Stojanović, Dubravka 246

Index

Stojanović, Ljubomir 201
Stojanović, Svetozar 112
Štoll, Ladislav 44
Stomma, Stanisław 103–4
Strossmayer, Josip Juraj 261, 279
Štúr, Ľudovít 231
Sturdza, Mihail, Prince of Moldova 196
Subtelny, Orest 246
Šufflay, Milan 209–10, 221, 224
Šuhaj, Nikola 146–7
Sundhaussen, Holm 63, 216
Supek, Rudi 112
Surowiecki, Wawrzyniec 260n22
Šusta, Josef 213, 222, 224–5
Švābe, Arveds 217–18
Szabó, Dezső 40, 159, 161
Szabó, István 236
Szacki, Jerzy 245
Szakasits, Árpád 108
Szathmári, Sándor 152, 157–9
Széchenyi, István 135
Szekfű, Gyula 117–19, 205–7, 214, 226, 234, 238
Szelényi, Iván 98
Szemlér, Ferenc 161
Szép, Ernő 136
Szostak, Sylwia 312
Szporluk, Roman 246
Szűcs, Jenő 50, 52–3, 80, 243
Szujski, Józef 4–5
Szyfman, Arnold 136
Szymborska, Wisława 133

Tábor, Béla 103
Tadić, Ljubomir 112
Tarde, Gabriel 119
Tazbir, Janusz 244
Teige, Karel 107–8
Teleki, Pál 215–16
Tentelis, Augusts 217
Țepeneag, Dumitru 180
Tham, Karel 264
Theodorescu, Barbu 204
Thompson, E. P. 113
Tigrid, Pavel 111–12, 180
Tischner, Józef 105
Tišma, Aleksandar 173–4, 176–8
Tiso, Jozef 169, 277
Tisza, István 161–2, 249
Tito, Josip Broz 77, 178, 286n167, 295n236, 296, 298, 349
Todorov, Nikolai 239
Todorova, Maria 63
Tokarska-Bakir, Joanna 251
Tőkés, László 298
Tokin, Boško 15
Toller, Ernst 152
Tomalevski, Georgy 24

Tomka, Miklós 294–5
Tömpe, István 342
Topolski, Jerzy 242
Tóth, István György 244
Treitz, Péter 216
Trentkowski, Bronisław 5
Troebst, Stefan 65
Troeltsch, Ernst 32–3
Trotsky, Leon 75, 179
Trubetzkoy, Nikolai 10
Truska, Liudas 252
Tsankov, Aleksandar 91, 210
Tsankov, Stefan 102
Tudjman, Franjo 302–3
Turowicz, Jerzy 103–4
Tymieniecki, Kazimierz 213, 221

Ugrešić, Dubravka 178
Updike, John 185

Vajda, Mihály 50, 58
Vályi, Péter 333–4
Varga, Jenő (Eugen) 76
Varga, Lucie 237
Varsik, Branislav 215
Vartanov, Anri 354
Vecsei, Marietta 355
Vekerdi, László 236
Velimirović, Nikolaj 100–1
Velmar-Janković, Vladimir 12
Venizelos, Eleftherios 82
Viková-Kunětická, Božena 96
Vode, Angela 97
Voinea, Șerban 90, 210
Vörös, Károly 245
Vrána, Josef 293
Vranicki, Predrag 112
Vujić, Vladimir 3, 13–14, 18
Vulcănescu, Mircea 120–1, 124

Wagner, Richard 178
Wajda, Andrzej 169
Walicki, Andrzej 5, 70, 245
Wallerstein, Immanuel 48, 241
Wandycz, Piotr S. 62
Wasilewska, Wanda 97
Wasowski, Jerzy 340–1
Weber, Max 106, 257n5
Wehler, Hans-Ulrich 244
Wells, H.G. 152
Wereszycki, Henryk 230, 247
Werfel, Franz 151
Werstadt, Jaroslav 222
Wierzyński, Kazimierz 151
Wiesel, Elie 133
Williams, Raymond 312
Winter, Eduard 78

Index

Witkiewicz, Stanisław Ignacy 152, 156–7
Wittram, Reinhard 216
Wojciechowski, Marian 221
Wojtyła, Karol (later, Pope John Paul II) 290–1
Wollman, František (Frank) 35
Wundt, Wilhelm 117
Wyczański, Andrzej 236, 244
Wyspiański, Stanisław 135
Wyszyński, Cardinal Stefan 104, 289–91, 294

Xenopol, Alexandru D. 199, 201–2, 204–5, 223, 233

Yanev, Yanko 14, 24–5, 42n184
Yotsov, Boris 24

Zaharia, Valerian 298
Żarnowski, Janusz 235, 244
Żeleński-Boy, Tadeusz 136
Zeletin, Ştefan 94, 210
Zhivkova, Lyudmila 229
Zientara, Benedykt 243
Zillich, Heinrich 160–1
Zimmermann, Susan 356
Zlatarski, Vasil N. 208, 224
Żmigrodzka, Maria 245
Zogu, Ahmet (ruled as Zog I, King of Albania) 81–2, 234
Zsurzs, Éva 355
Županić, Niko 198, 220–1
Zweig, Ferdynand 95
Zweig, Stefan 52, 151
Zwitter, Fran 79, 219, 242n240

Taylor & Francis eBooks

www.taylorfrancis.com

A single destination for eBooks from Taylor & Francis with increased functionality and an improved user experience to meet the needs of our customers.

90,000+ eBooks of award-winning academic content in Humanities, Social Science, Science, Technology, Engineering, and Medical written by a global network of editors and authors.

TAYLOR & FRANCIS EBOOKS OFFERS:

- A streamlined experience for our library customers
- A single point of discovery for all of our eBook content
- Improved search and discovery of content at both book and chapter level

REQUEST A FREE TRIAL
support@taylorfrancis.com